THE FAR SIDE GALLERY

by GARY LARSON

Pete —
Get Well
Soon!
10/89
The Givens Gang

Andrews and McMeel
A Universal Press Syndicate Company
Kansas City • New York

The Far Side Gallery copyright © 1980, 1981, 1982, 1983, 1984 by the Chronicle Publishing Company. All rights reserved. Printed in the United States of America. No part of this book may be used or reproduced in any manner whatsoever without written permission except in the case of reprints in the context of reviews. For information write Andrews and McMeel, a Universal Press Syndicate Company, 4900 Main Street, Kansas City, Missouri 64112.

ISBN: 0-8362-2062-5
Library of Congress Catalog Card Number: 84-81550

First Printing, September 1984
Fifteenth Printing, August 1988

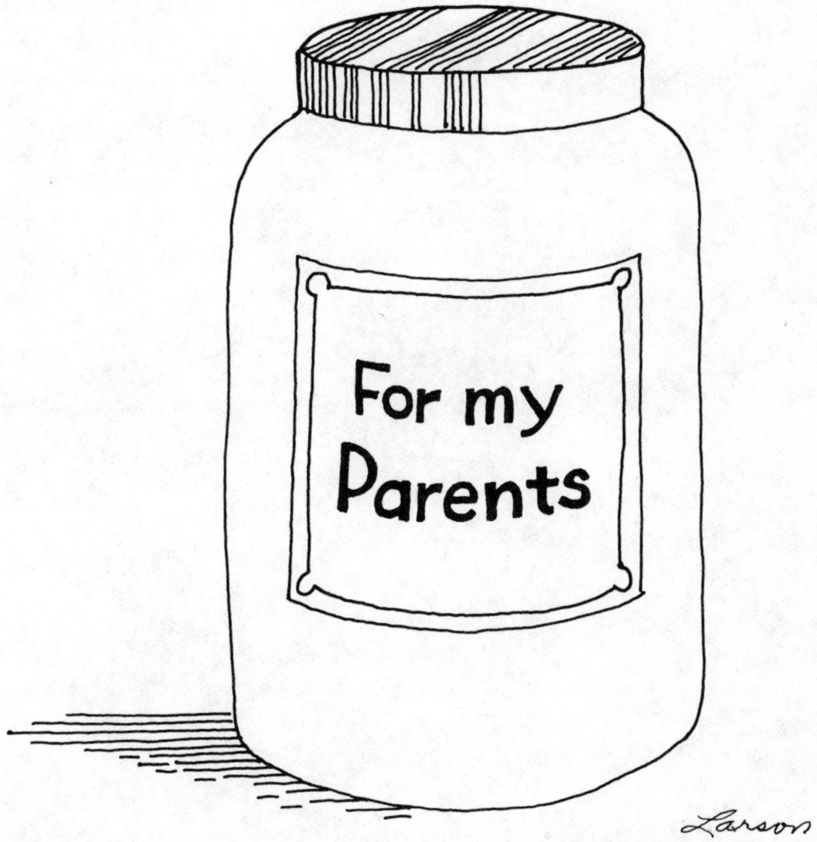
For my Parents
Larson

Labels on jars: Brach... | Homo dementicus | Metridau m

This is my brother's fault.

As a young boy, I was plagued with an overactive imagination — compounded by the fact that we lived in a house with your standard, monster-infested basement. Occasionally, I would hear my father's command that never failed to horrify me: "Go down to the basement, Gary, and bring up some firewood." Death.

And so down I'd go, certain I was about to become the leading character in a story that would be told around campfires for generations to come. ("Say, has anyone here heard, 'The Boy Who Went for Firewood'?")

My task nearly completed, I would begin my quick ascent back to the world of the living. And then, as it had countless times before, it would happen. With an audible click, followed by sinister laughter, the lights would go off.

Engulfed in blackness, I would scramble my way to the top of the stairs only to find the door held firmly shut. From the other side, where the light switch was controlled, I would hear my older brother's voice begin to chant: "It's coming for you, Gary! It's coming! Do you hear it? Do you hear it breathing, Gary?"

Unbeknownst to my parents the deep grooves in that side of the door were not caused by the dog.

Now, many years later, here I am a cartoonist. And if the cartoons I draw seem a little — well — different, I hope this story has scratched the surface of understanding my childhood: a sort of "Theodore Cleaver Meets the Thing."

So, without further ado, let my brother's handiwork be revealed. I hear something coming.

— Gary Larson

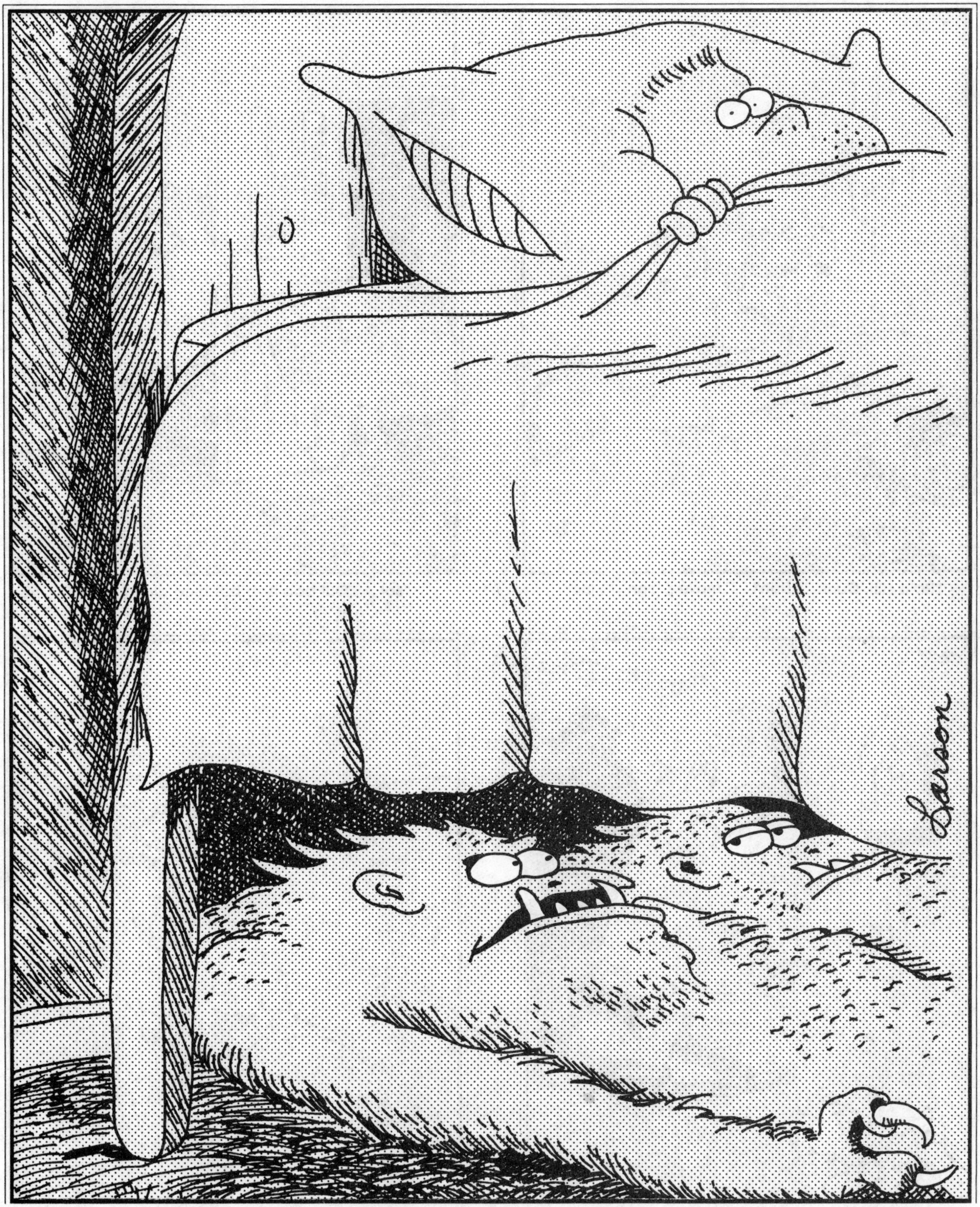
Larson

"I've got it again, Larry . . . an eerie feeling like there's something on top of the bed."

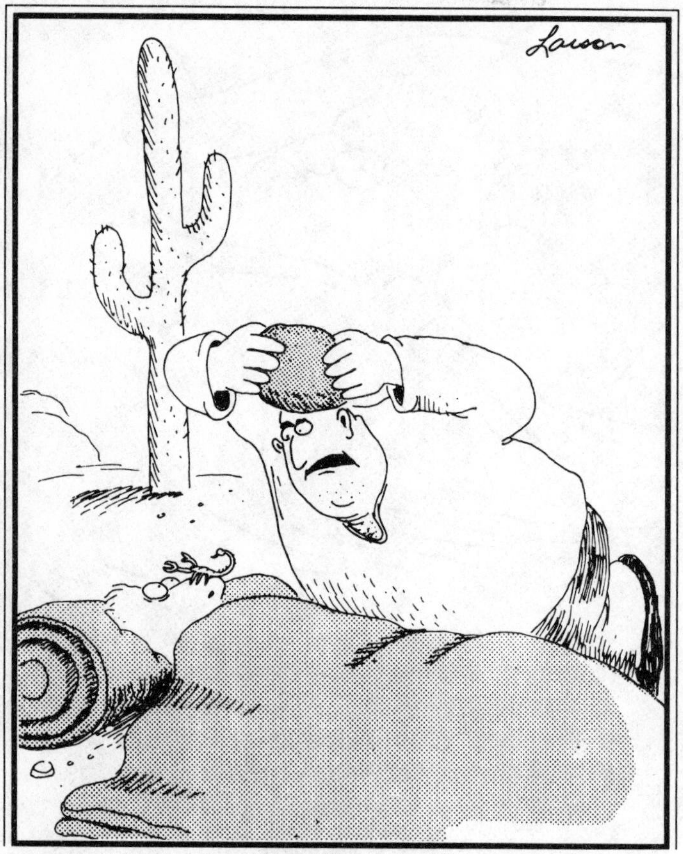
Larson

"Hold still, Carl! . . . Don't . . . move . . . an . . . inch!"

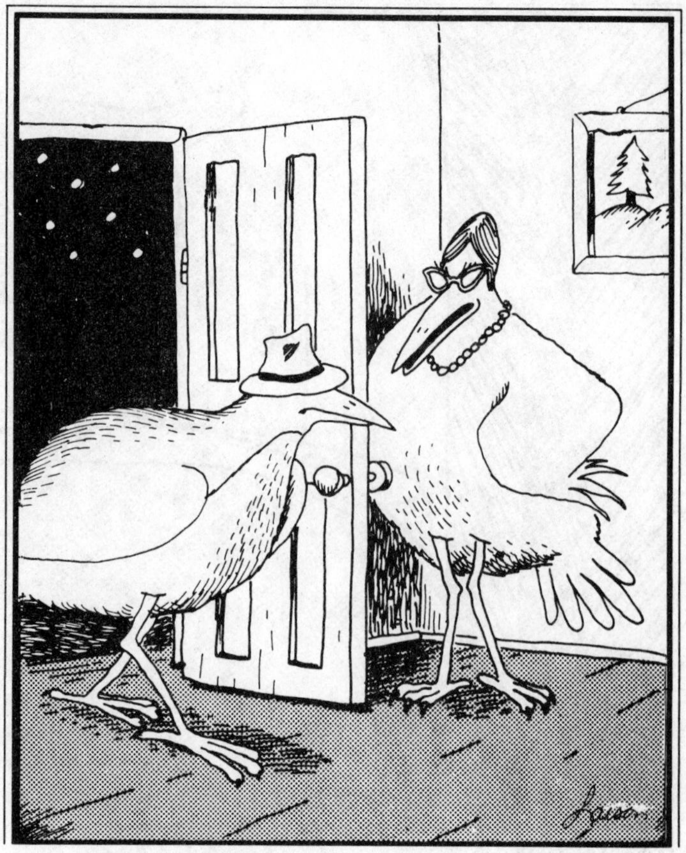
Larson

"So! . . . Out bob bob bobbing along again!"

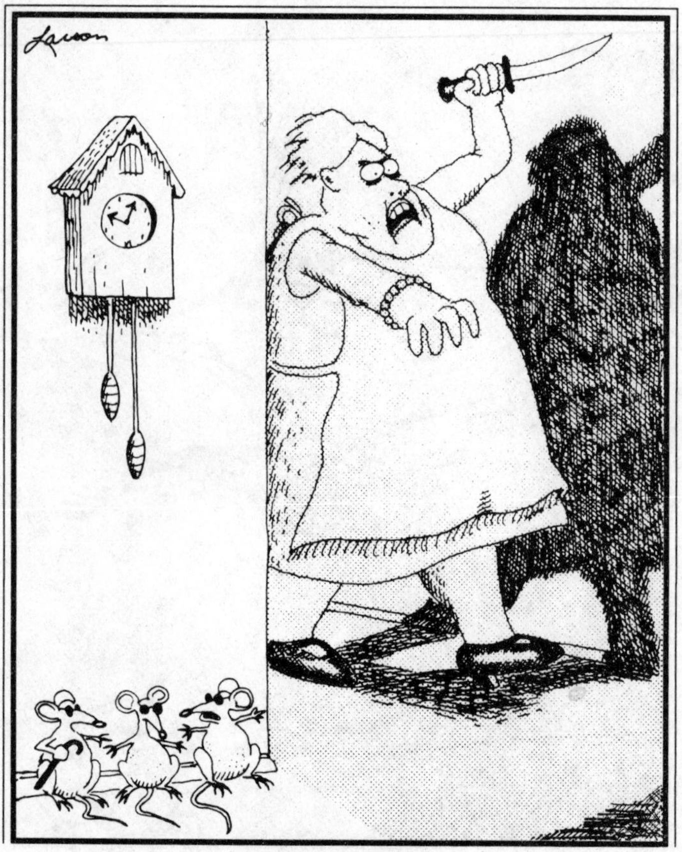
Larson

"Egad! . . . Sounds like the farmer's wife has really flipped out this time!"

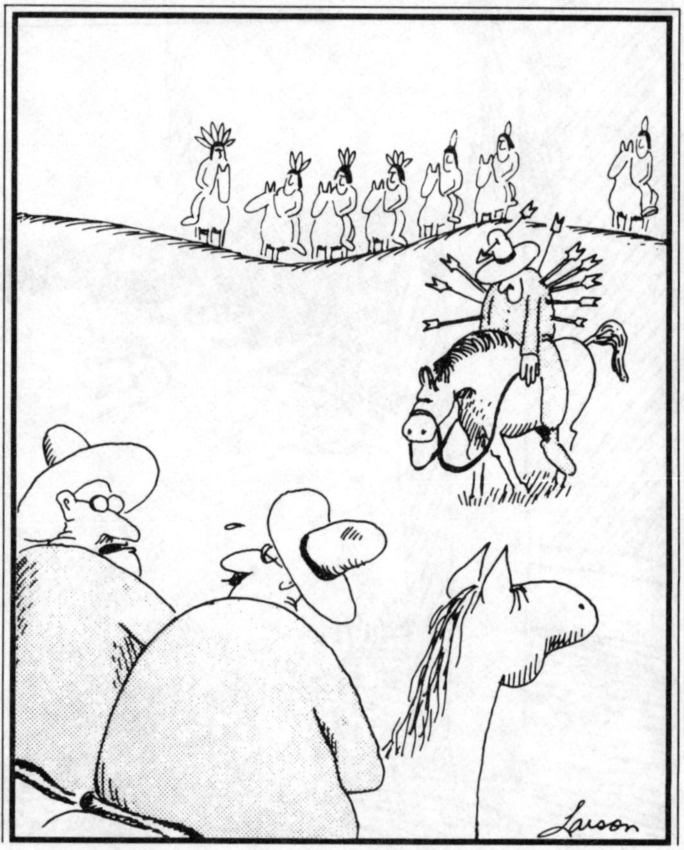
Larson

"Now stay calm . . . Let's hear what they said to Bill."

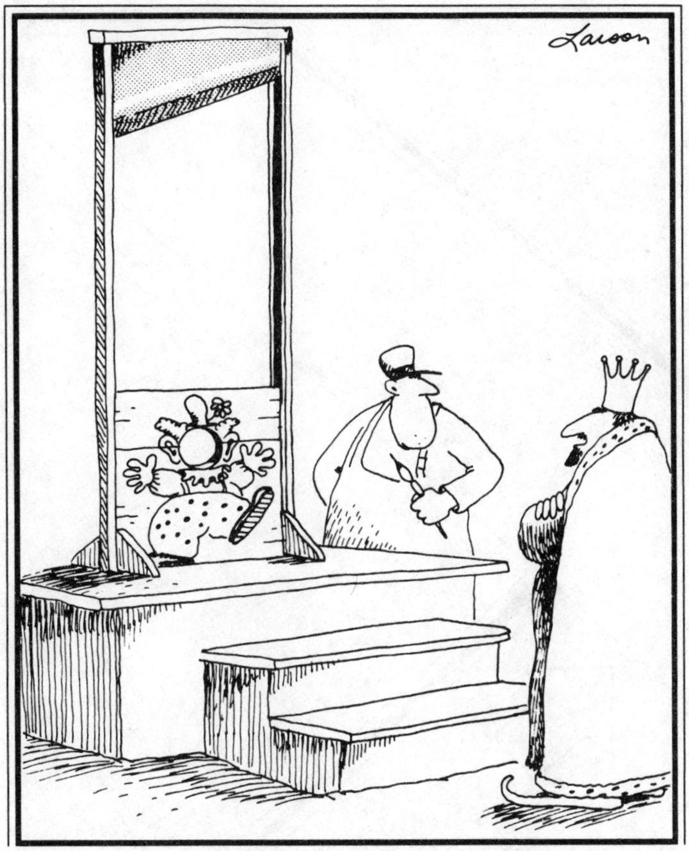

"I like it . . . I like it."

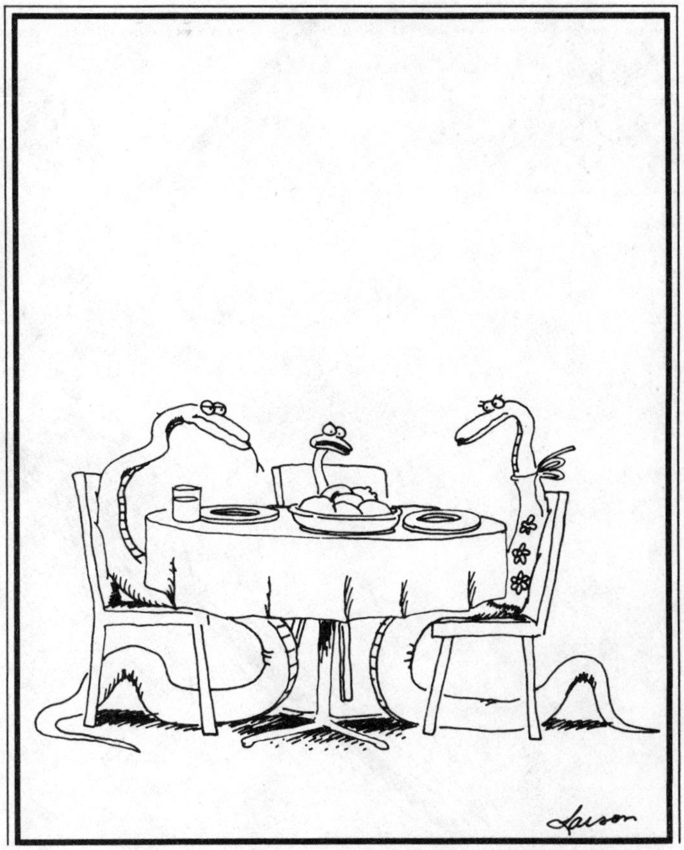

"Oh, brother! . . . Not hamsters again!"

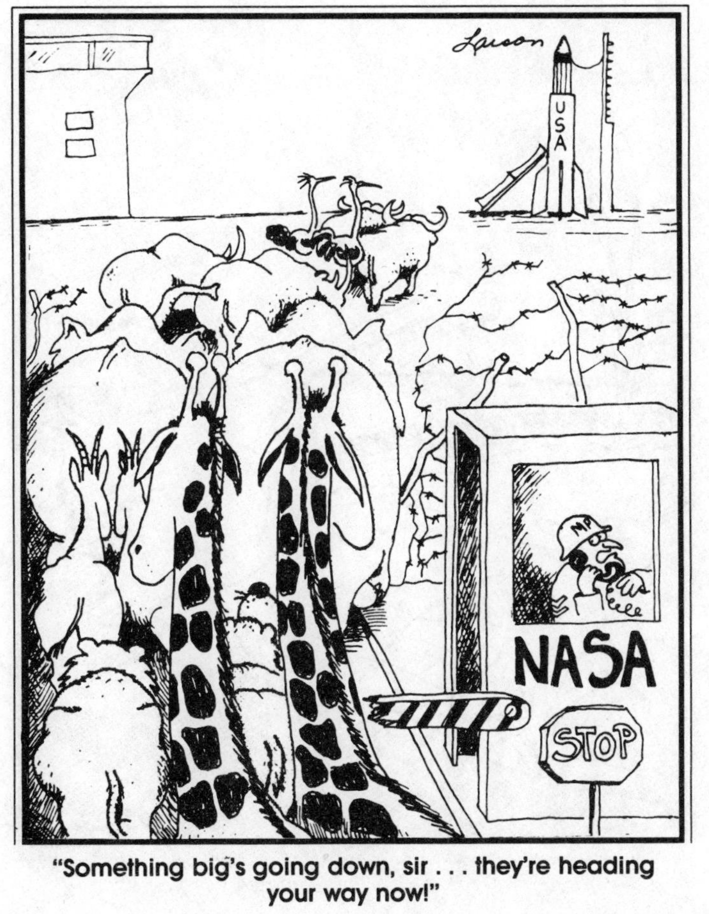
USA
MP
NASA
STOP

"Something big's going down, sir . . . they're heading your way now!"

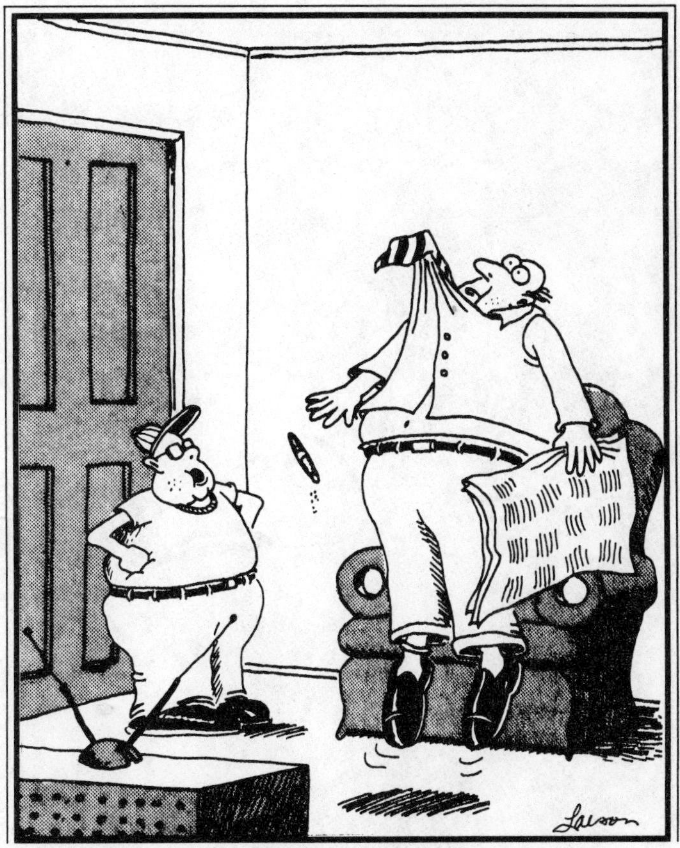

"Big Bob says he's getting tired of you saying he doesn't really exist."

Larson

Larson

Larson

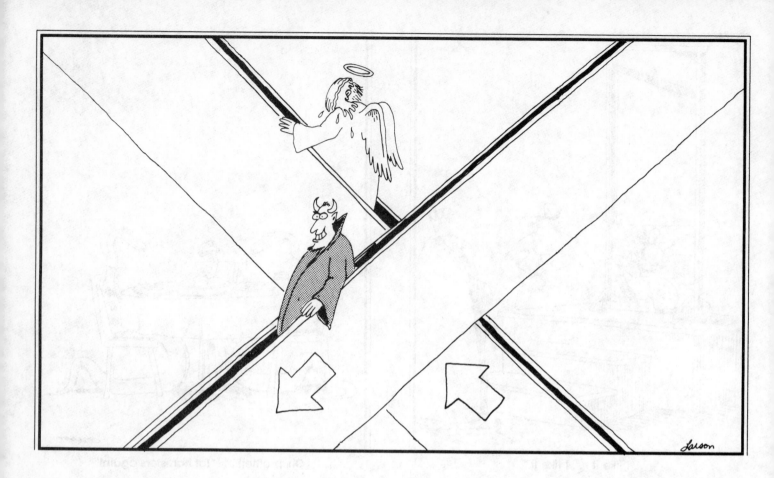

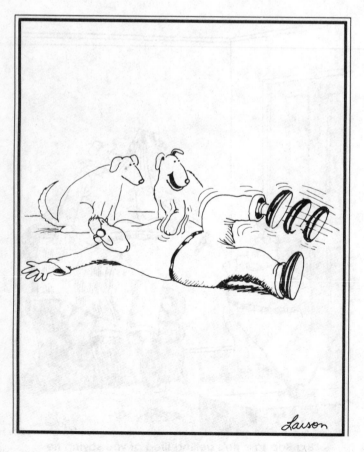

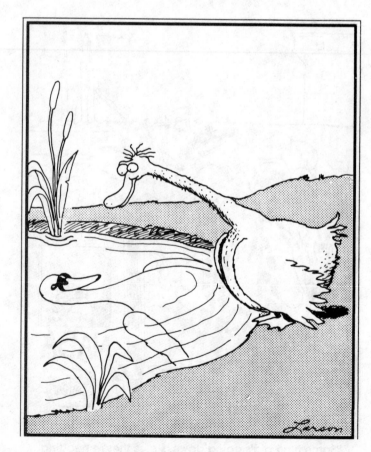

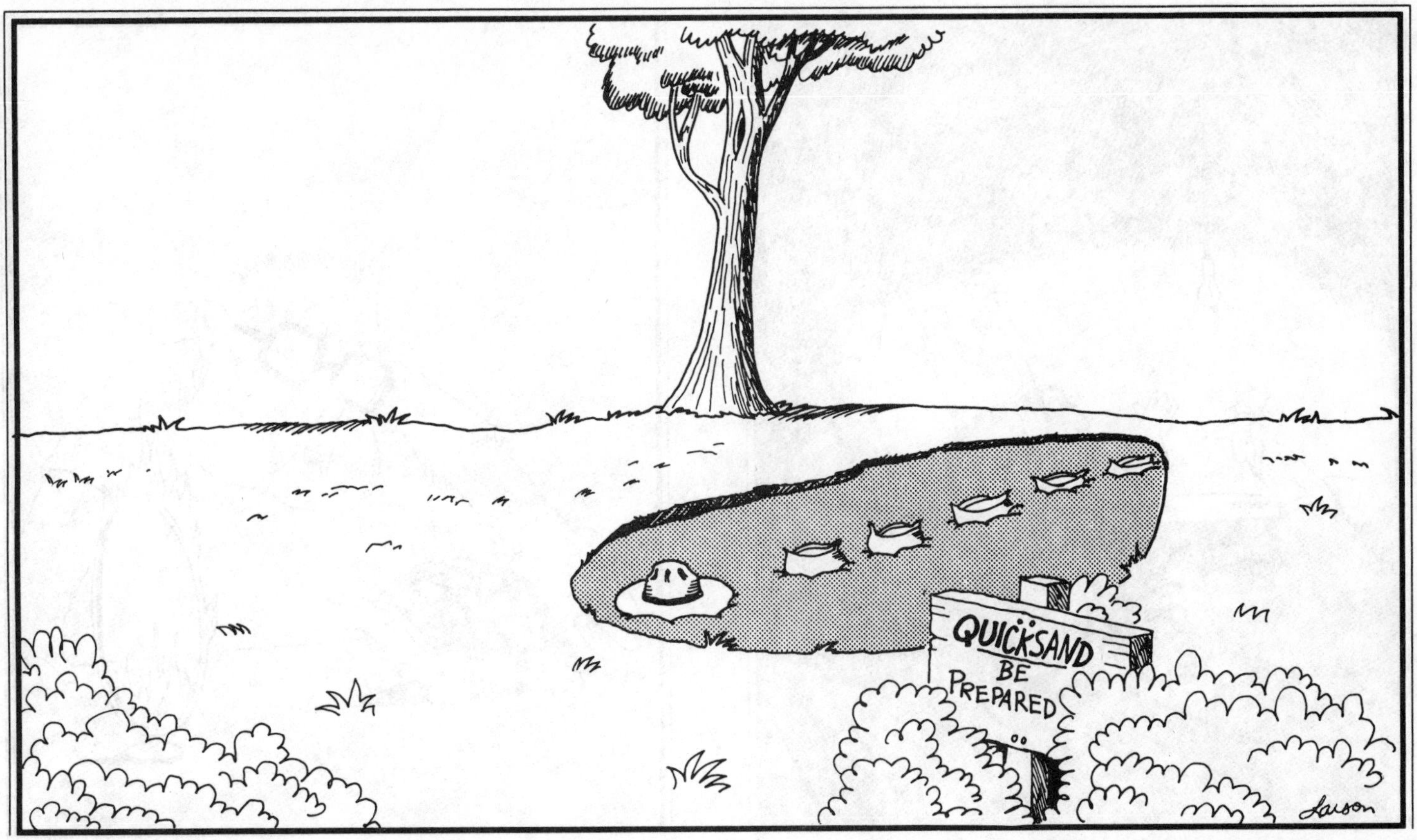
QUICKSAND
BE
PREPARED
Larson

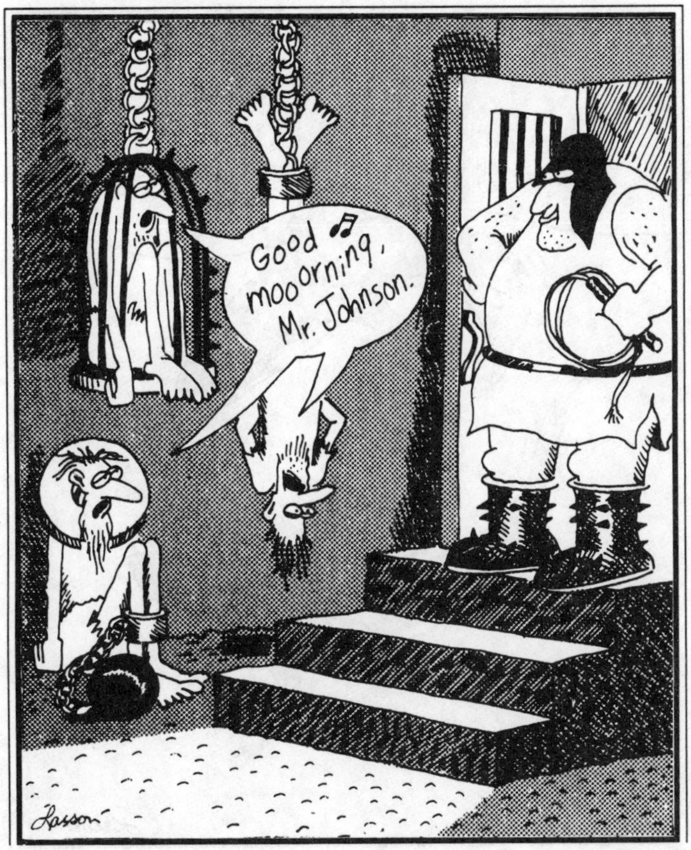
Good moo orning, Mr. Johnson.
Larson

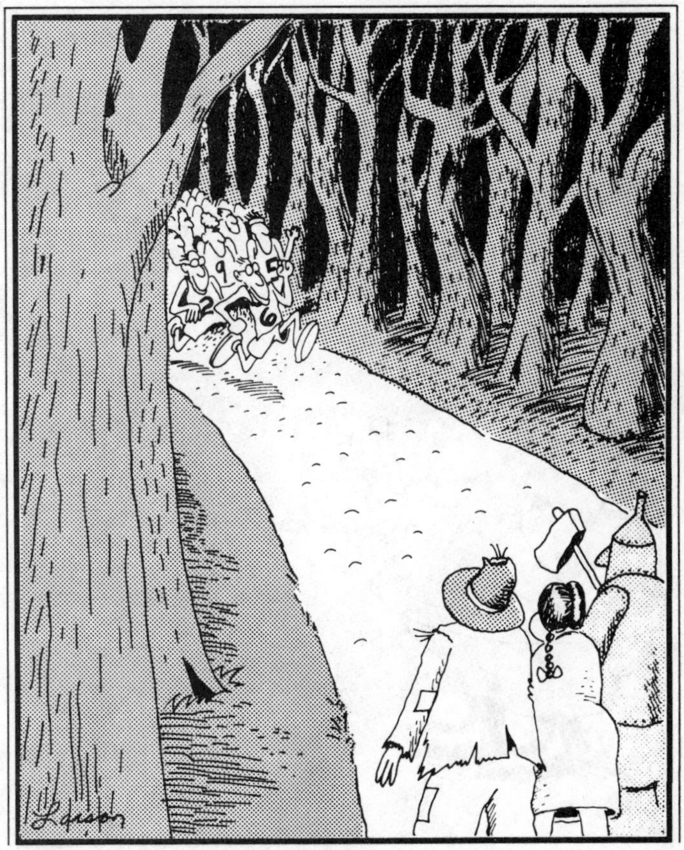
Larson

"Okay, buddy. Then how 'bout the right arm?"

"Through the hoop, Bob! Through the hoop!"

"And I've only one thing to say about all these complaints I've been hearing about . . . venison!"

"Say, honey . . . didn't I meet you last night at the feeding-frenzy?"

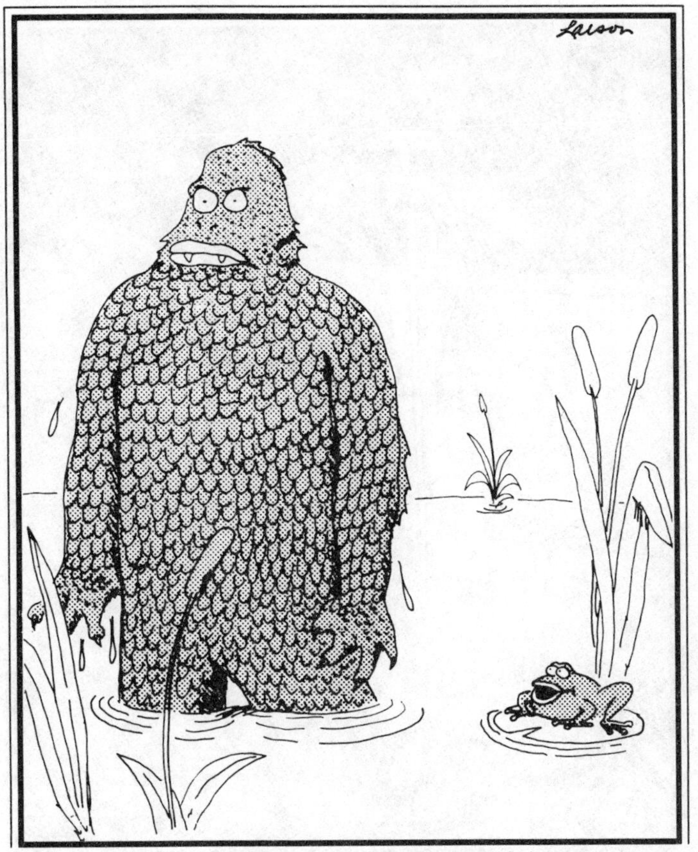
Larson

"Go get 'em, brother."

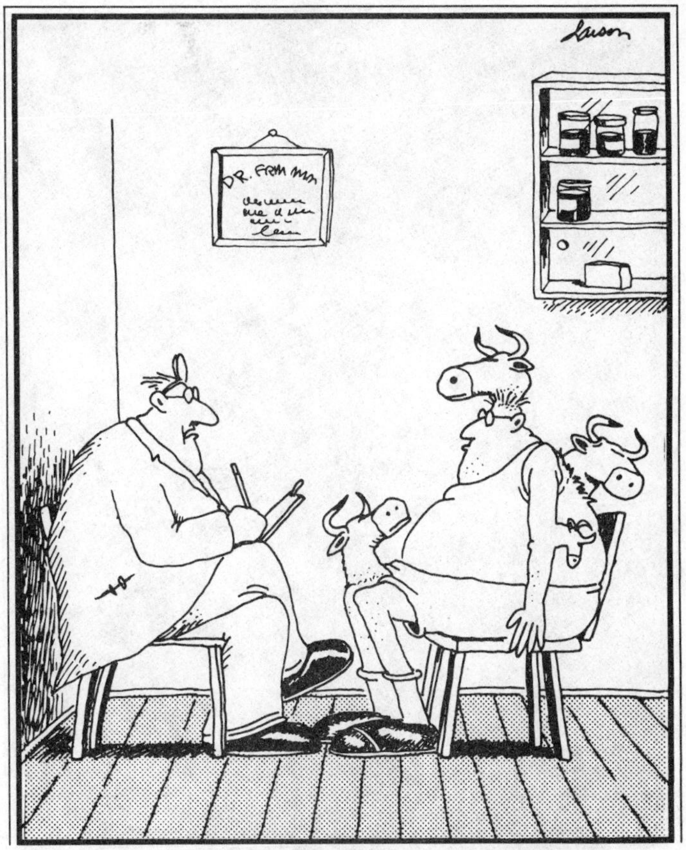
Larson

"I'm afraid you've got cows, Mr. Farnsworth."

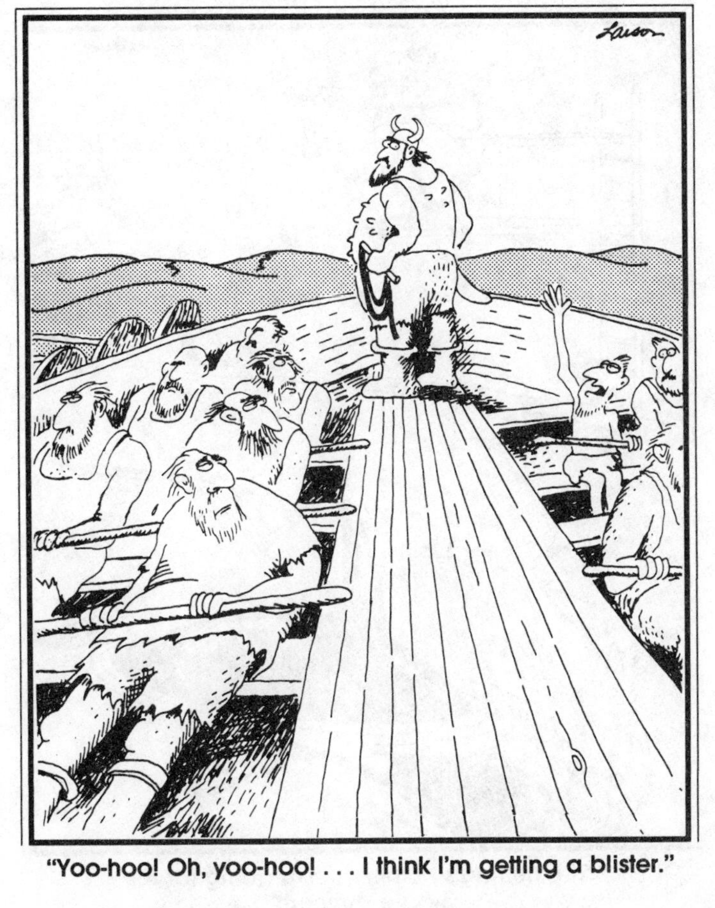
Larson

"Yoo-hoo! Oh, yoo-hoo! . . . I think I'm getting a blister."

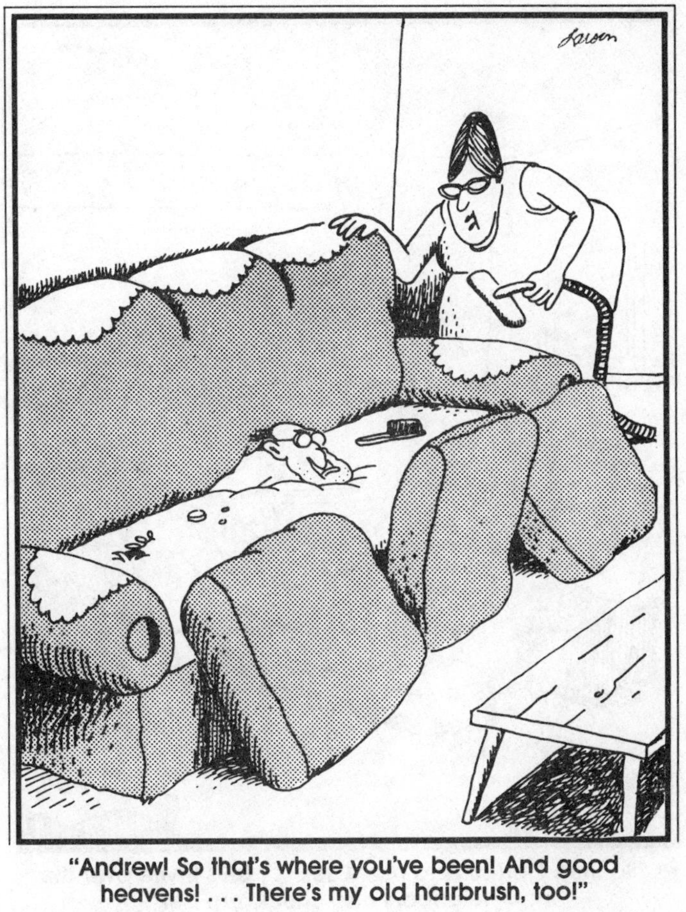
Larson

"Andrew! So that's where you've been! And good heavens! . . . There's my old hairbrush, too!"

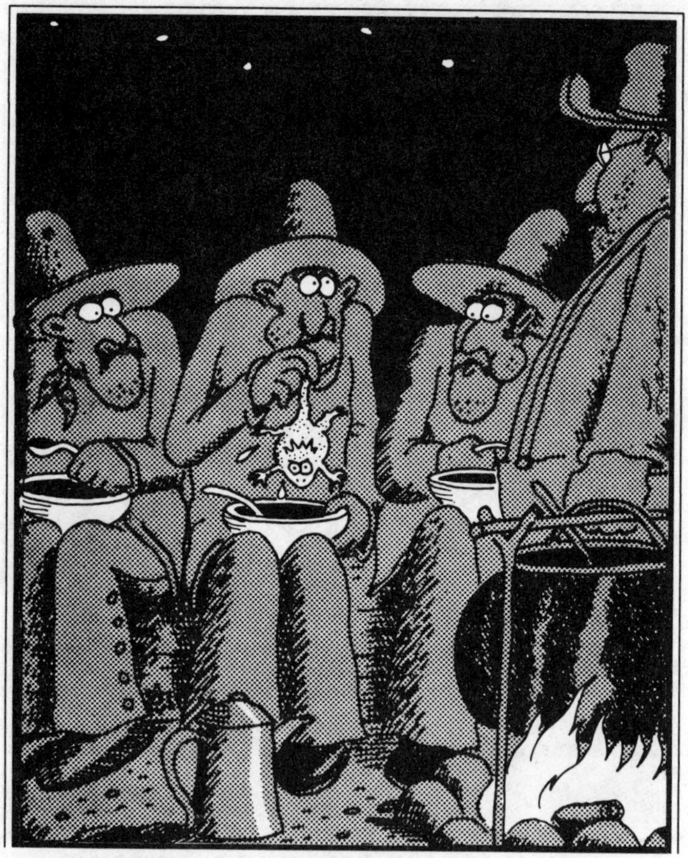

"Well, I'll be! Eggbeater must have missed that one."

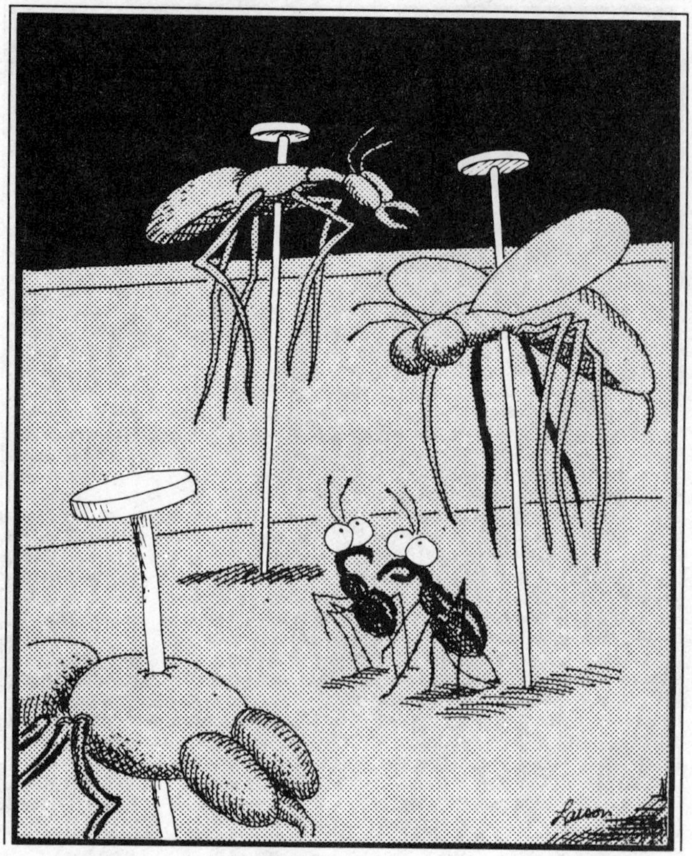

"Gad, I hate walking through this place at night."

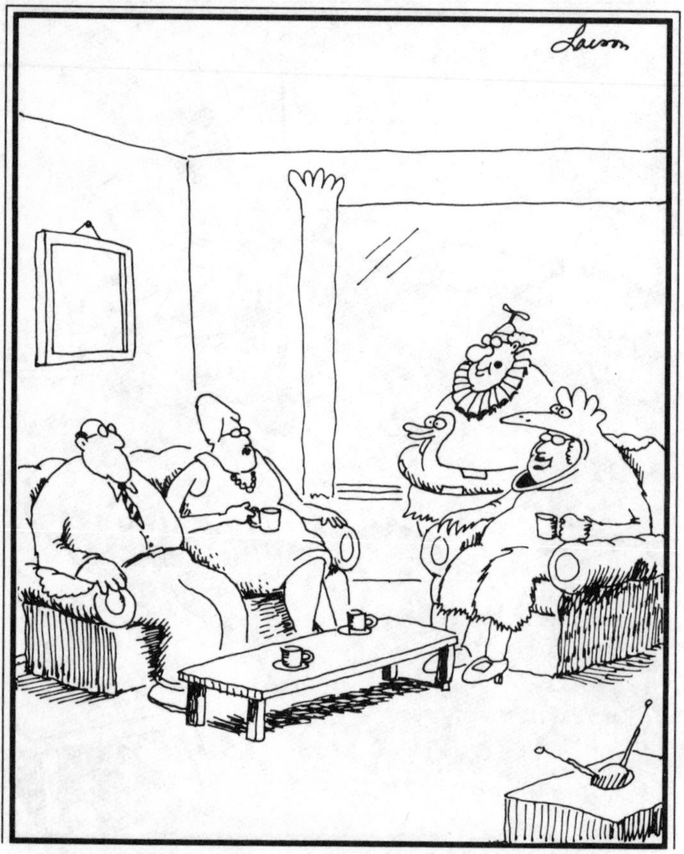

"So then Carl says to me, 'Look . . . Let's invite over the new neighbors and check 'em out.'"

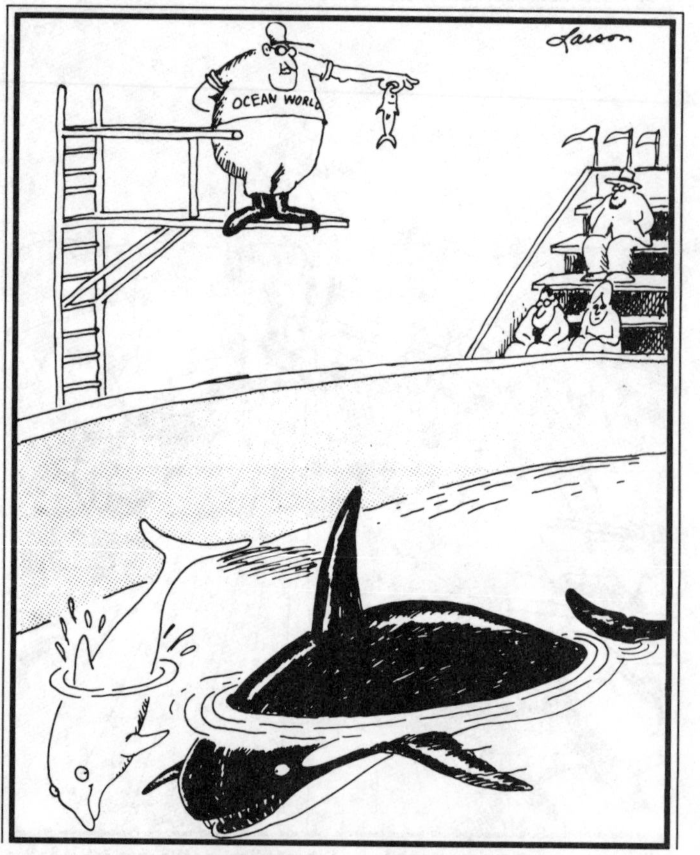
OCEAN WORLD

"The herring's nothin' . . . I'm going for the whole shmeer!"

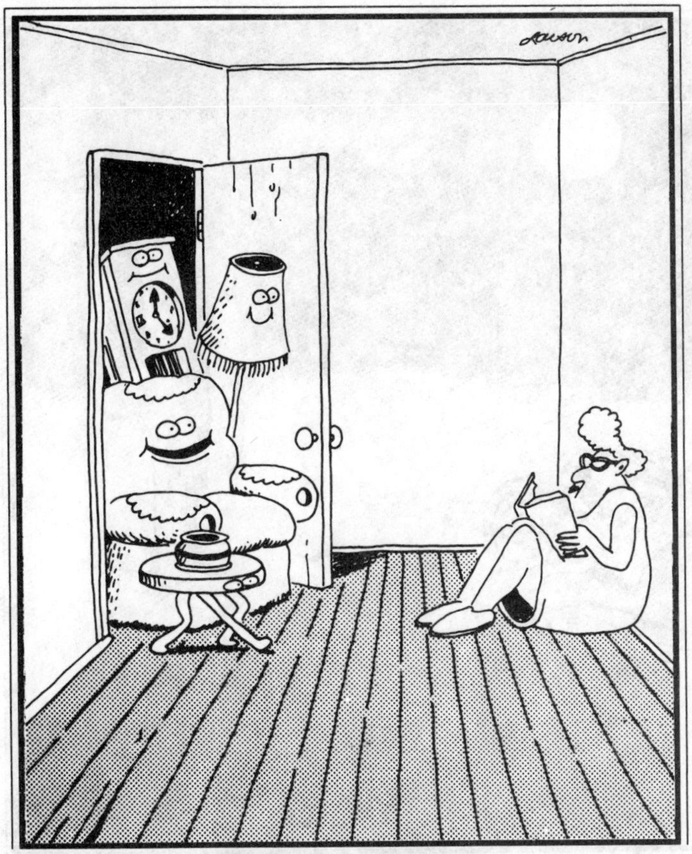

"Well, we're back!"

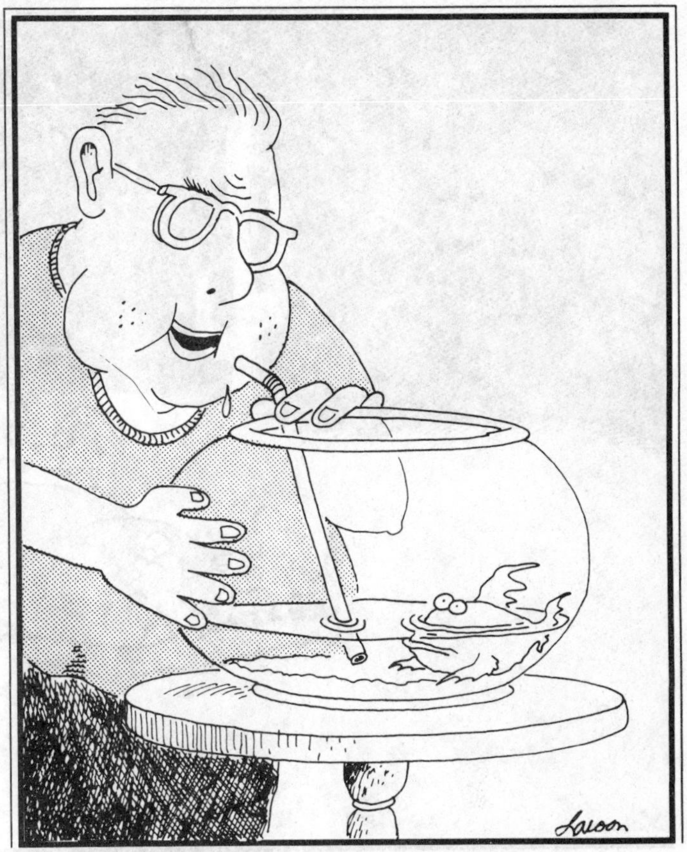
Larson

"So! . . . you STILL won't talk, eh?"

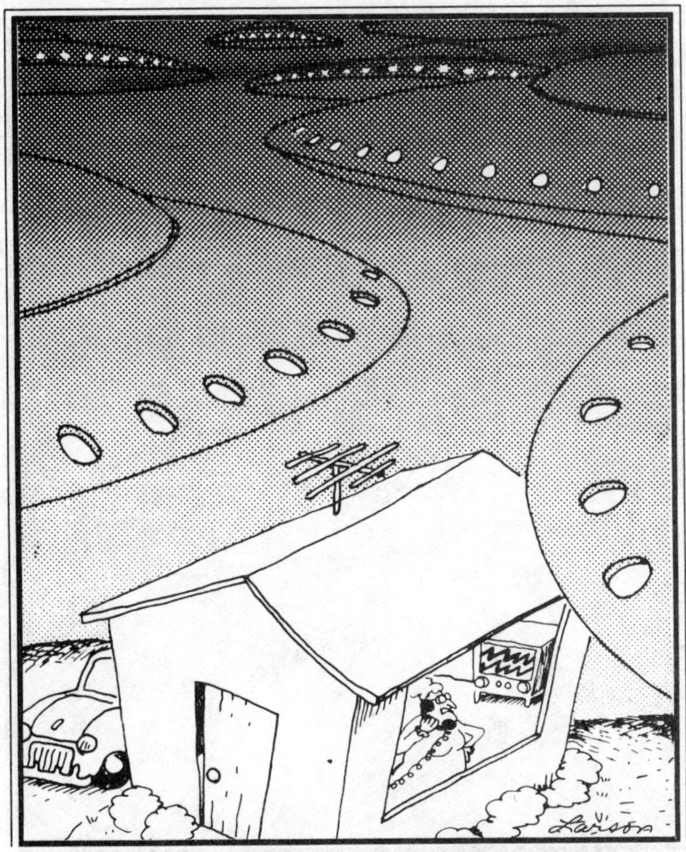
Larson

"Yeah, Sylvia . . . my set too . . . and in the middle of 'Laverne and Shirley.'"

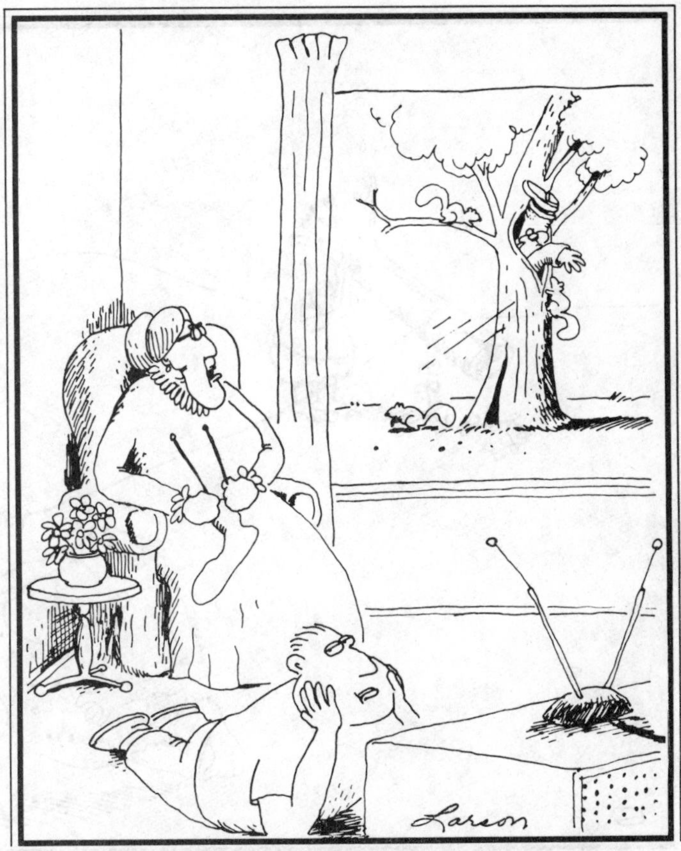
Larson

"Andrew, go out and get your grandfather . . . the squirrels have got him again."

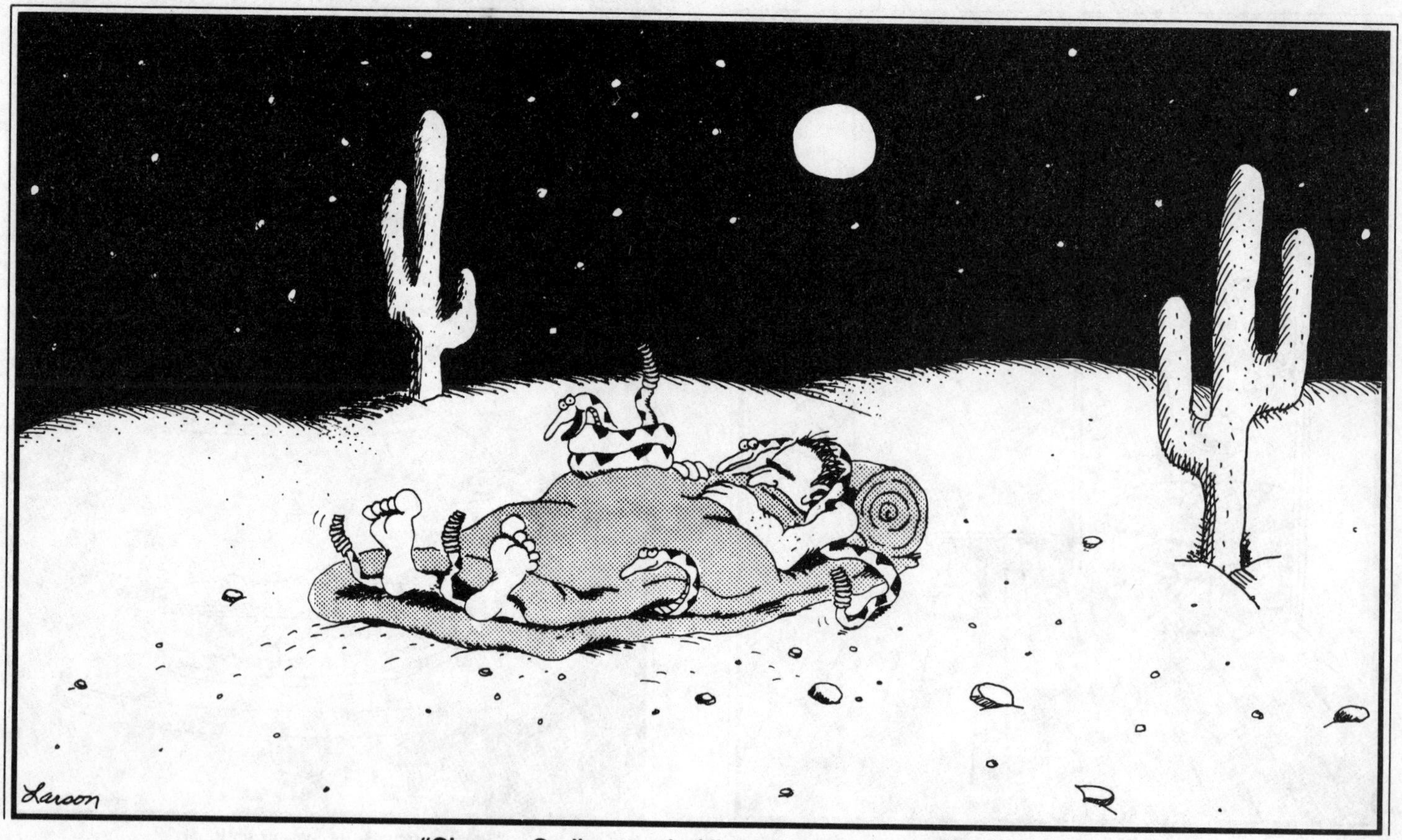
Larson

"Okay . . . On the count of three everybody rattles."

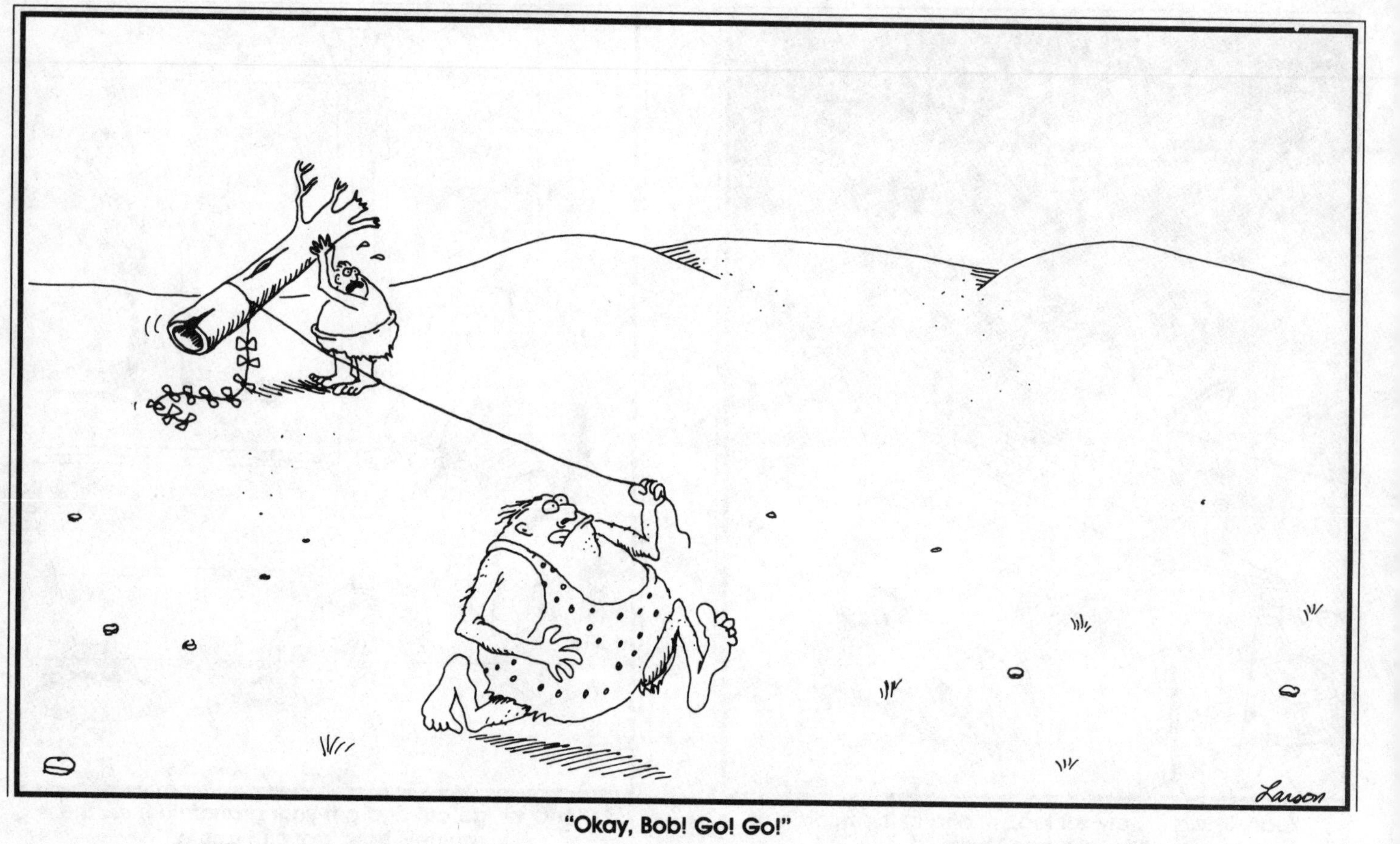
Larson

"Okay, Bob! Go! Go!"

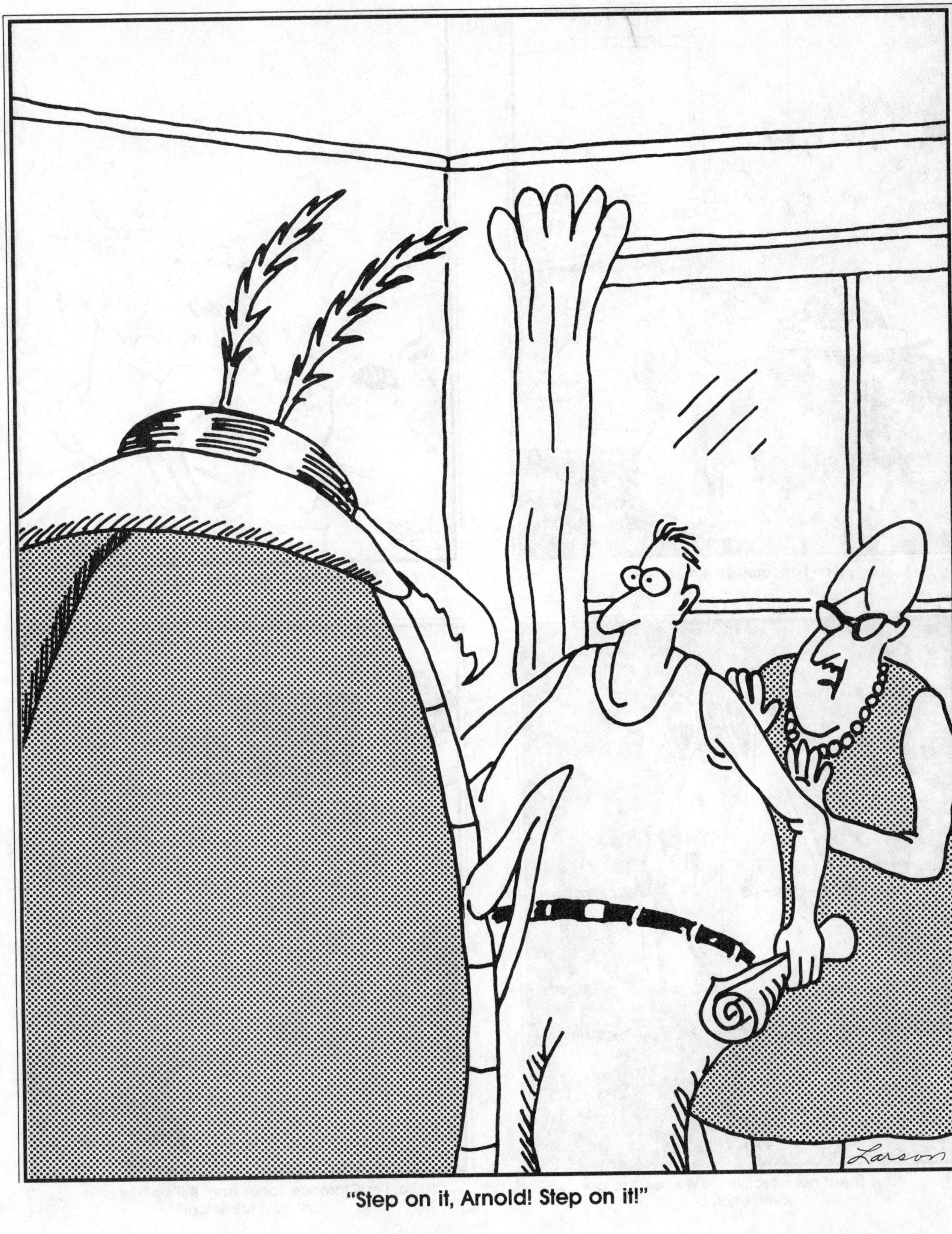
Larson

"Step on it, Arnold! Step on it!"

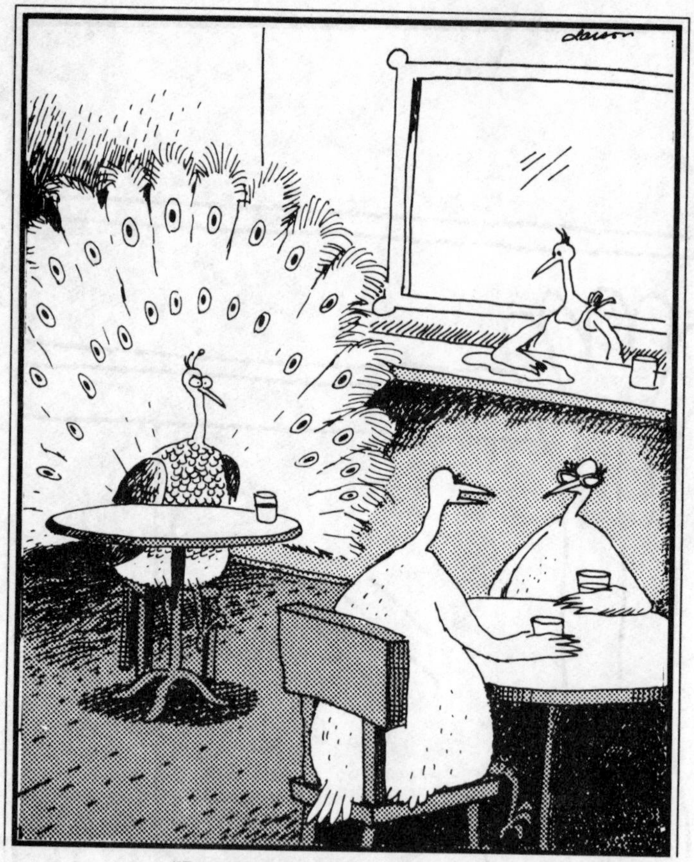

"Don't encourage him, Sylvia."

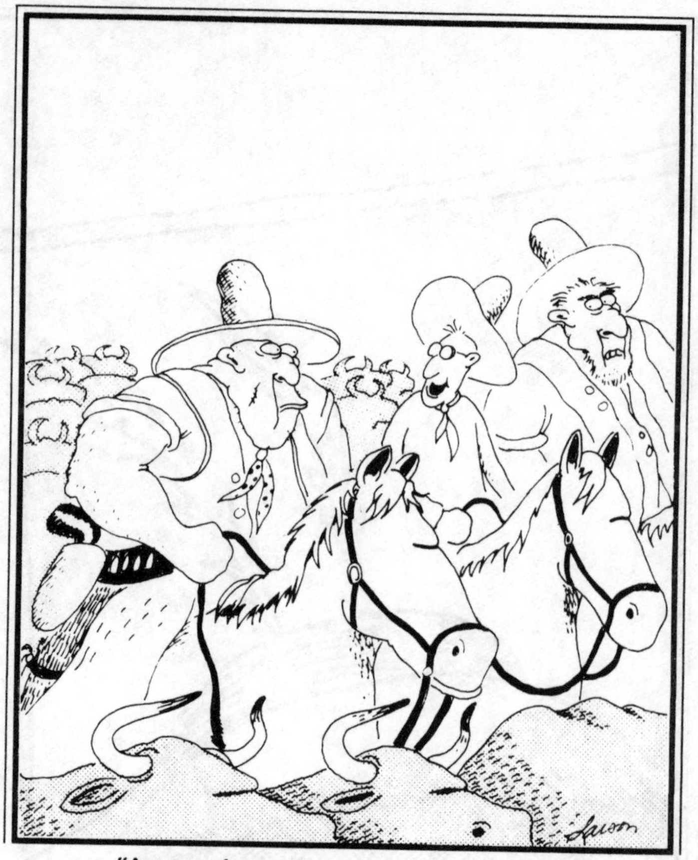

"Anyone for a chorus of 'Happy Trails'?"

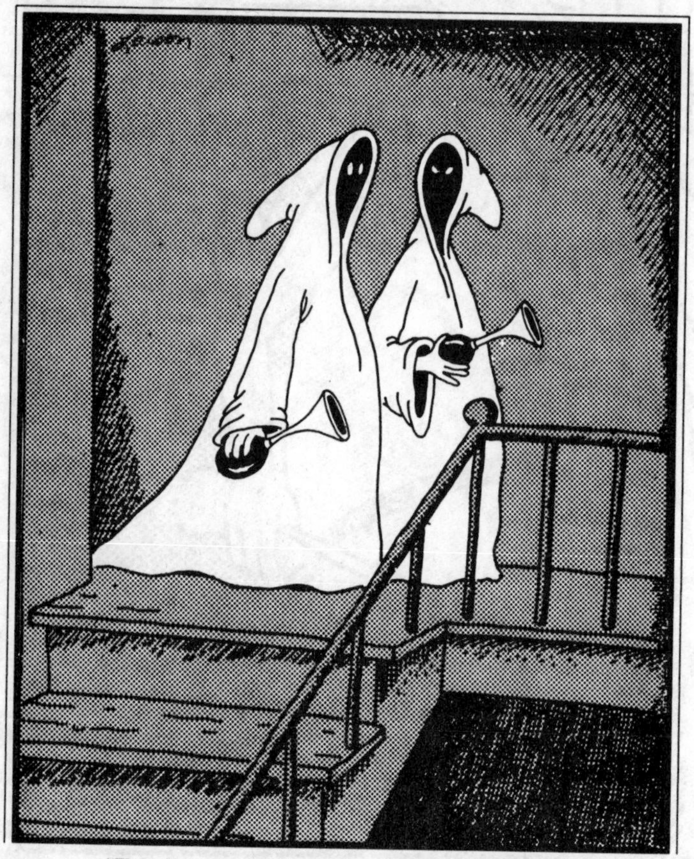

"This is just not effective . . . We need to get some chains."

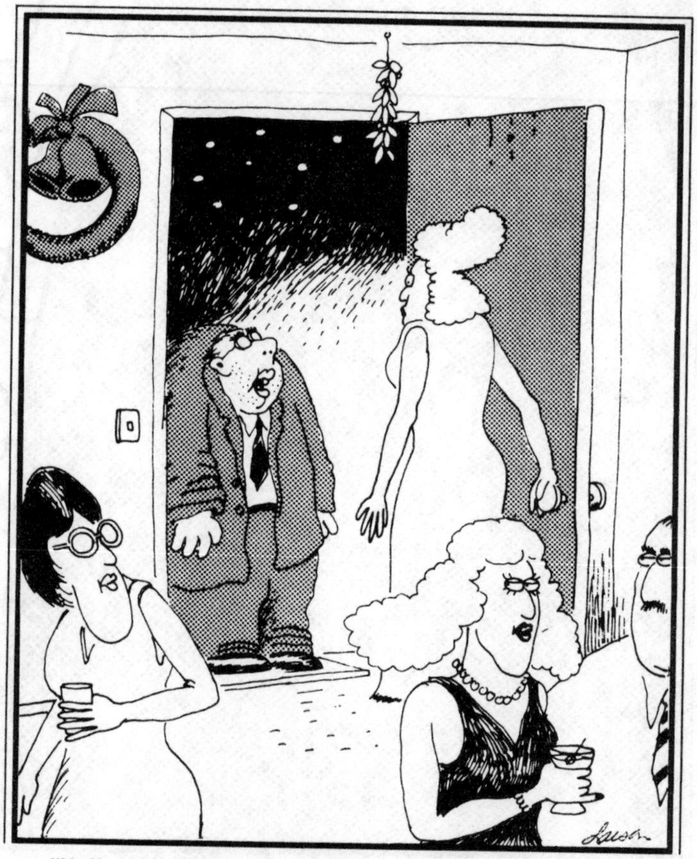

"Hello, I'm Clarence Jones from Bill's office and . . . Oh! Hey! Mistletoe!"

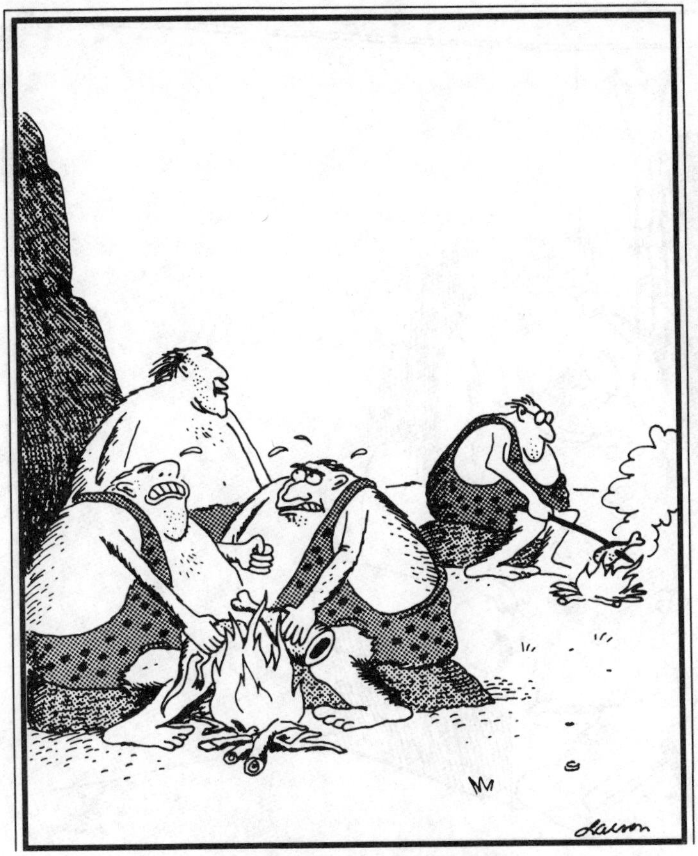

"Hey! Look what Zog do!"

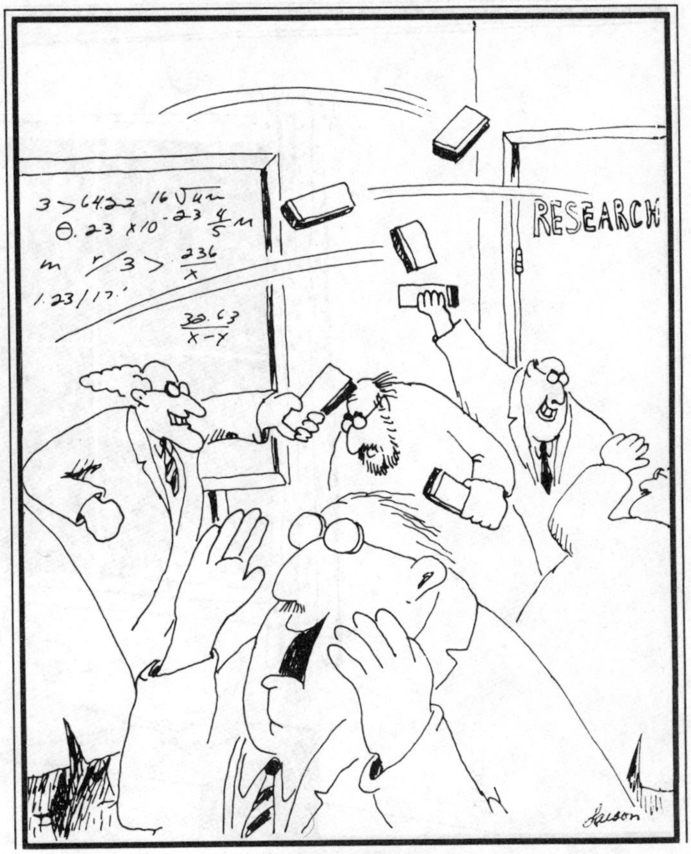
RESEARCH

"Eraser fight!"

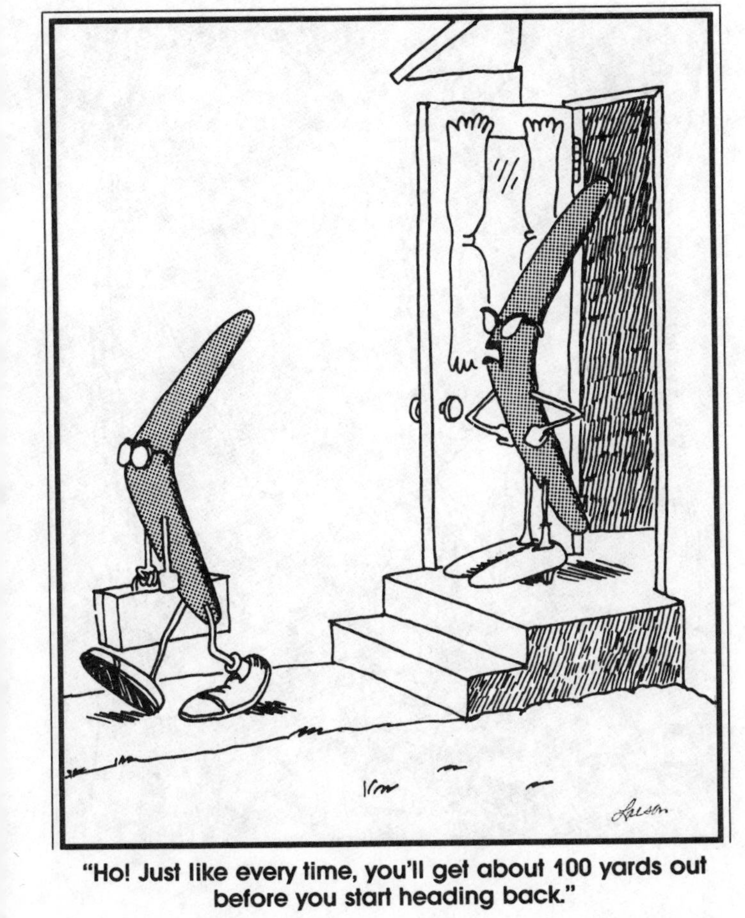

"Ho! Just like every time, you'll get about 100 yards out before you start heading back."

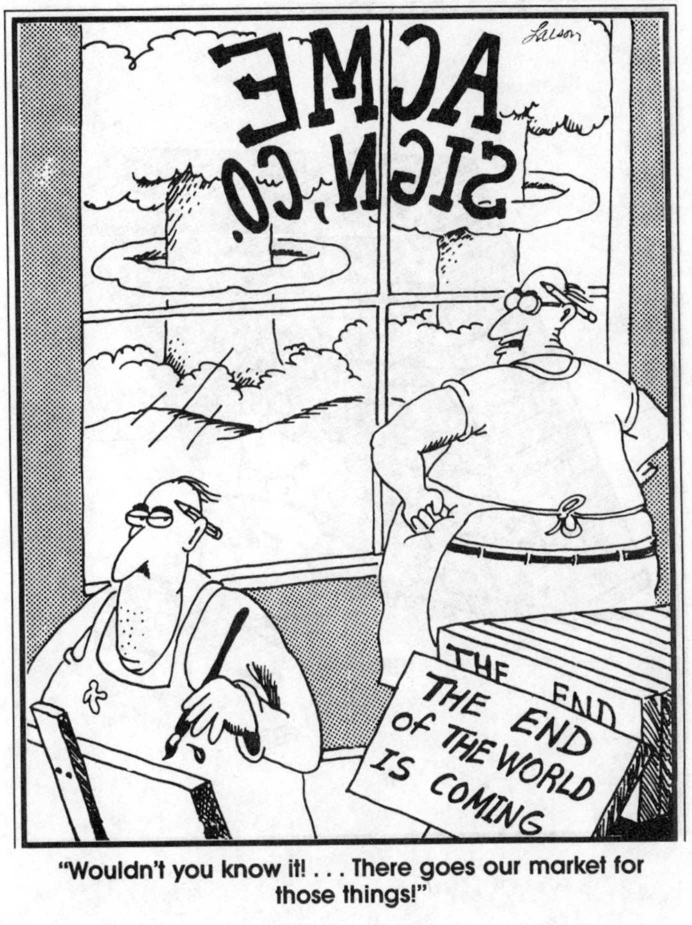
ACME SIGN, CO.
THE END
THE END OF THE WORLD IS COMING

"Wouldn't you know it! . . . There goes our market for those things!"

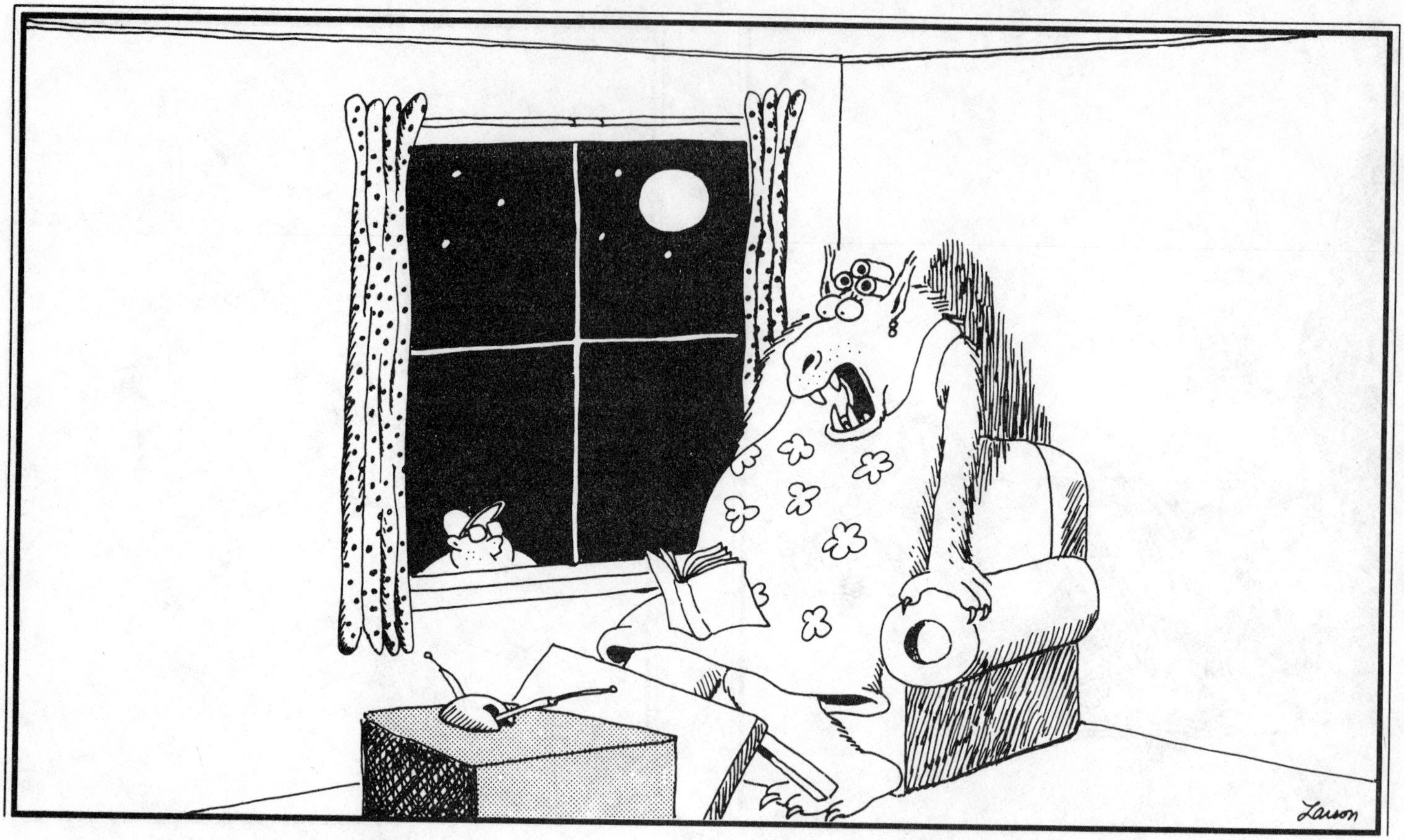
Larson

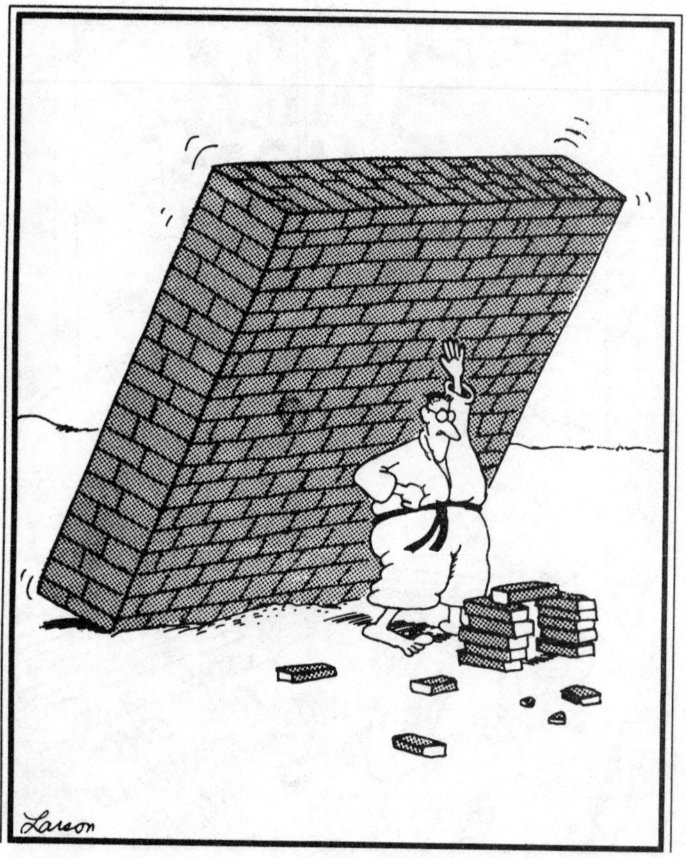
Larson

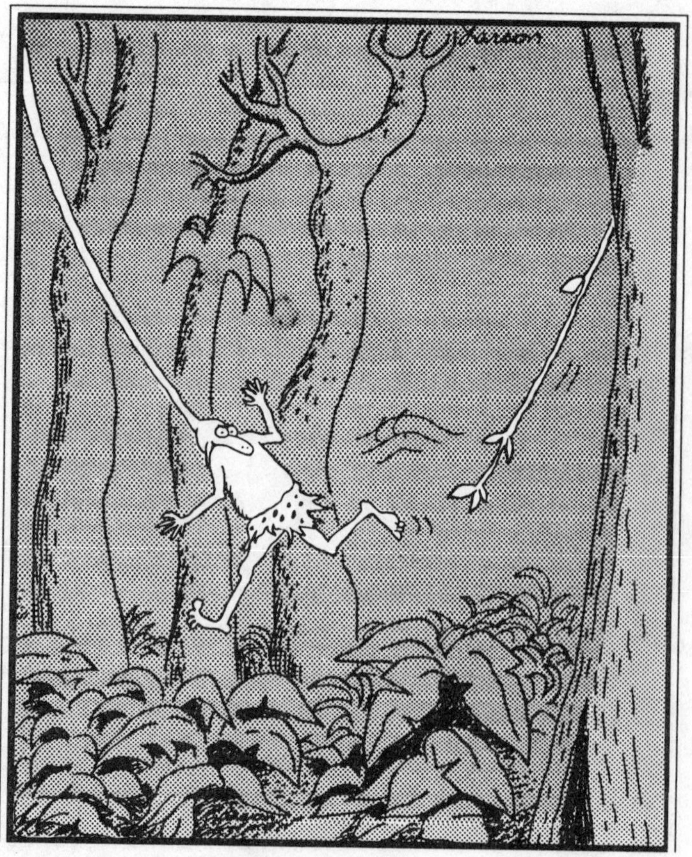
Larson

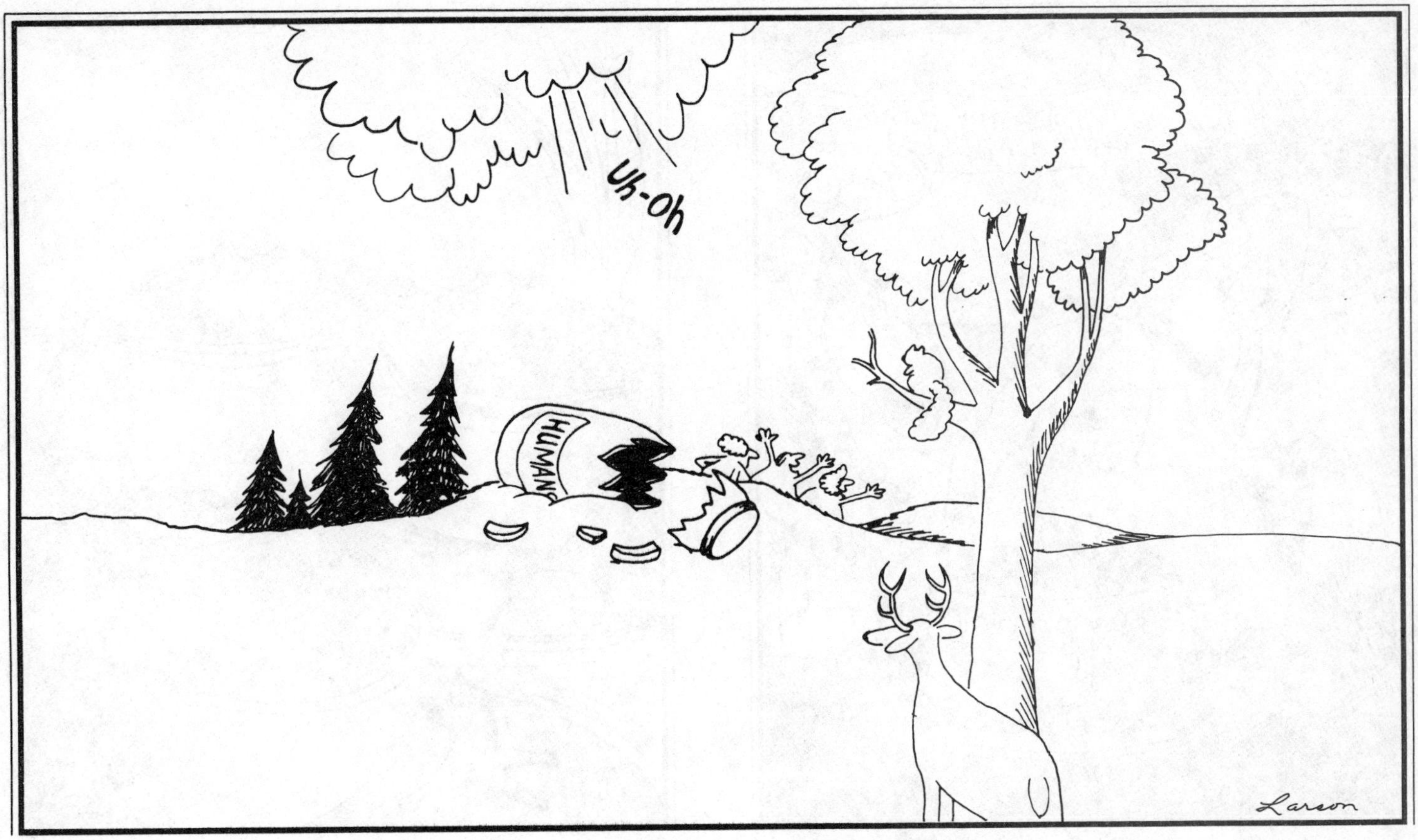
Uh-Oh
HUMANS
Larson

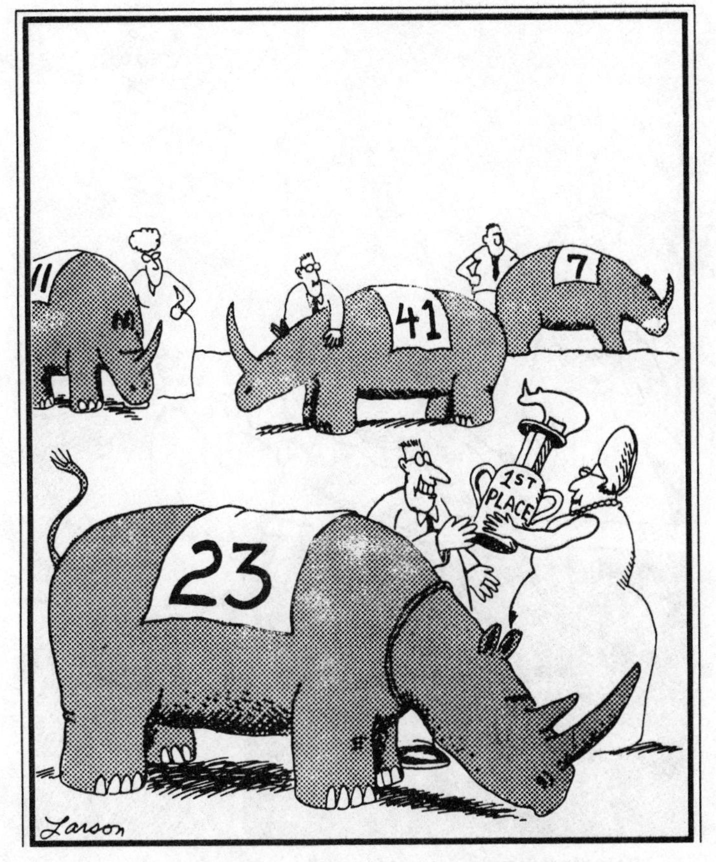
11
41
7
1ST PLACE
23
Larson

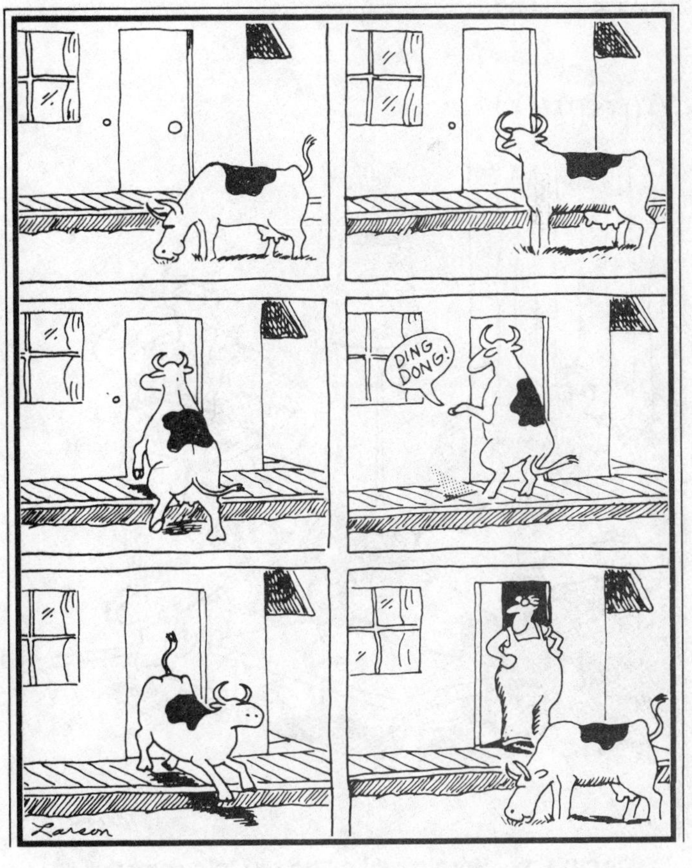
DING DONG!
Larson

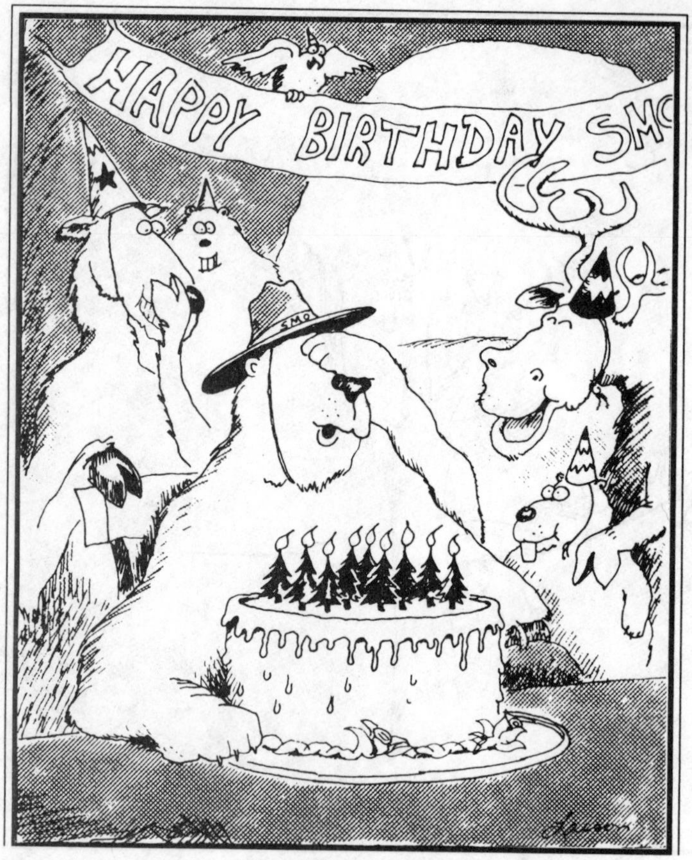
HAPPY BIRTHDAY SMO
SMO

"Can I look now?"

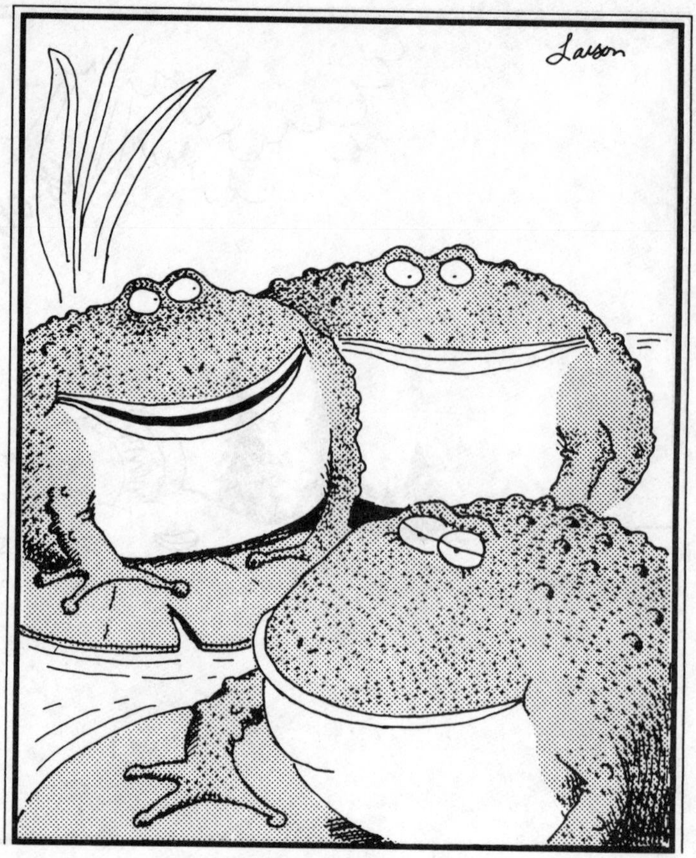

"Vive la difference."

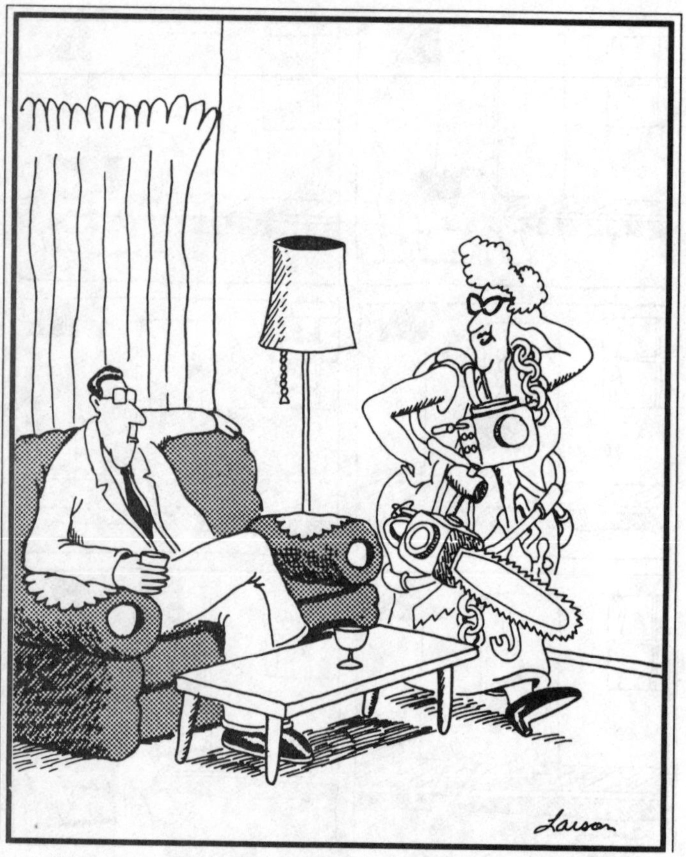

"Excuse me, Harold, while I go slip into something more comfortable."

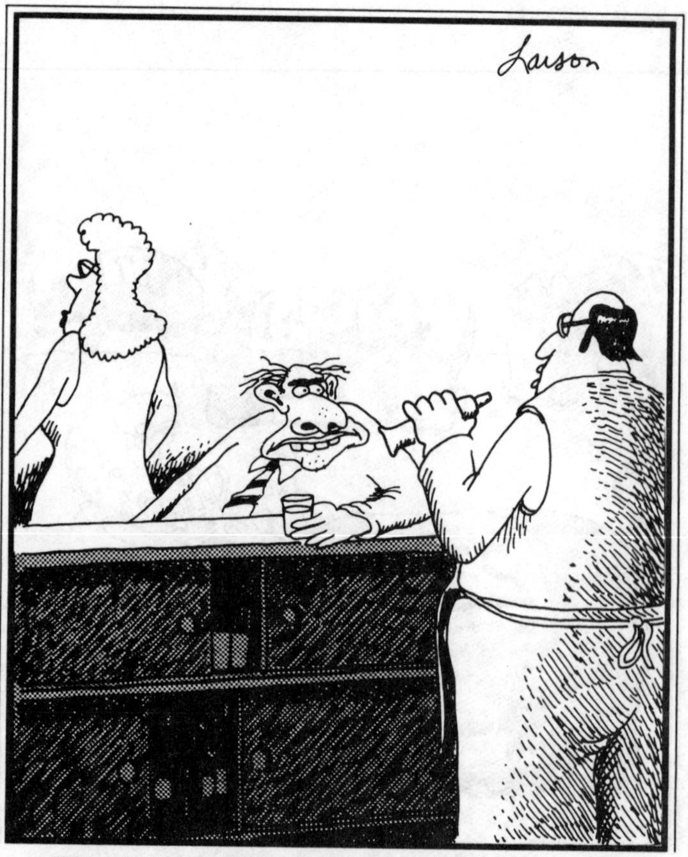

"Rejected again, huh, Murray? . . . Have you heard about this new breath-freshening toothpaste?"

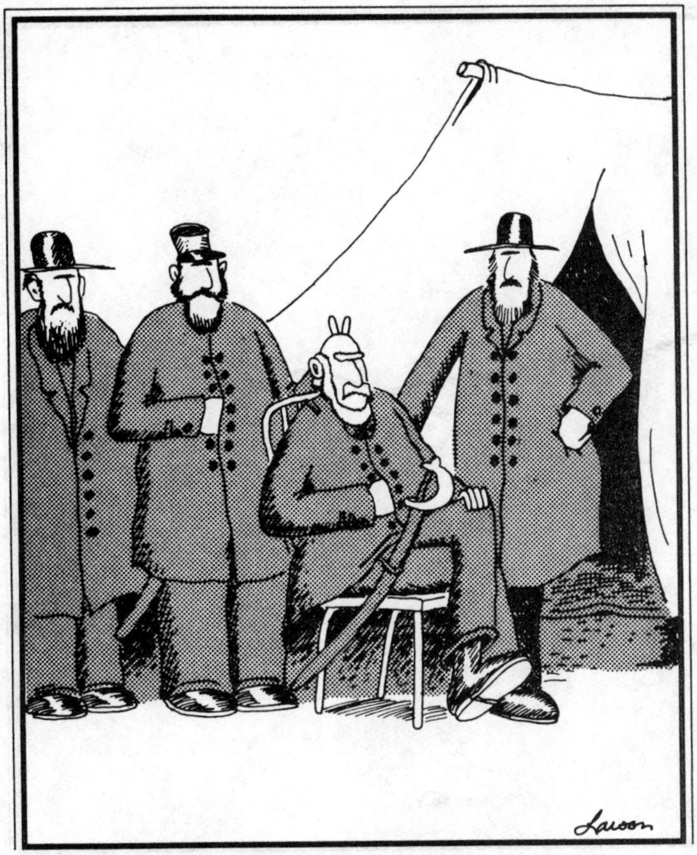
Larson

Near Gettysburg, 1863: A reflective moment.

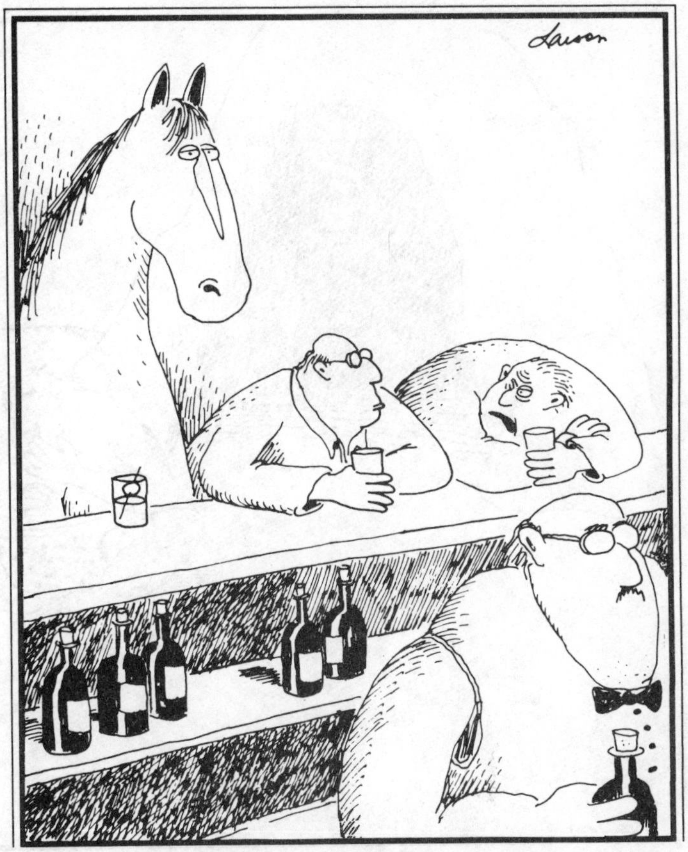
Larson

"Sure — but can you make him drink?"

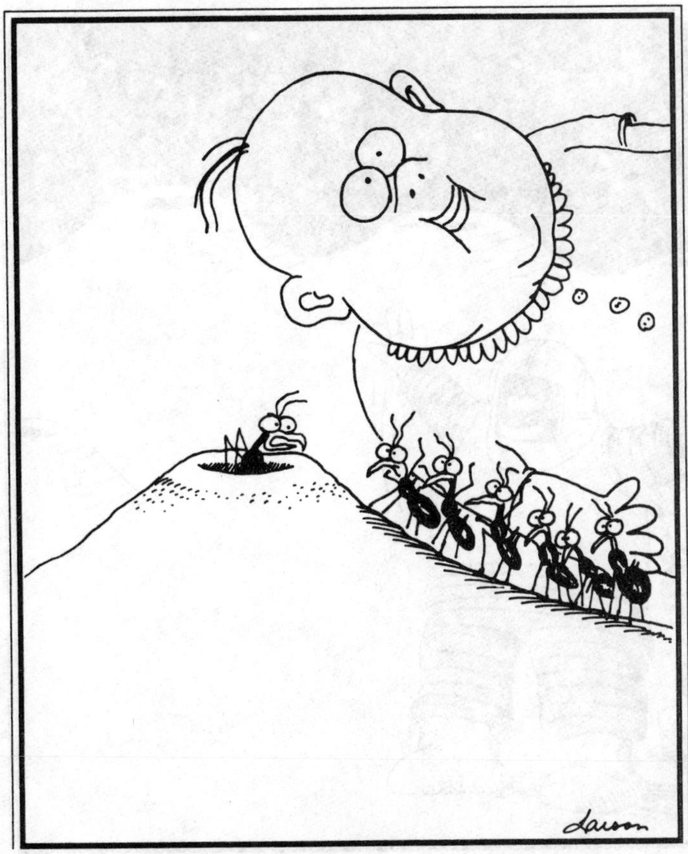
Larson

"You idiots! . . . We'll never get that thing down the hole!"

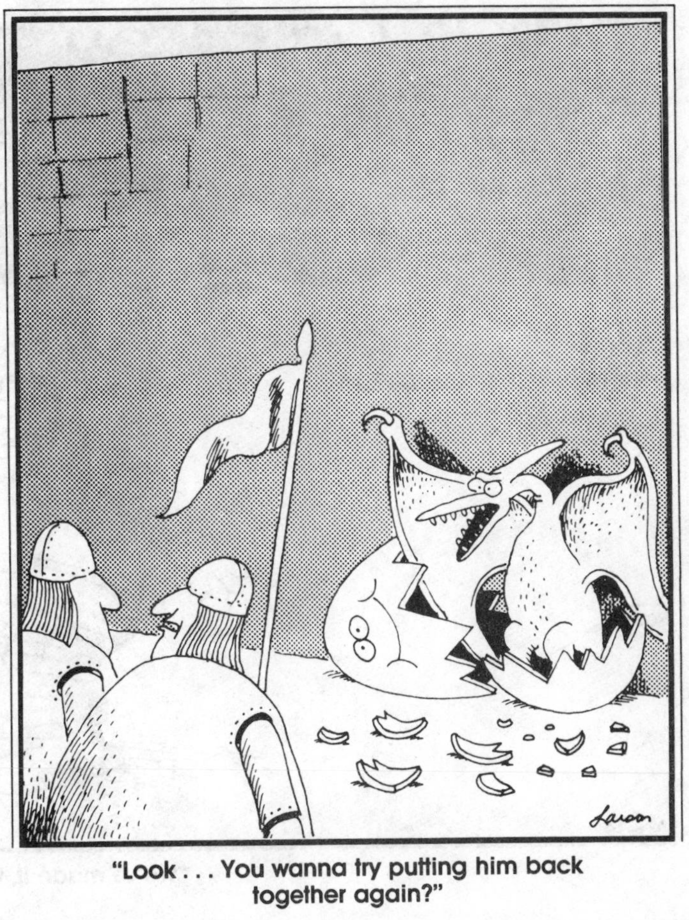
Larson

"Look . . . You wanna try putting him back together again?"

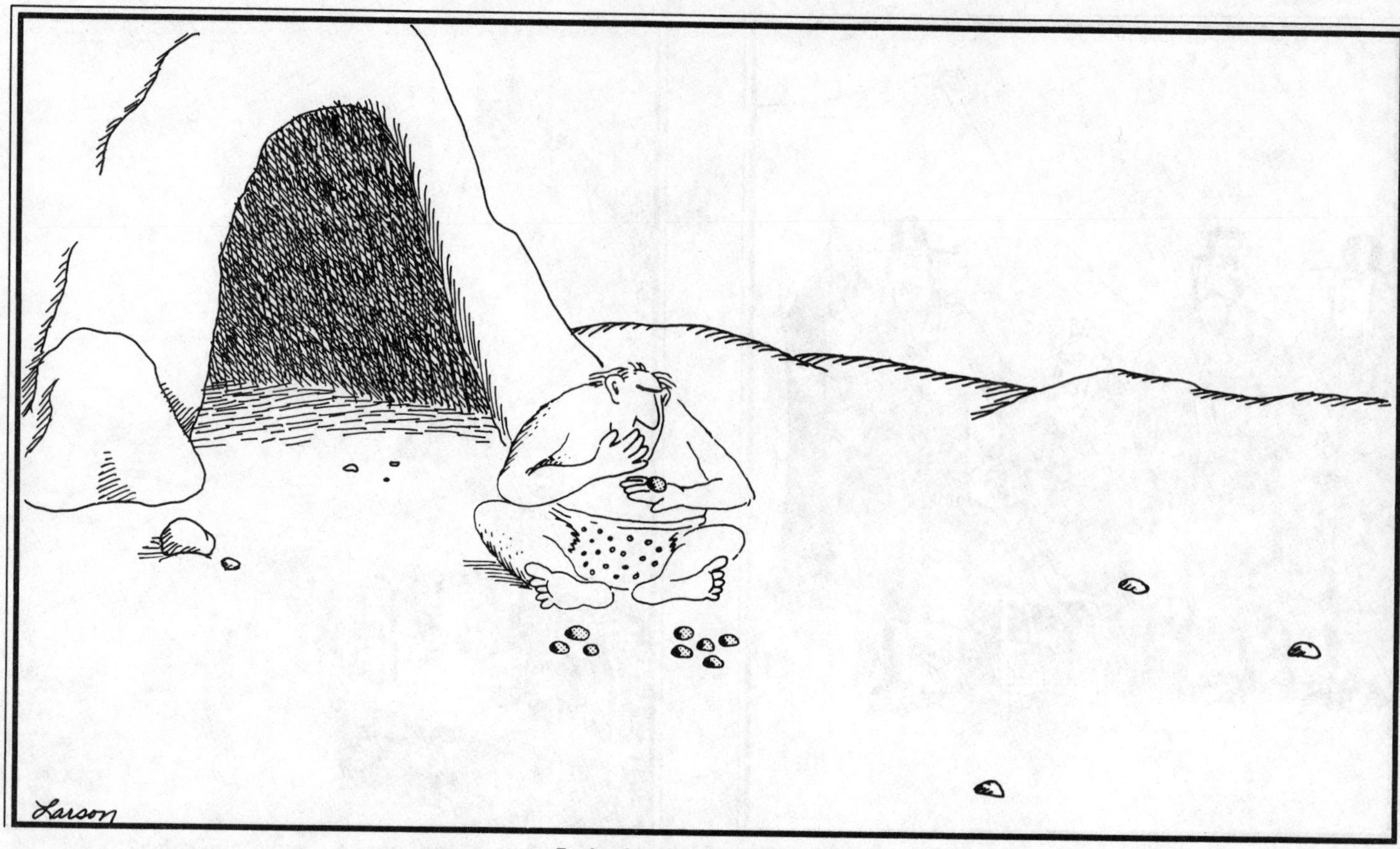
Larson

Early stages of math anxiety

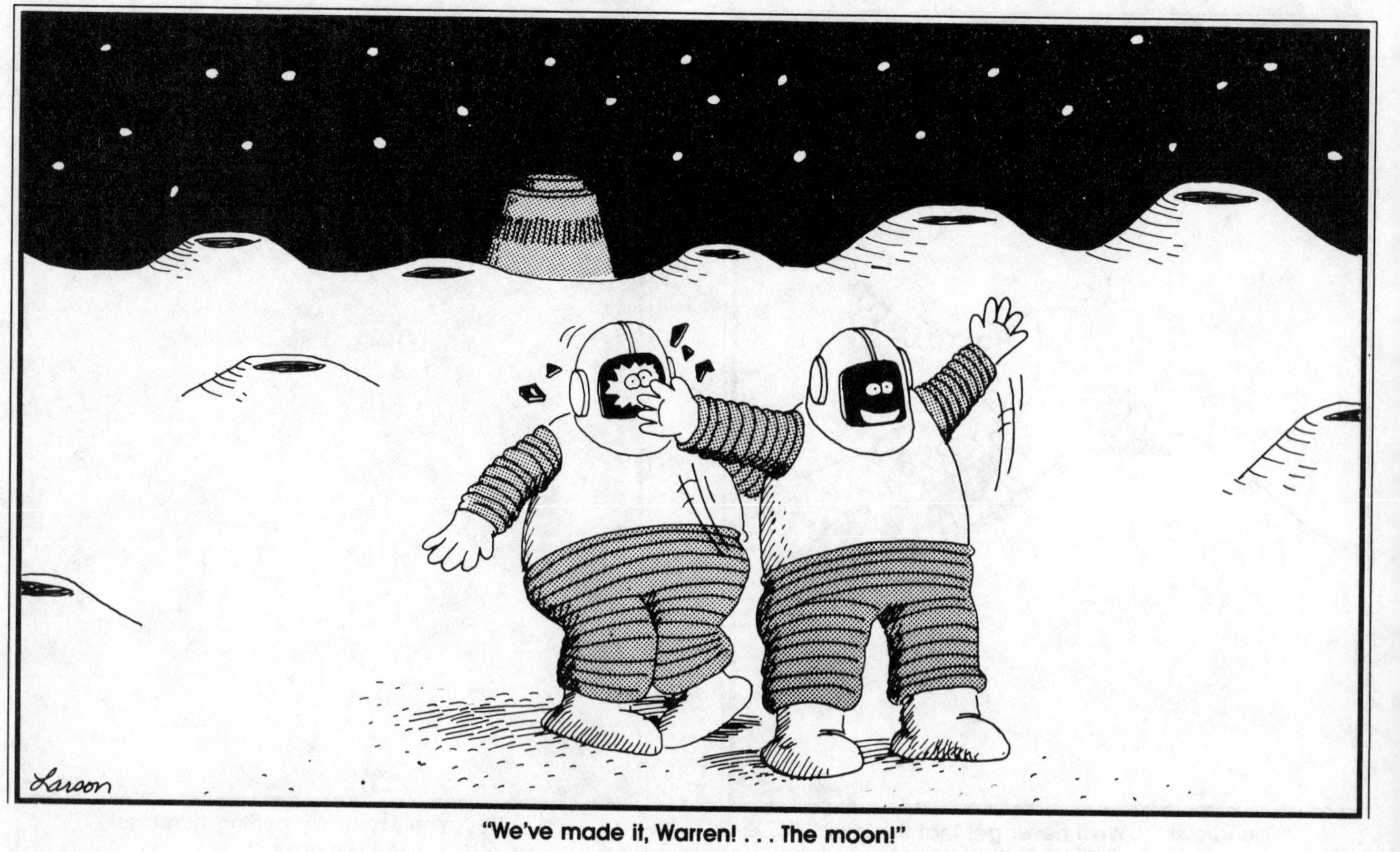
Larson

"We've made it, Warren! . . . The moon!"

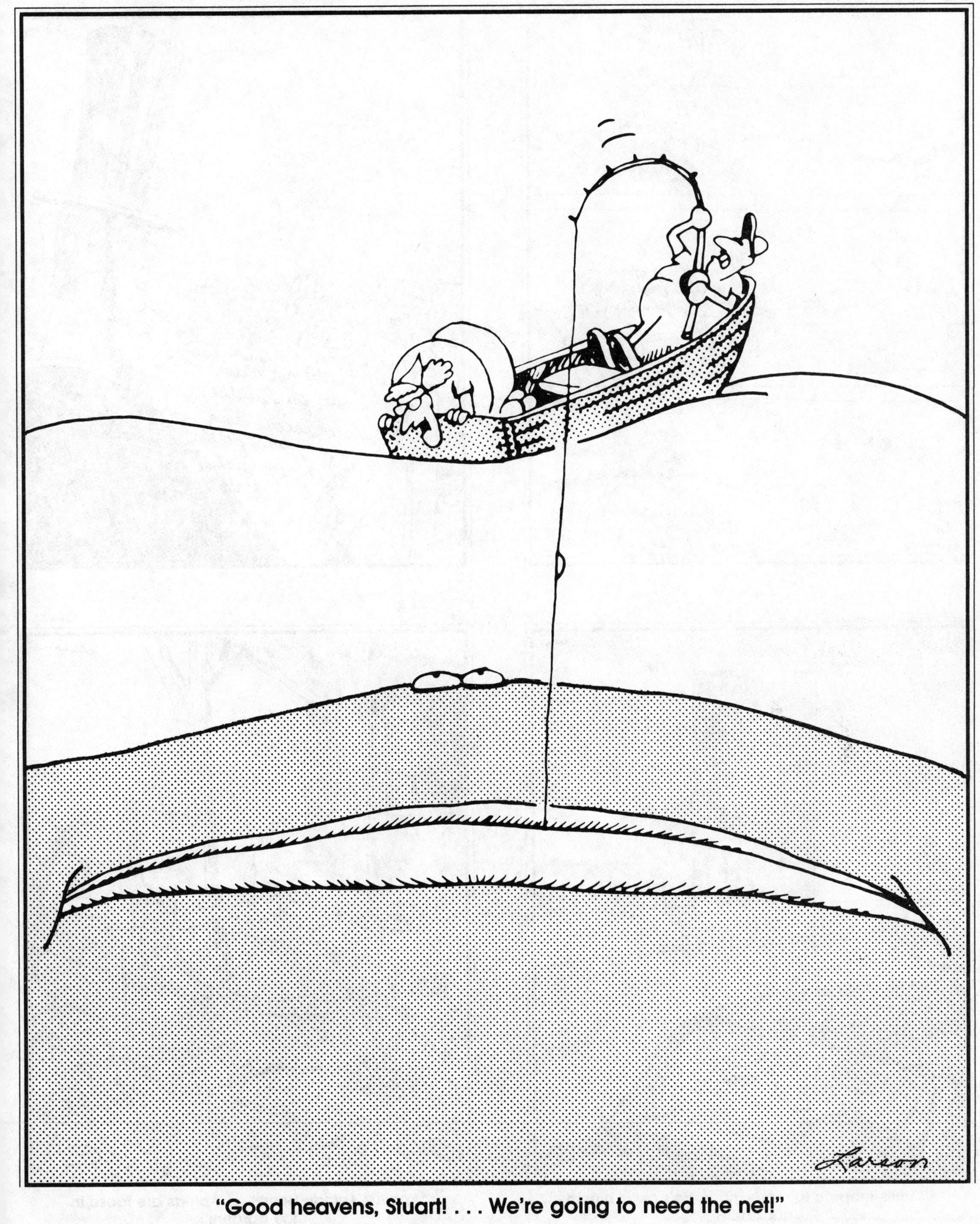
Larson

"Good heavens, Stuart! . . . We're going to need the net!"

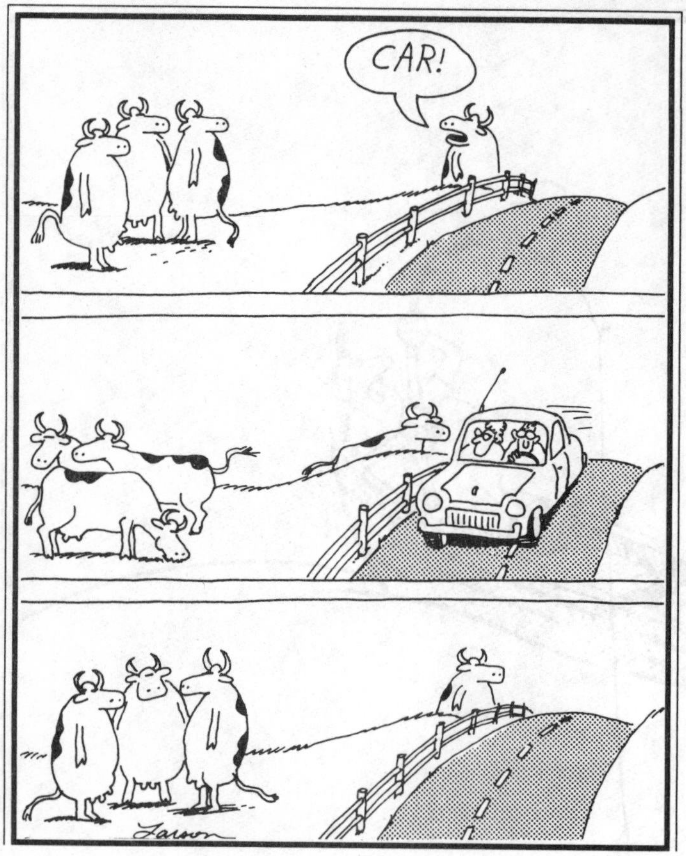
CAR!
Larson

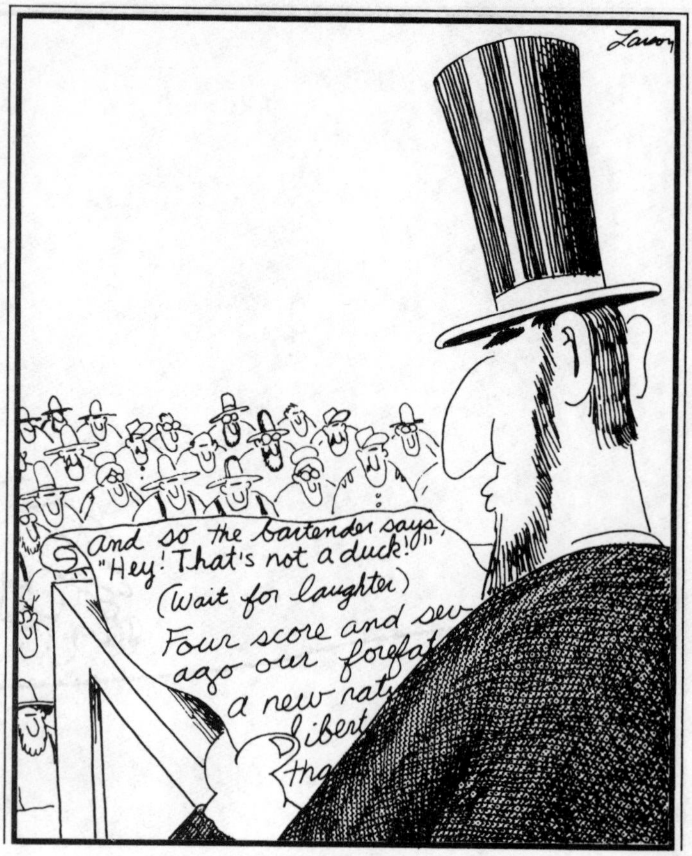
Larson
and so the bartender says
"Hey! That's not a duck!"
(Wait for laughter)
Four score and sev
ago our forefat
a new nat
Libert
tha

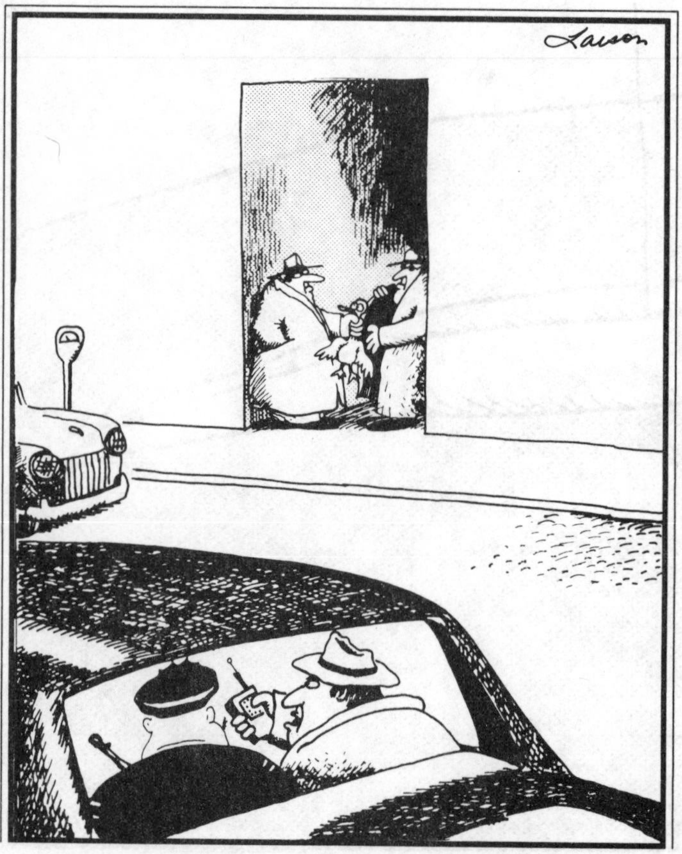
Larson

"All units prepare to move in! . . . He's givin' him the duck now!"

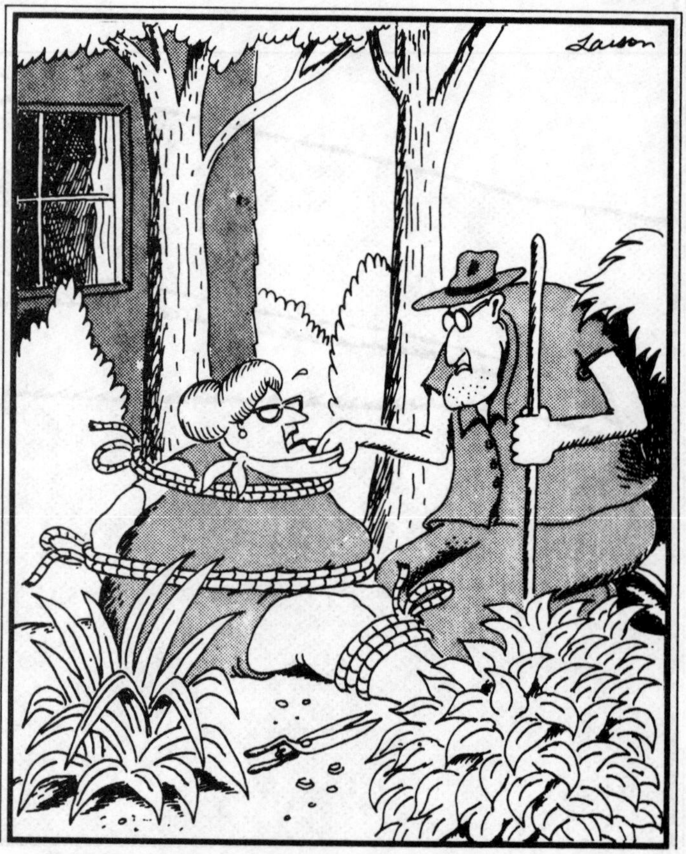
Larson

"Aphids! Aphids, Henry! . . . Aphids are loose in the garden!"

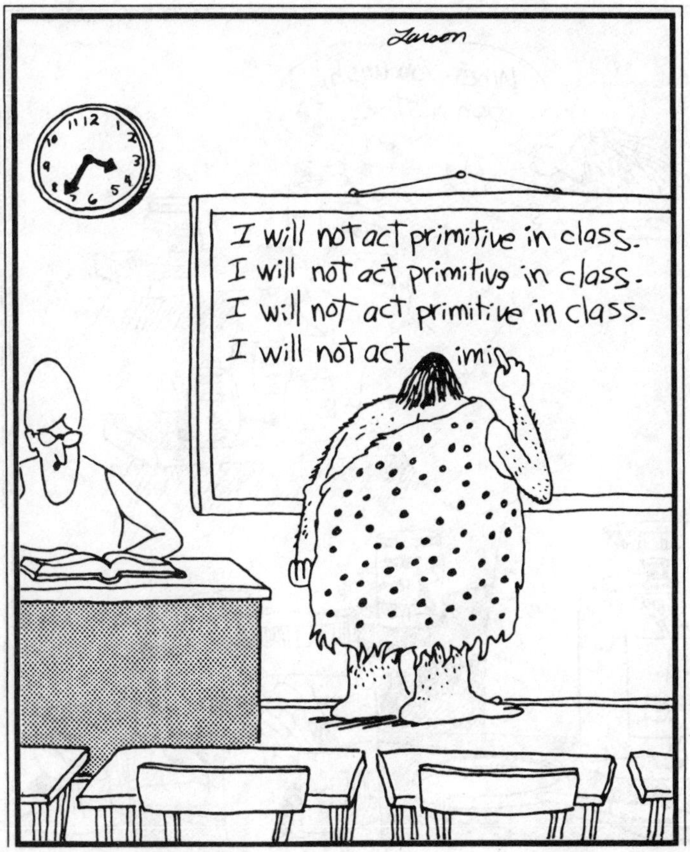
Larson
I will not act primitive in class.
I will not act primitive in class.
I will not act primitive in class.
I will not act imi

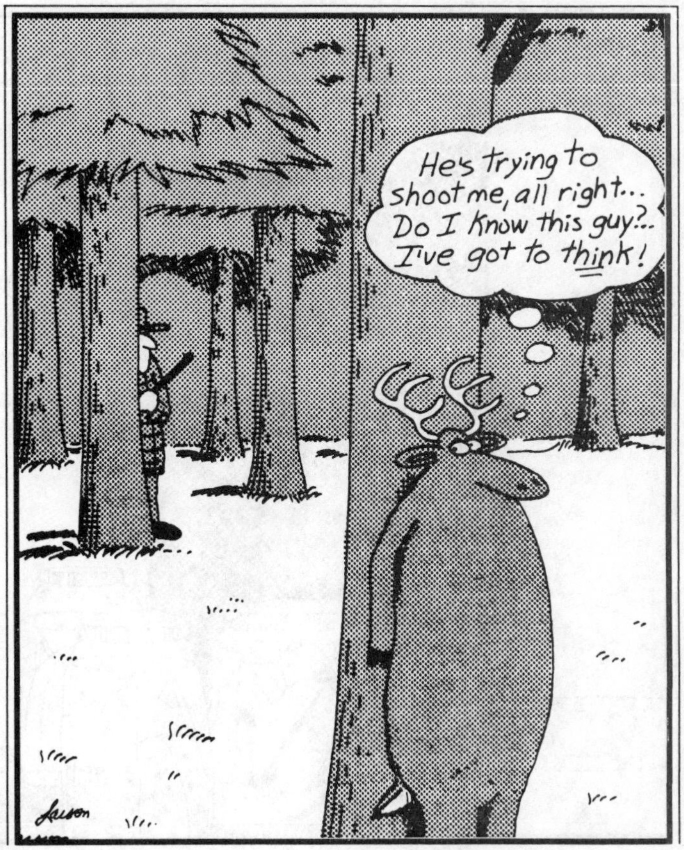
He's trying to shoot me, all right... Do I know this guy?.. I've got to think!
Larson

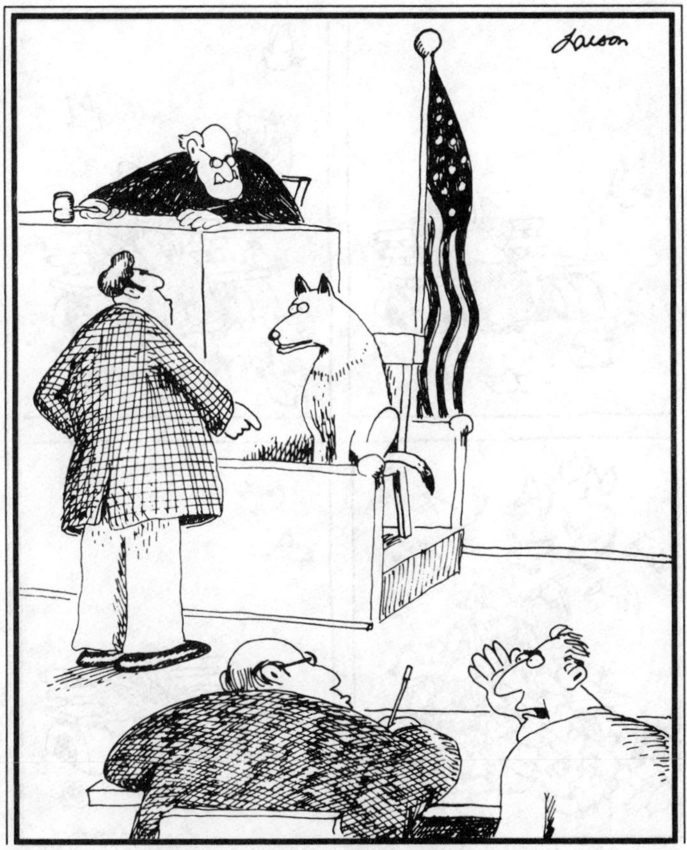
Larson

"I could have guessed . . . my friends all warned me that this breed will sometimes turn on you."

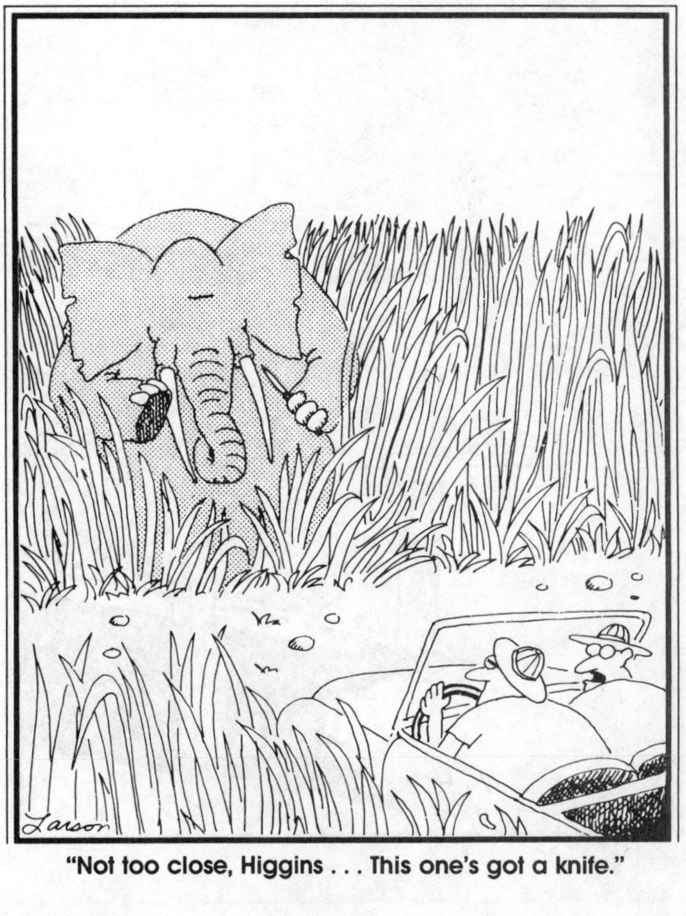
Larson

"Not too close, Higgins . . . This one's got a knife."

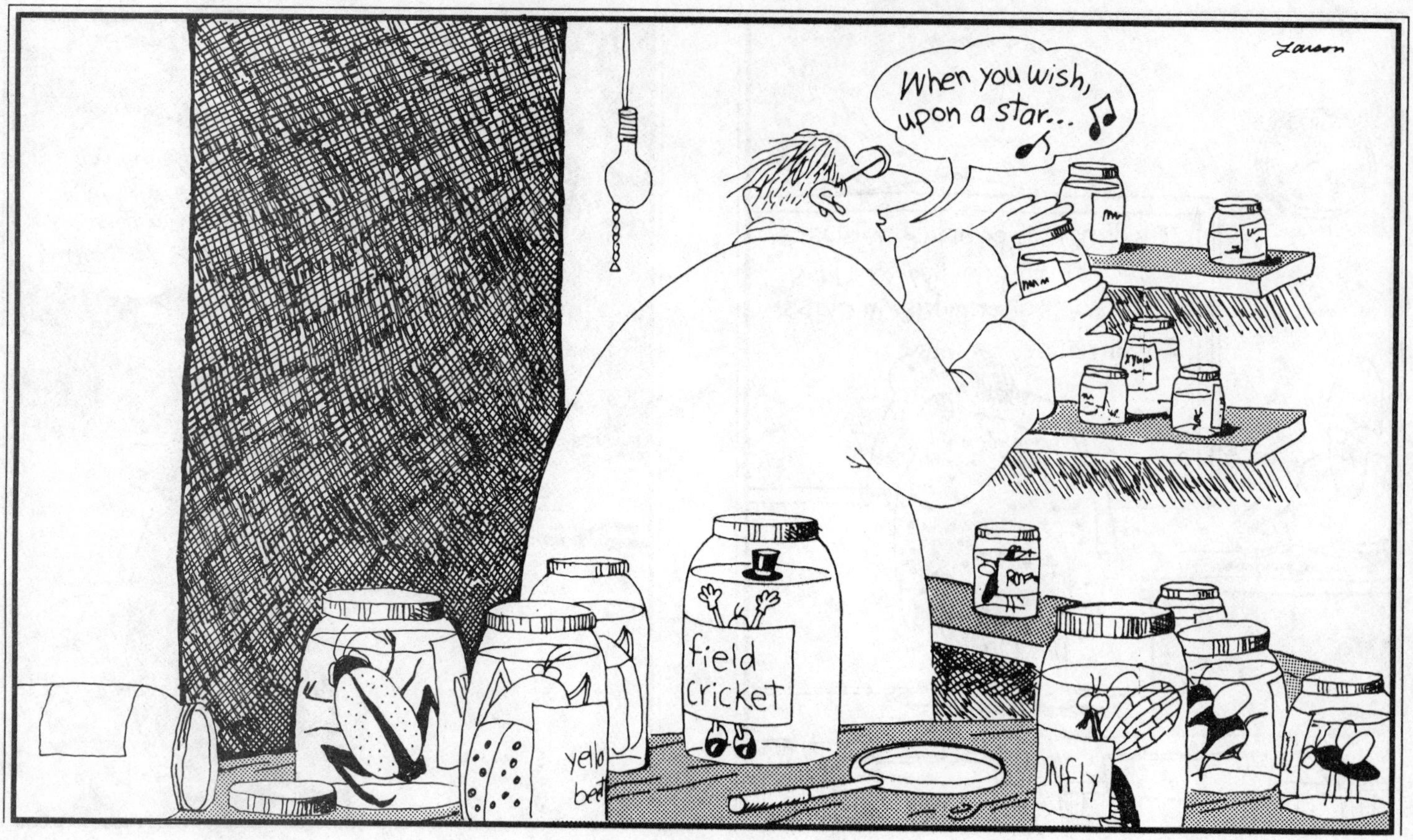
Larson
When you wish, upon a star...
field Cricket
yello bee
ONfly

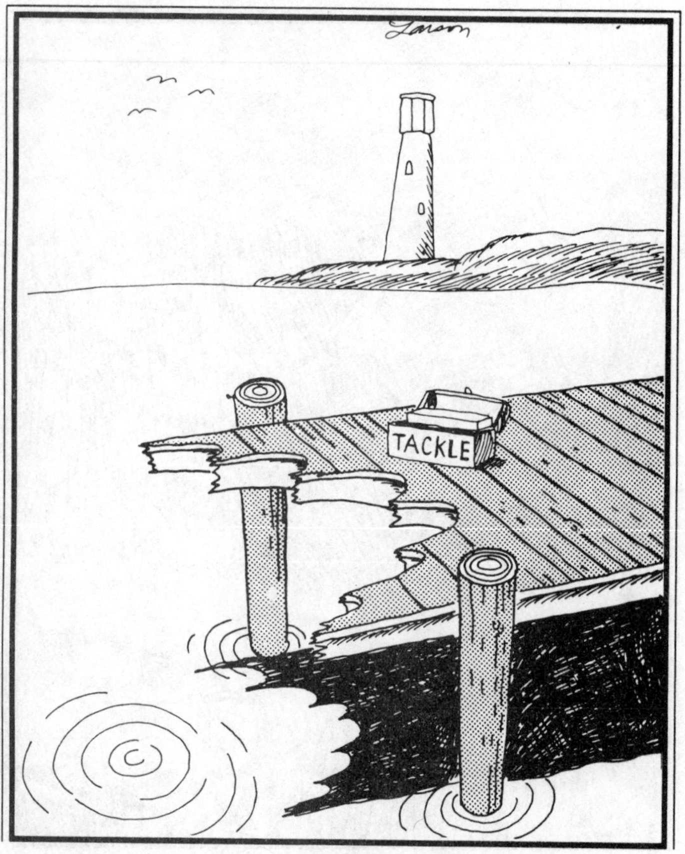
Larson
TACKLE

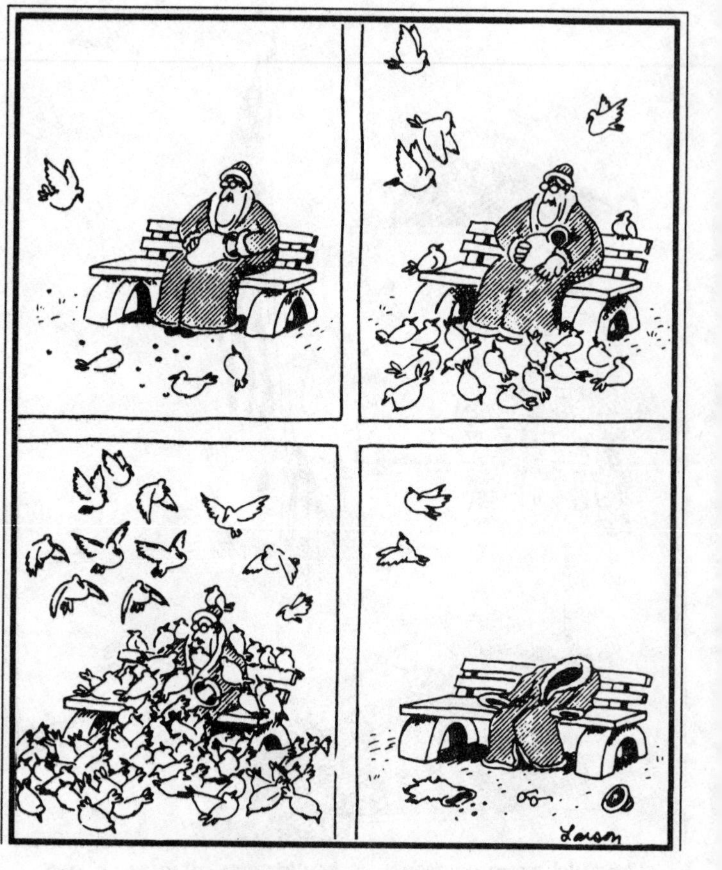
Larson

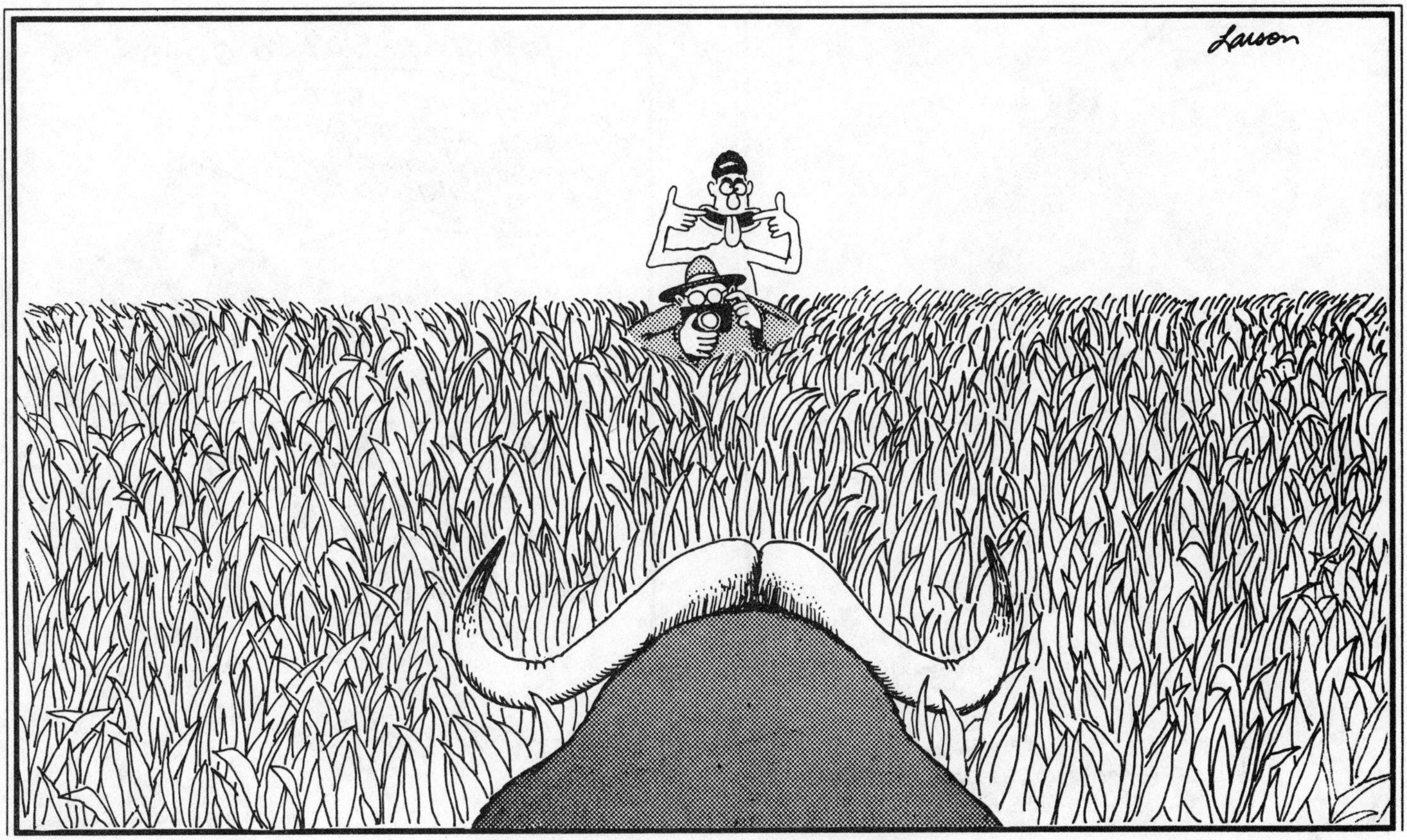
Larson

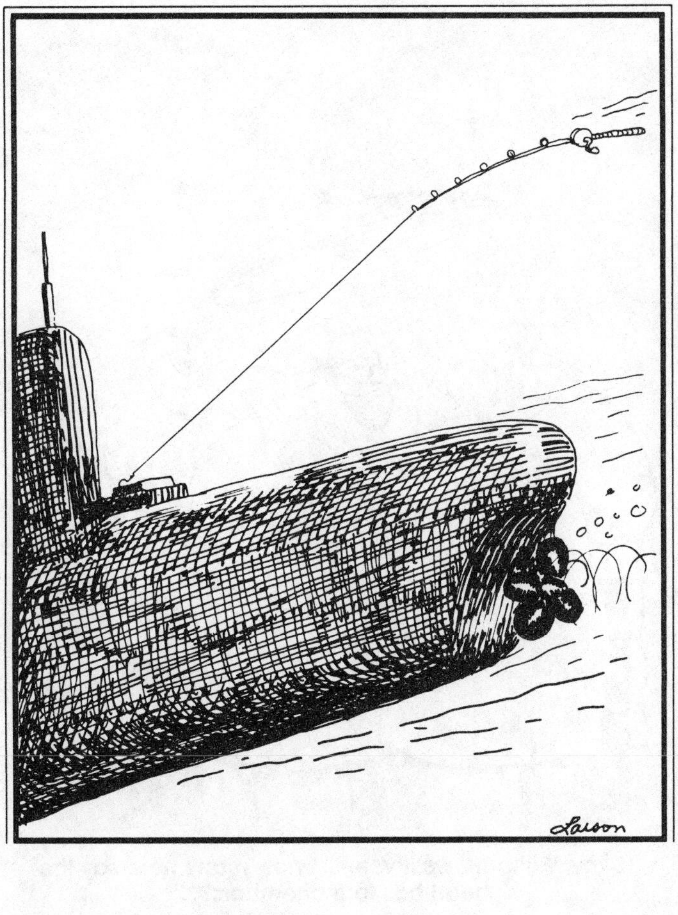
Larson

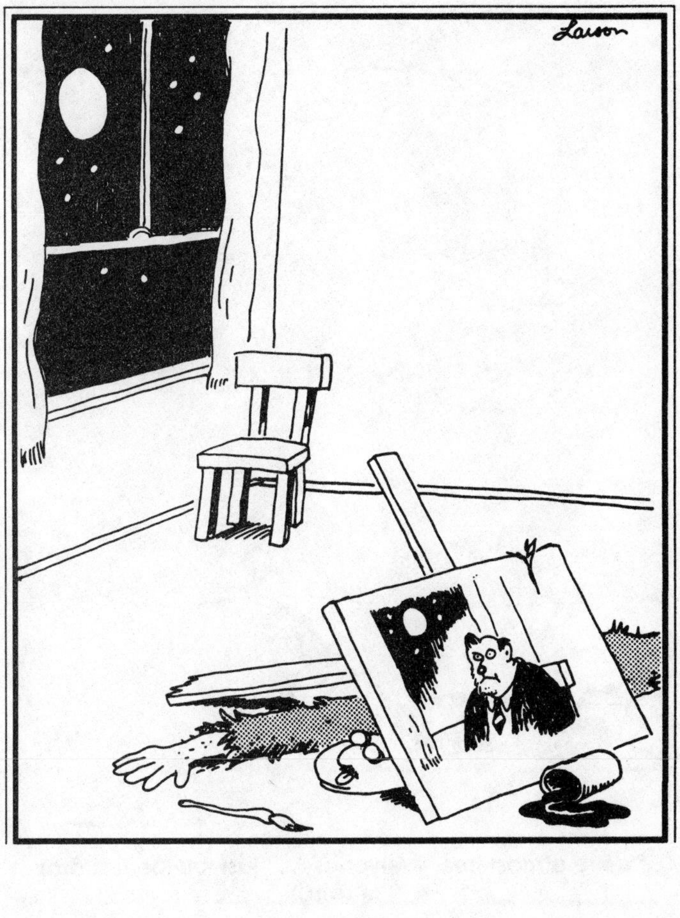
Larson

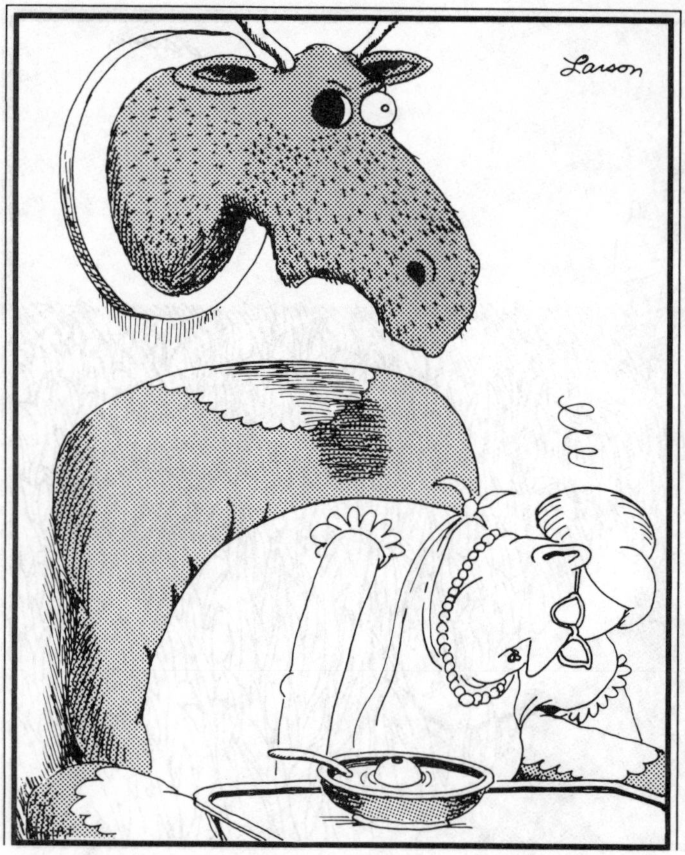

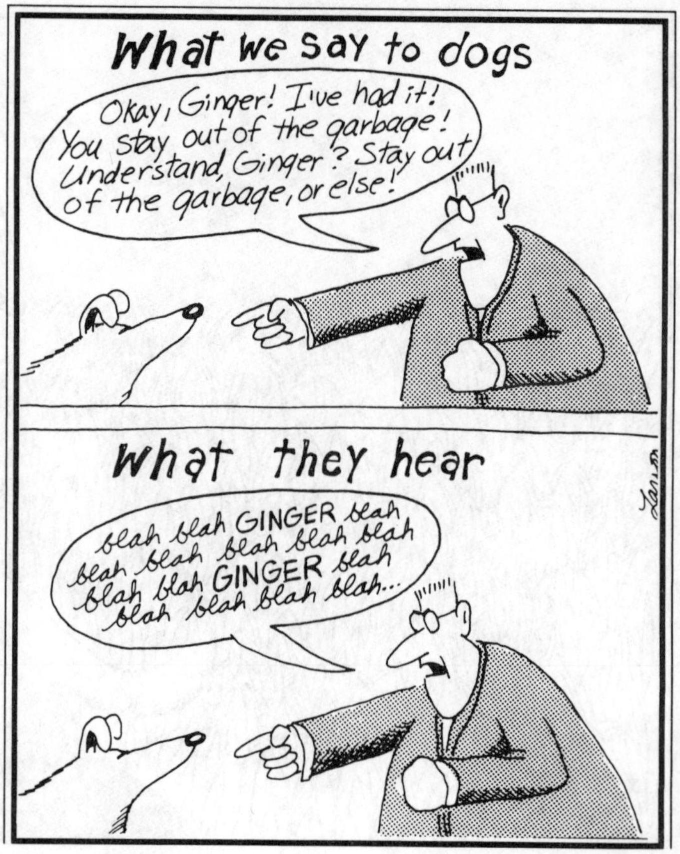
What we say to dogs
Okay, Ginger! I've had it! You stay out of the garbage! Understand, Ginger? Stay out of the garbage, or else!
What they hear
blah blah GINGER blah blah blah blah blah blah blah blah GINGER blah blah blah blah blah...

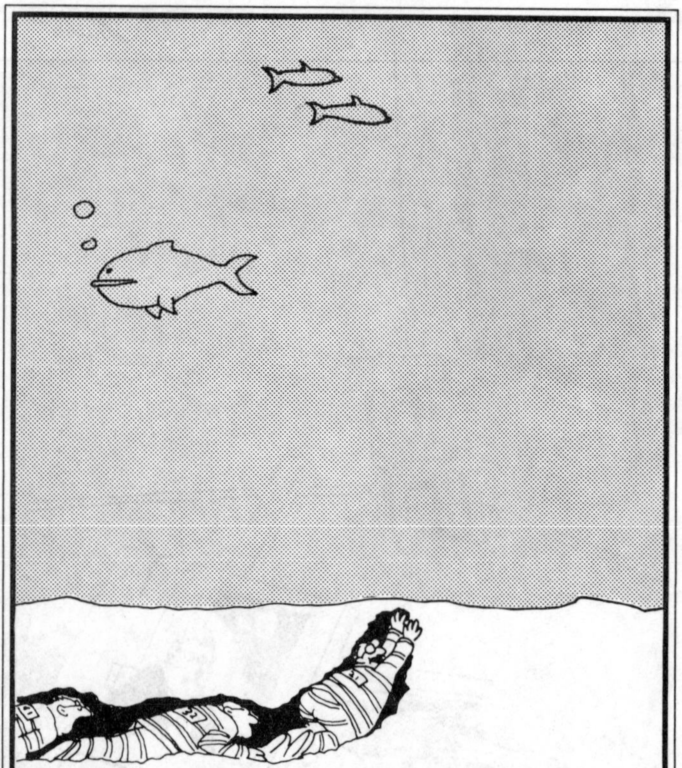

"We're almost free, everyone! . . . I just felt the first drop of rain."

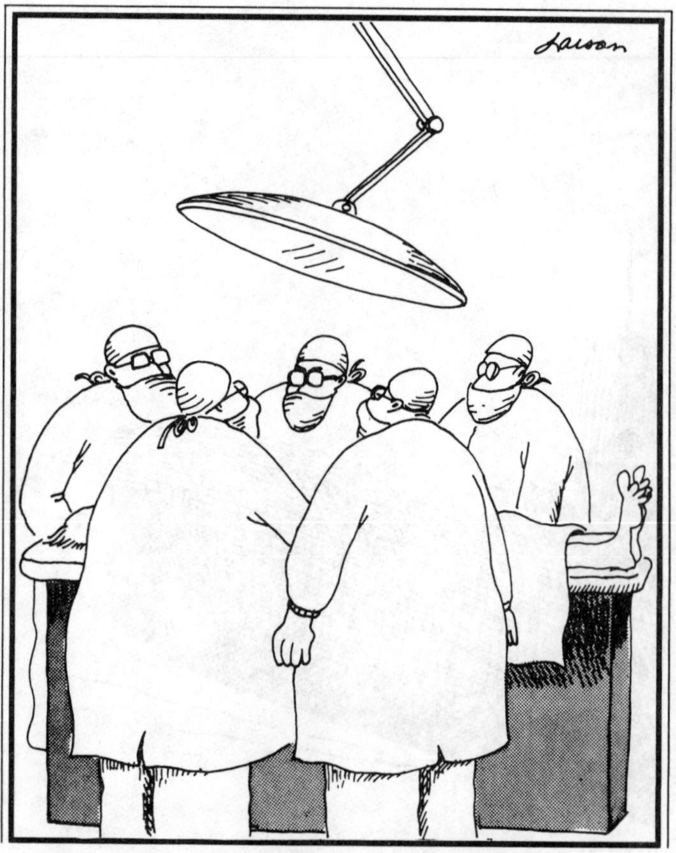

"Okay, Williams, we'll vote . . . how many here say the heart has four chambers?"

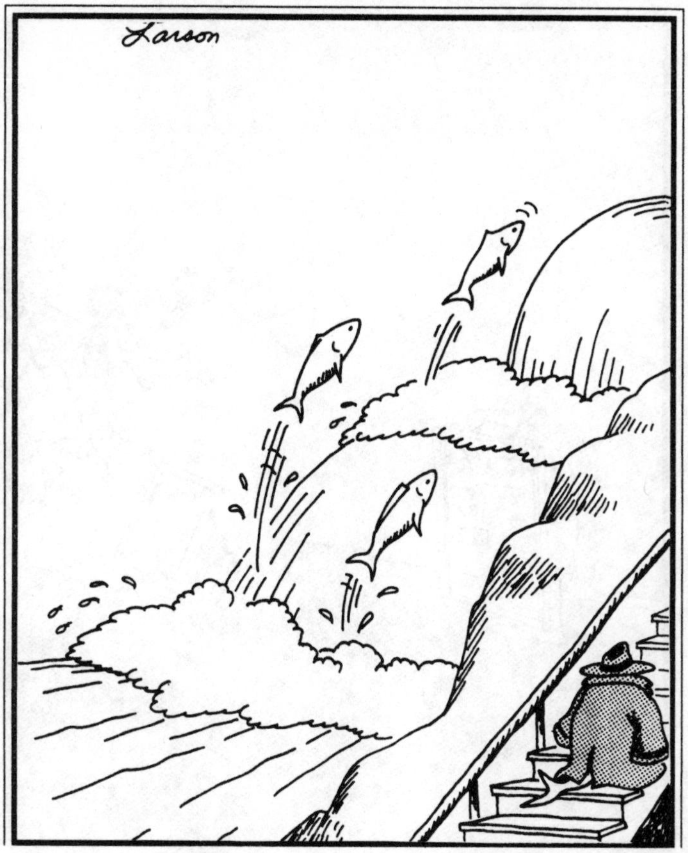
Larson

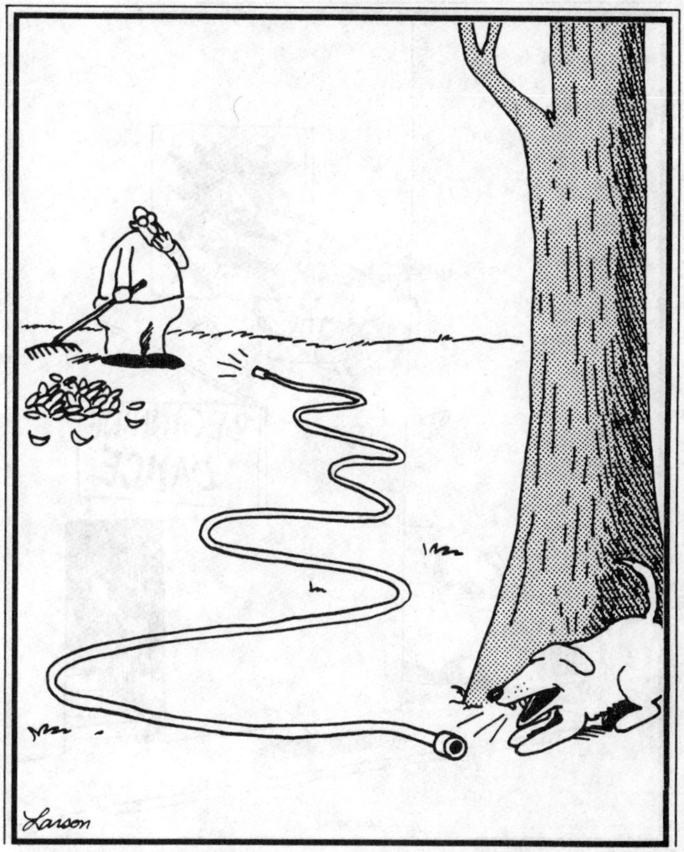
Larson

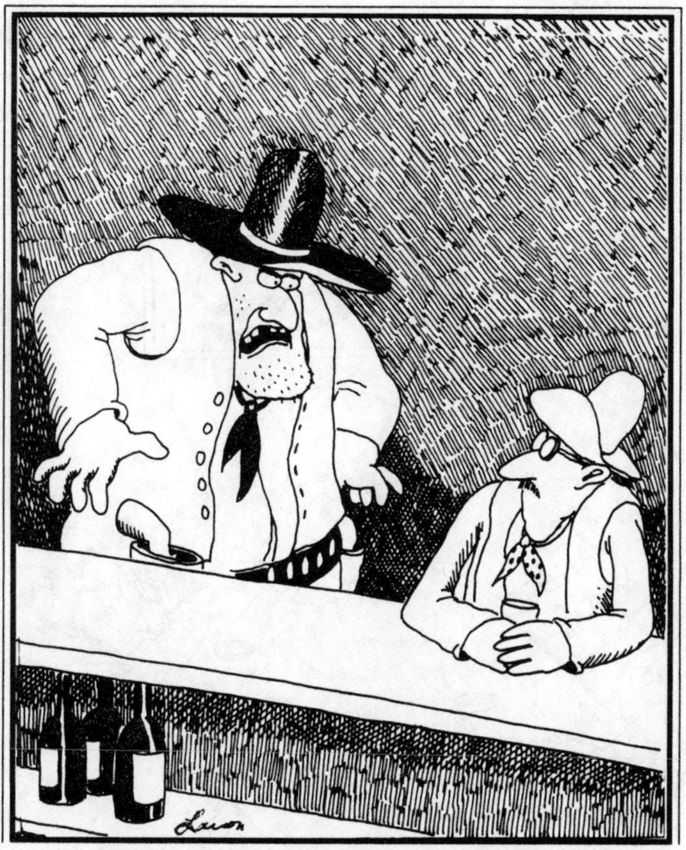
Larson

"I asked you a question, buddy . . . What's the square root of 5,248?"

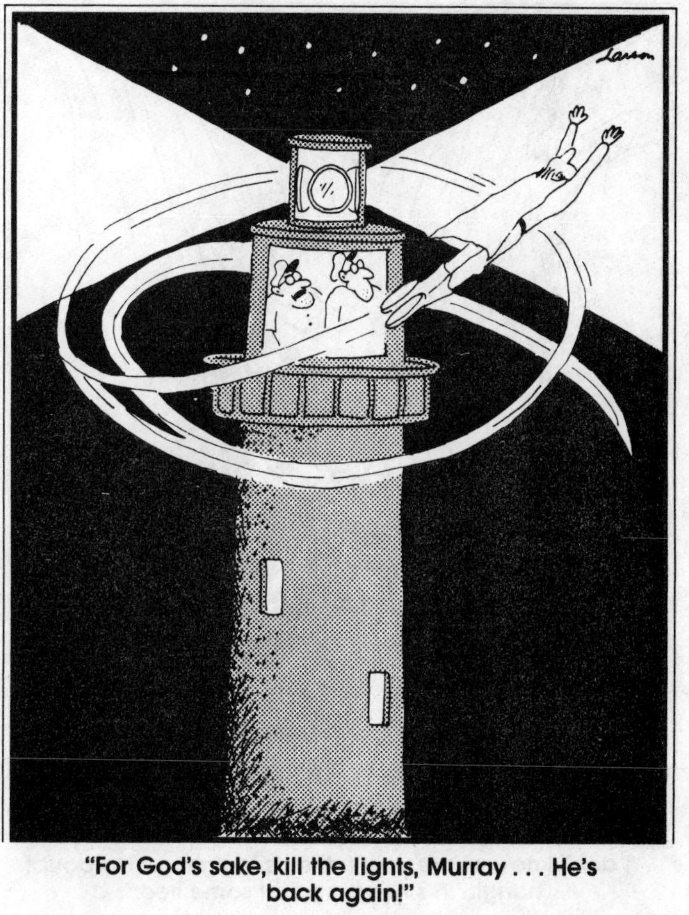
Larson

"For God's sake, kill the lights, Murray . . . He's back again!"

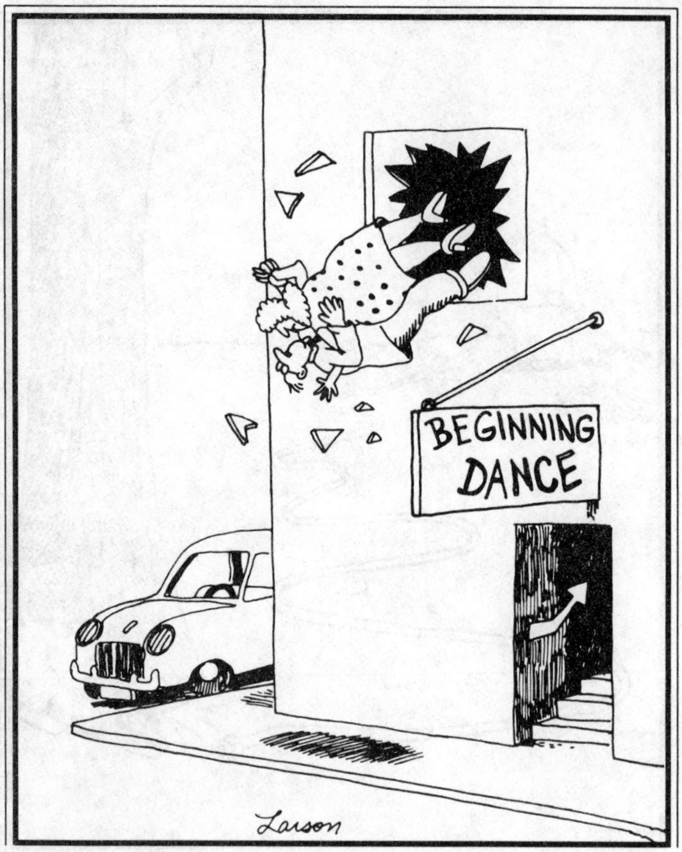
BEGINNING
DANCE
Larson

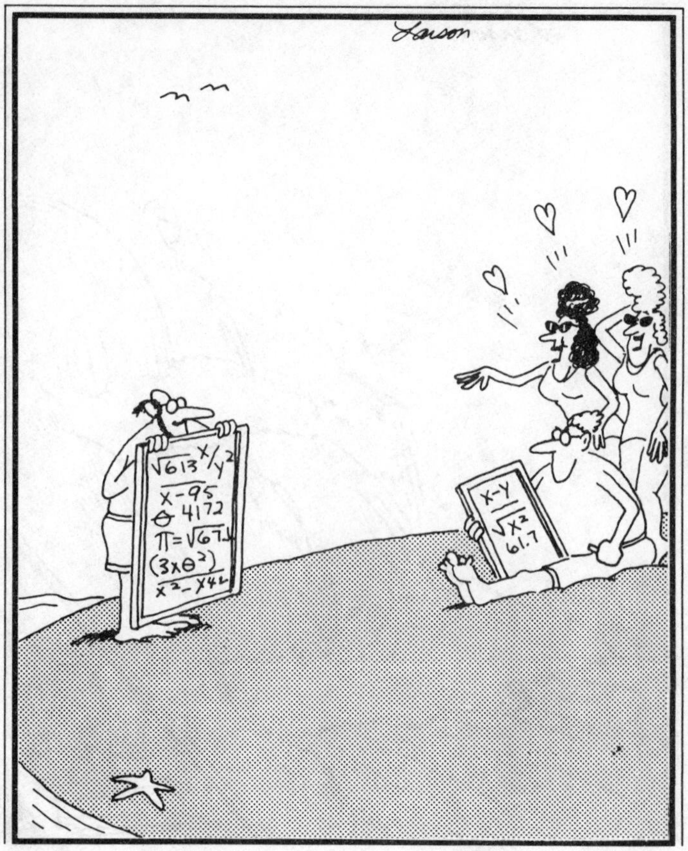
Larson

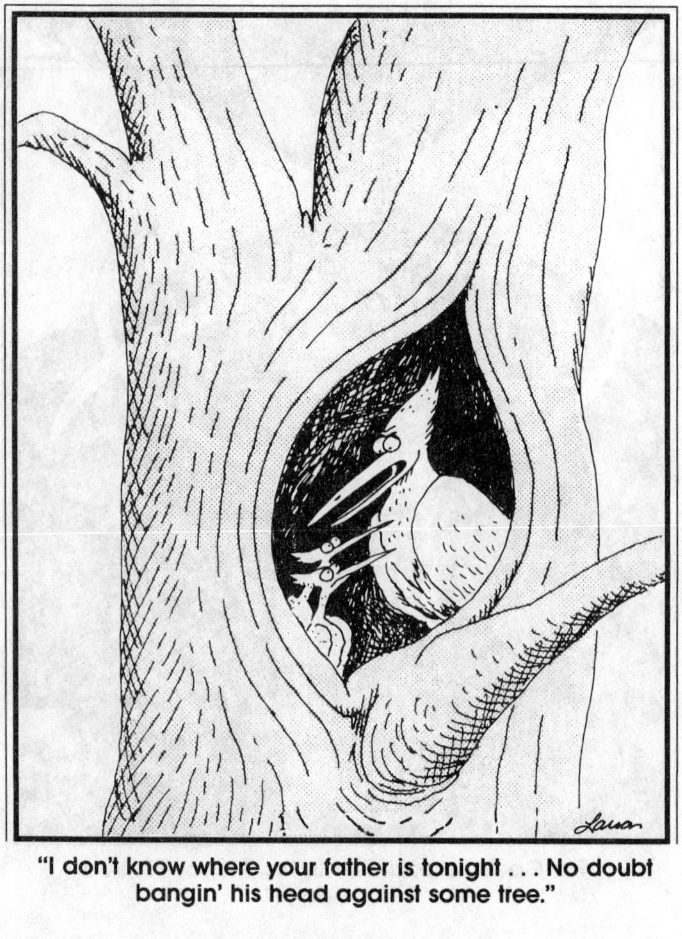
Larson

"I don't know where your father is tonight . . . No doubt bangin' his head against some tree."

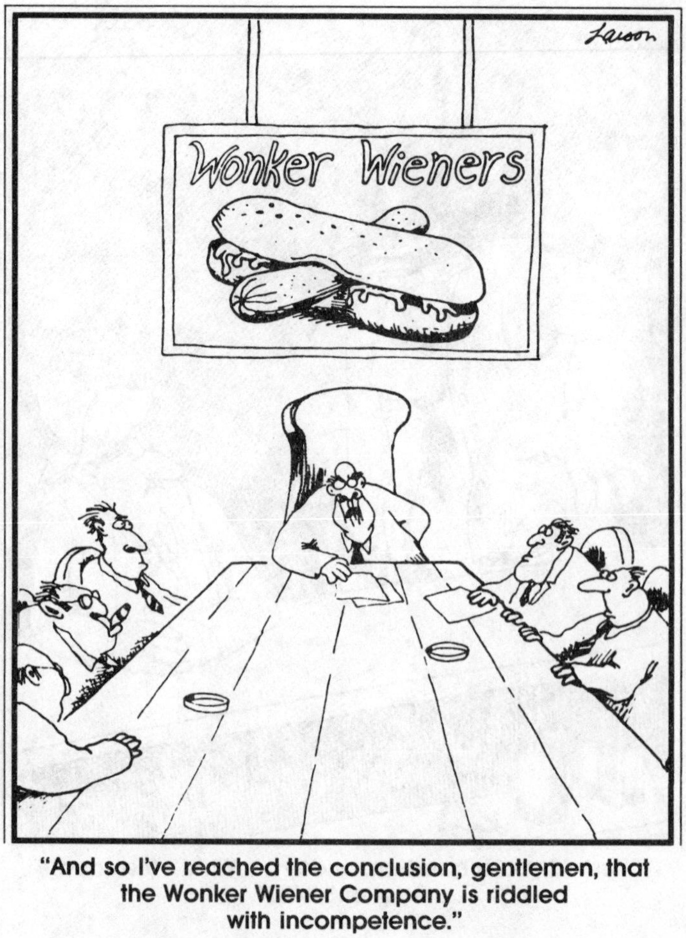
Larson
Wonker Wieners

"And so I've reached the conclusion, gentlemen, that the Wonker Wiener Company is riddled with incompetence."

U.S. MAIL
Larson

What to do today... what to do...
Larson

Larson

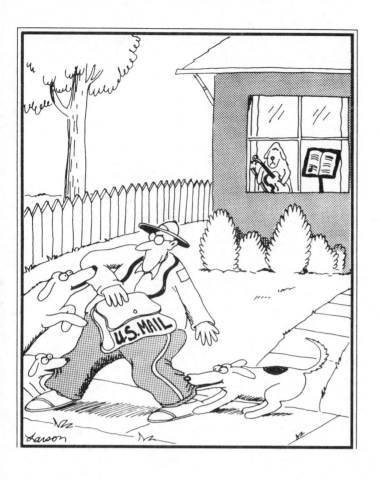

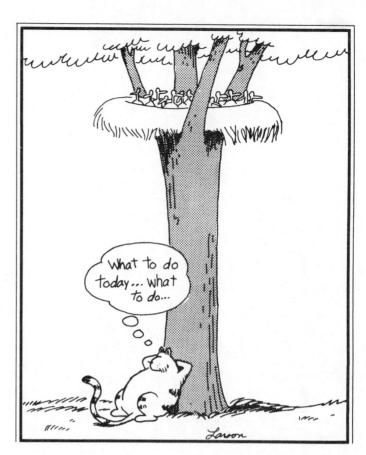

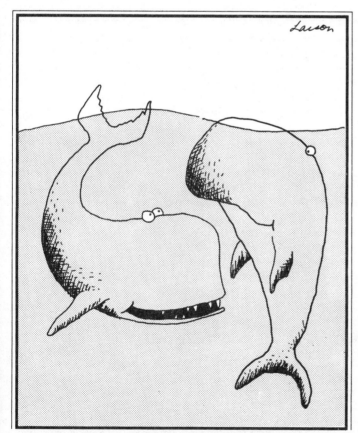

"I don't know . . . how many college students do you think you could eat at one time?"

Larson

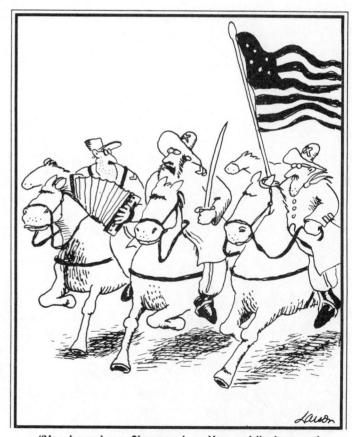

"You heard me, Simmons! . . . You get that cursed bugle fixed!"

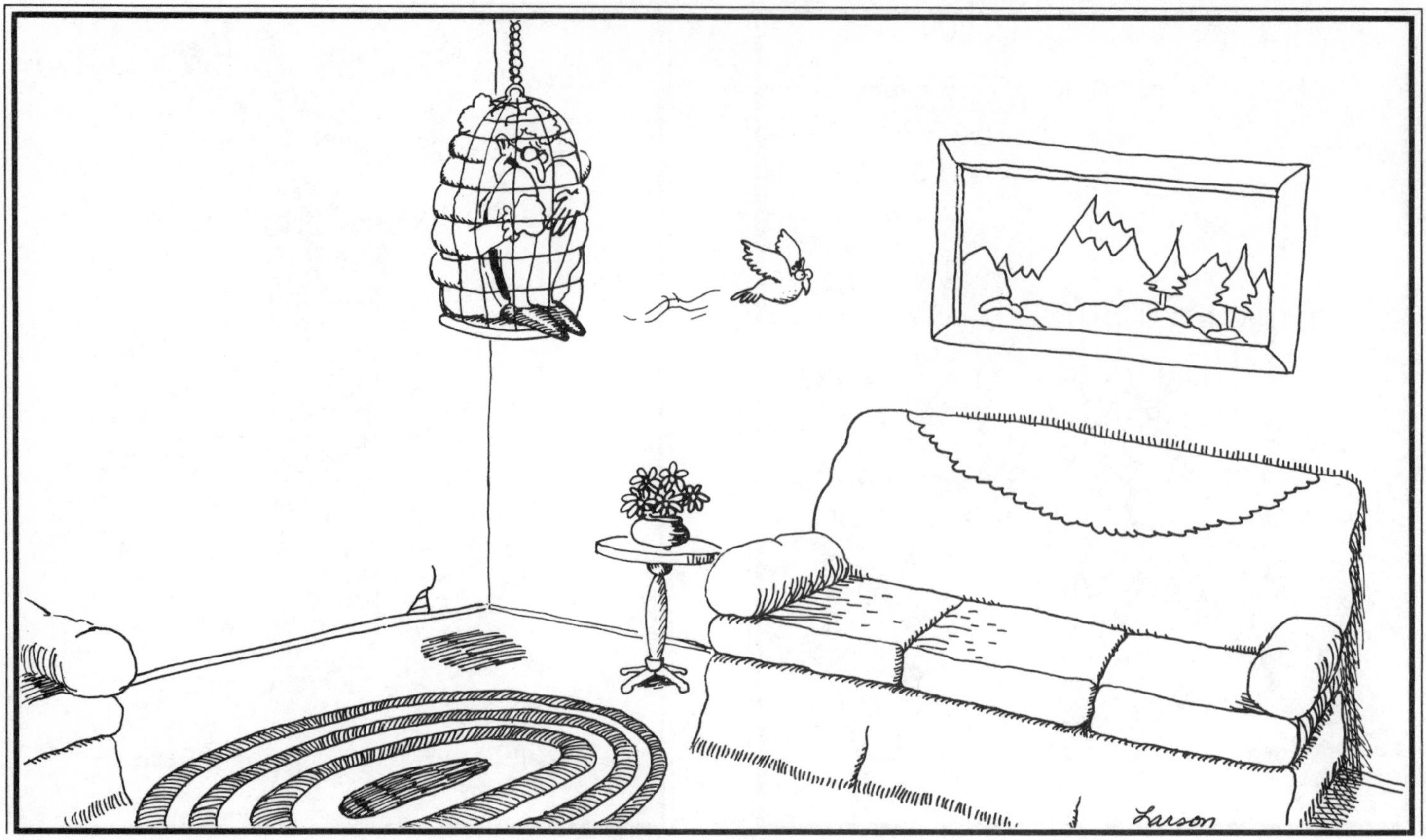
Larson

"You'll never get away with this!"

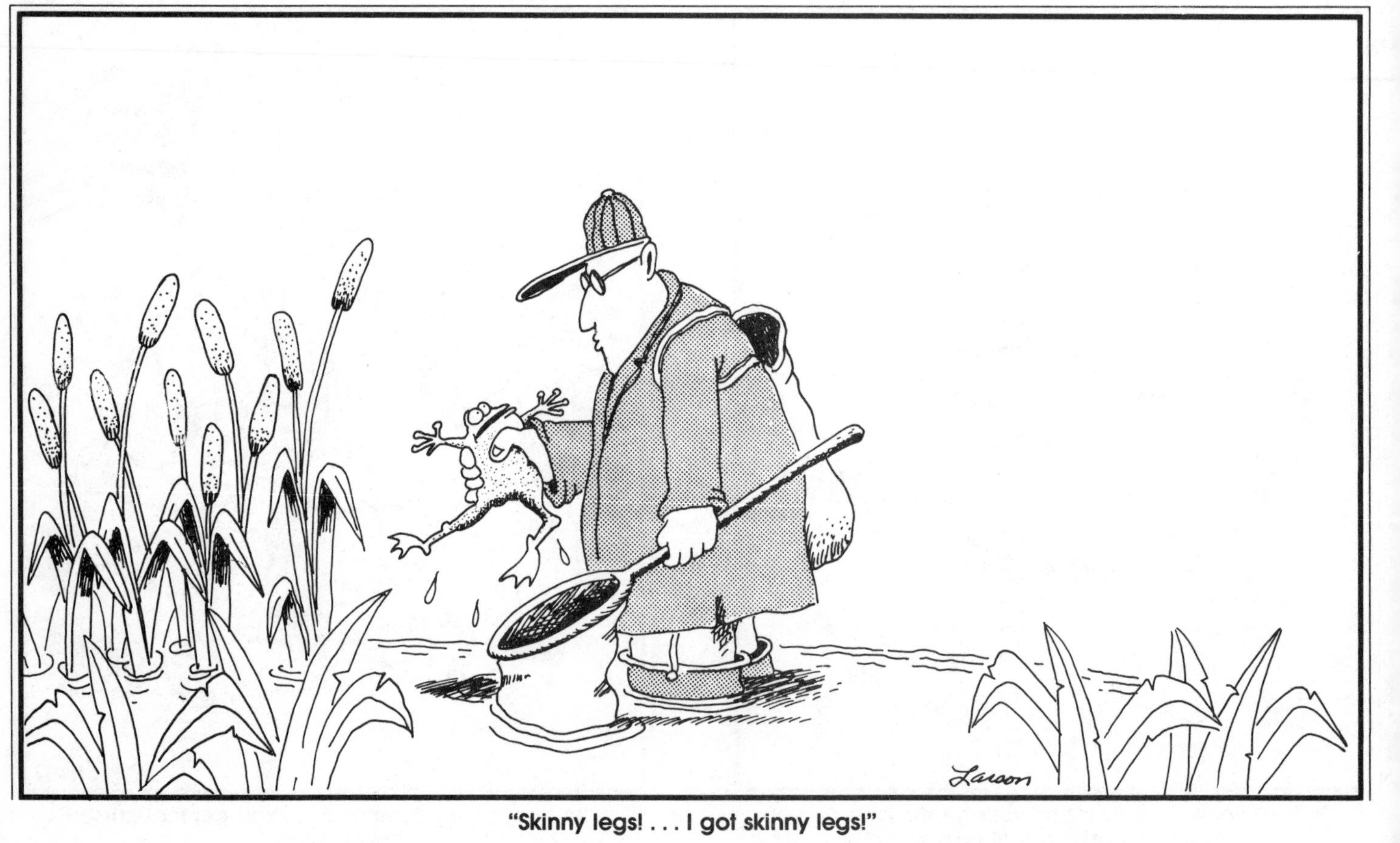
Larson

"Skinny legs! . . . I got skinny legs!"

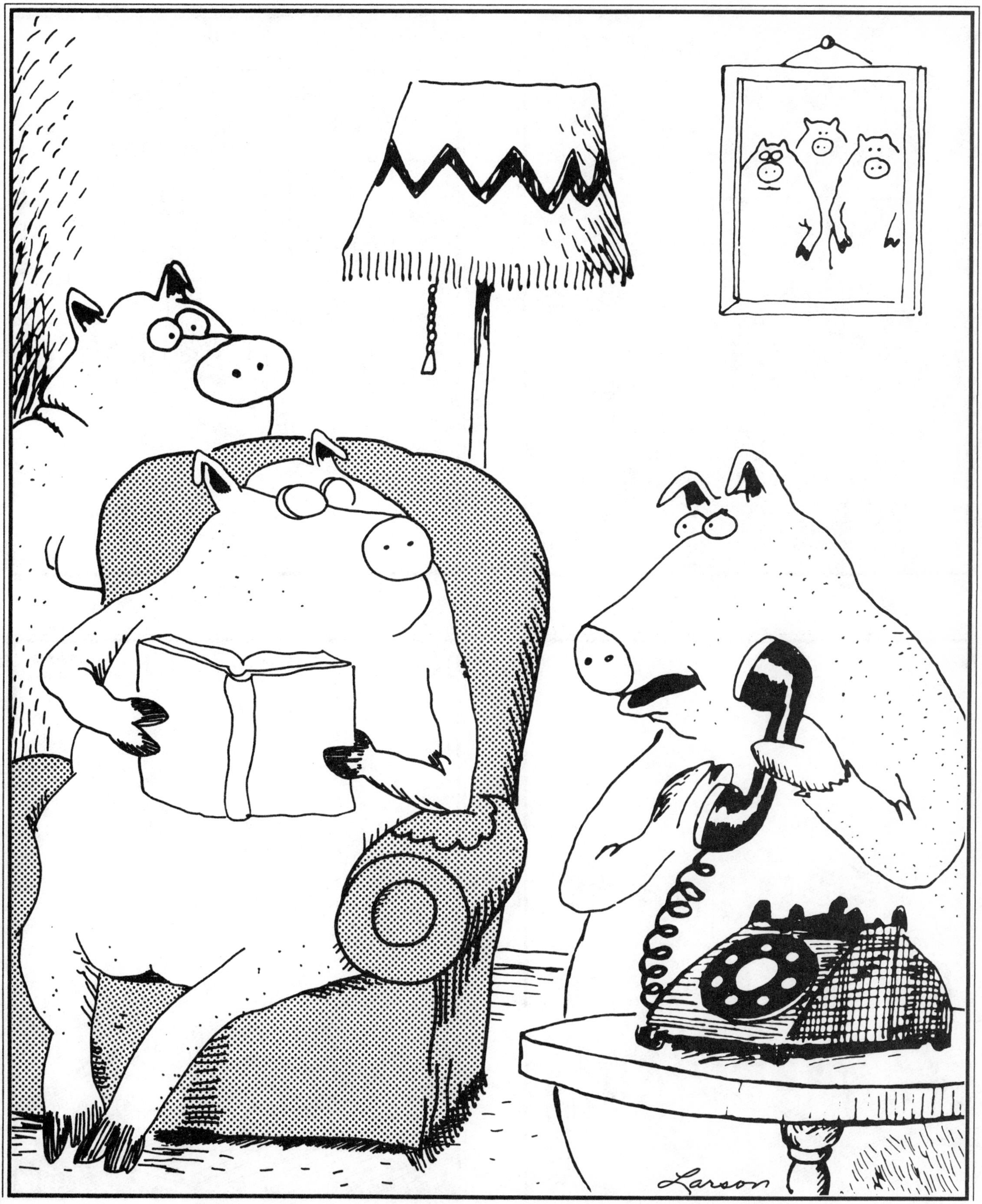
Larson

"Disgusting . . . It's just a sort of heavy huffing and puffing."

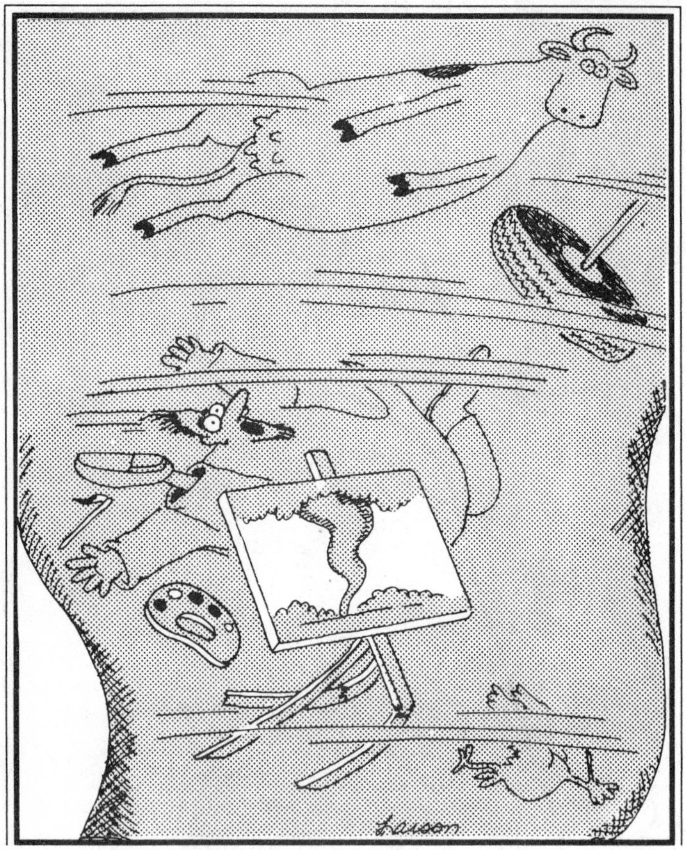

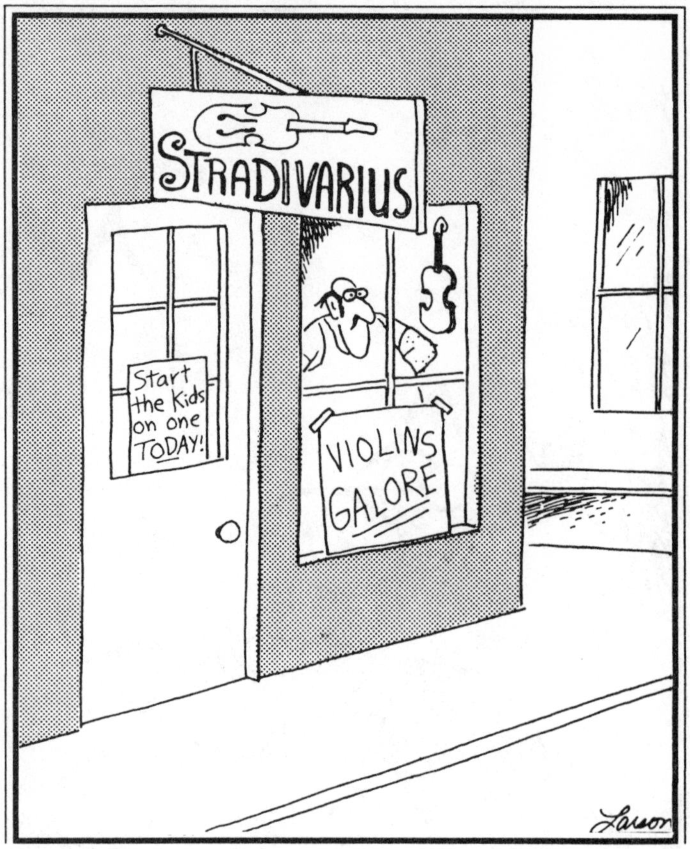
STRADIVARIUS
Start the Kids on one TODAY!
VIOLINS GALORE

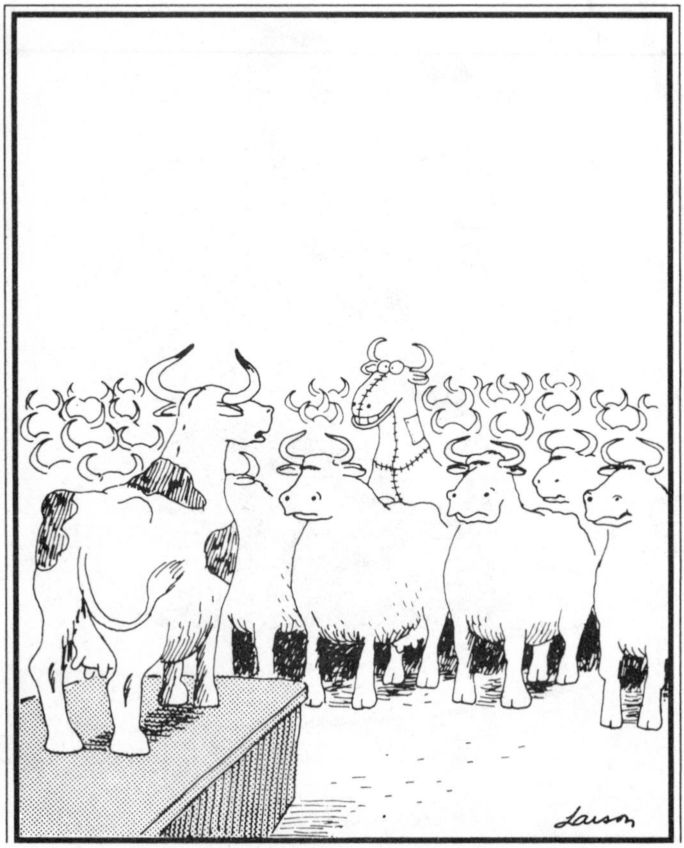

"The revolution has been postponed . . . We've discovered a leak."

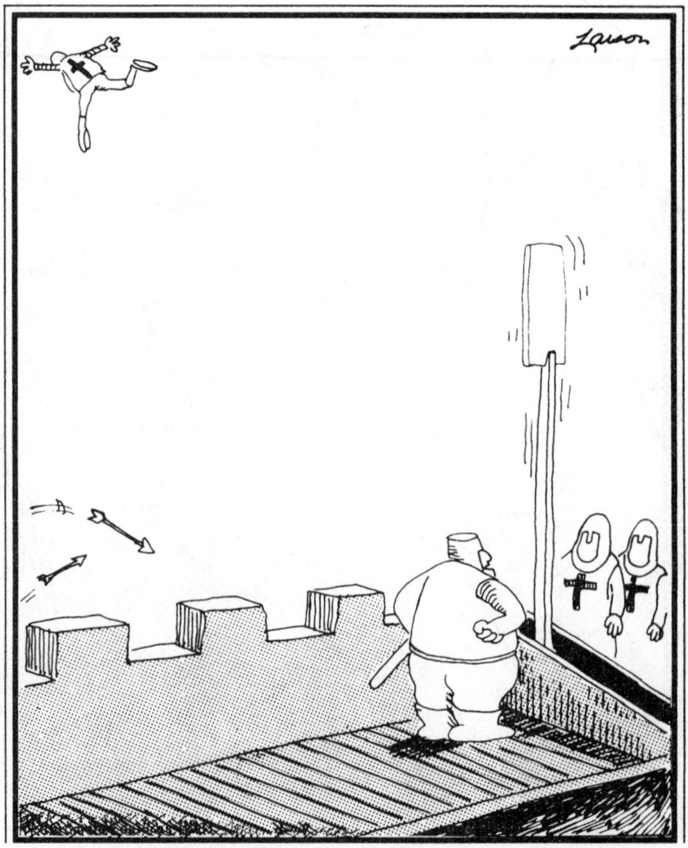

"I told you guys to slow down and take it easy or something like this would happen."

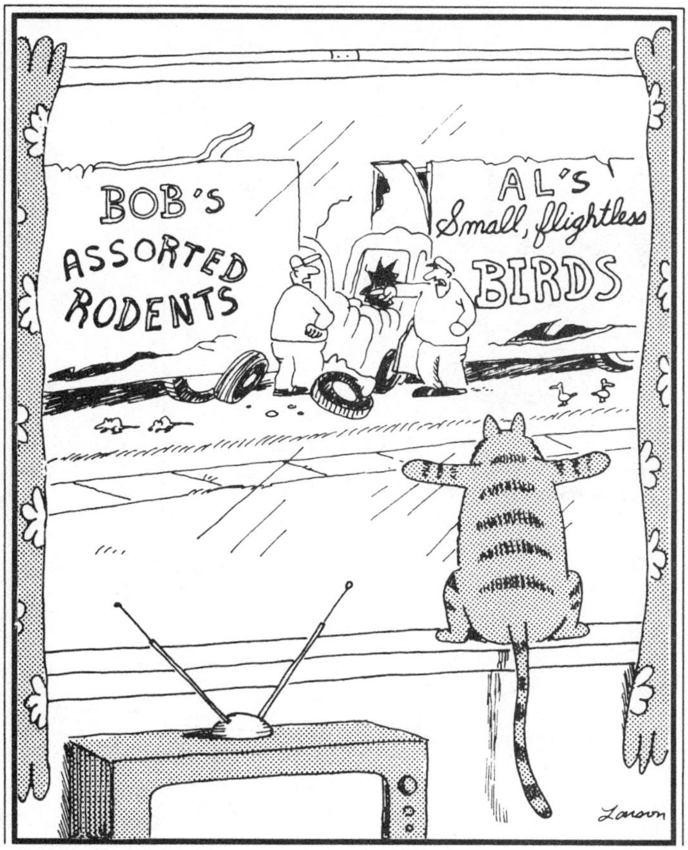
BOB'S
ASSORTED
RODENTS
AL'S
Small, flightless
BIRDS
Larson

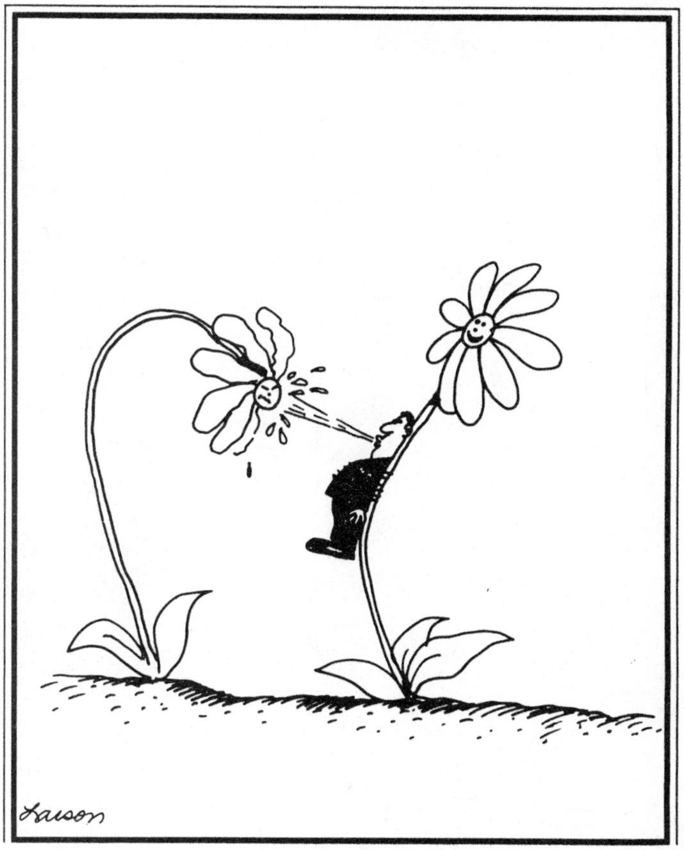
Larson

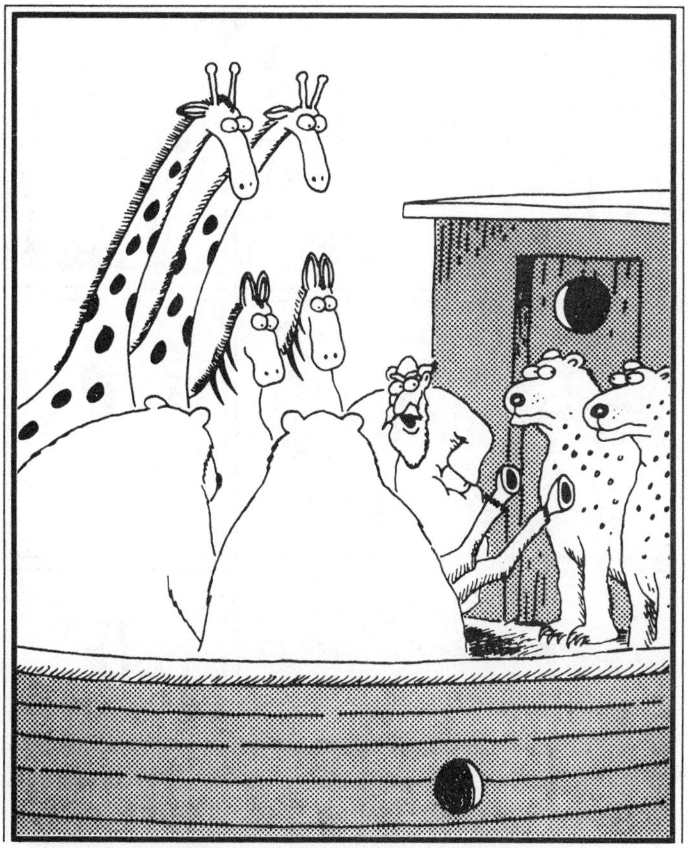

"Well, so much for the unicorns . . . But from now on, all carnivores will be confined to 'C' deck."

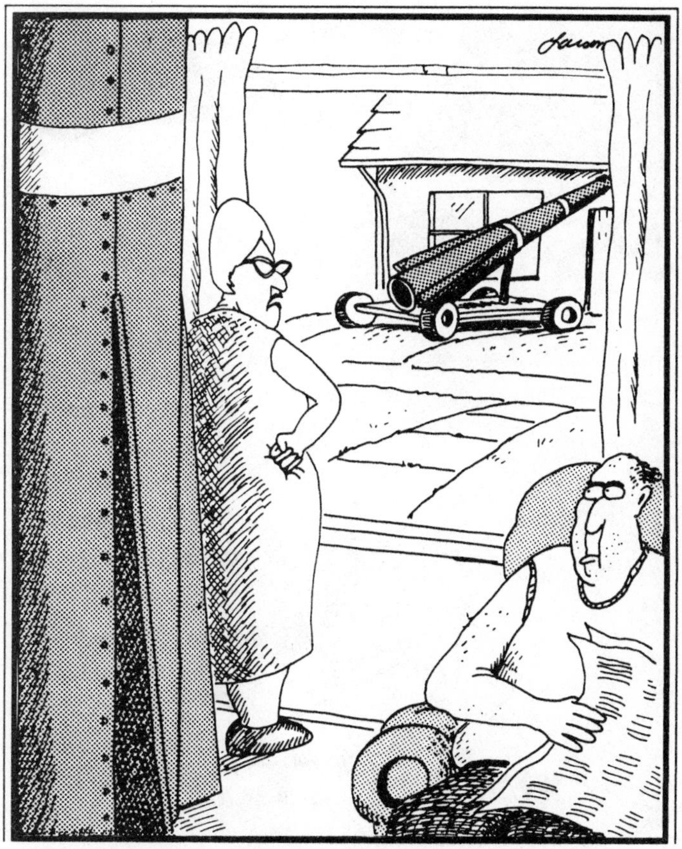
Larson

"Wouldn't you know it! Now the Hendersons have the bomb."

UNNATURAL
FOODS
Larson

CAREERS
IN
COMPUTERS
Larson

Larson

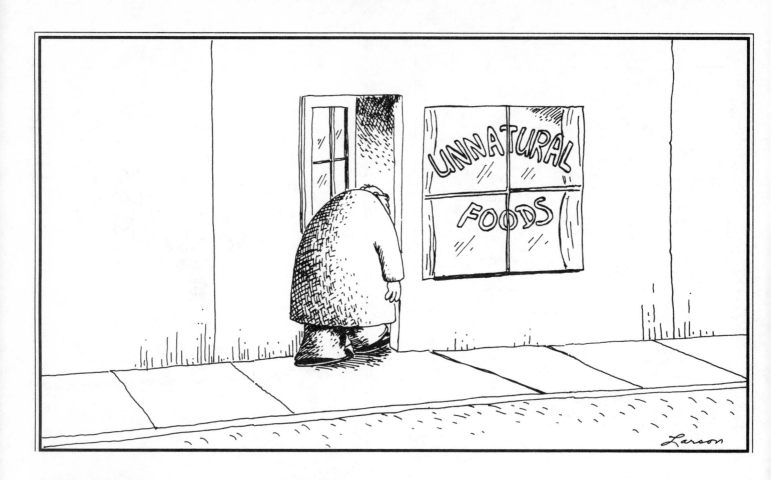

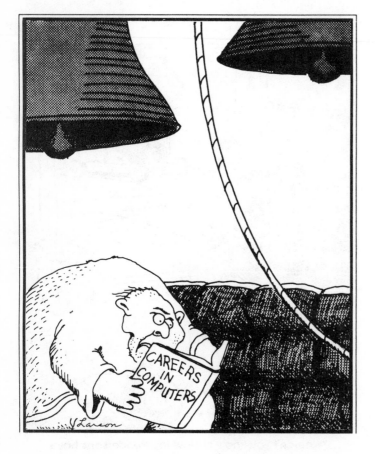

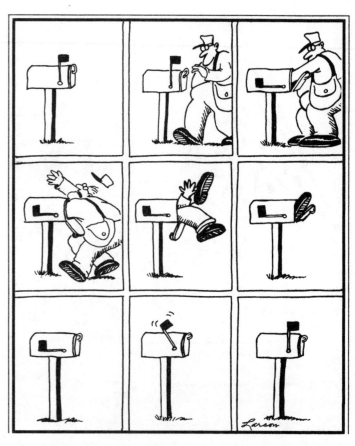

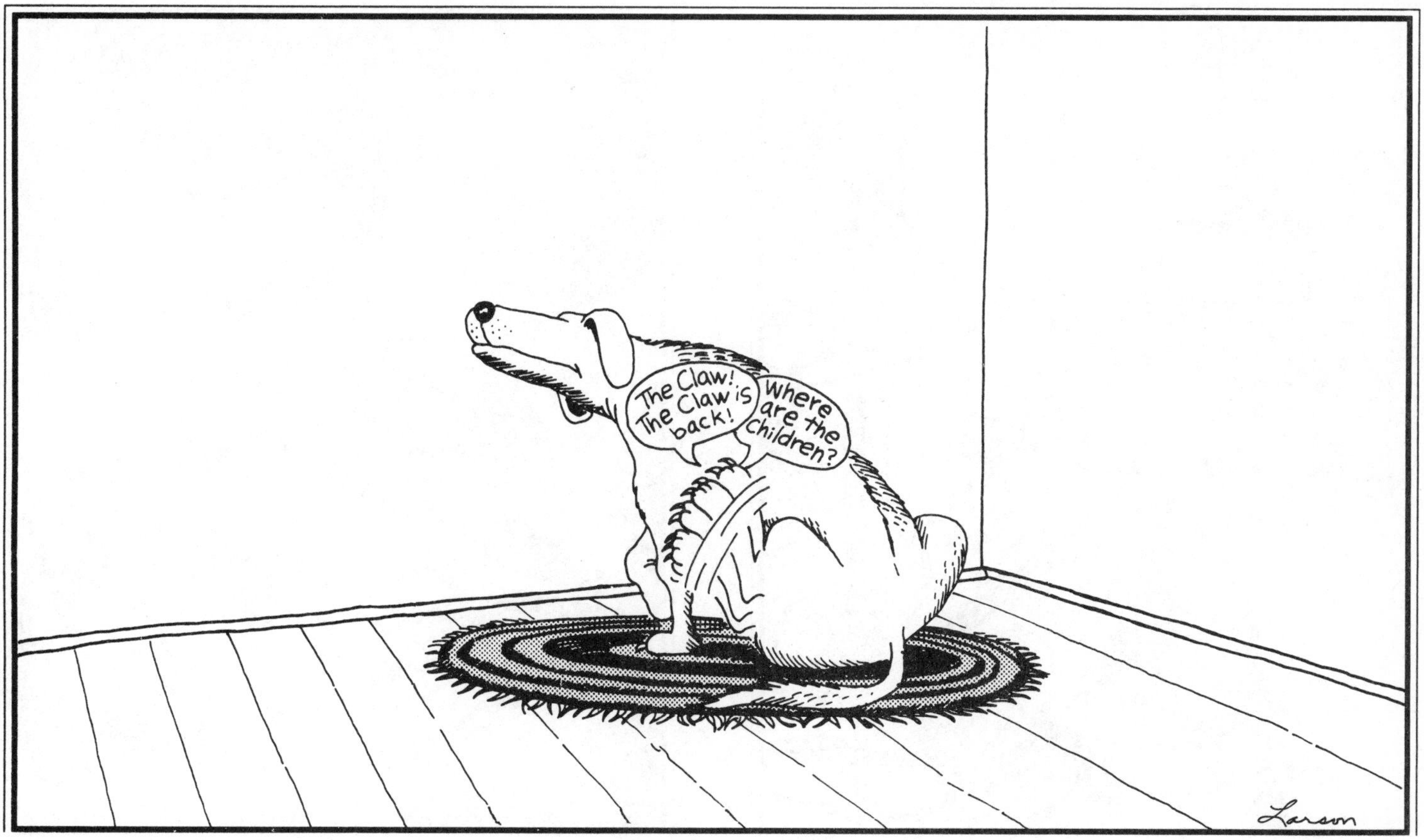
The Claw! The Claw is back!
Where are the children?
Larson

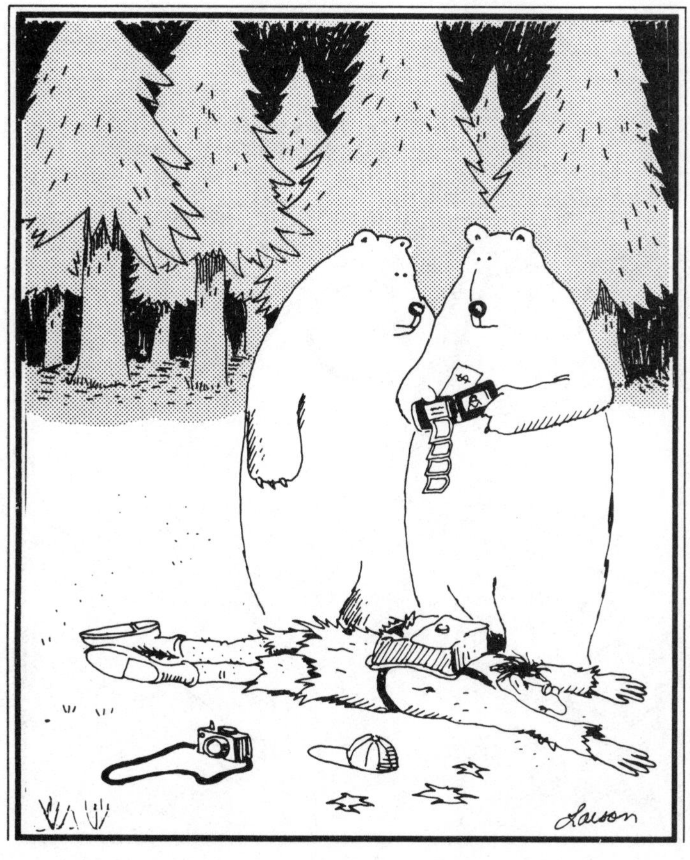
Larson

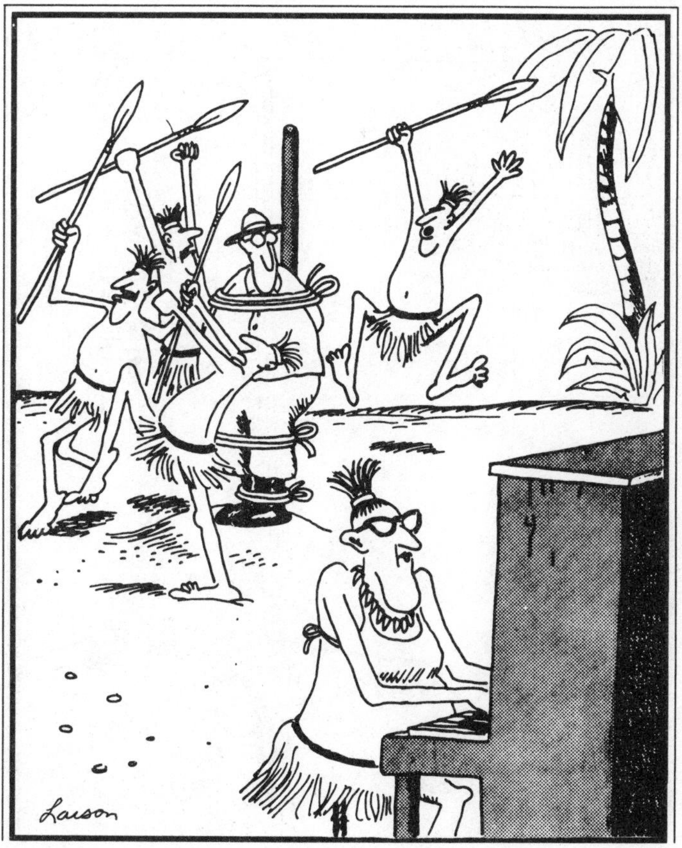
Larson

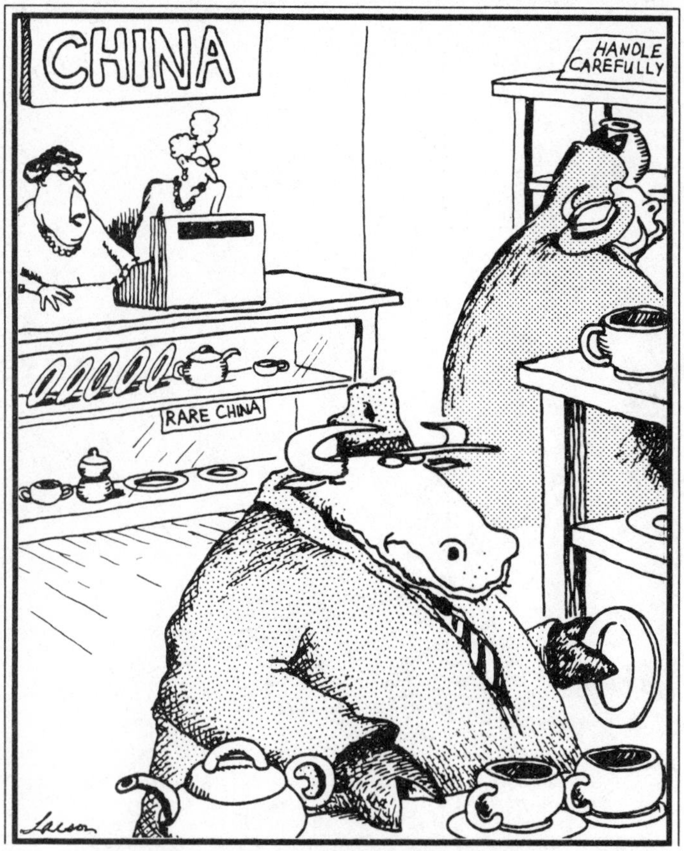
CHINA
HANDLE CAREFULLY
RARE CHINA

"I got a bad feeling about this, Harriet."

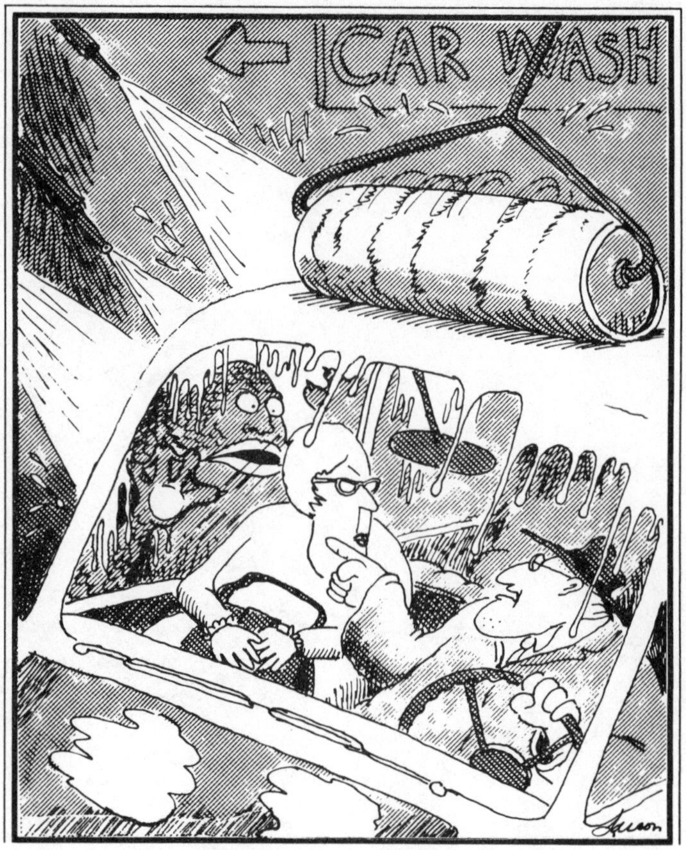
CAR WASH

"Quick, Agnes! Look! . . . There it is again!"

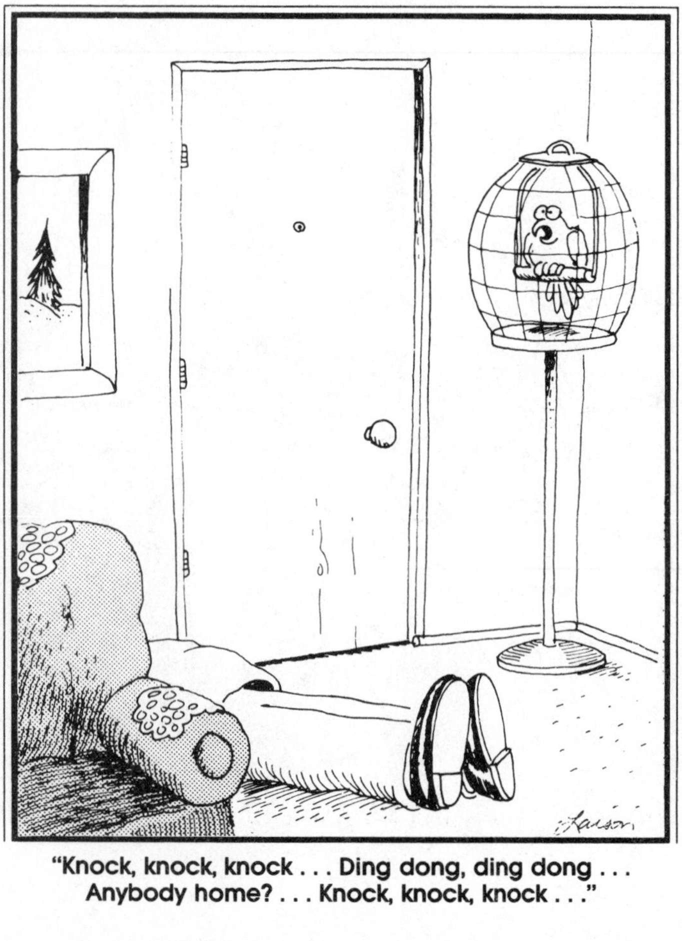

"Knock, knock, knock . . . Ding dong, ding dong . . . Anybody home? . . . Knock, knock, knock . . ."

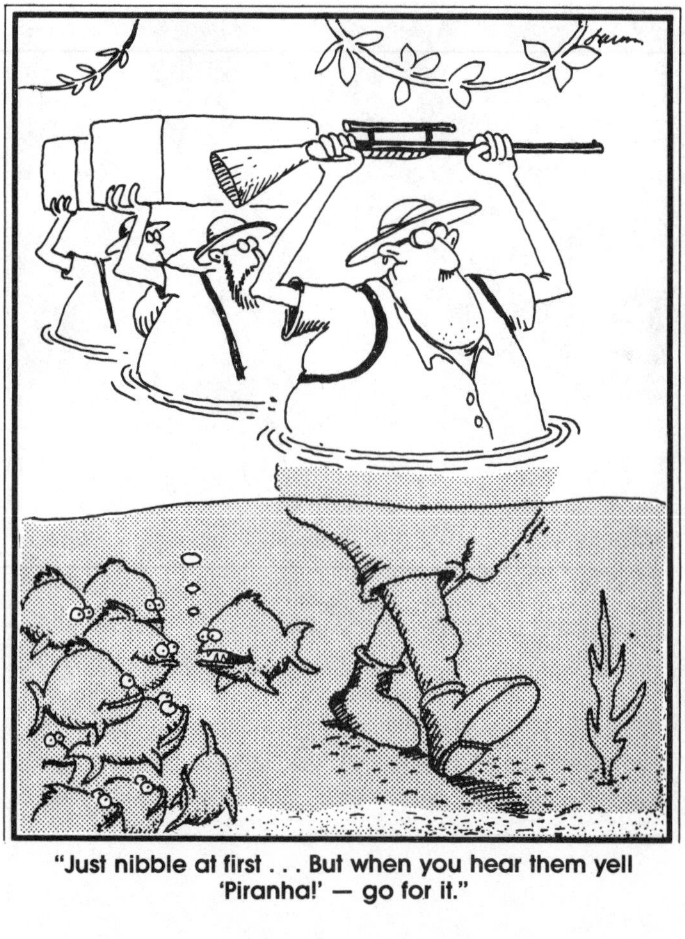

"Just nibble at first . . . But when you hear them yell 'Piranha!' — go for it."

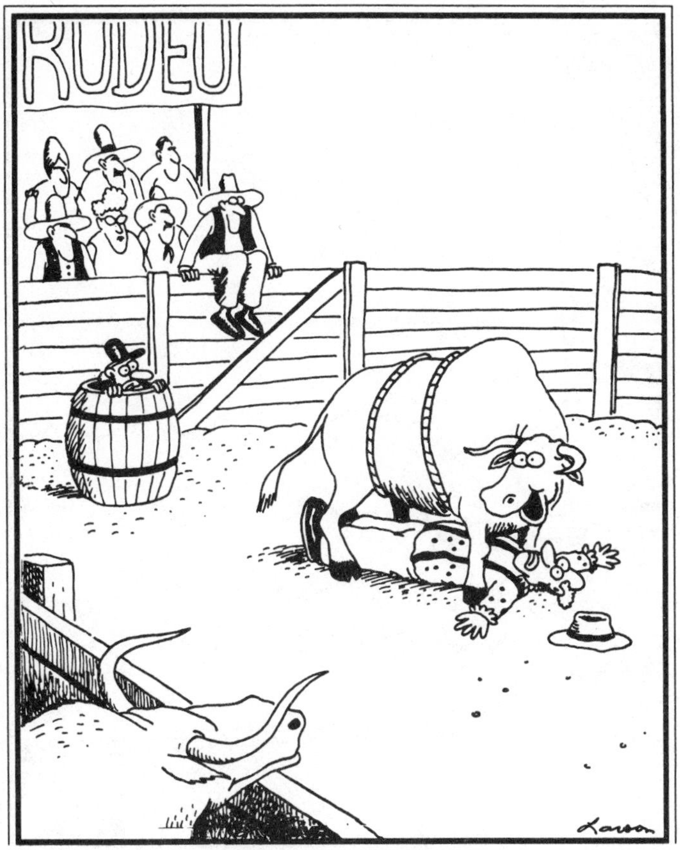
RODEO
Larson

"Hey! I got one! I got one!"

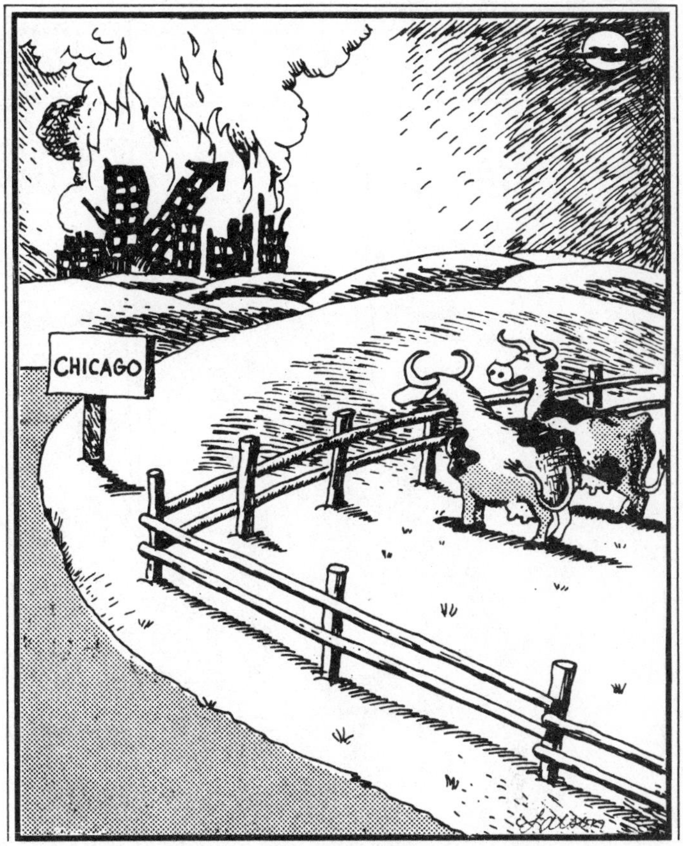
CHICAGO

"It seems that agent 6373 has accomplished her mission."

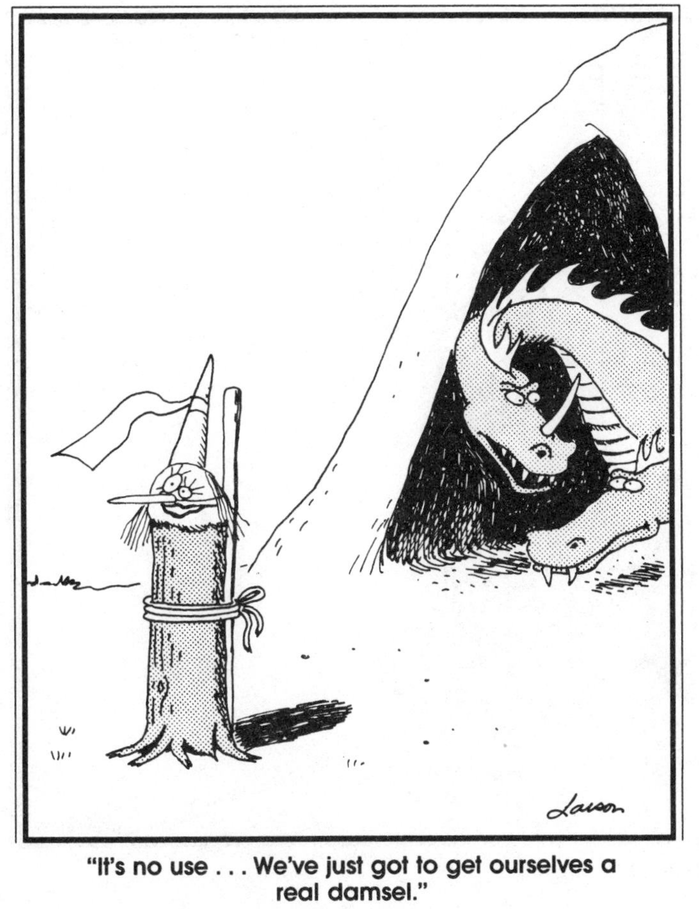
Larson

"It's no use . . . We've just got to get ourselves a real damsel."

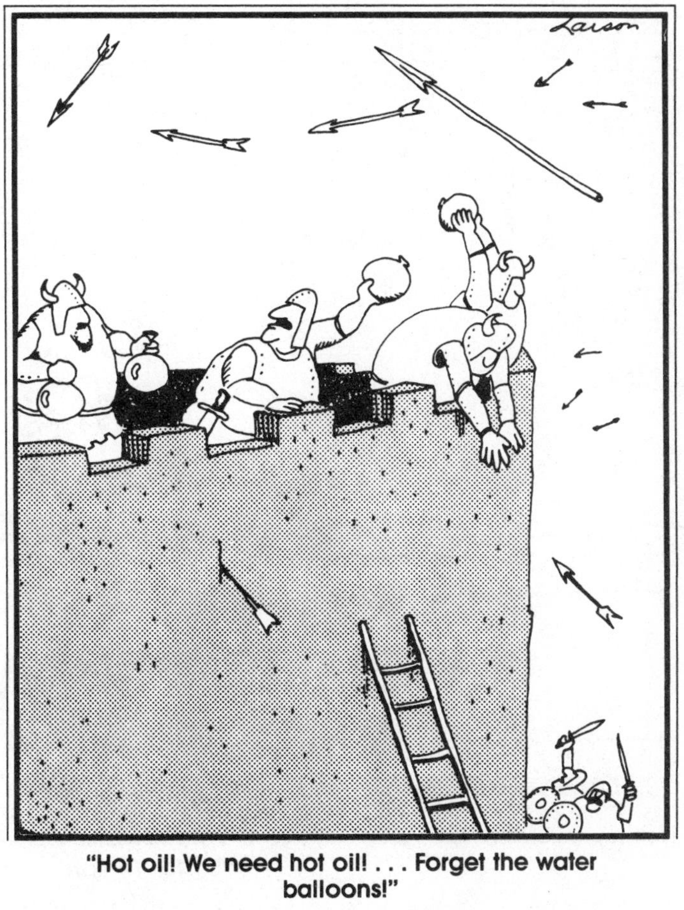
Larson

"Hot oil! We need hot oil! . . . Forget the water balloons!"

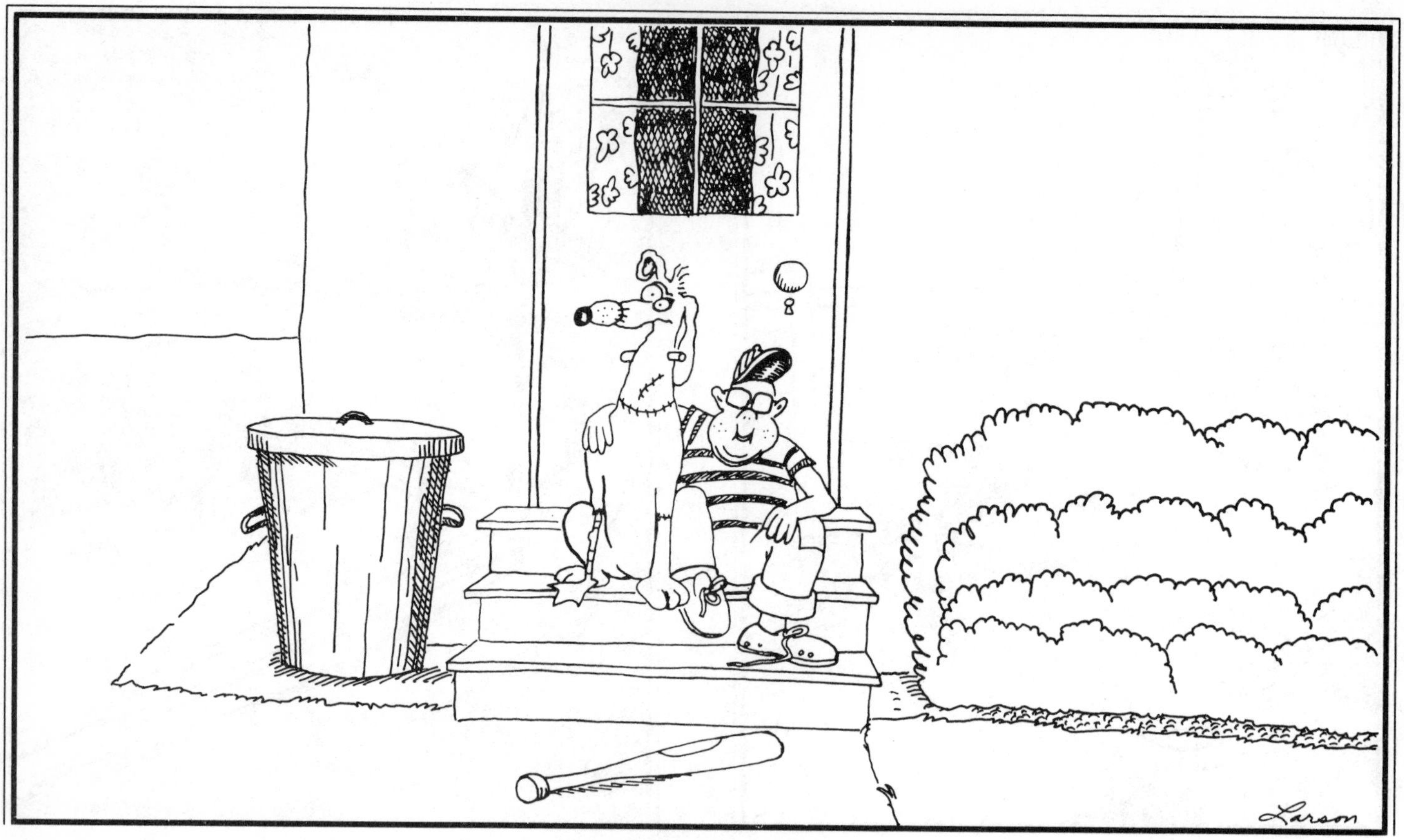

Young Jimmy Frankenstein

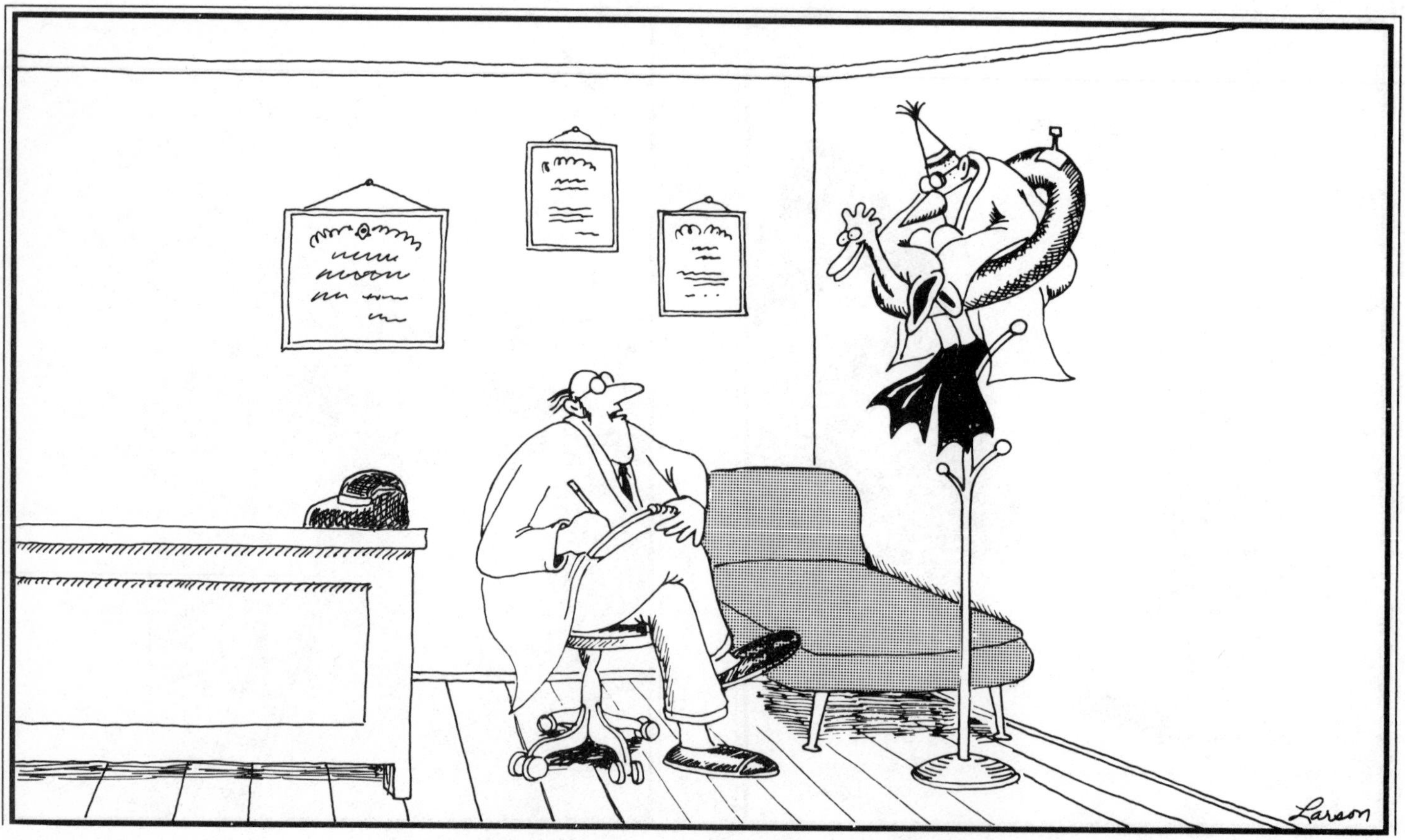

"So, Mr. Fenton . . . Let's begin with your mother."

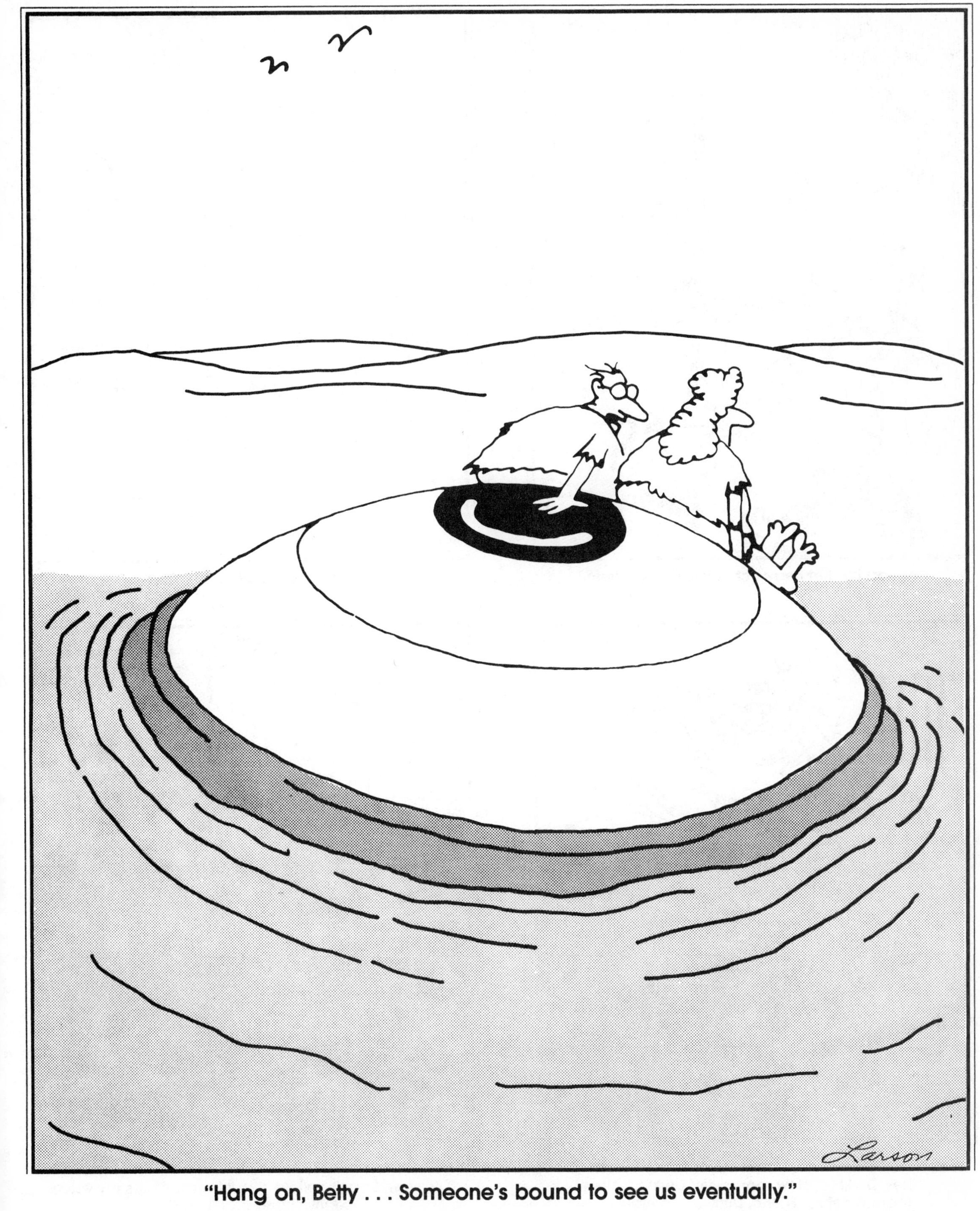
Larson

"Hang on, Betty . . . Someone's bound to see us eventually."

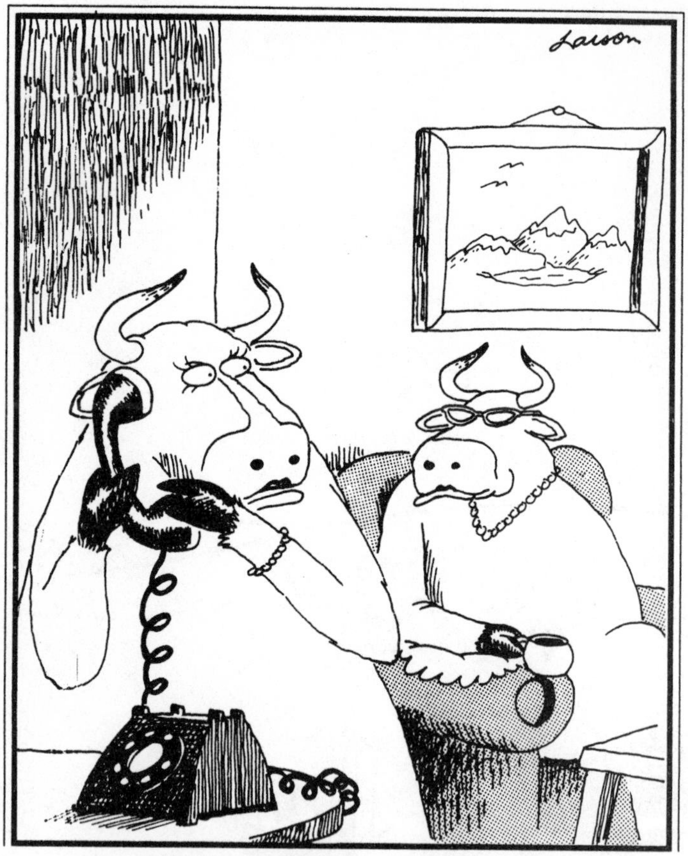
Larson

"Agnes! It's that heavy, chewing sound again!"

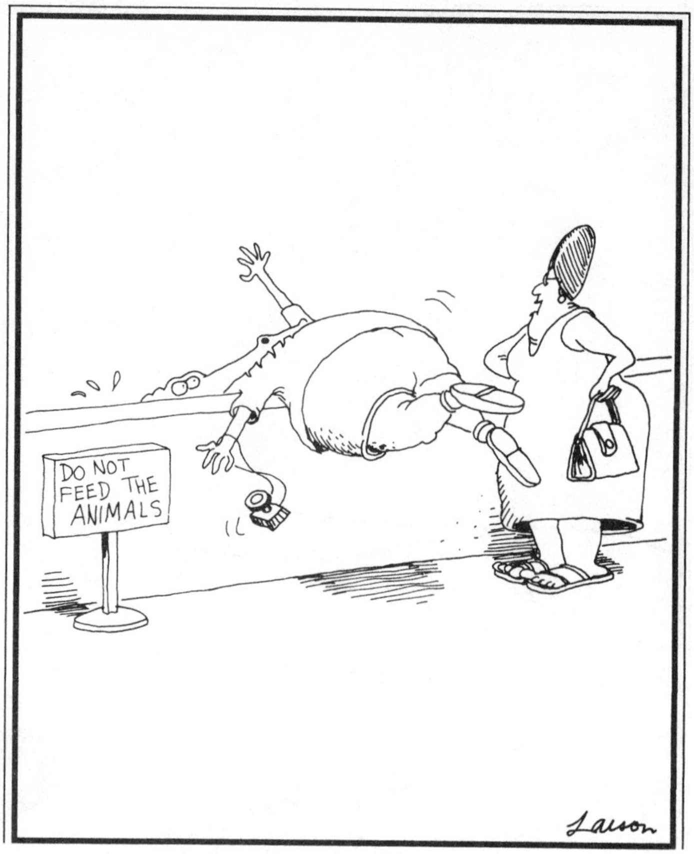
DO NOT
FEED THE
ANIMALS
Larson

"You're embarrassing me, Warren."

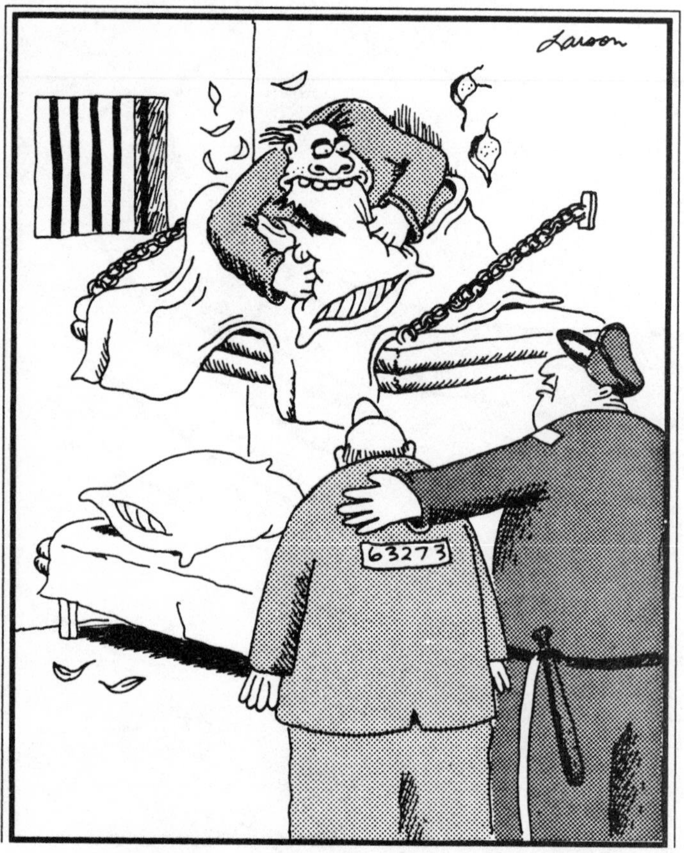
Larson
63273

"Hey, Durk! . . . New roommate, Durk! . . . New roommate! . . . Friend, Durk! . . . Friend! . . ."

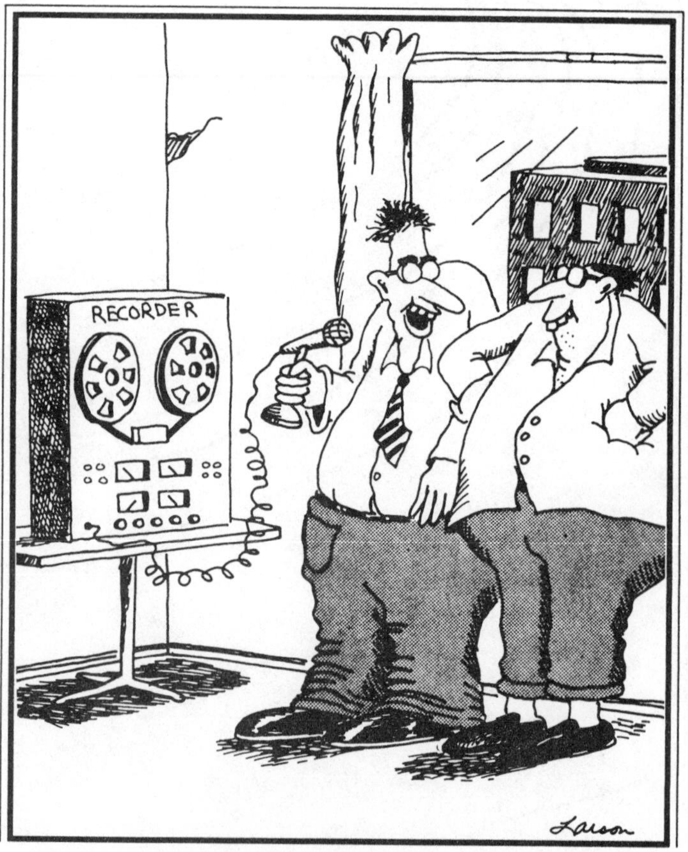
RECORDER
Larson

"Oh, wow! I can't believe this thing! . . . Does my voice really sound that funny?"

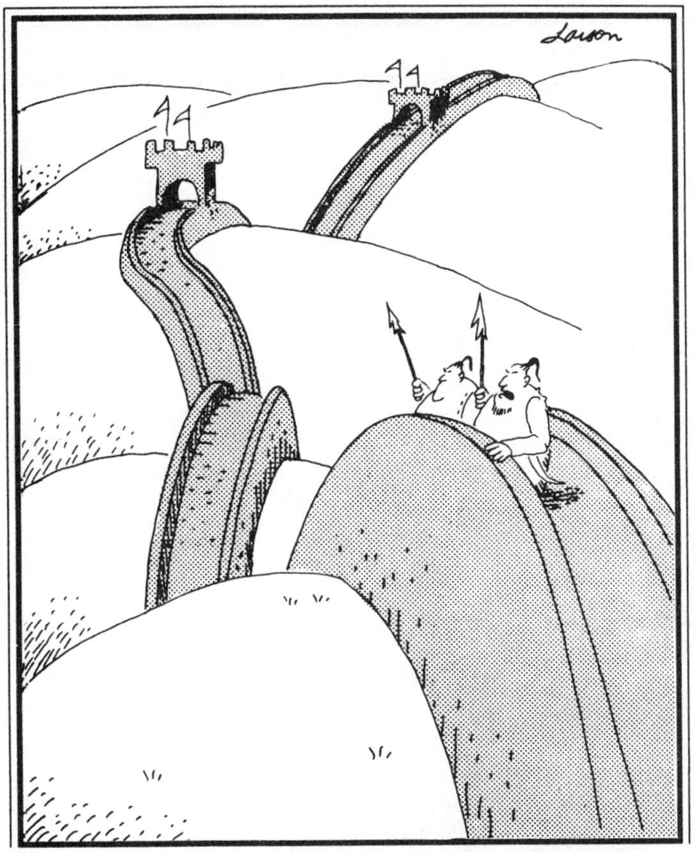
Larson

"NOW we'll see if that dog can get in here!"

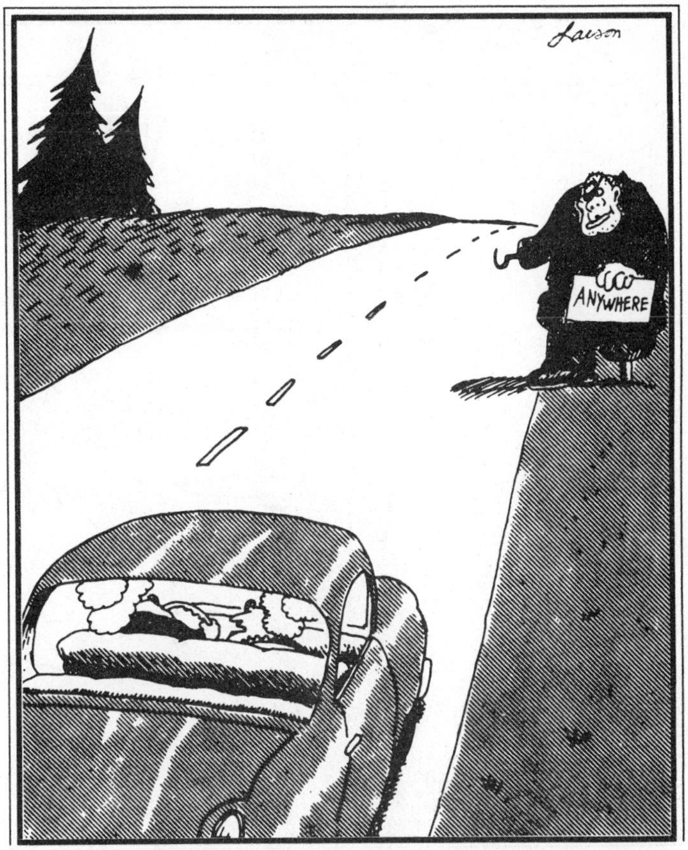
Larson
ANYWHERE

"C'mon, Sylvia . . . where's your spirit of adventure?"

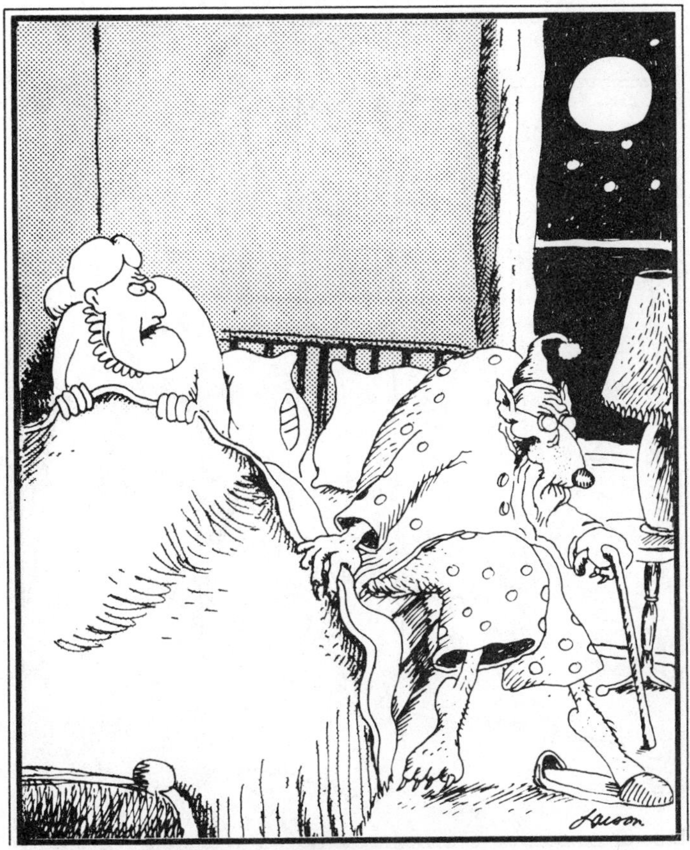
Larson

"Well, I just think I've been putting up with this silly curse of yours long enough!"

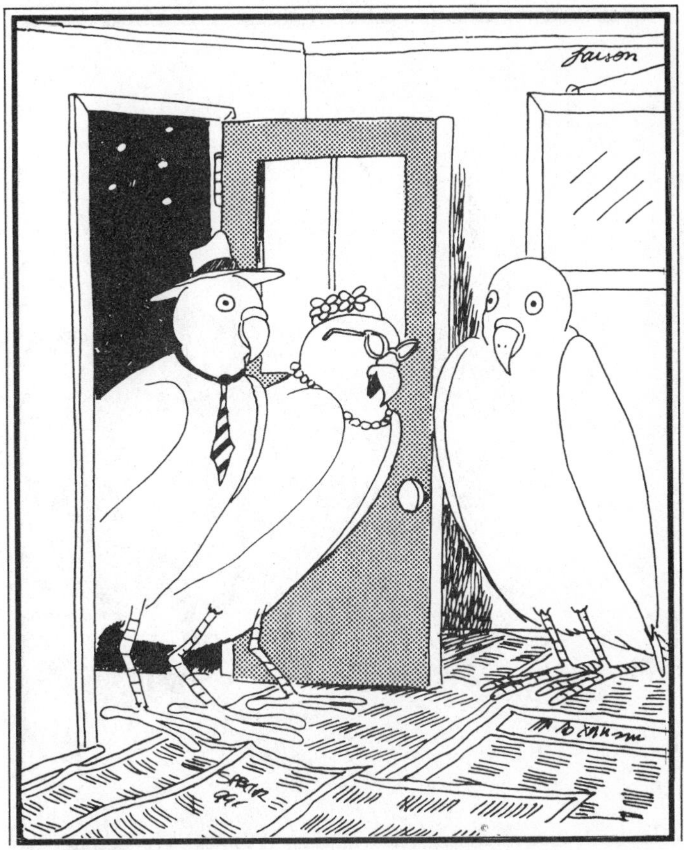
Larson

"What a lovely home, Edna! . . . And look at the fresh newspaper, Stanley!"

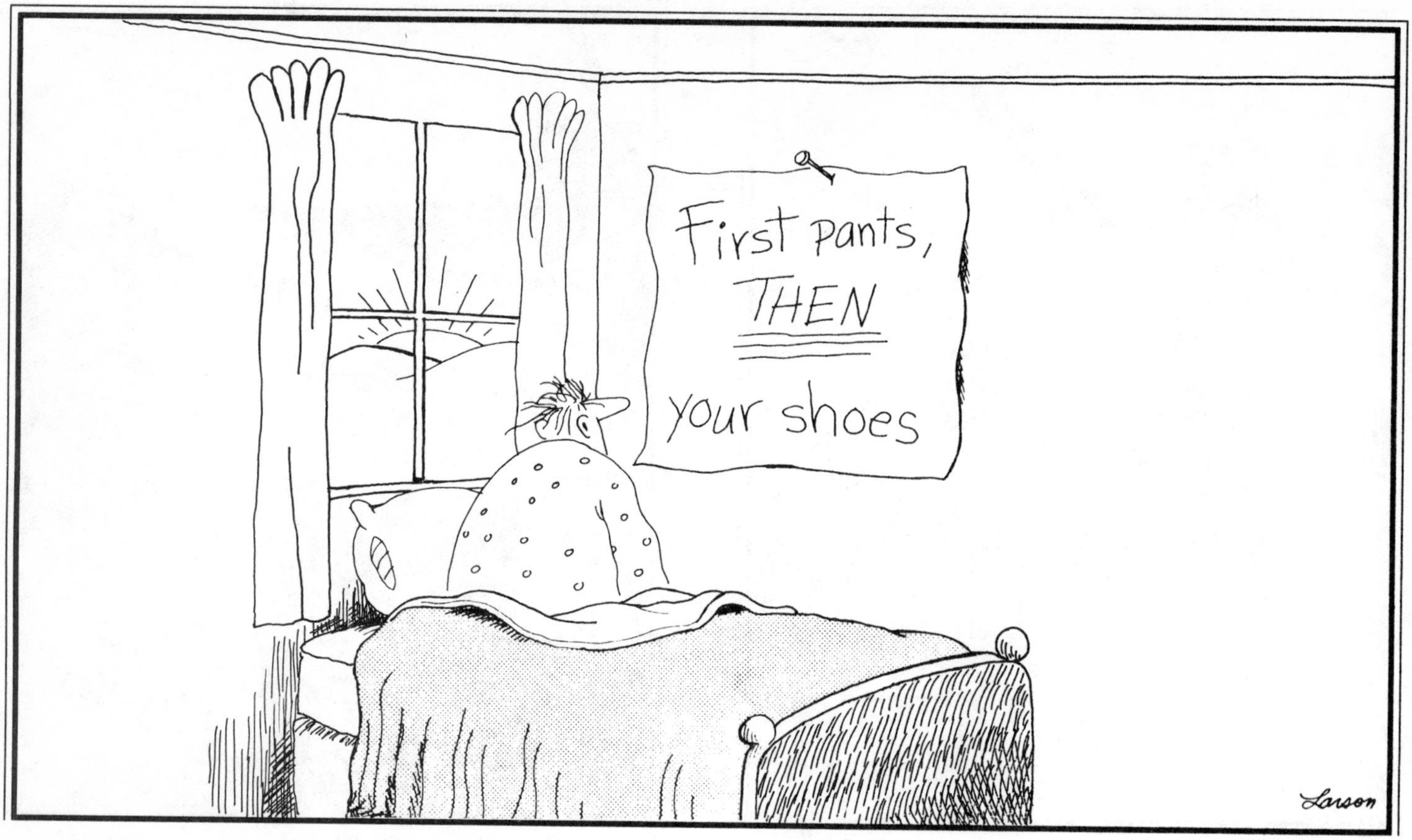
First pants,
THEN
your shoes
Larson

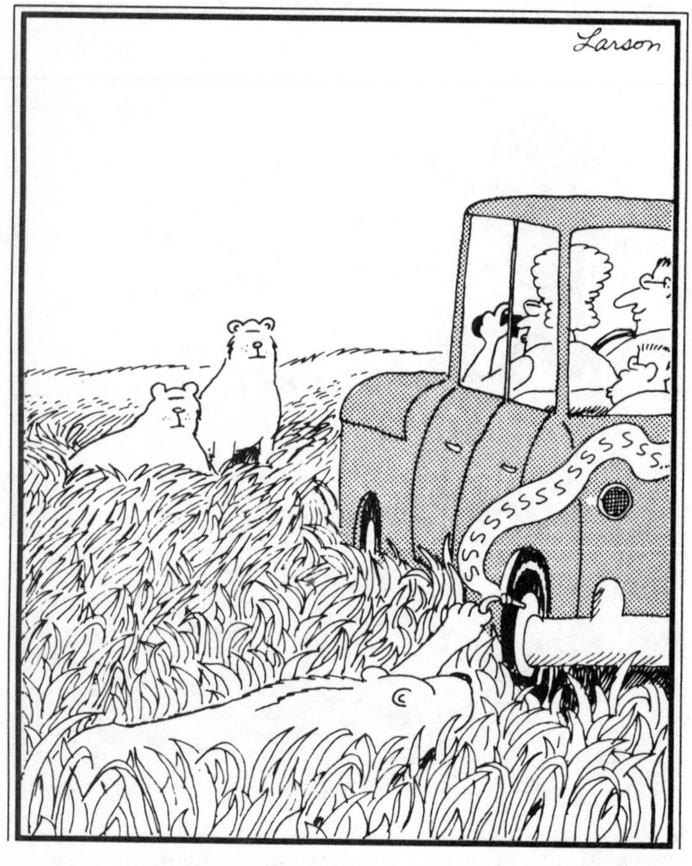
Larson

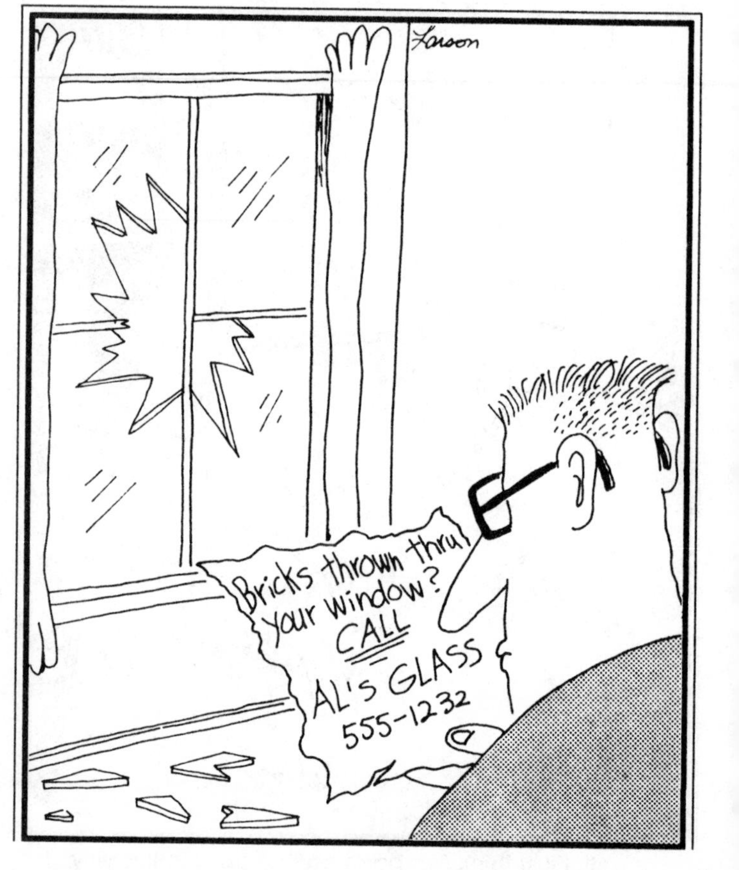
Larson
Bricks thrown thru your window? CALL AL's GLASS 555-1232

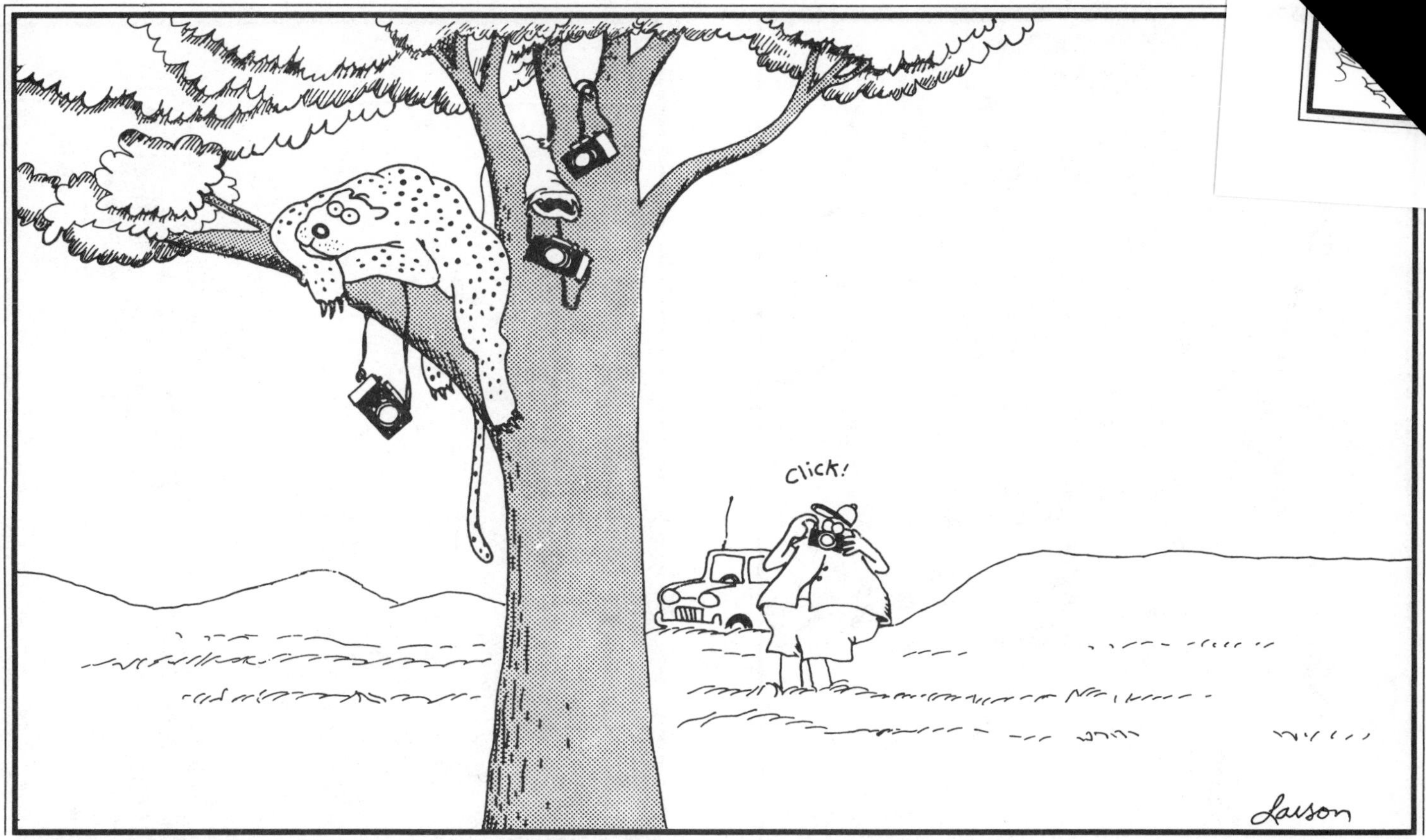
Click!
Larson

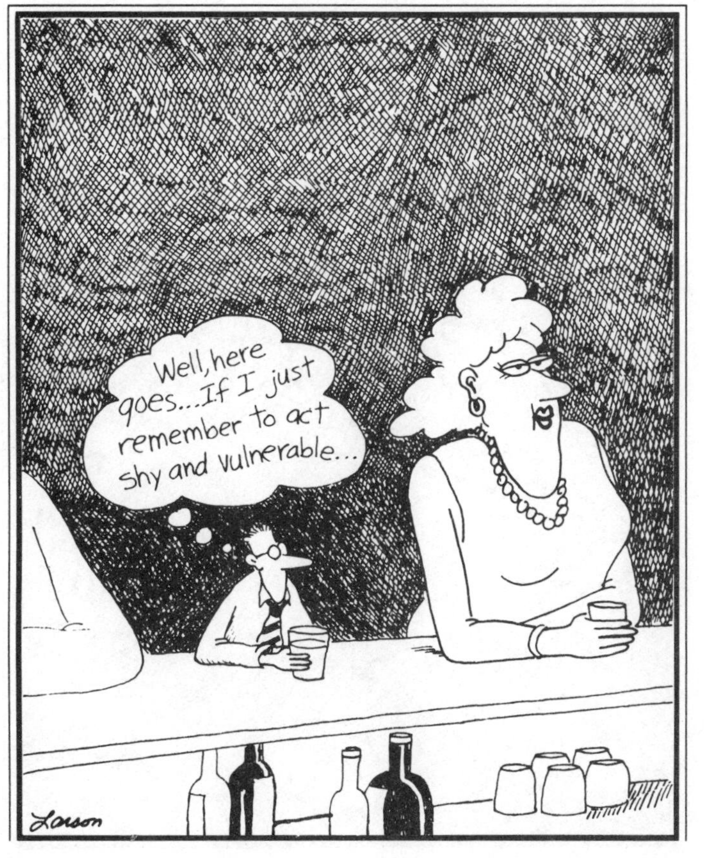
Well, here goes... If I just remember to act shy and vulnerable...
Larson

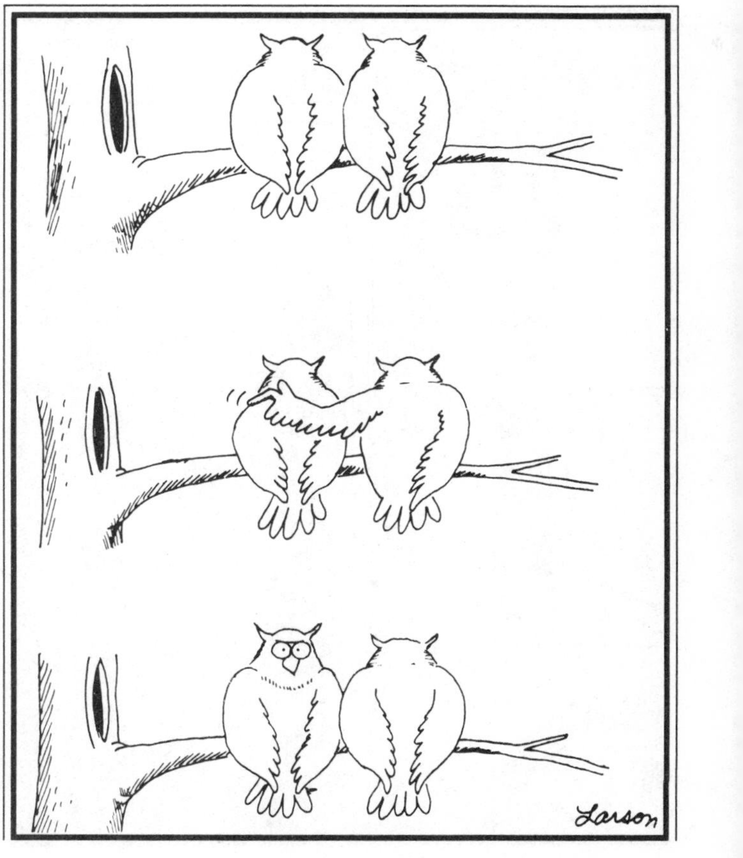
Larson

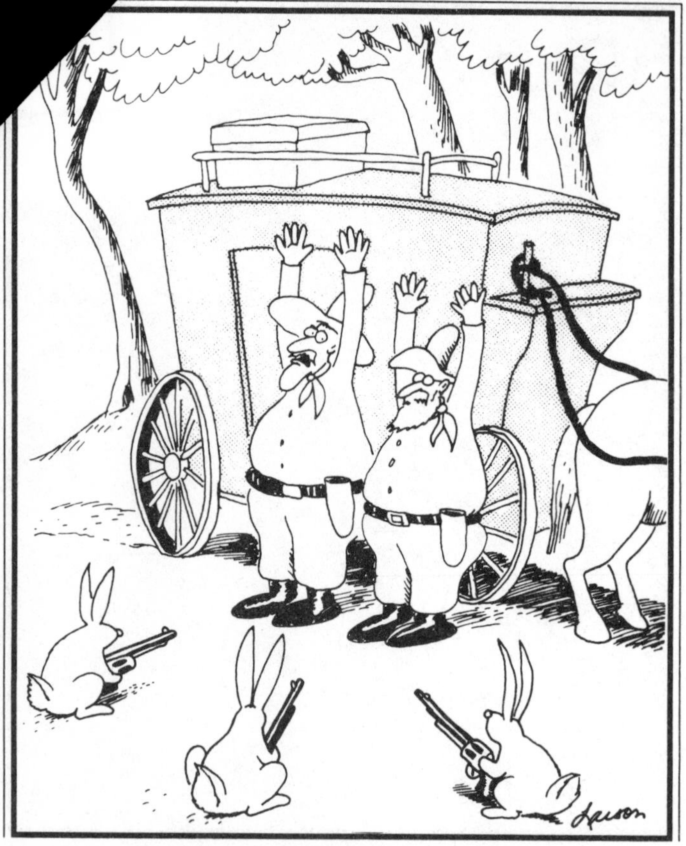
Larson

"This ain't gonna look good on our report, Leroy."

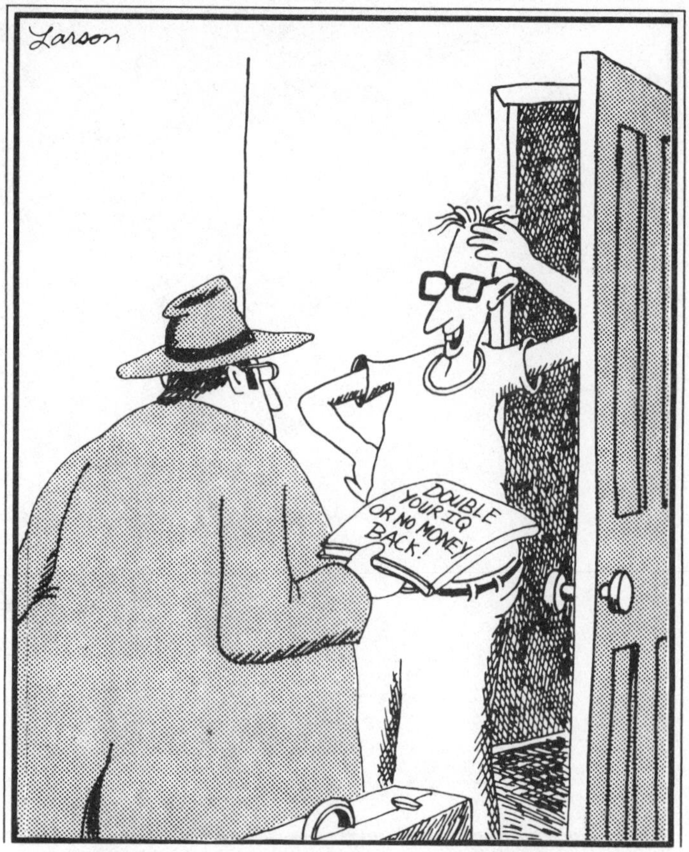
Larson
DOUBLE YOUR IQ OR NO MONEY BACK!

"Well, I dunno . . . Okay, sounds good to me."

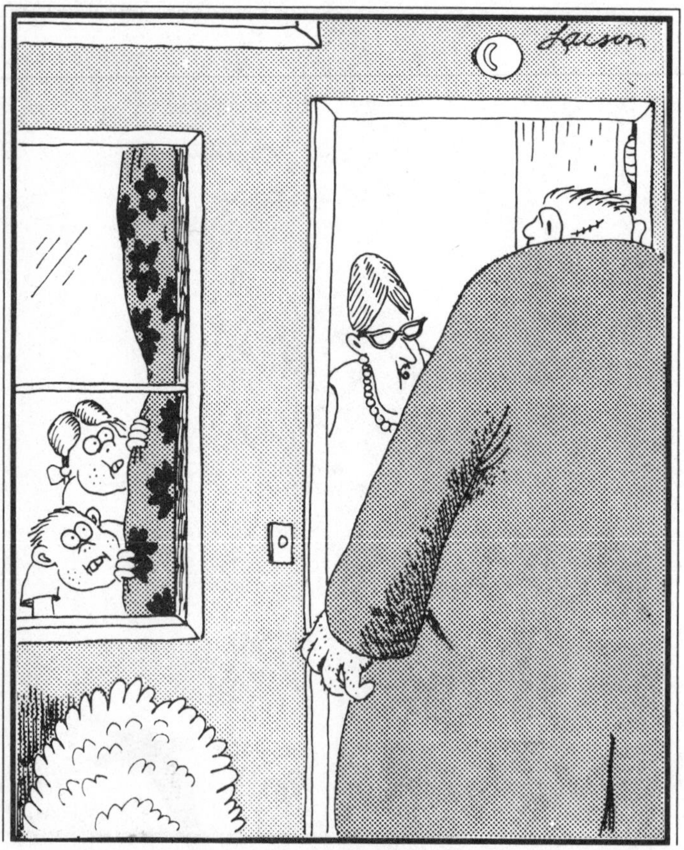
Larson

"Why, yes . . . we do have two children who won't eat their vegetables."

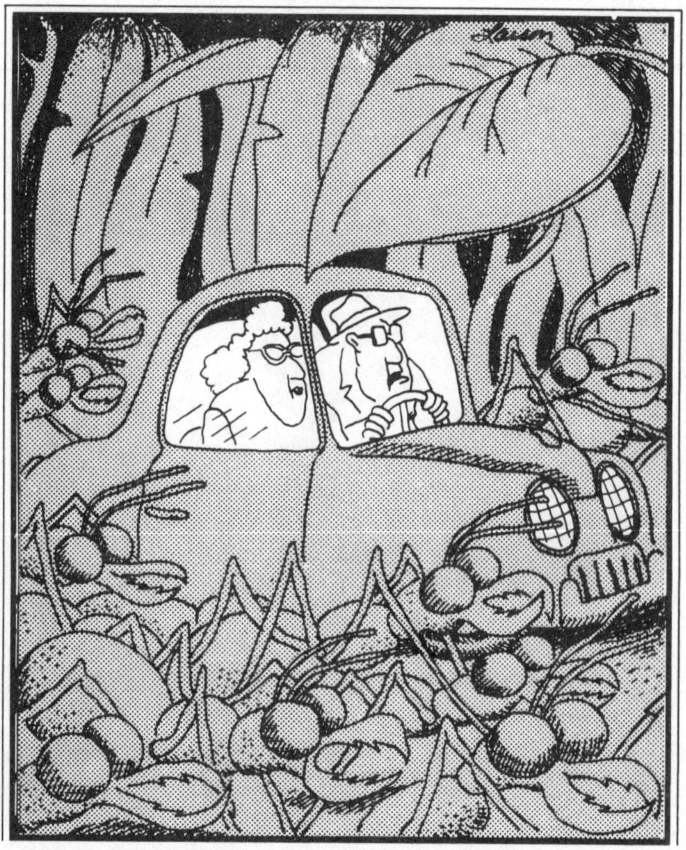
Larson

"Something's wrong here, Harriet . . . This is starting to look less and less like Interstate 95."

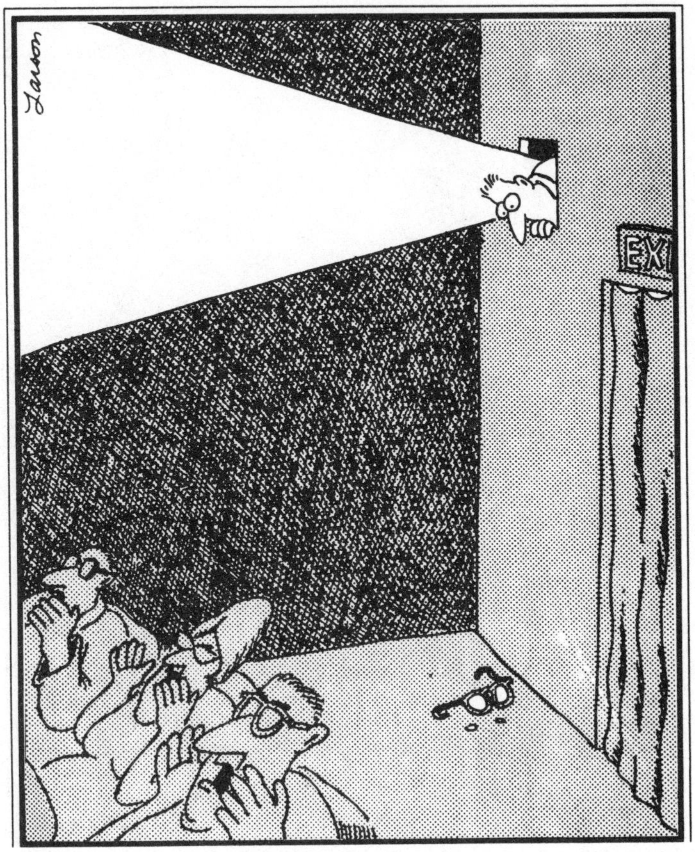
Larson
EXI

"Focus! . . . Focus!"

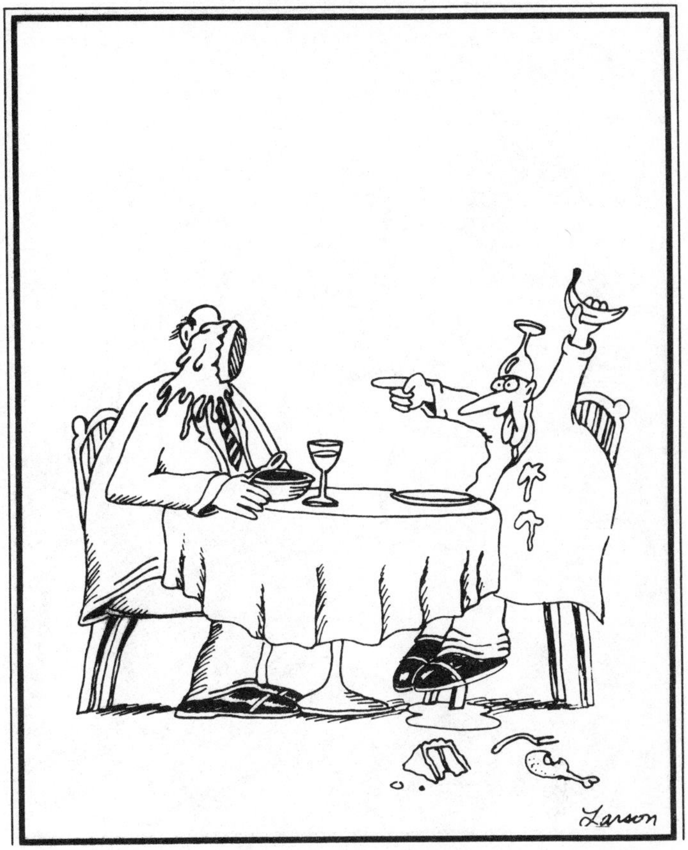
Larson

My dinner with Andy

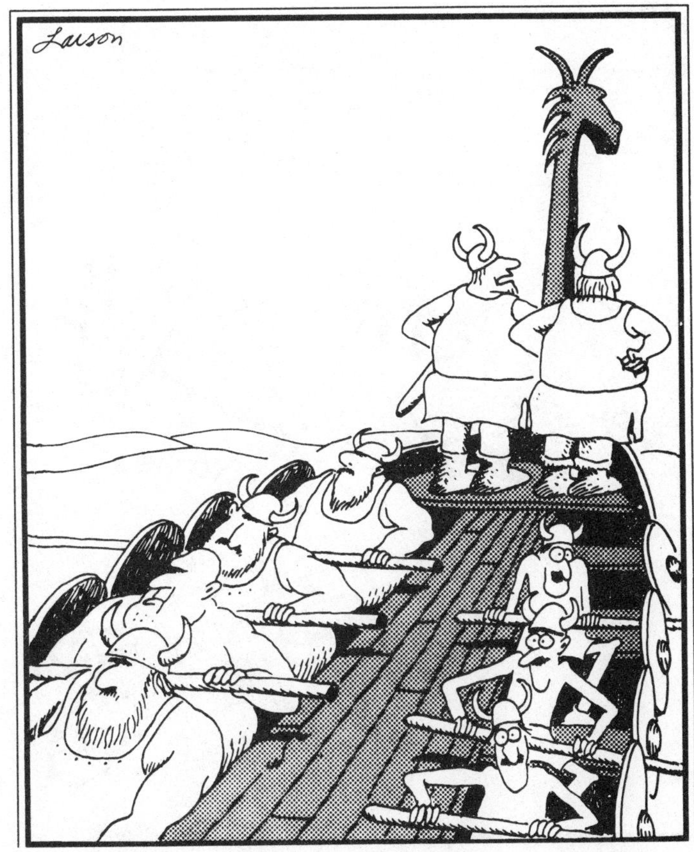
Larson

"I've got it, too, Omar . . . a strange feeling like we've just been going in circles."

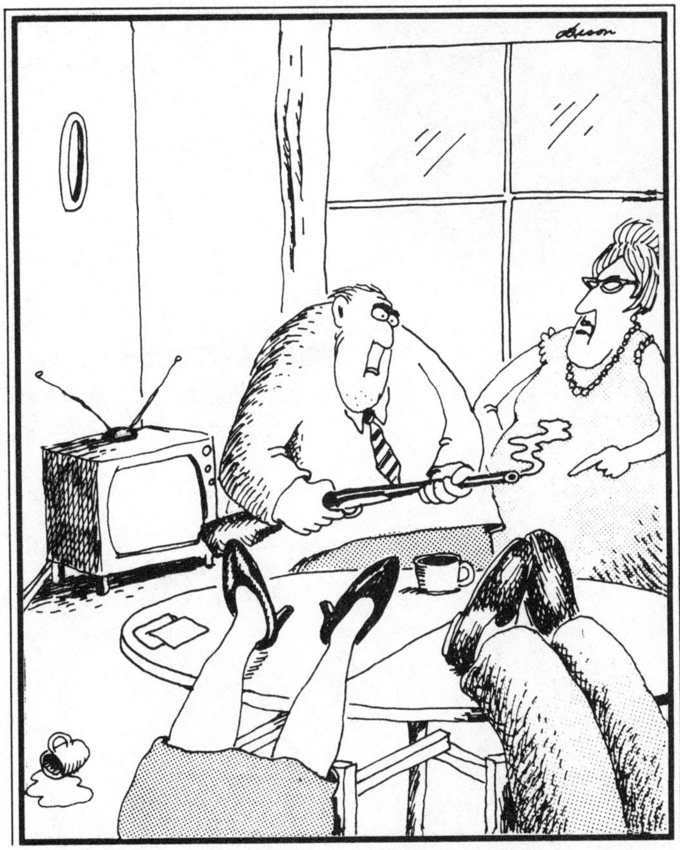

"That settles it, Carl! . . . From now on, you're getting only decaffeinated coffee!"

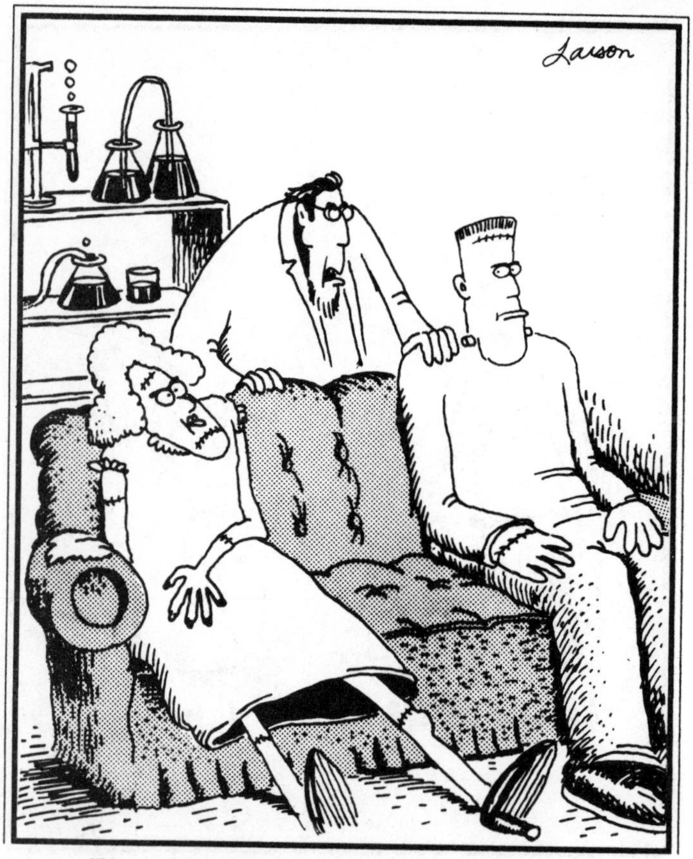
Larson

"Hey, c'mon now! . . . You two were MADE for each other!"

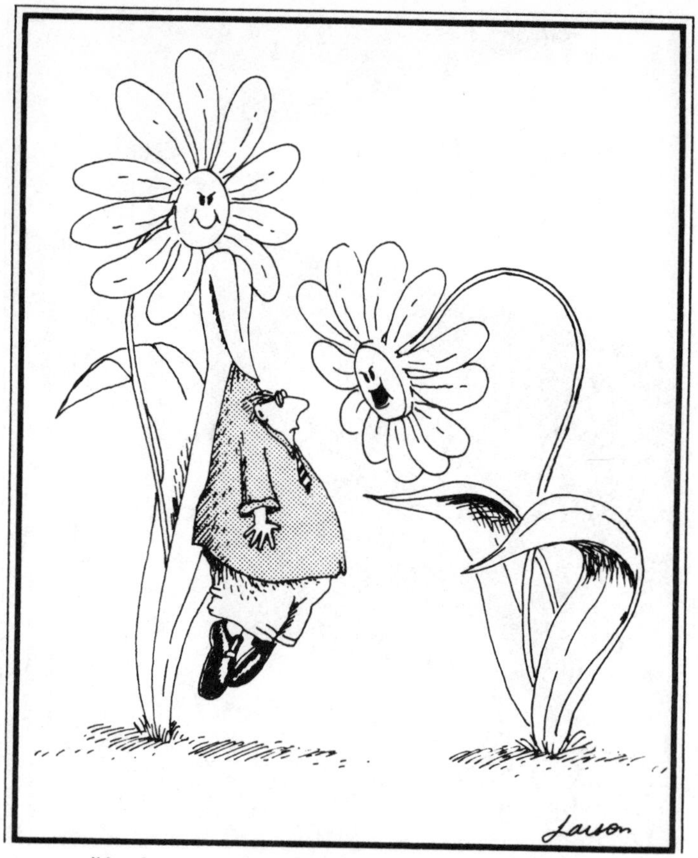
Larson

"And now we're going to play she-loves-me, she-loves-me-not!"

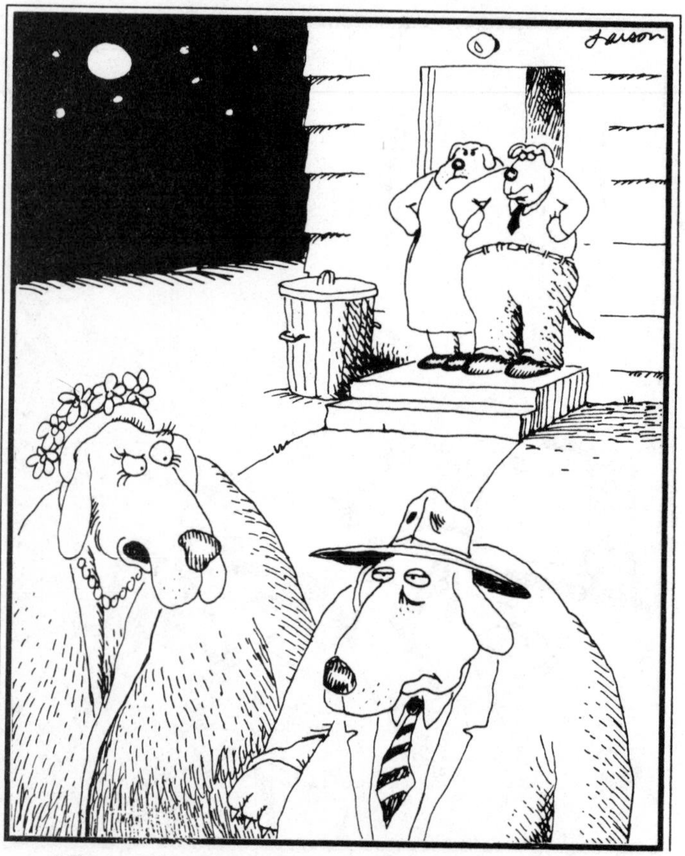
Larson

"One of the nicest evenings I've ever spent at the Wilson's . . . and then you had to go and do that on the rug!"

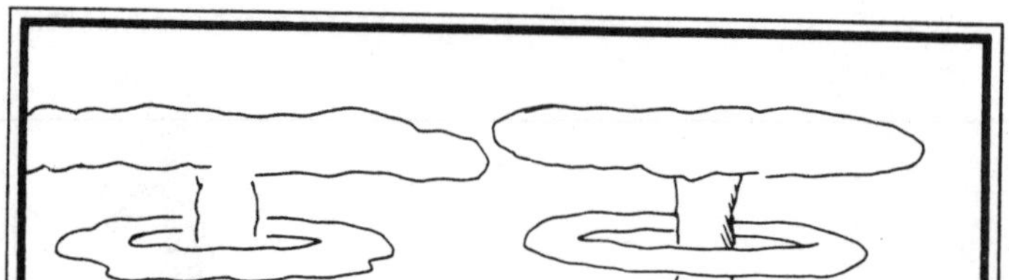
Larson

"This is a test. For the next thirty seconds, this station will conduct a test of the emergency broadcast system . . ."

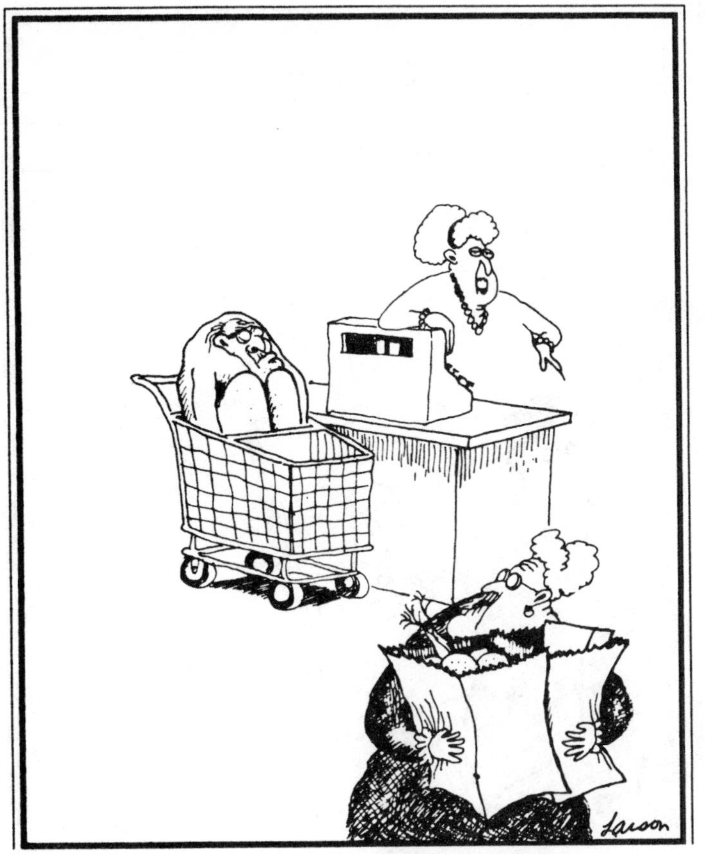
Larson

"Oh, Mrs. Oswald . . . you've forgotten something again."

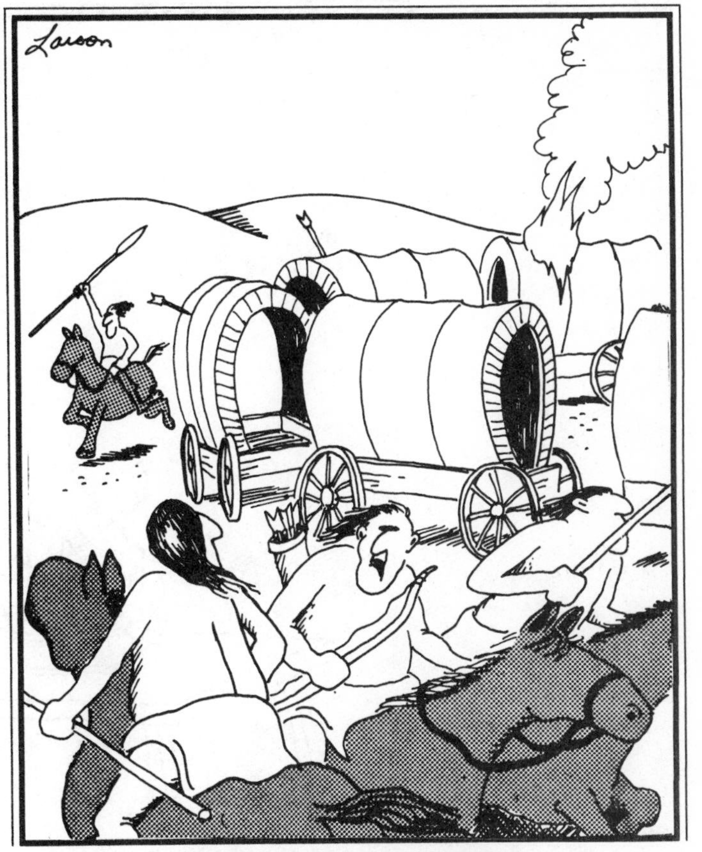
Larson

"Counterclockwise, Red Eagle! Always counterclockwise!"

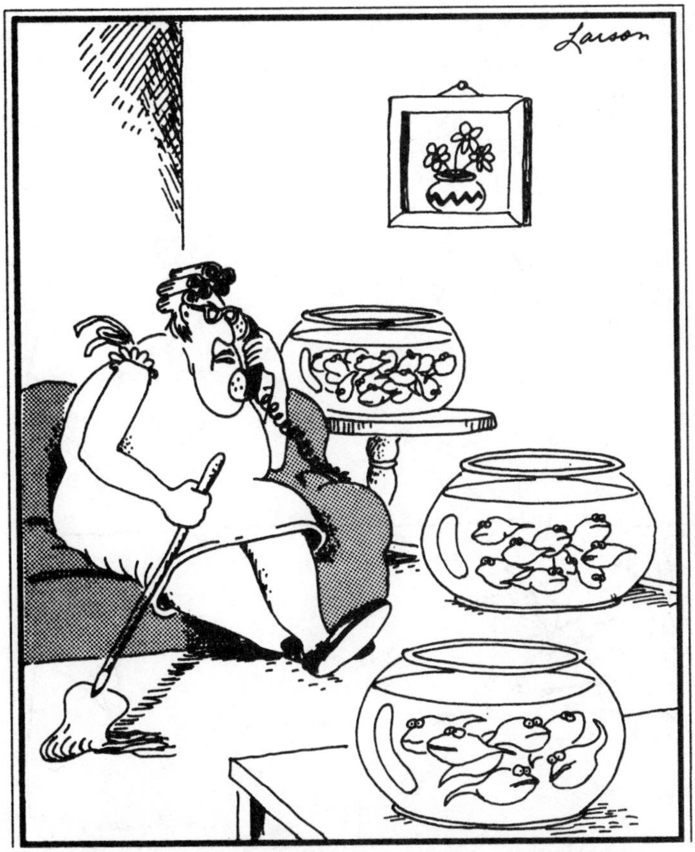
Larson

"Well that's how it happened, Sylvia . . . I kissed this frog, he turns into a prince, we get married and wham! . . . I'm stuck at home with a bunch of pollywogs."

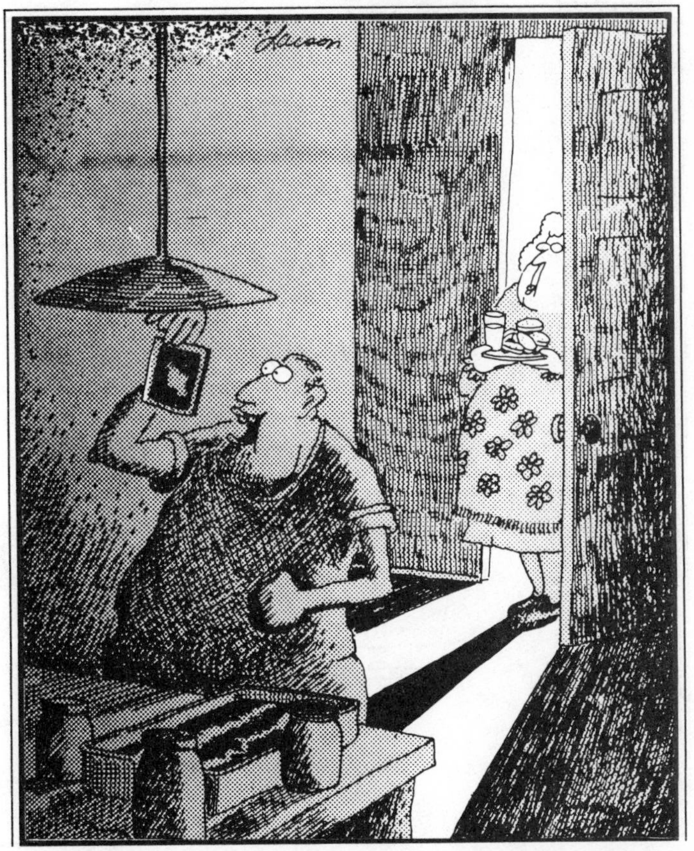
Larson

"I've done it! The first real evidence of a UFO! . . . And with my own camera, in my own darkroom, and in my own . . ."

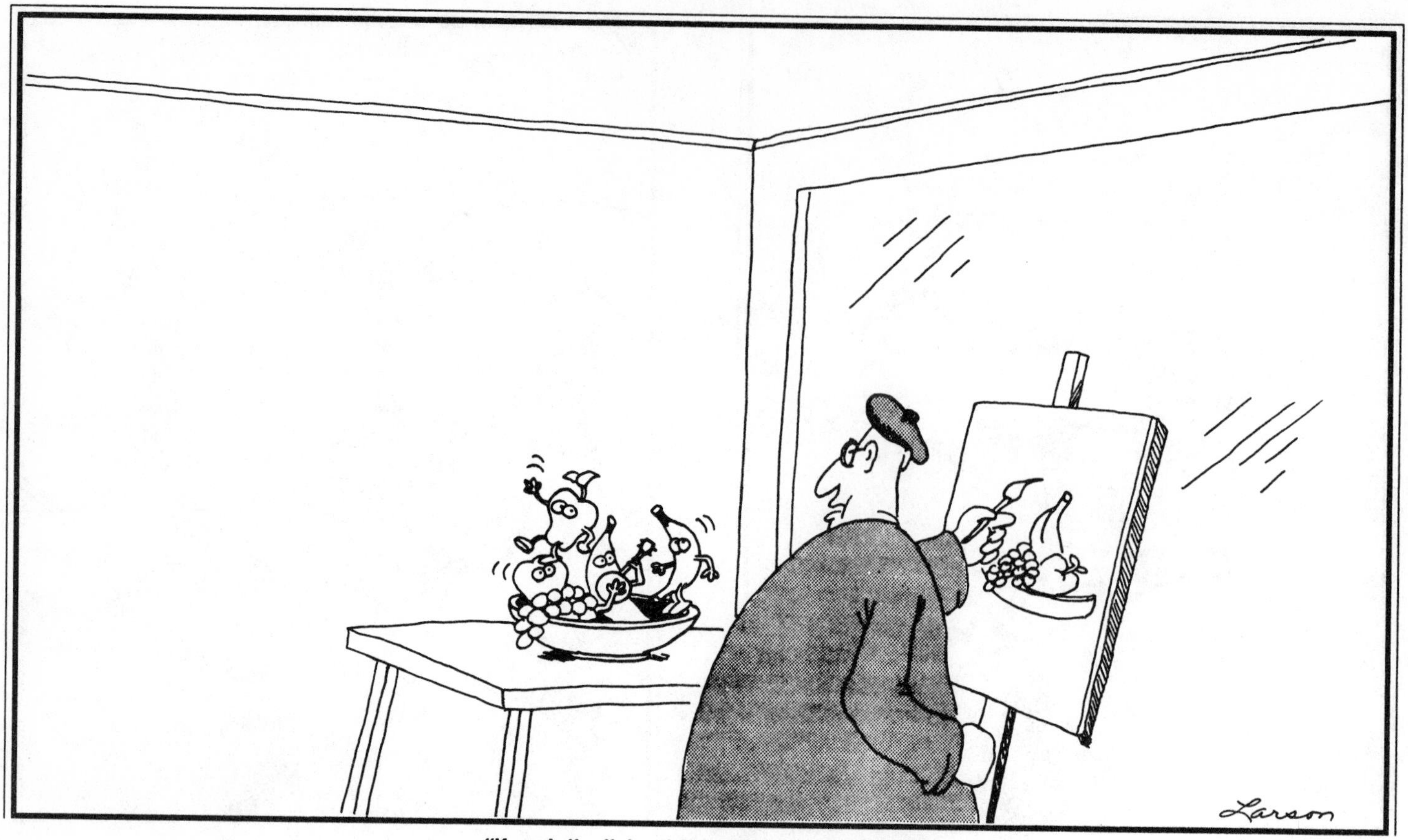
Larson
"Knock it off, I said! . . . This is a still life!"

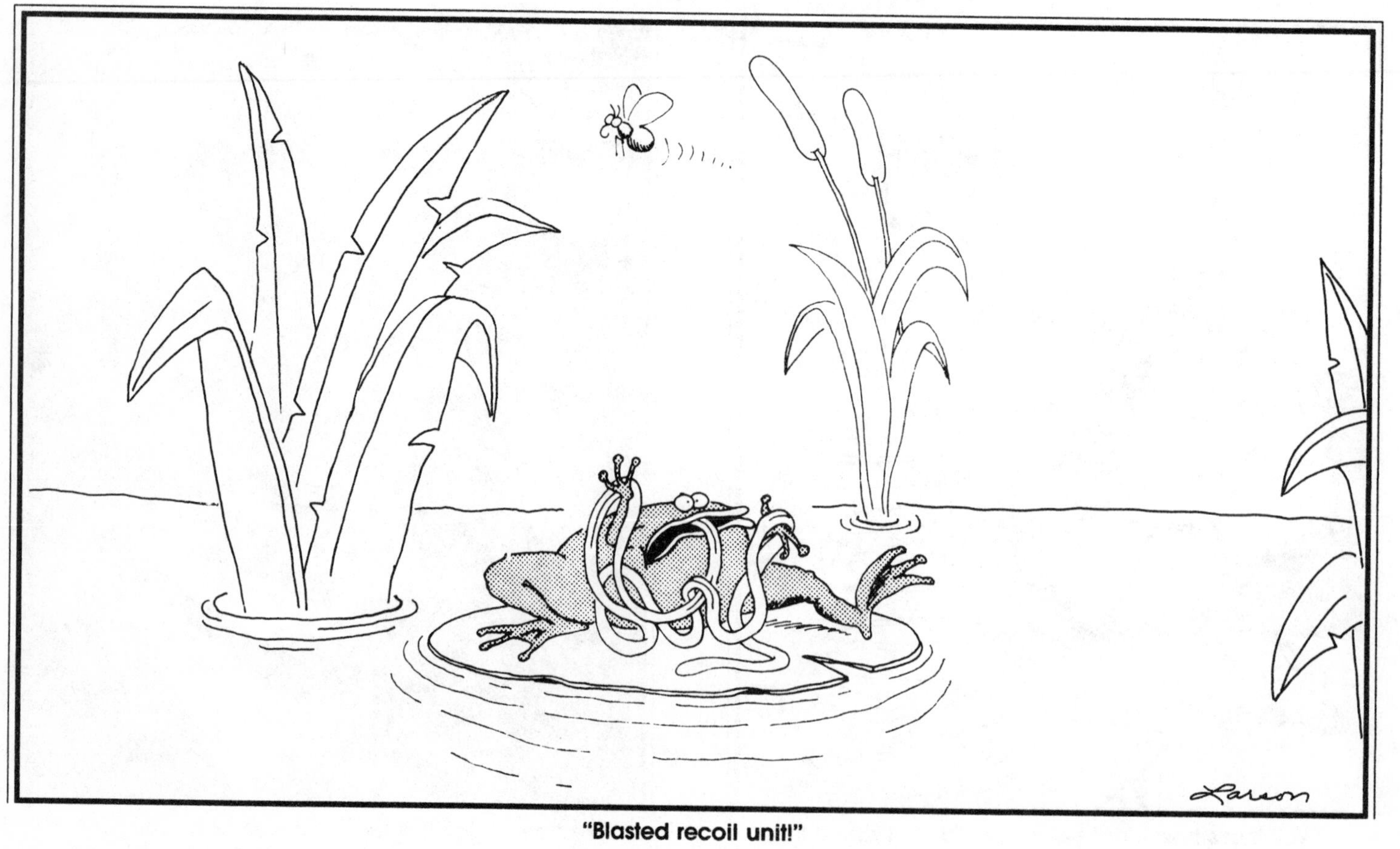
Larson
"Blasted recoil unit!"

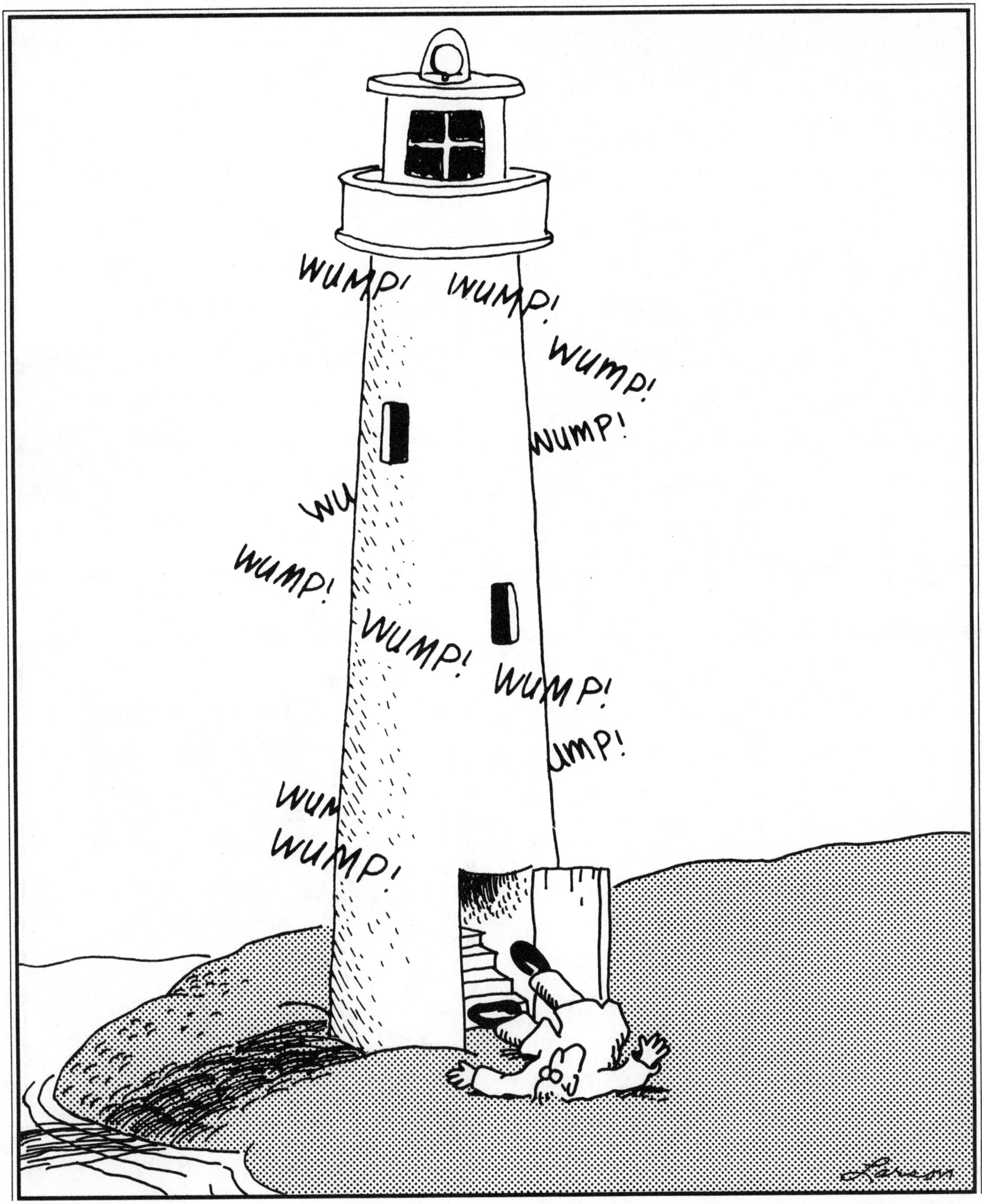
WUMP!
WUMP!
WUMP!
WUMP!
WU
WUMP!
WUMP!
WUMP!
UMP!
WUM
WUMP!

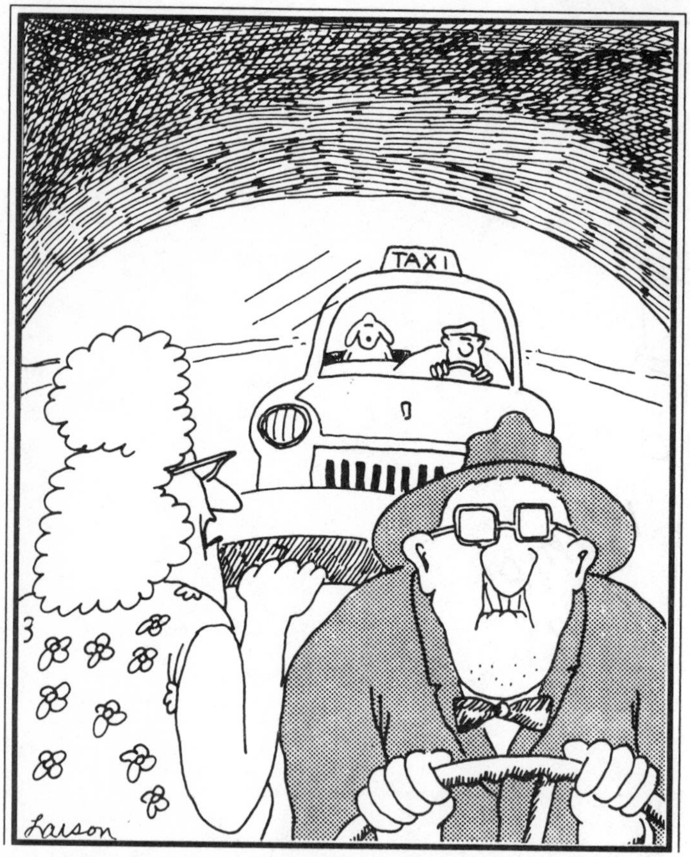
TAXI
Larson

"Blast it, Henry! . . . I think the dog is following us."

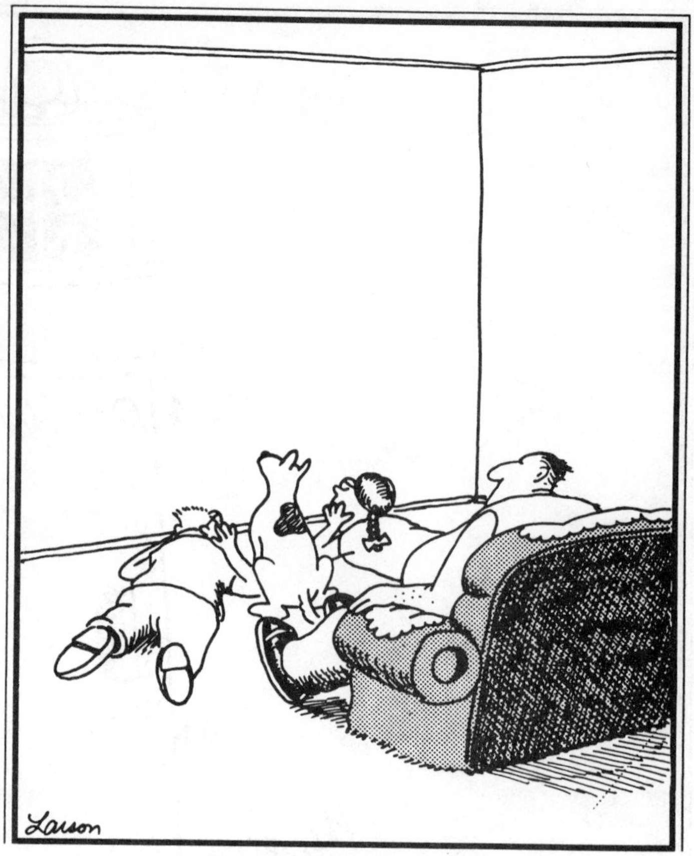
Larson

In the days before television

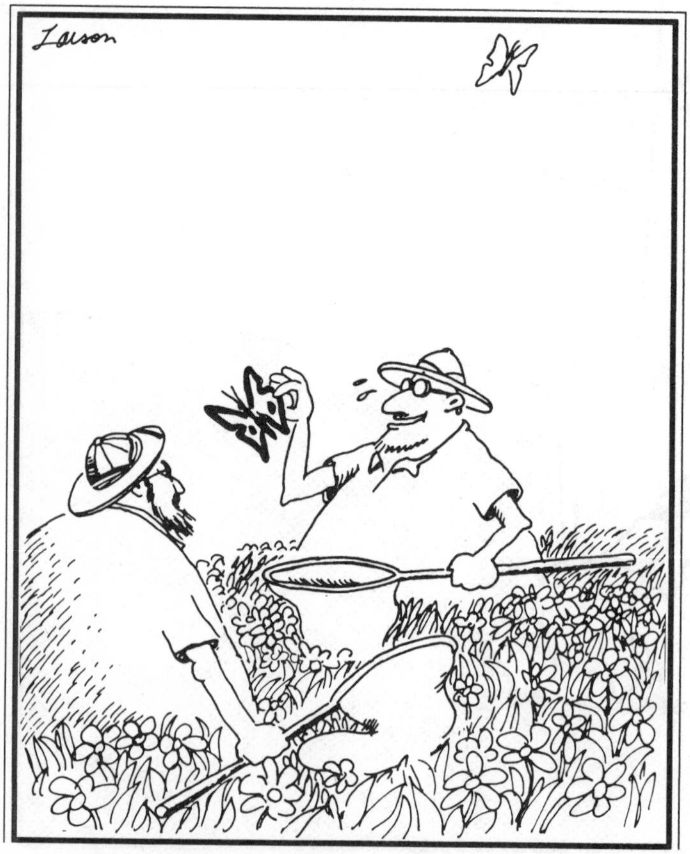
Larson

"An excellent specimen . . . symbol of beauty, innocence, and fragile life . . . hand me the jar of ether."

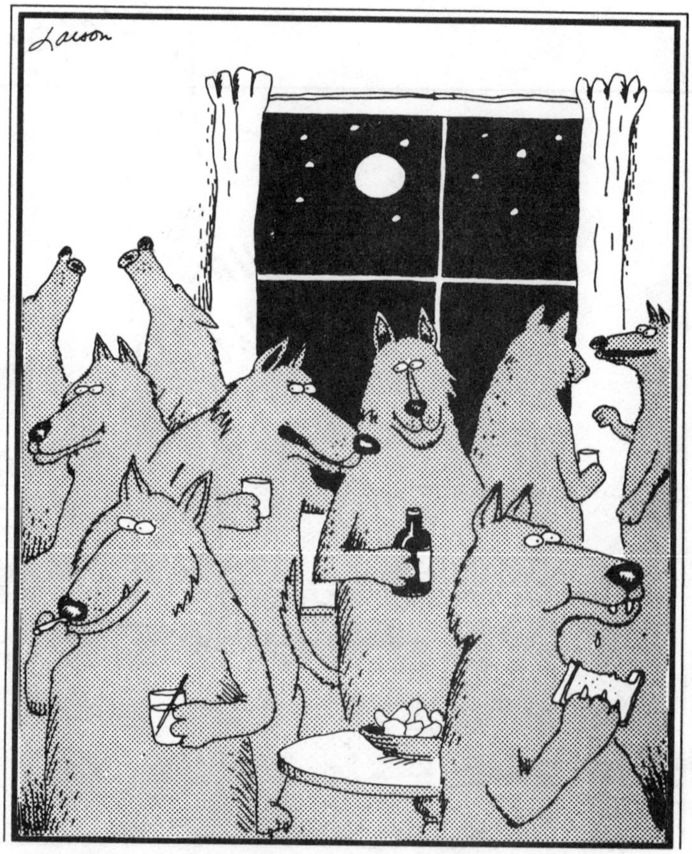
Larson

"Listen . . . this party's a drag. But later on, Floyd, Warren, and myself are going over to Farmer Brown's and slaughter some chickens."

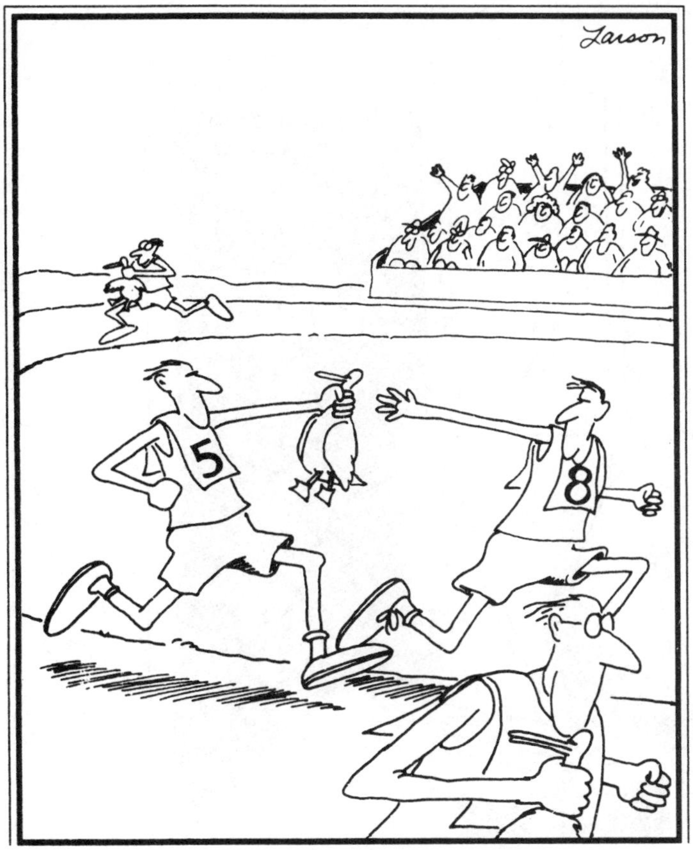
Larson
5
8

The duck relays

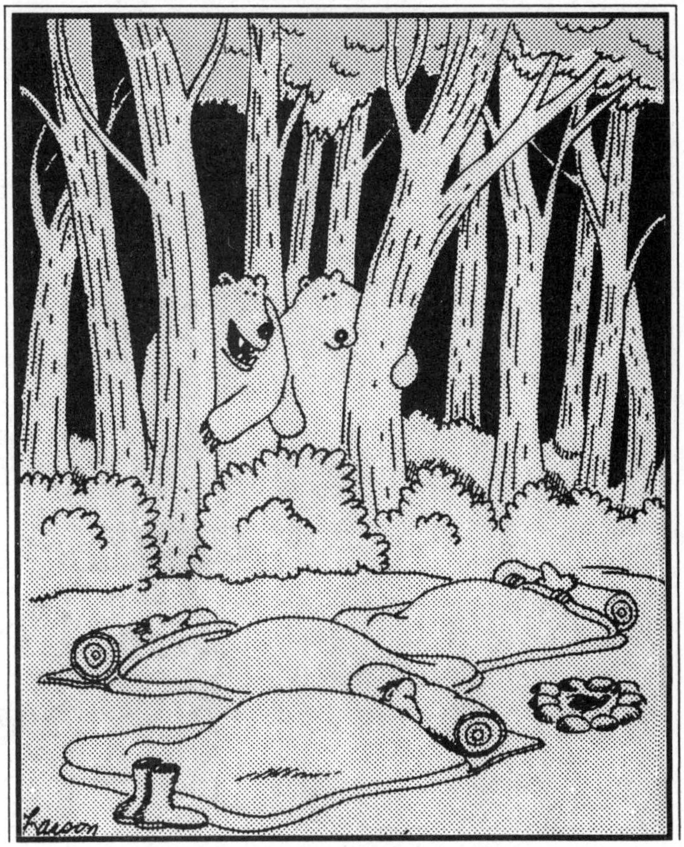
Larson

"Sandwiches!"

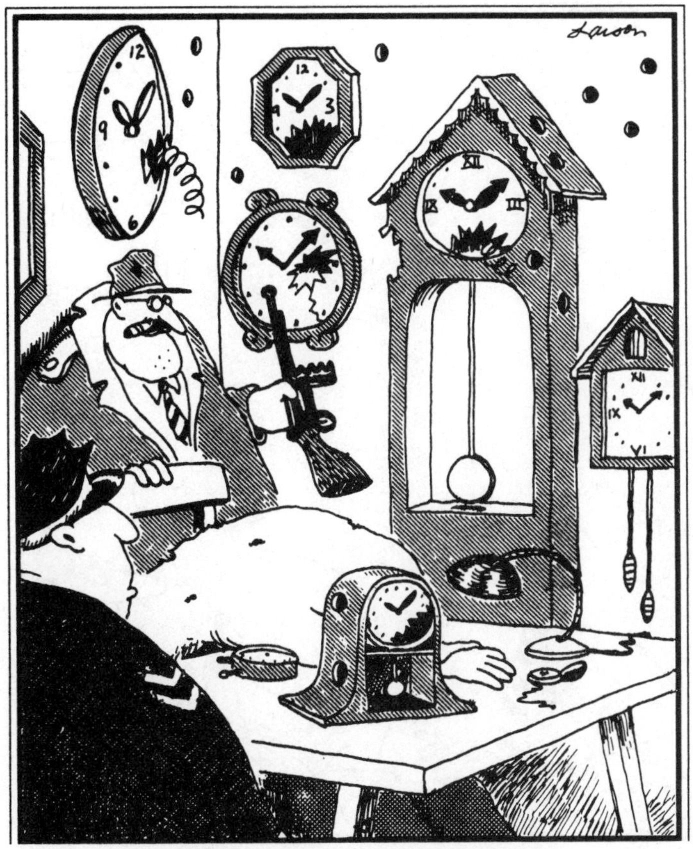
Larson

"We've got the murder weapon and the motive . . . now if we can just establish time-of-death."

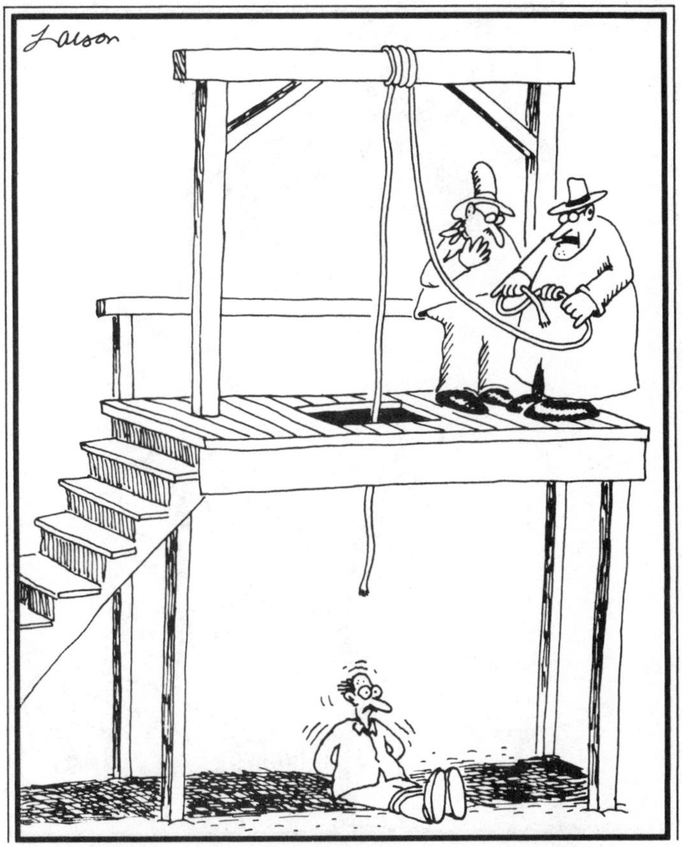
Larson

"You meathead! Now watch! . . . The rabbit goes through the hole, around the tree five or six times . . ."

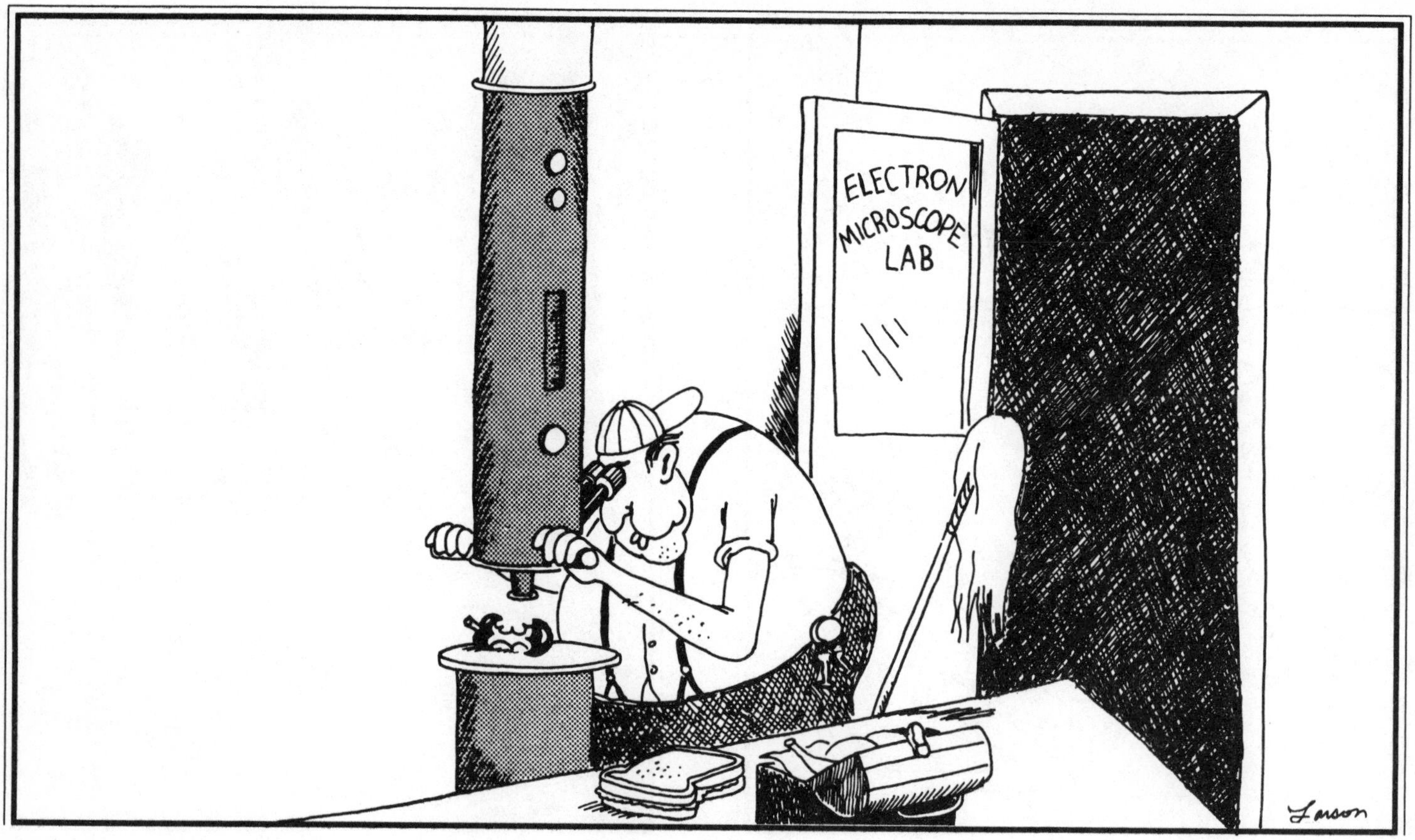
ELECTRON
MICROSCOPE
LAB
Larson

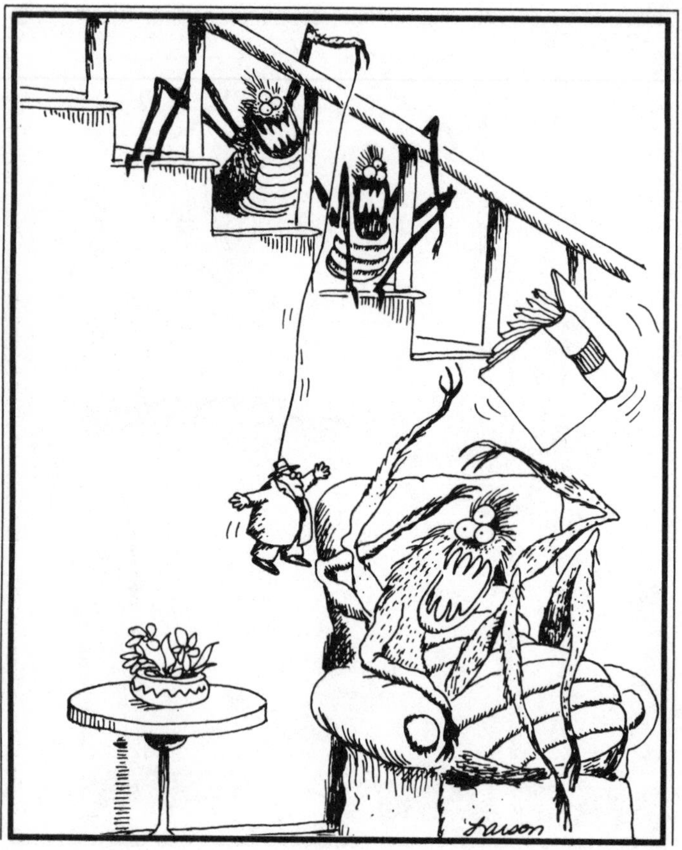
Larson

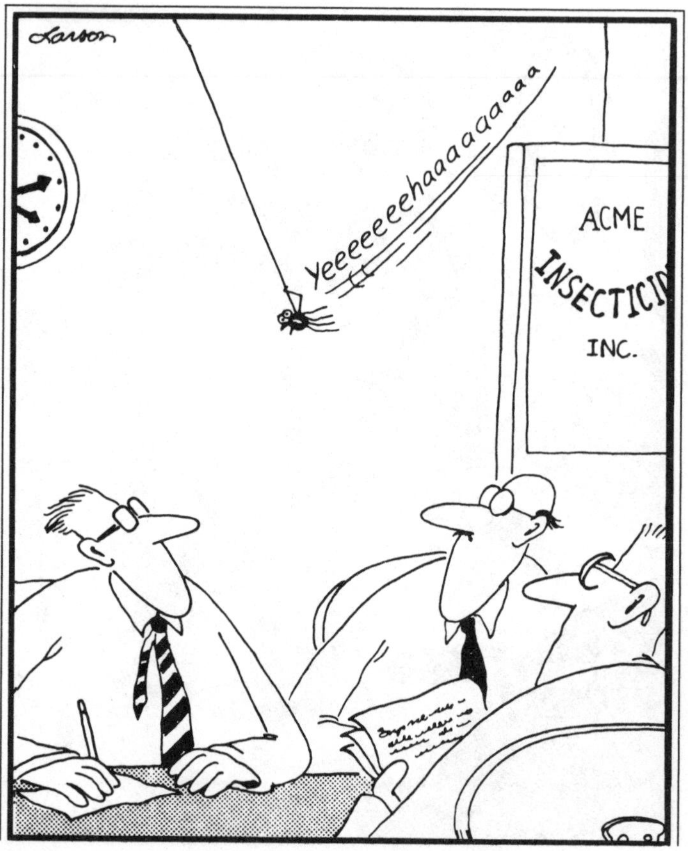
Larson
Yeeeeeeehaaaaaaaaa
ACME
INSECTICID
INC.

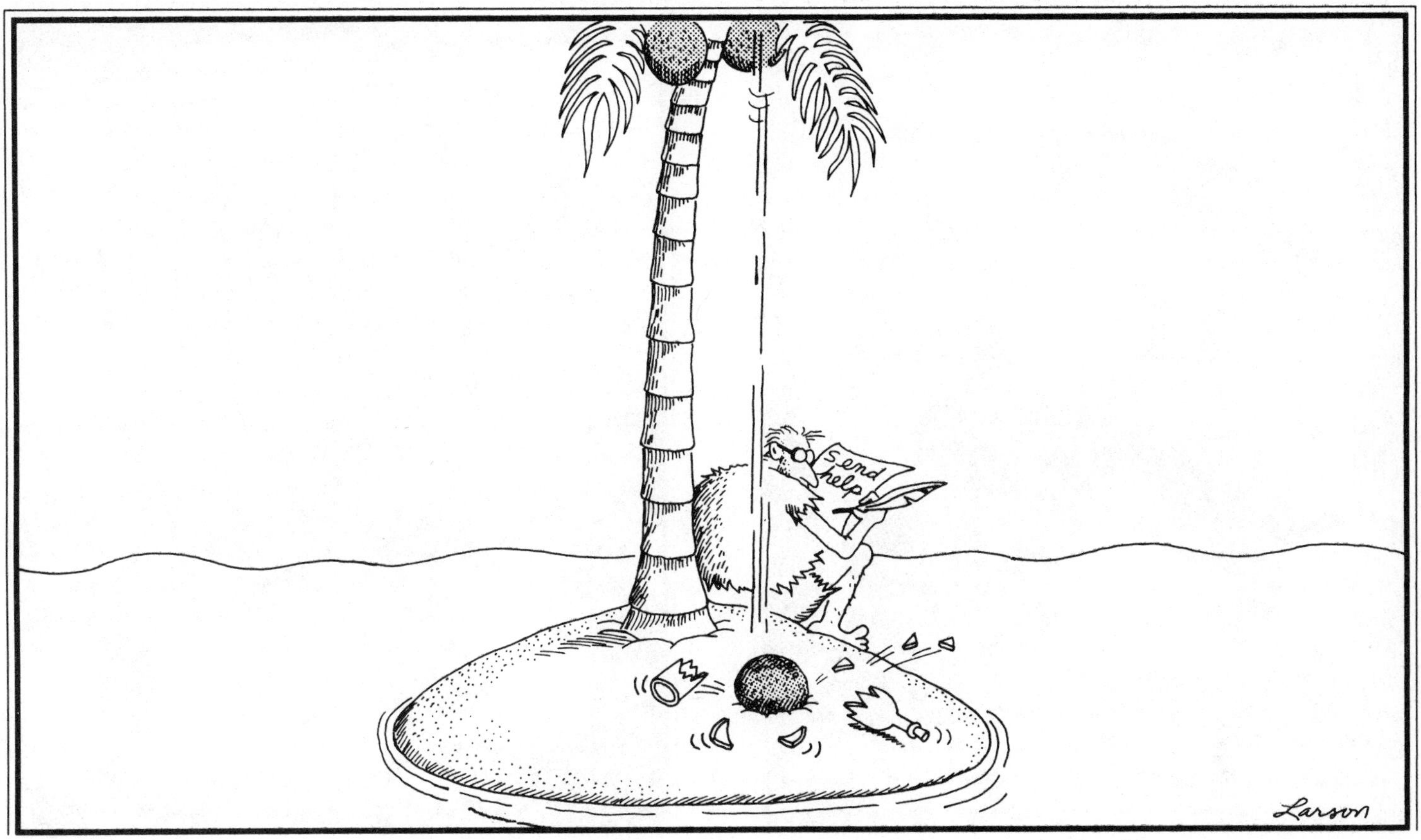
Send help
Larson

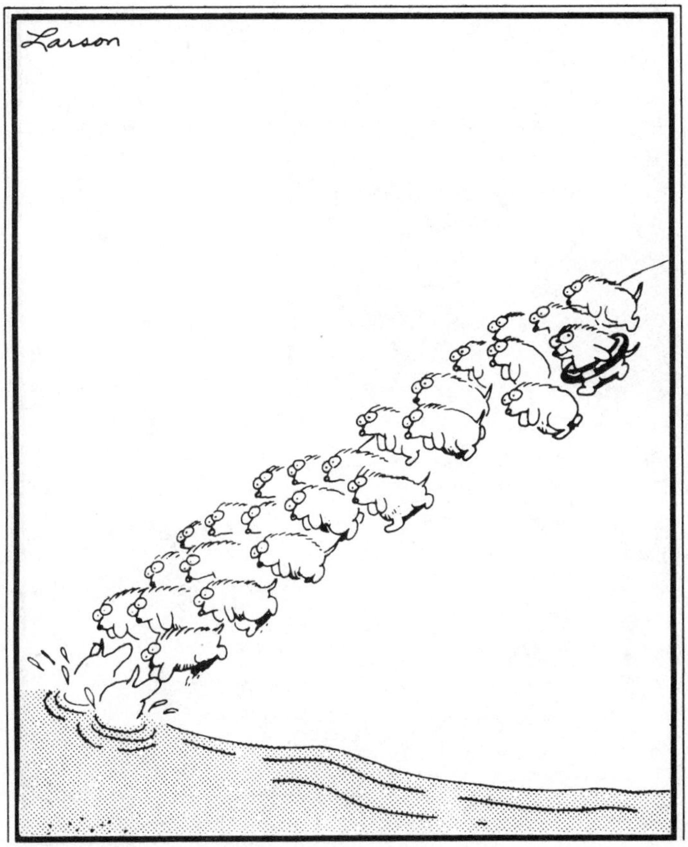
Larson

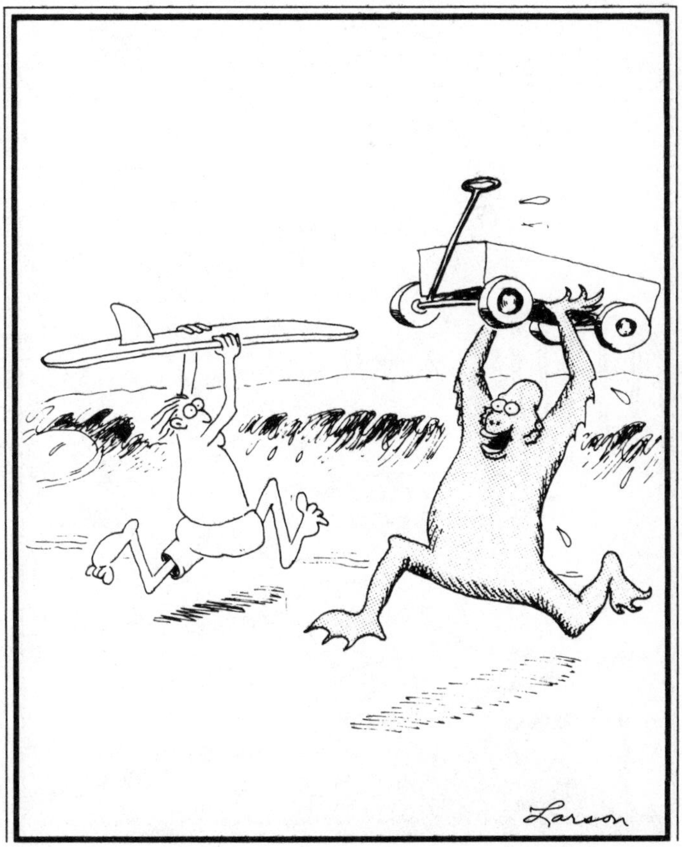
Larson

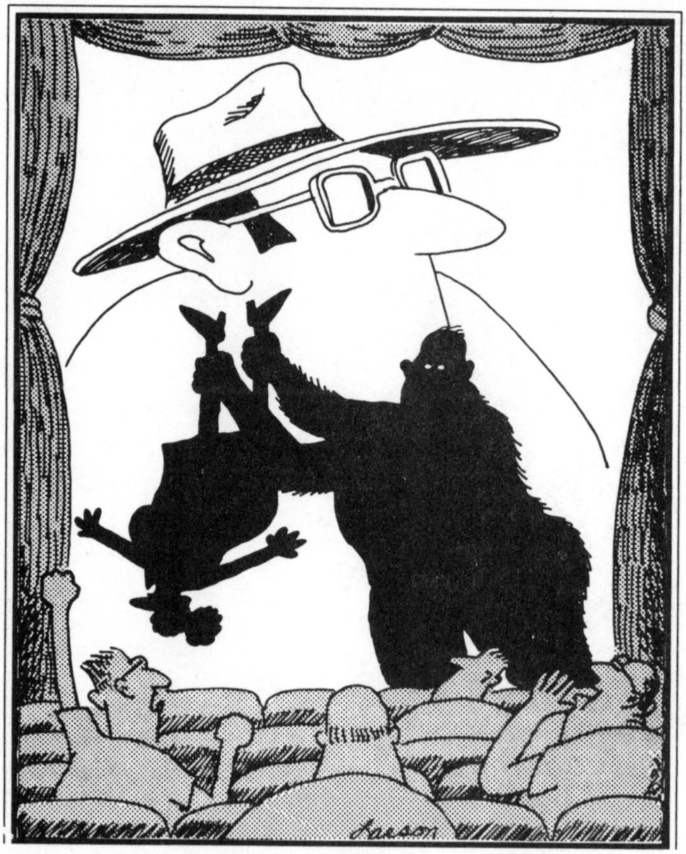
Larson

"Down in front! . . . Sit down! . . . Sit down!"

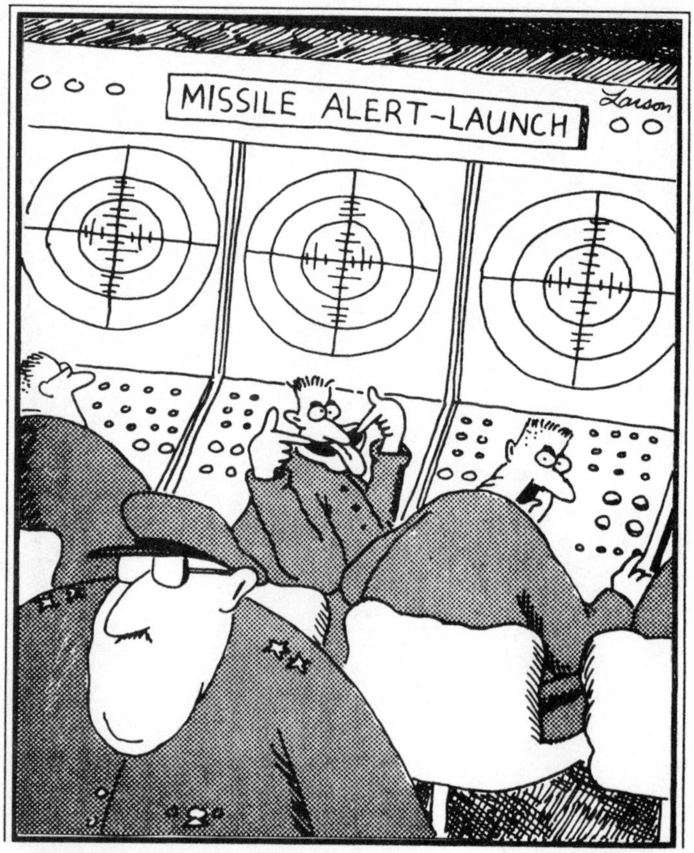
MISSILE ALERT-LAUNCH
Larson

"General! Quick! Look! . . . Henderson is doing it again!"

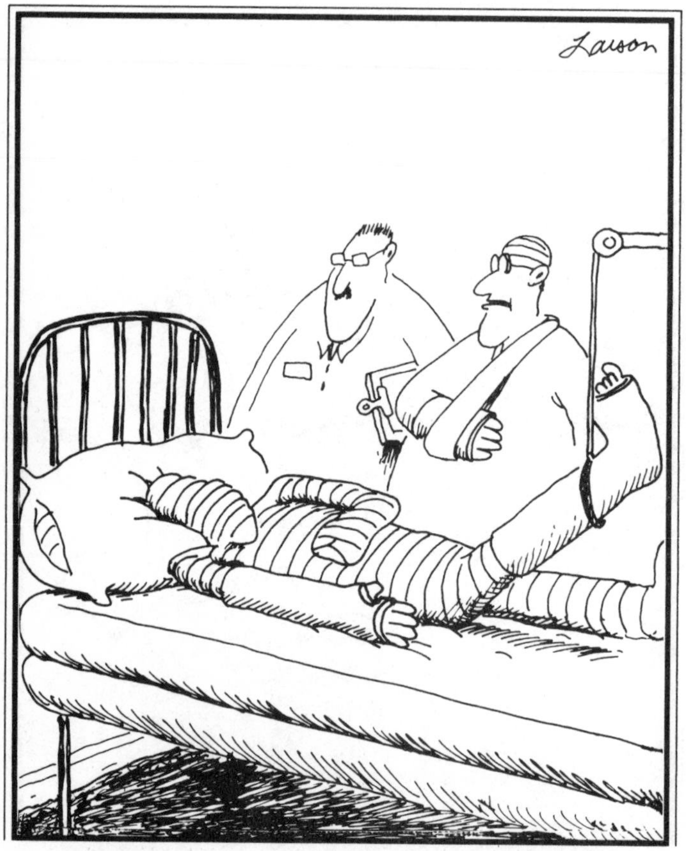
Larson

"So there he was — this big gorilla just laying there. And Jim says, 'Do you suppose it's dead or just asleep?' "

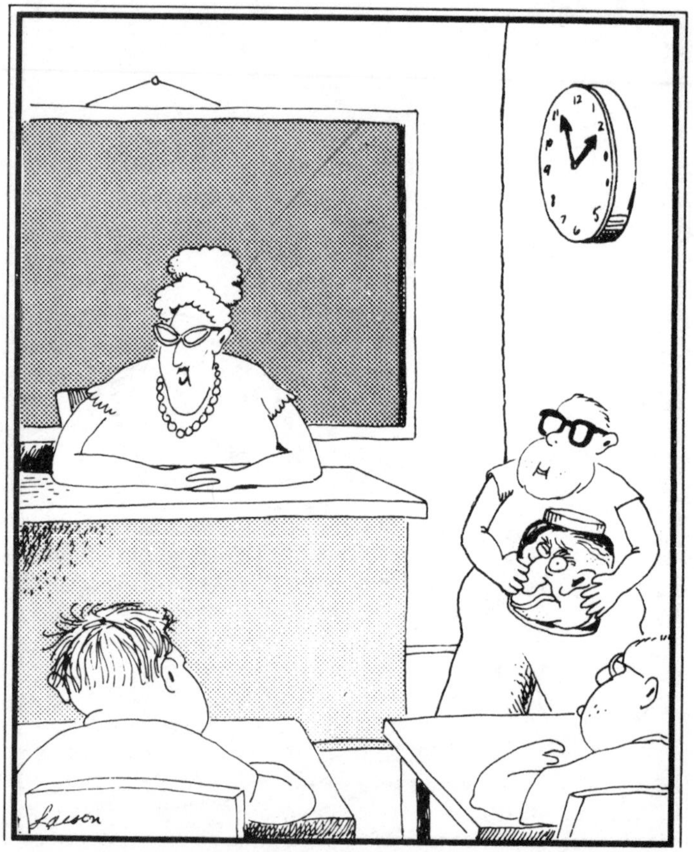
Larson

"And next, for show and tell, Bobby Henderson says he has something he found on the beach last summer . . ."

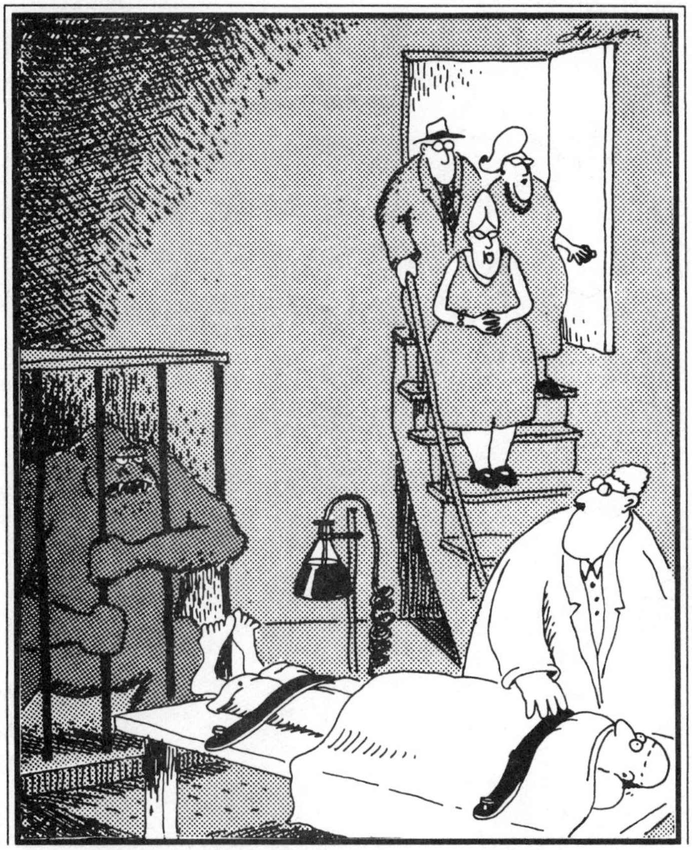
Larson

"Honey, the Merrimonts are here . . . They'd like to come down and see your ape-man project."

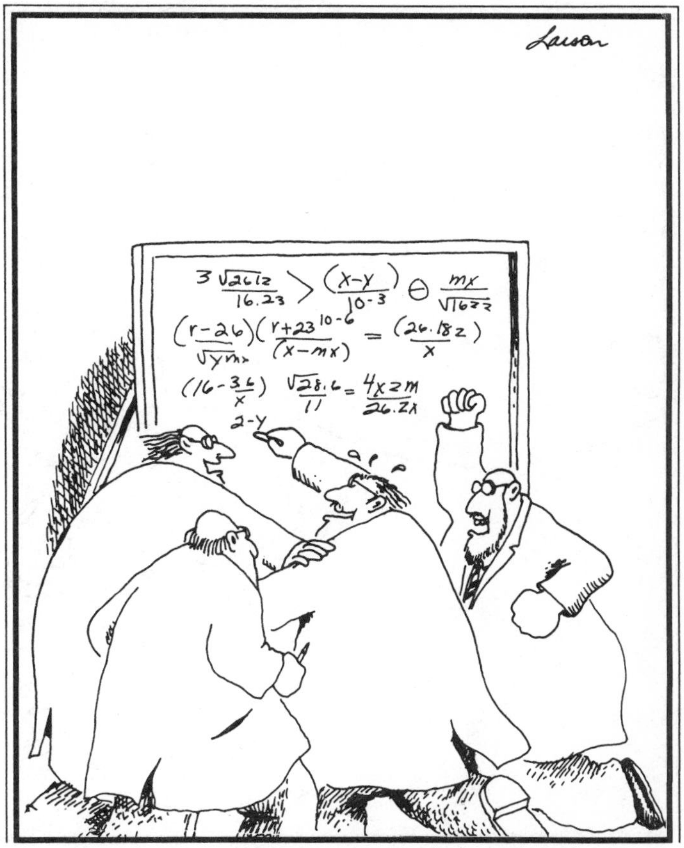
Larson

"Go for it, Sidney! You've got it! You've got it! Good hands! Don't choke!"

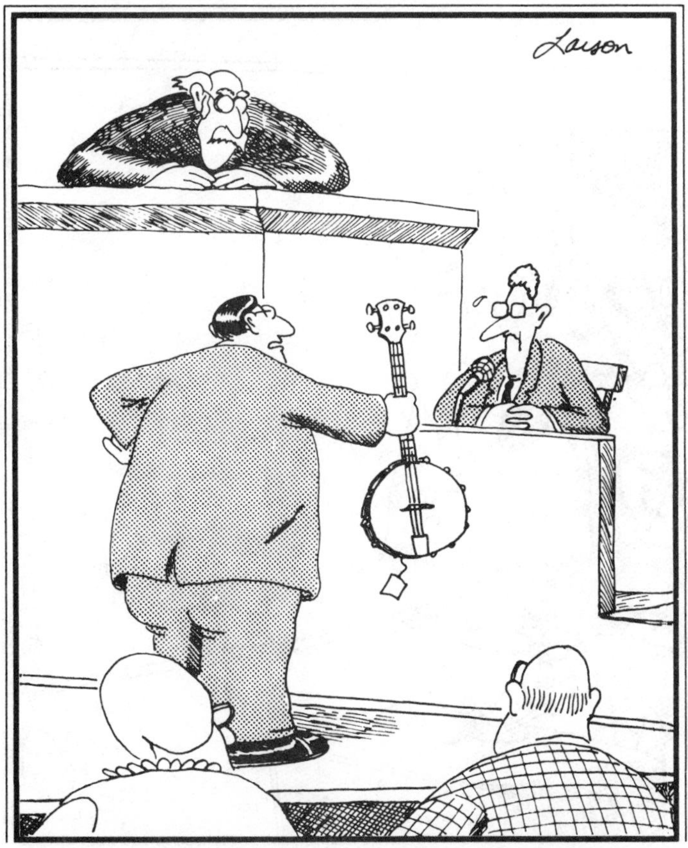
Larson

"So! You admit that this is, indeed, your banjo the police found at the scene . . . But, you expect this jury to believe you were never in the kitchen with Dinah?"

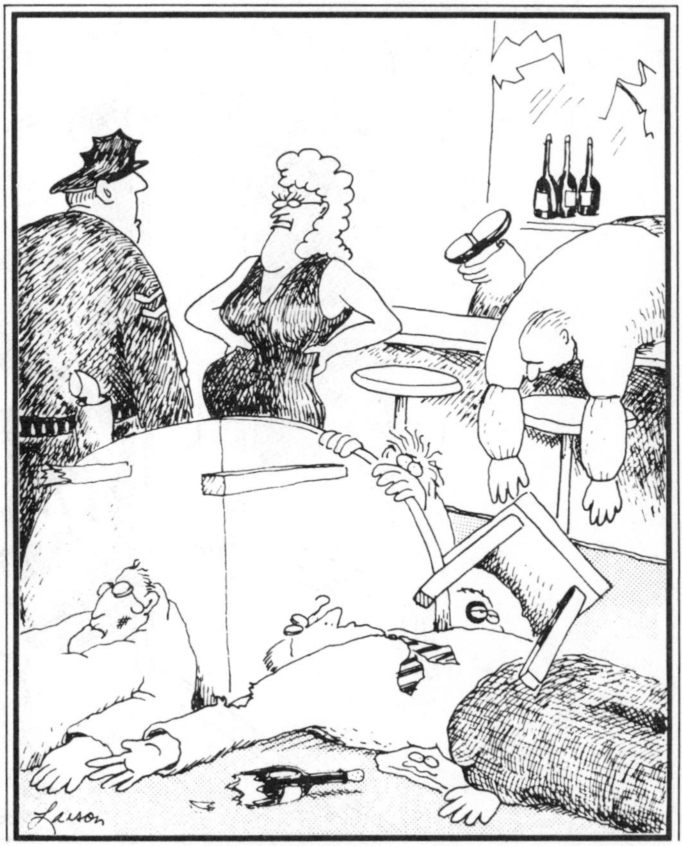
Larson

"So then this little sailor dude whips out a can of spinach, this crazy music starts playin', and . . . well, just look at this place."

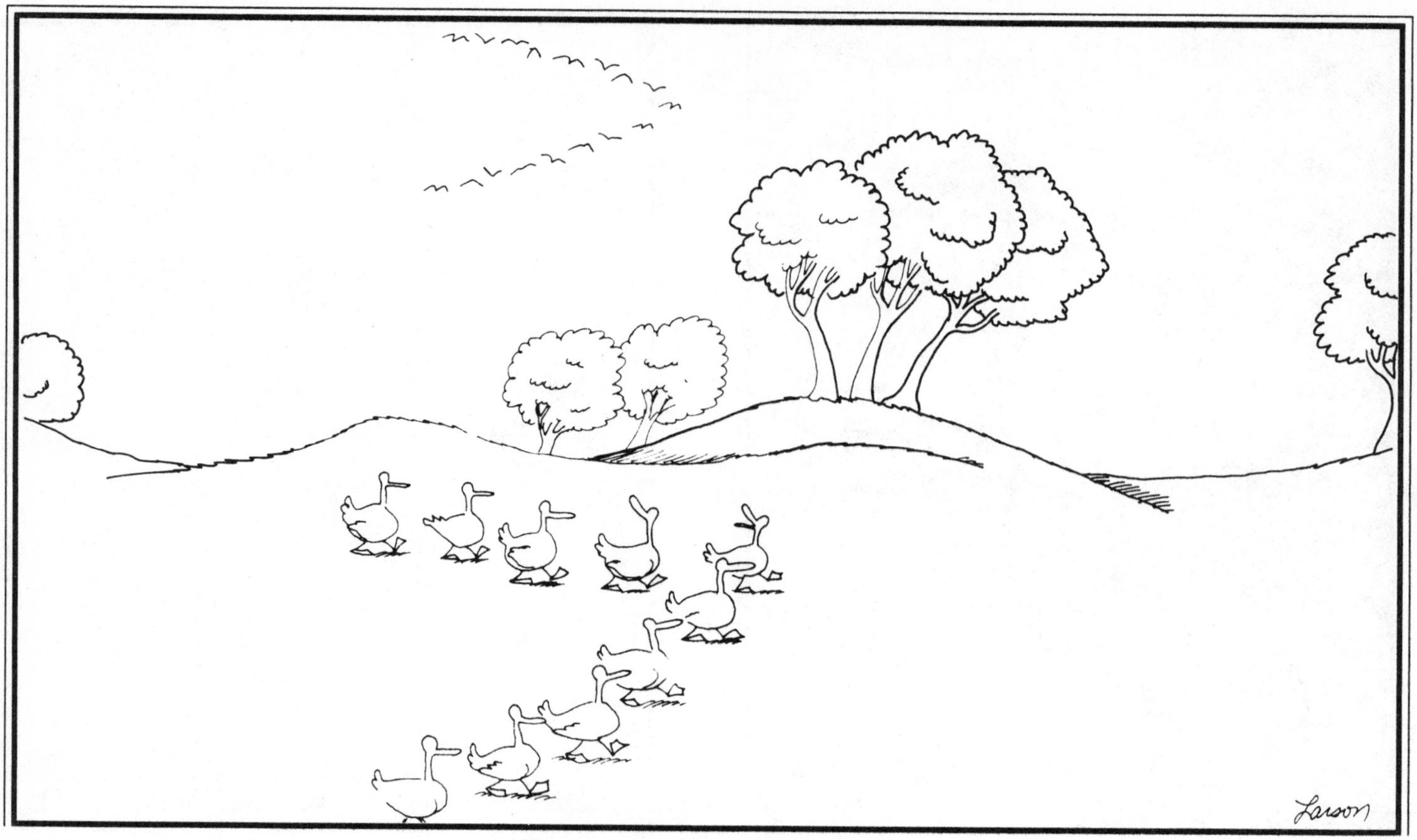
Larson

"Say . . . Look what THEY'RE doing."

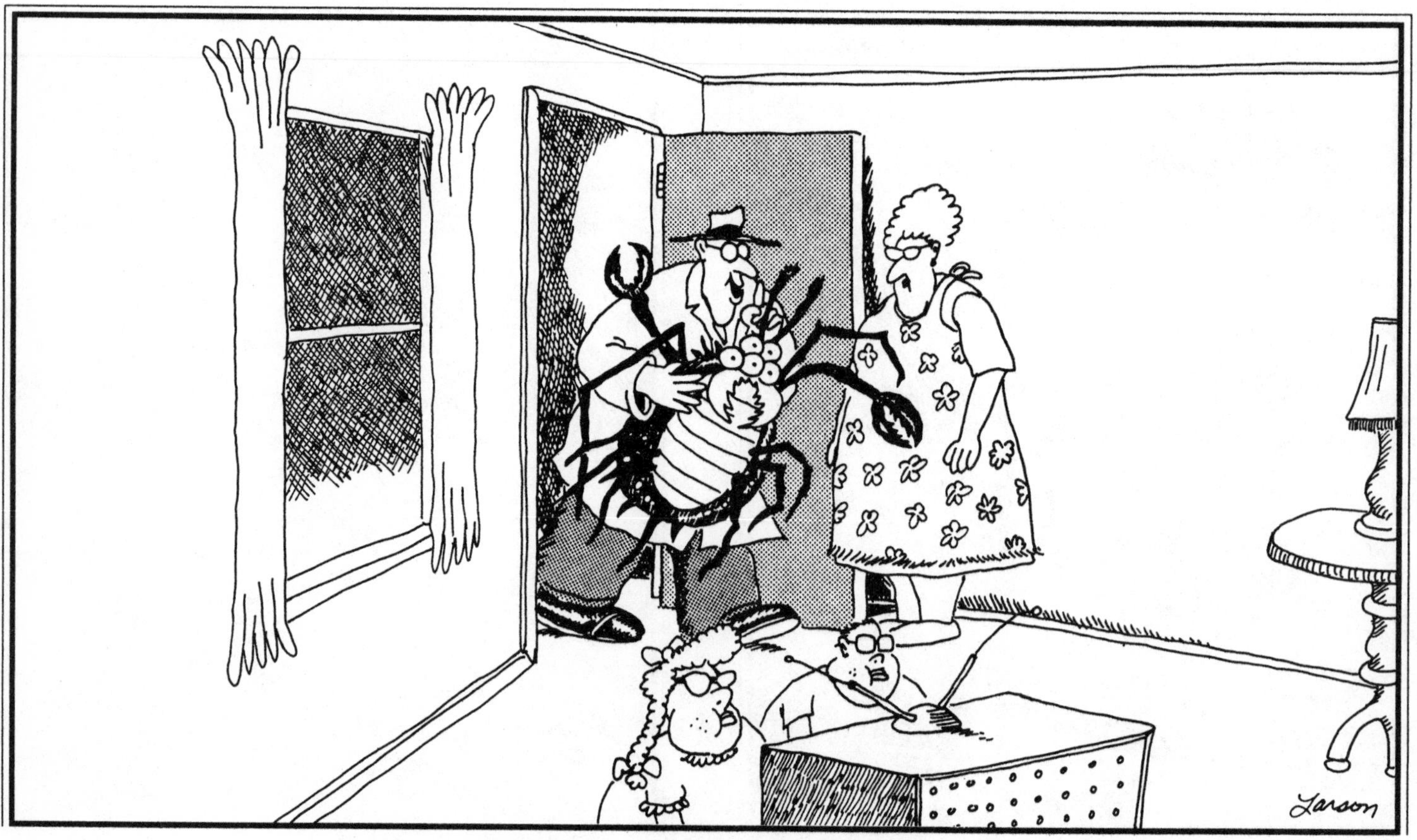
Larson

"Shhhhhhh . . . I wanna surprise the kids."

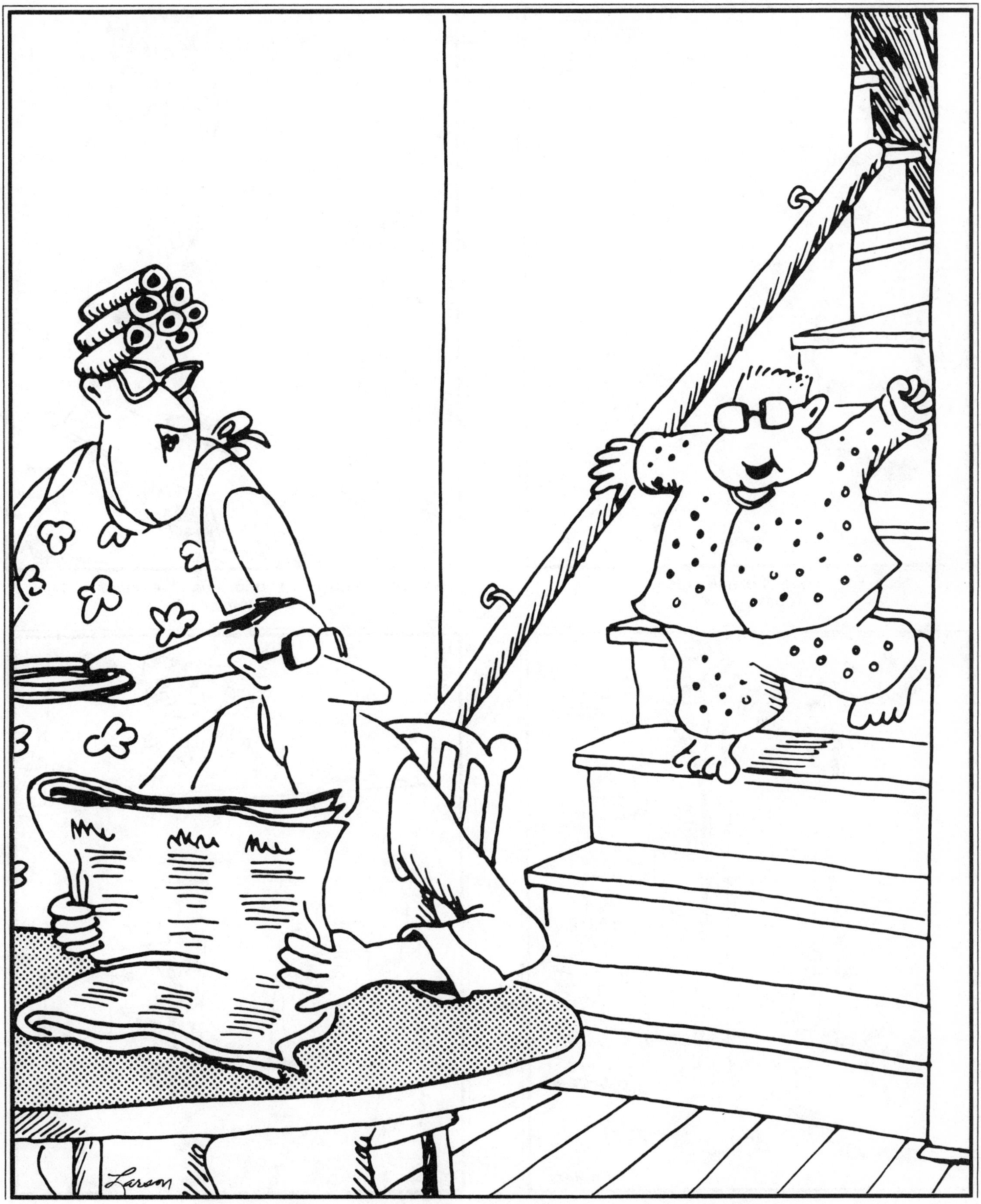
Larson

"Mom! Dad! . . . The nose fairy left me a whole quarter!"

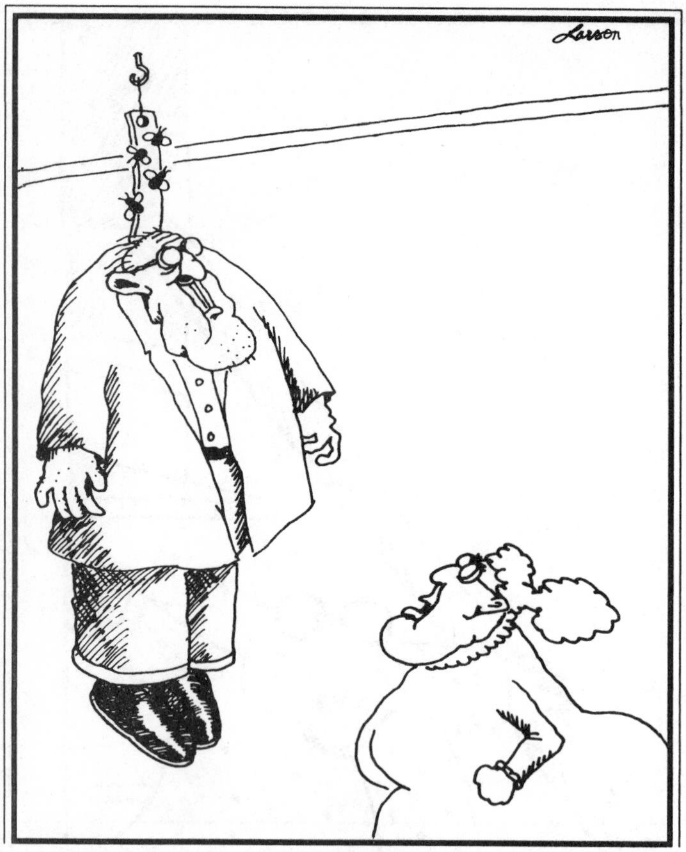
Larson

"So! . . . You've been buzzing around the living room again!"

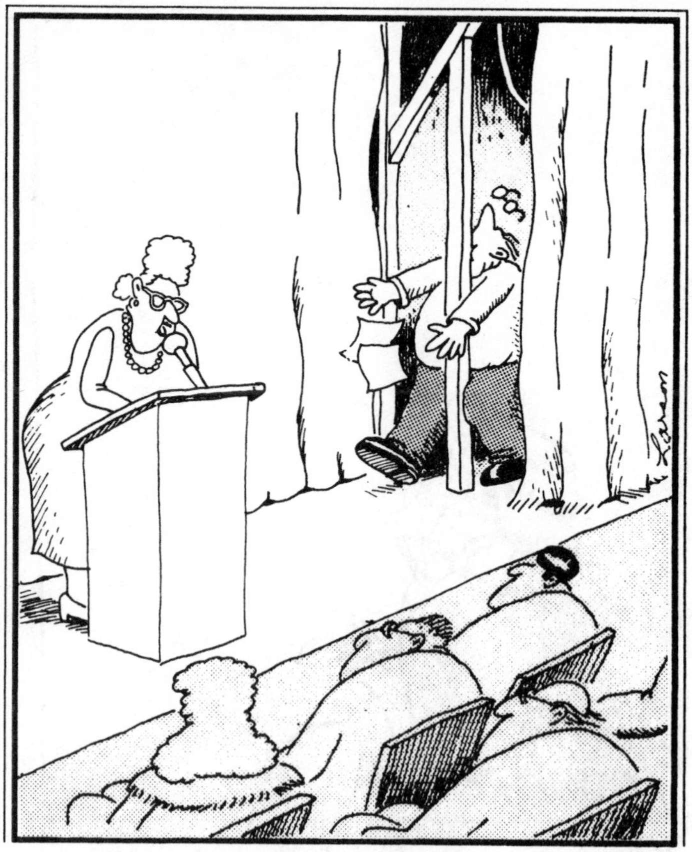
Larson

"And so, without further ado, here's the author of 'Mind over Matter' . . ."

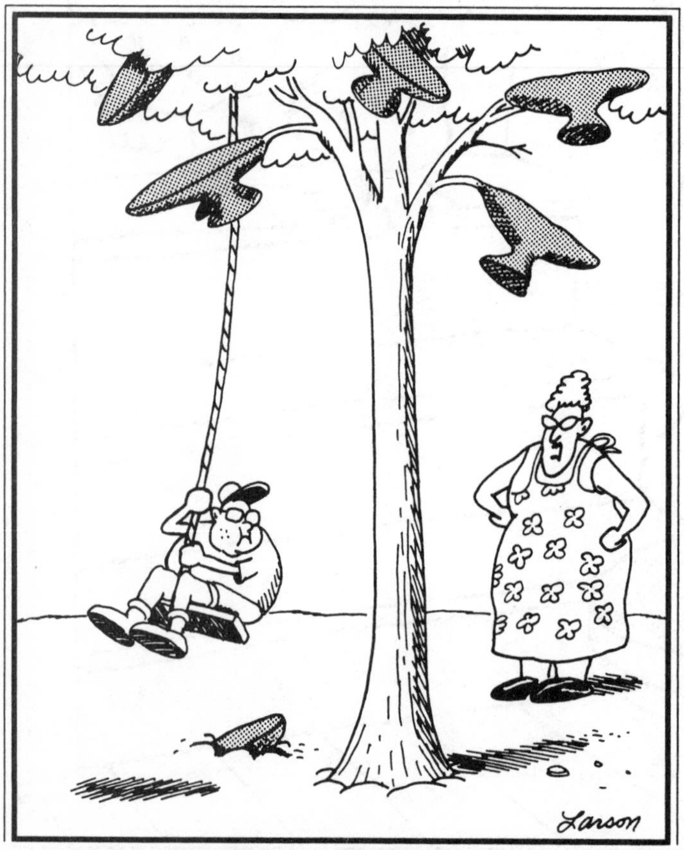
Larson

"All right, Billy, you just go right ahead! . . . I've warned you enough times about playing under the anvil tree!"

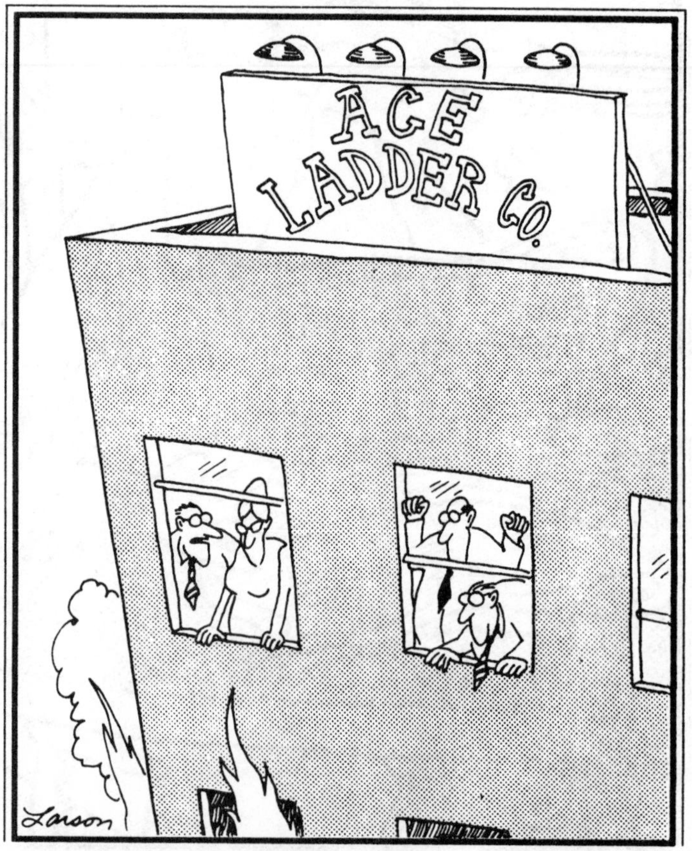
ACE
LADDER CO.
Larson

"Wait a minute! Say that again, Doris! . . . You know, the part about, 'If only we had some means of climbing down.'"

"Say . . . Now I'M starting to feel kinda warm!"

"You know, we're just not reaching that guy."

"And another thing . . . I want you to be more assertive!
I'm tired of everyone calling you Alexander the
Pretty-Good!"

"Of course, living in an all-glass house has its
disadvantages . . . but you should see the birds
smack it."

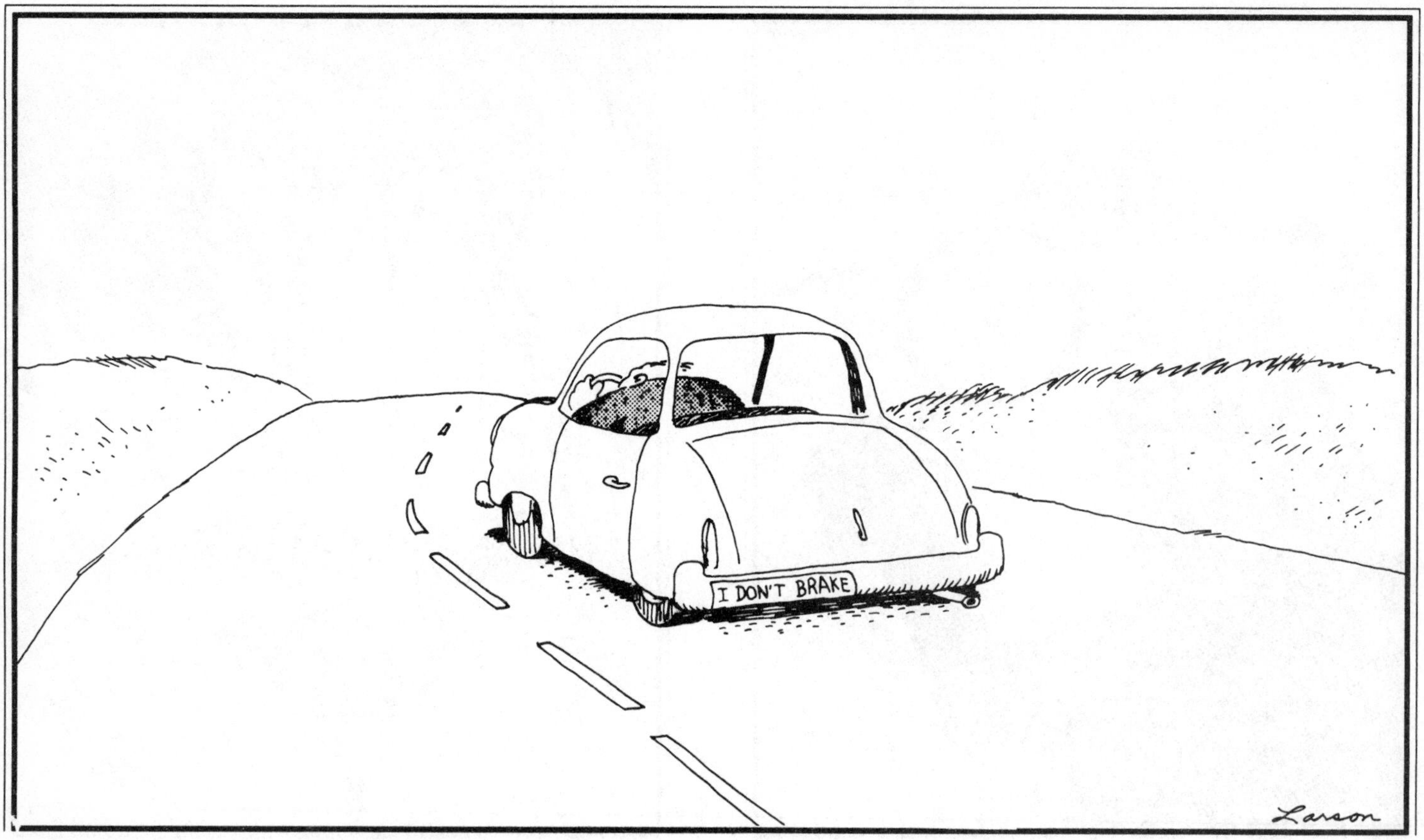
I DON'T BRAKE
Larson

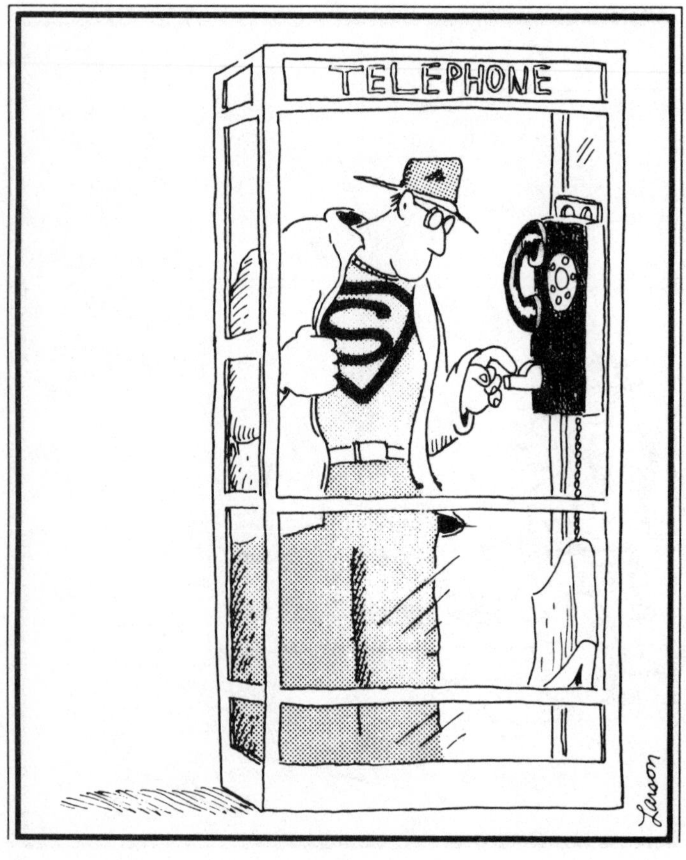
TELEPHONE
Larson

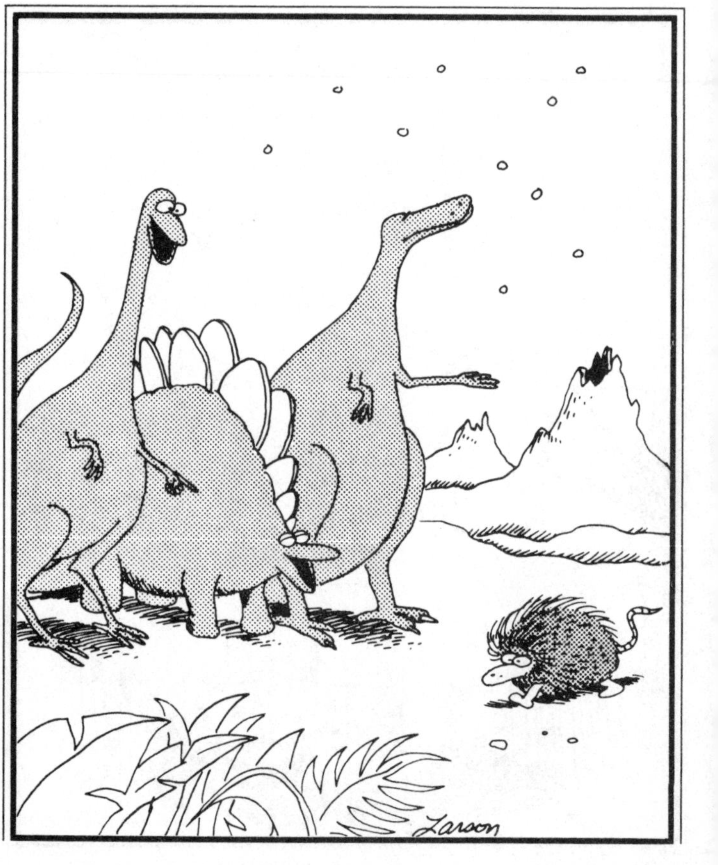
Larson

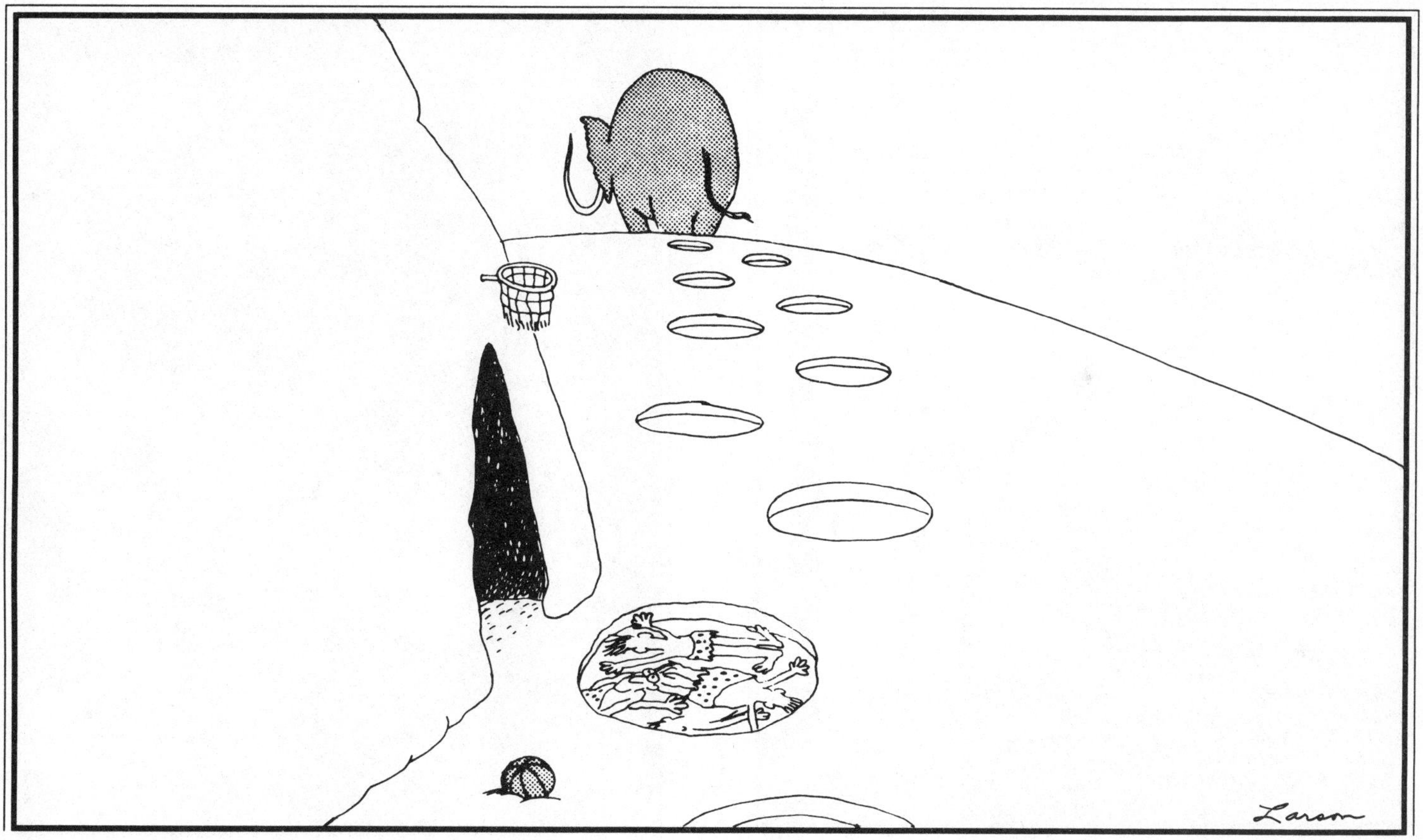
Larson

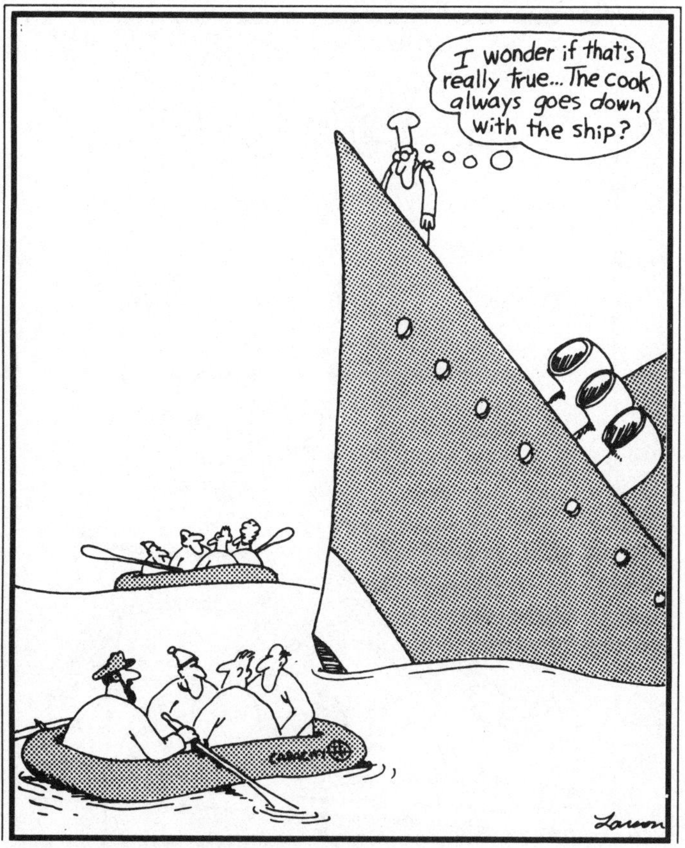
I wonder if that's really true... The cook always goes down with the ship?
Larson

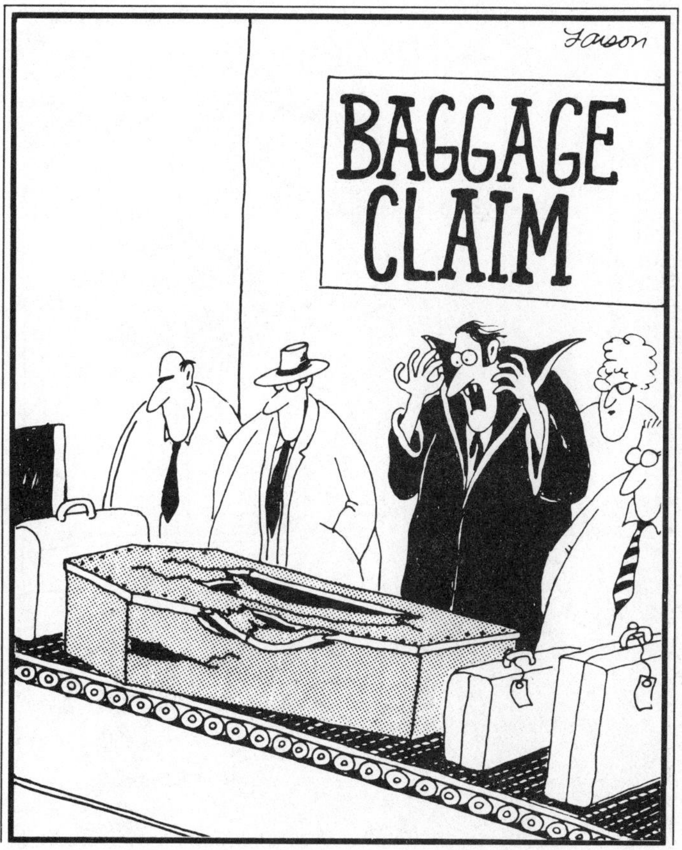
Larson
BAGGAGE CLAIM

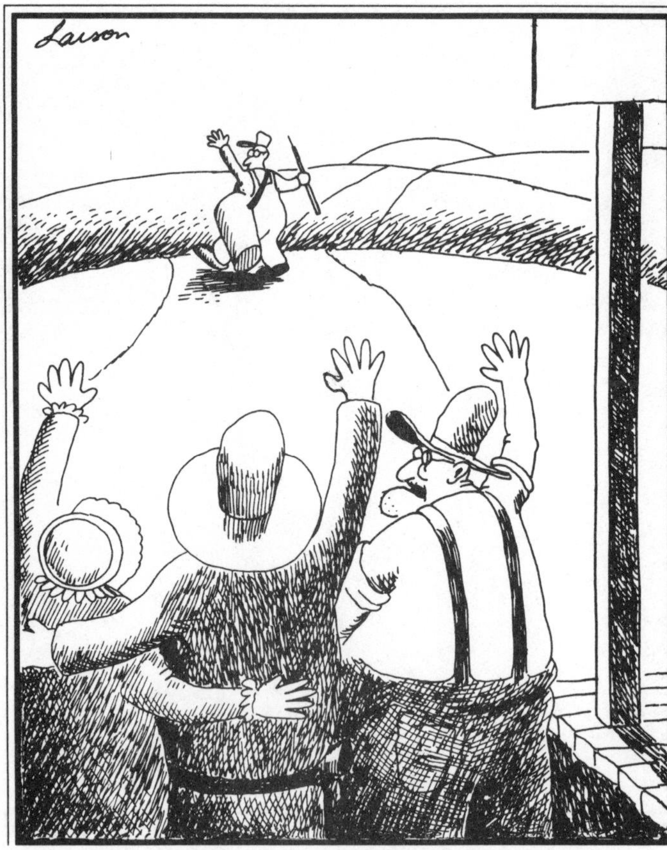
Larson

"I never got his name . . . but he sure cleaned up this town."

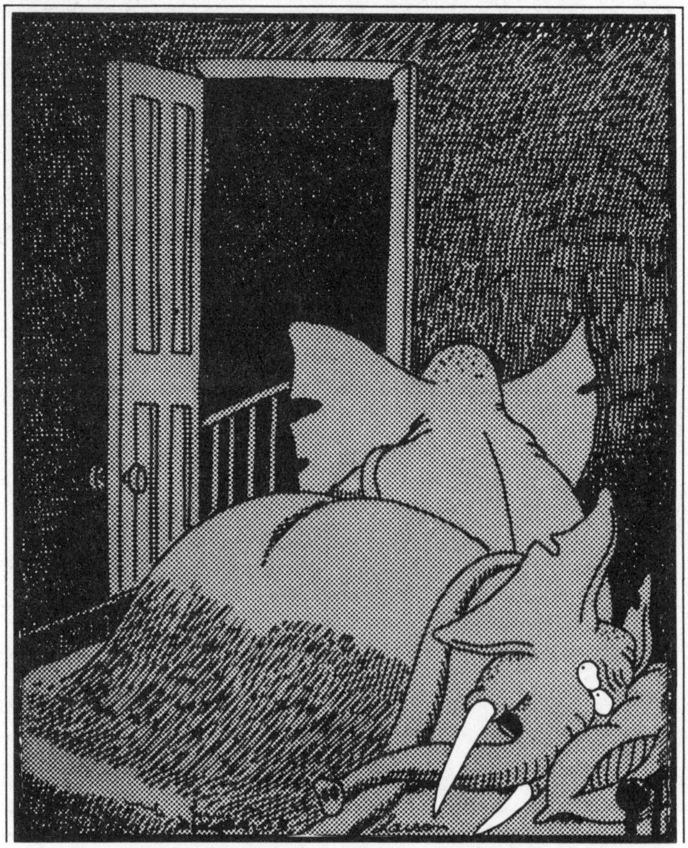

"For crying out loud! . . . You're ALWAYS hearing something moving around downstairs!"

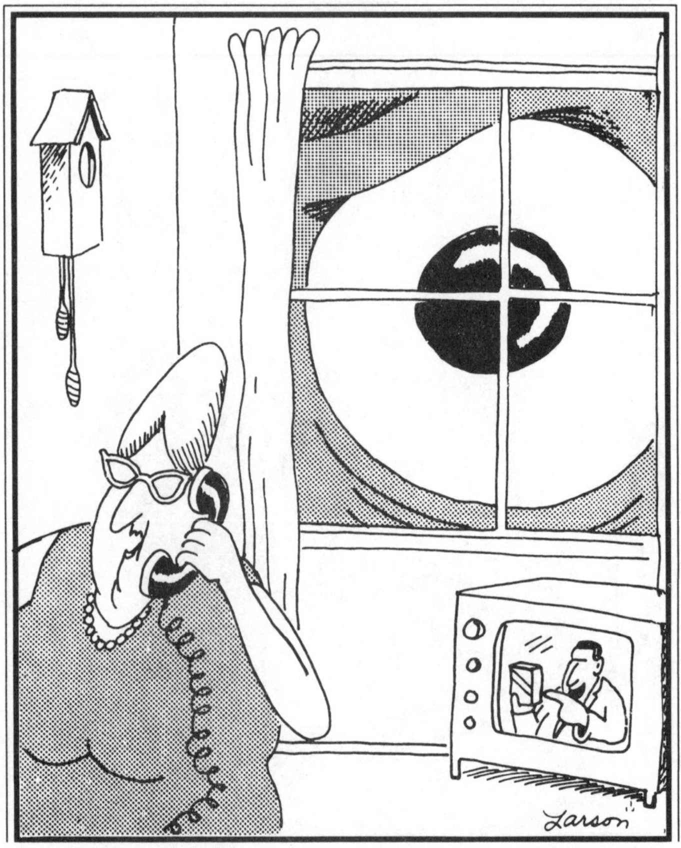
Larson

"Hello, Emily. This is Gladys Murphy up the street. Fine, thanks . . . Say, could you go to your window and describe what's in my front yard?"

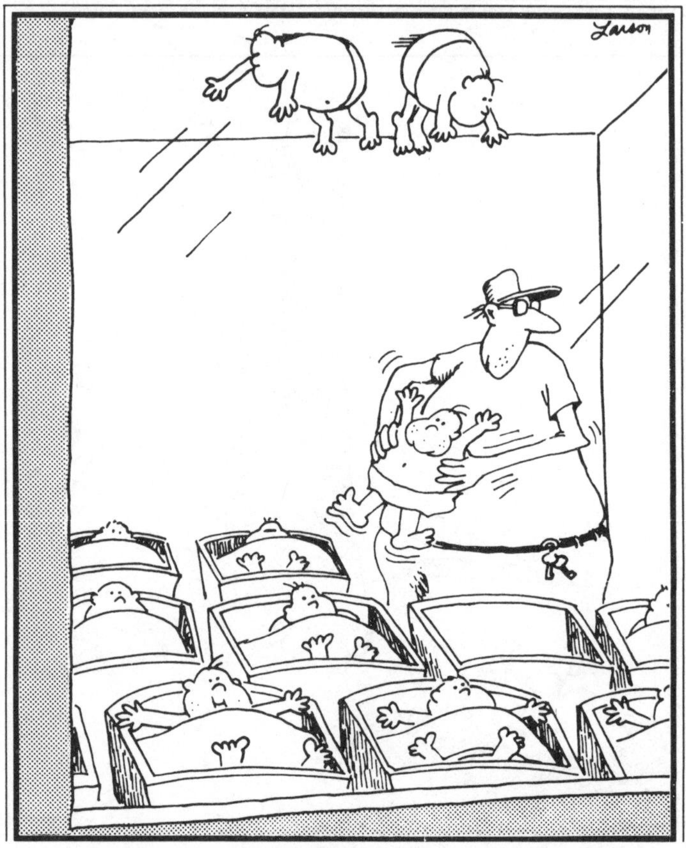
Larson

Late at night, and without permission, Reuben would often enter the nursery and conduct experiments in static electricity.

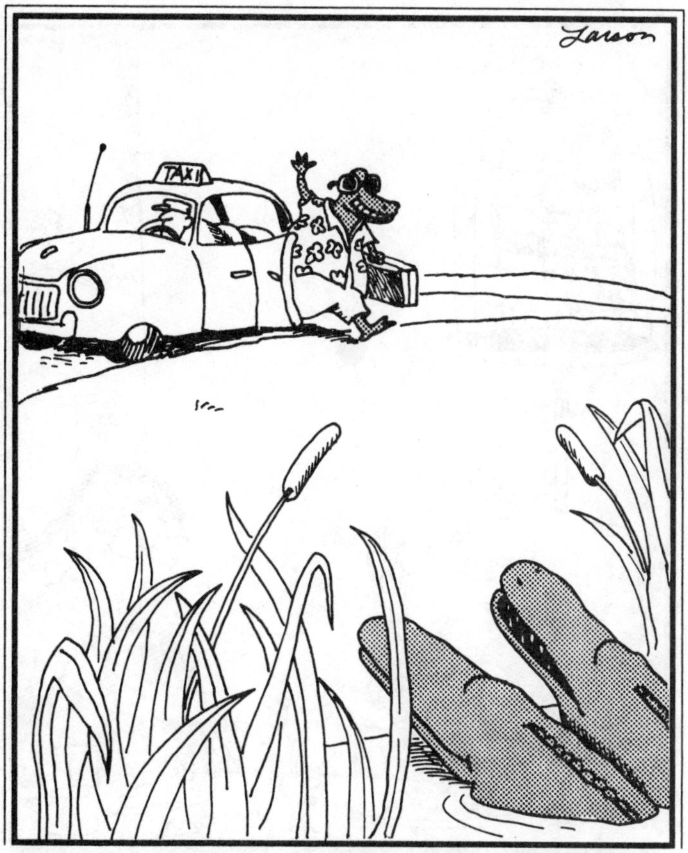
TAXI
Larson

"Well, for crying out loud! . . . It's Uncle Irwin from the city sewer!"

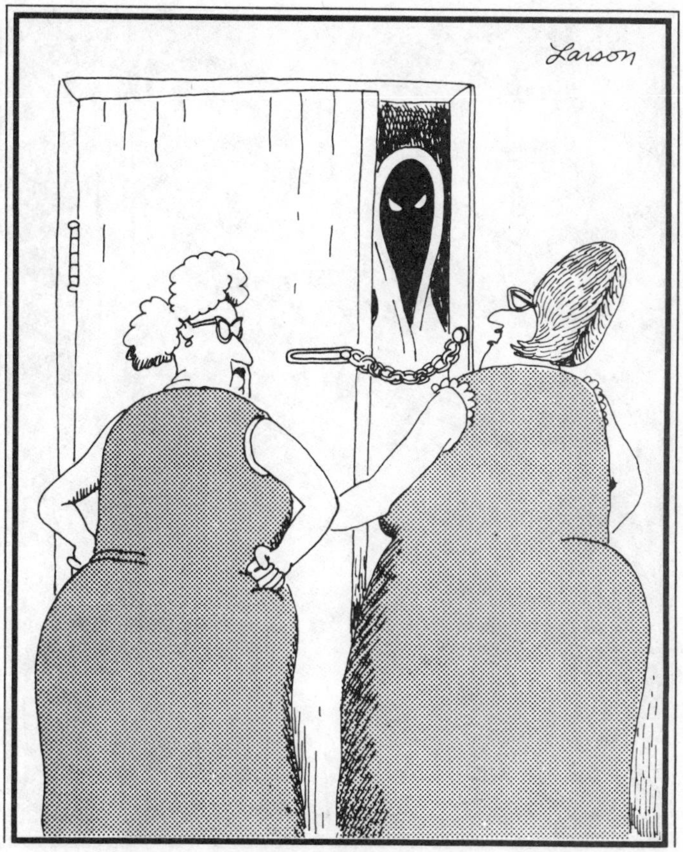
Larson

"Now wait just a minute here . . . How are we supposed to know you're the REAL Angel of Death?"

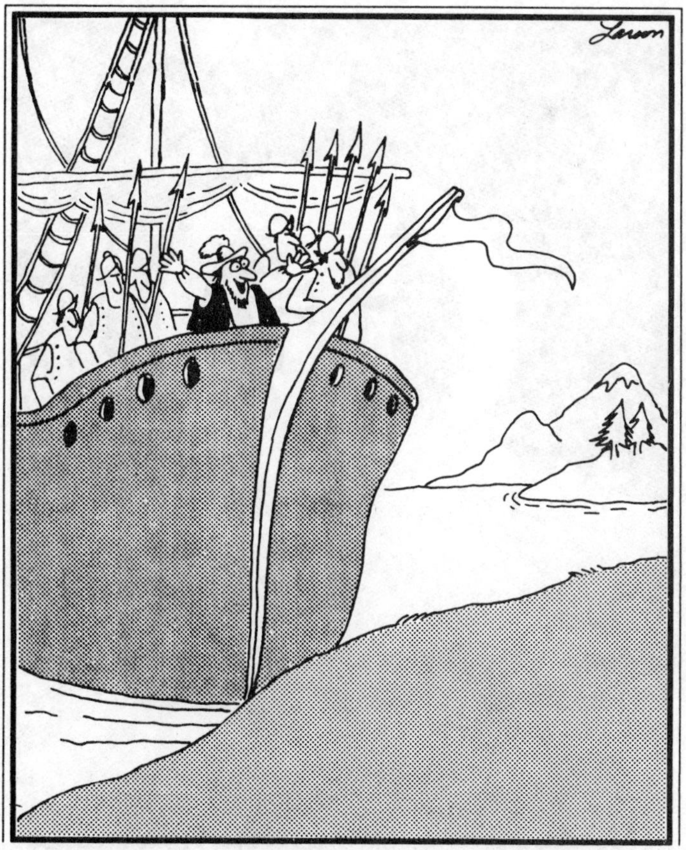
Larson

"Look! Look, gentlemen! . . . Purple mountains! Spacious skies! Fruited plains! . . . Is someone writing this down?"

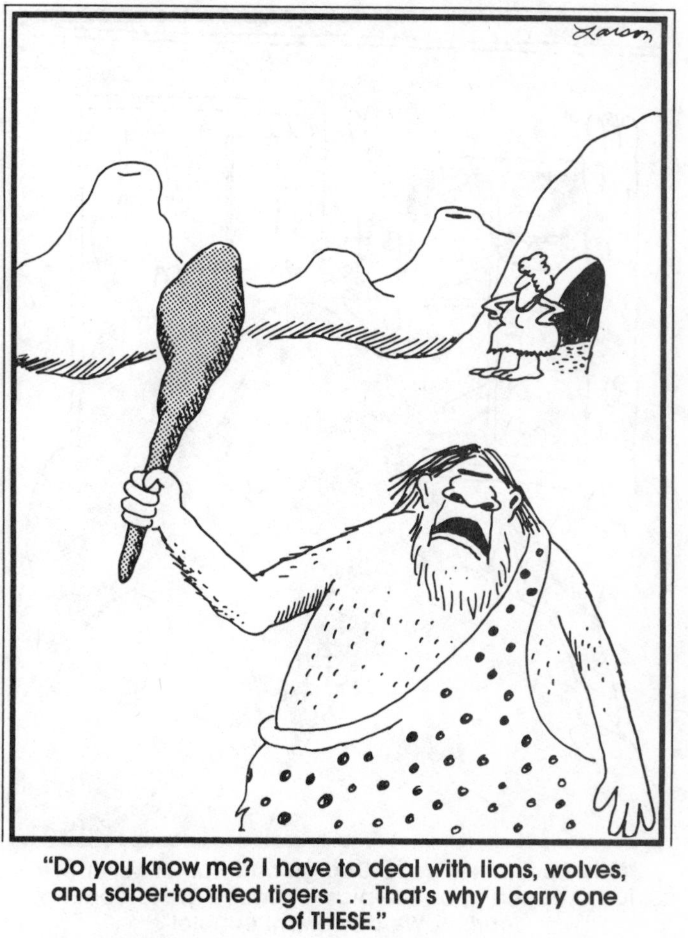
Larson

"Do you know me? I have to deal with lions, wolves, and saber-toothed tigers . . . That's why I carry one of THESE."

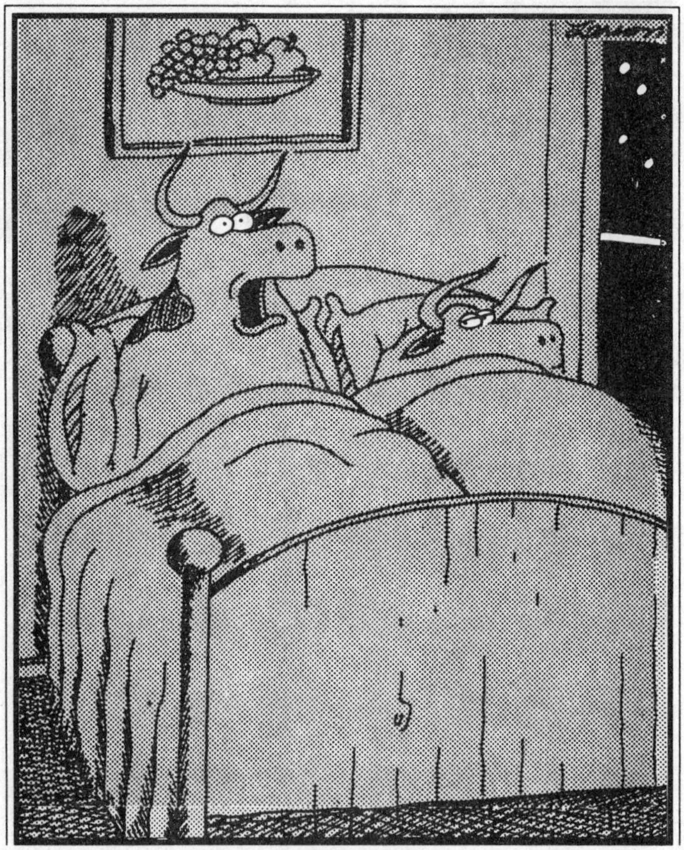

"The golden arches! The golden arches got me!"

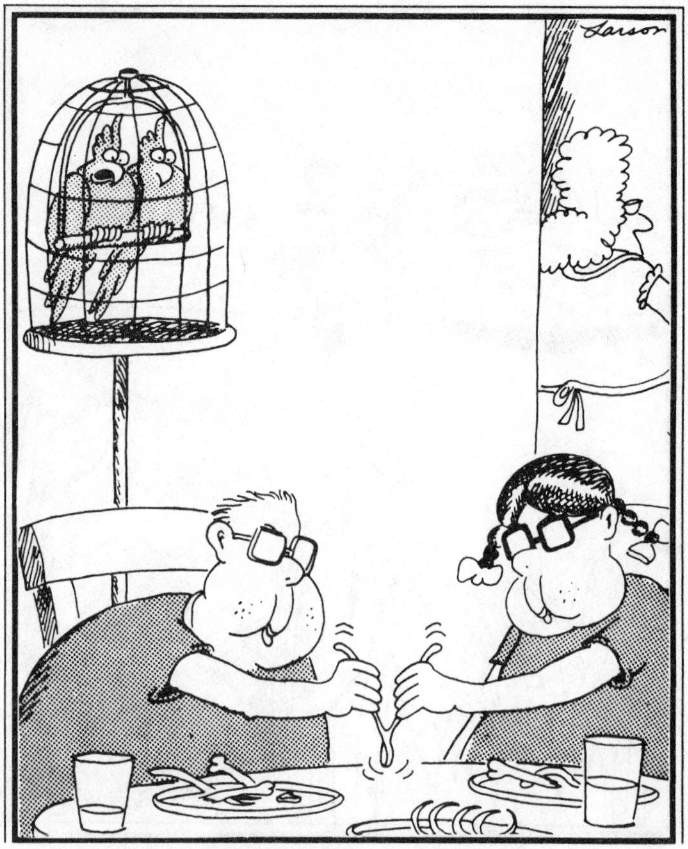

"Now here comes the barbaric finale."

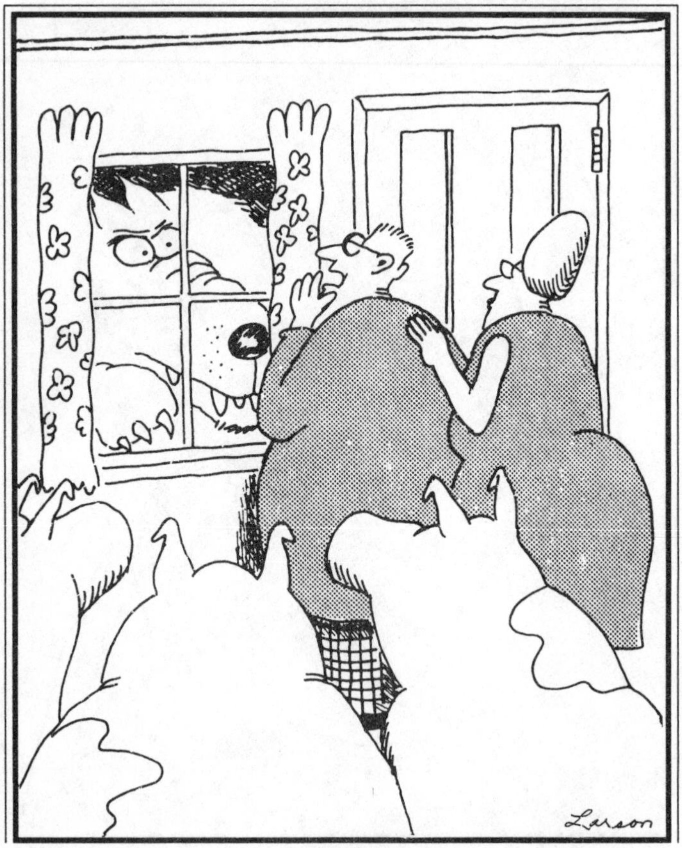

"Listen out there! We're George and Harriet Miller! We just dropped in on the pigs for coffee! We're coming out! . . . We don't want trouble!"

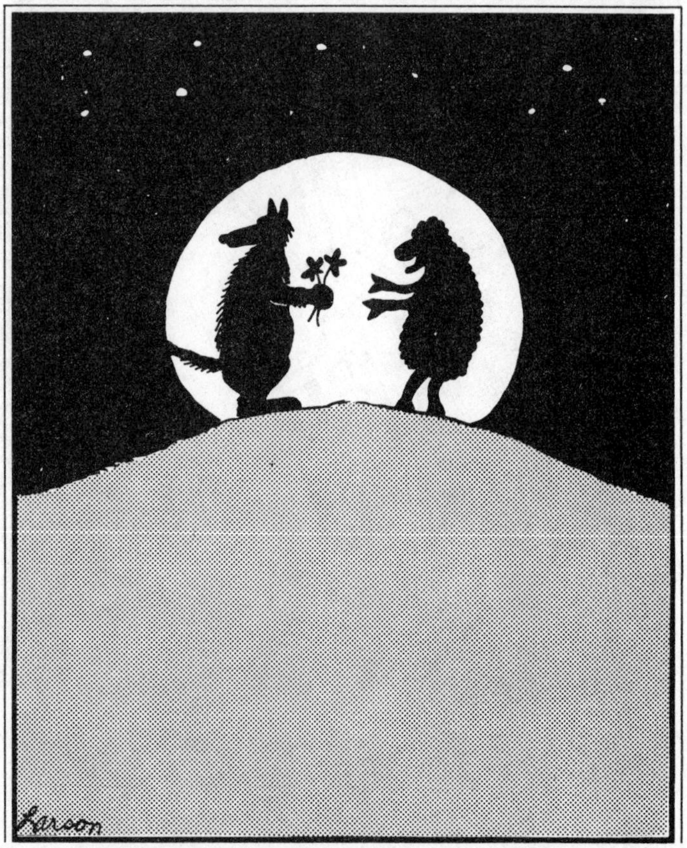

Inevitably, their affair ended: Howard worried excessively about what the pack would think, and Agnes simply ate the flowers.

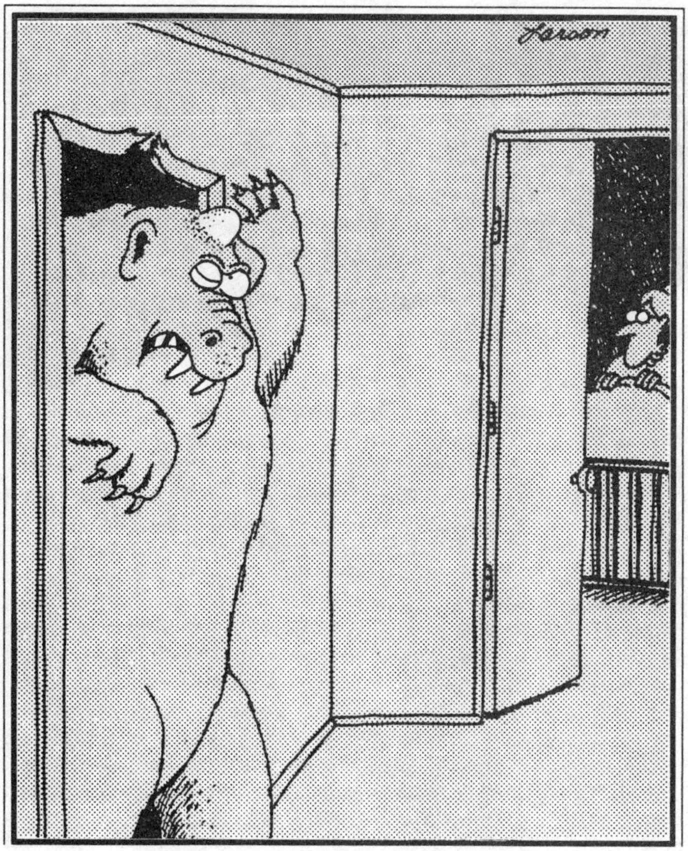
Larson

Things that go bump in the night

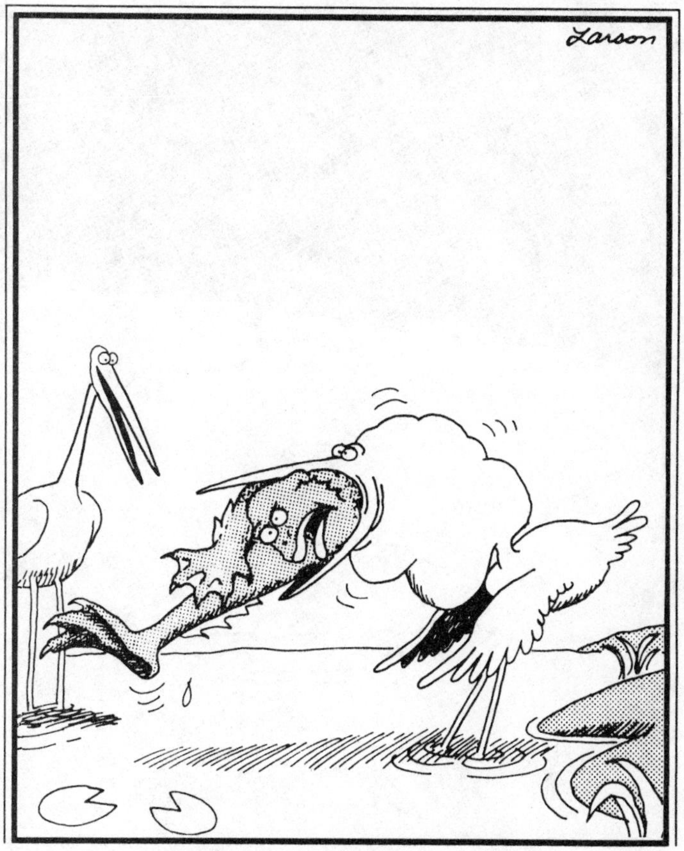
Larson

"NOW, you've got him, Vinnie!"

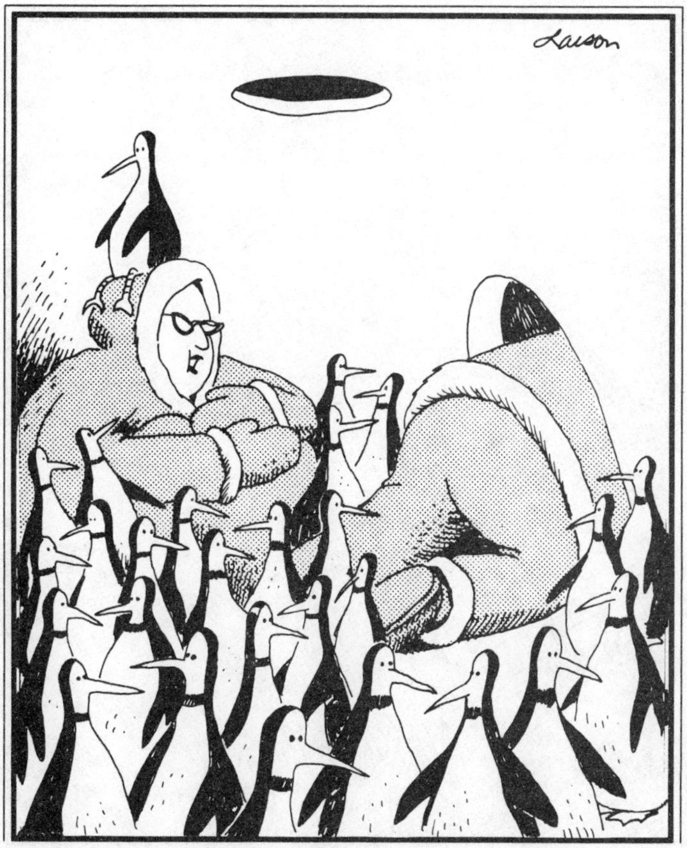
Larson

"Remember, milk, eggs, loaf of bread . . . and pick up one of those No-Penguin-Strips."

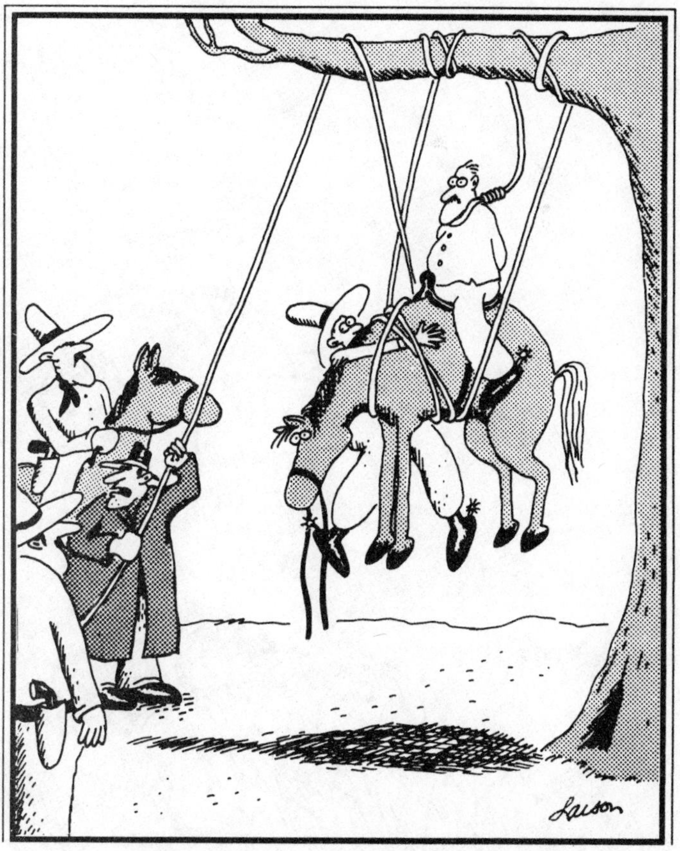
Larson

"Okay, okay, okay . . . Everyone just calm down and we'll try this thing one more time."

"Well, once again, here we are."

"You know? . . . I think I'd like a salad."

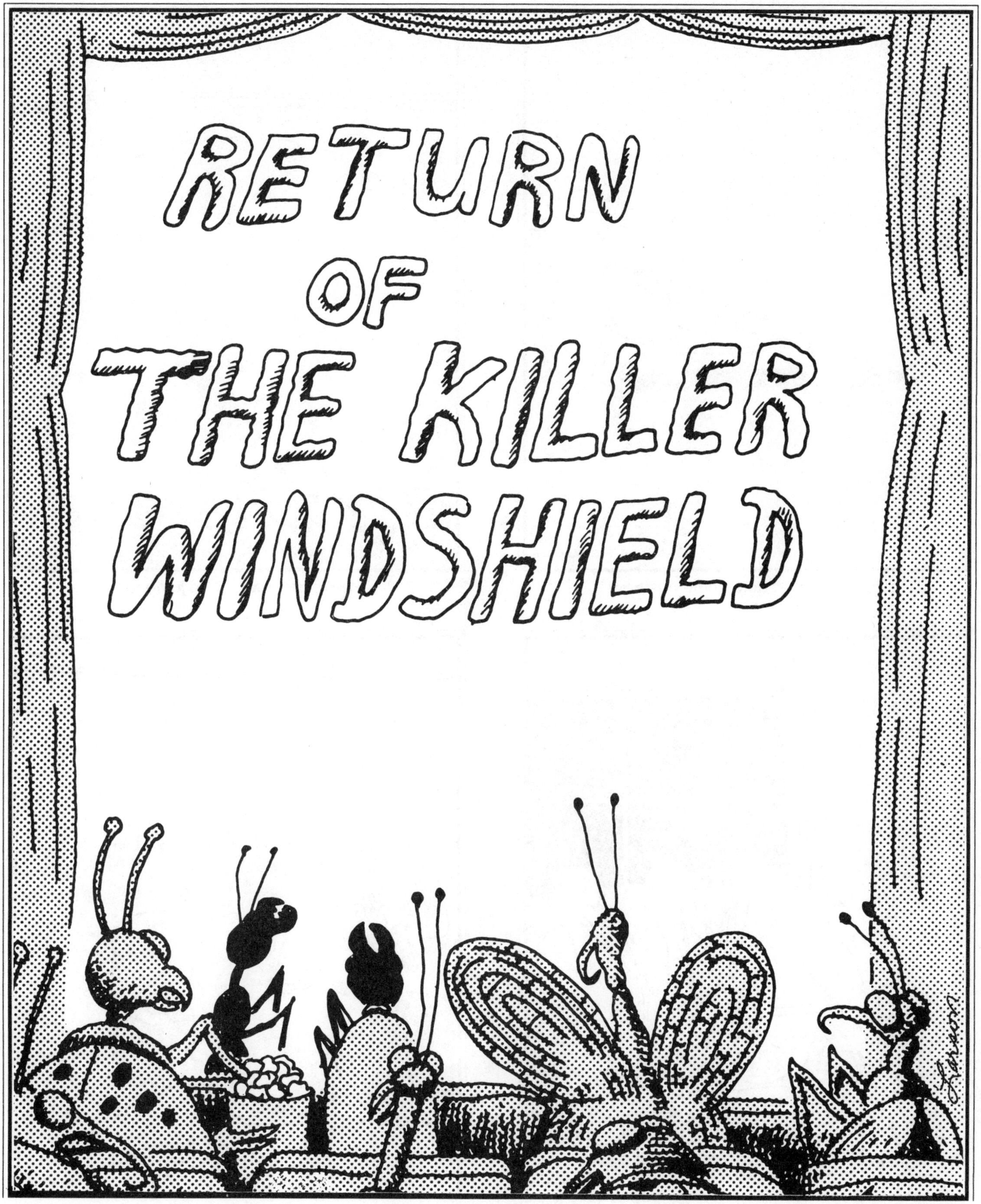
RETURN
OF
THE KILLER
WINDSHIELD

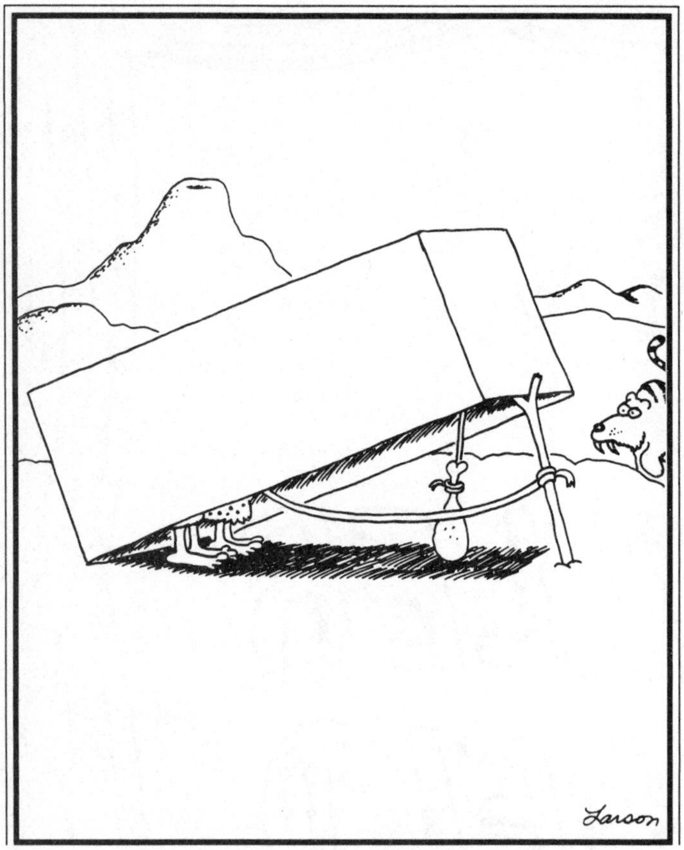
Larson

"Shhhh, Zog! . . . Here come one now!"

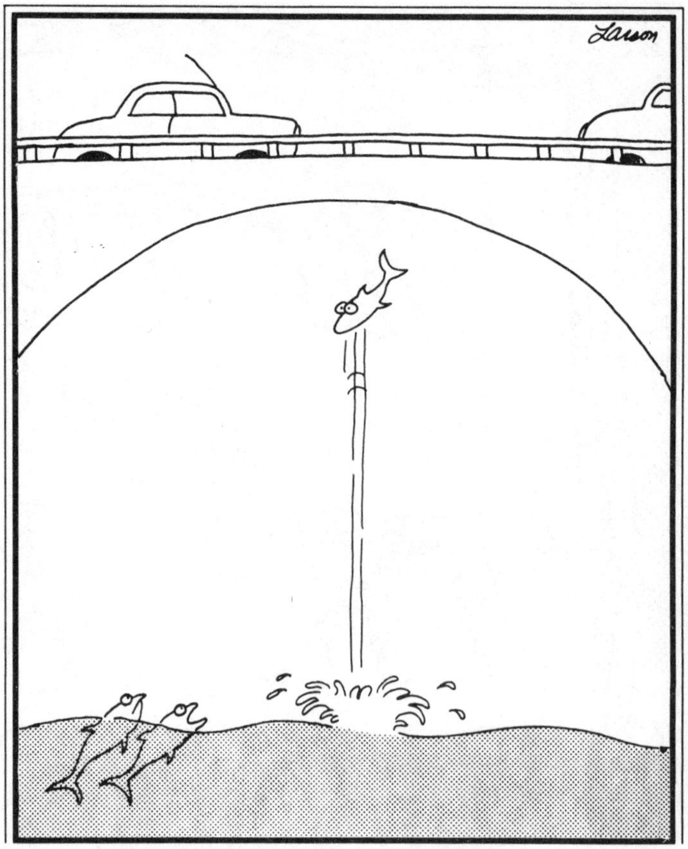
Larson

"We're too late! . . . He jumped!"

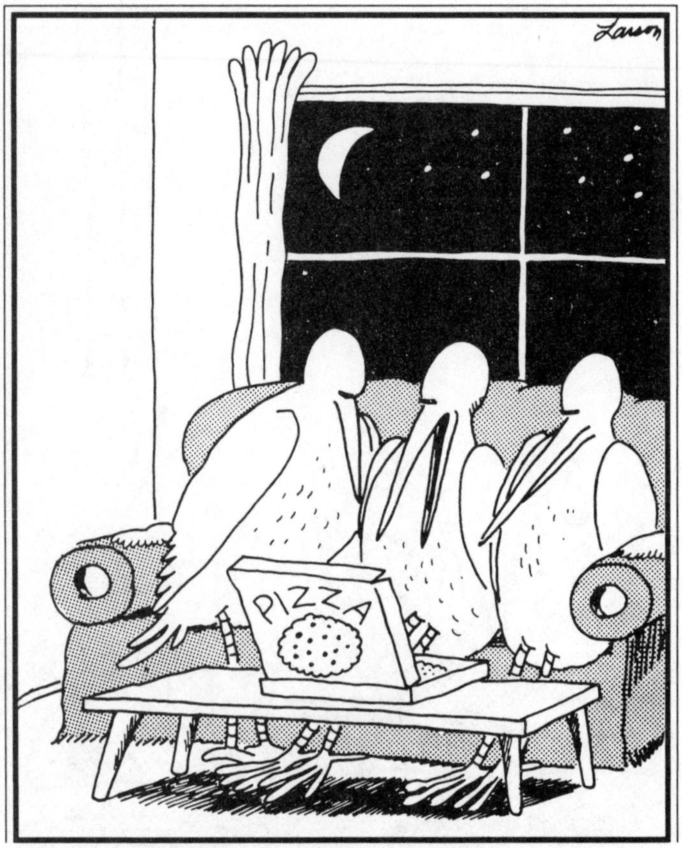
Larson
PIZZA

"Let's see — Mosquitos, gnats, flies, ants . . . What the? . . . Those jerks! We didn't order stink bugs on this thing!"

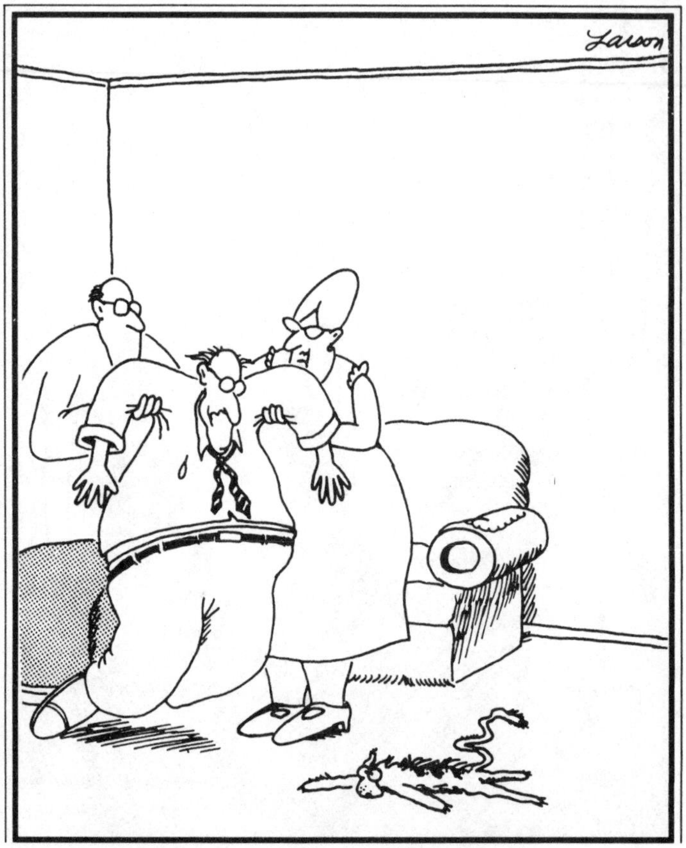
Larson

"Well, I guess both Warren and the cat are okay . . . But thank goodness for the Heimlich maneuver!"

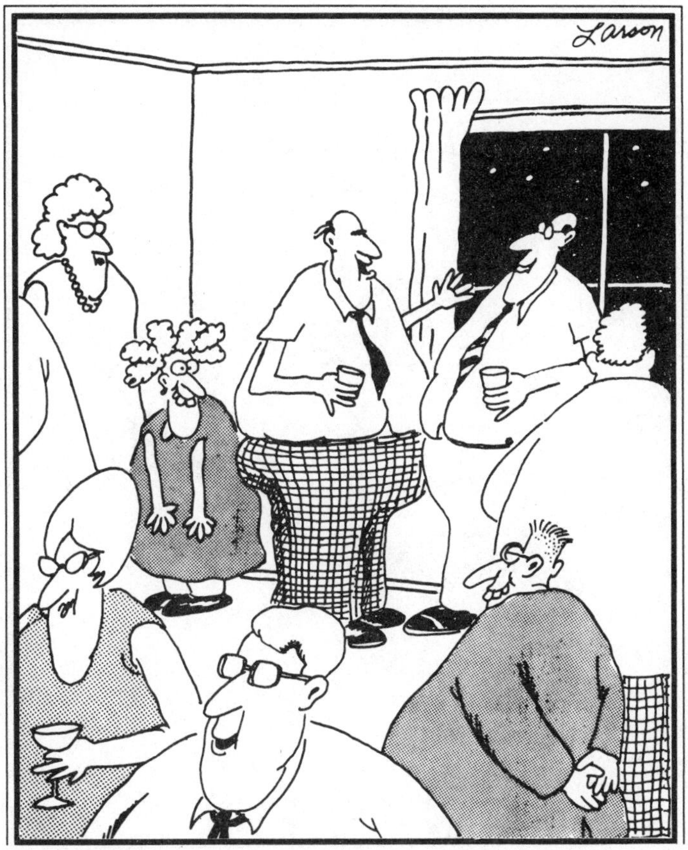
Larson

And then, from across the room, their eyes met.

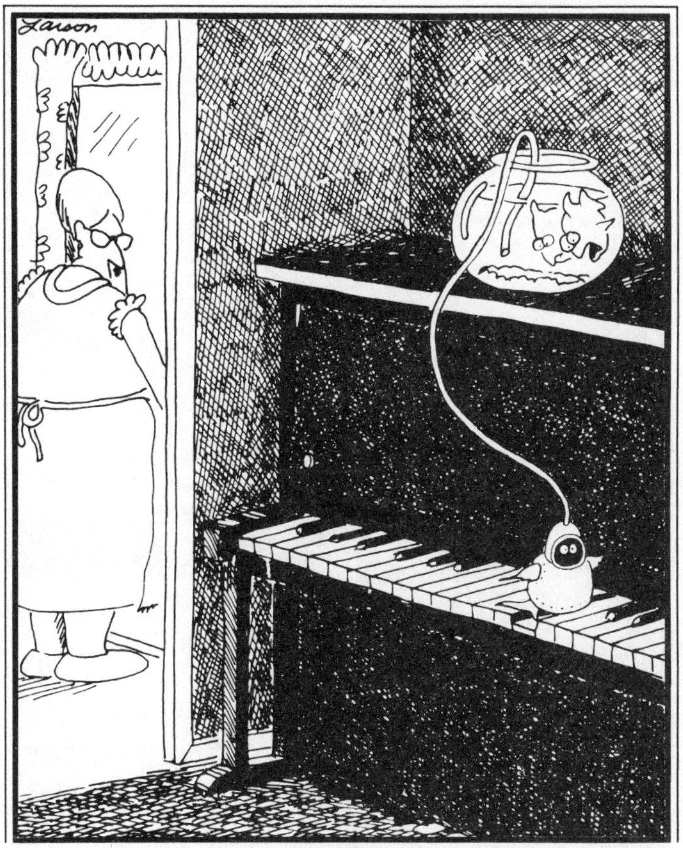
Larson

"The fool! . . . He's on the keyboard!"

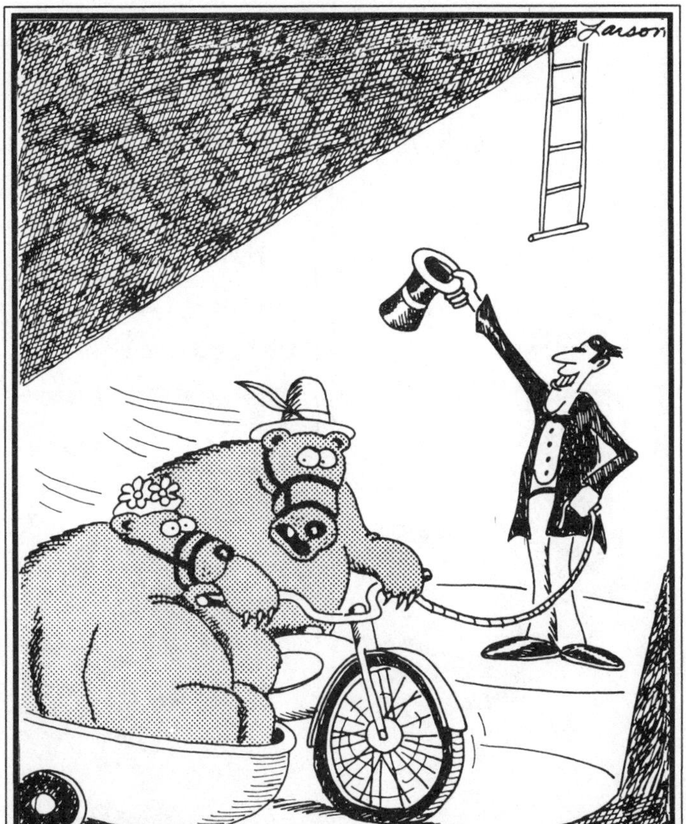
Larson

"'Looks like a trap,' I said. 'Nonsense,' you said. 'No one would set a trap way out here in the woods,' you said."

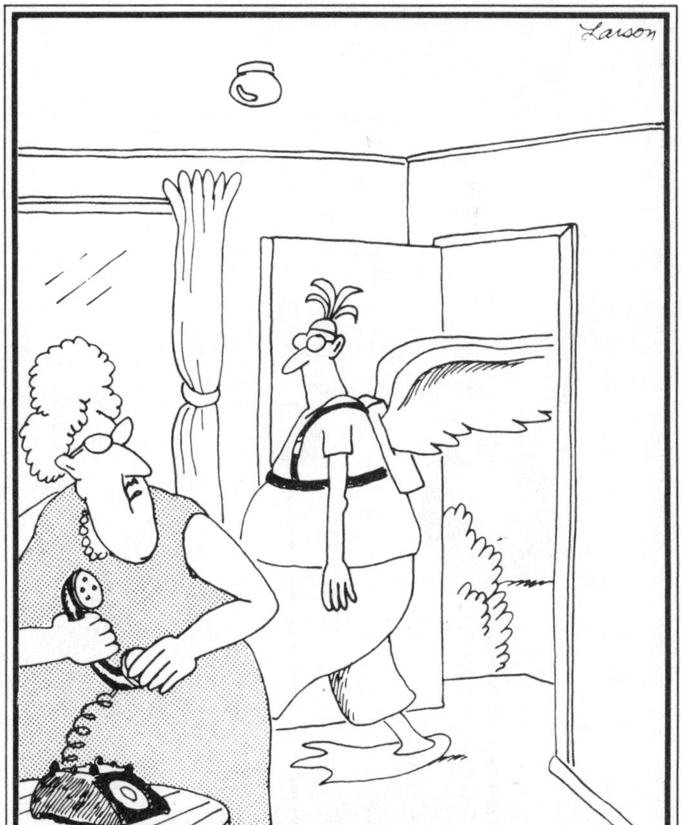
Larson

"Arnold, it's Mr. Wimberly on the phone . . . He says the next time you buzz his house, he'll have his 12-gauge ready."

GROCERY
Larson

Larson

Larson

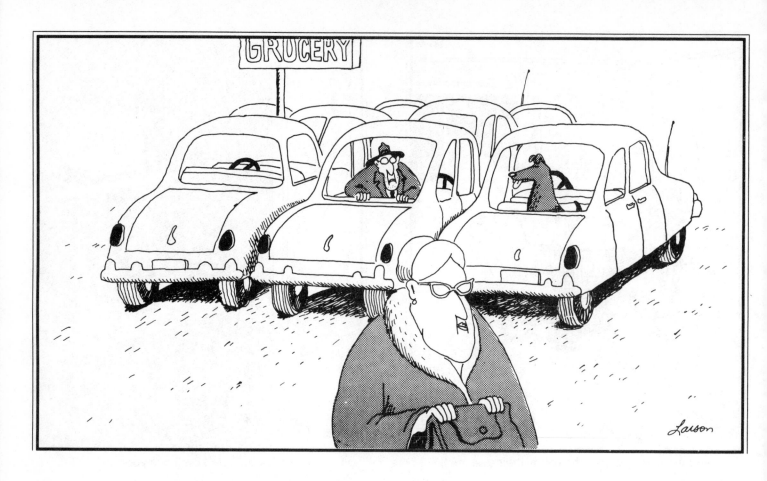

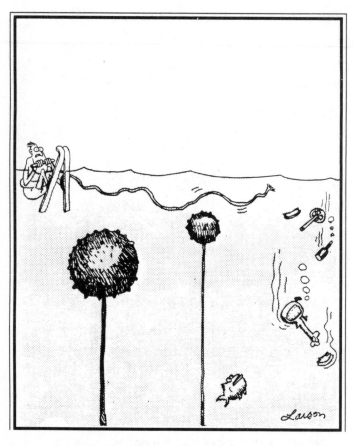

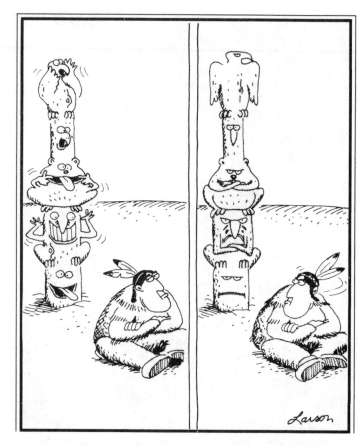

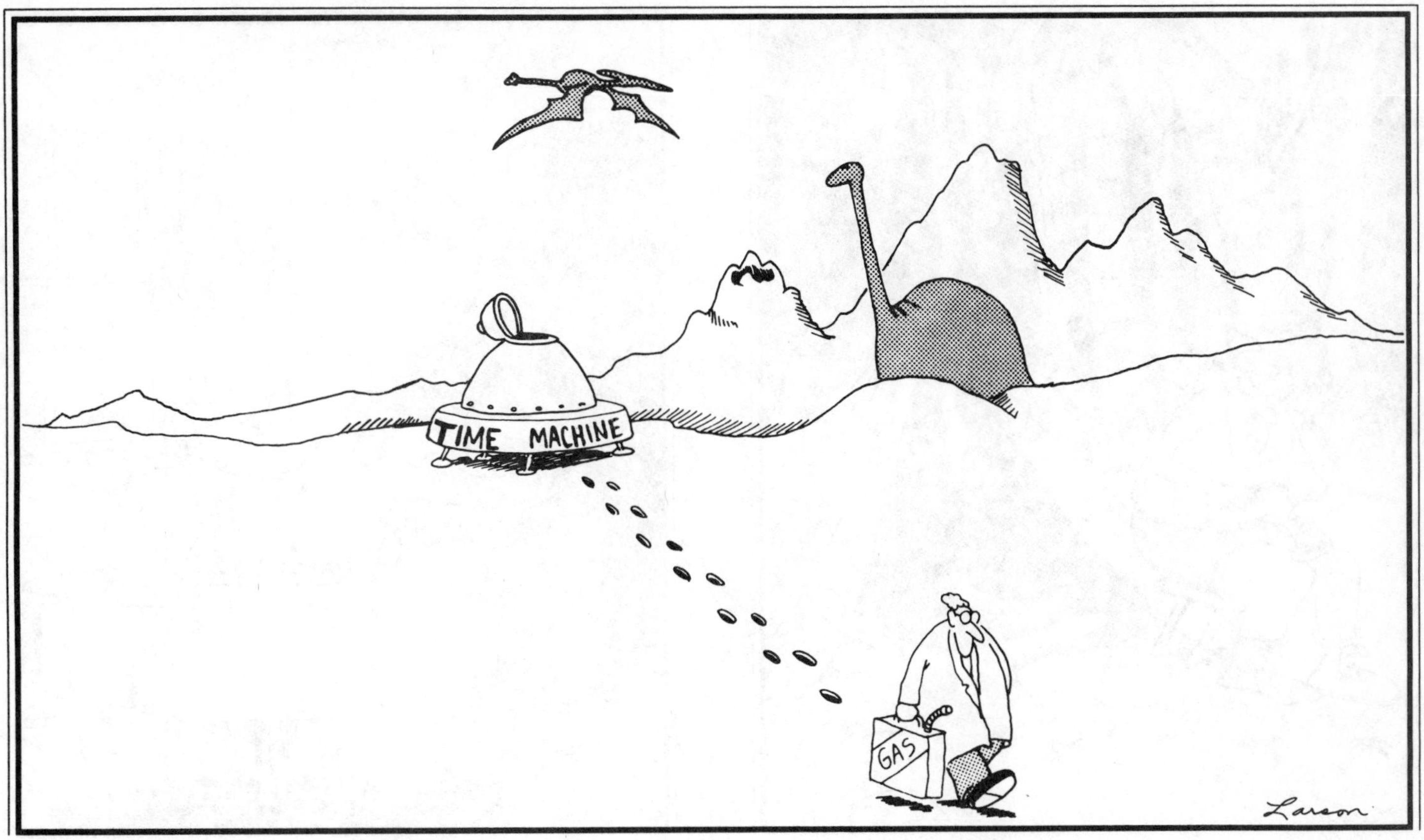
TIME MACHINE
GAS
Larson

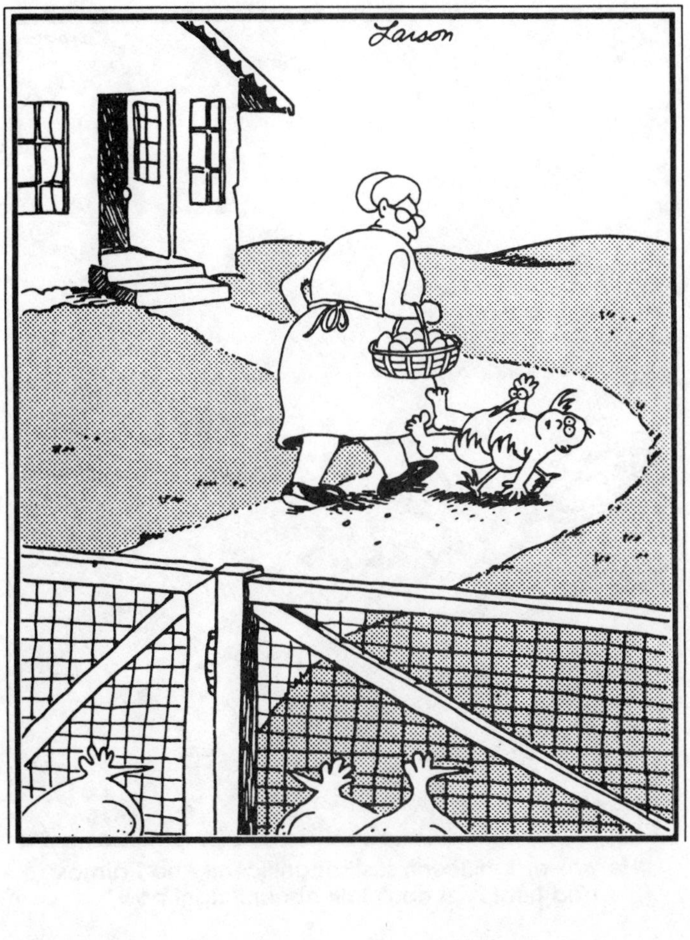
Larson

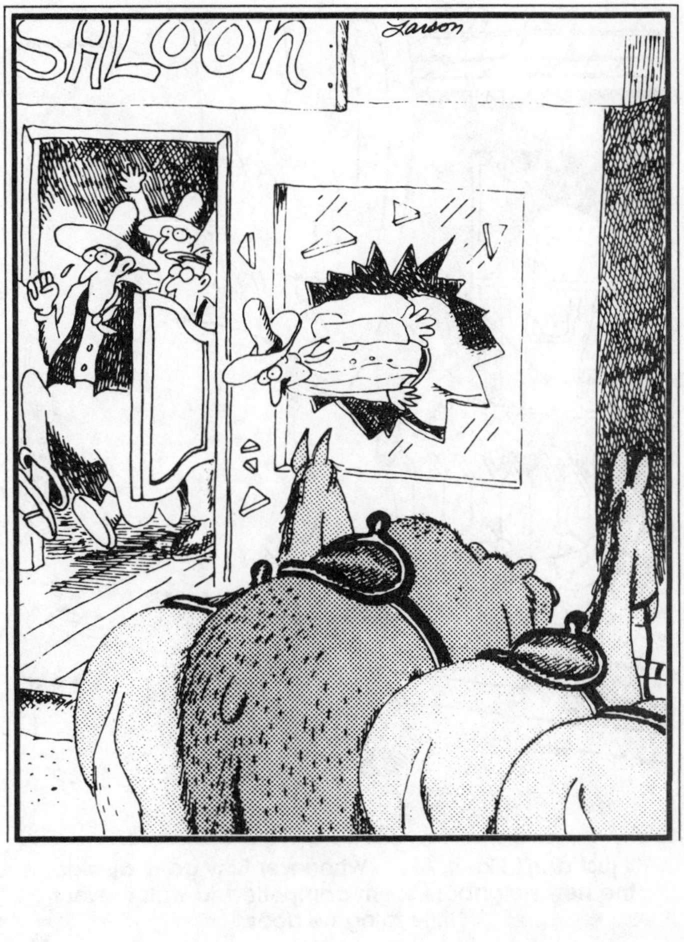
SALOON
Larson

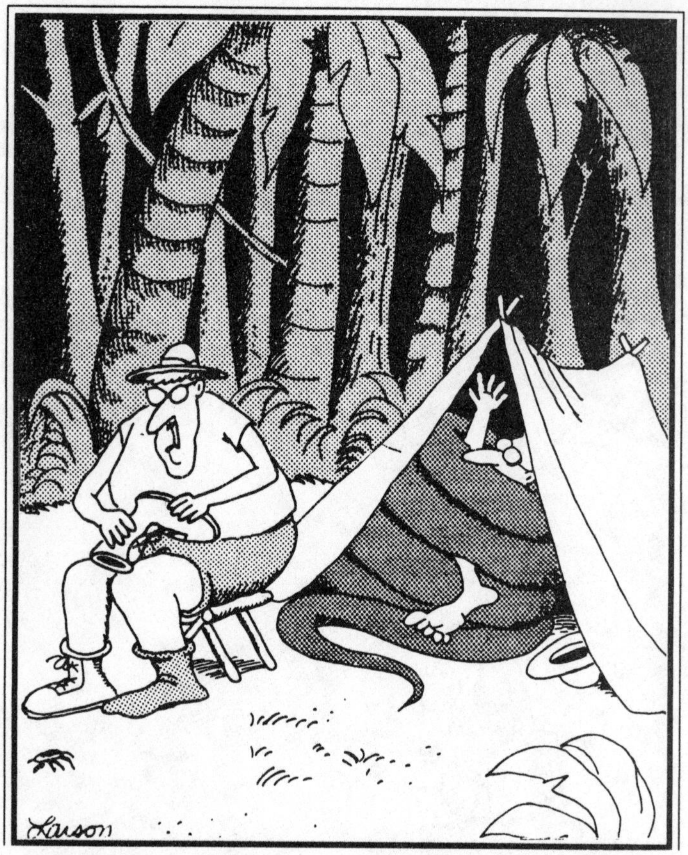
Larson

"Aaaaaaaaa! Murray! . . . A spider was in my shoe!"

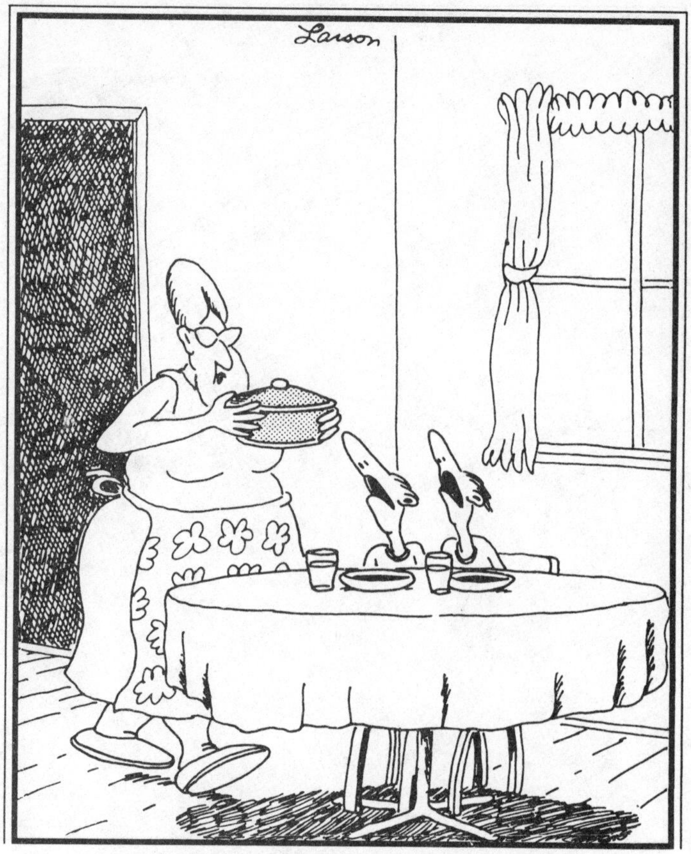
Larson

Dinner time for the young Wright brothers

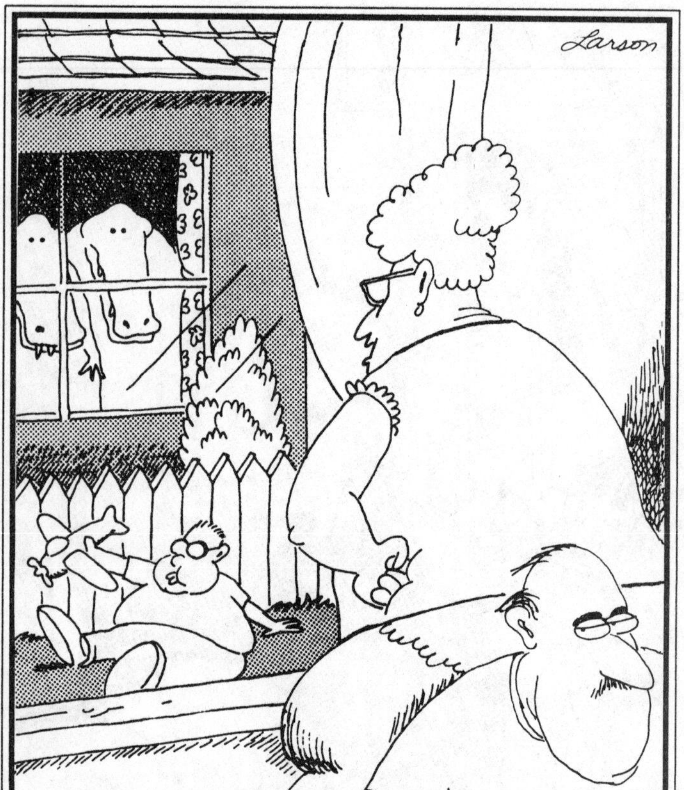
Larson

"I just don't like it, Al . . . Whenever Billy goes outside, the new neighbors seem compelled to watch every little thing he does."

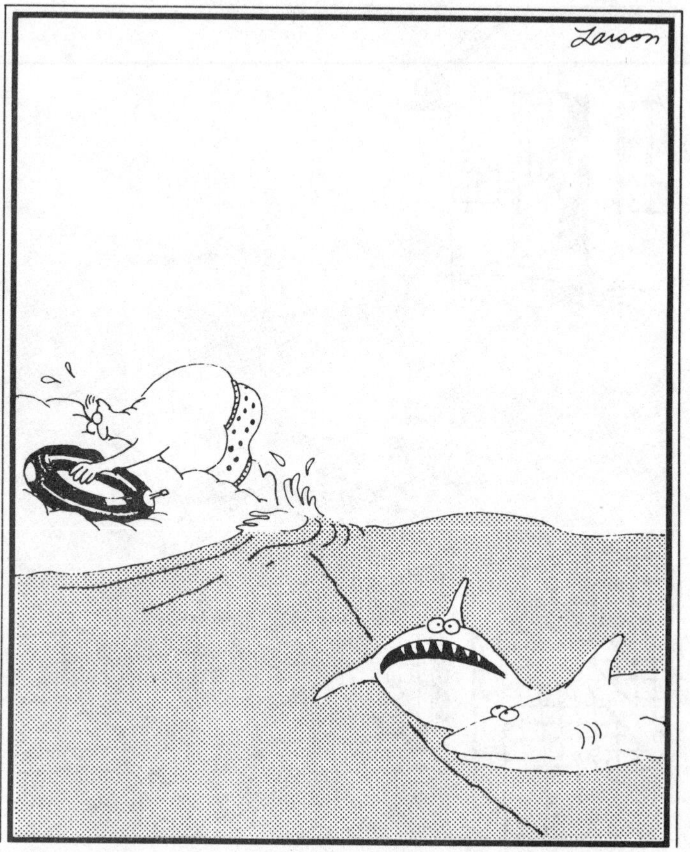
Larson

"He was magnificent! Just magnificent! And I almost had him! . . . I can't talk about it right now."

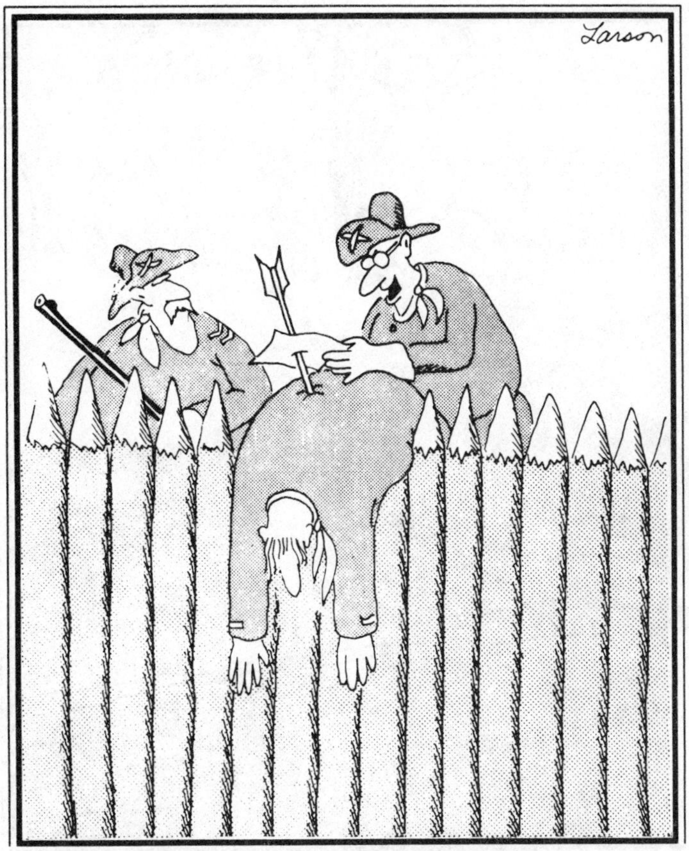

"Ha! The idiots spelled 'surrender' with only one 'r'!"

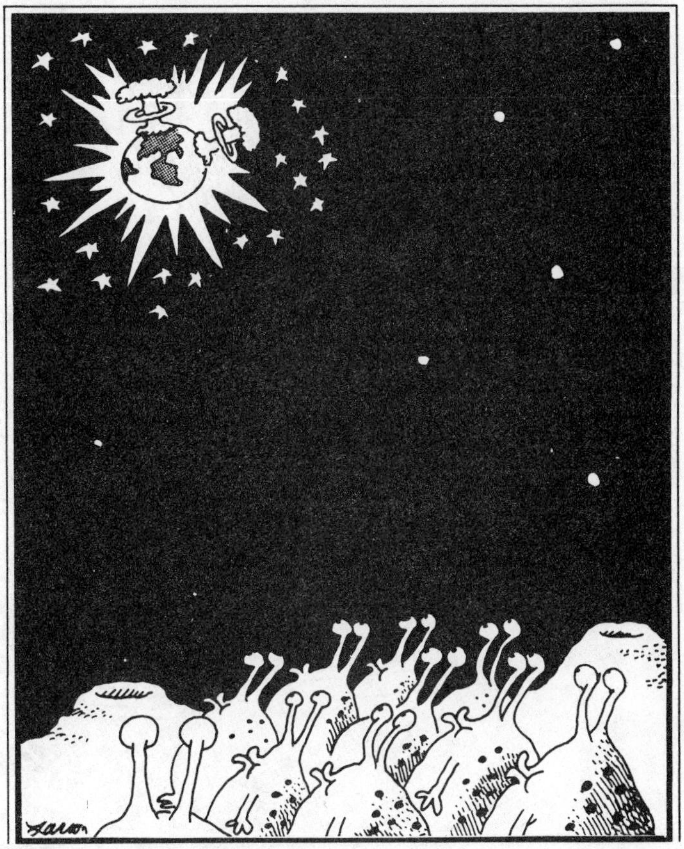

"Oooooooooooooo!"

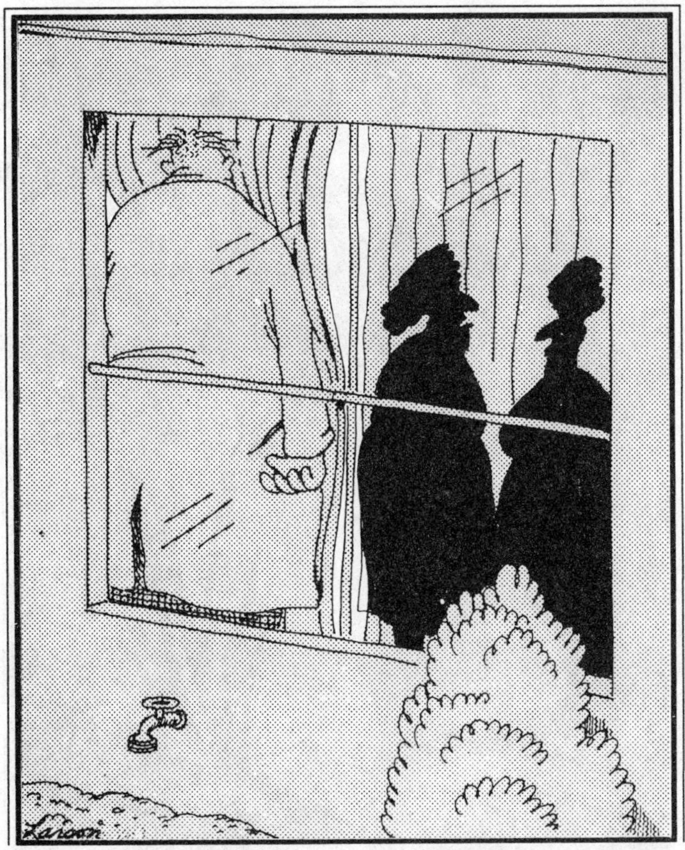

"See, Barbara? There's no one in here, no one outside . . . I'll even open the drapes and have a look."

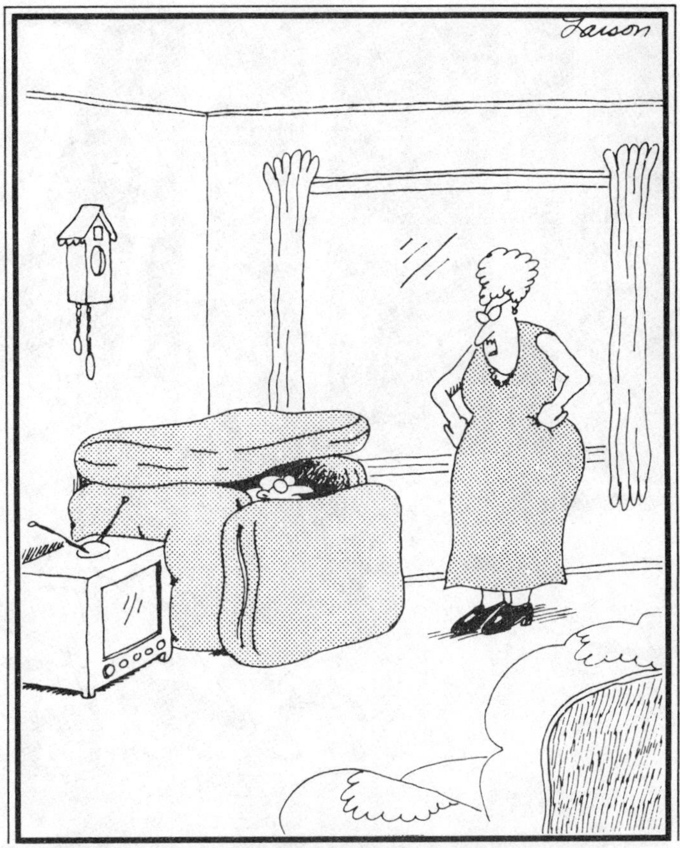

"Well, you can just rebuild the fort later, Harold . . . Phyllis and Shirley are coming over and I'll need the cushions."

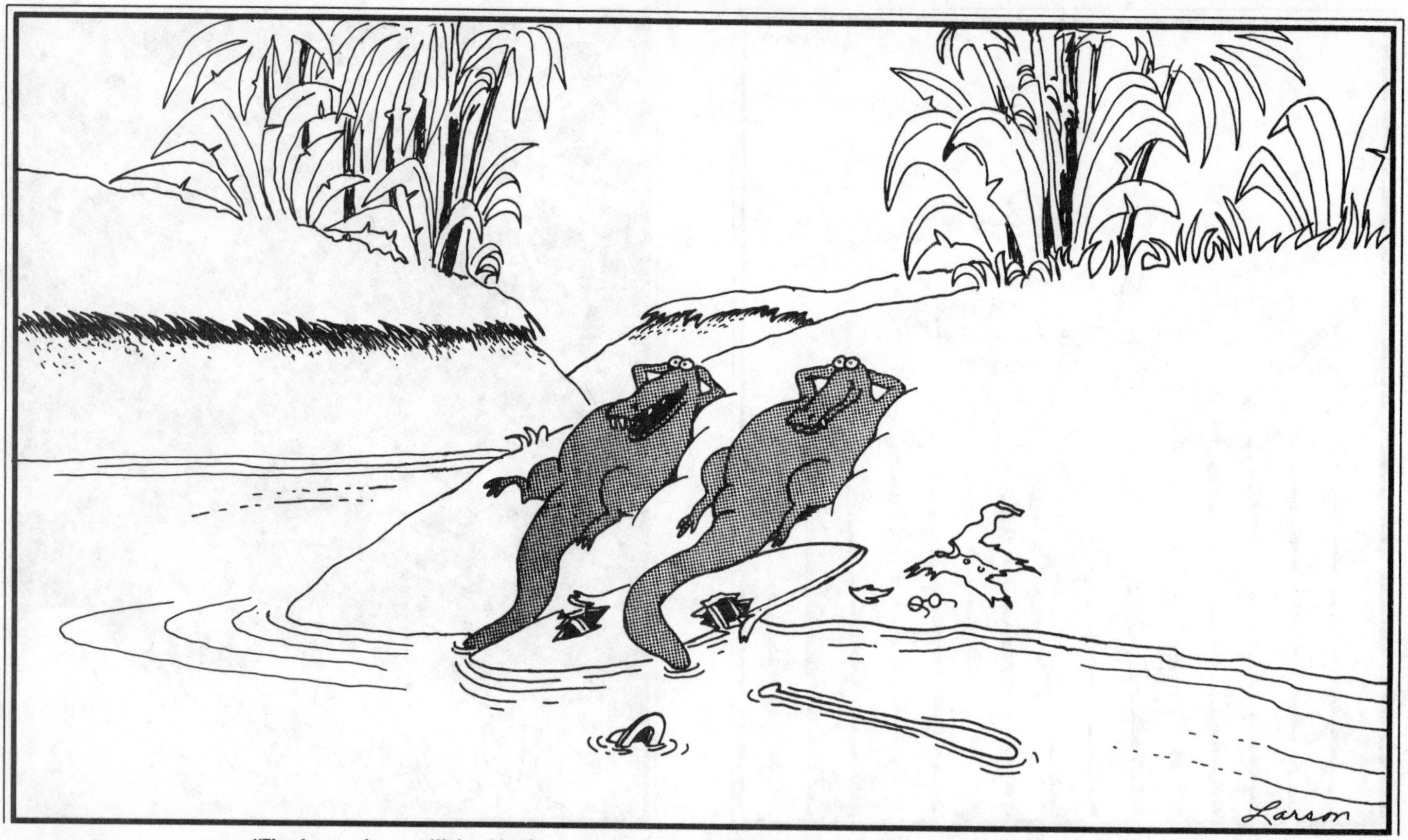
Larson

"That was incredible. No fur, claws, horns, antlers, or nothin' . . . Just soft and pink."

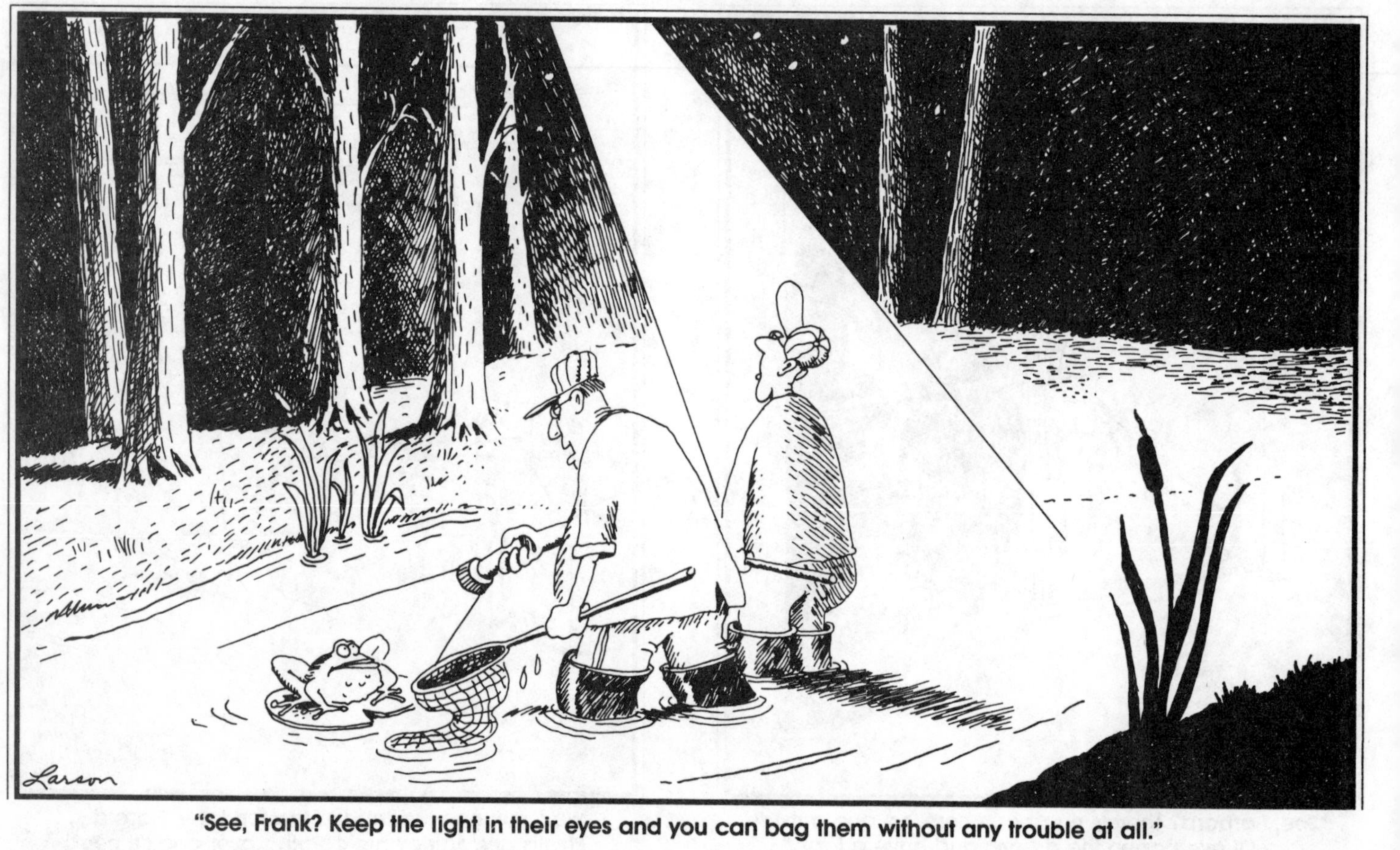
Larson

"See, Frank? Keep the light in their eyes and you can bag them without any trouble at all."

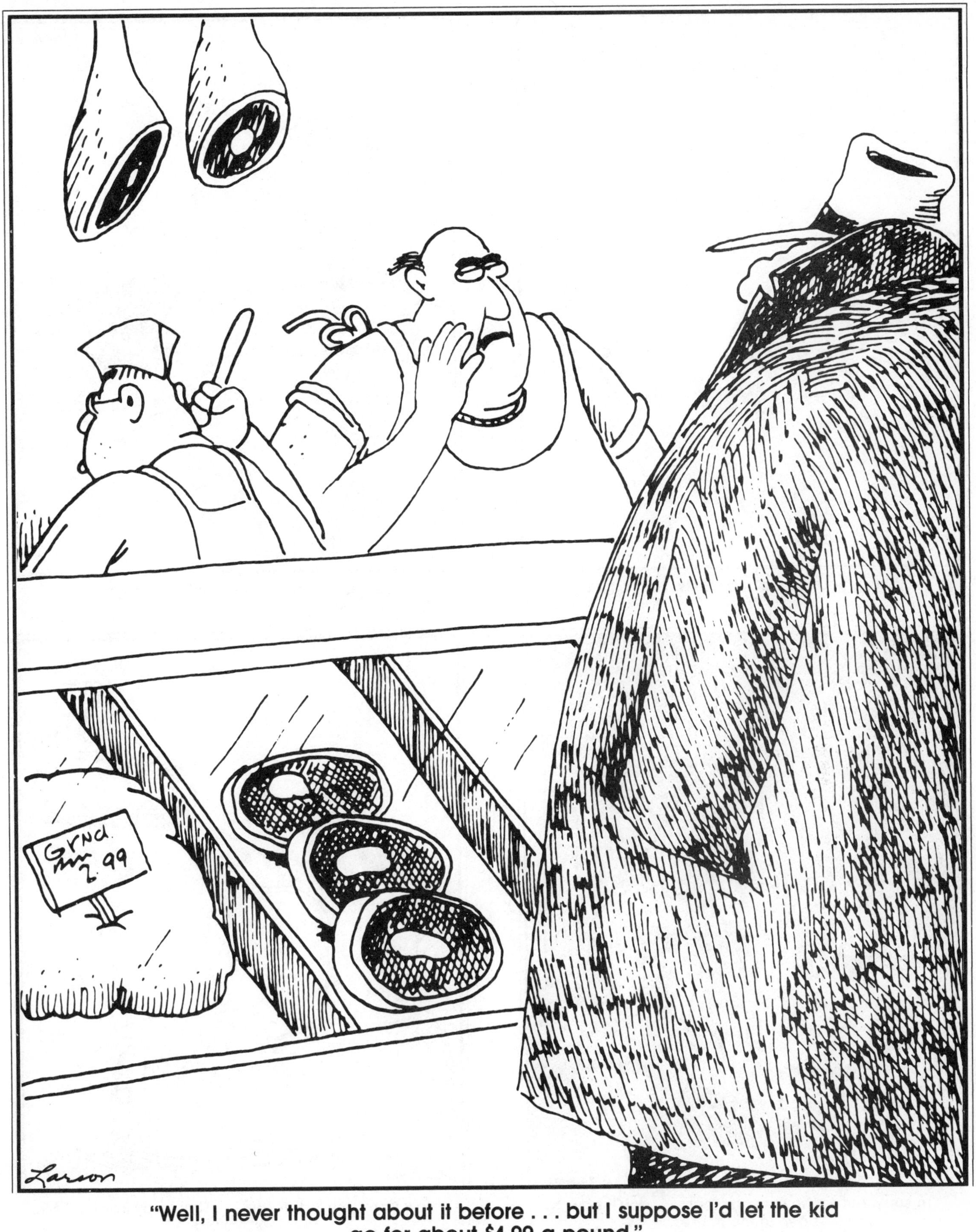
Grnd
2.99
Larson

"Well, I never thought about it before . . . but I suppose I'd let the kid go for about $1.99 a pound."

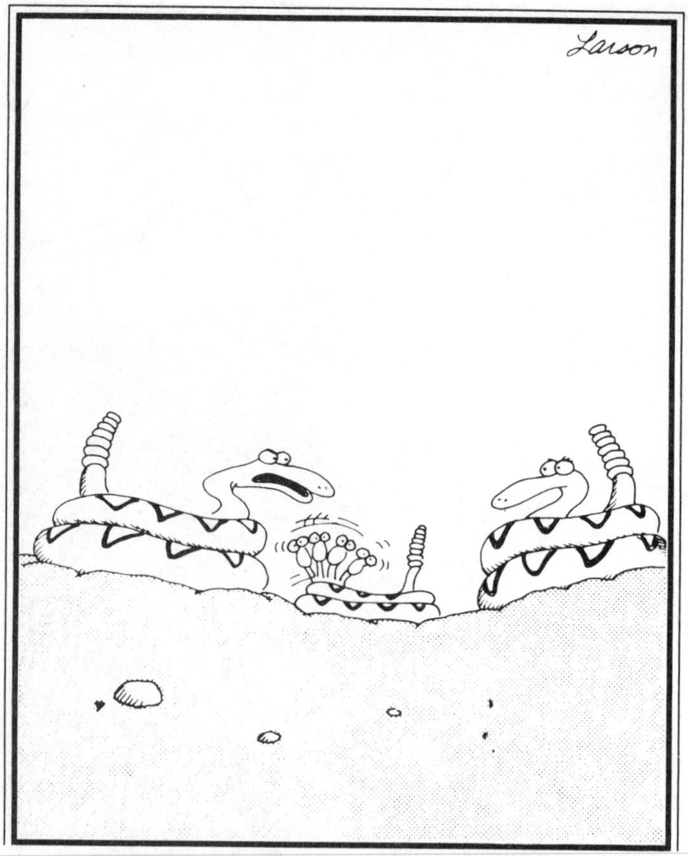
Larson

"This is your side of the family, you realize."

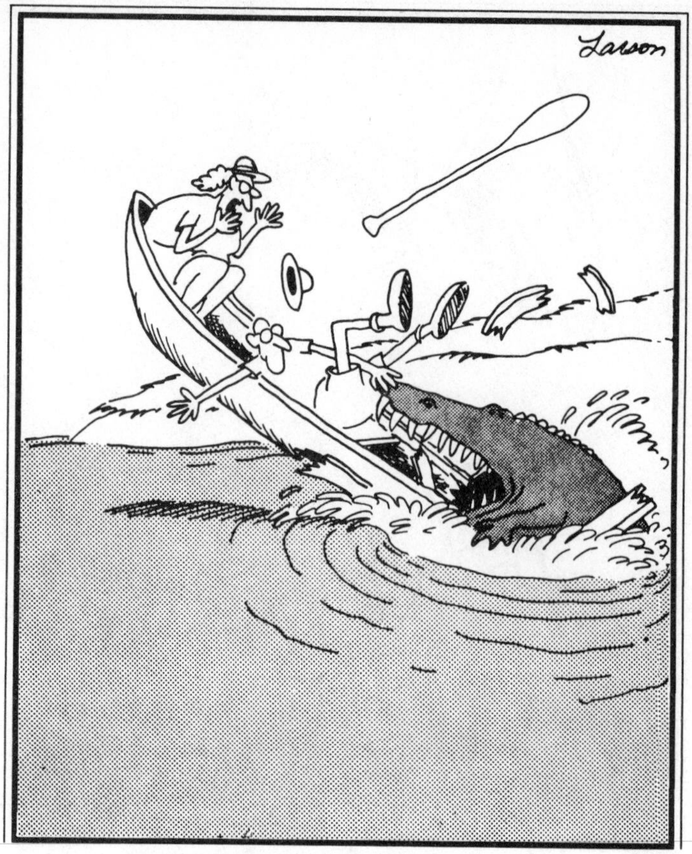
Larson

"Rub his belly, Ernie! Rub his belly!"

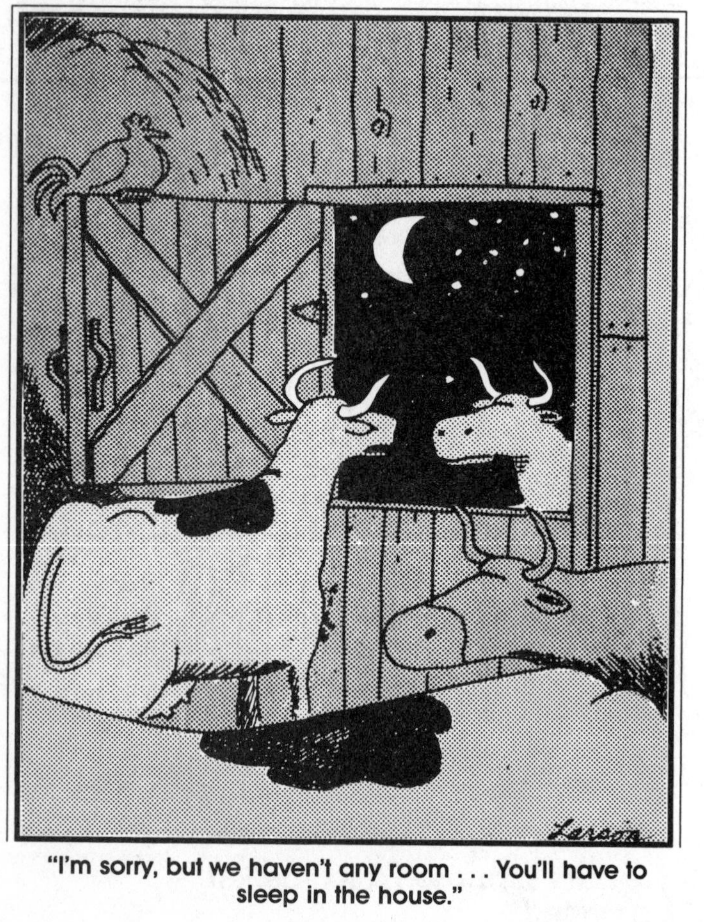
Larson

"I'm sorry, but we haven't any room . . . You'll have to sleep in the house."

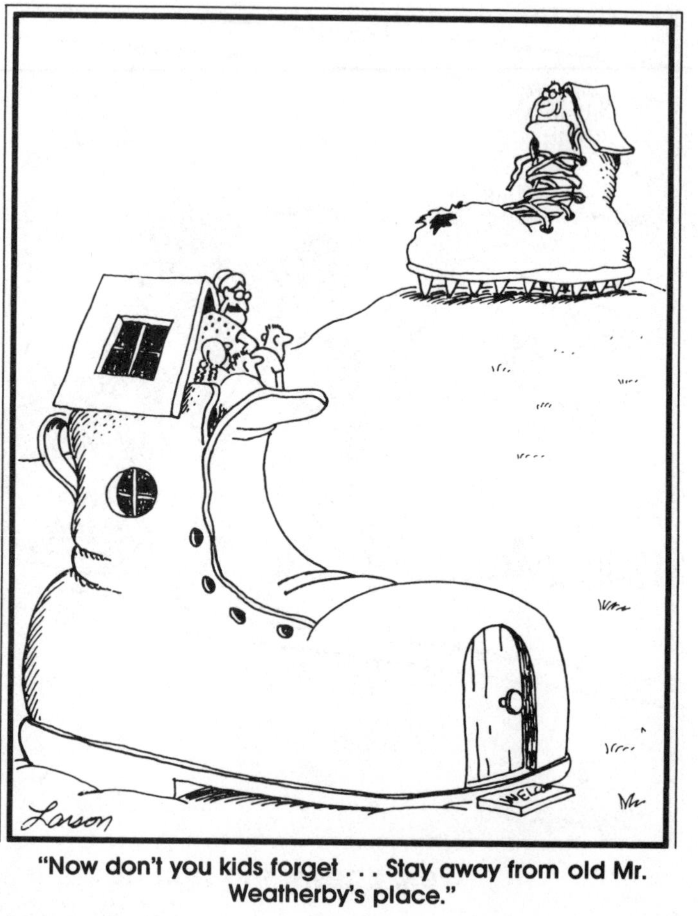
Larson

"Now don't you kids forget . . . Stay away from old Mr. Weatherby's place."

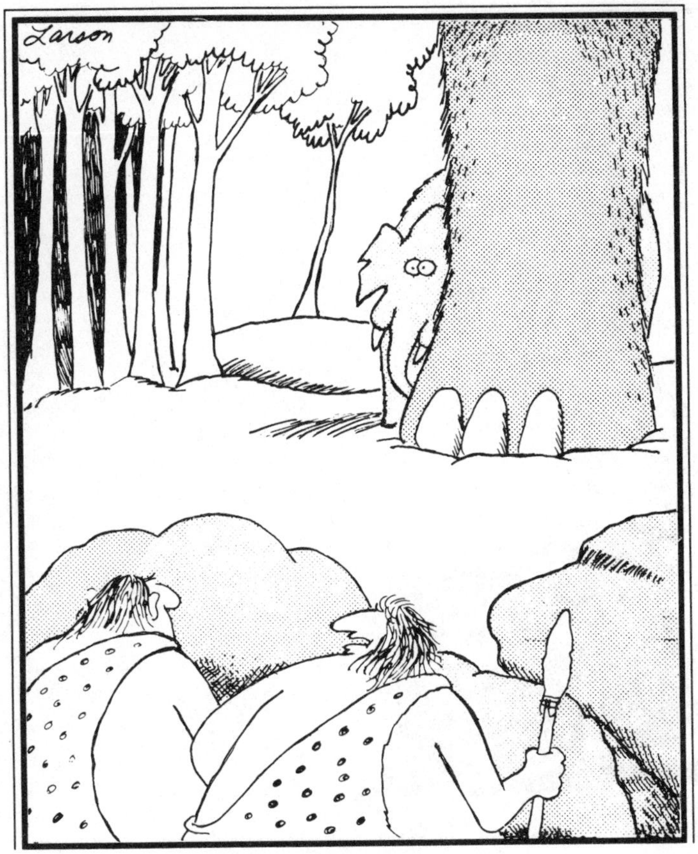

"Ha! We got him now!"

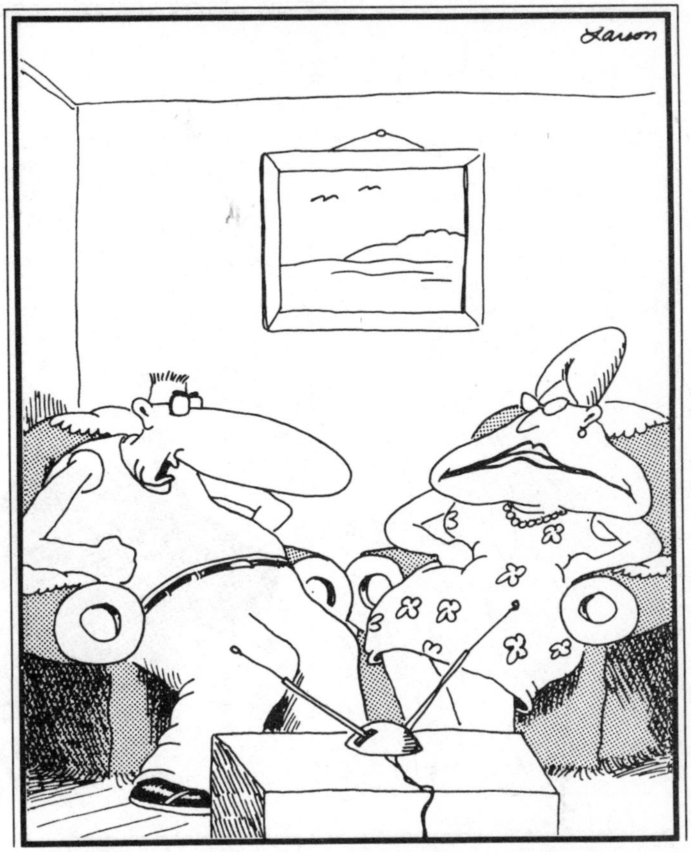

"Oh! Is that so? . . . Well, YOU'VE got a big MOUTH!"

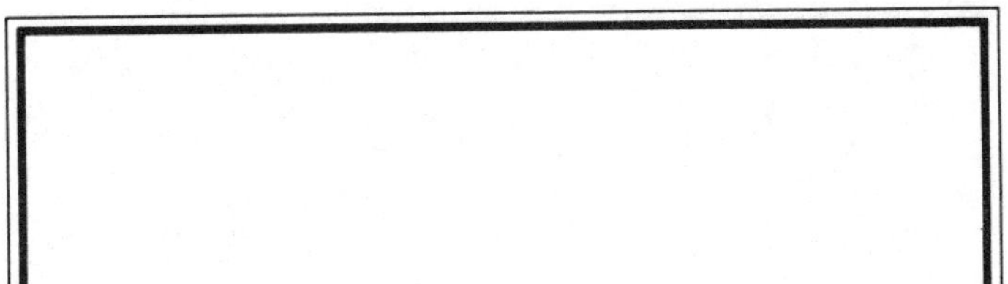

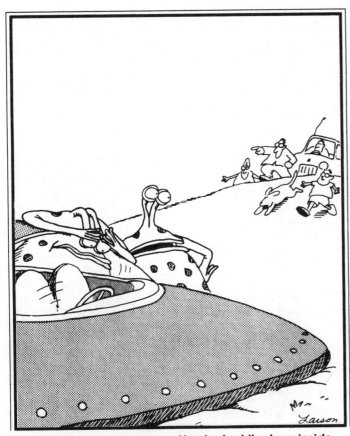

"Well, here they come . . . You locked the keys inside, you do the talkin'."

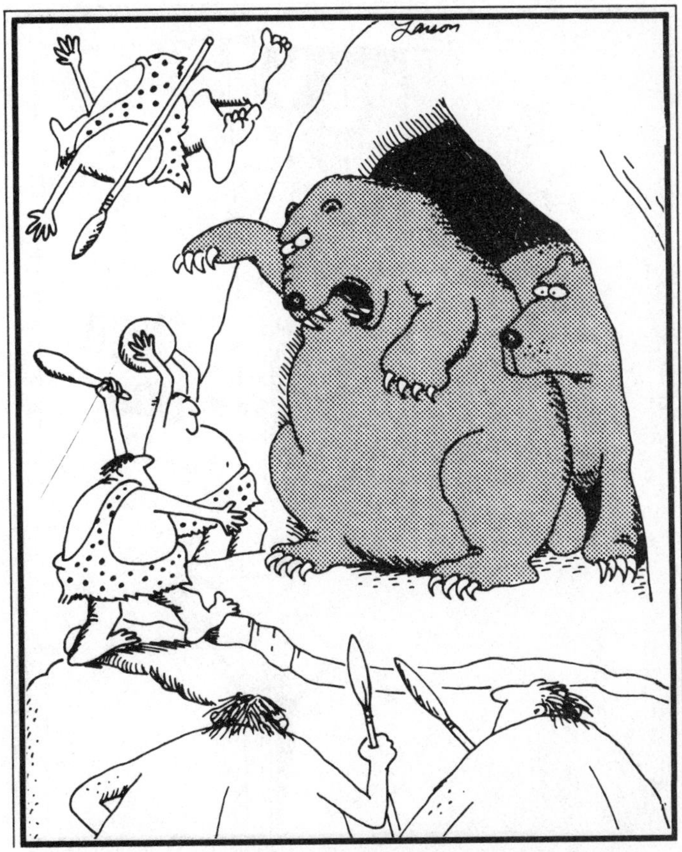

"Criminy! . . . It seems like every summer there's more and more of these things around!"

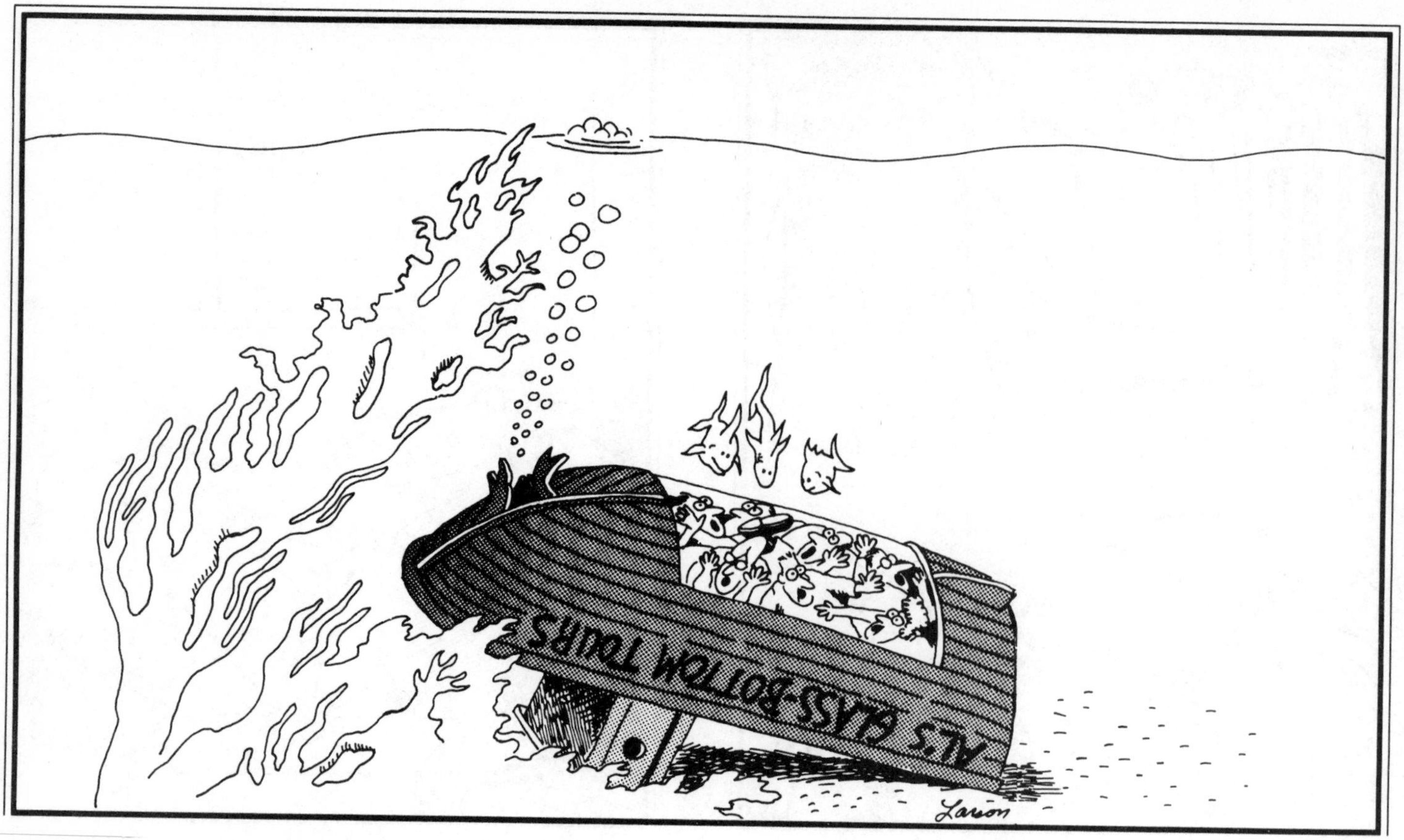
AL'S GLASS-BOTTOM TOURS
Larson

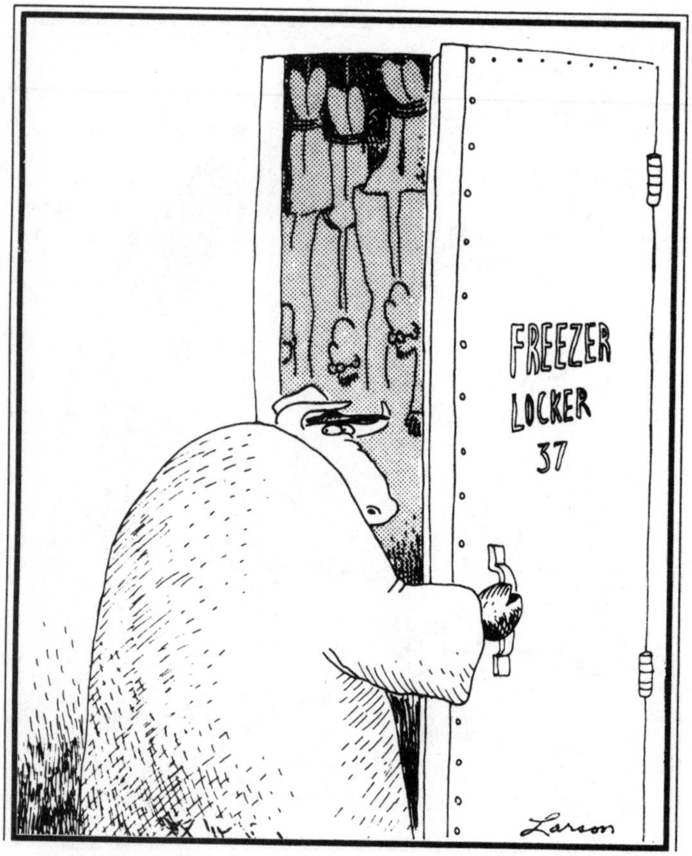
FREEZER
LOCKER
37
Larson

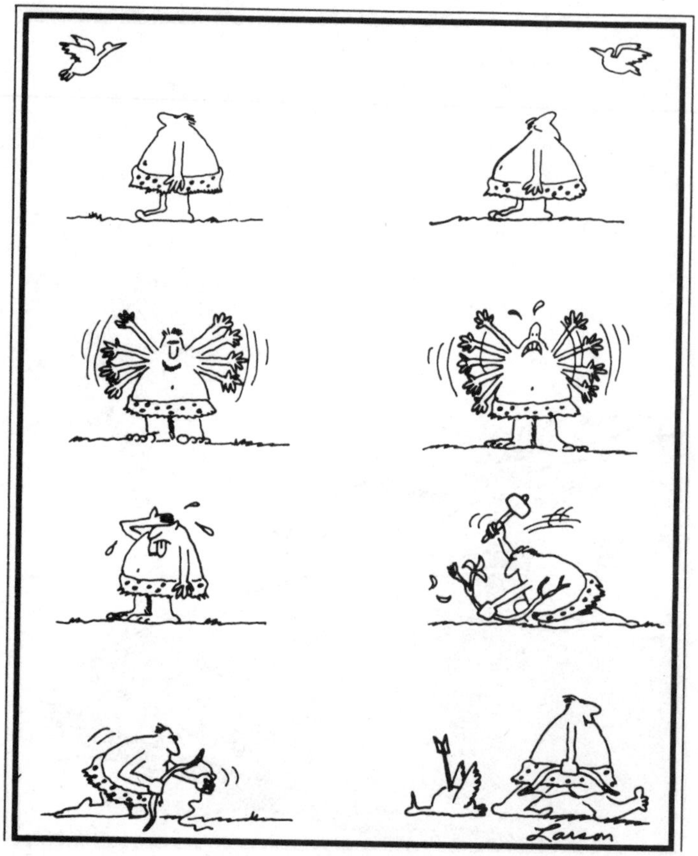
Larson

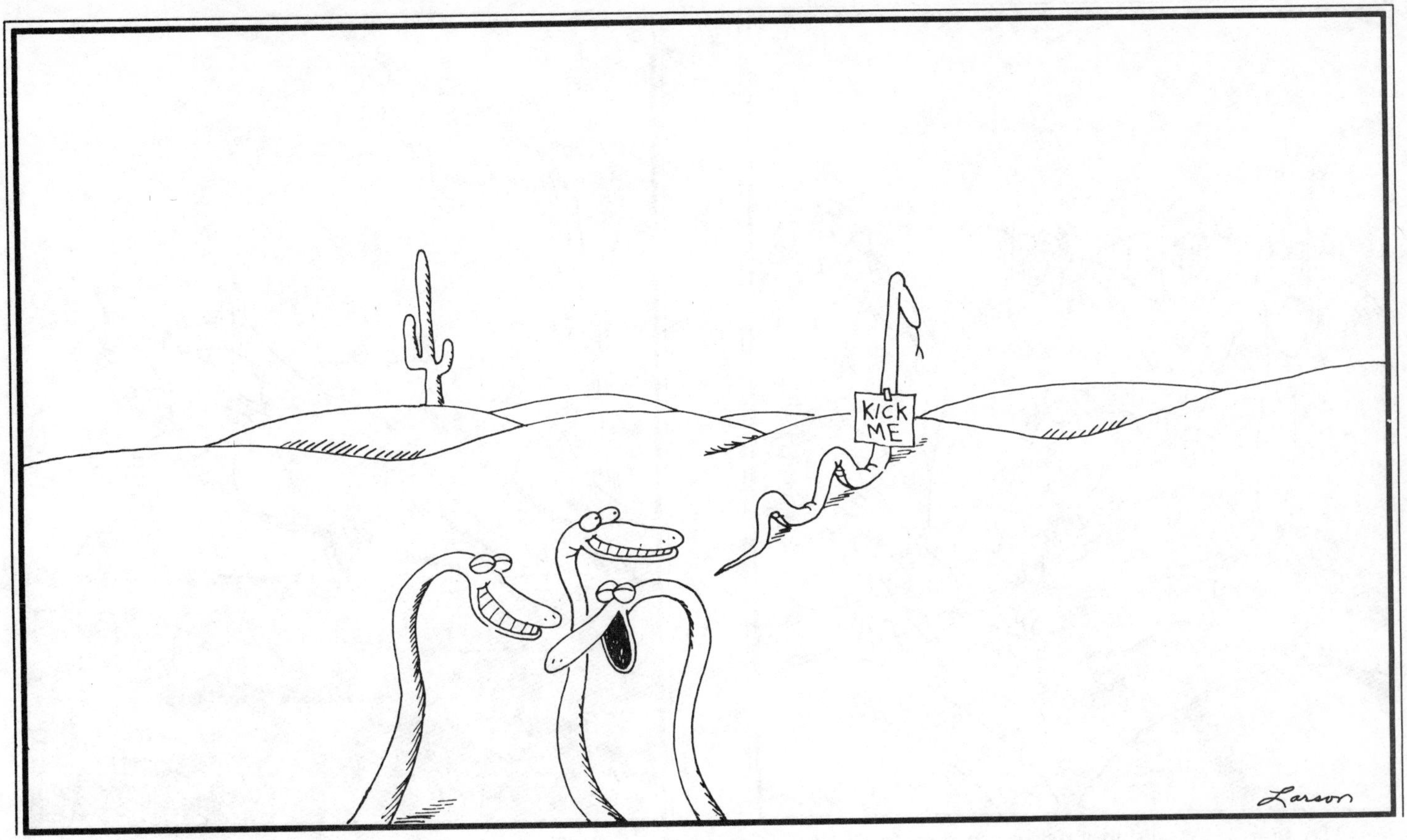
KICK ME
Larson

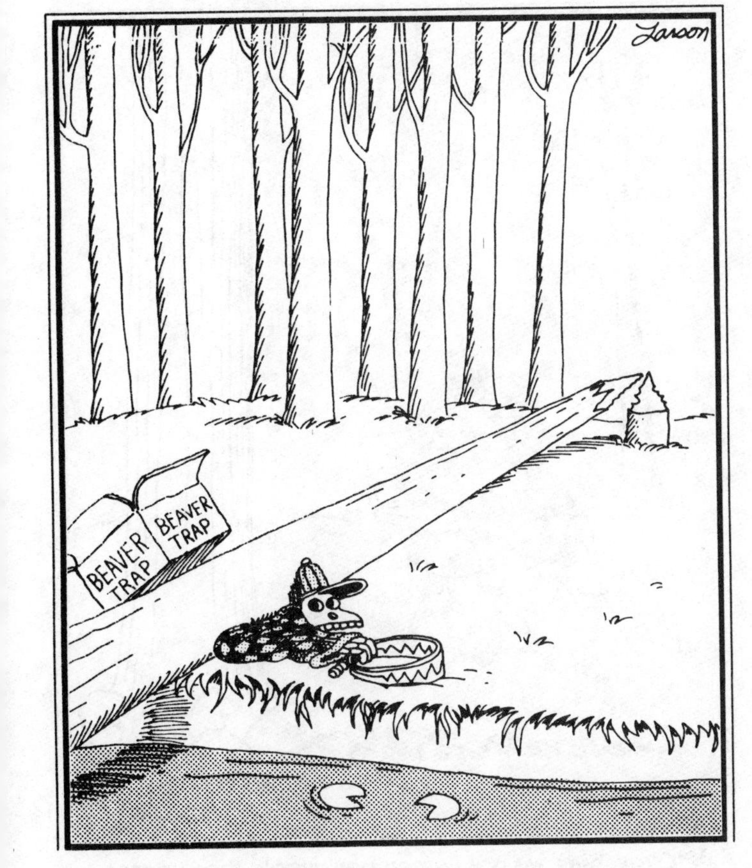
Larson
BEAVER TRAP
BEAVER TRAP

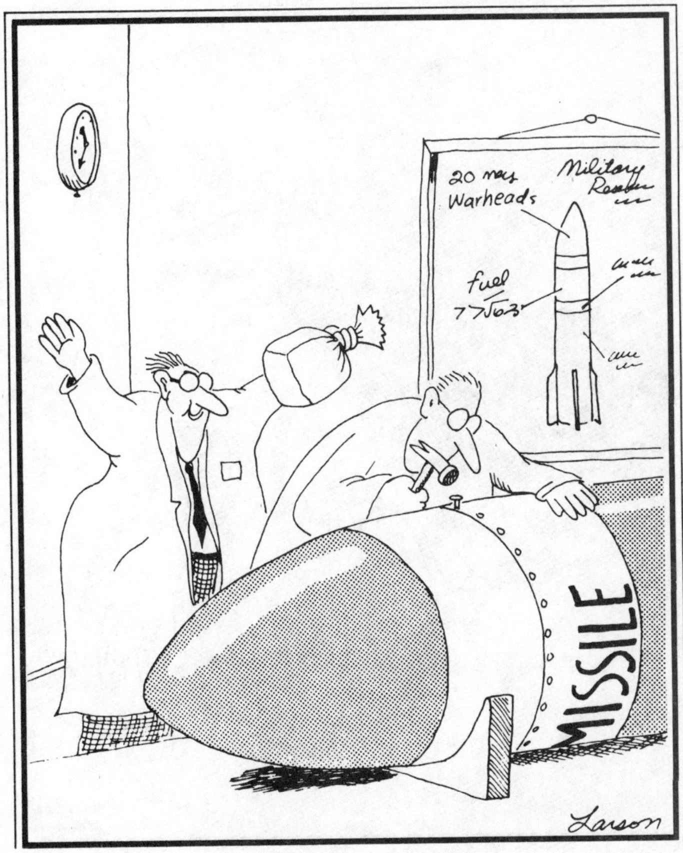
Military
Warheads
fuel
MISSILE
Larson

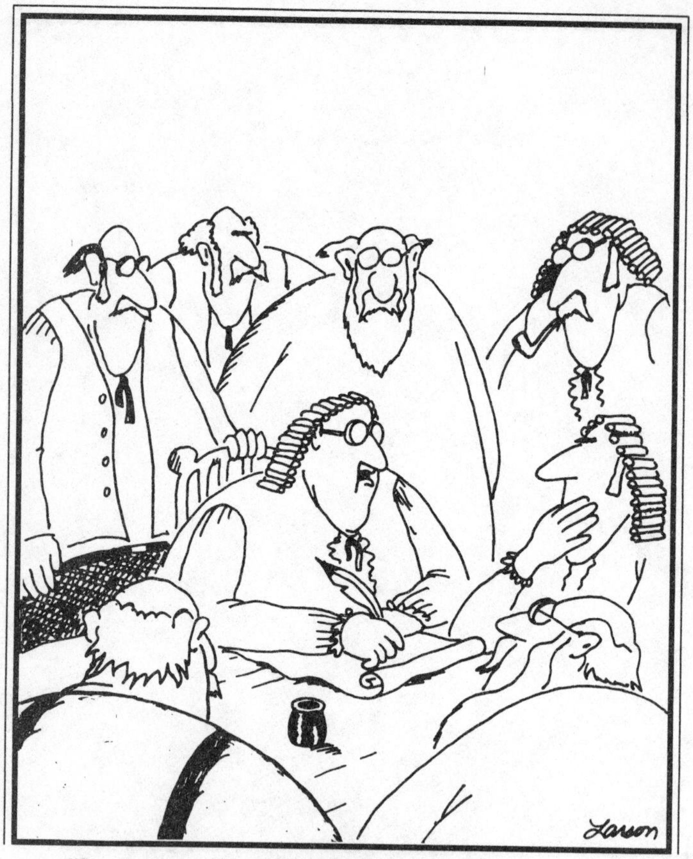
Larson

"So, then . . . Would that be 'us the people' or 'we the people'?"

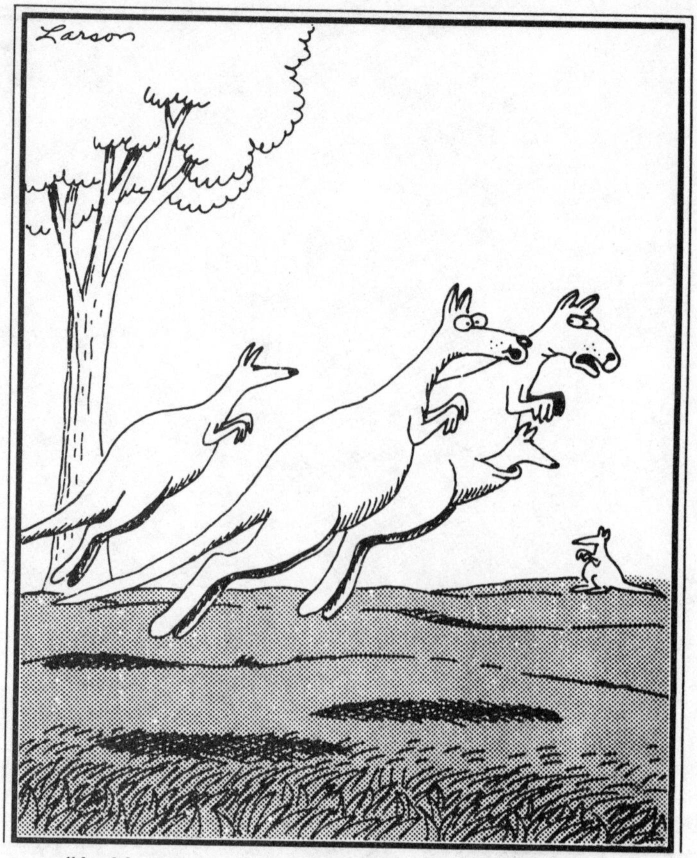
Larson

"Just jump, fool! . . . You don't have to go, 'Boing, boing, boing'!"

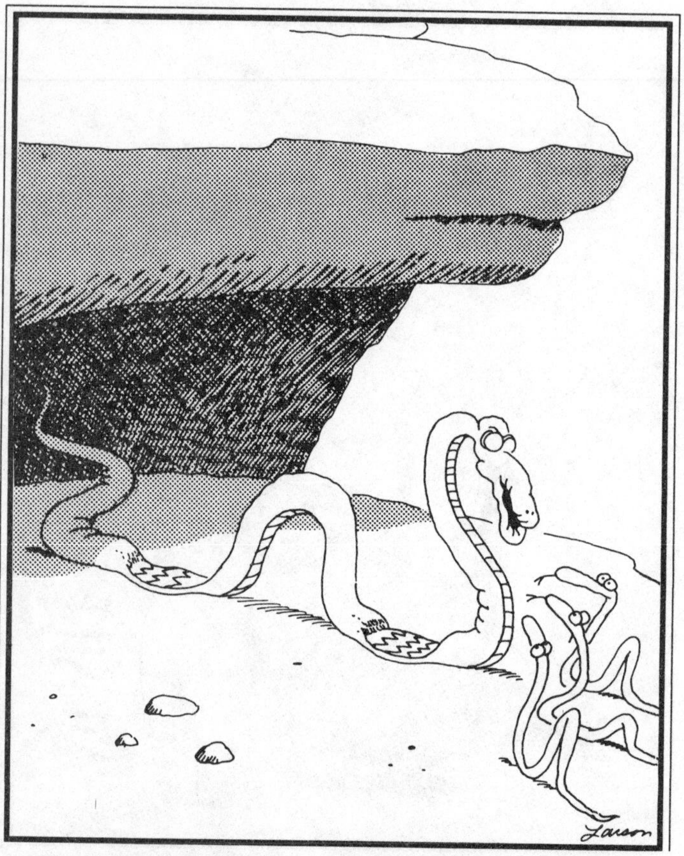
Larson

"Again? Oh, all right . . . One warm, summer evening many years ago, I was basking on a stretch of Interstate 95 not far from here . . ."

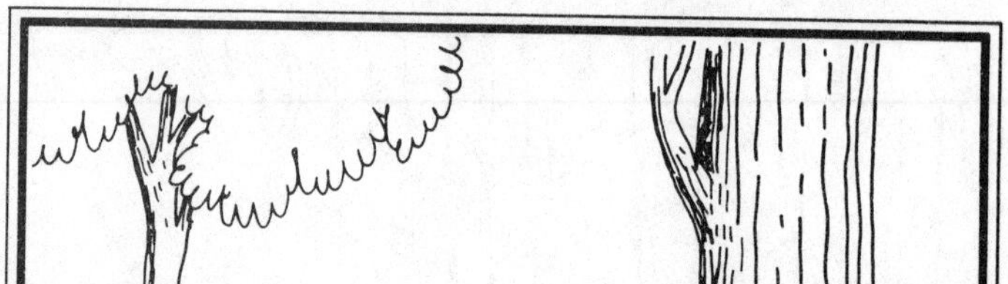
Larson

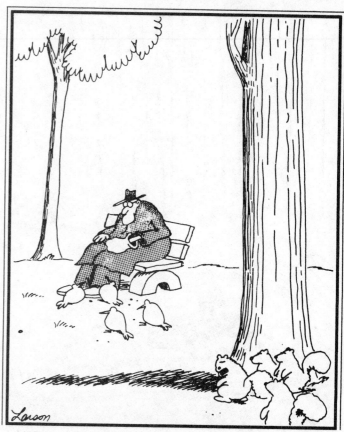

"Okay, here we go! Remember, wiggle those noses, stuff those cheeks, and act cute — and no smoking, Carl."

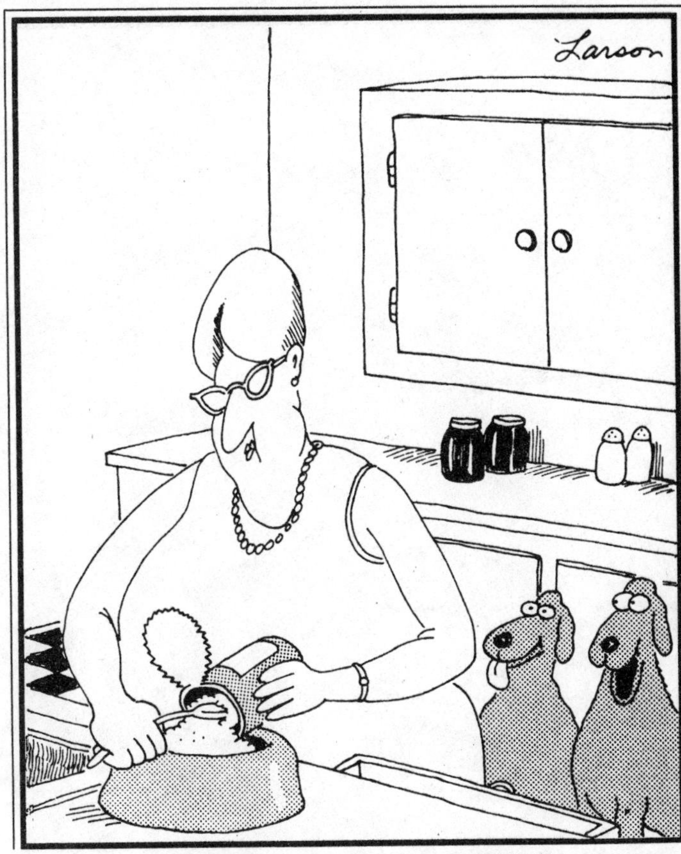
Larson

"Oh boy! . . . It's dog food AGAIN!"

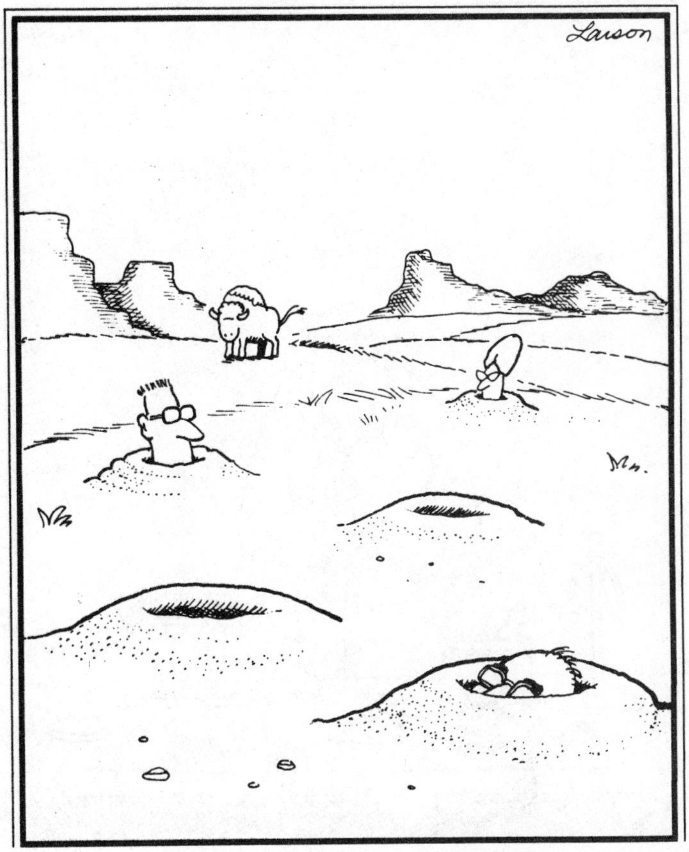
Larson

The rare and timid prairie people

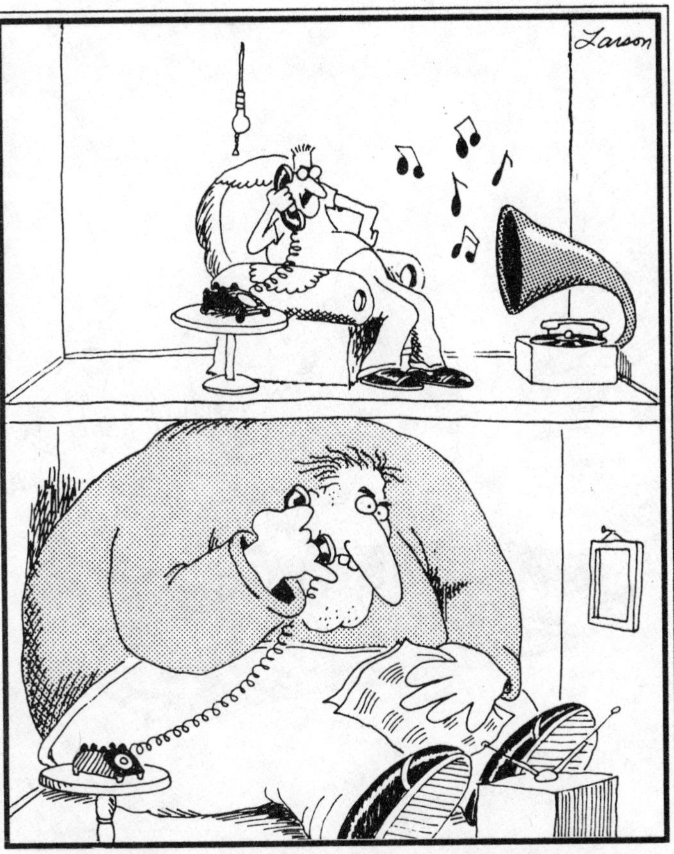
Larson

"Well, why don't you come up here and MAKE me turn it down . . . or do you just TALK big, fellah?"

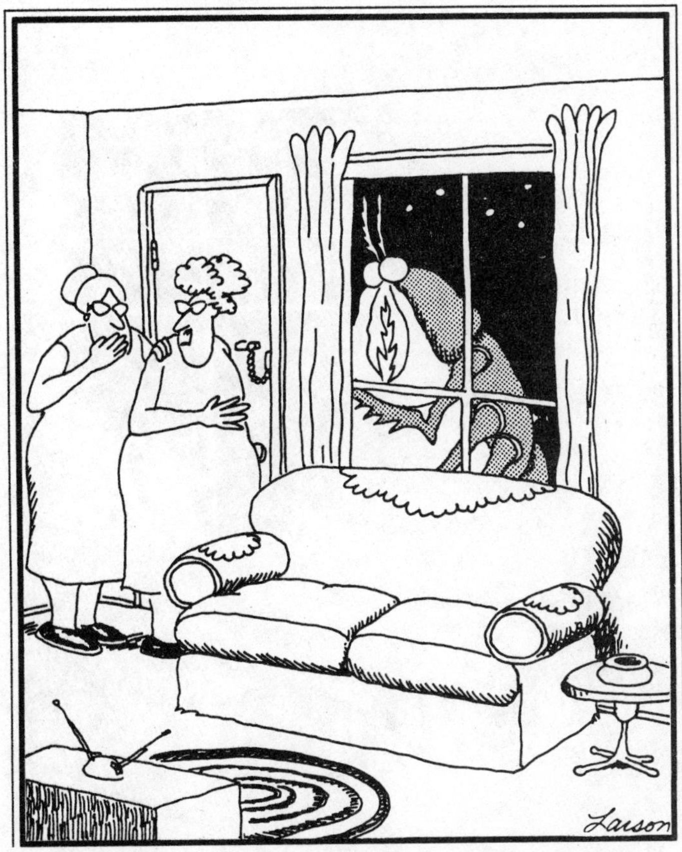
Larson

"Calm down, Edna . . . Yes, it's some giant, hideous insect . . . but it could be some giant, hideous insect in need of help."

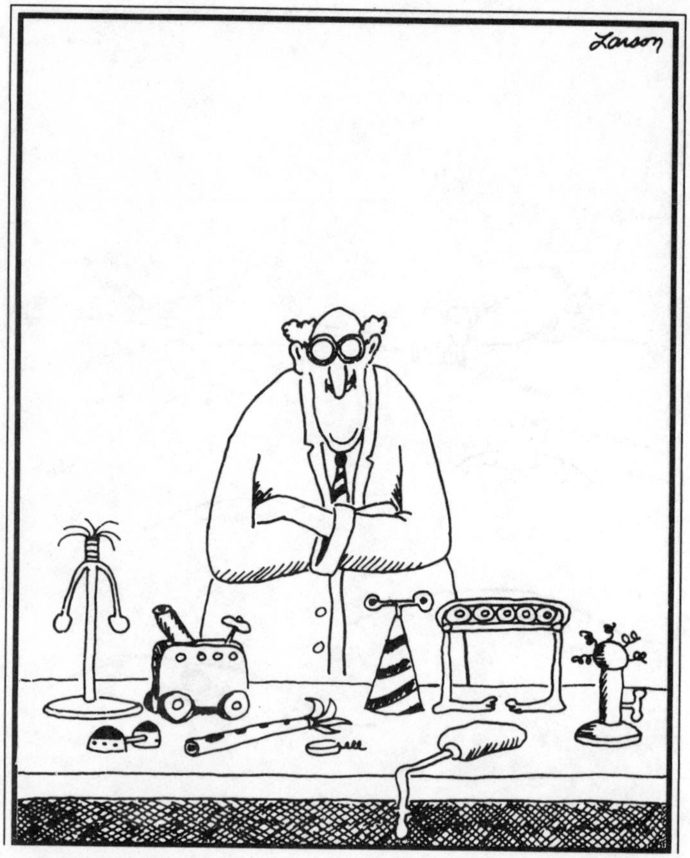
Larson

Professor E. F. Gizmo and some of his many inventions

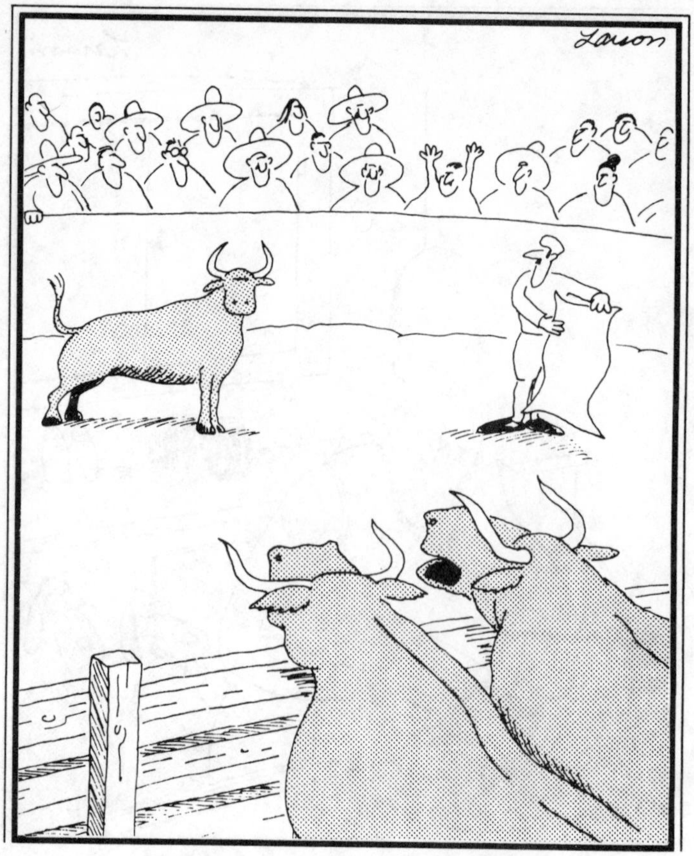
Larson

"The cape, Larry! Go for the cape!"

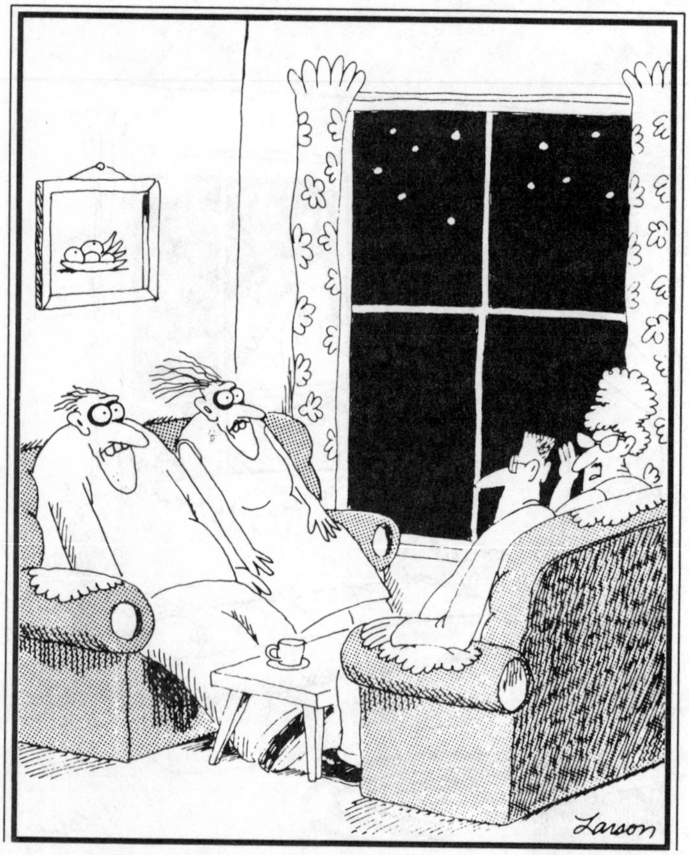
Larson

"What did I say, Alex? . . . Every time we invite the Zombies over, we all end up just sitting around staring at each other."

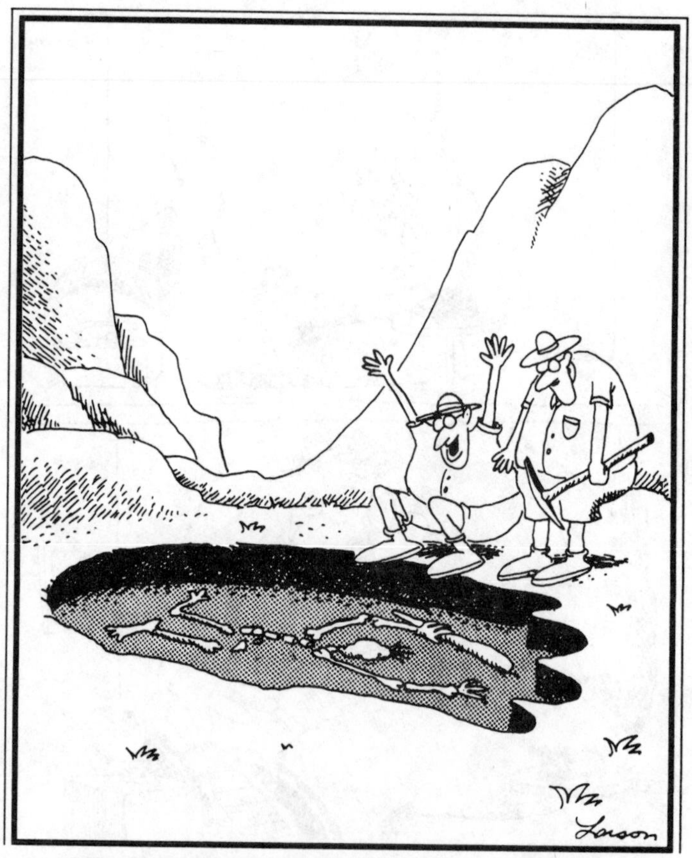
Larson

"What a find, Williams! The fossilized footprint of a brachiosaurus! . . . And a Homo habilus thrown in to boot!"

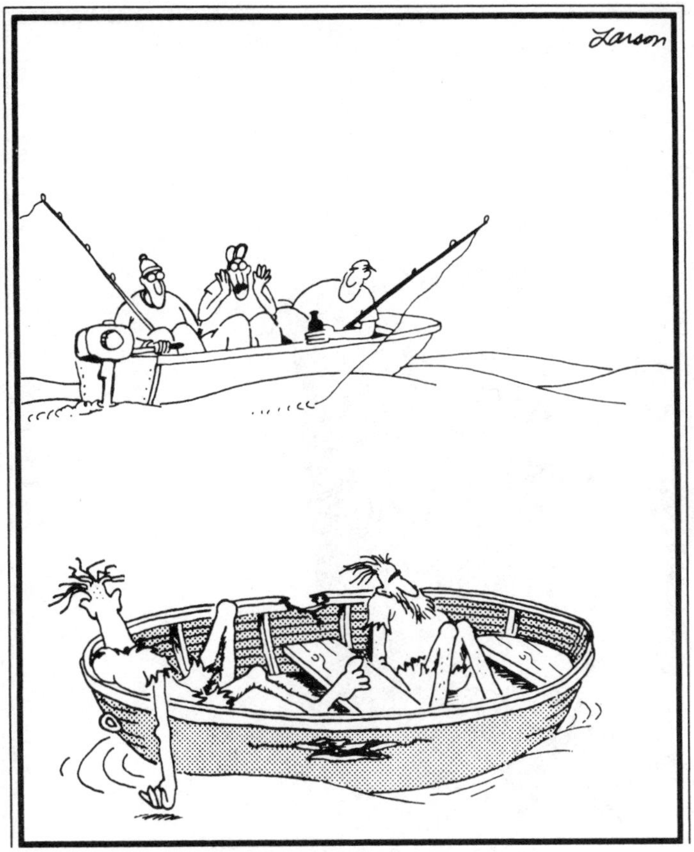
Larson

"You boys gotta bottle-opener?"

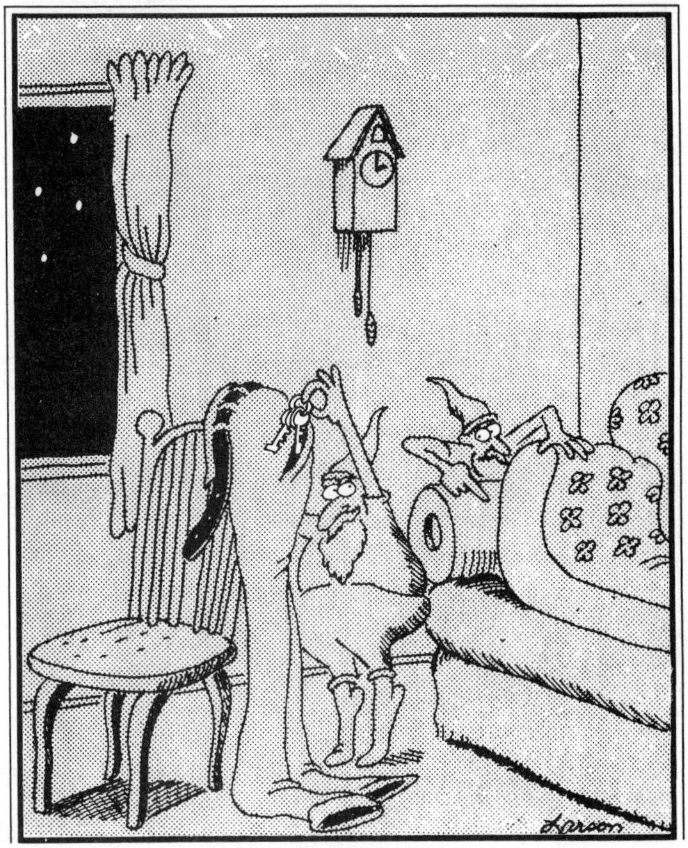
Larson

Car key gnomes

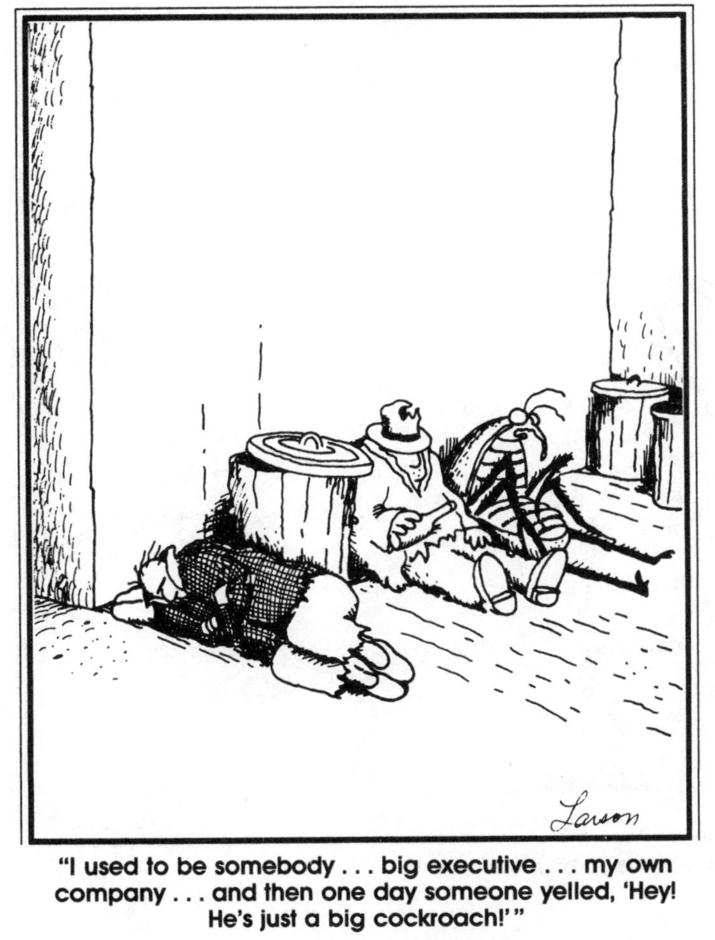
Larson

"I used to be somebody . . . big executive . . . my own company . . . and then one day someone yelled, 'Hey! He's just a big cockroach!' "

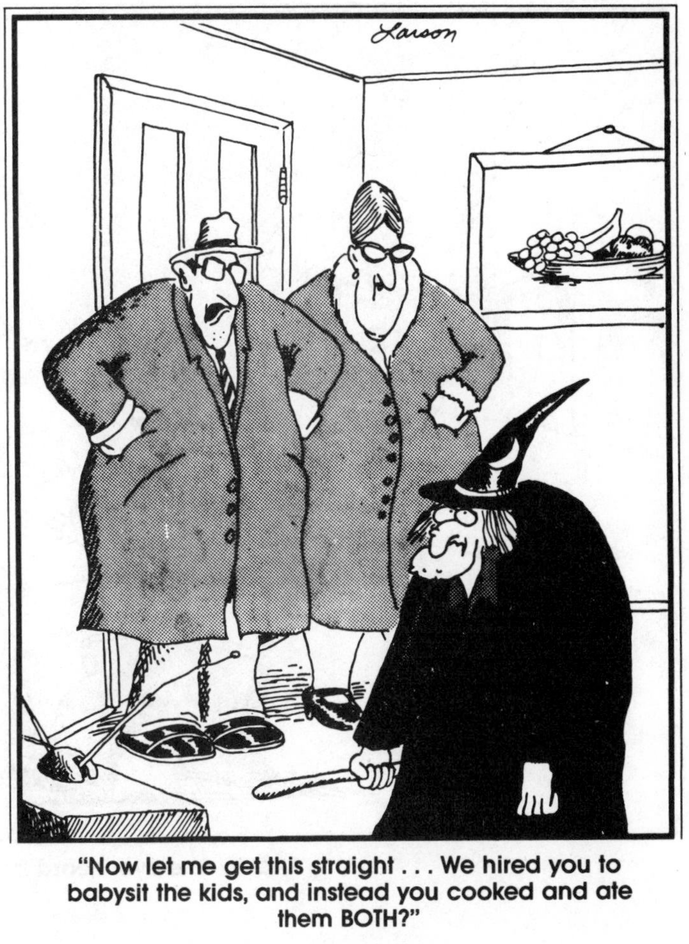
Larson

"Now let me get this straight . . . We hired you to babysit the kids, and instead you cooked and ate them BOTH?"

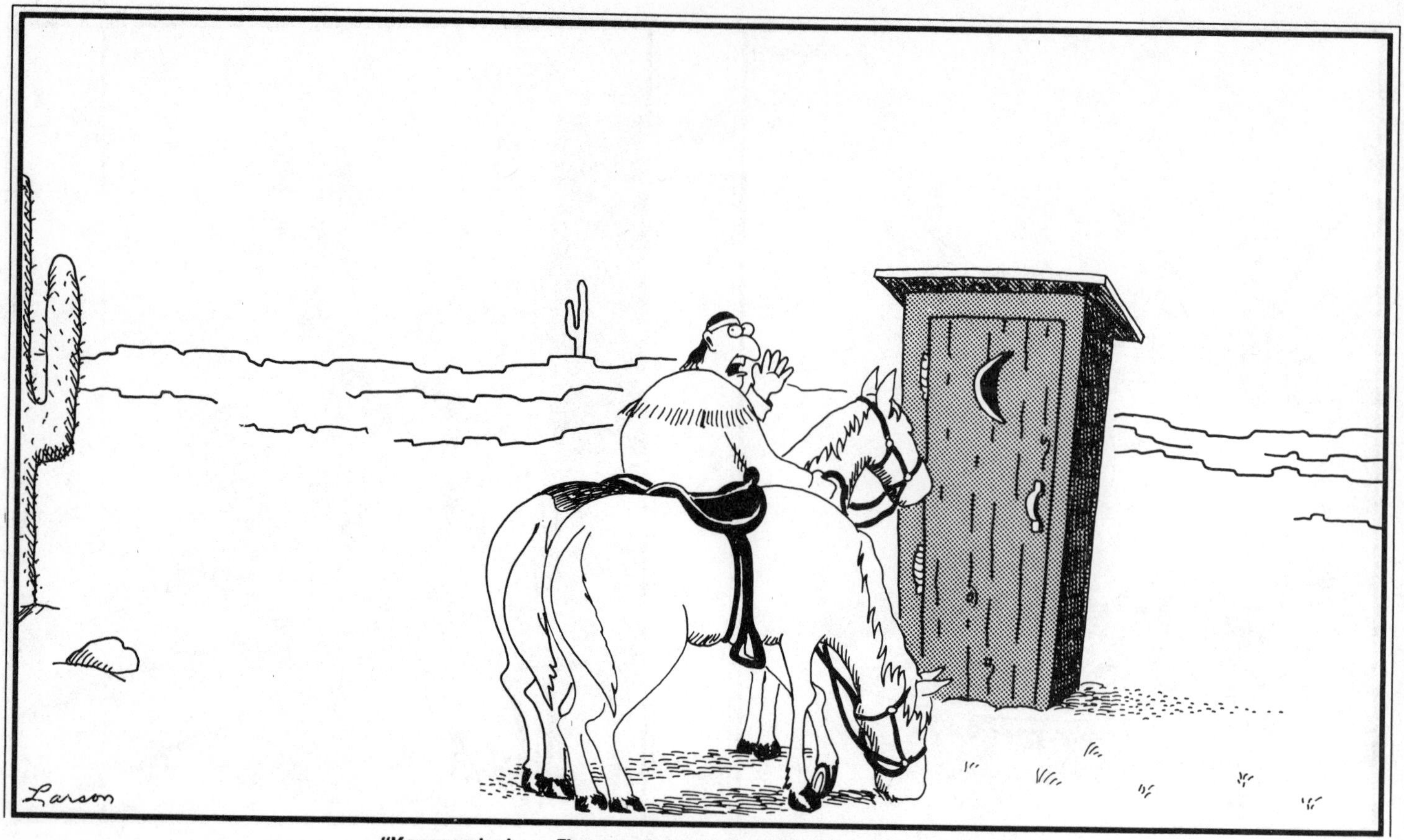
Larson

"Kemosabe! . . . The music's starting! The music's starting!"

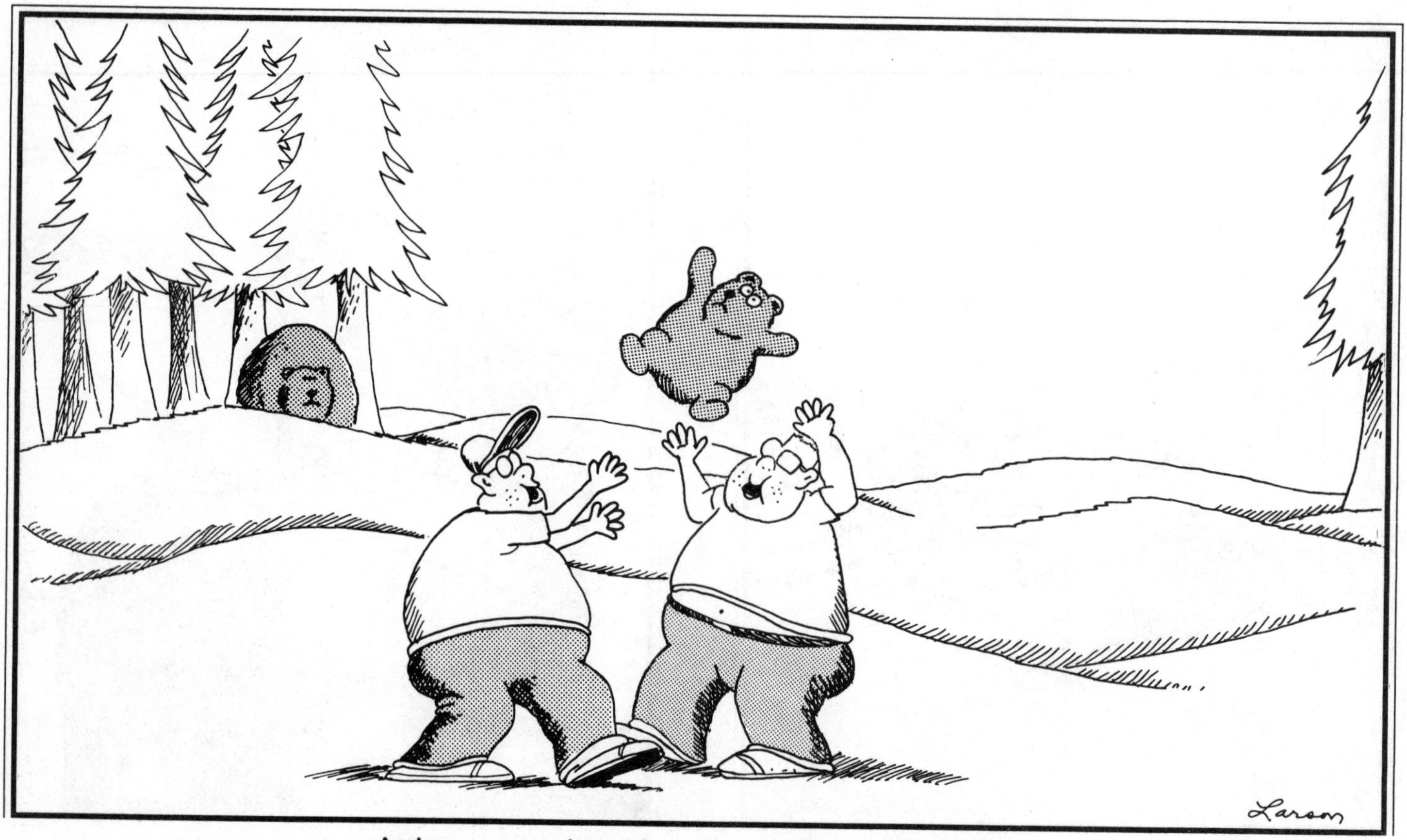
Larson

And no one ever heard from the Anderson brothers again.

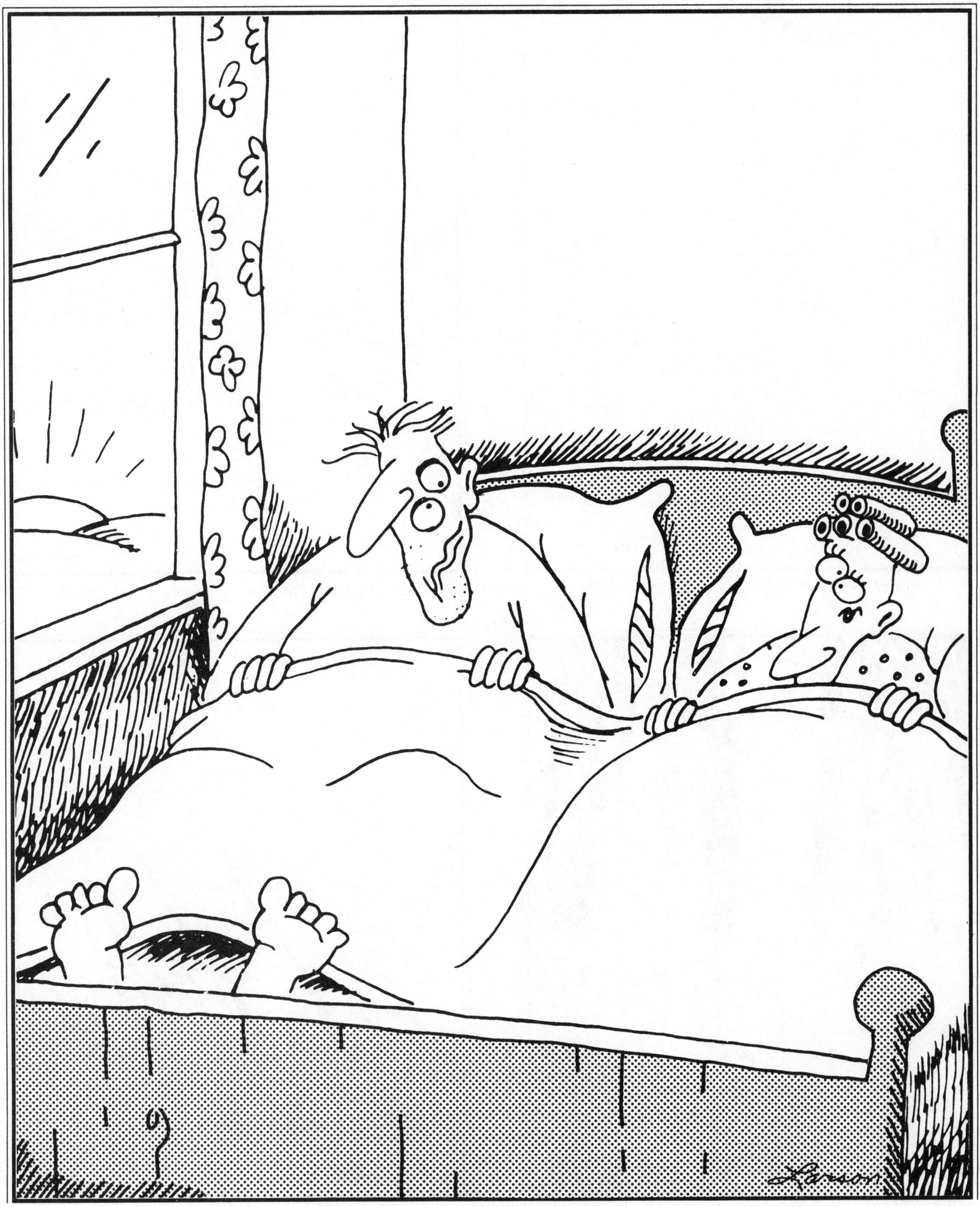
Larson

The embarrassment of "morning face"

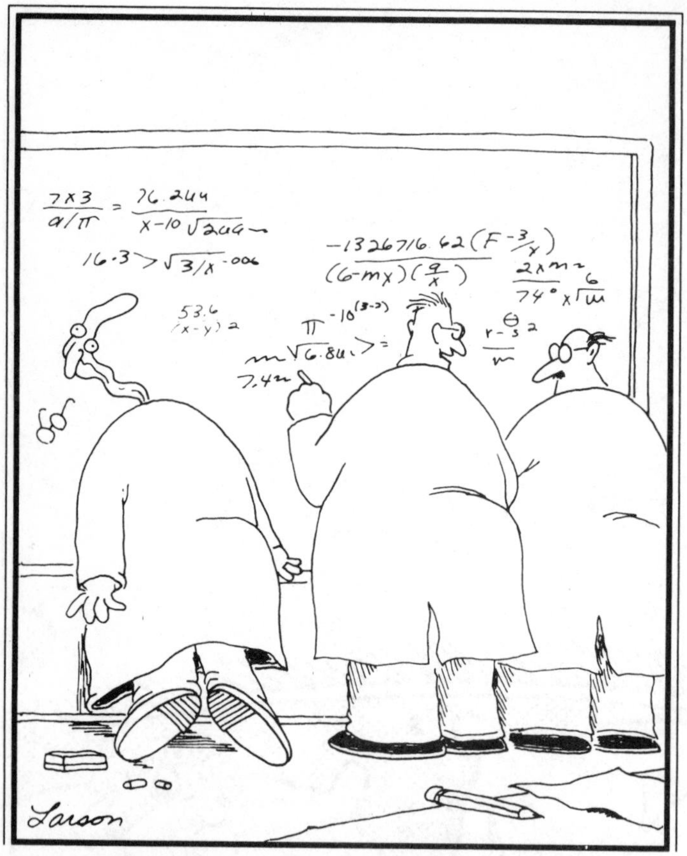
Larson

"Ha! Webster's blown his cerebral cortex."

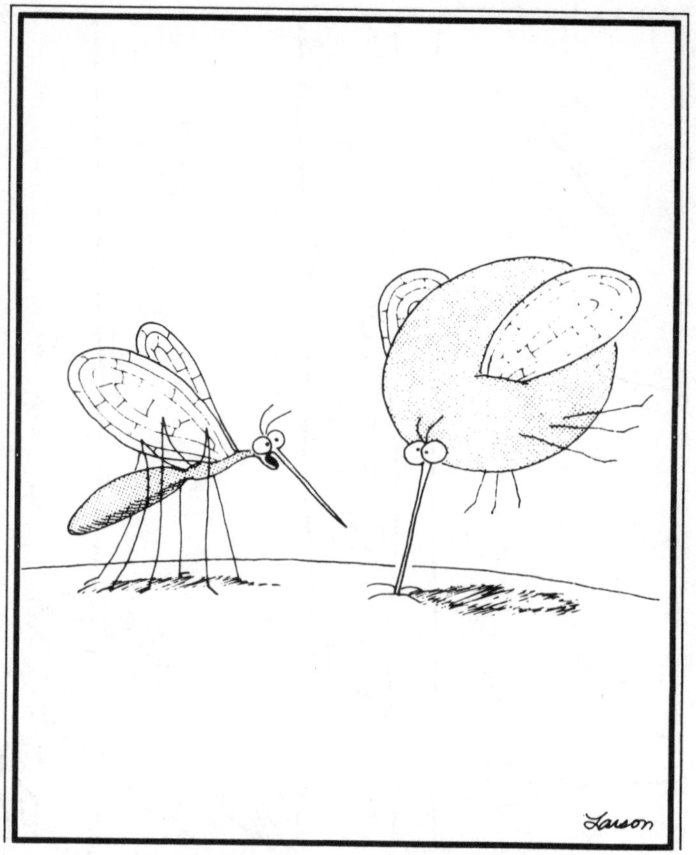
Larson

"Pull out, Betty! Pull out! . . . You've hit an artery!"

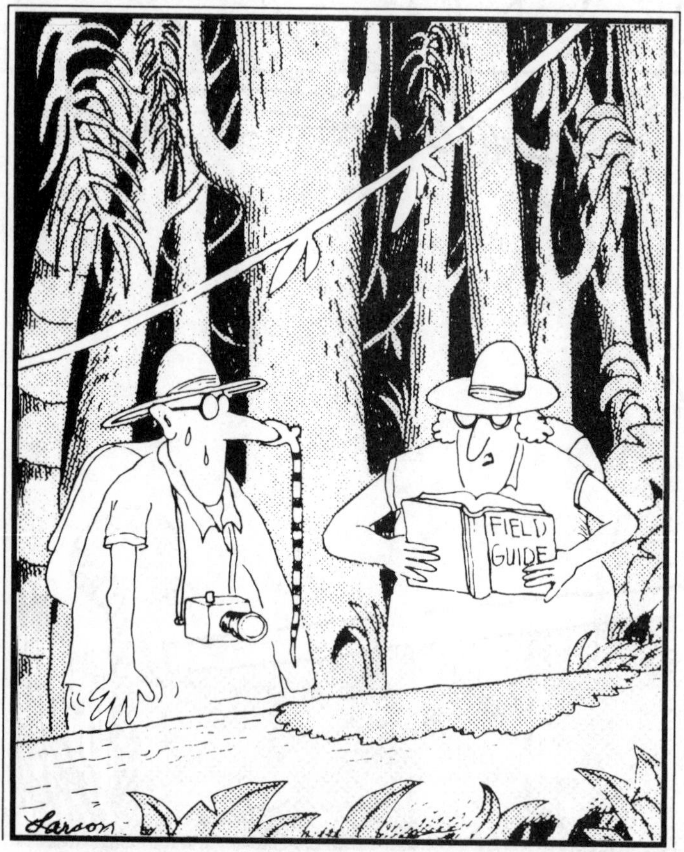
FIELD GUIDE
Larson

"'This dangerous viper, known for its peculiar habit of tenaciously hanging from one's nose, is vividly colored.' Oo! Murray! Look! . . . Here's a picture of it!"

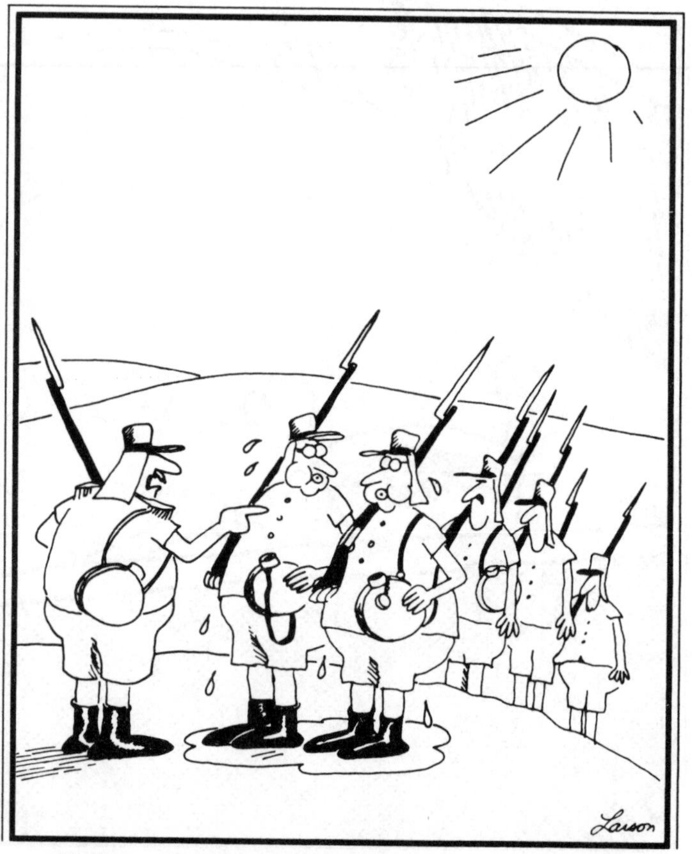
Larson

"Halt! . . . Okay! Johnson! Higgins! . . . You both just swallow what you've got and knock off these water fights once and for all!"

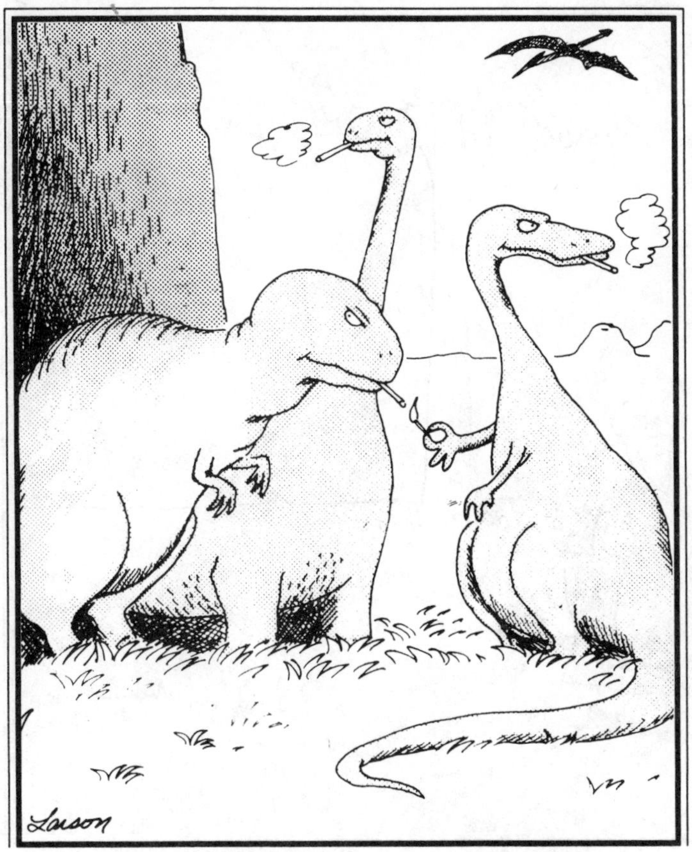
Larson

The real reason dinosaurs became extinct

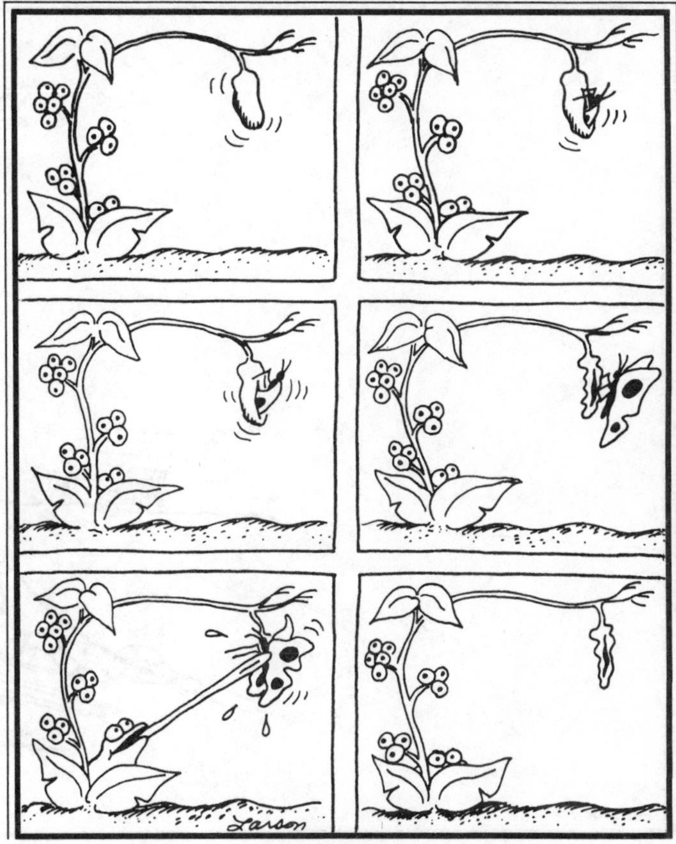
Larson

Metamorphosis

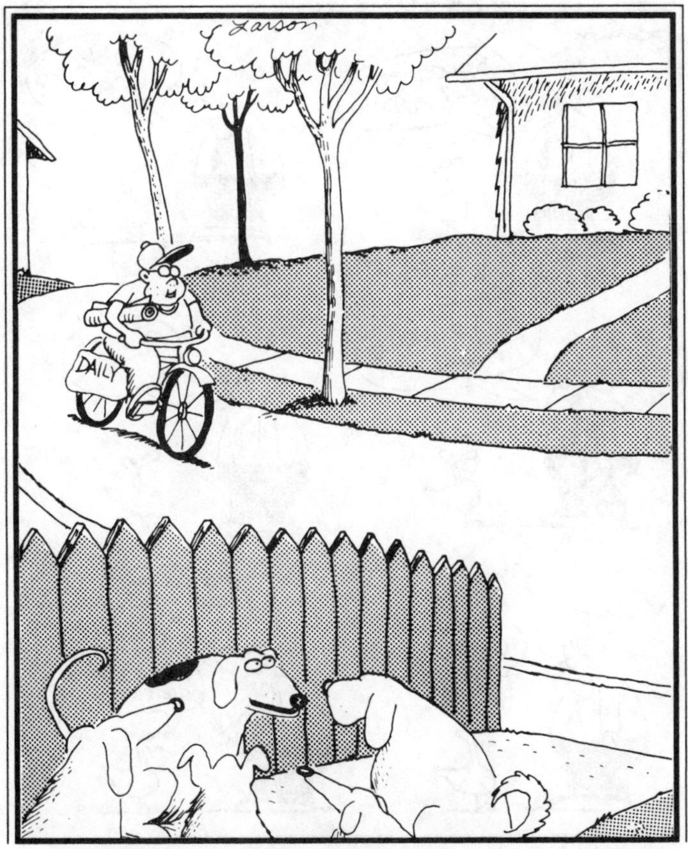
Larson
DAILY

"Okay, this time Rex and Zeke will be the wolves, Fifi and Muffin will be the coyotes, and . . . Listen! . . . Here comes the deer!"

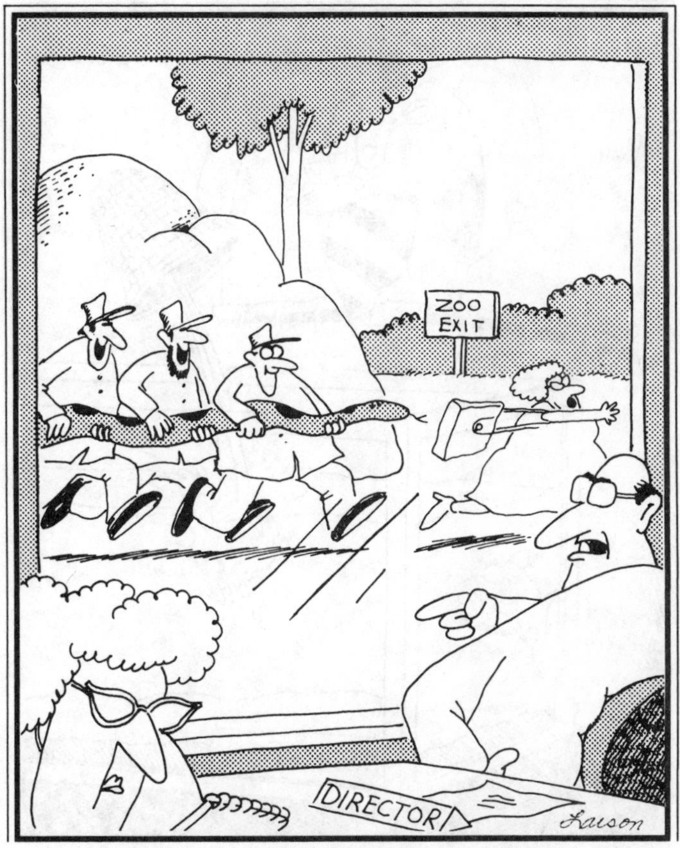
ZOO
EXIT
DIRECTOR
Larson

"Take another memo, Miss Wilkens . . . I want to see all reptile personnel in my office first thing tomorrow morning!"

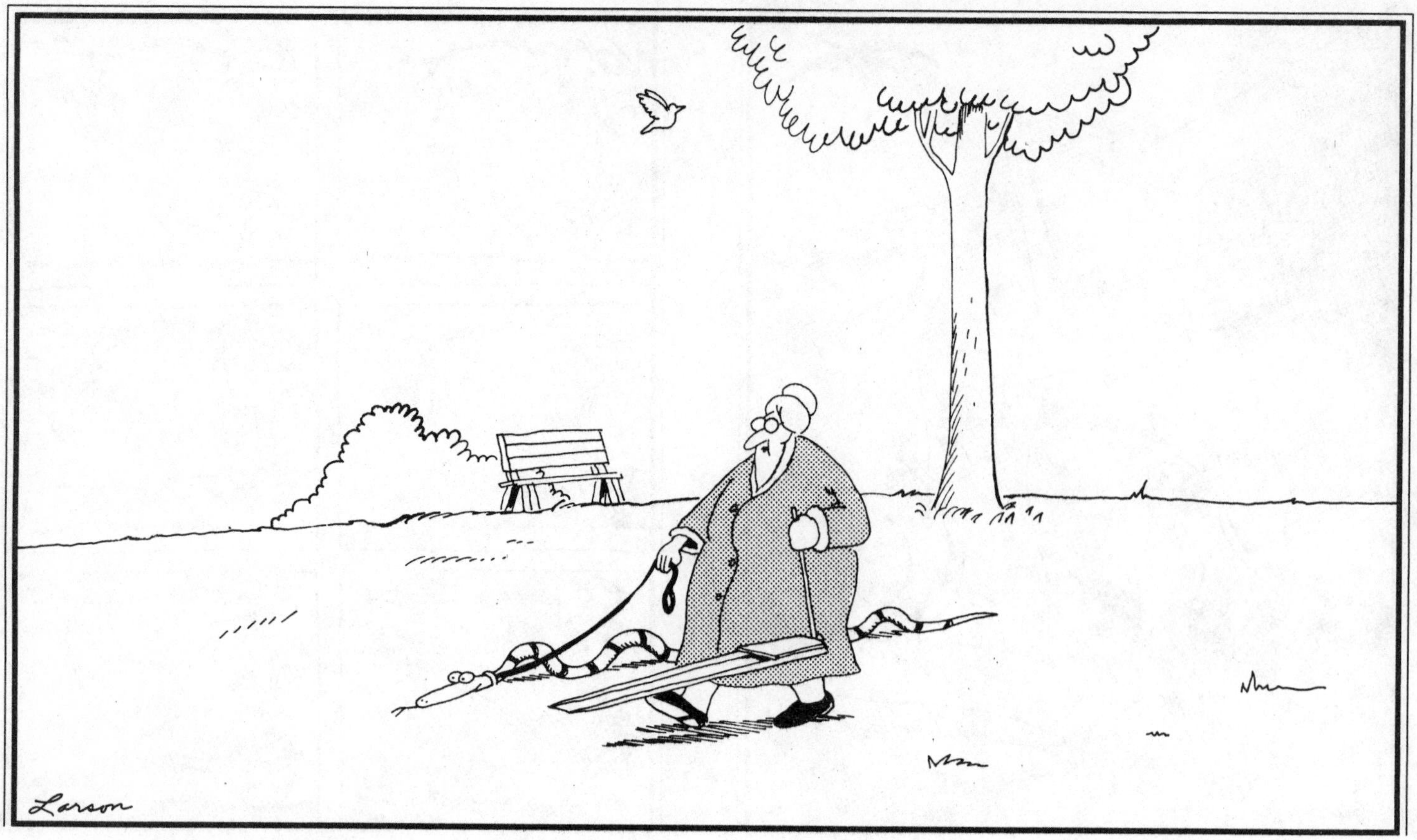
Larson

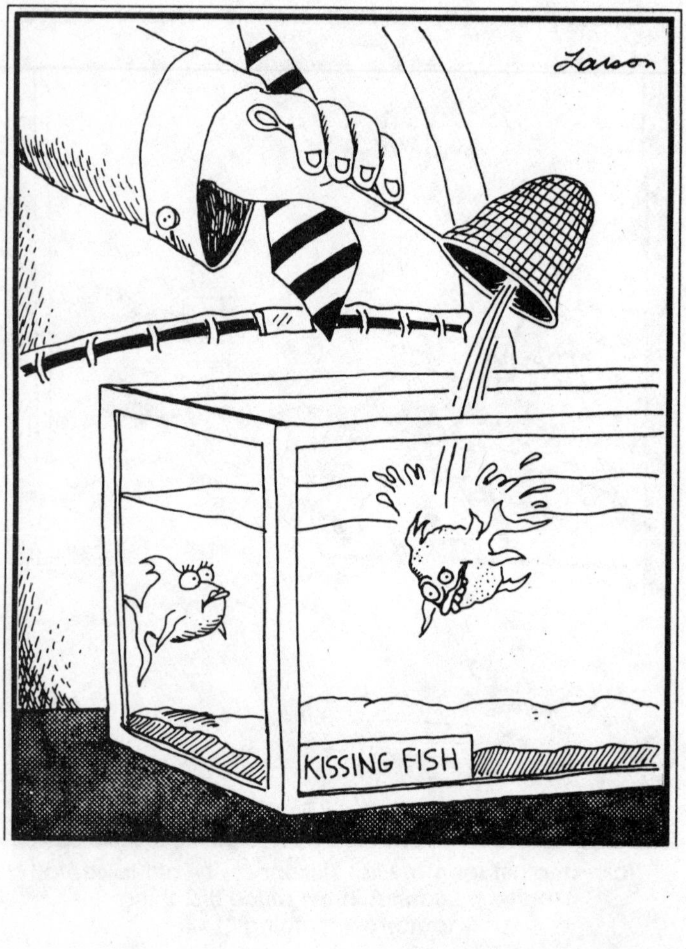
Larson
KISSING FISH

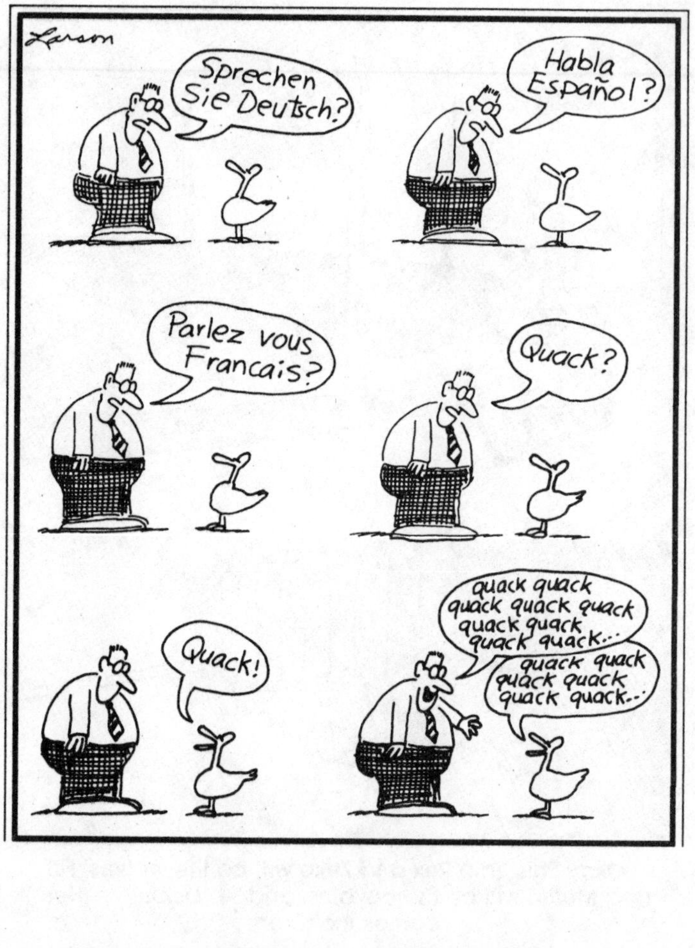
Larson
Sprechen Sie Deutsch?
Habla Español?
Parlez vous Francais?
Quack?
Quack!
quack quack quack quack quack quack quack quack quack quack...
quack quack quack quack quack quack...

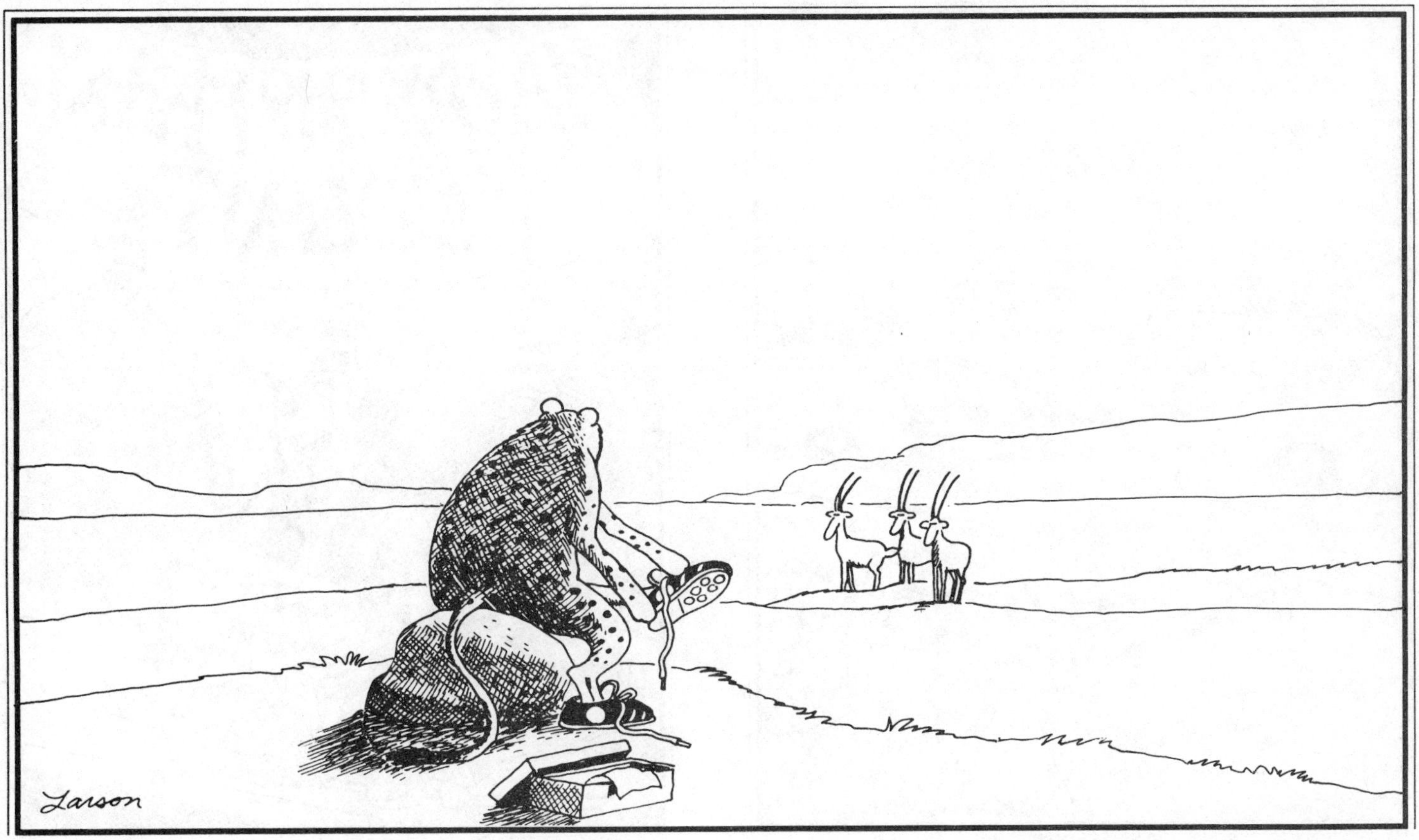
Larson

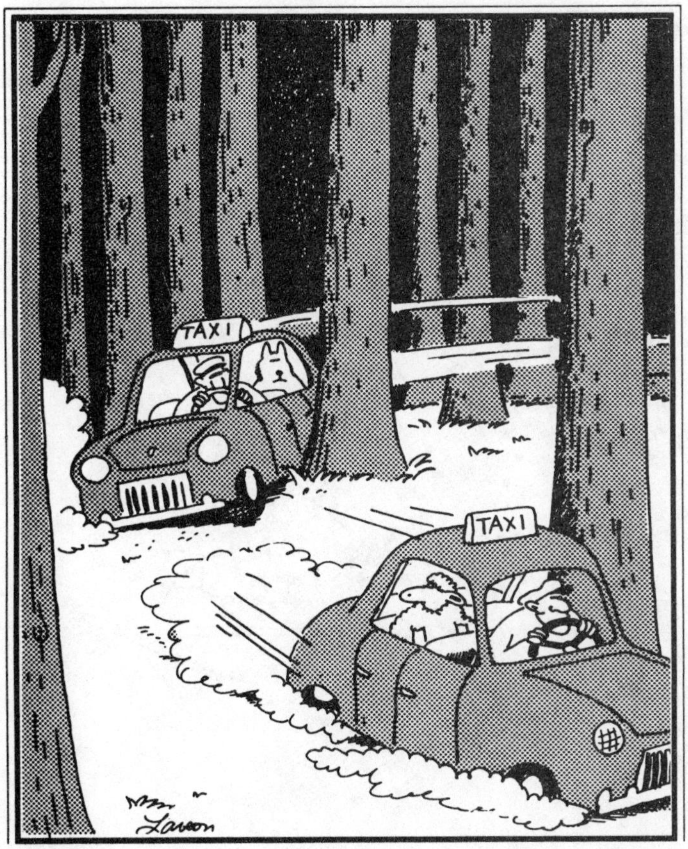
TAXI
TAXI
Larson

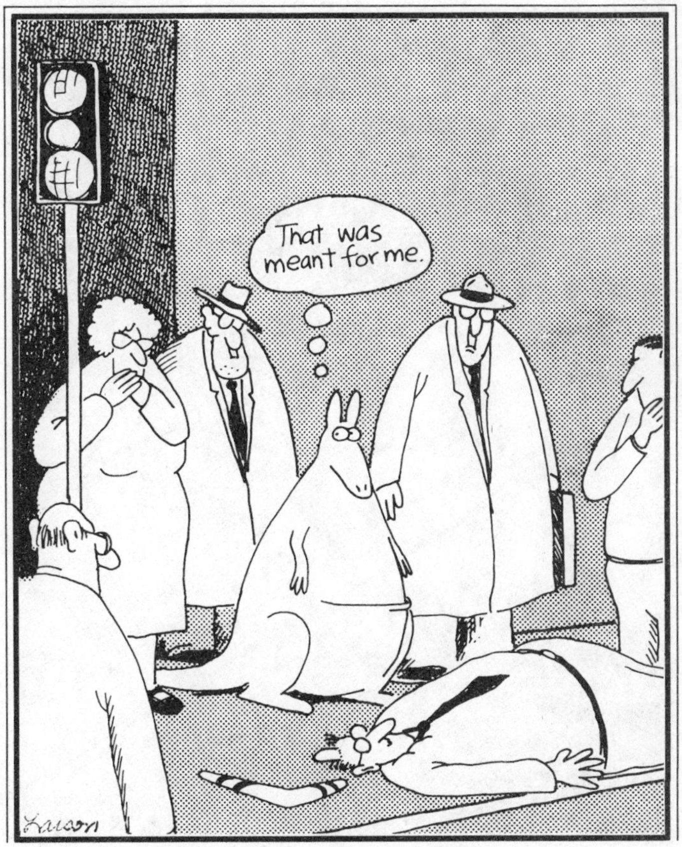
That was meant for me.
Larson

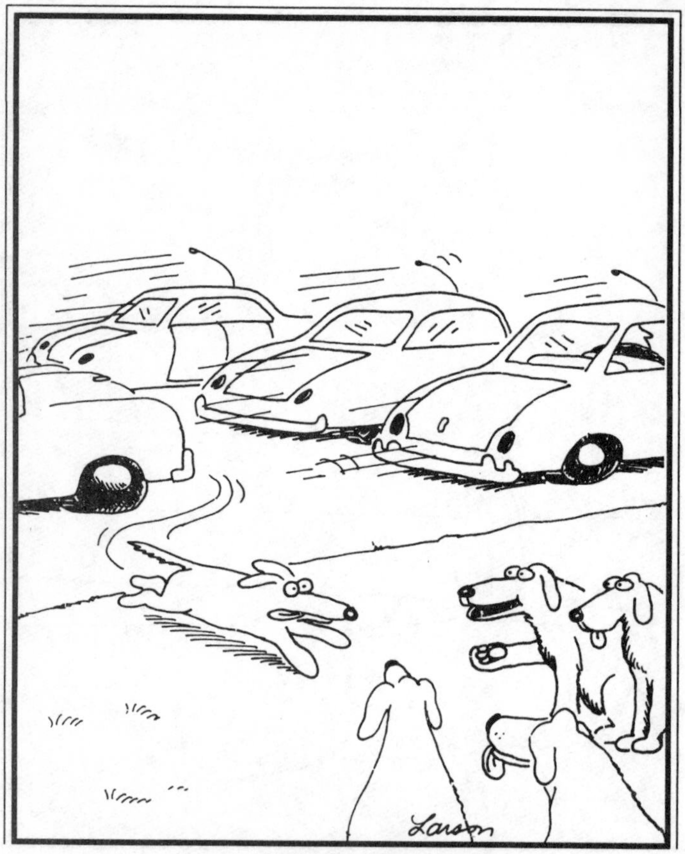
Larson

"All right! Rusty's in the club!"

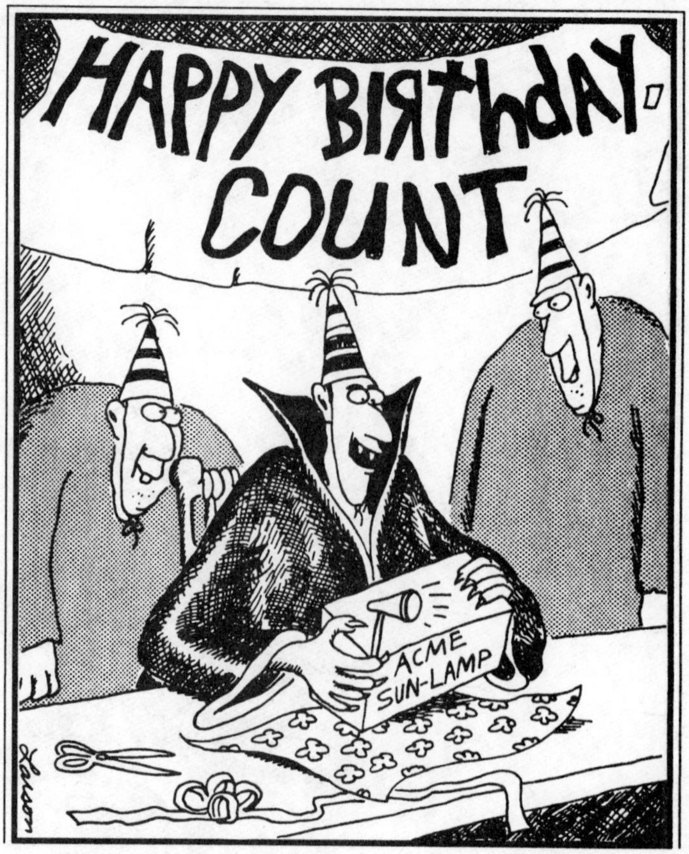
HAPPY BIRTHDAY COUNT
ACME SUN-LAMP
Larson

"Well, for goodness sakes! . . . What is this thing?"

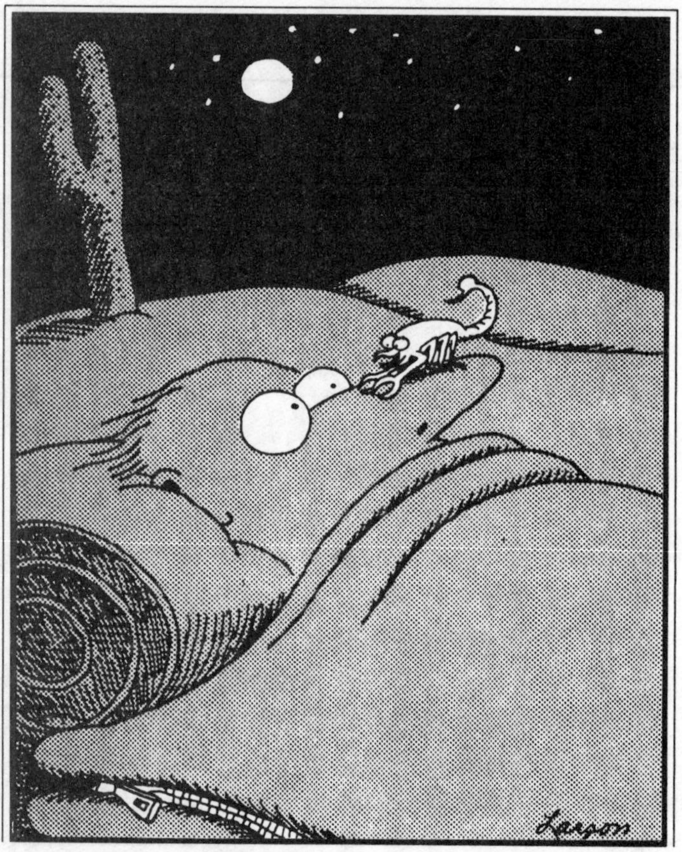
Larson

"Excuse me, but the others sent me up here to ask you not to roll around so much."

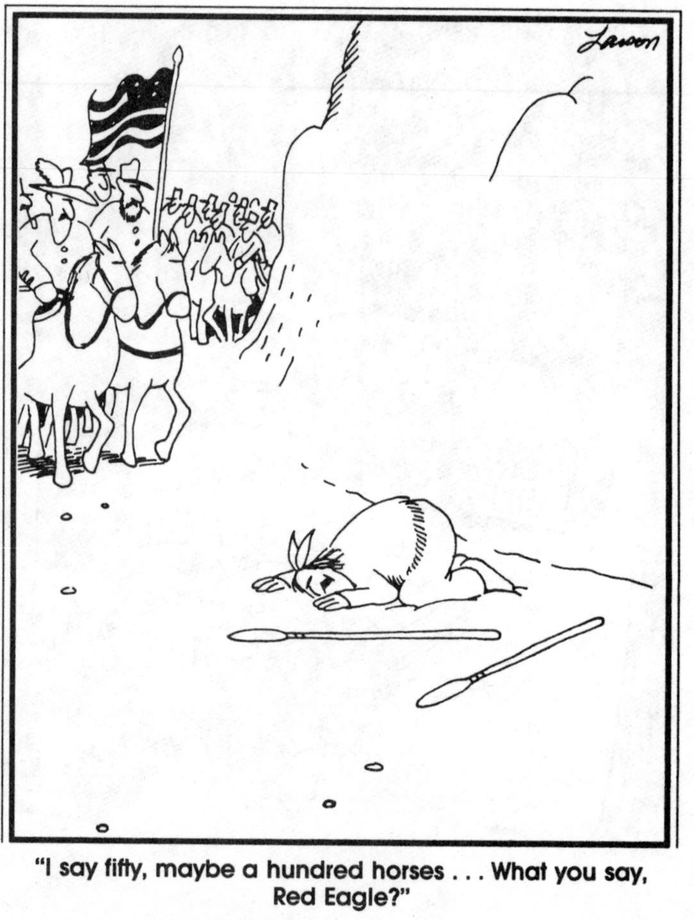
Larson

"I say fifty, maybe a hundred horses . . . What you say, Red Eagle?"

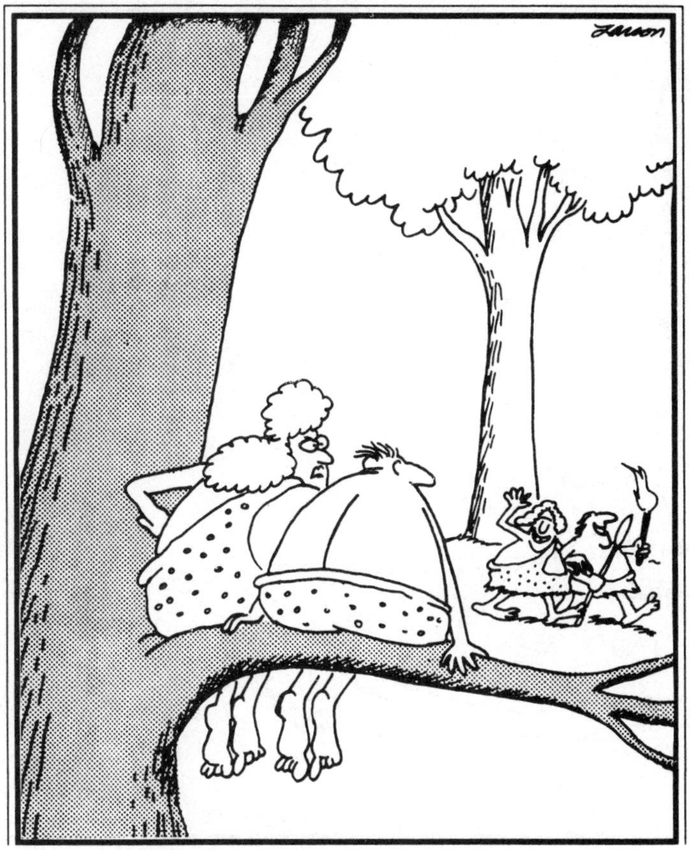
Larson

"And now there go the Wilsons! . . . Seems like everyone's evolving except us!"

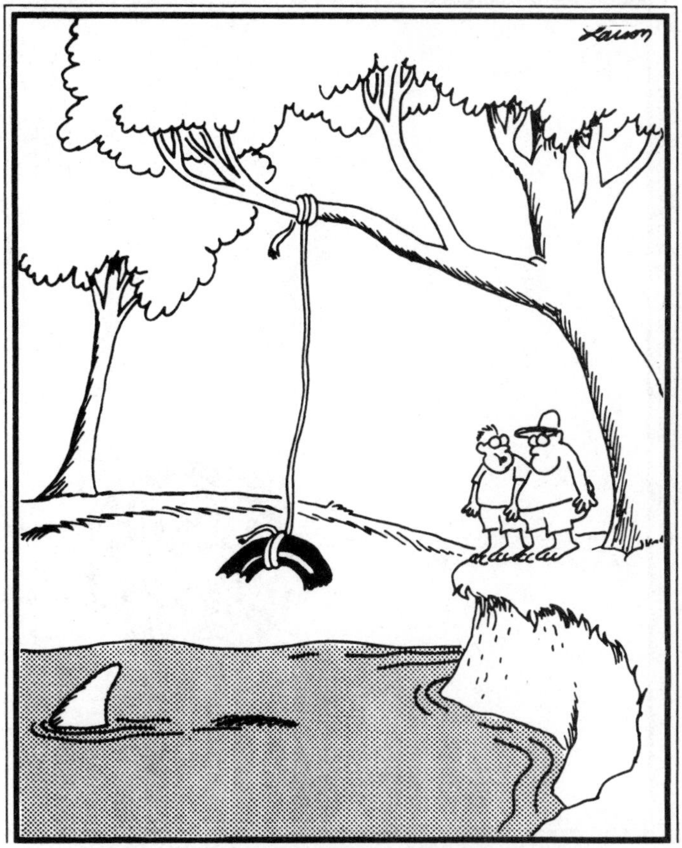
Larson

"Listen . . . You go tell Billy's mother, and I'll start looking for another old tire."

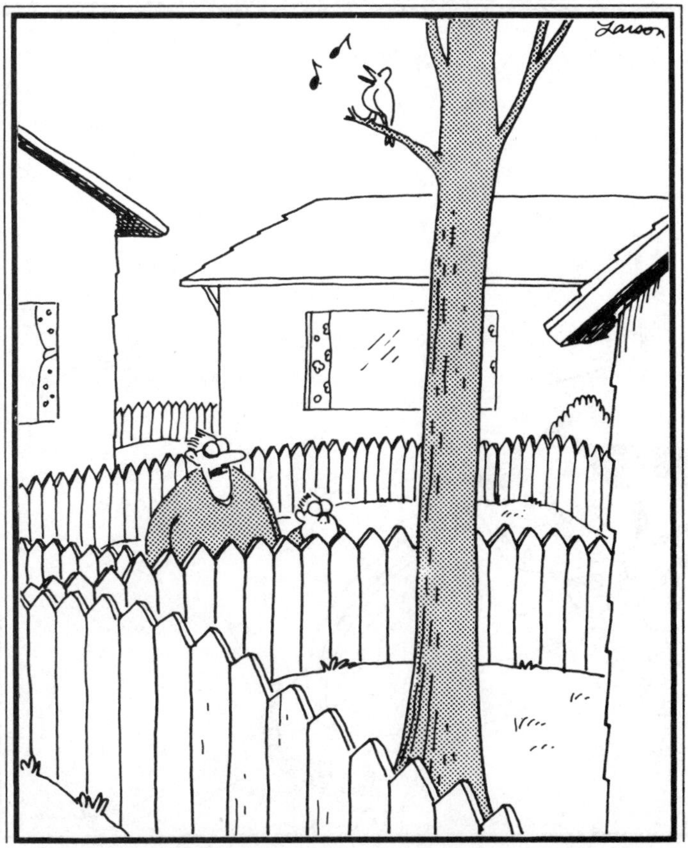
Larson

"And now, Randy, by use of song, the male sparrow will stake out his territory . . . an instinct common in the lower animals."

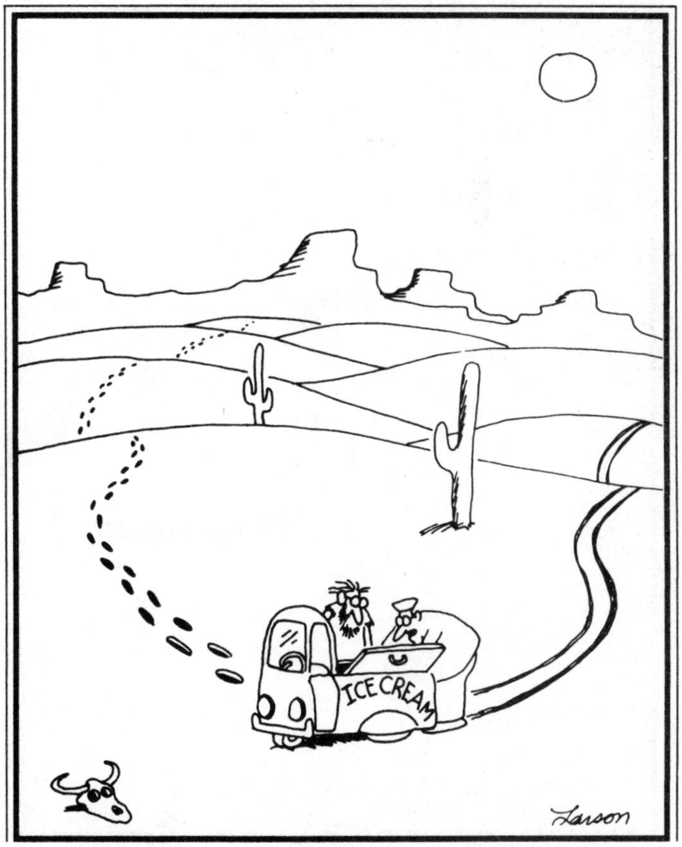
ICE CREAM
Larson

"Let's see . . . No orange . . . no root beer . . . no Fudgsicles . . . Well, for crying out loud! . . . Am I out of everything?"

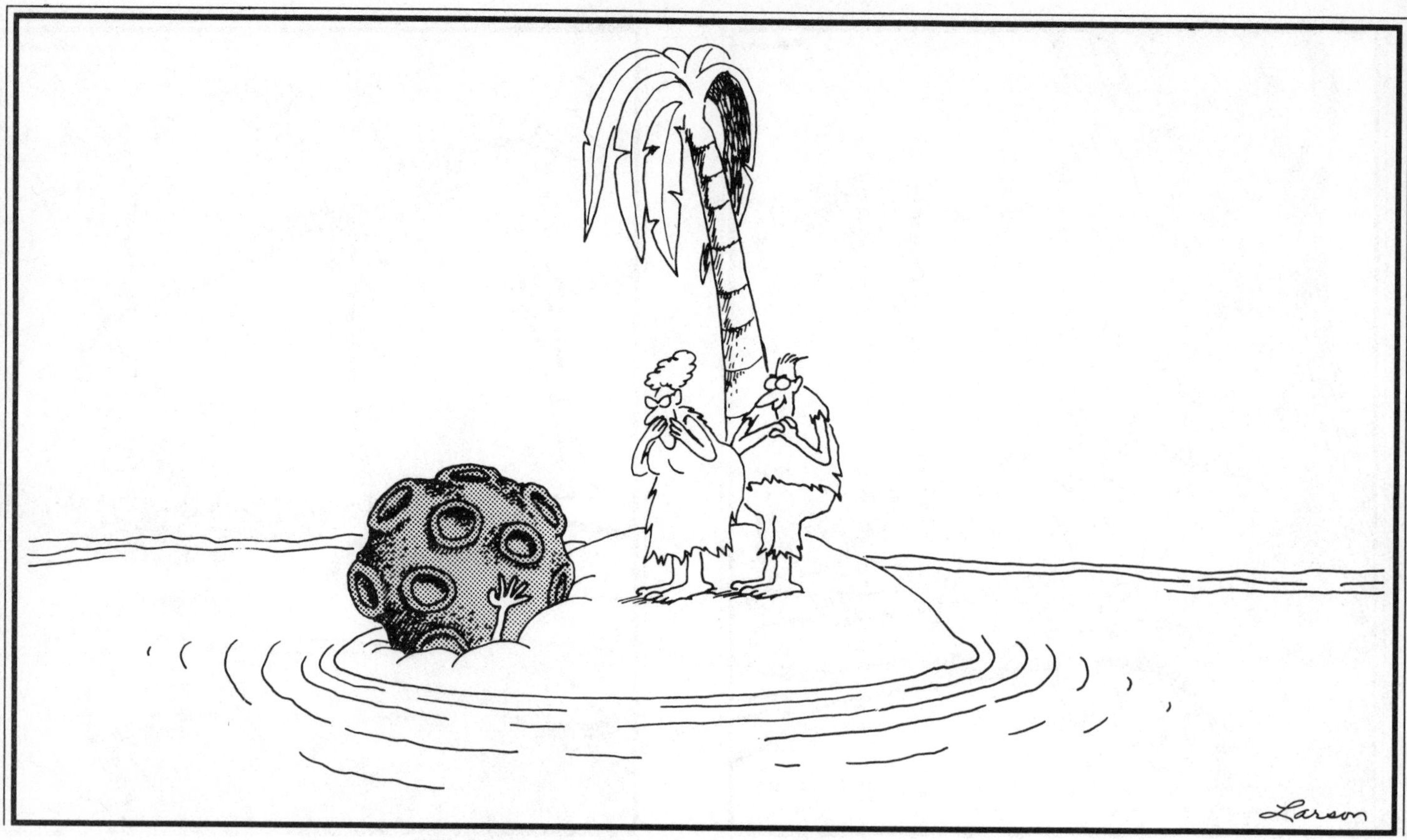
Larson

With Roger out of the way, it was Sidney's big chance.

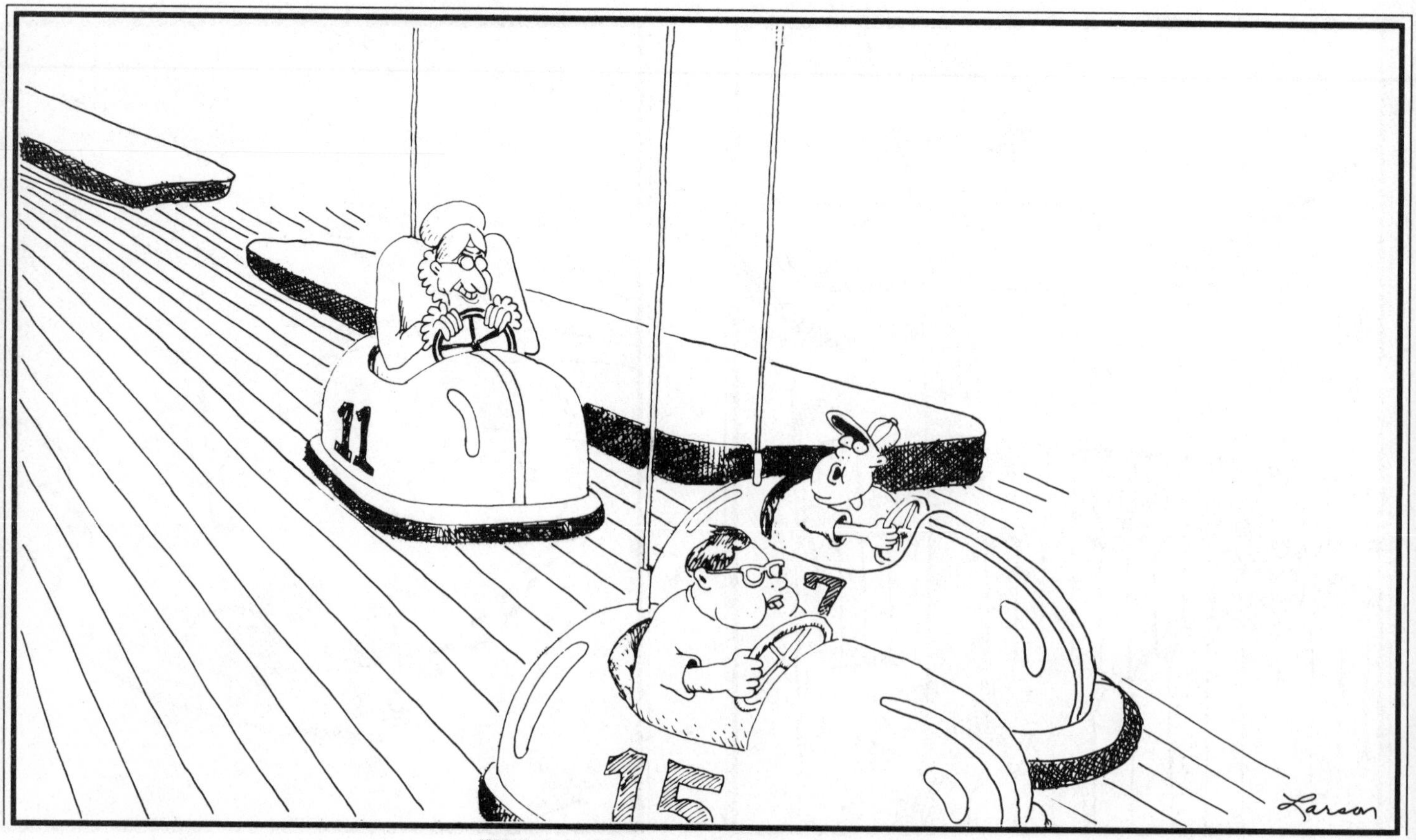
11
7
15
Larson

"Watch it, Randy! . . . She's on your case!"

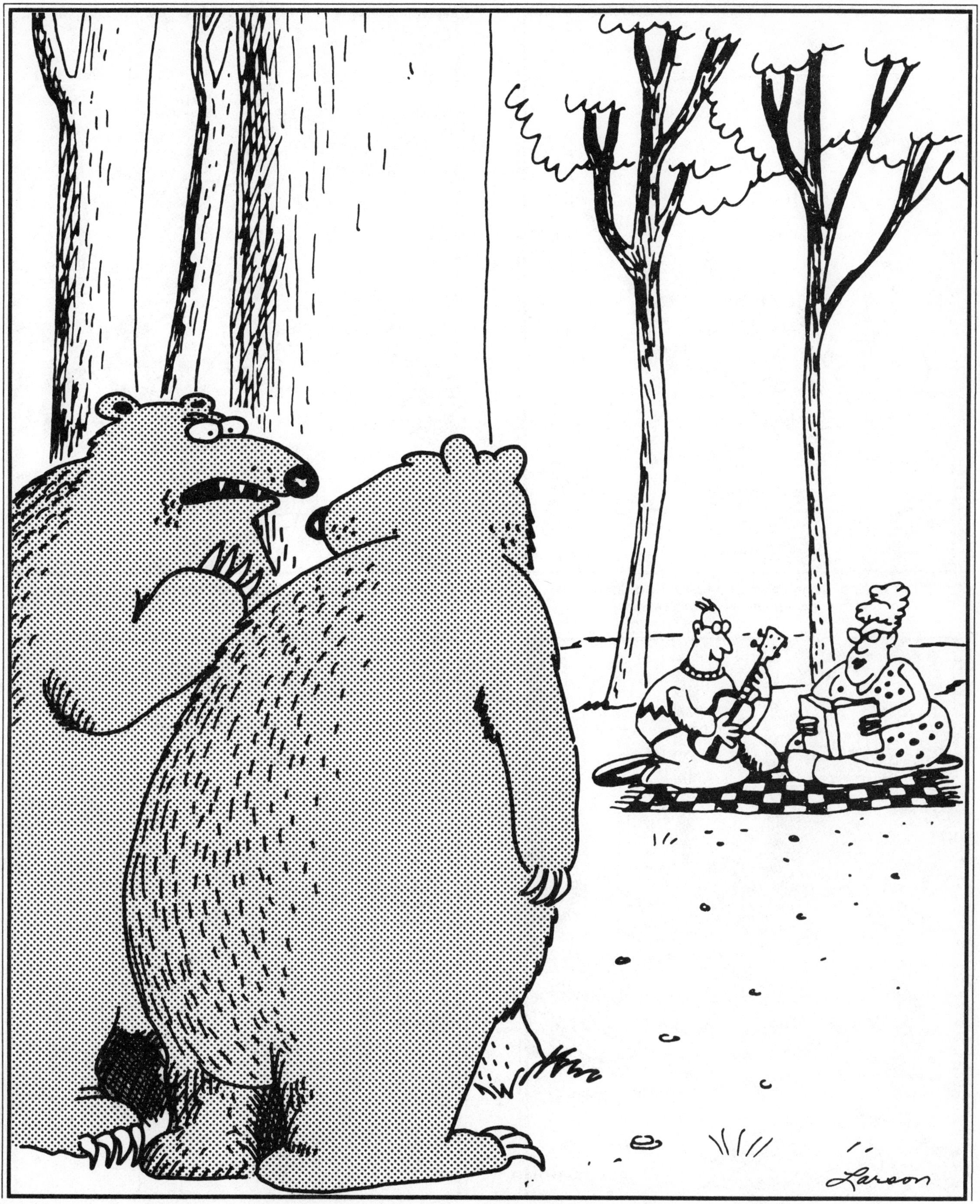
Larson

"C'mon! Look at these fangs! . . . Look at these claws! . . . You think we're supposed to eat just honey and berries?"

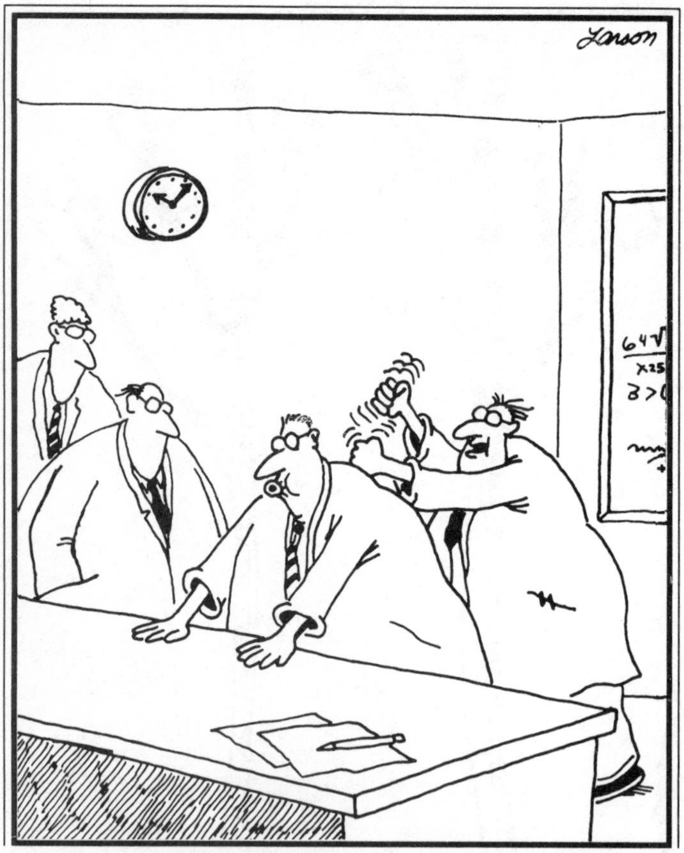
Larson

"And notice, gentlemen, the faster I go, the more Simmons sounds like a motorboat."

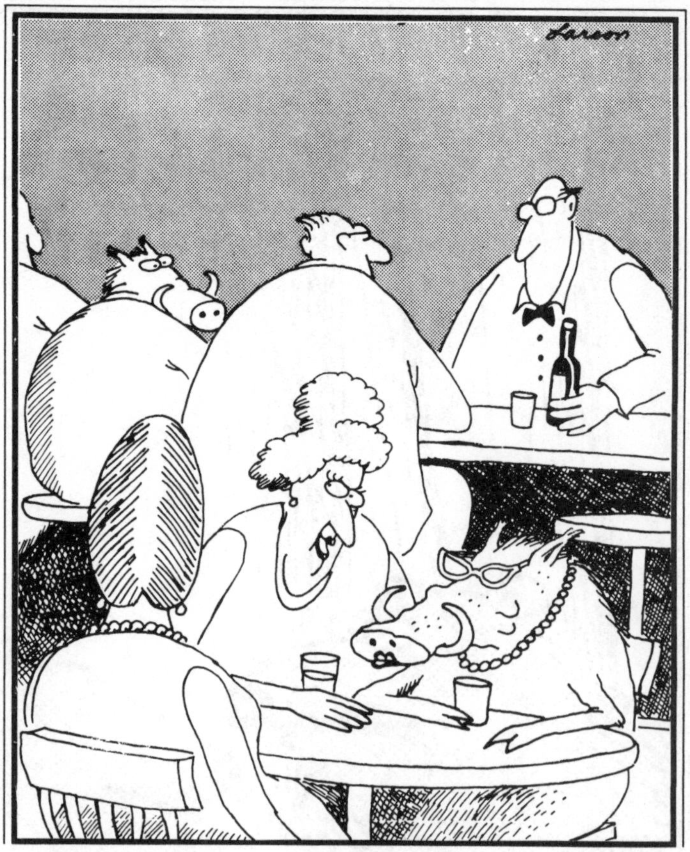
Larson

"Uh-oh, Lorraine . . . Someone seems to be checking you out."

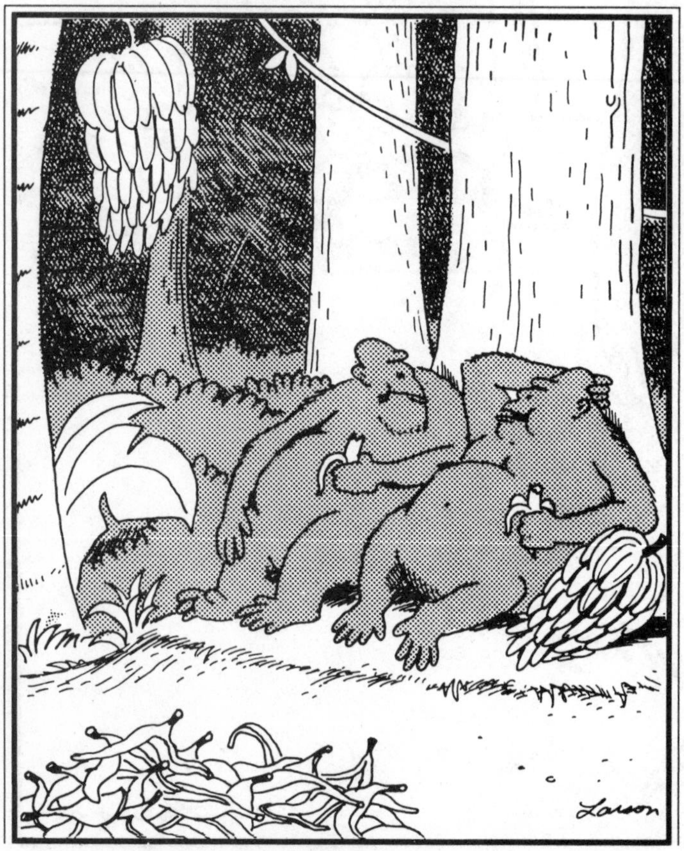
Larson

"You know, Sid, I really like bananas . . . I mean, I know that's not profound or nothin' . . . Heck! We ALL do . . . But for me, I think it goes much more beyond that."

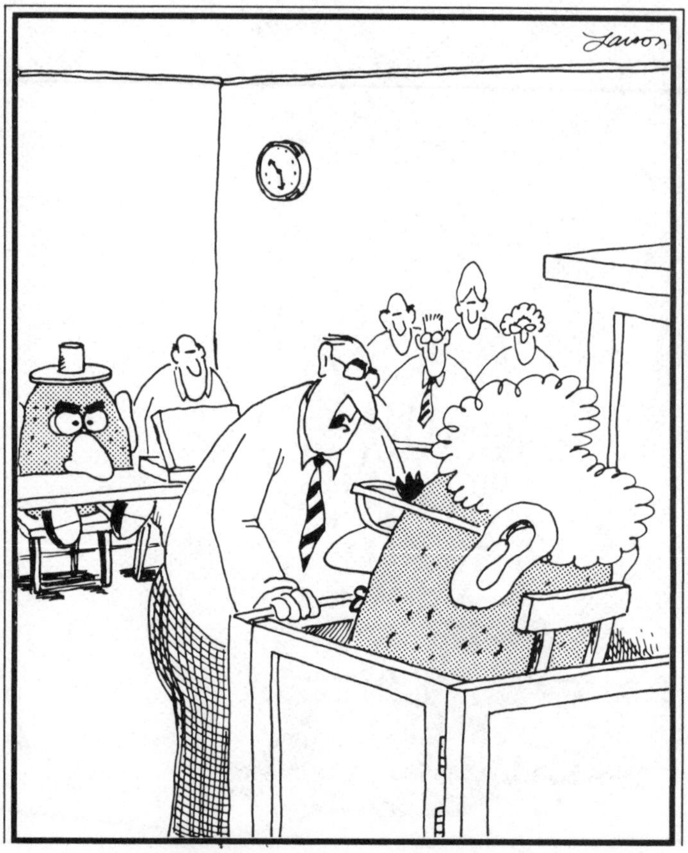
Larson

"So now tell the court, if you will, Mrs. Potato Head, exactly what transpired on the night your husband chased you with the Vegomatic."

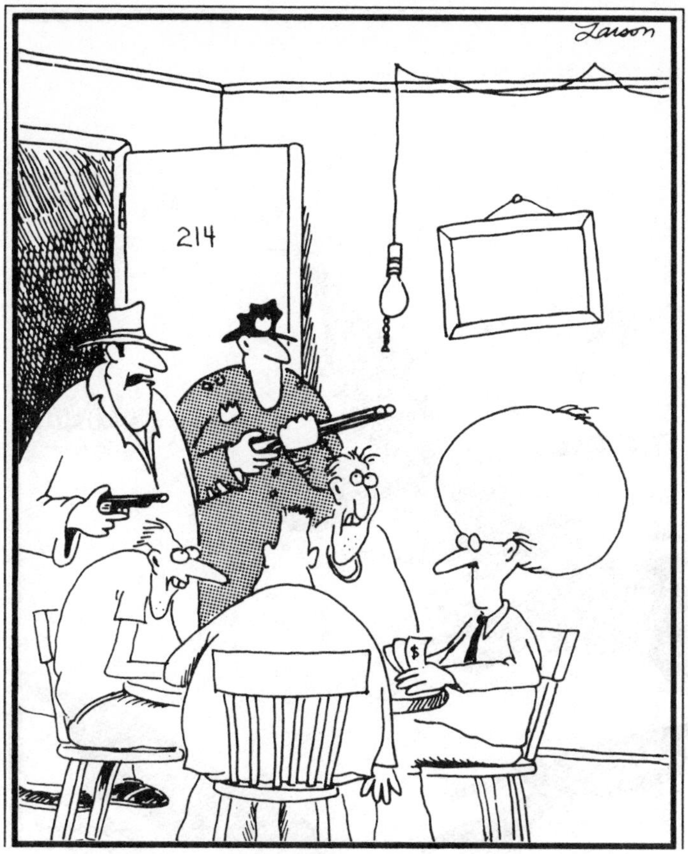
Larson
214

"Freeze! . . . Okay, now . . . Who's the brains of this outfit?"

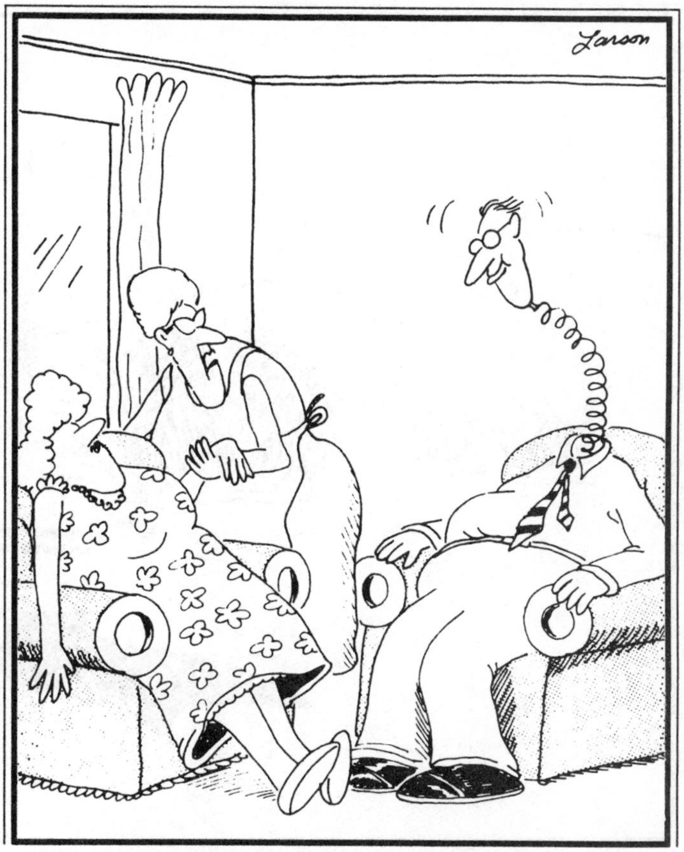
Larson

"Well, Emily is out like a light . . . Just can't resist pulling that little stunt of yours, can you, Earl!"

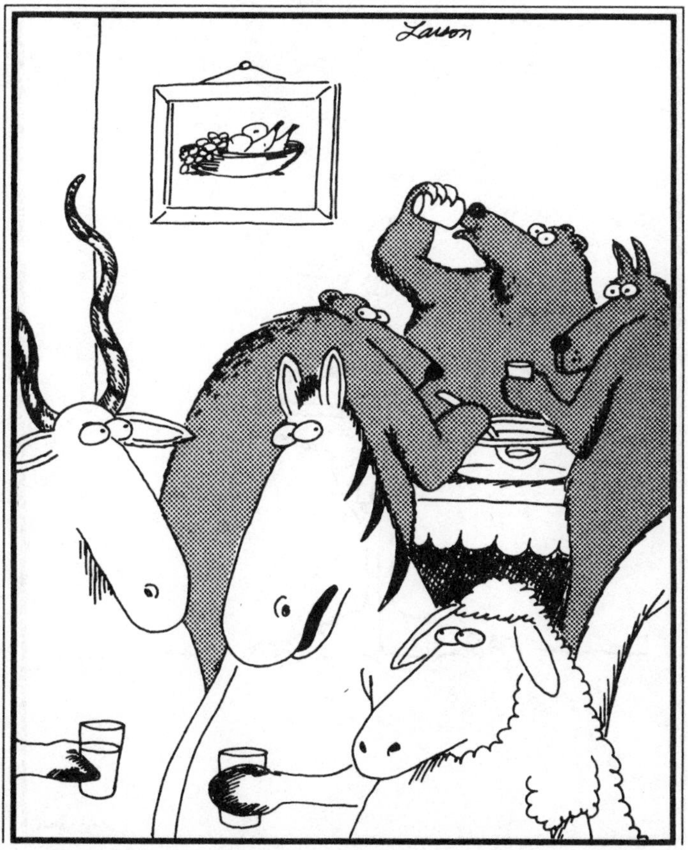
Larson

"I don't like this . . . The carnivores have been boozing it up at the punchbowl all night — drinking, looking around, drinking, looking around . . ."

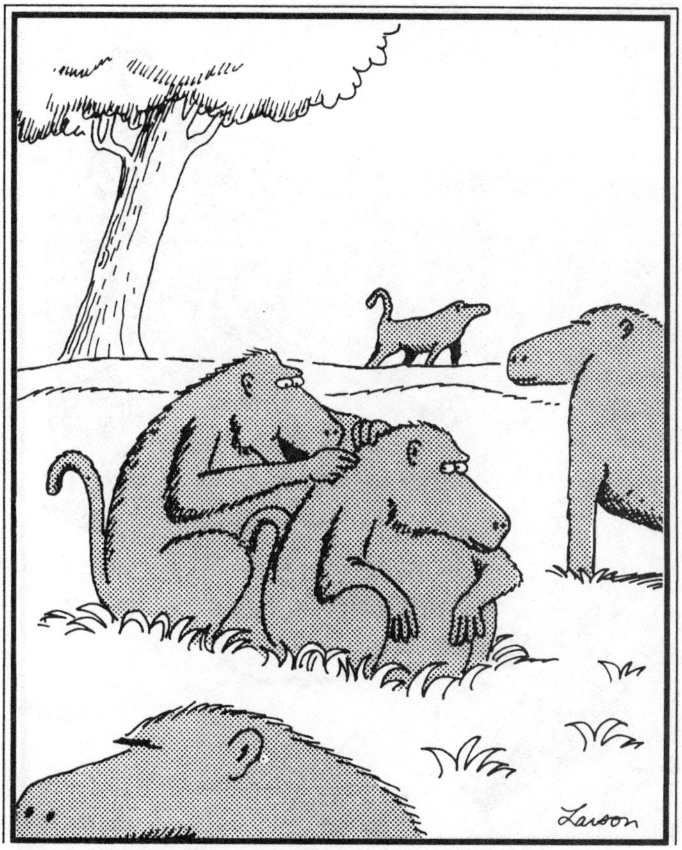
Larson

"So then Sheila says to Betty that Arnold told her what Harry was up to, but Betty told me she already heard it from Blanche, don't you know . . ."

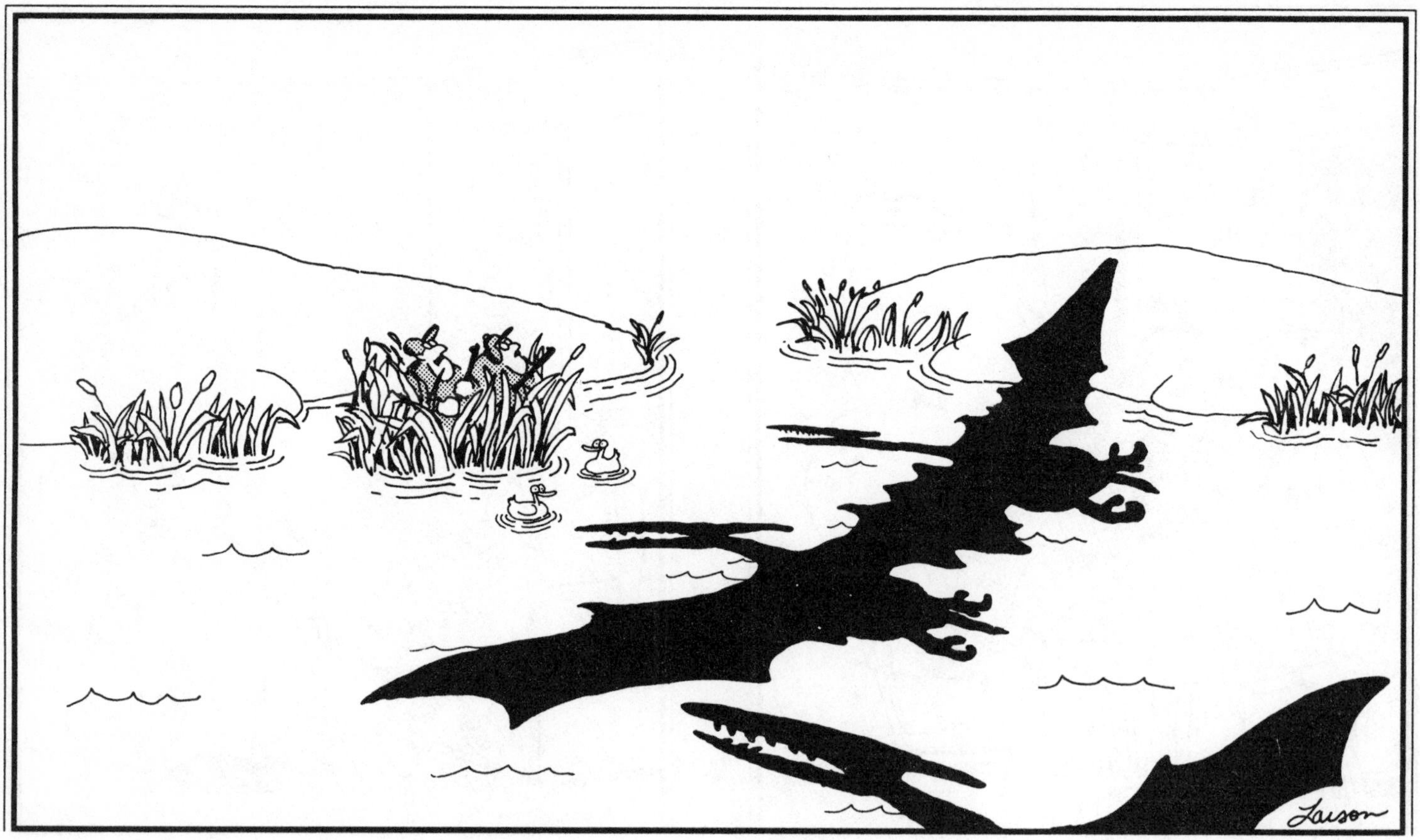
Larson

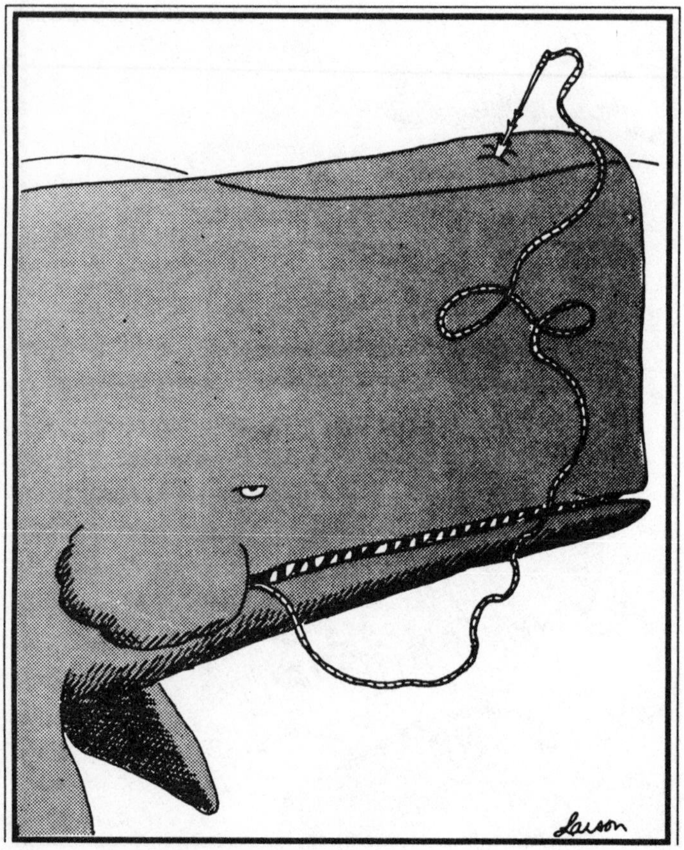
Larson

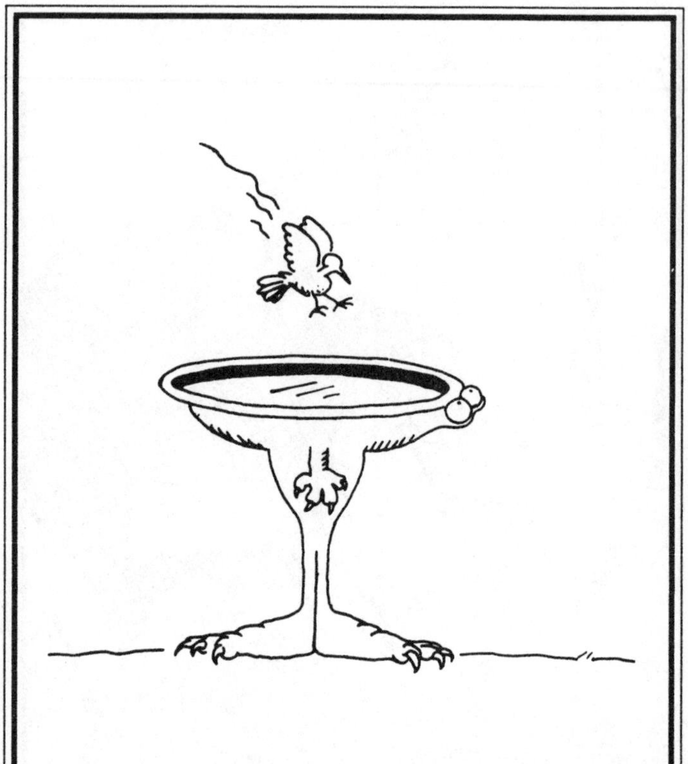
Larson

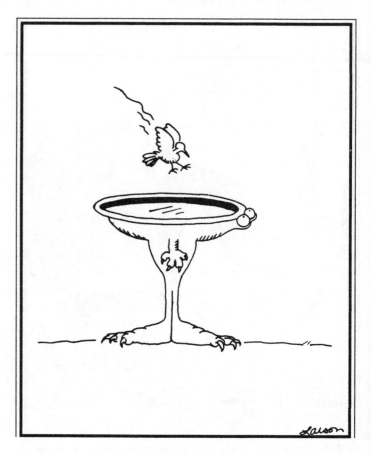

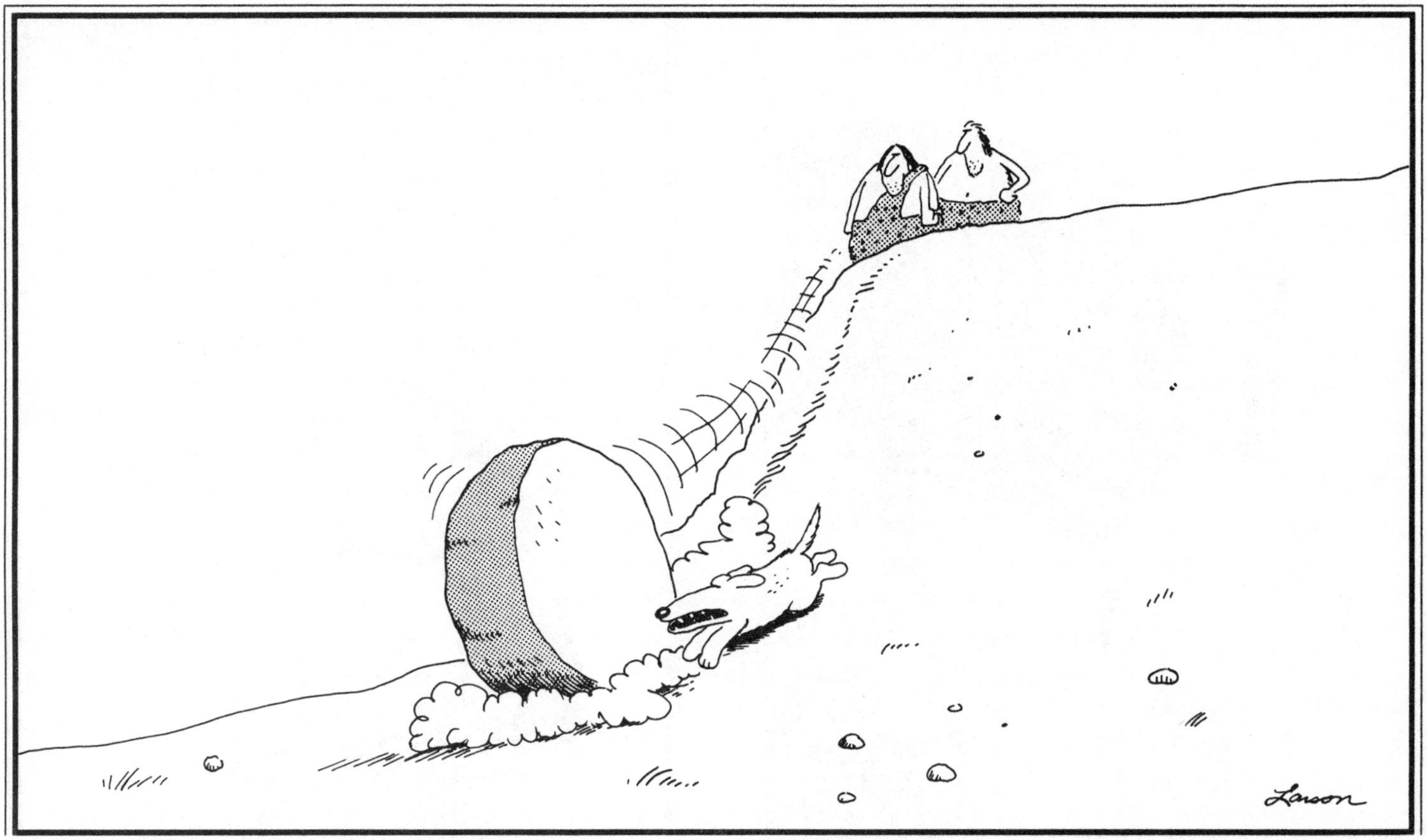

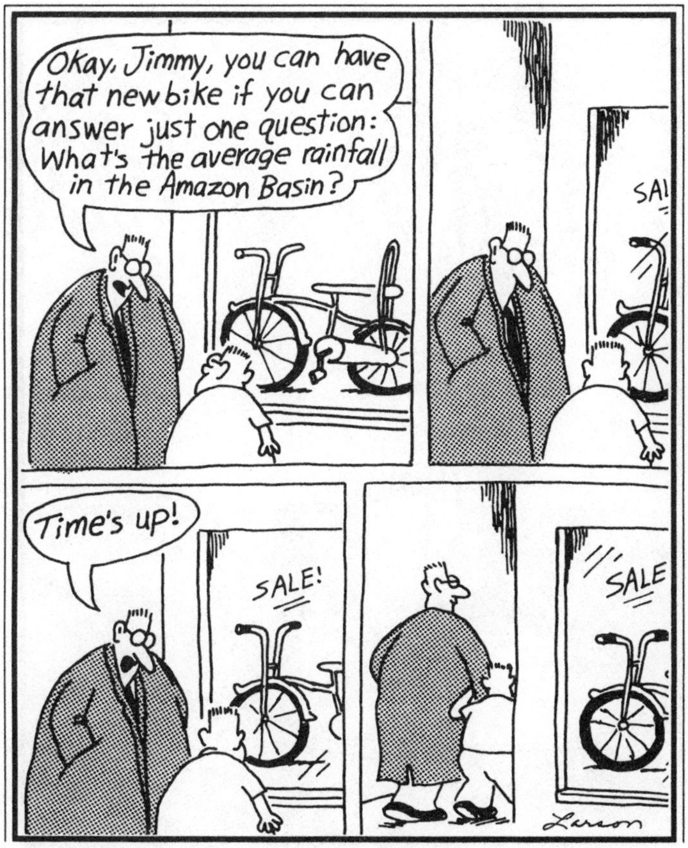
Okay, Jimmy, you can have that new bike if you can answer just one question: What's the average rainfall in the Amazon Basin?
SA!
Time's up!
SALE!
SALE

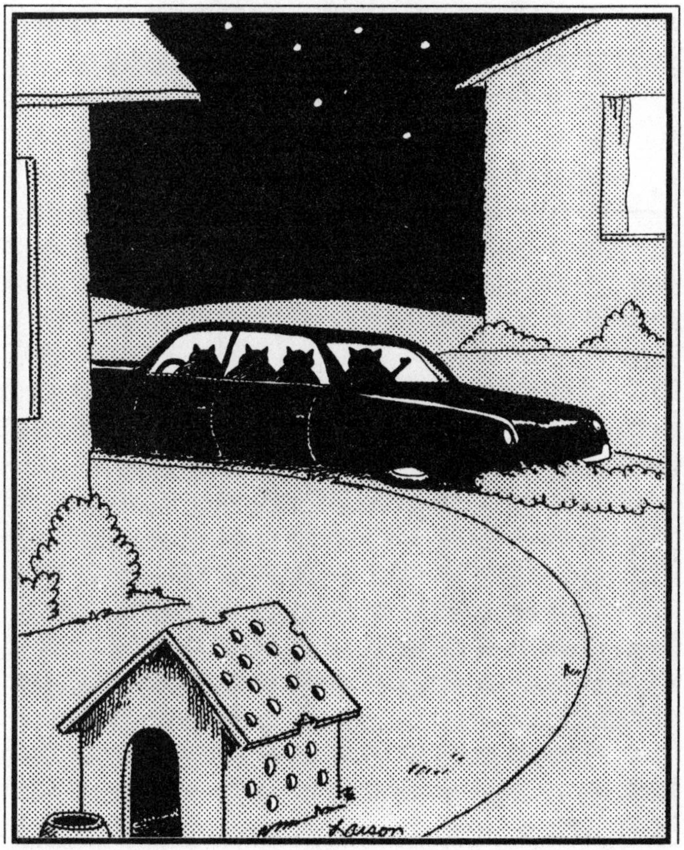

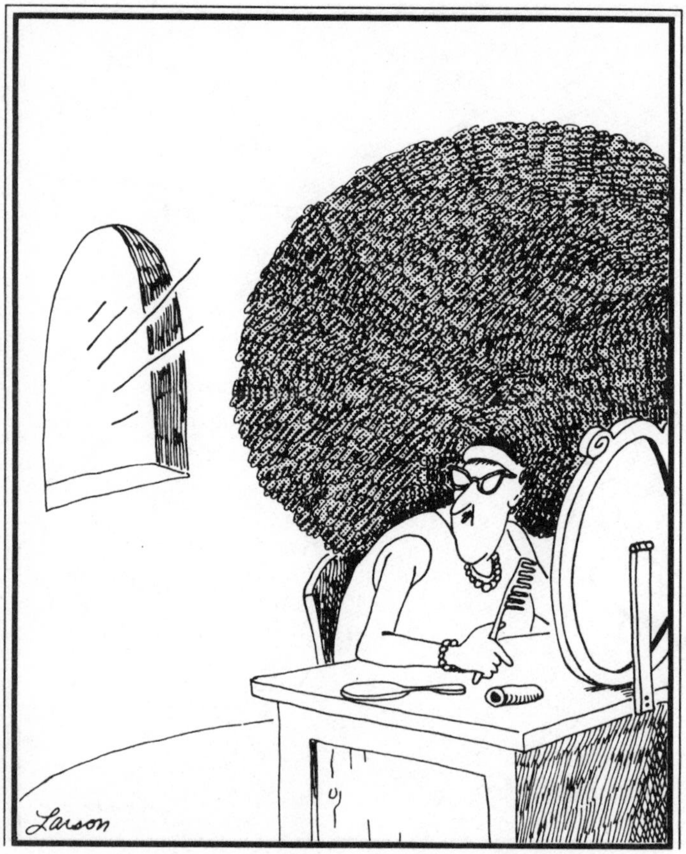
Larson

"Rapunzel, Rapunzel! . . . Let down your hair!"

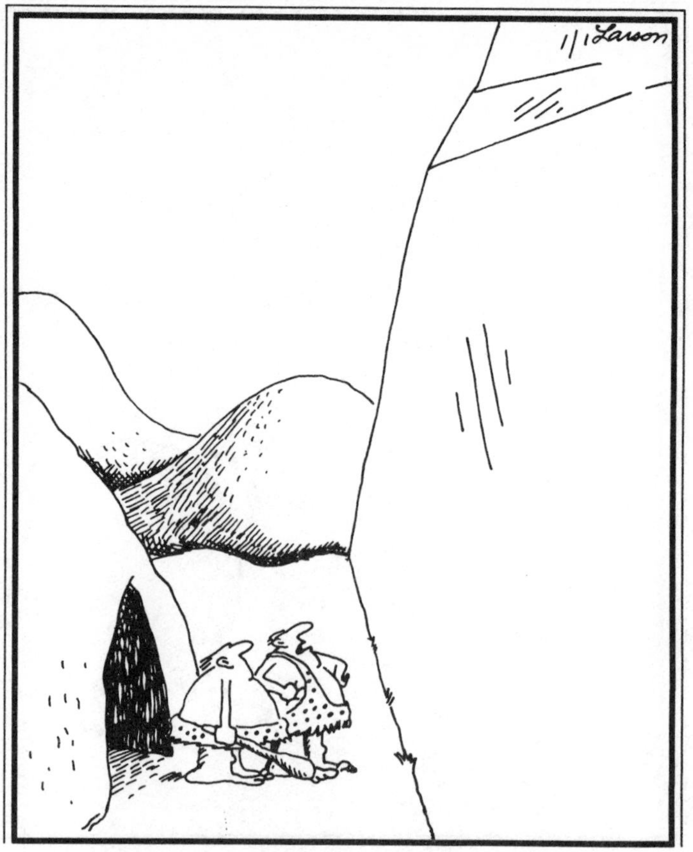
Larson

"Say, Thag . . . Wall of ice closer today?"

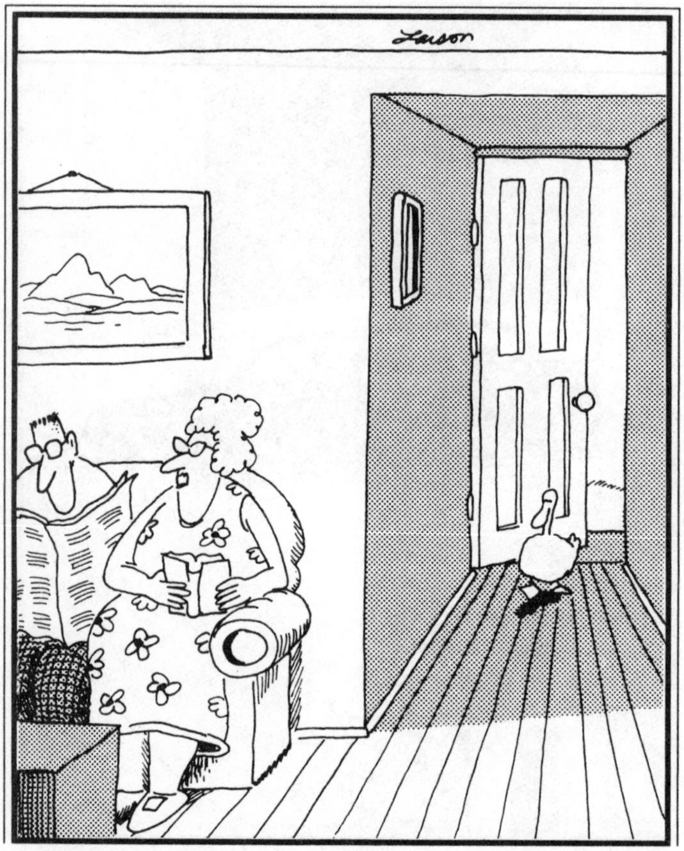
Larson

"Here he comes, Earl . . . Remember, be gentle but firm . . . we are absolutely, positively, NOT driving him south this winter."

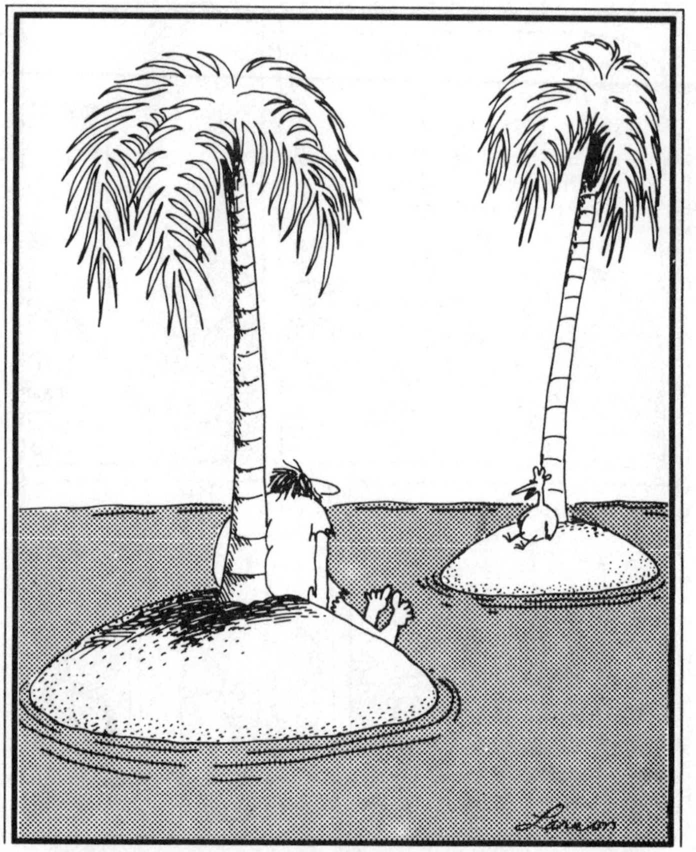
Larson

"Boy, there's sure a lot of sharks around here, aren't there? . . . Circling and circling . . . There goes another one! . . . Killers of the sea . . . yes siree . . ."

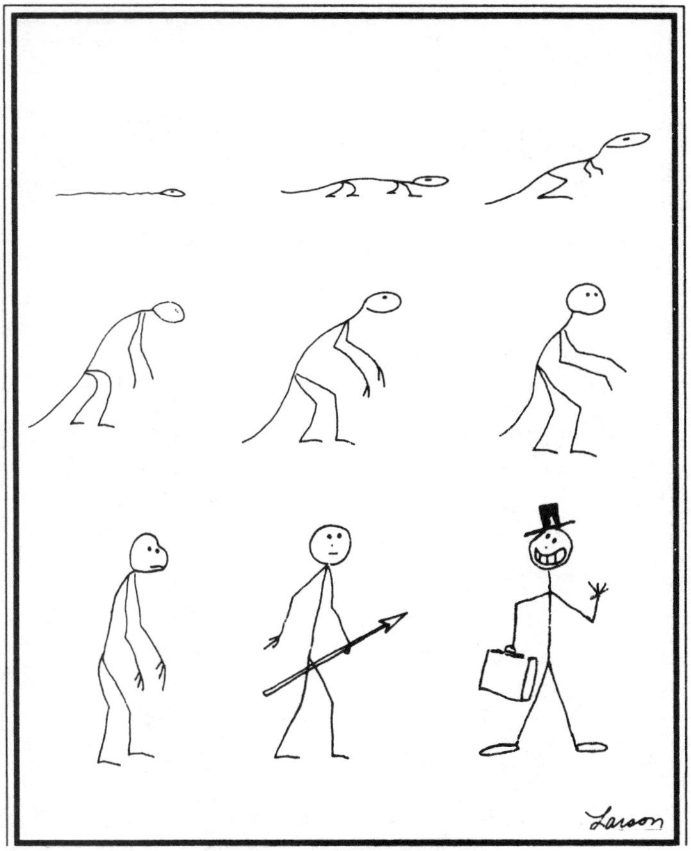
Larson

Evolution of the Stickman

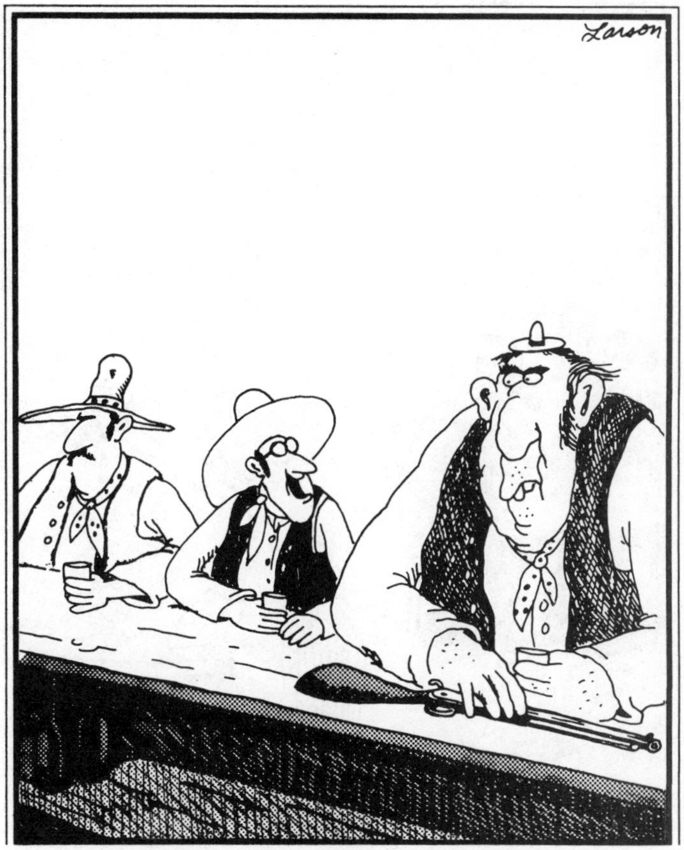
Larson

"Say . . . Now THERE'S a little hat!"

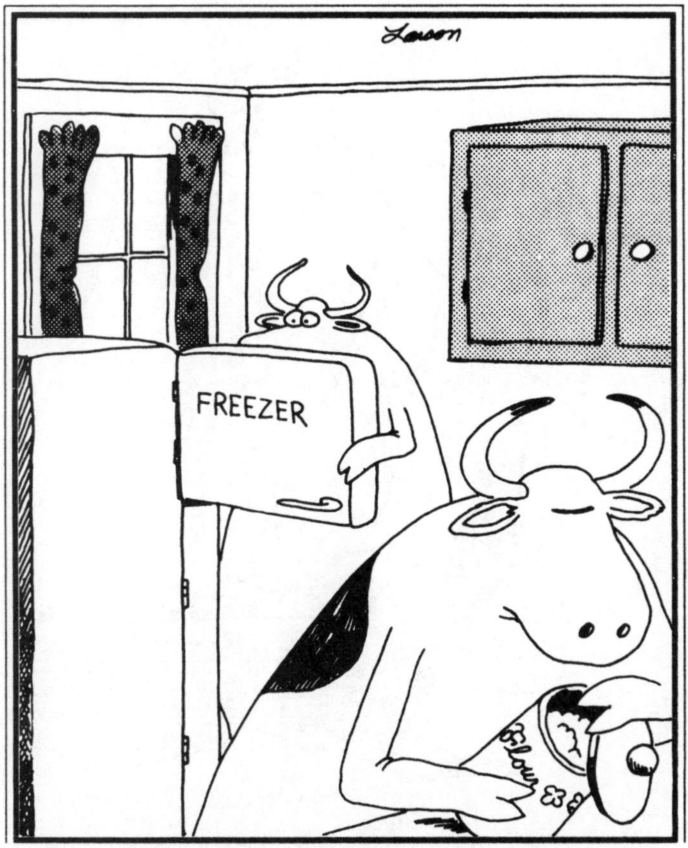
Larson
FREEZER

While Farmer Brown was away, the cows got into the kitchen and were having the time of their lives — until Betsy's unwitting discovery.

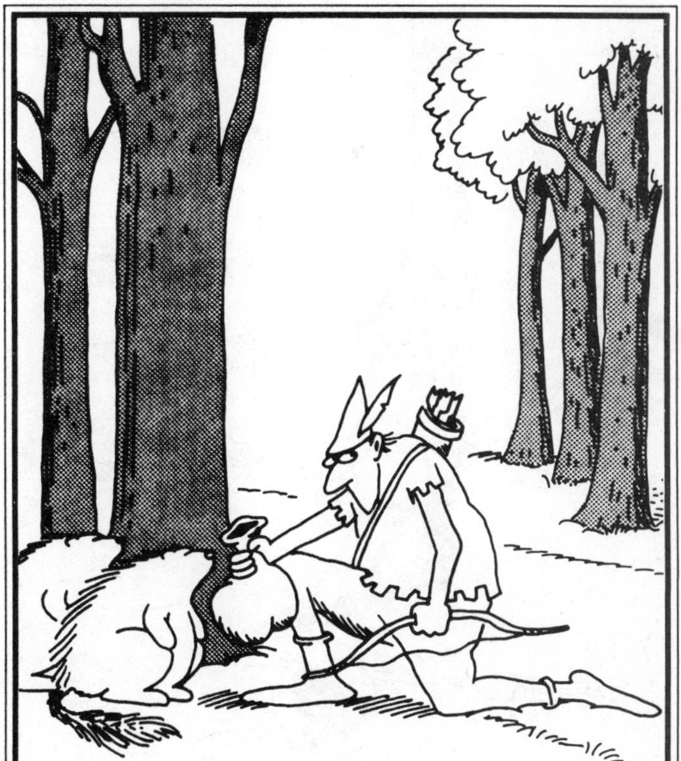
Larson

Historic note: Until his life's destiny was further clarified, Robin Hood spent several years robbing from the rich and giving to the porcupines.

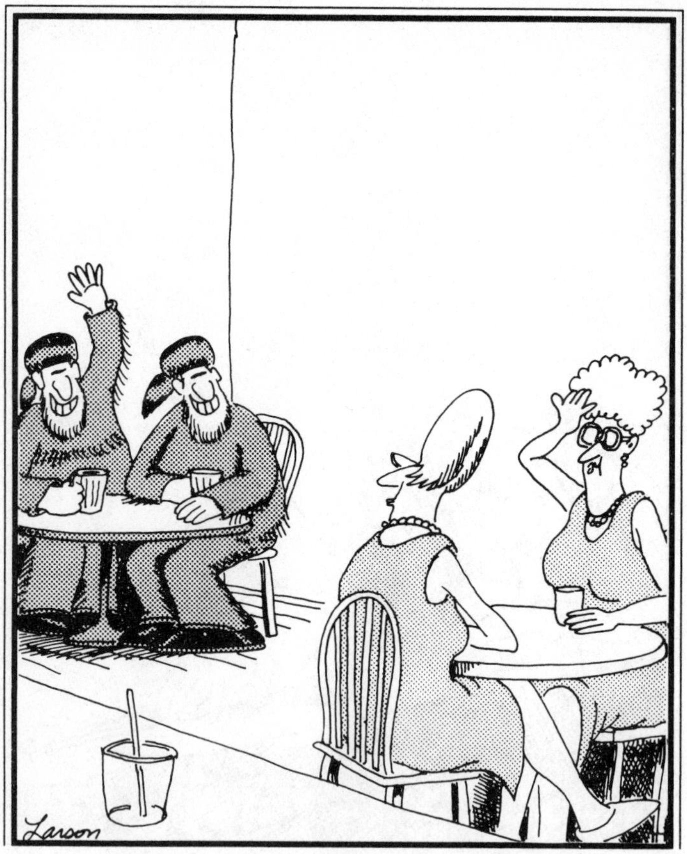
Larson

Lewis and Clark meet Sylvia and Rhonda.

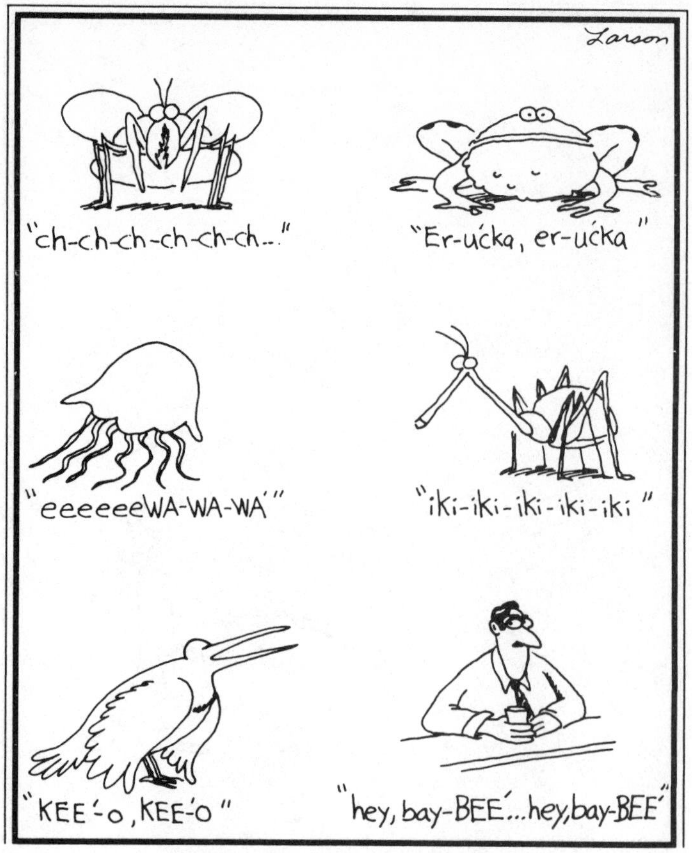
Larson
"ch-ch-ch-ch-ch-ch-ch..."
"Er-ucka, er-ucka"
"eeeeeeWA-WA-WA"
"iki-iki-iki-iki-iki"
"KEE-o, KEE-o"
"hey, bay-BEE...hey, bay-BEE"

Animals and their mating songs

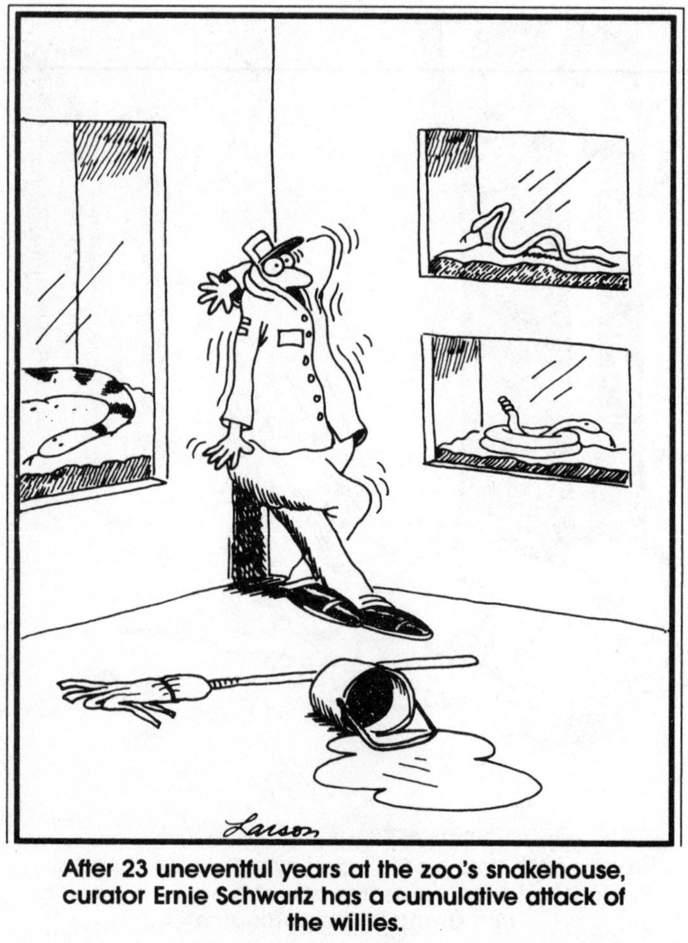
Larson

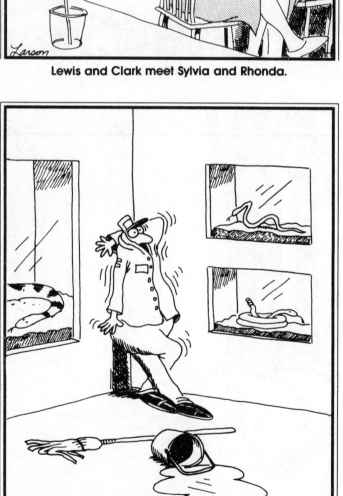

After 23 uneventful years at the zoo's snakehouse, curator Ernie Schwartz has a cumulative attack of the willies.

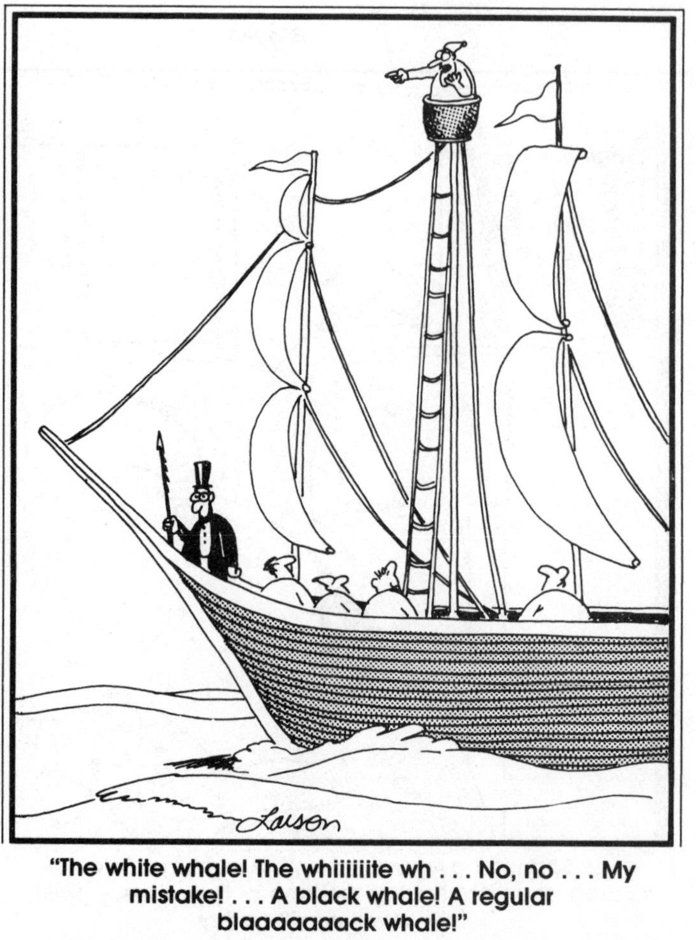
Larson

"The white whale! The whiiiiiite wh . . . No, no . . . My mistake! . . . A black whale! A regular blaaaaaaack whale!"

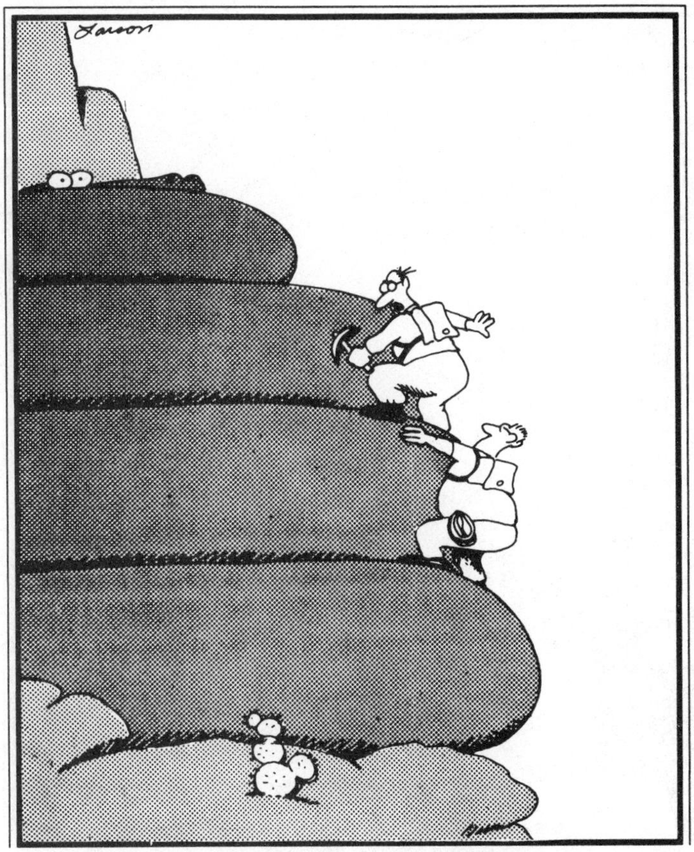
Larson

"Freeze, Earl! Freeze! . . . Something rattled!"

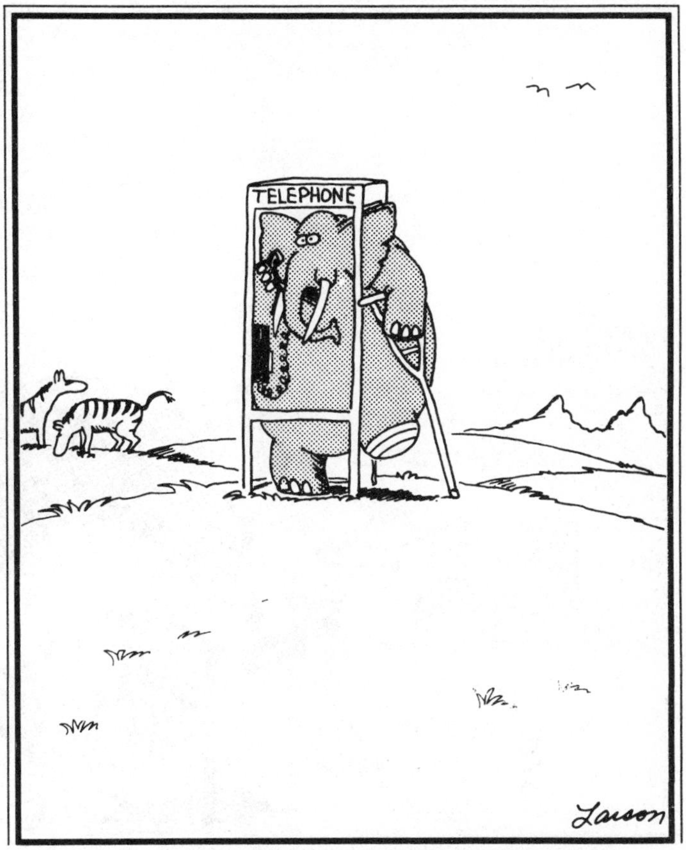
TELEPHONE
Larson

"What? . . . They turned it into a WASTEbasket?"

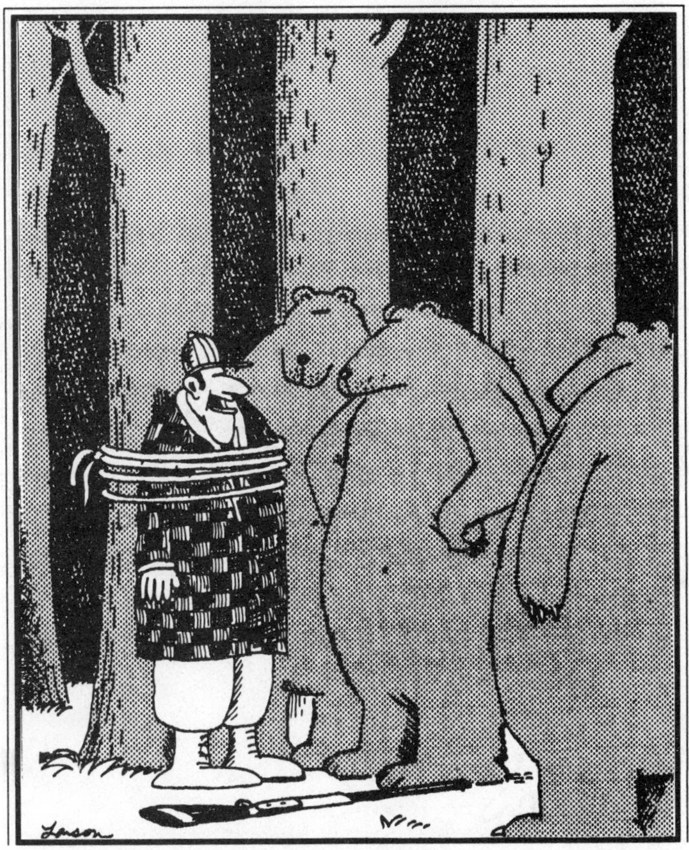
Larson

"Do what you will to me, but I'll never talk! . . . Never! And, after me, there'll come others — and others — and others! . . . Ha ha ha!"

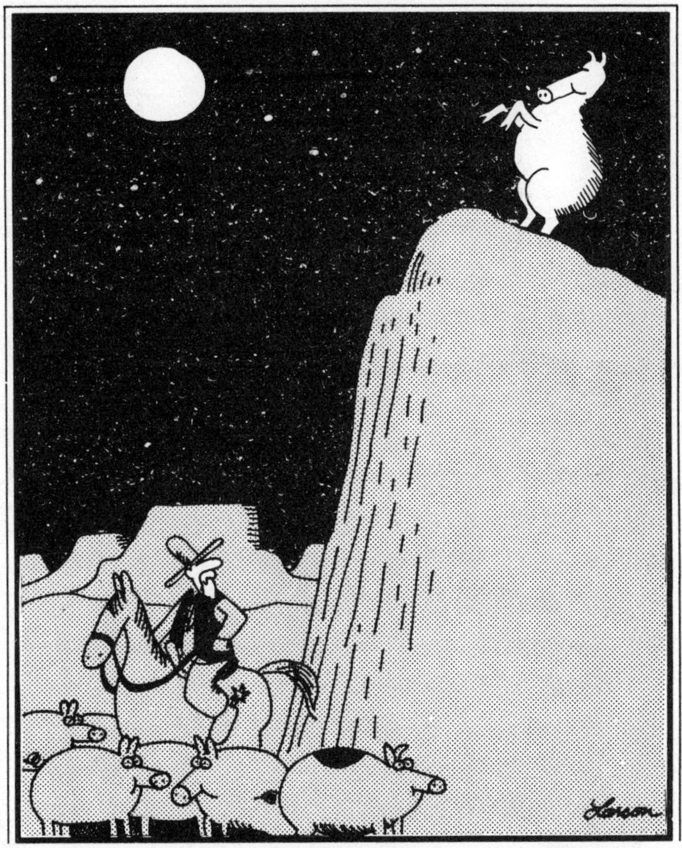
Larson

Trying to calm the herd, Jake himself was suddenly awestruck by the image of beauty and unbridled fury on the cliff above — Pink Shadow had returned.

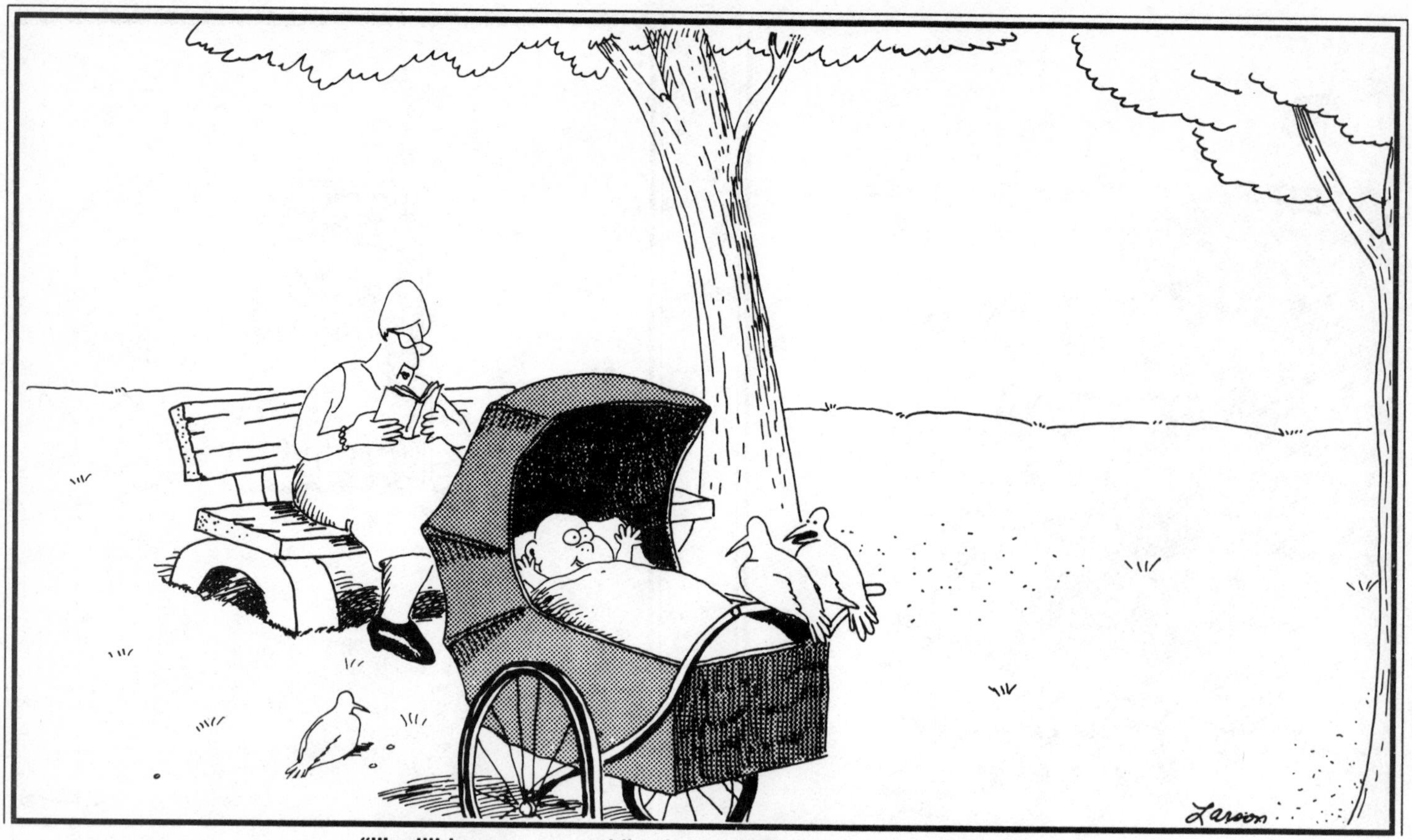
Larson

"It's still hungry . . . and I've been stuffing worms into it all day."

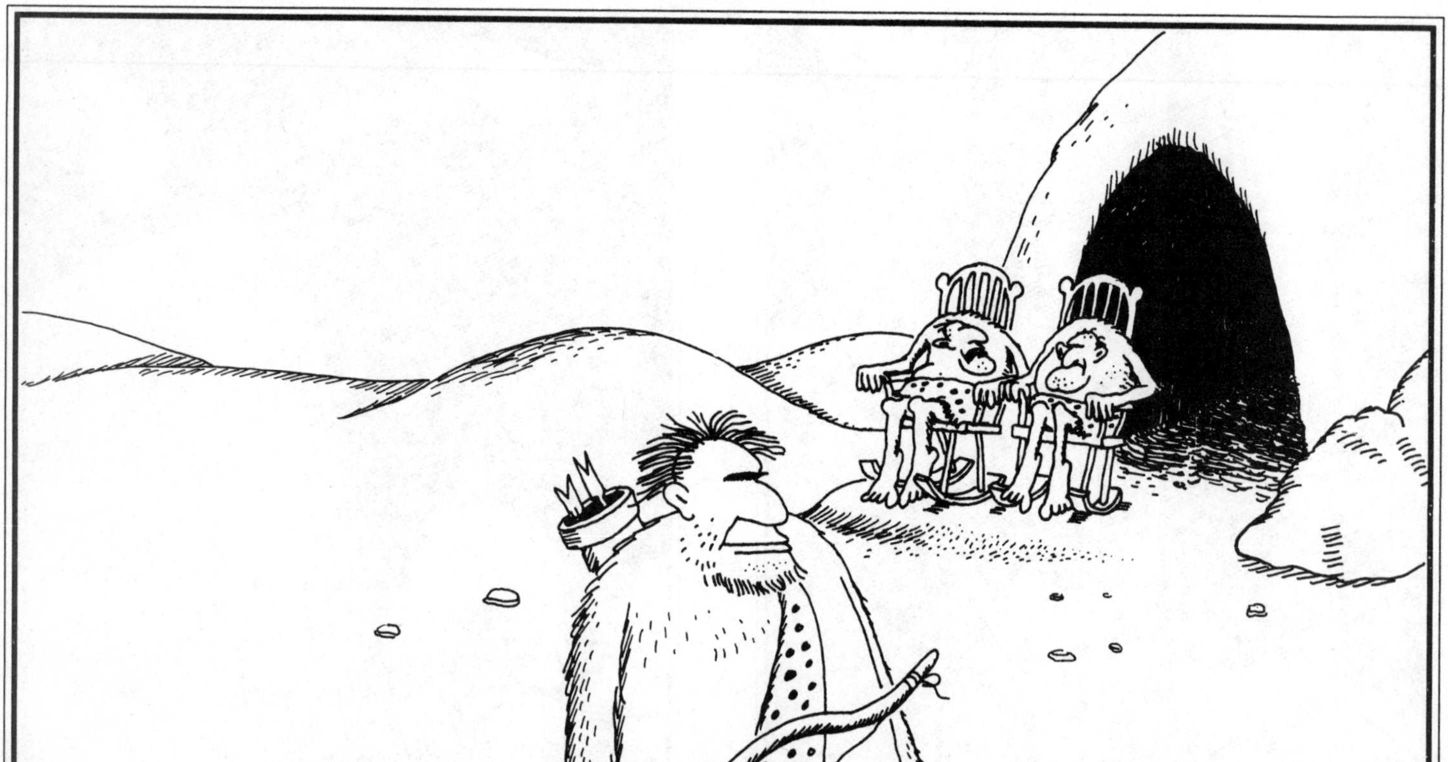
Larson

"Look at that! . . . Give me the good old days when a man carried a club and had a brain the size of a walnut."

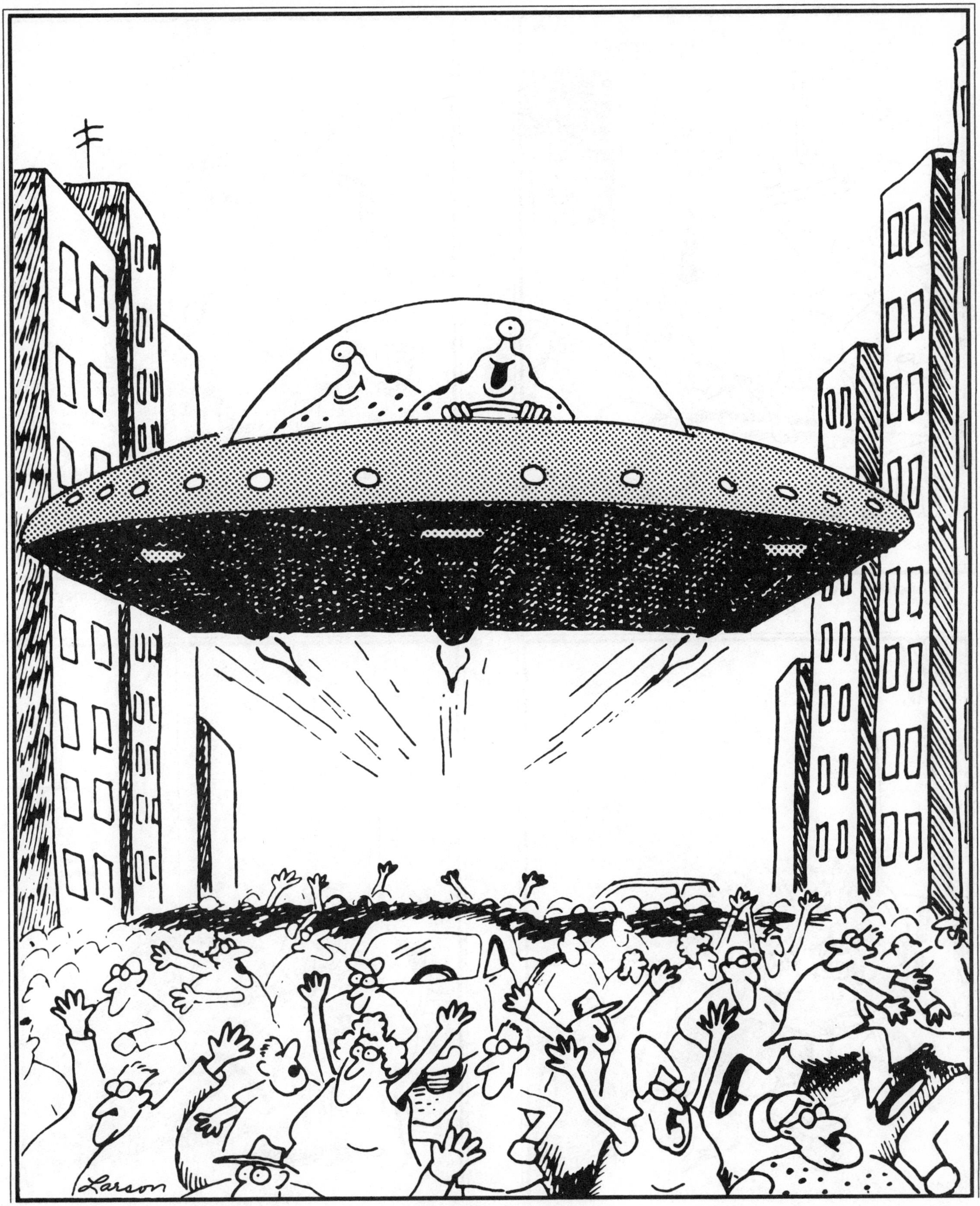
Larson

"Yeeeeeeeeeeeha!"

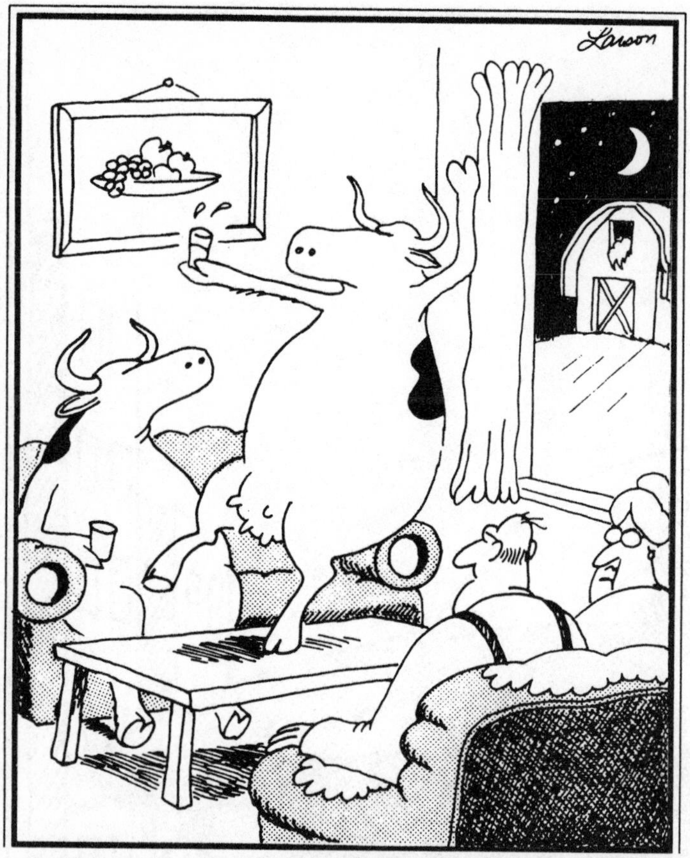
Larson

"Satisfied? . . . I warned you not to invite the cows in for a few drinks."

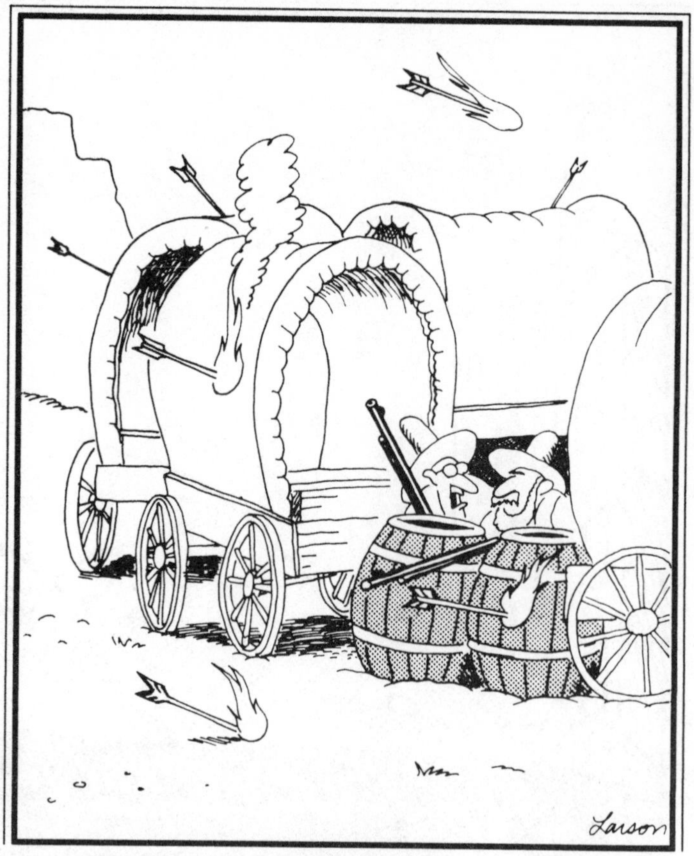
Larson

"Hey! They're lighting their arrows! . . . Can they DO that?"

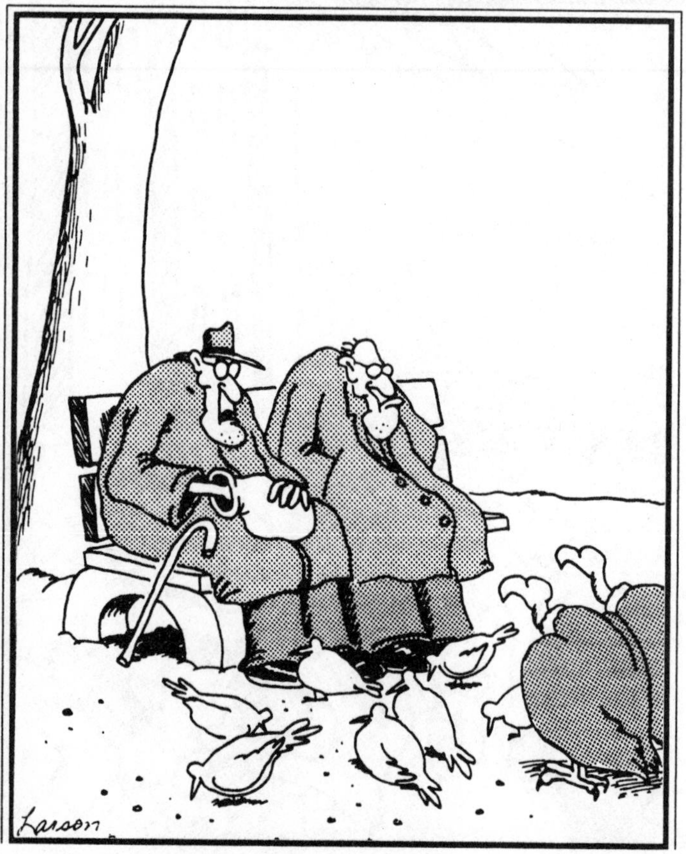
Larson

"Now take them big birds, Barnaby . . . Never eat a thing . . . Just sit and stare."

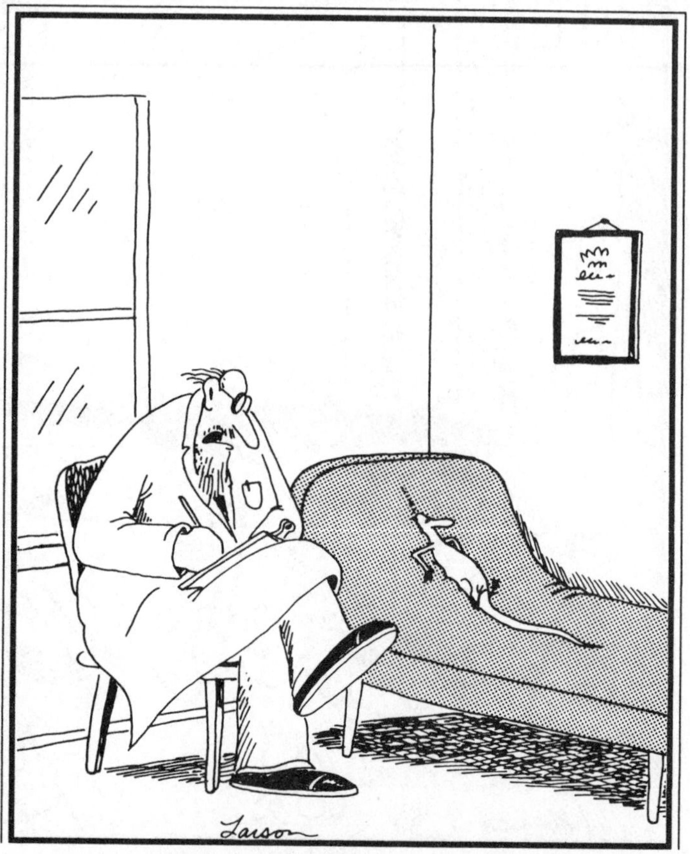
Larson

"Listen . . . You've got to relax . . . The more you think about changing colors, the less chance you'll succeed . . . Shall we try the green background again?"

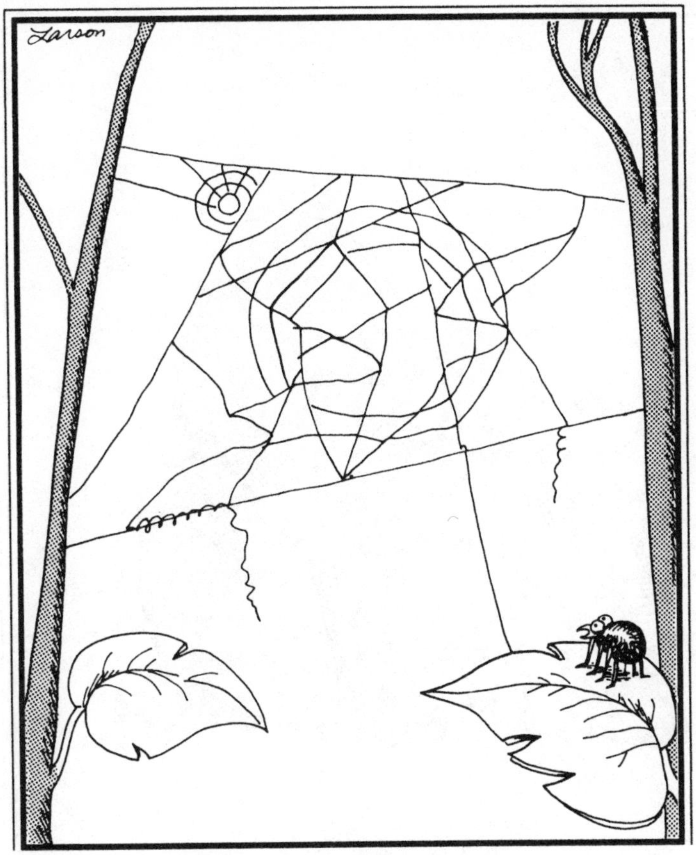
Larson

"Whoa! . . . That CAN'T be right!"

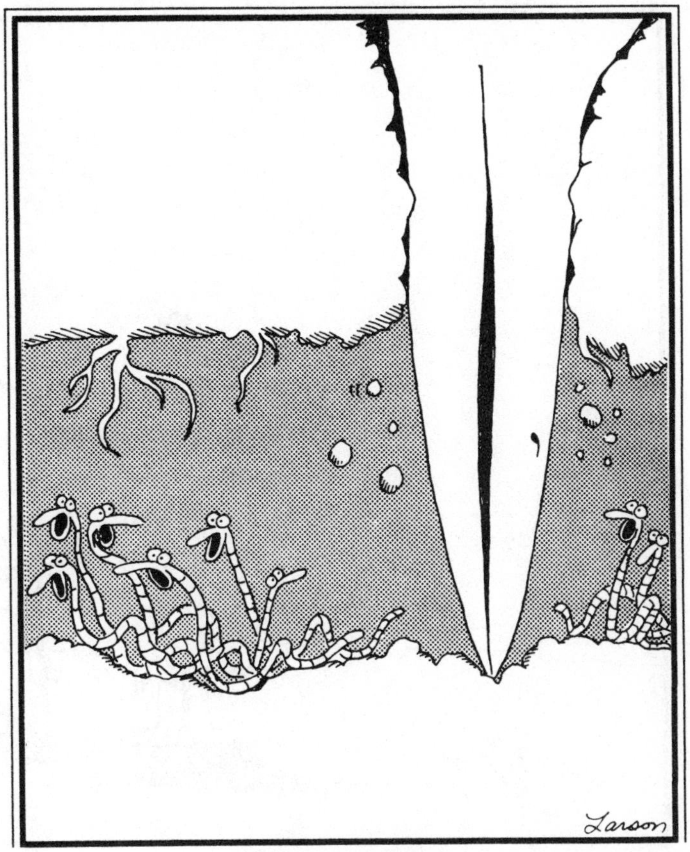
Larson

Night of the Robin

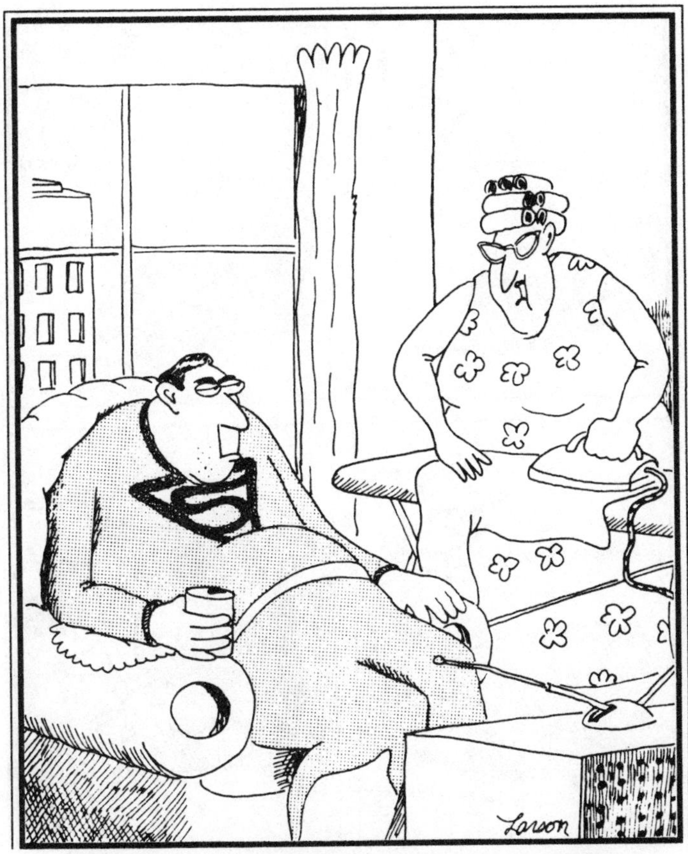
Larson

"By the way, we're playing cards with the Millers tonight . . . And Edna says if you promise not to use your X-ray vision, Warren promises not to bring his Kryptonite."

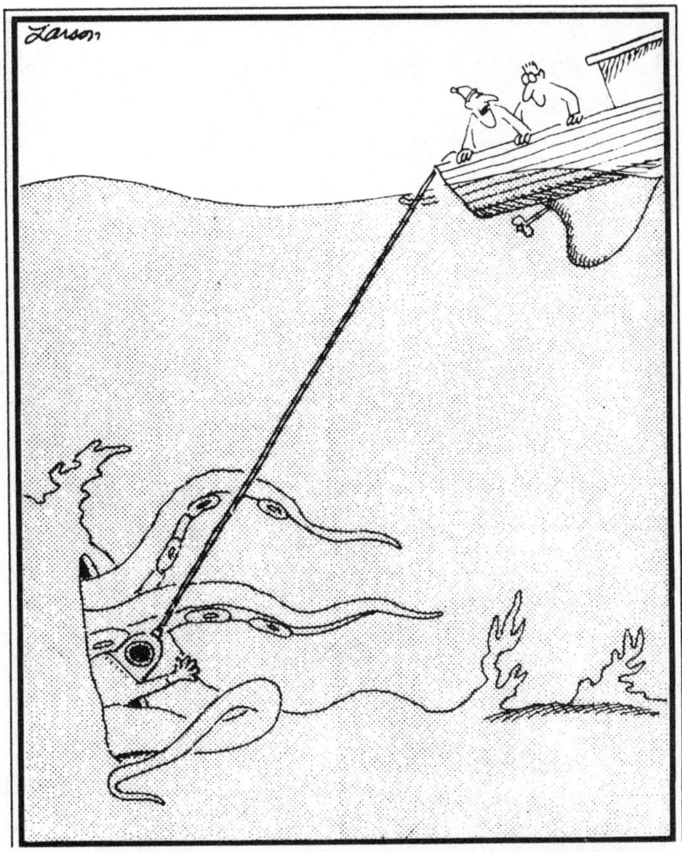
Larson

"Now wait a minute . . . He said two jerks means 'more slack' and three means 'come up' . . . but he never said nothin' about one long, steady pull."

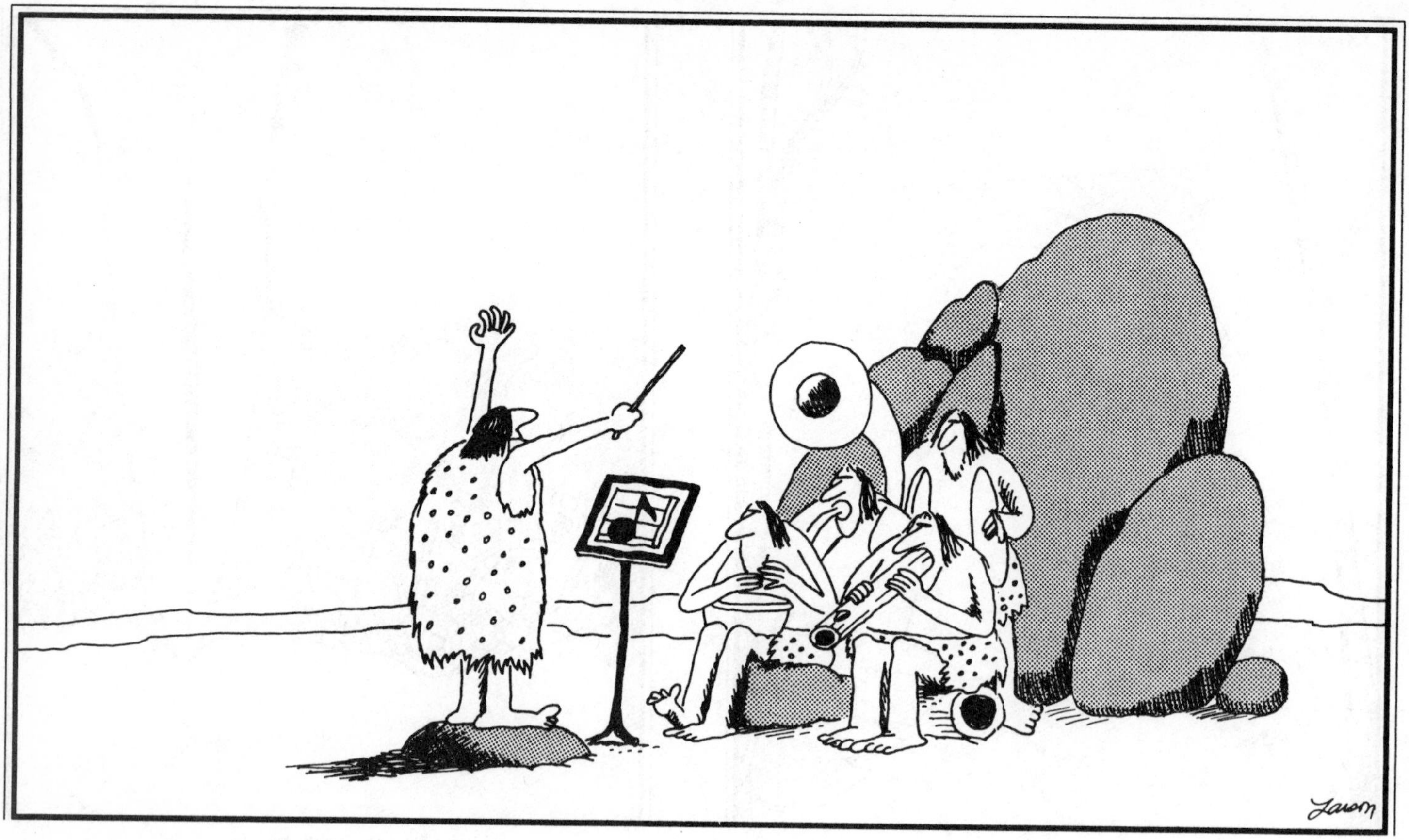
Larson

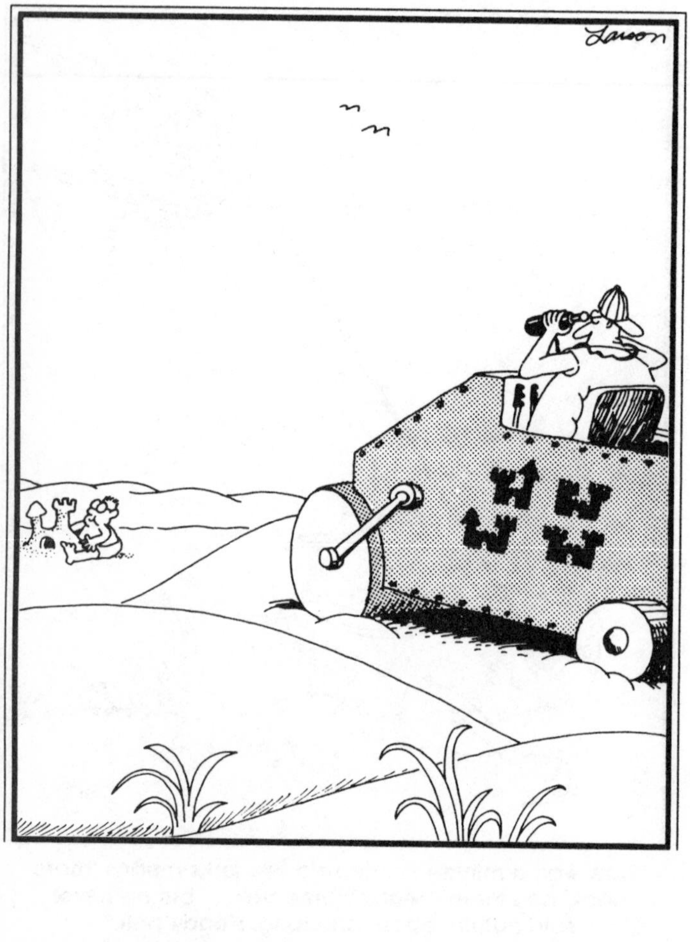
Larson

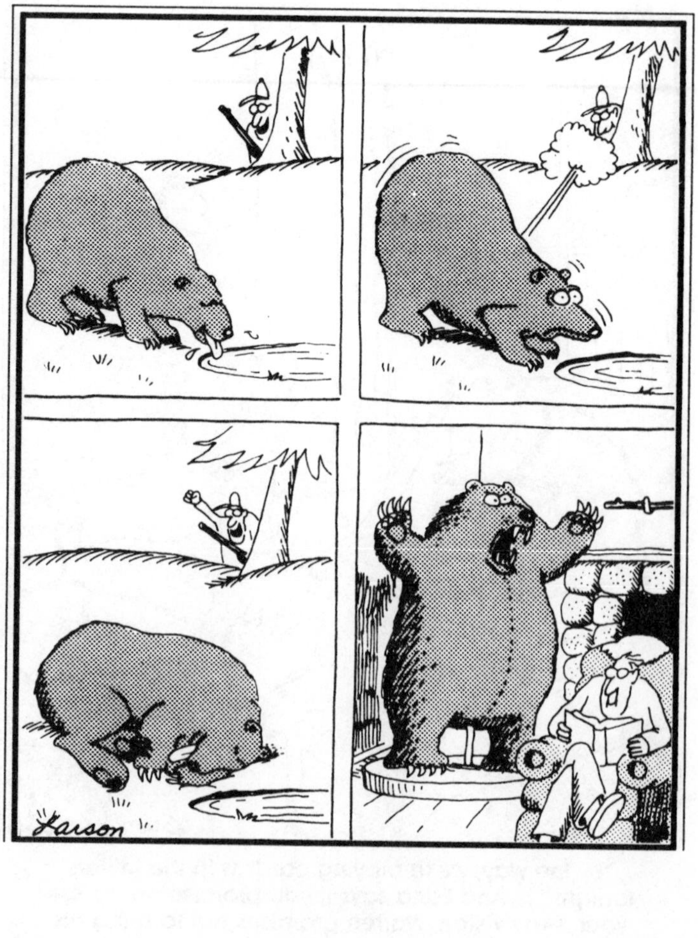
Larson

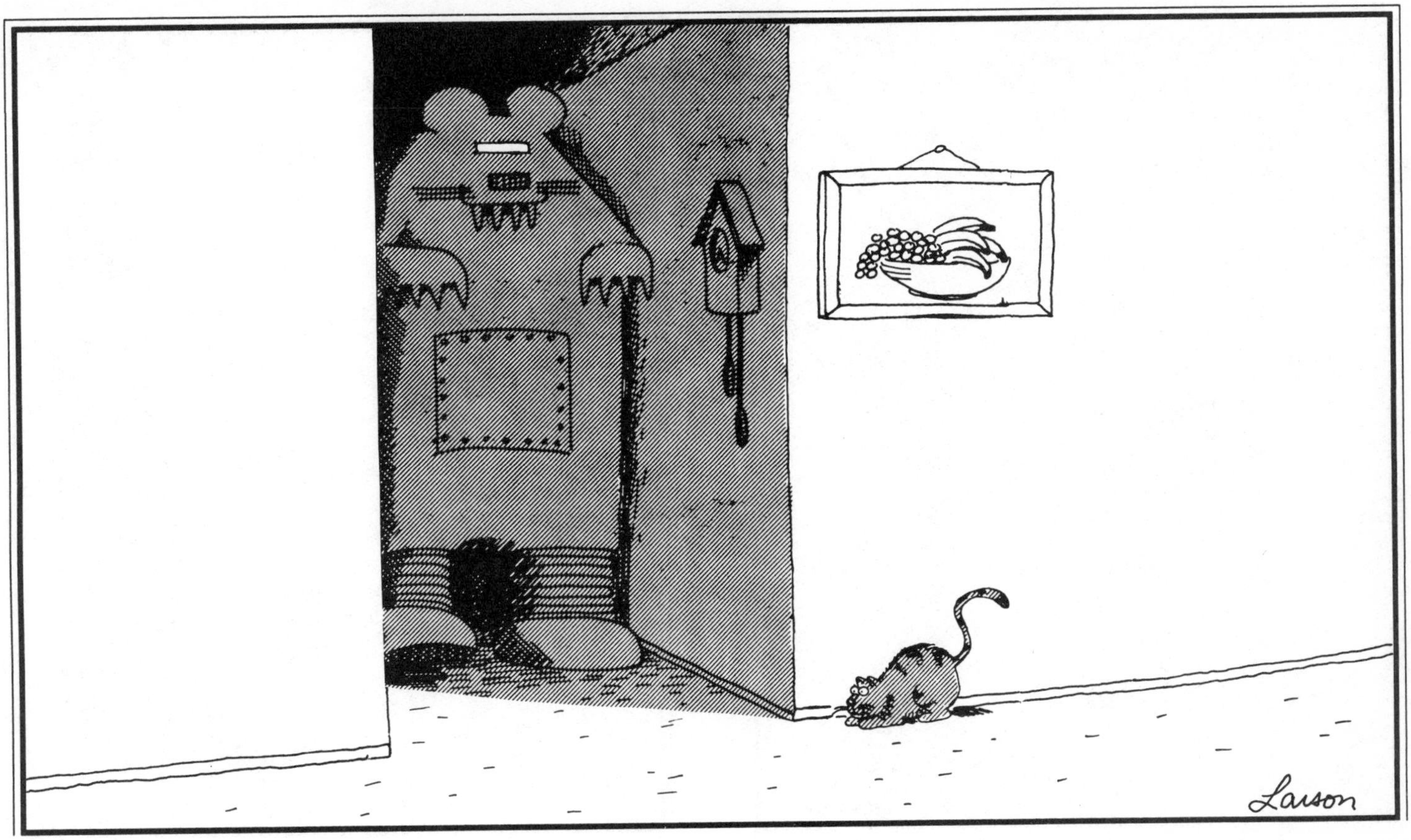
Larson

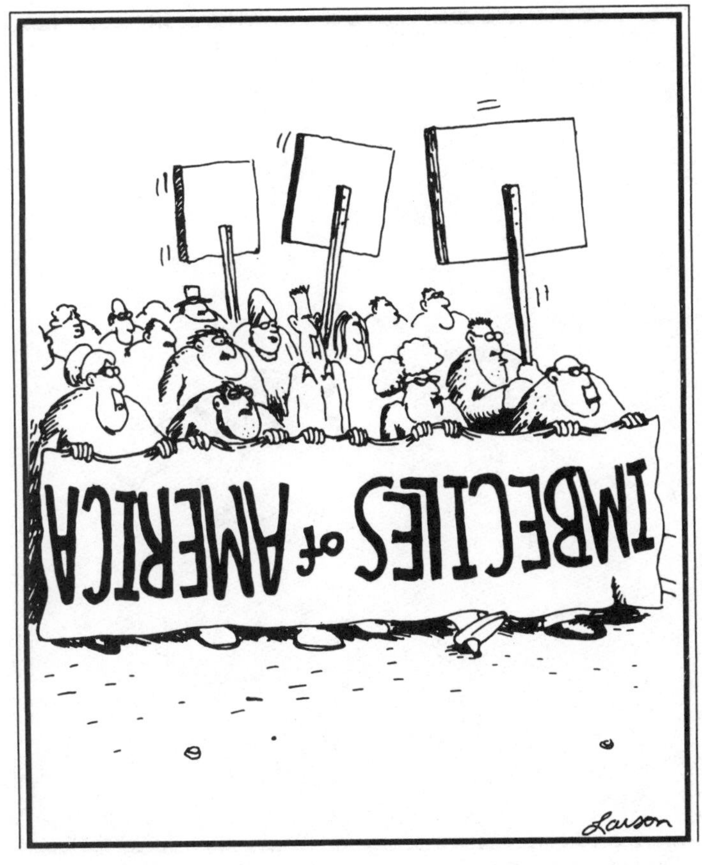
IMBECILES of AMERICA
Larson

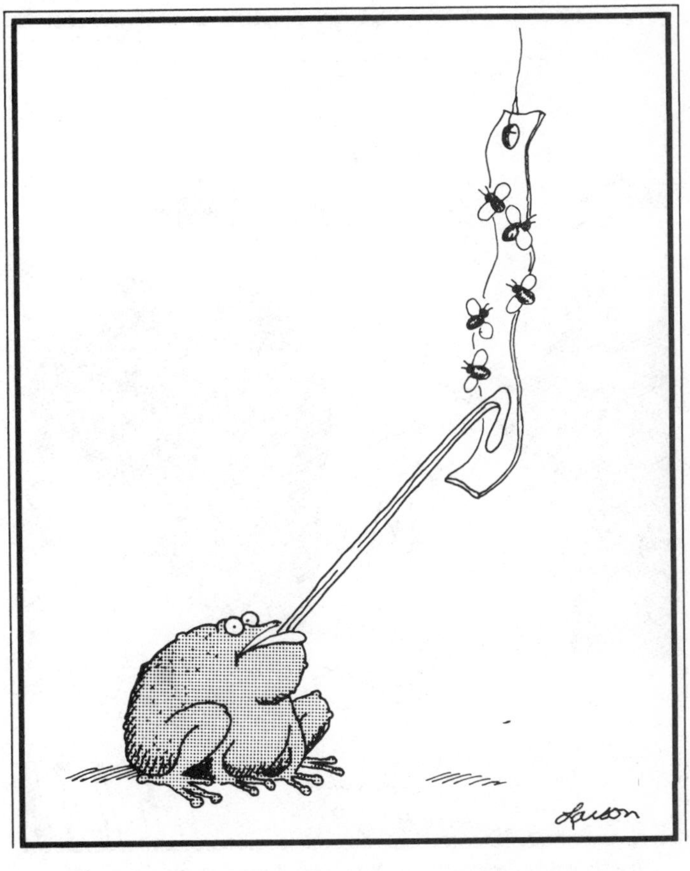
Larson

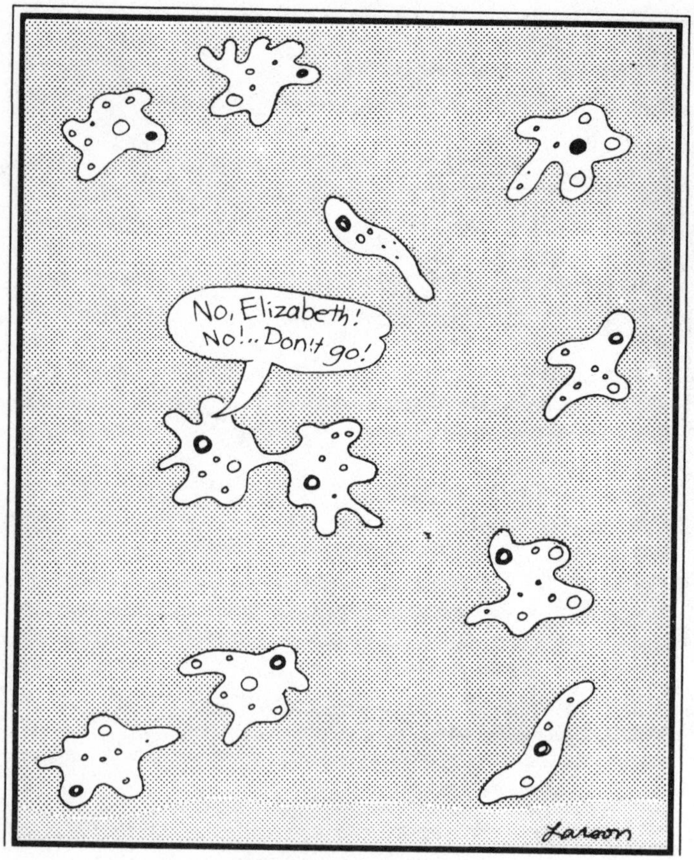
No, Elizabeth!
No!.. Don't go!
Larson

Life in the petri dish

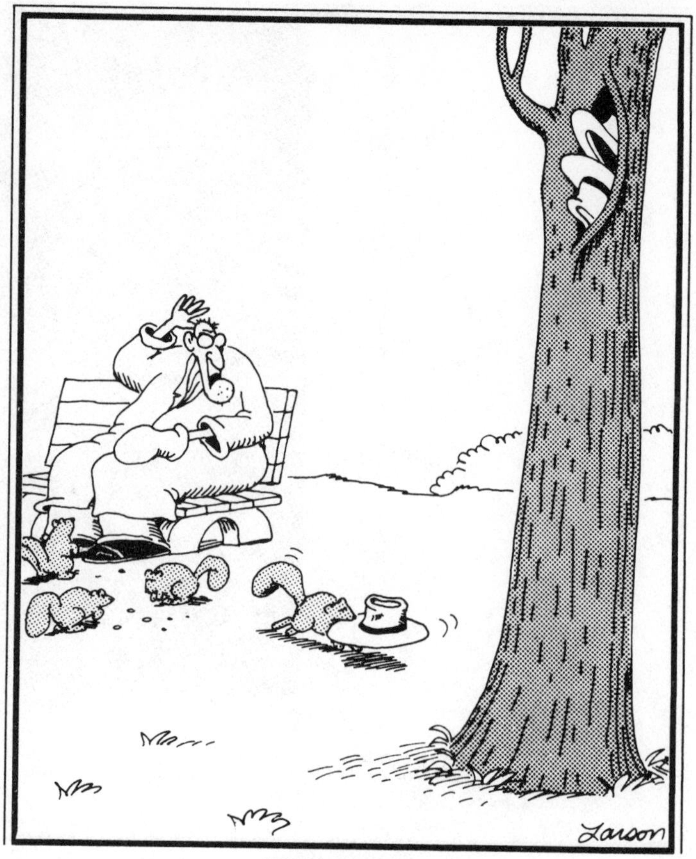
Larson

"YOU again!"

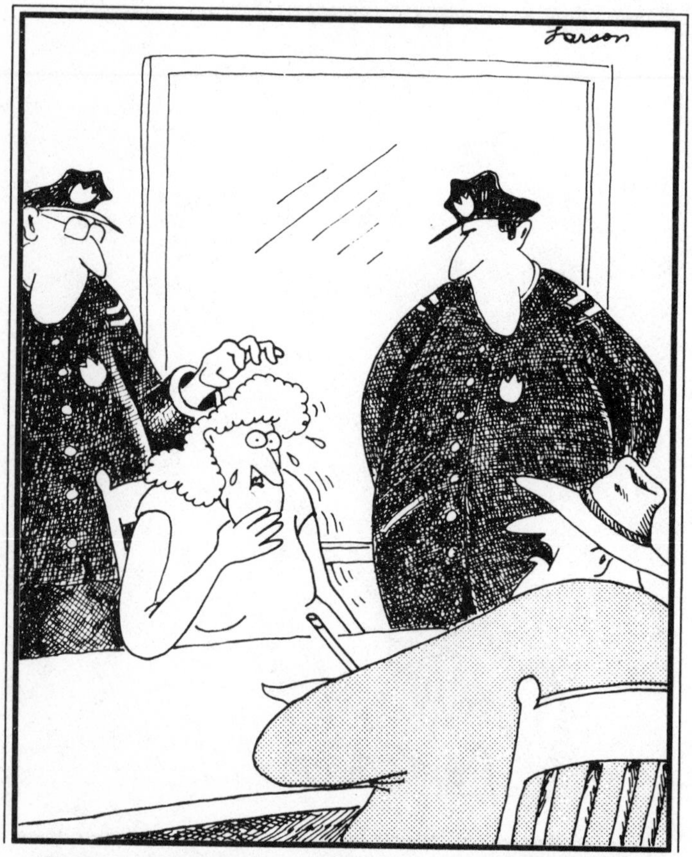
Larson

"Try to relax, ma'am . . . You say it was dark; you were alone in the house, when suddenly you felt a hand reaching from behind and . . . JOHNSON! Knock it off!"

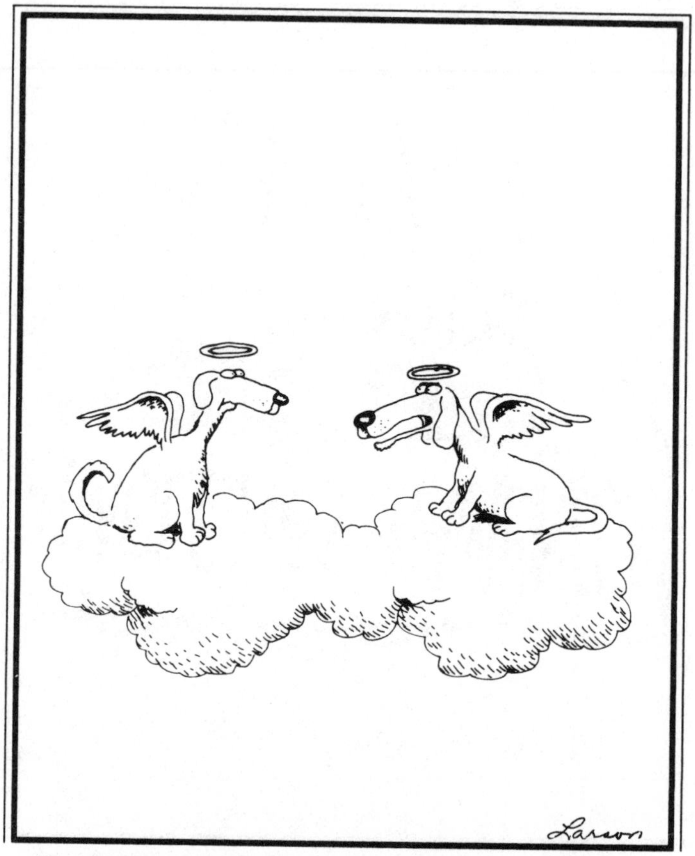
Larson

"For twelve perfect years I was a car-chaser. Pontiacs, Fords, Chryslers . . . I took them all on . . . and yesterday my stupid owner backs over me in the driveway."

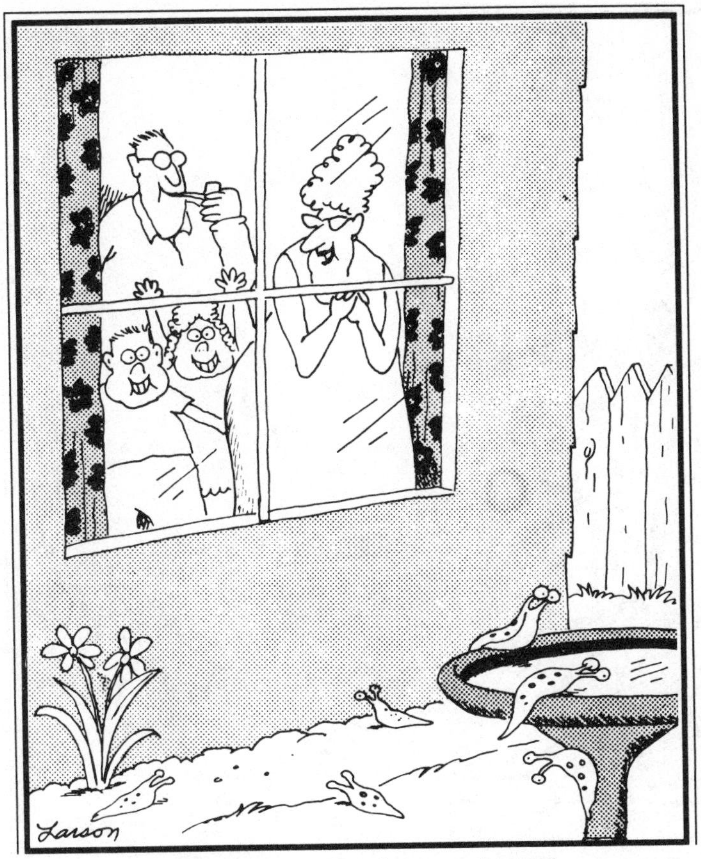

"Kids! Kids! . . . The slugs are back!"

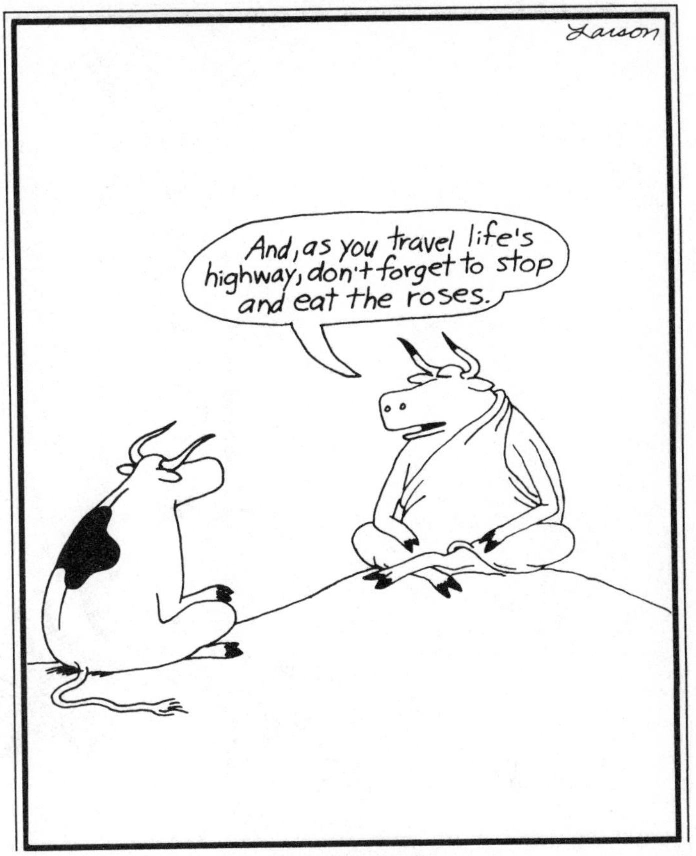
And, as you travel life's highway, don't forget to stop and eat the roses.

Cow philosophy

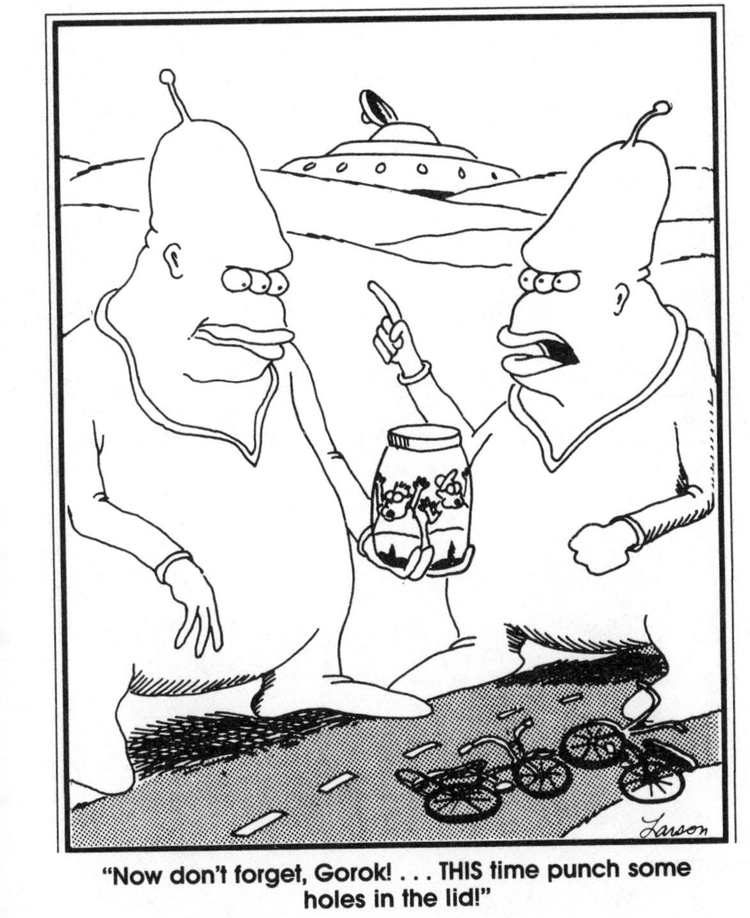

"Now don't forget, Gorok! . . . THIS time punch some holes in the lid!"

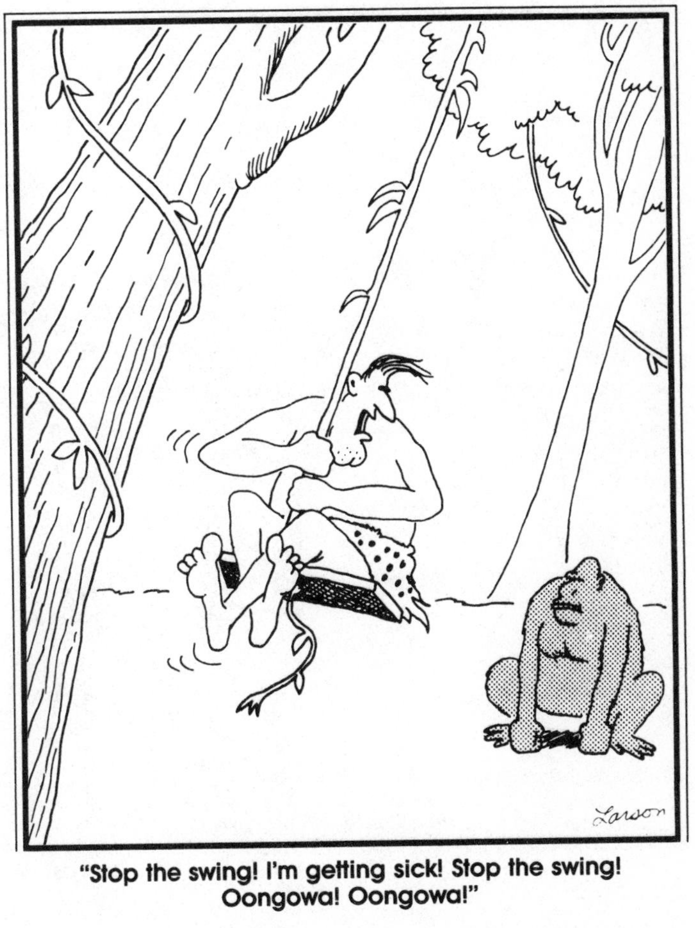

"Stop the swing! I'm getting sick! Stop the swing! Oongowa! Oongowa!"

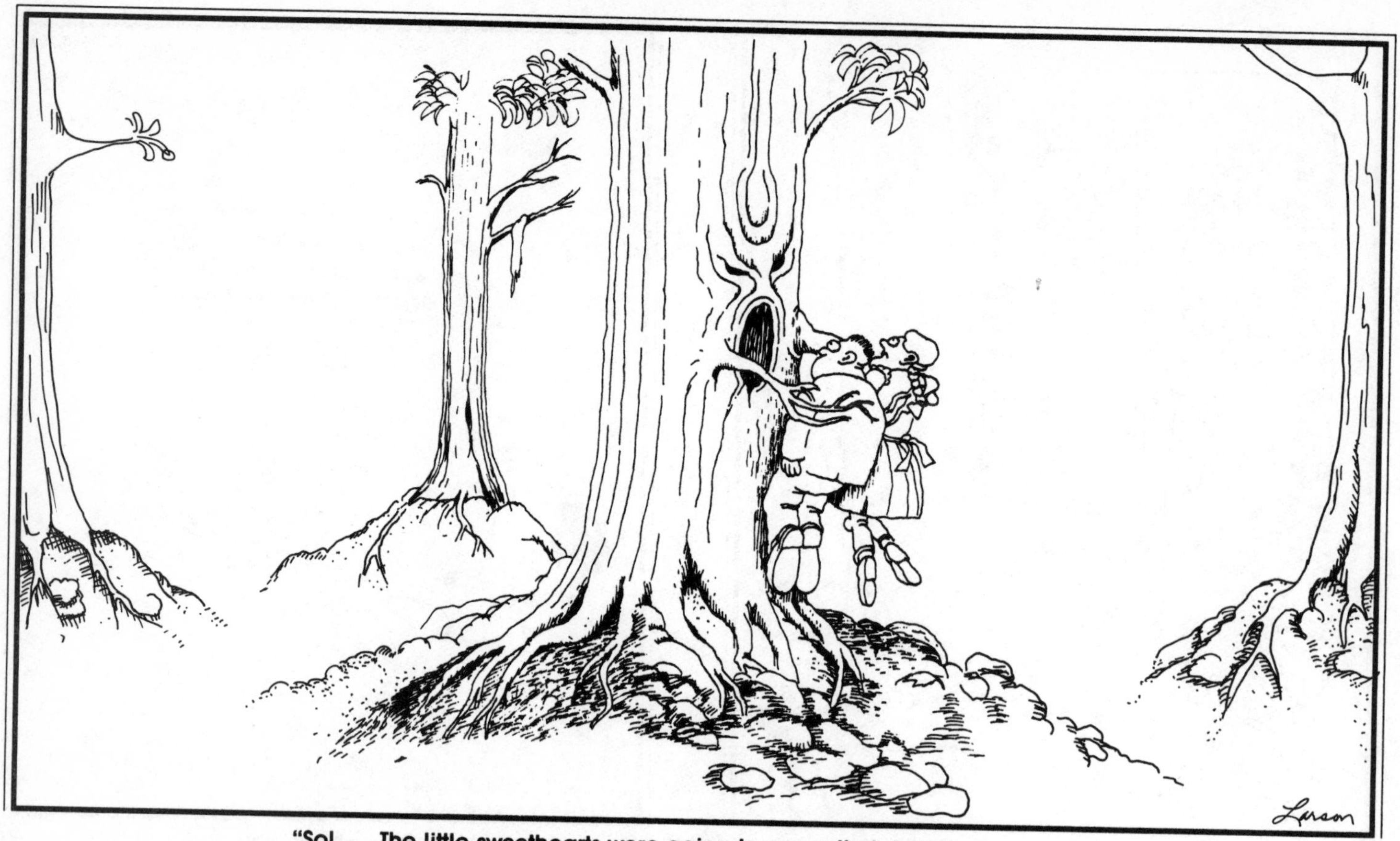

"So! . . . The little sweethearts were going to carve their initials on me, eh?"

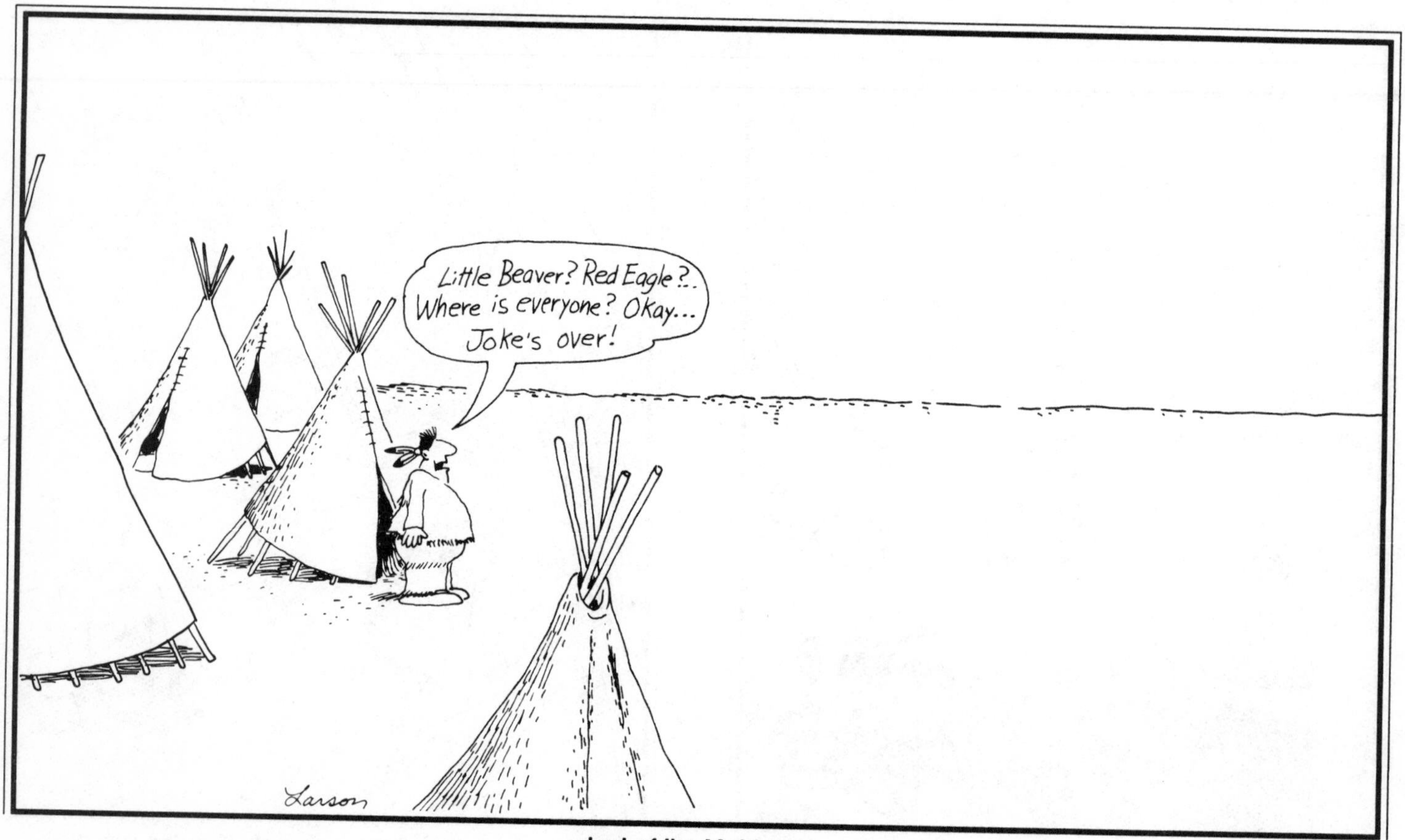
Little Beaver? Red Eagle?.. Where is everyone? Okay... Joke's over!

Last of the Mohicans

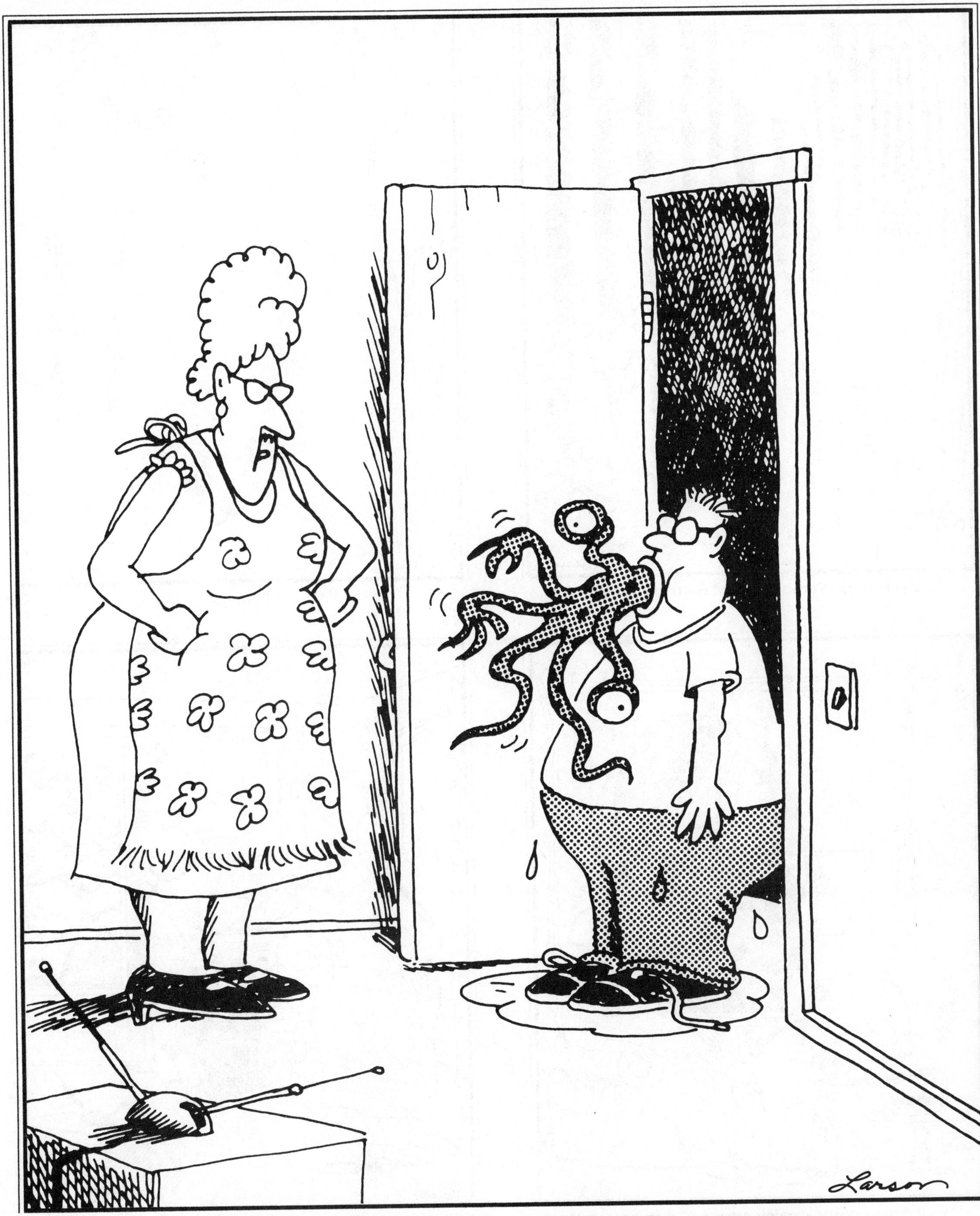
Larson

"Well, just look at you, Jimmy! . . . Soaking wet, hair mussed up, shoes untied . . . and take that horrible thing out of your mouth!"

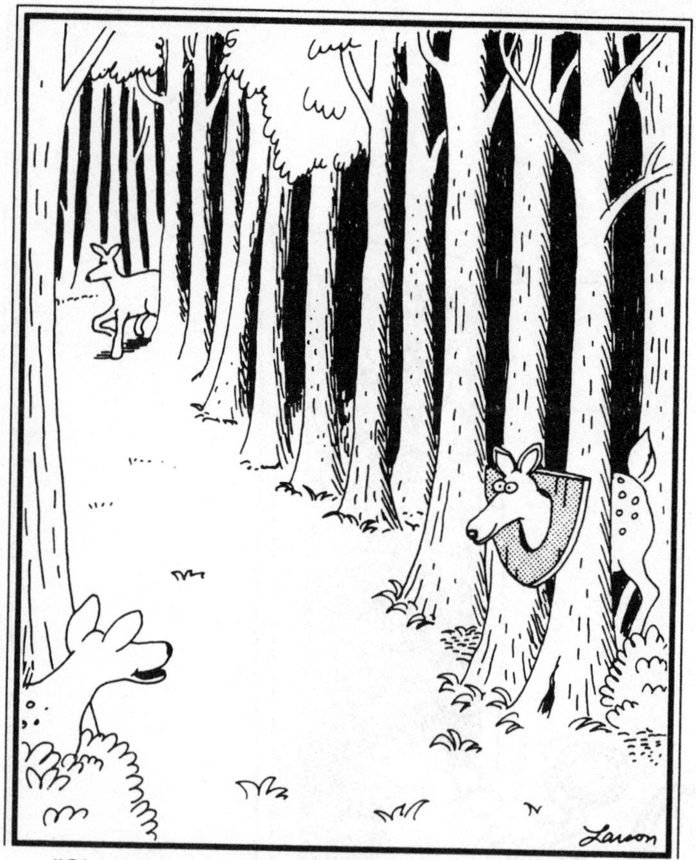
Larson

"Okay! Now don't move, Andy! Here comes Mom!"

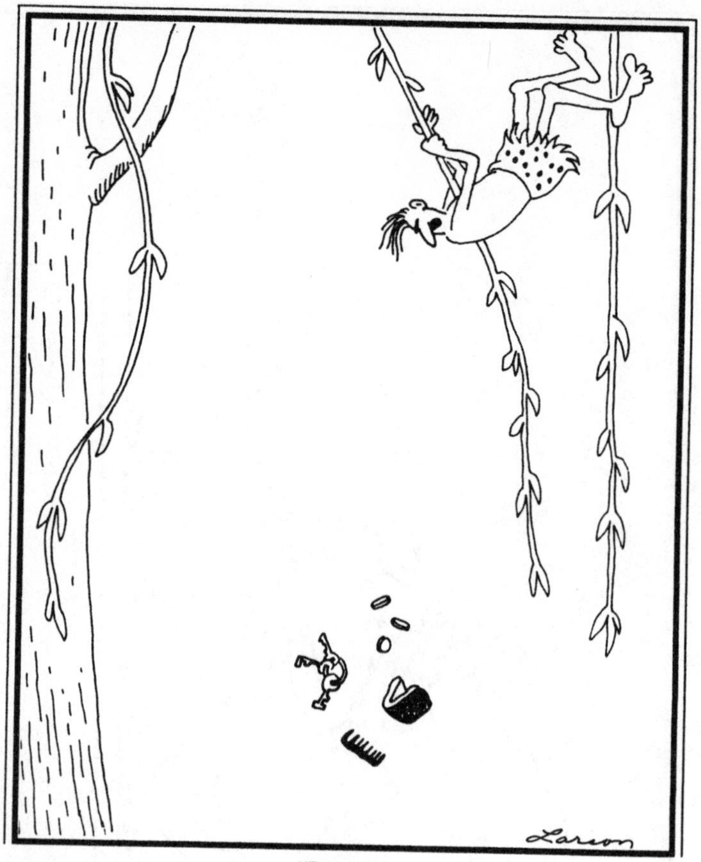
Larson

"Dang!"

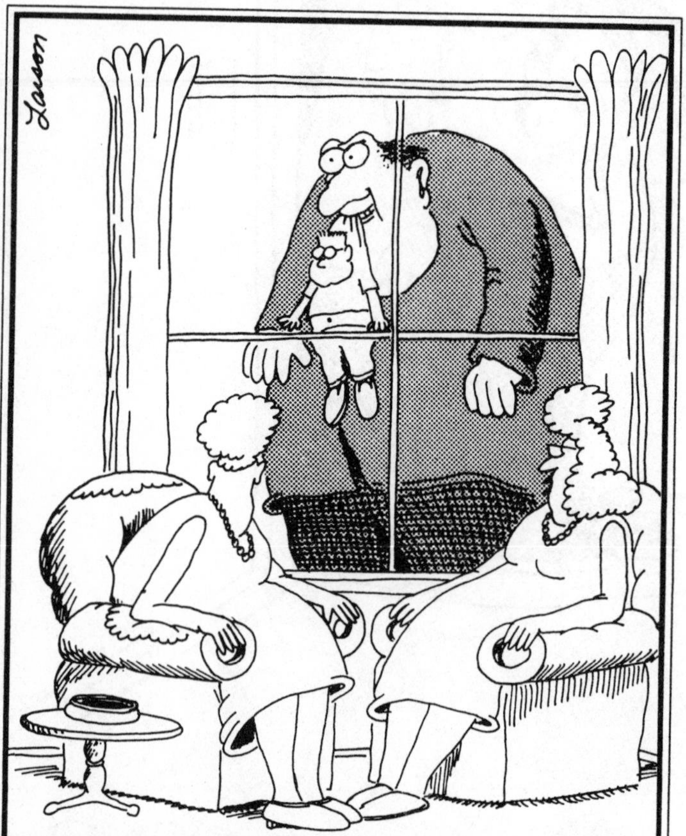
Larson

"Well, here comes Stanley now . . . Good heavens! What's he caught THIS time?"

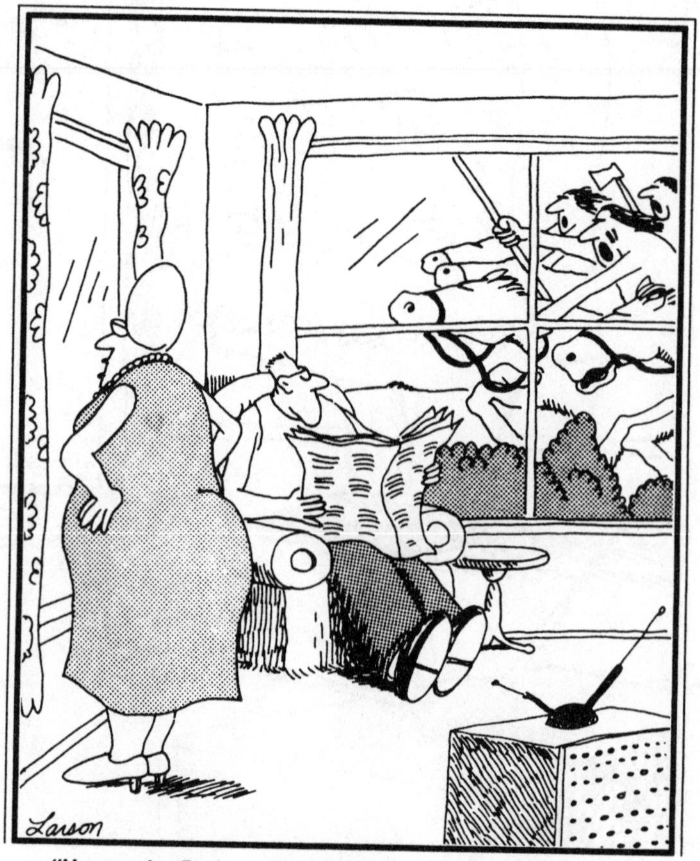
Larson

"How cute, Earl . . . The kids have built a little fort in the backyard."

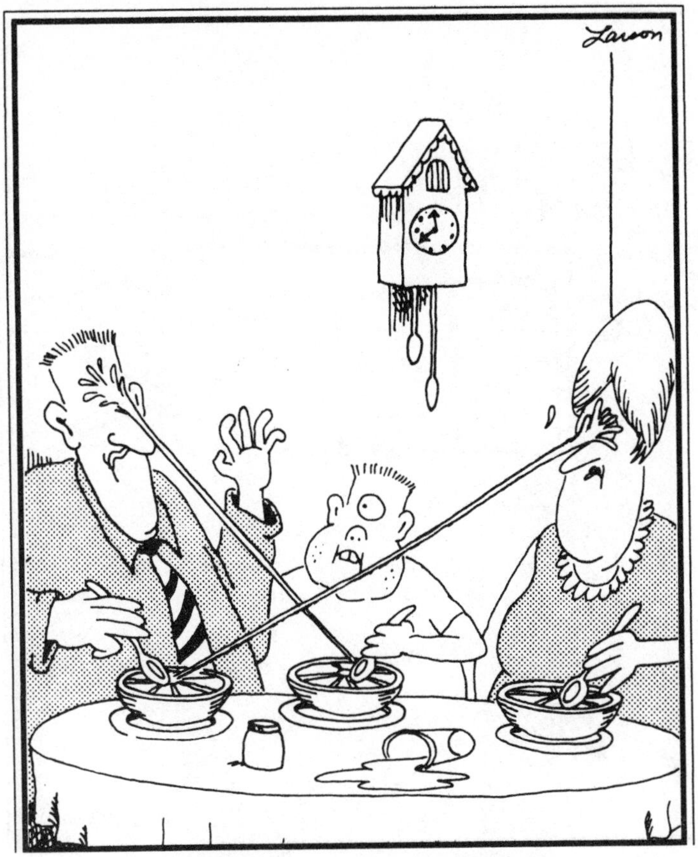
Larson

The Cyclops family at breakfast

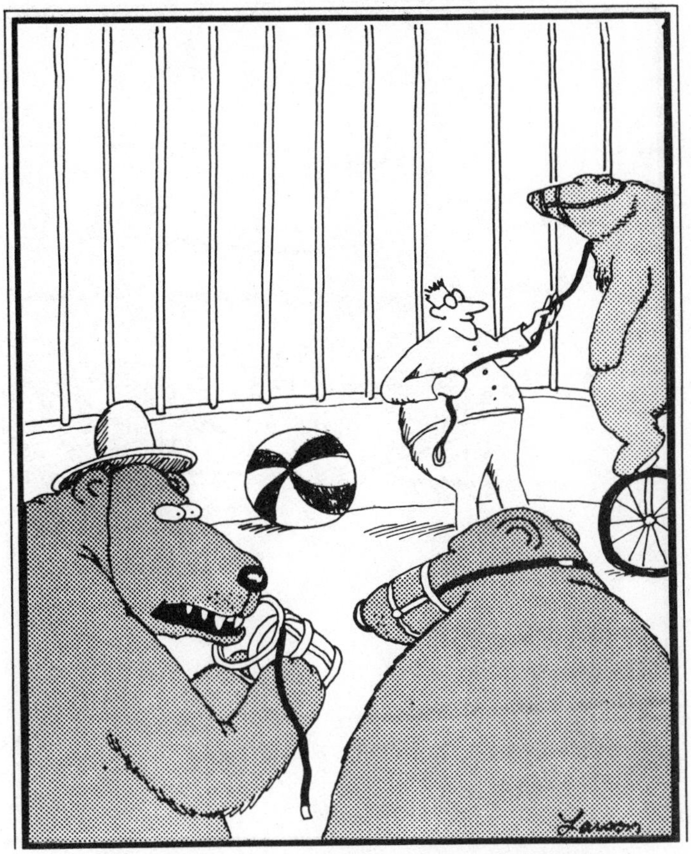
Larson

"Well, hey . . . These things just snap right off."

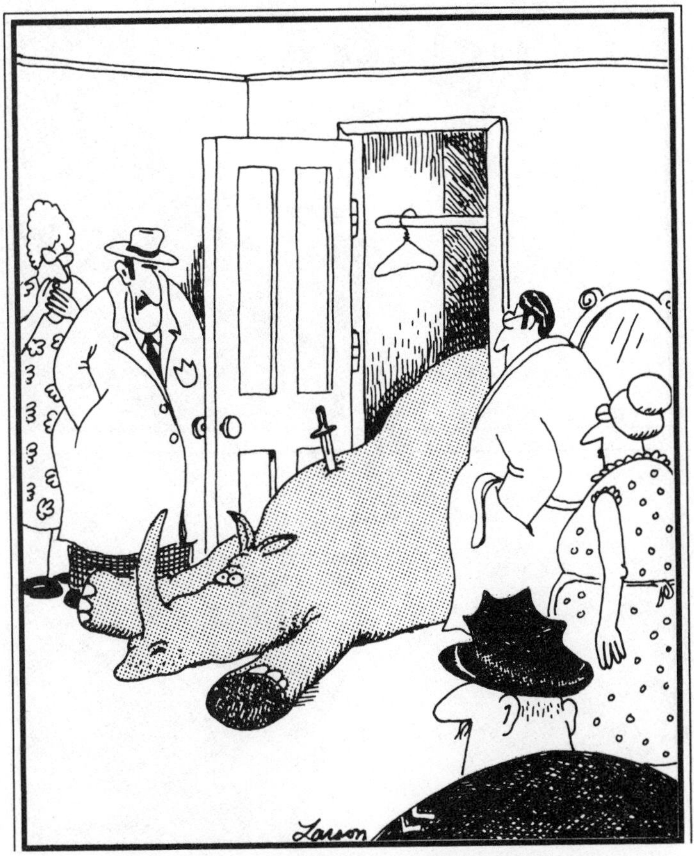
Larson

"Blast! Up to now, the rhino was one of my prime suspects."

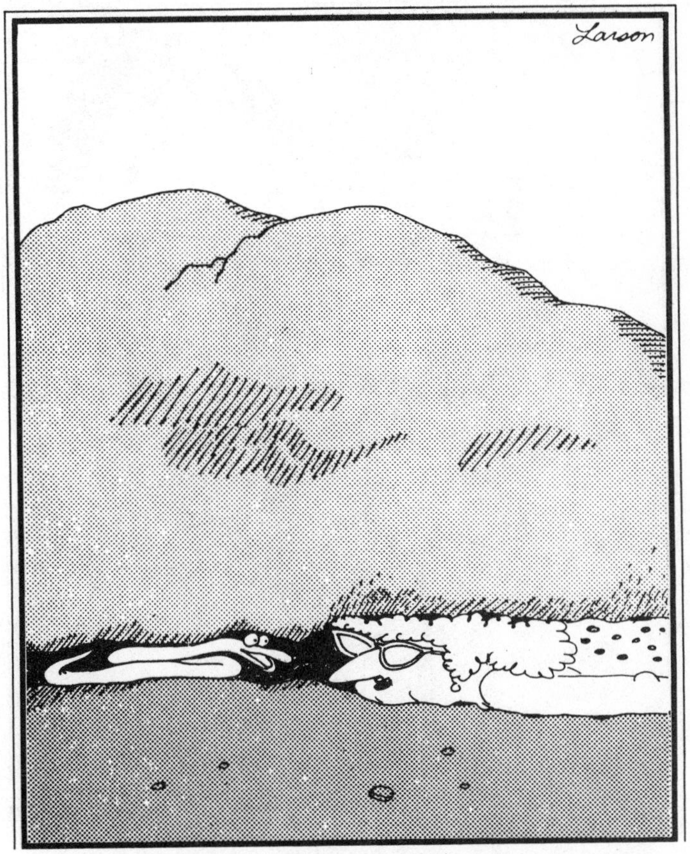
Larson

"It's true, Barbara . . . You're the first woman I've ever brought here."

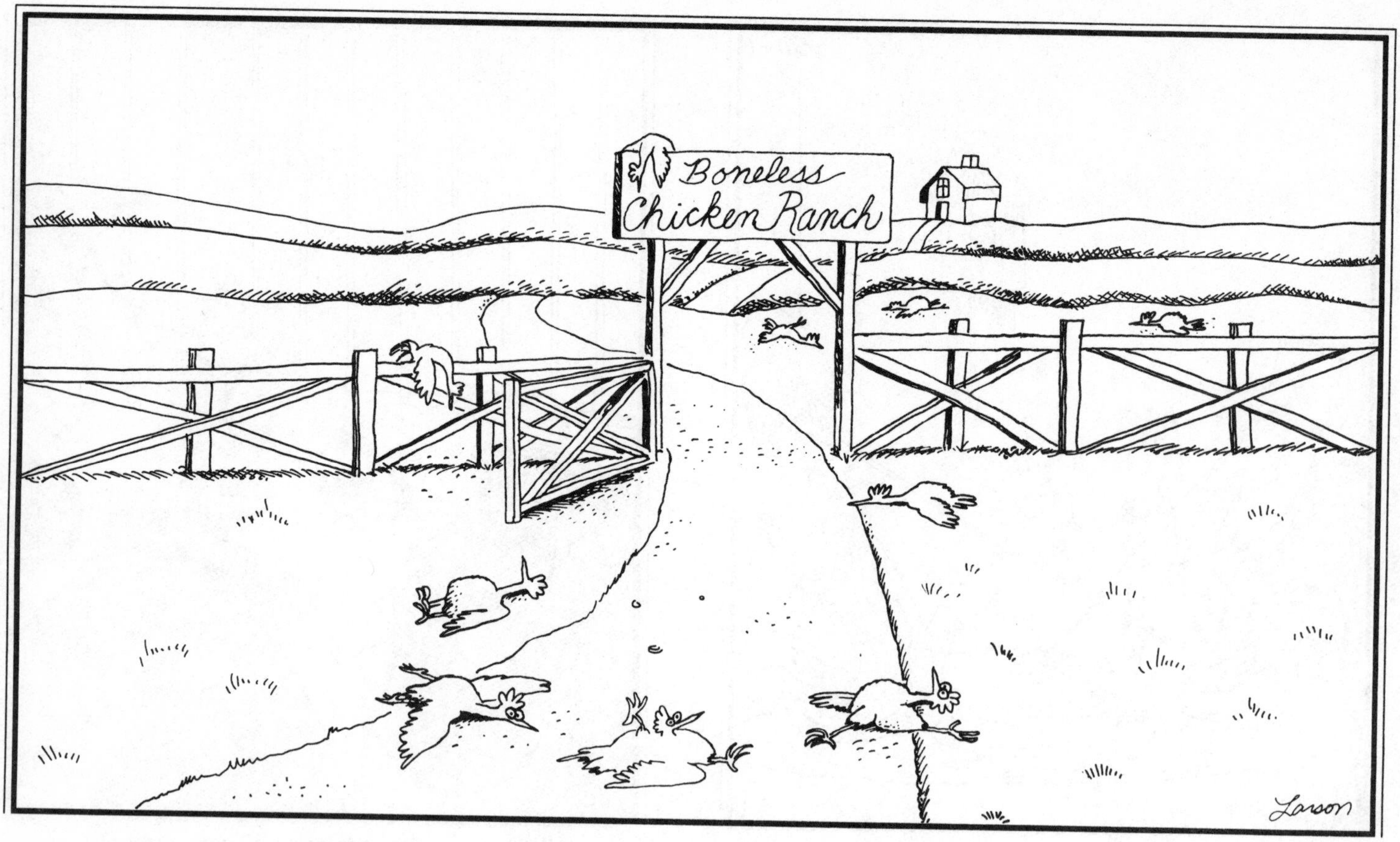
Boneless
Chicken Ranch
Larson

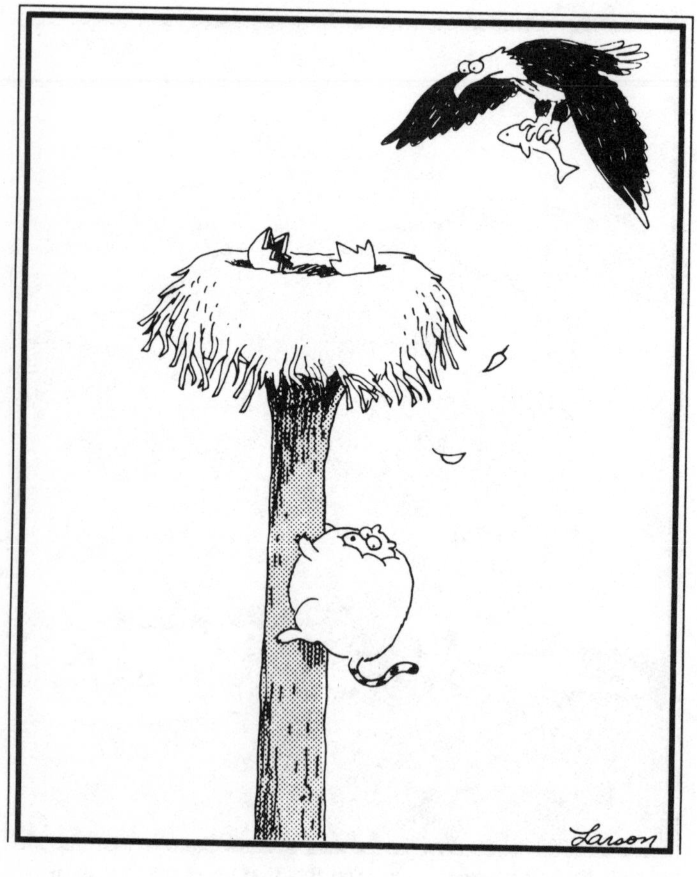
Larson

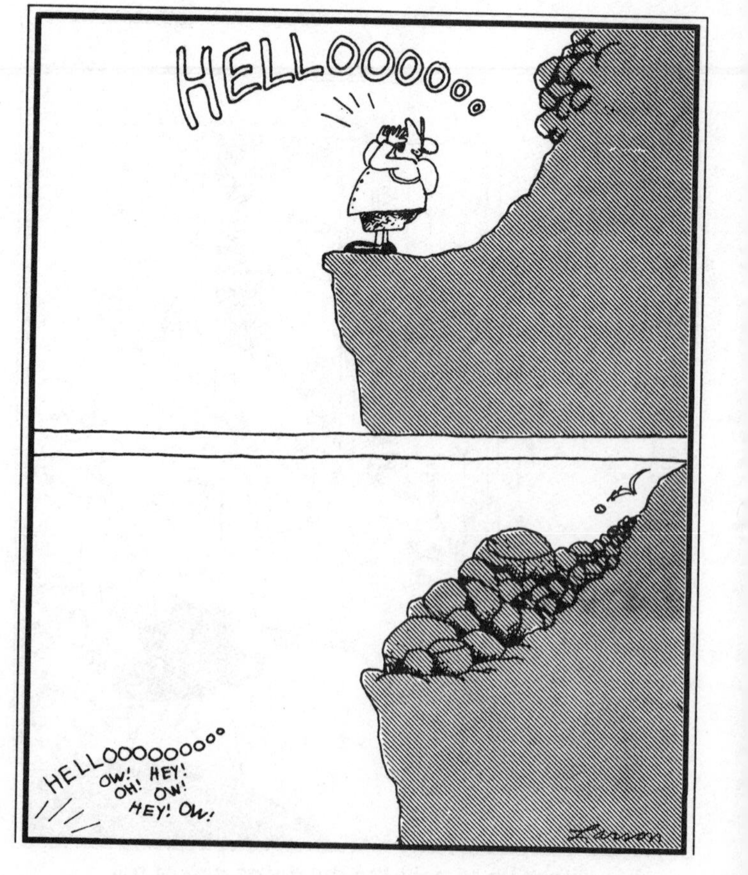
HELLOOOOo
HELLOOOOOOOOo
OW! HEY!
OH! OW!
HEY! OW!
Larson

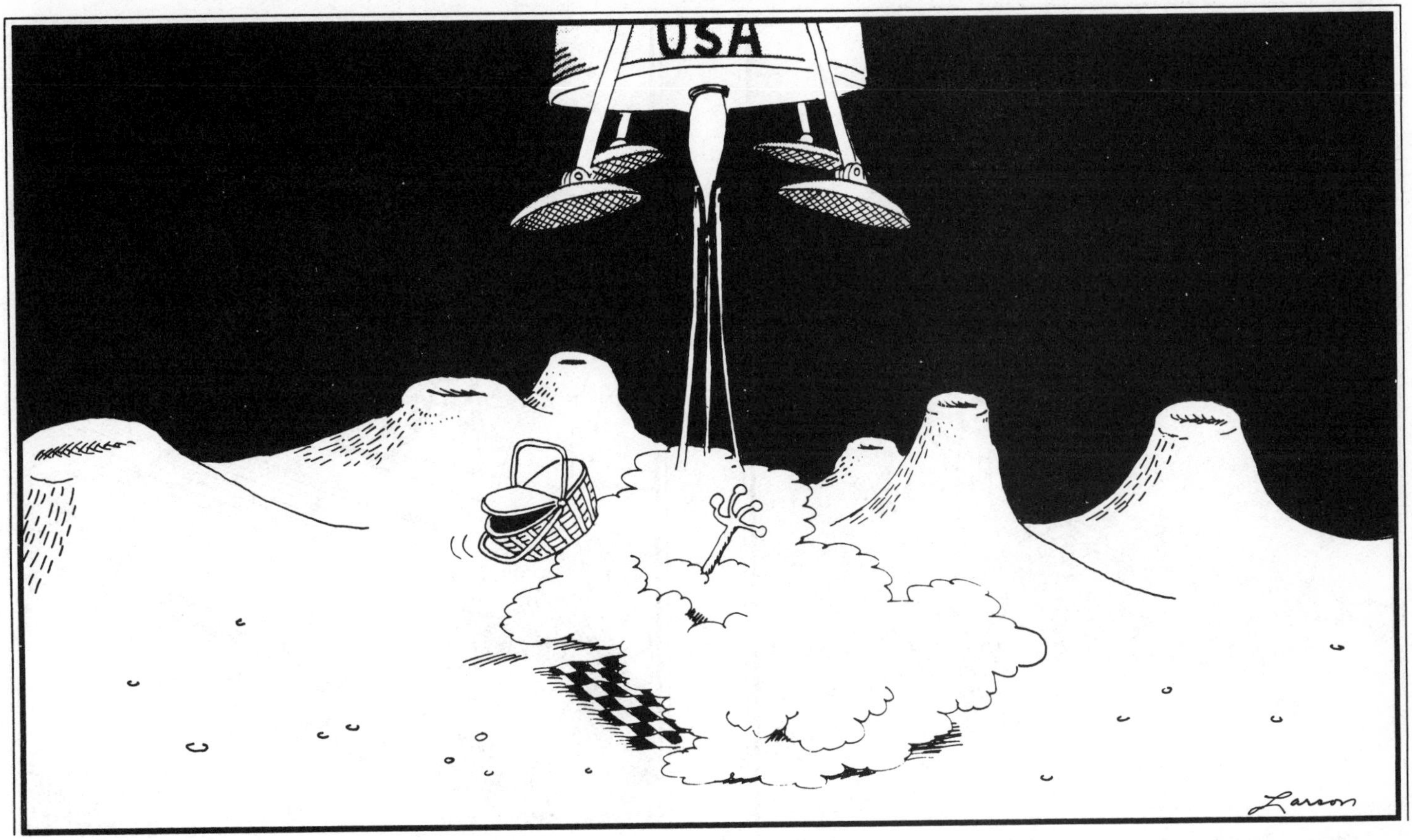
USA
Larson

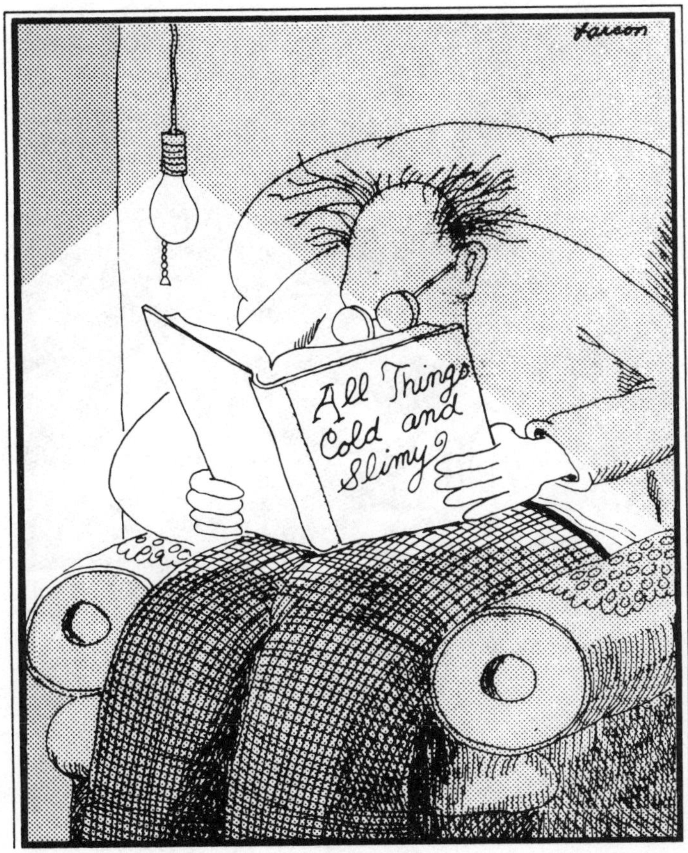
Larson
All Things Cold and Slimy?

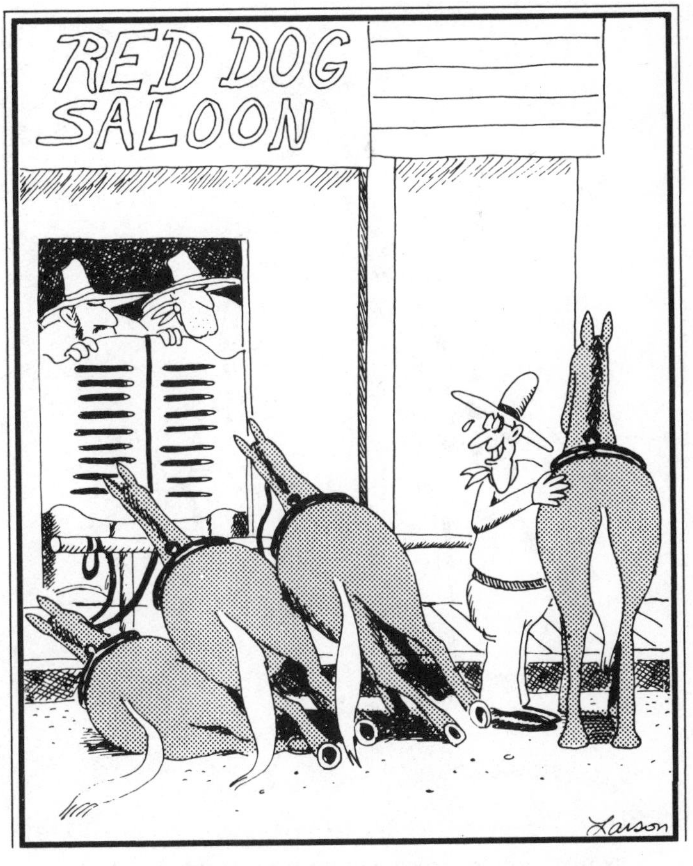
RED DOG SALOON
Larson

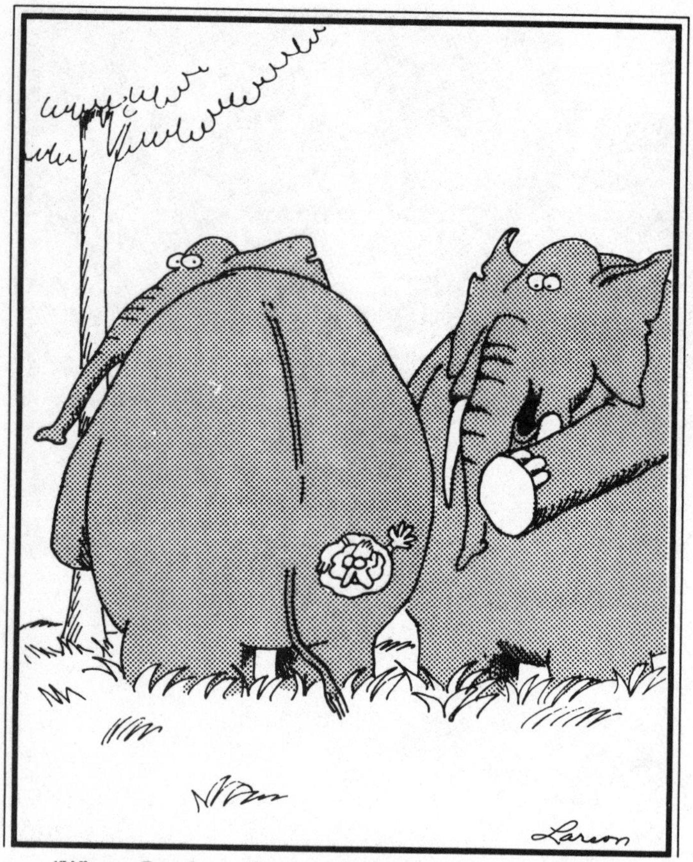

"Whoa, Frank . . . Guess what youuuuuuuuu sat in!"

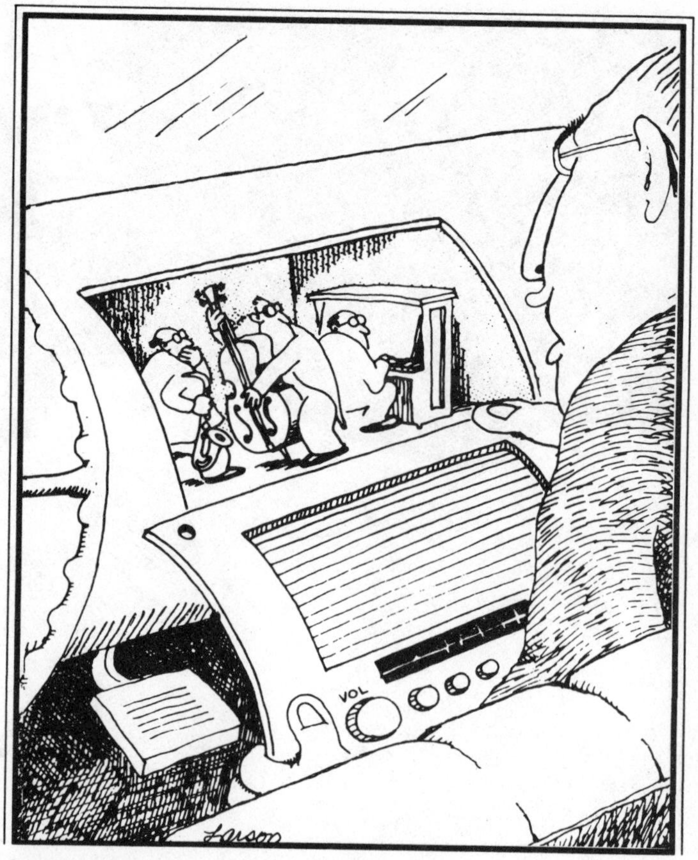
VOL

"Aha!"

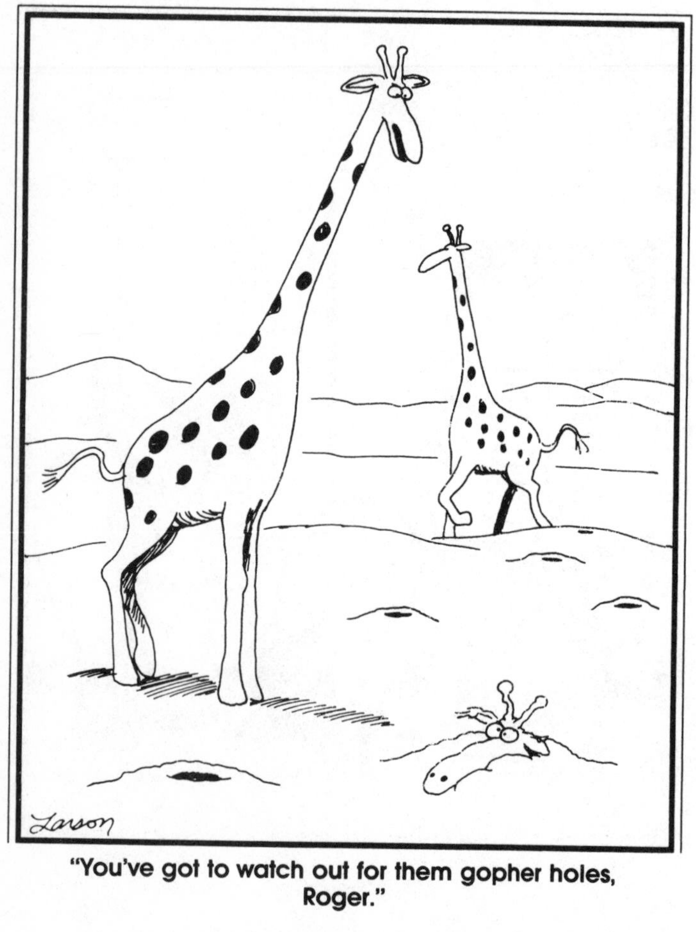

"You've got to watch out for them gopher holes, Roger."

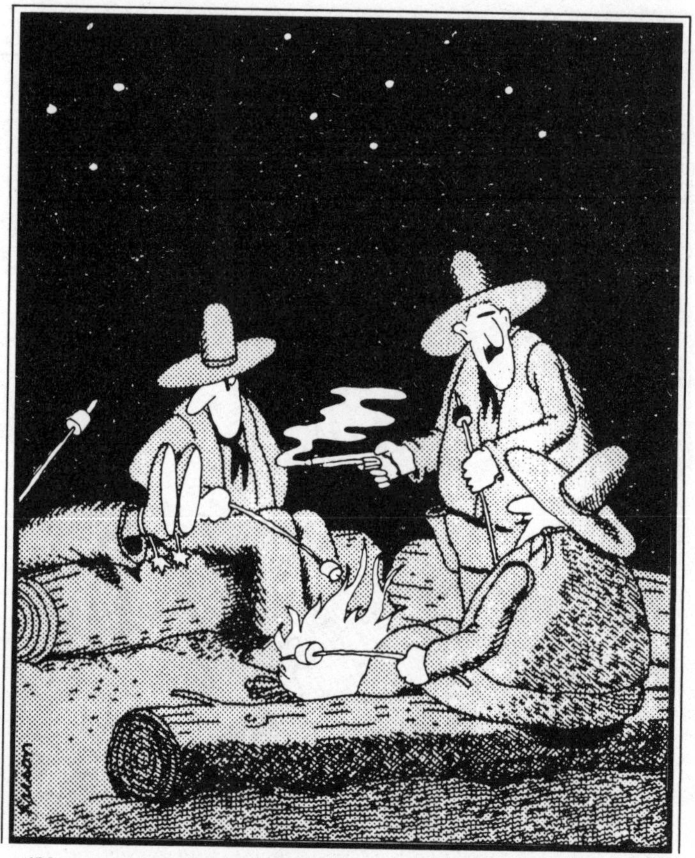

"You guys are both witnesses . . . He laughed when my marshmallow caught fire."

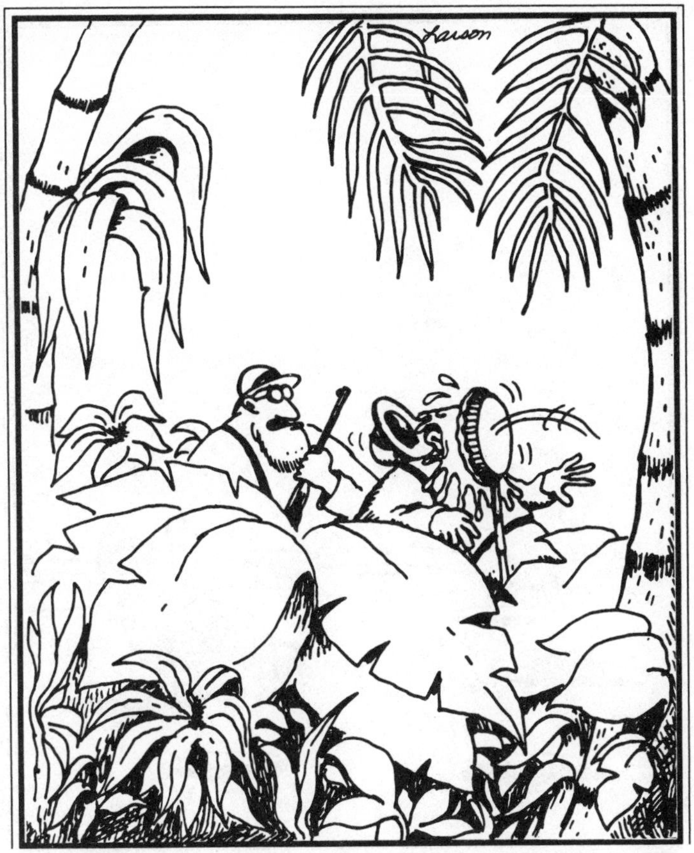
Larson

"Pie trap! . . . We're in Zubutu country, all right."

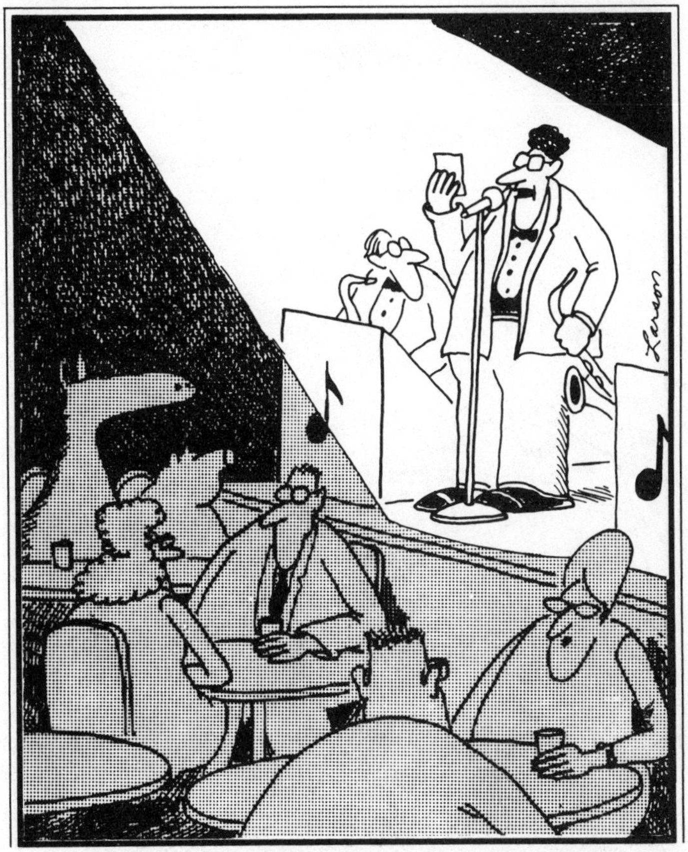
Larson

"What? . . . Another request for 'Old McDonald'?"

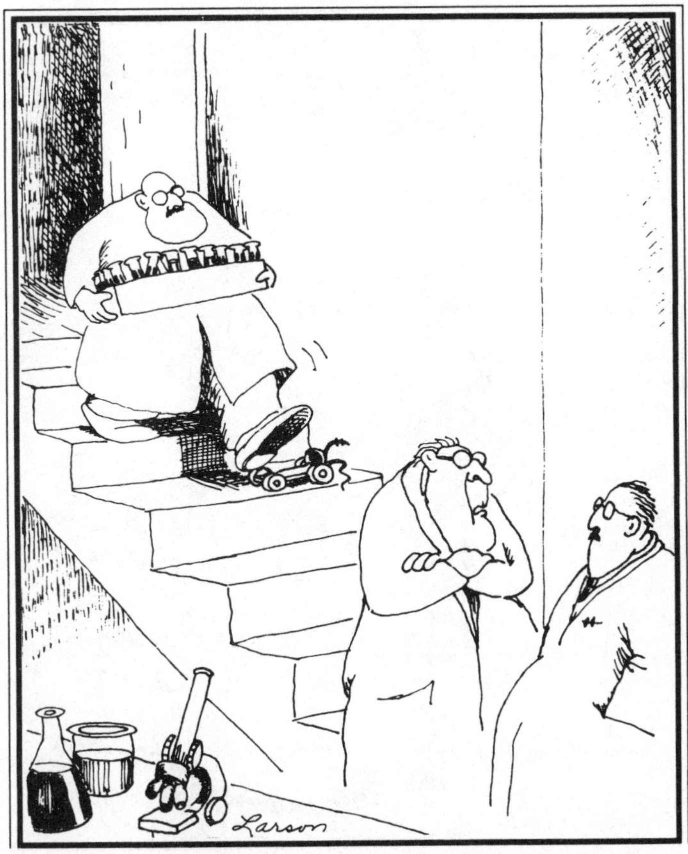
Larson

"And, as you shall soon observe, we are quite proud of our test tube baby progress."

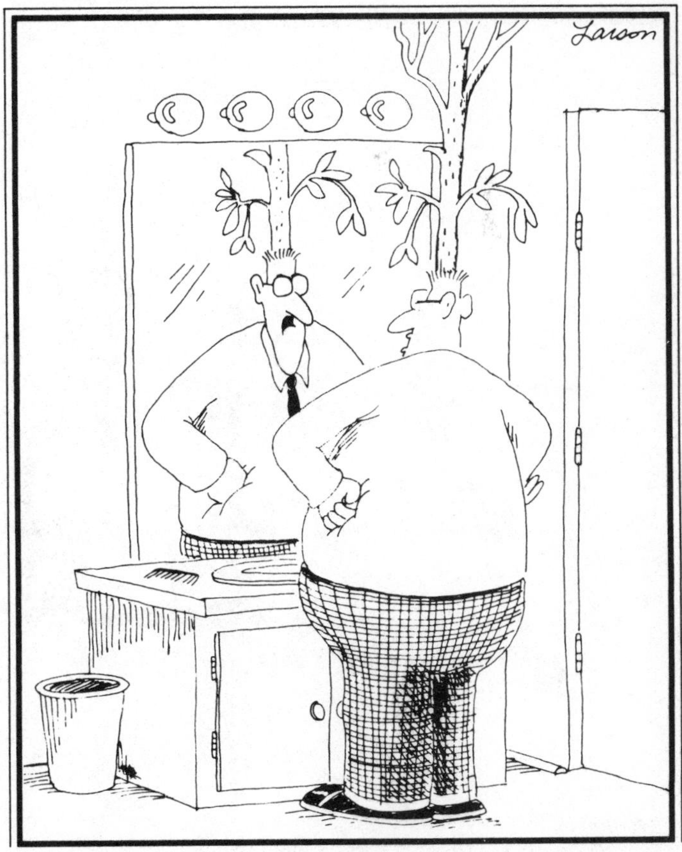
Larson

"Wouldn't you know it! . . . And always just before a big date!"

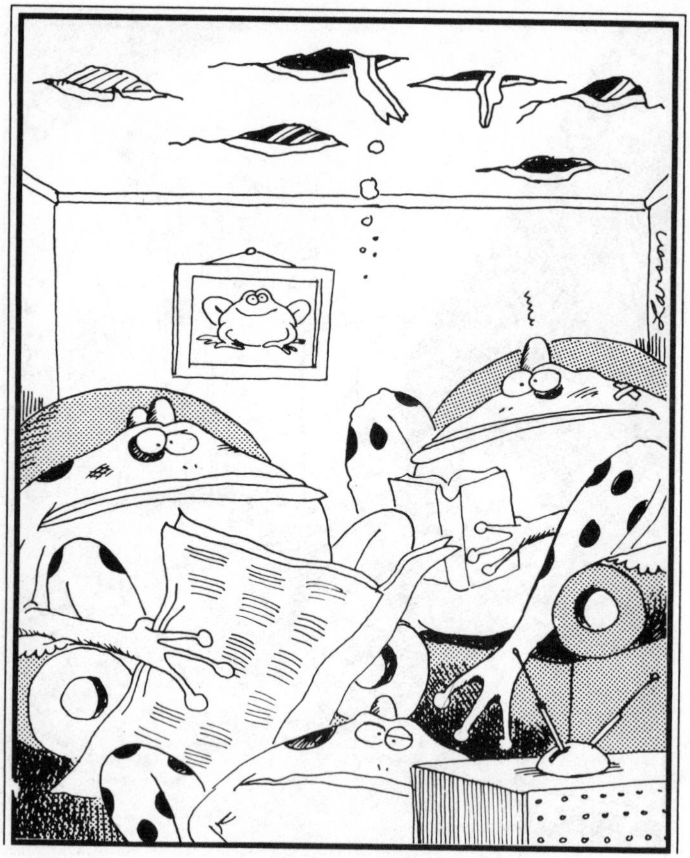
Larson

The frogs at home

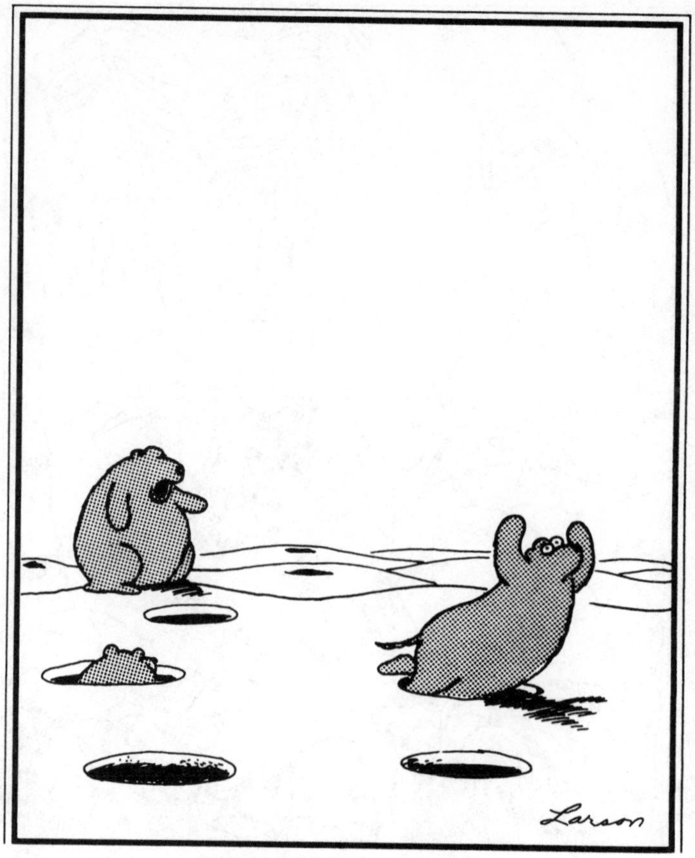
Larson

"Carl! Watch for holes!"

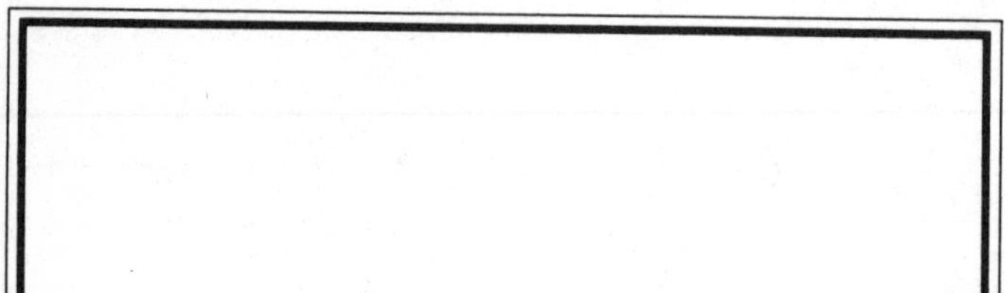
Larson

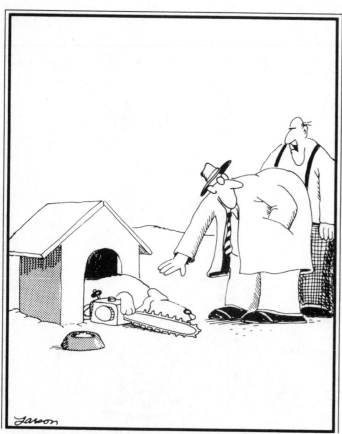

"I wouldn't do that, mister . . . Old Zeek's liable to fire that sucker up."

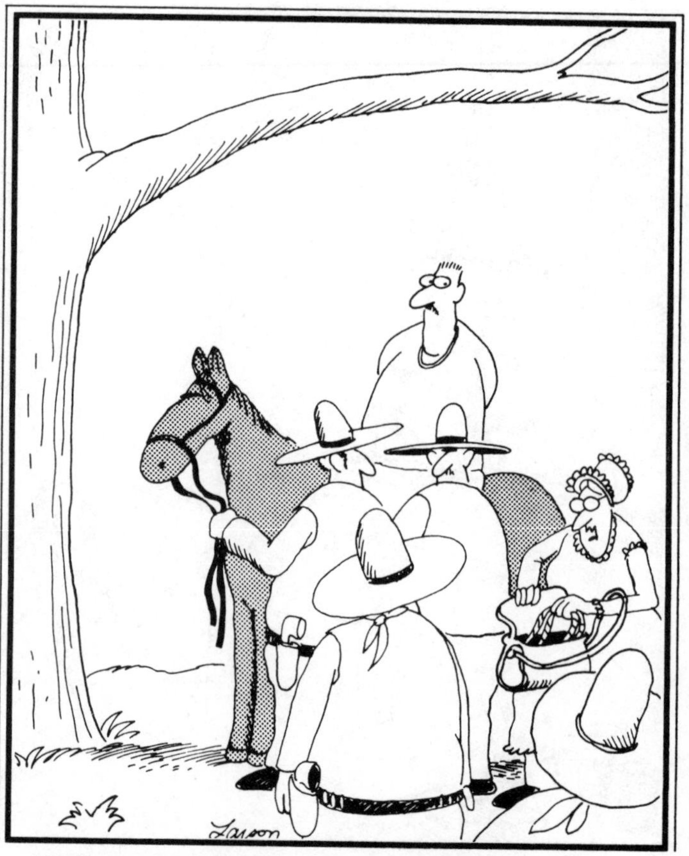
Larson

"Well, good heavens! . . . I can't believe you men . . . I'VE got some rope!"

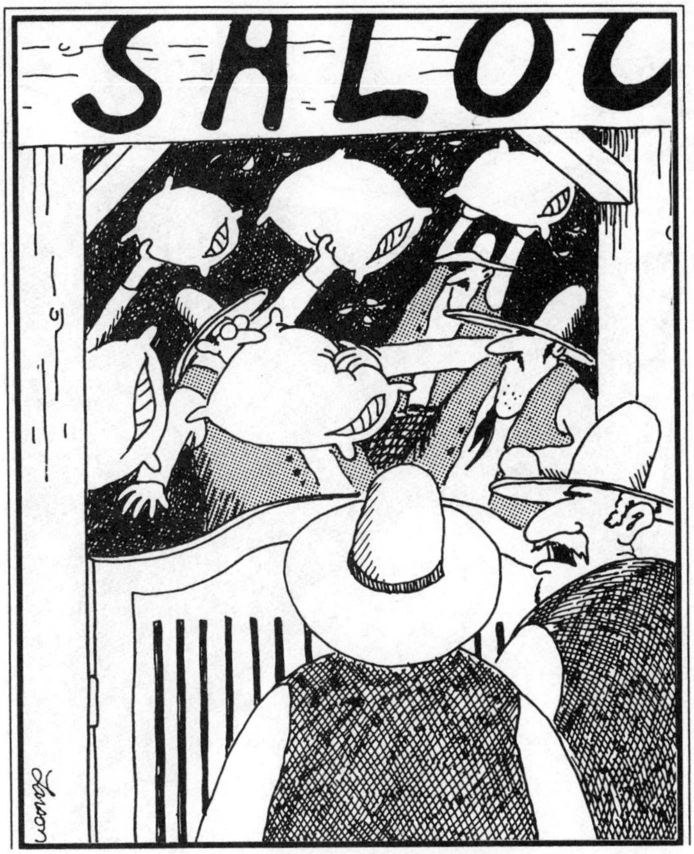
SALO
Larson

"Somebody better run fetch the sheriff."

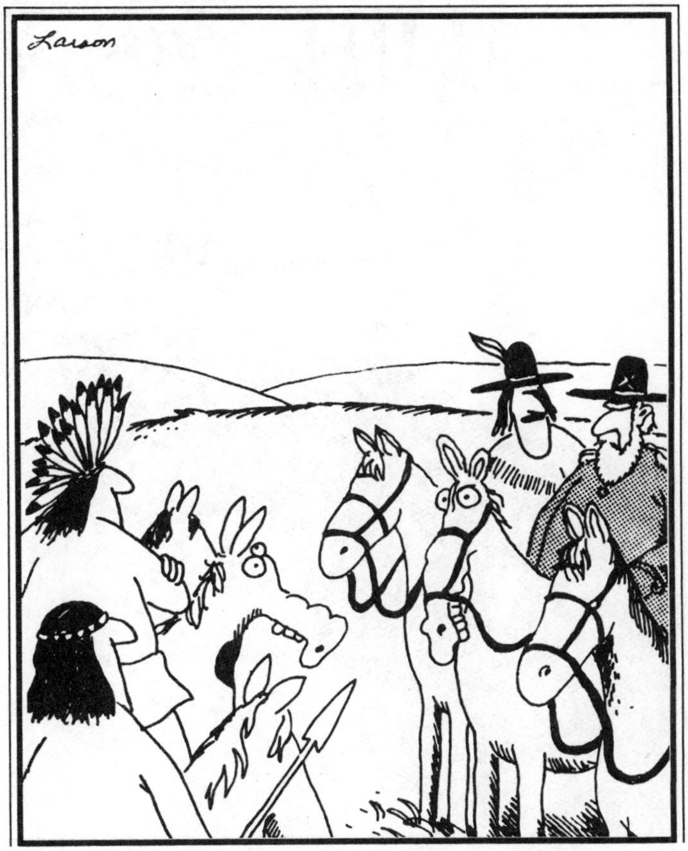
Larson

"Chief say, 'Oh, yeah? . . . YOUR horse ugly.'"

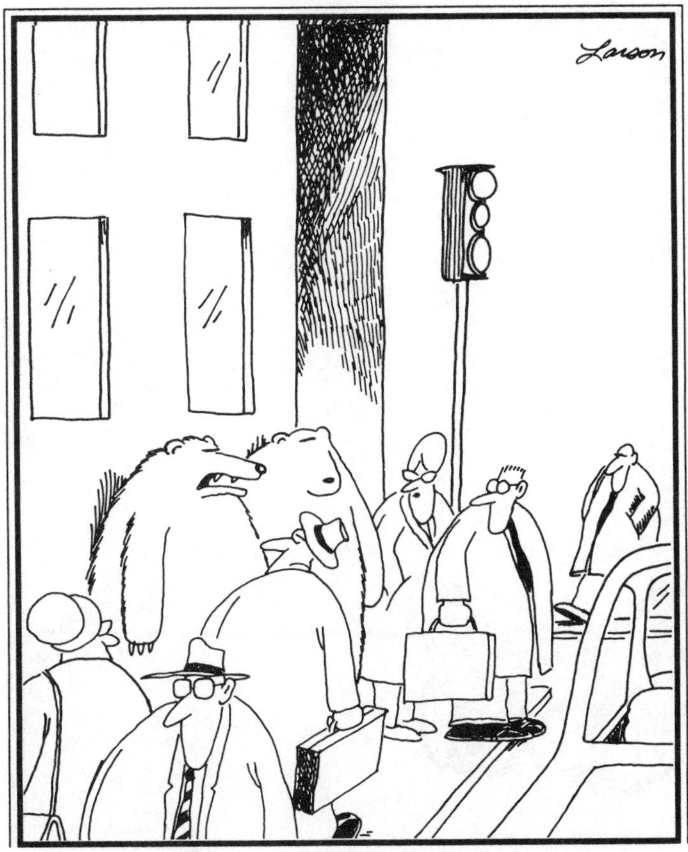
Larson

"Well, we're lost . . . And it's probably just a matter of time before someone decides to shoot us."

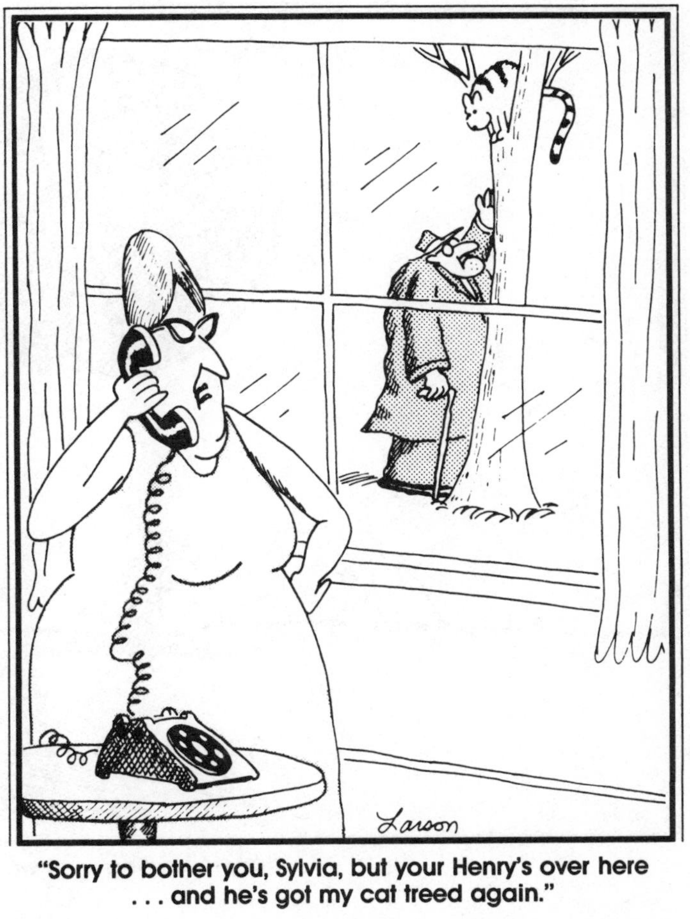
Larson

"Sorry to bother you, Sylvia, but your Henry's over here . . . and he's got my cat treed again."

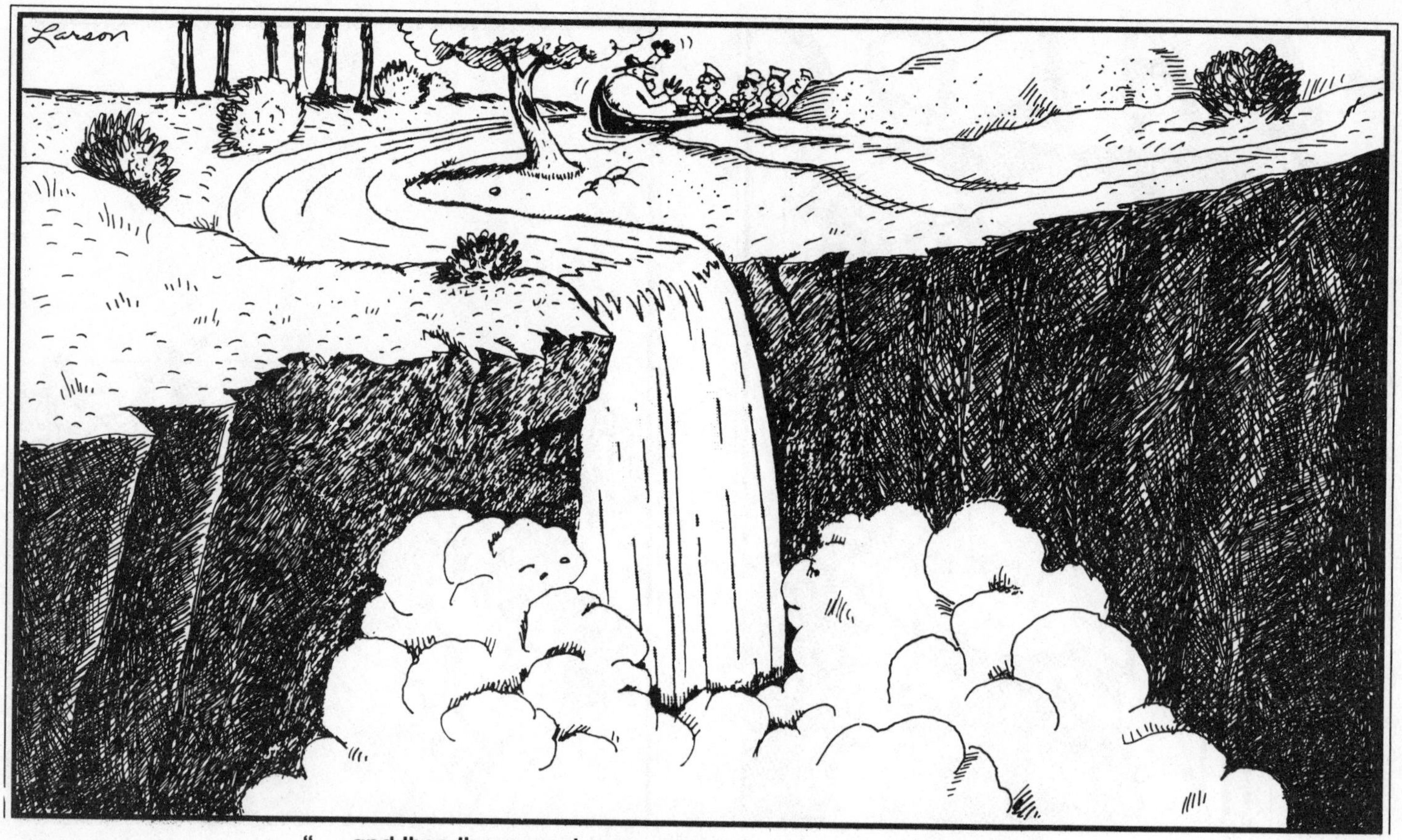
Larson

"... and then the second group comes in — 'row, row, row your boat' ..."

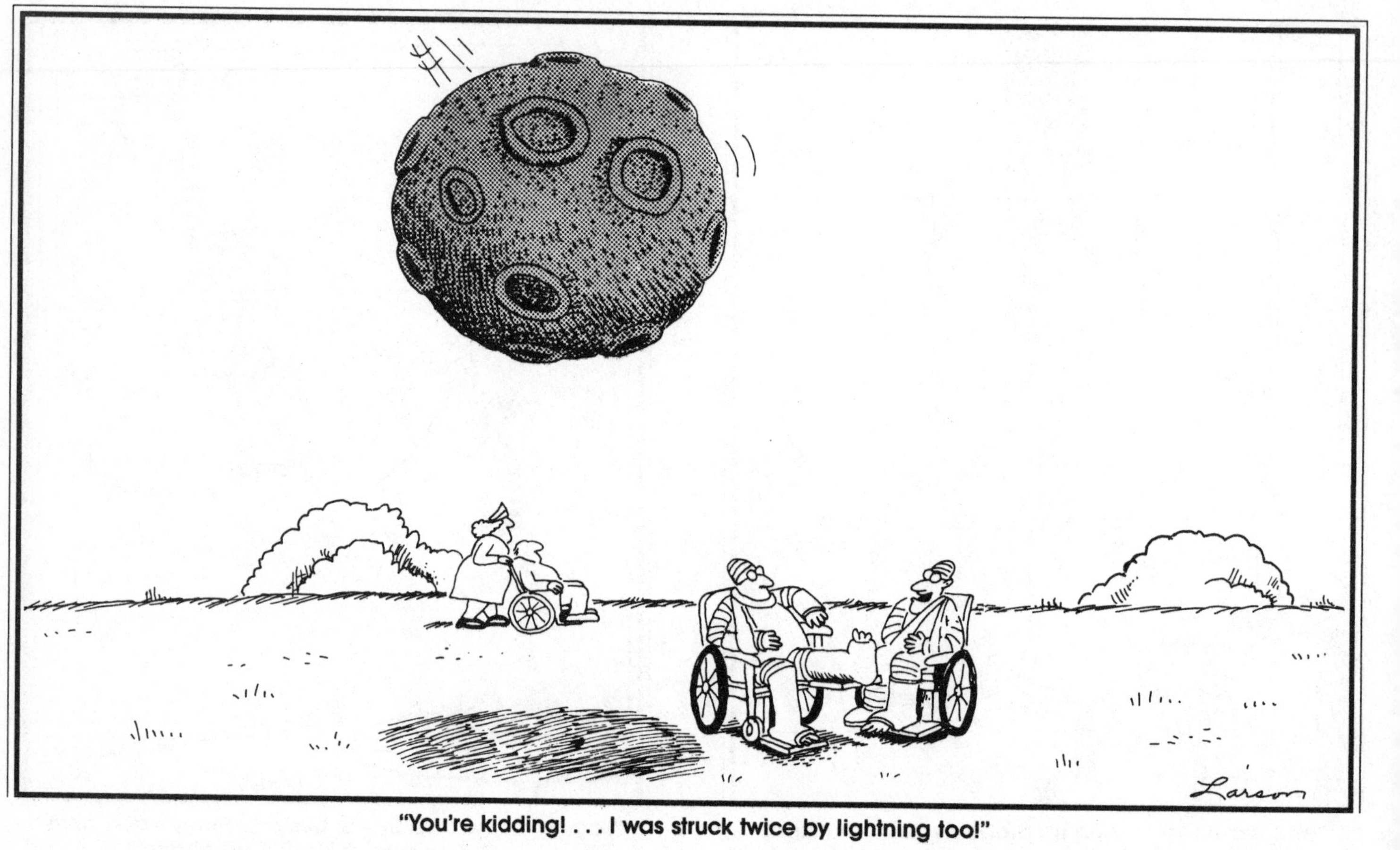
Larson

"You're kidding! ... I was struck twice by lightning too!"

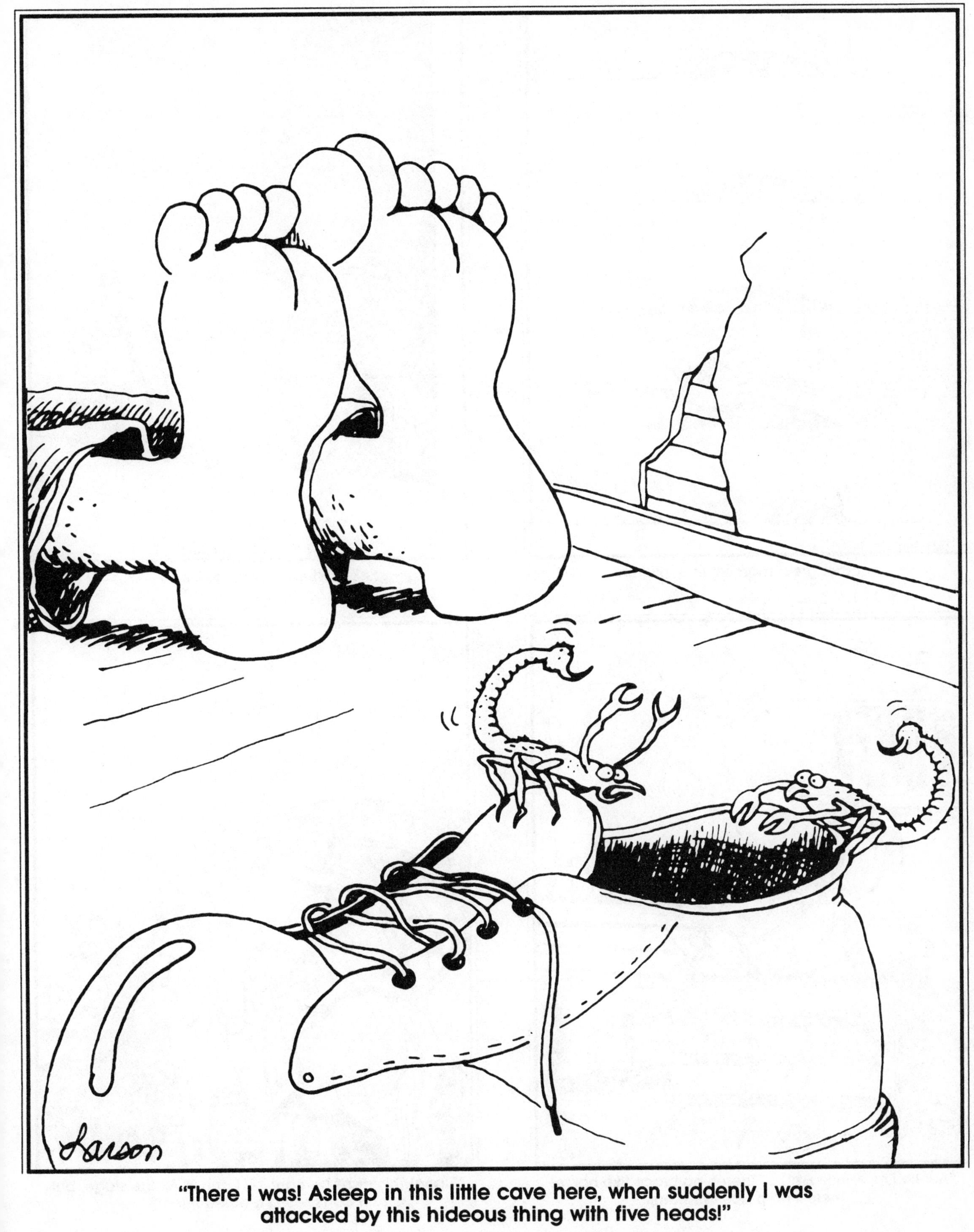
Larson

"There I was! Asleep in this little cave here, when suddenly I was attacked by this hideous thing with five heads!"

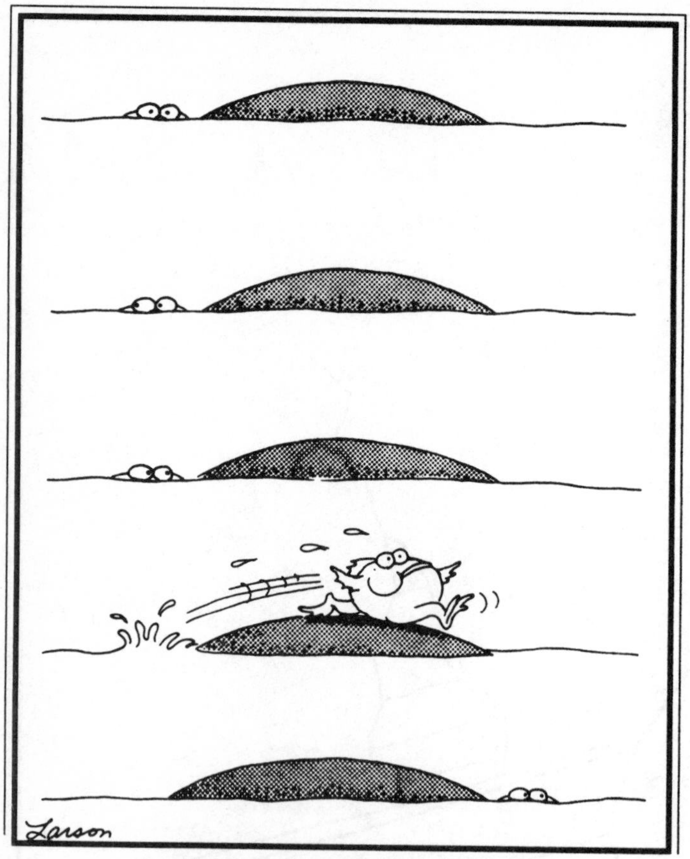
Larson

Another great moment in evolution

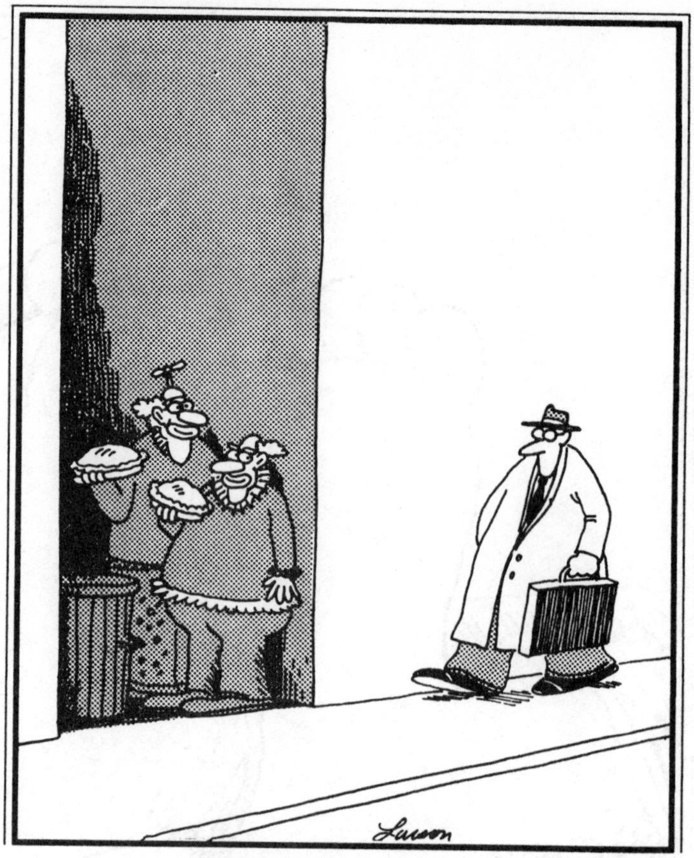
Larson

When clowns go bad

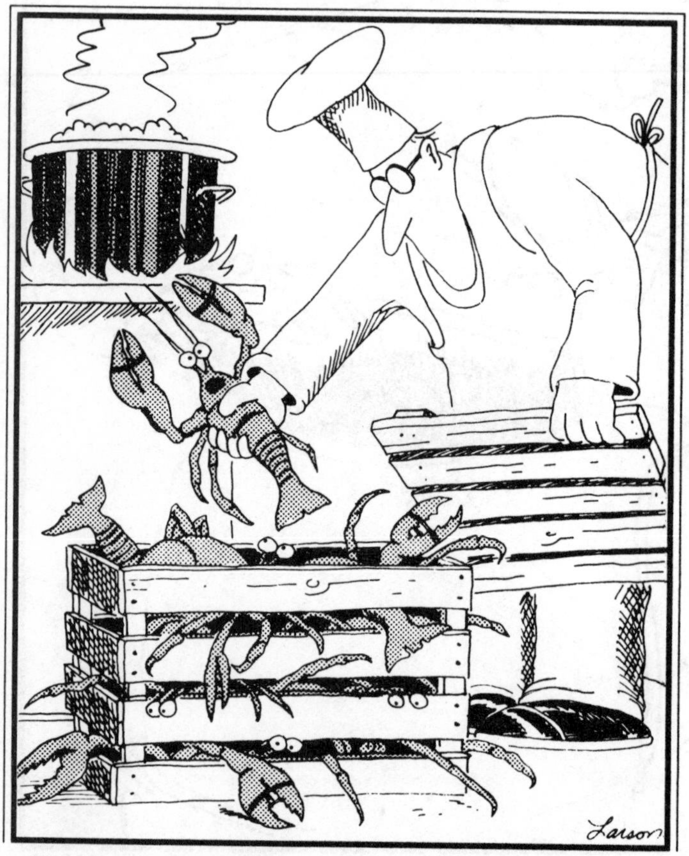
Larson

"Auntie Em, Auntie Em! . . . There's no place like home! . . . There's no place like home."

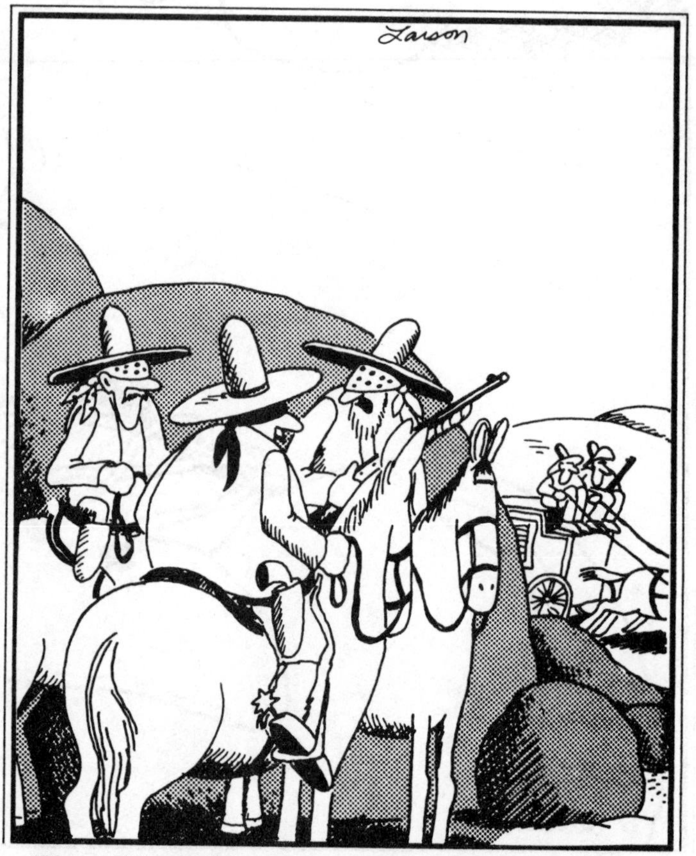
Larson

"Dang! This can't be right . . . I can HEAR the stage, but I can't see a blamed thing!"

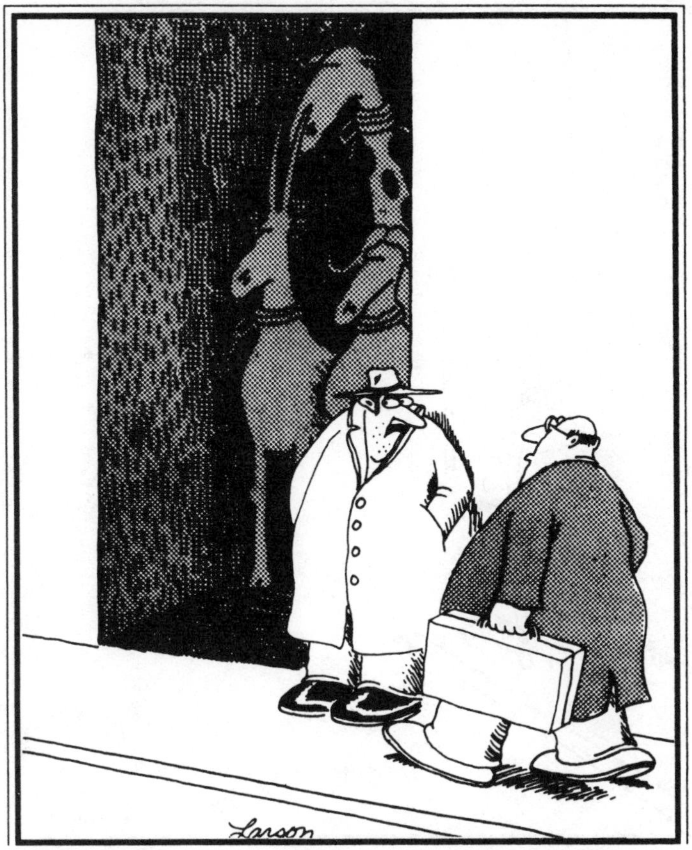
Larson

"Hey, buddy . . . You wanna buy a hoofed mammal?"

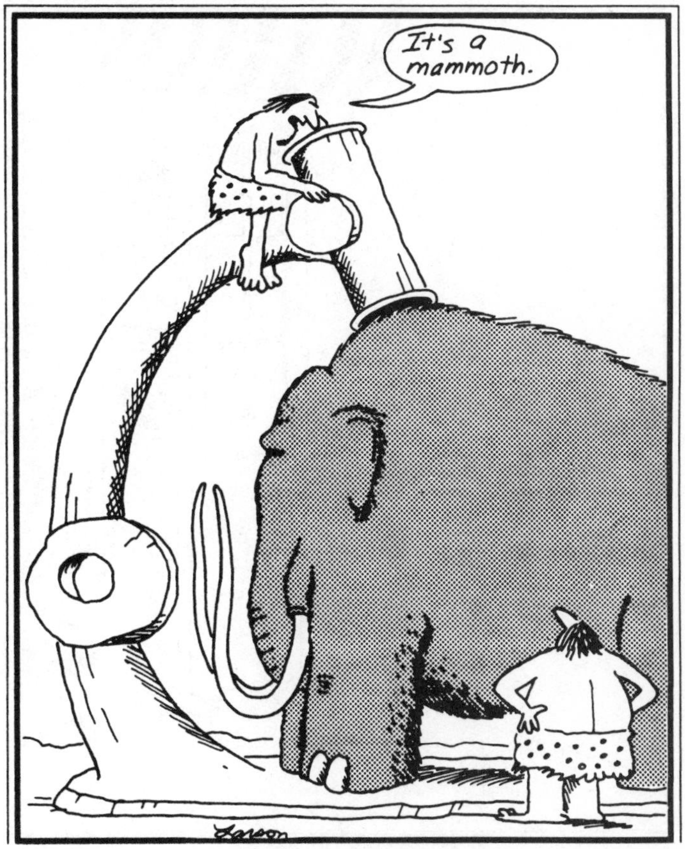
It's a mammoth.
Larson

Early microscope

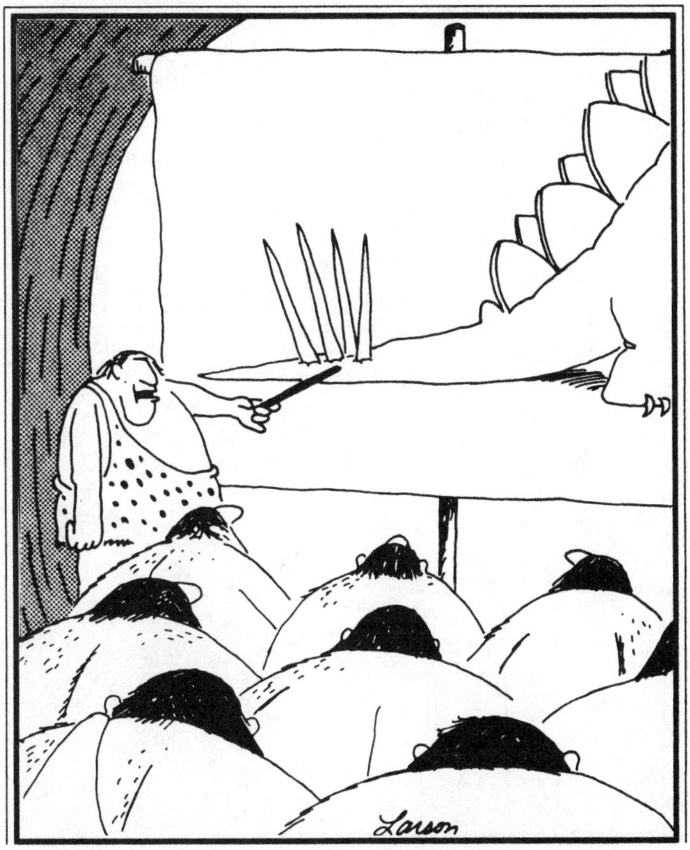
Larson

"Now this end is called the thagomizer . . . after the late Thag Simmons."

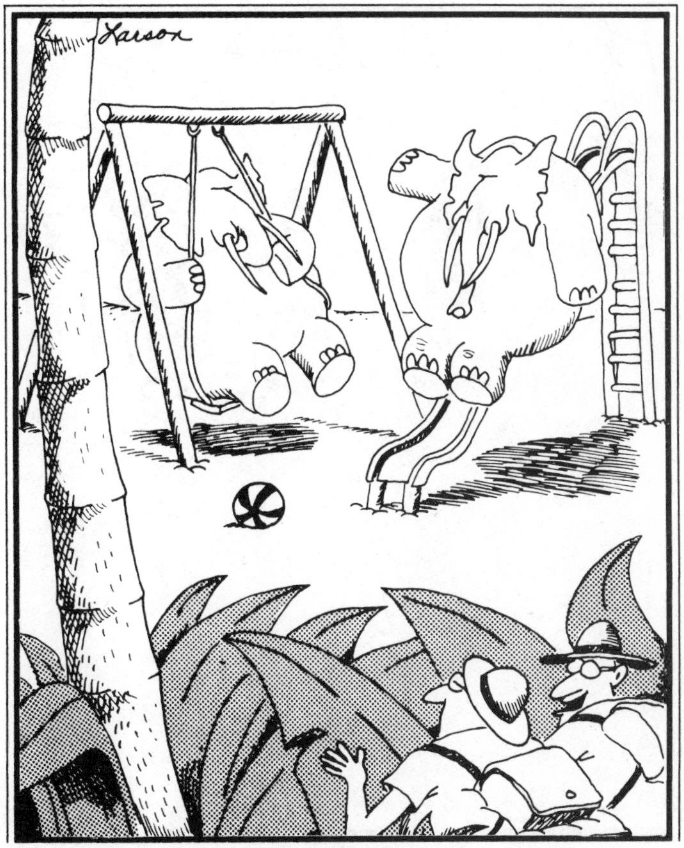
Larson

"By Jove! We've found it, Simmons! . . . The Secret Elephant Playground!"

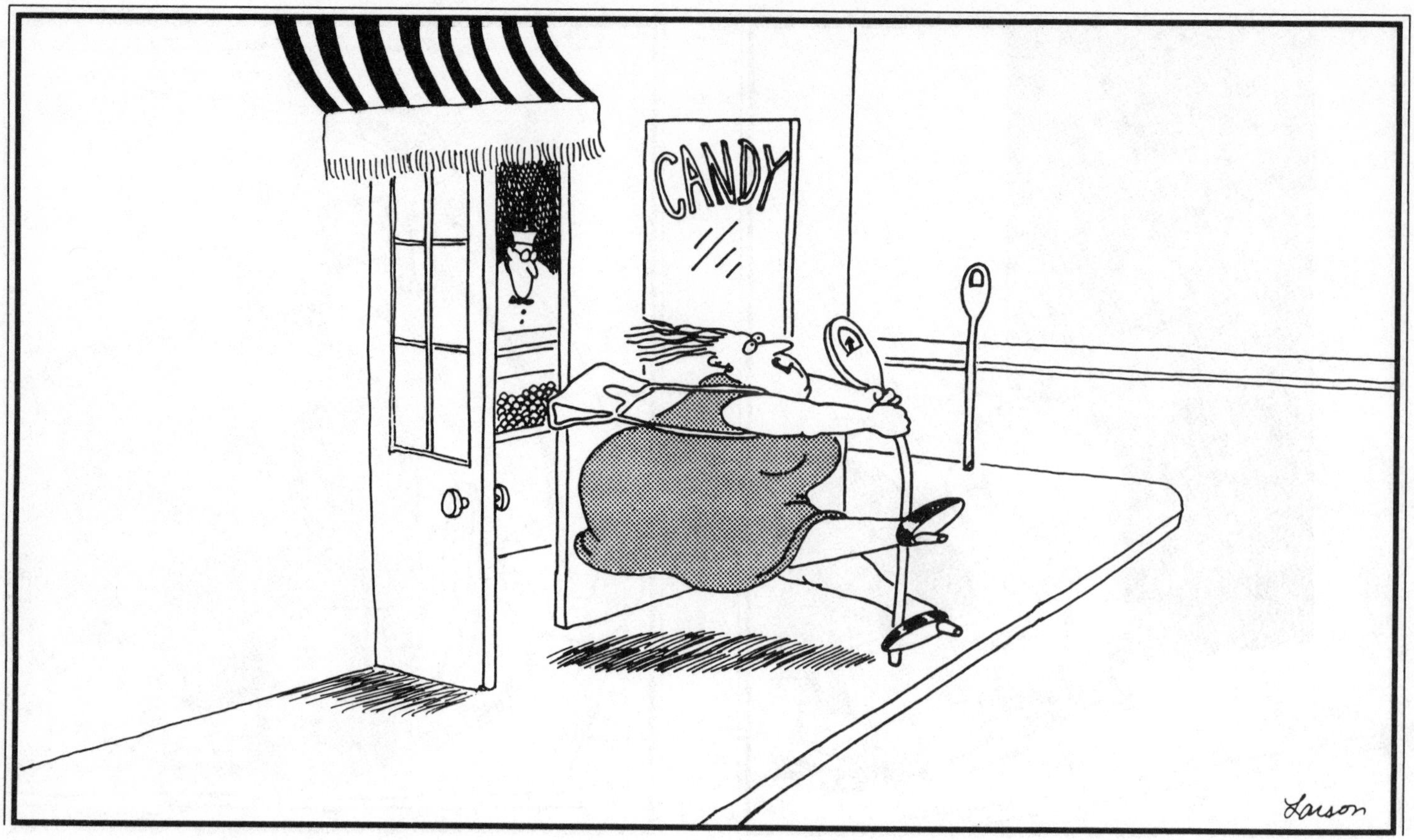
CANDY
Larson

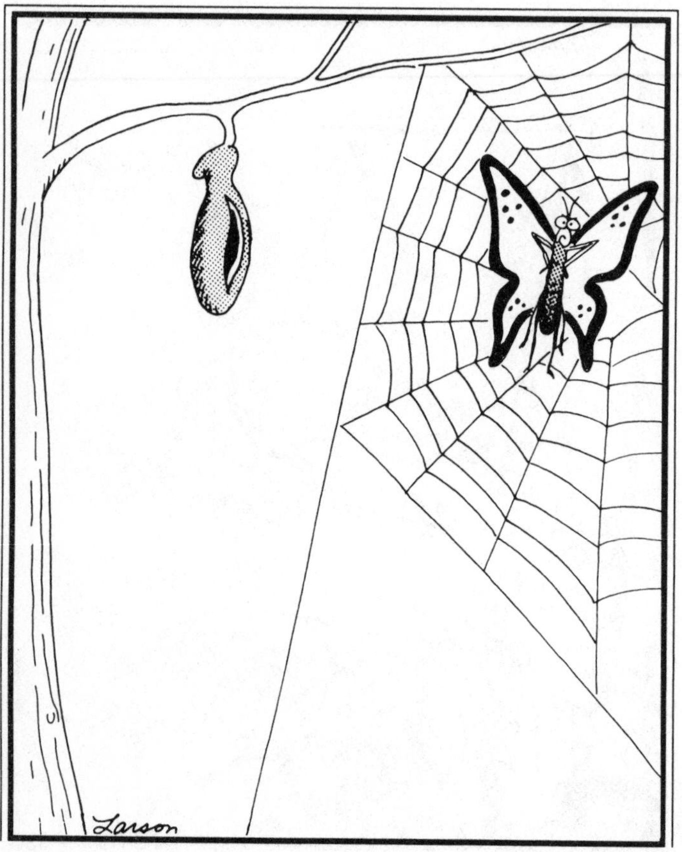
Larson

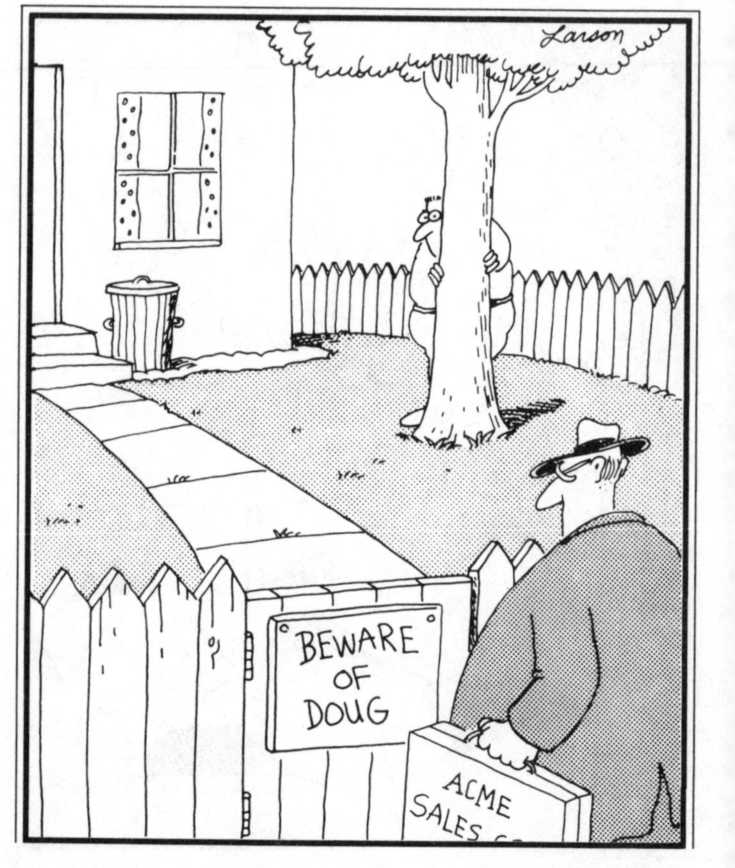
Larson
BEWARE OF DOUG
ACME SALES

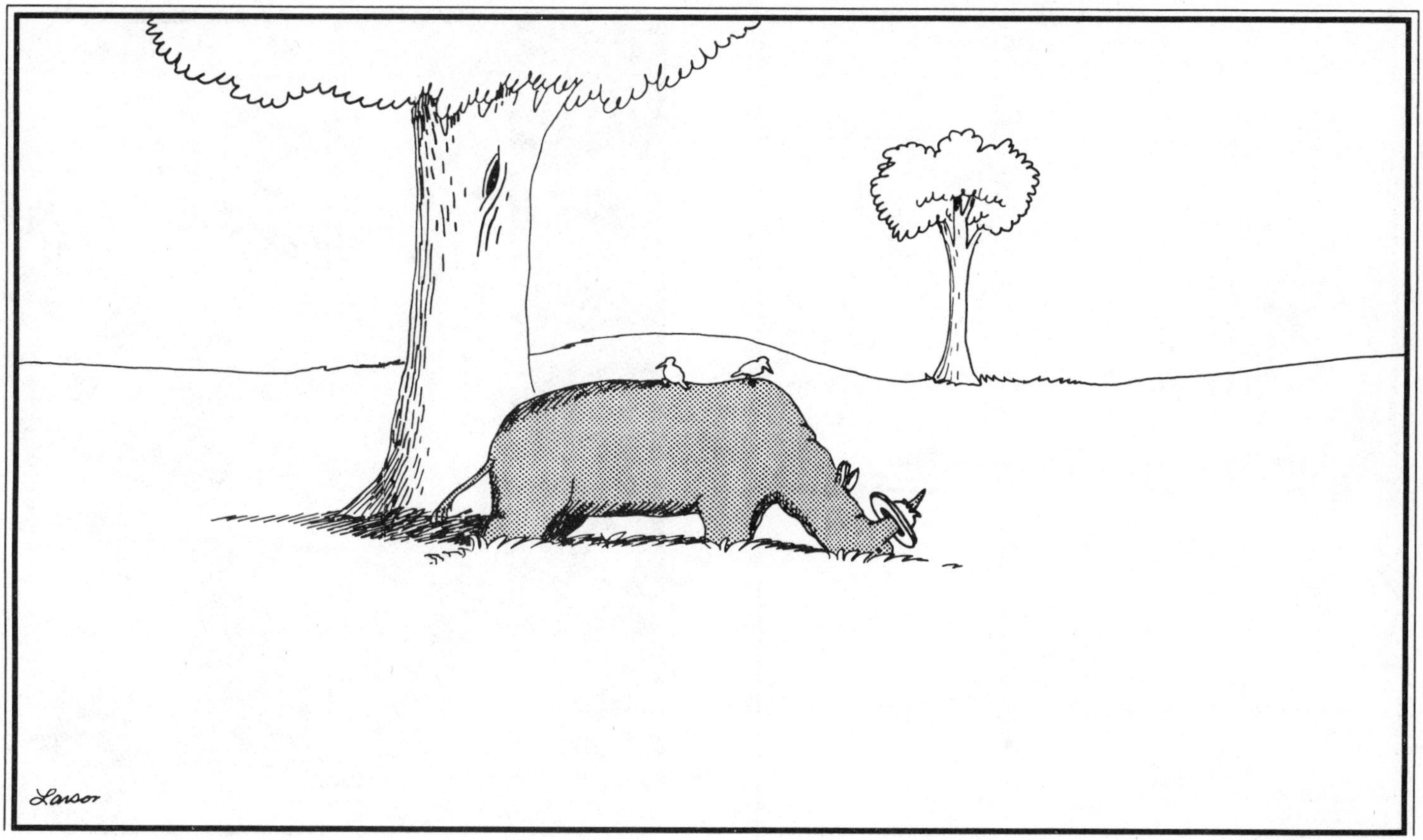
Larson

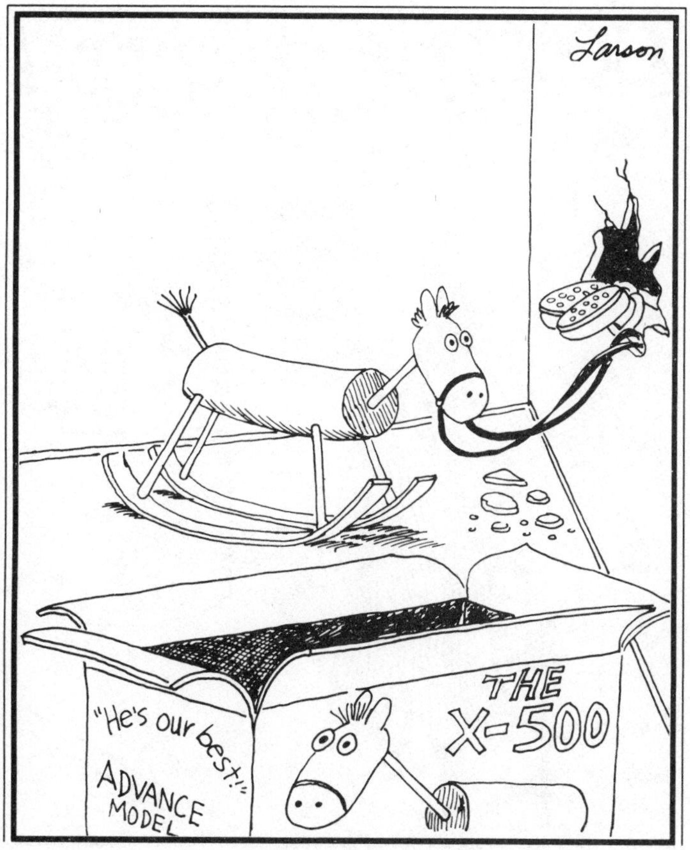
Larson
THE
X-500
"He's our best!"
ADVANCE
MODEL

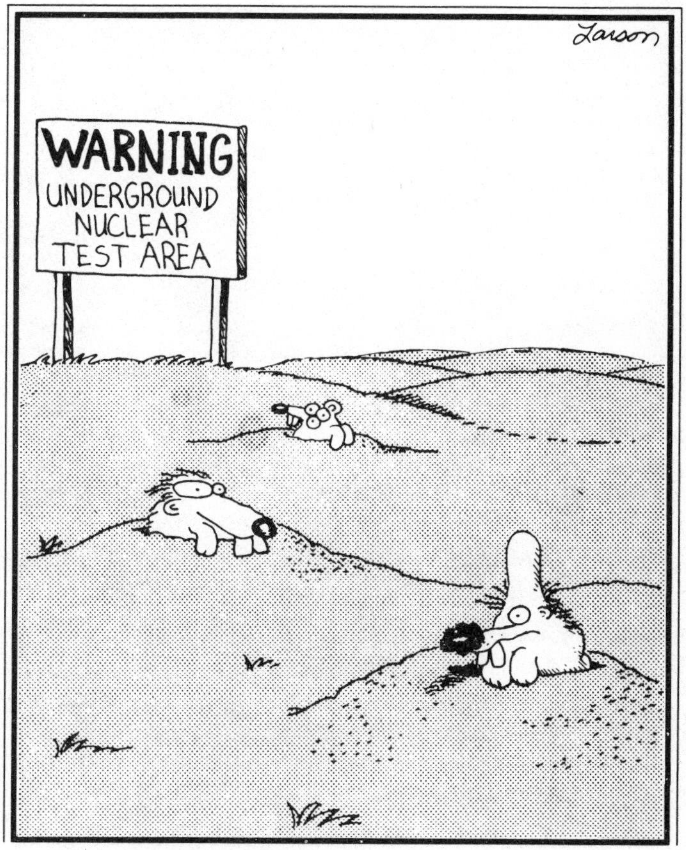
Larson
WARNING
UNDERGROUND
NUCLEAR
TEST AREA

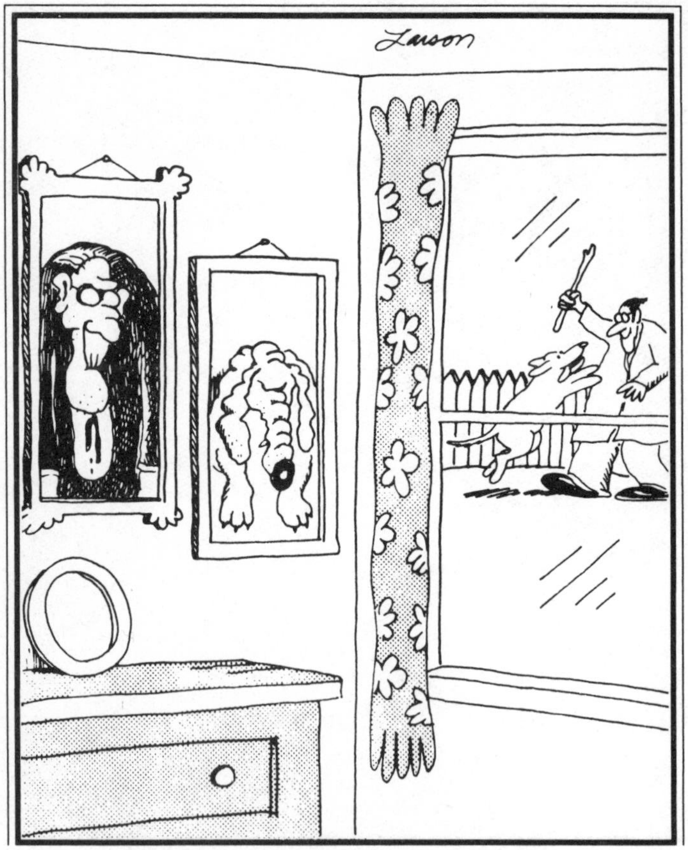
Larson

The Portrait of Dorian Gray and his dog

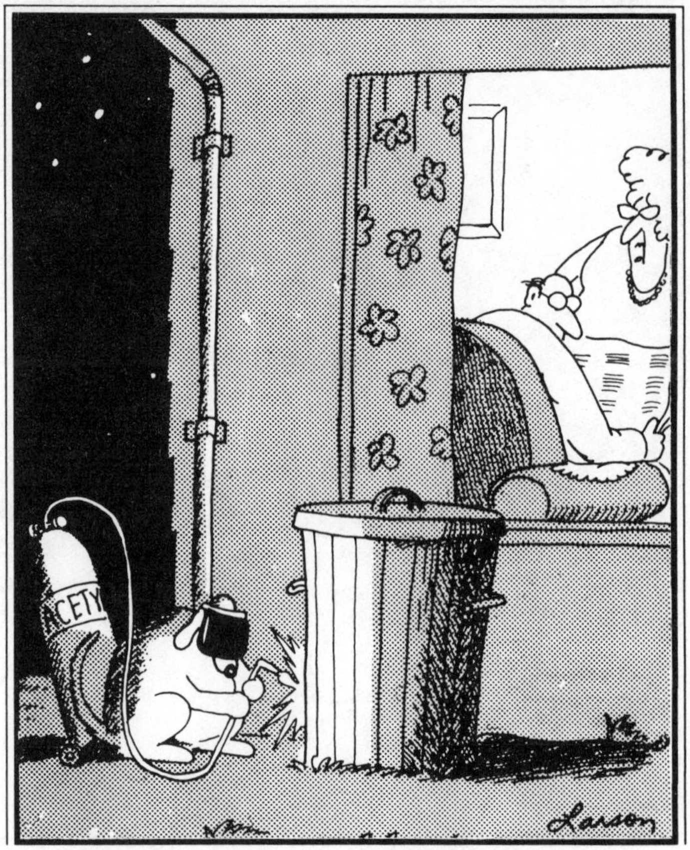
ACETY
Larson

"Vernon! That light! . . . The Jeffersons' dog is back!"

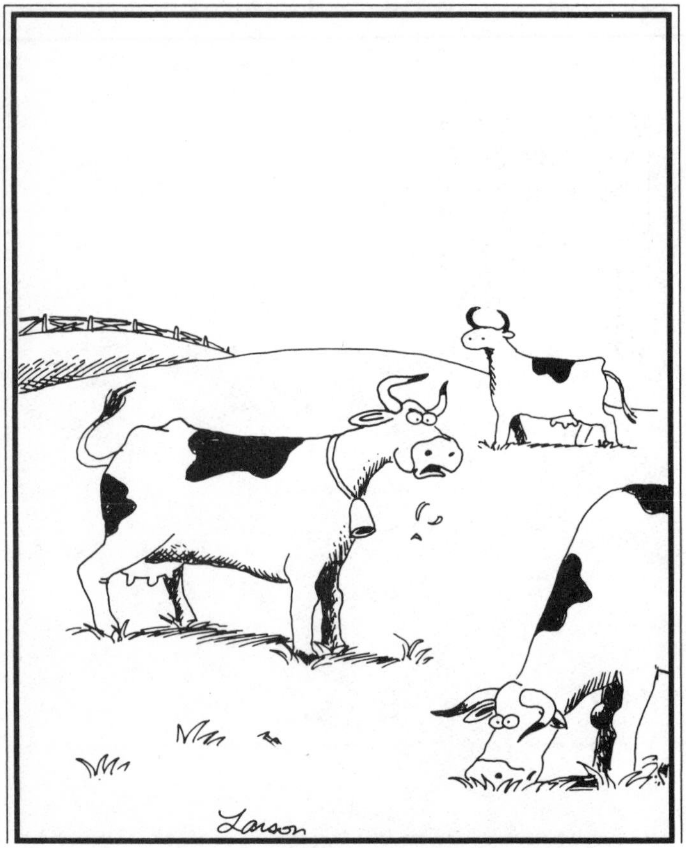
Larson

"Hey, wait a minute! This is grass! We've been eating grass!"

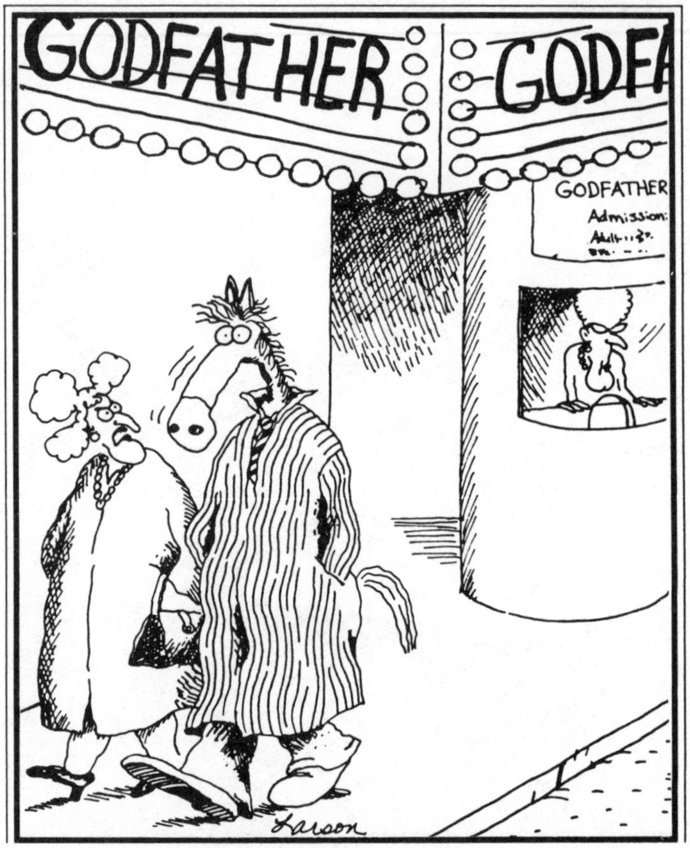
GODFATHER
GODFA
GODFATHER
Admission:
Larson

"Get a hold of yourself! . . . It was only a movie, for crying out loud!"

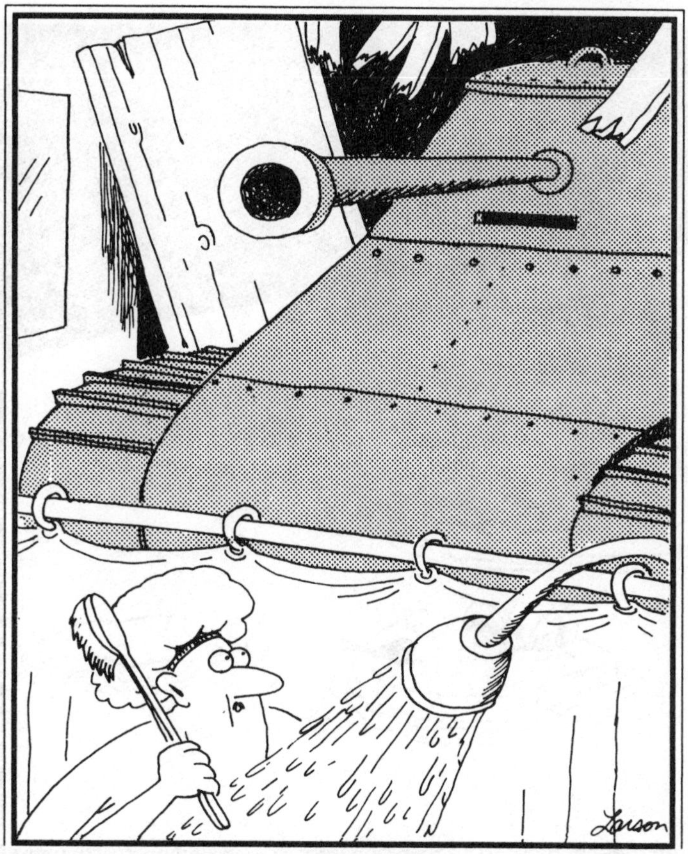
Larson

Psycho III

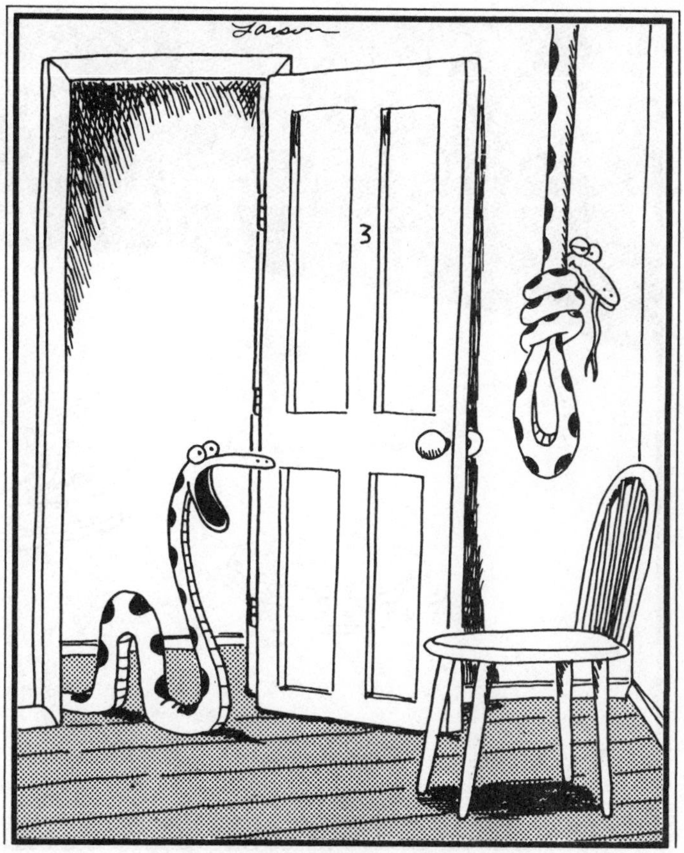
Larson
3

"Oh no, Elliott! Why? . . . Why? . . ."

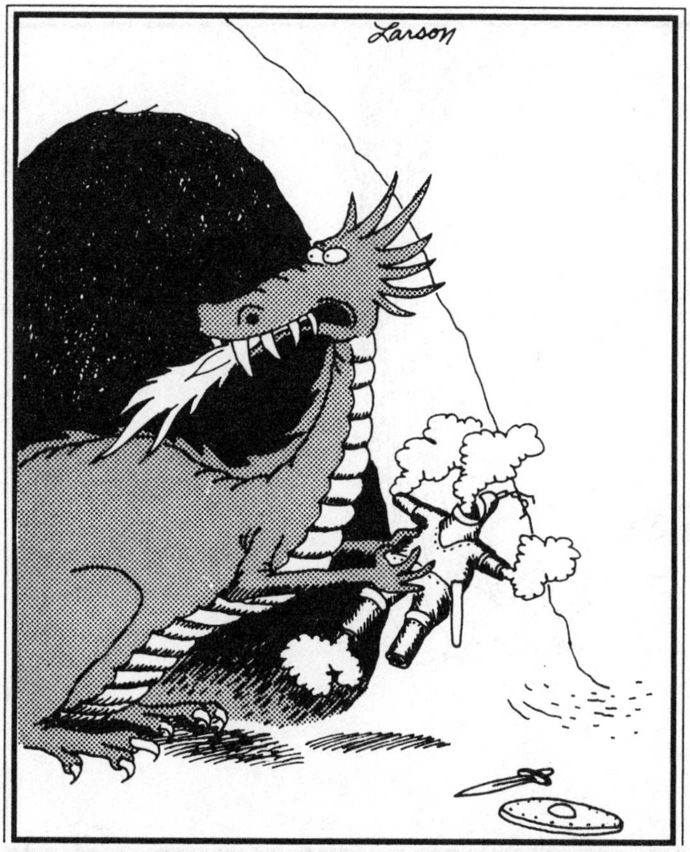
Larson

"Ooo! Ow! Blast it, Phyllis! . . . Hurry up with them hot pads!"

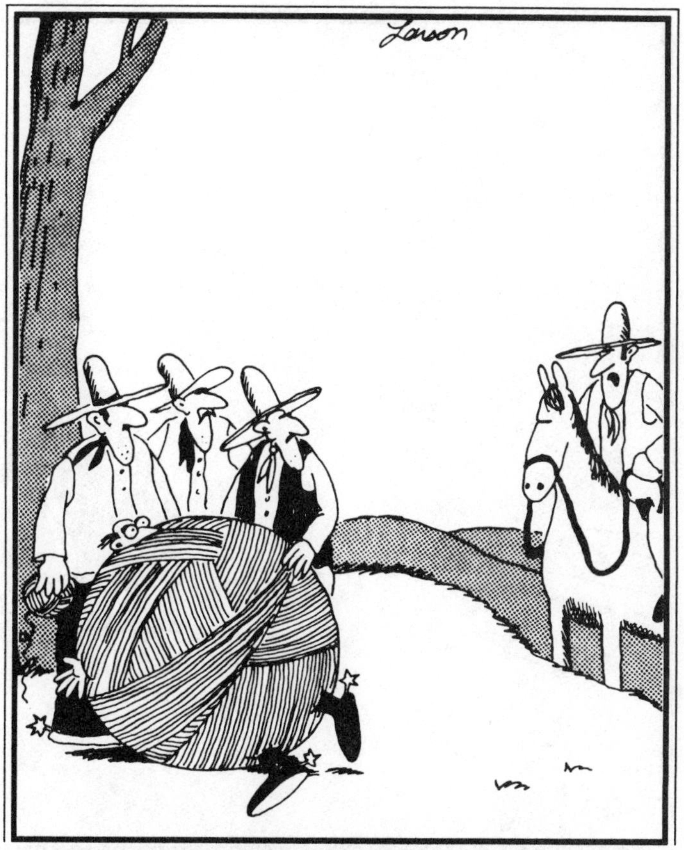
Larson

"Hang him, you idiots! Hang him! . . . 'String-him-up' is a figure of speech!"

"You imbecile! . . . We flew 12,000 miles for THIS?"

"I can't stand it . . . They're so CUTE when they sit like that."

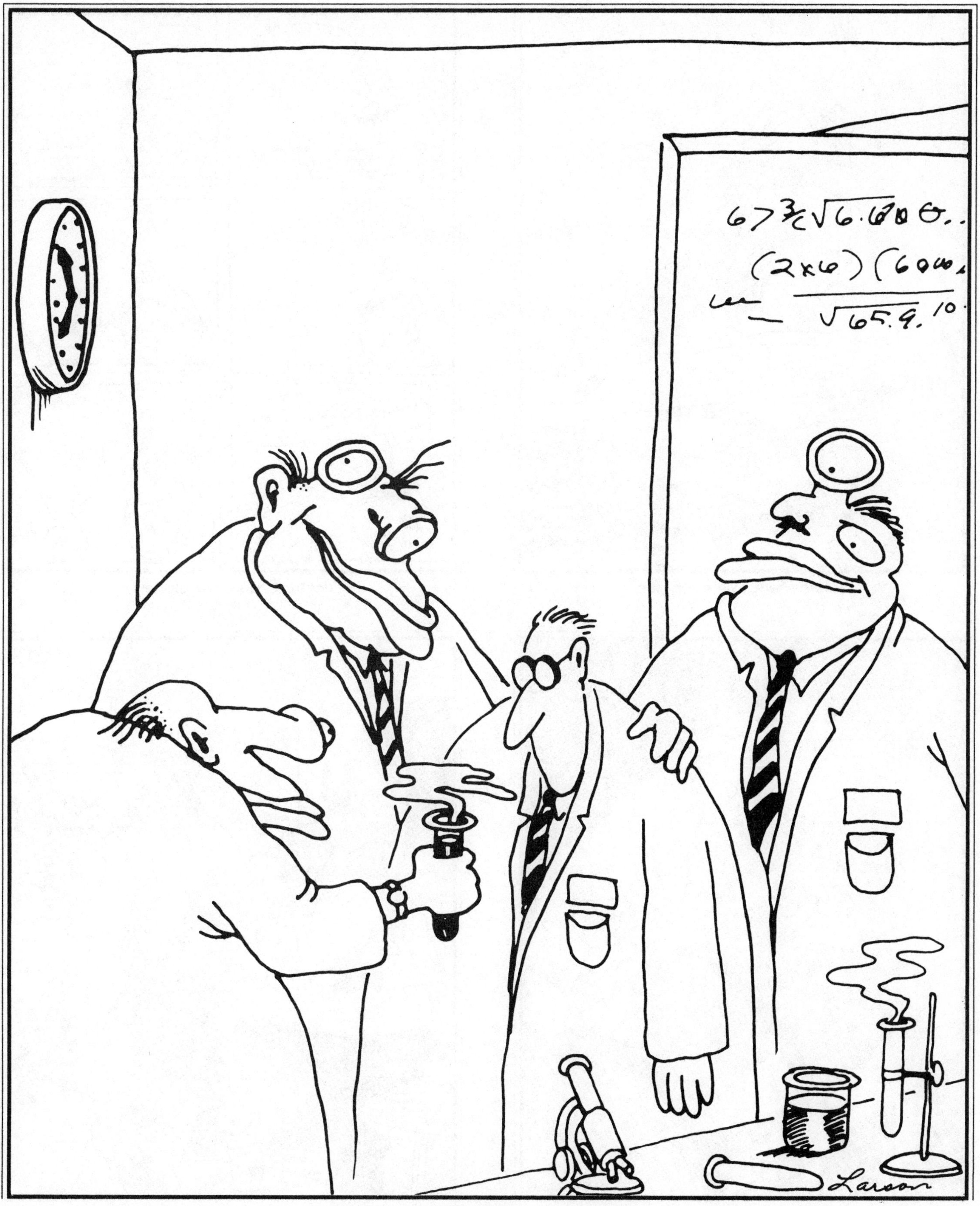
Larson

Laboratory peer pressure

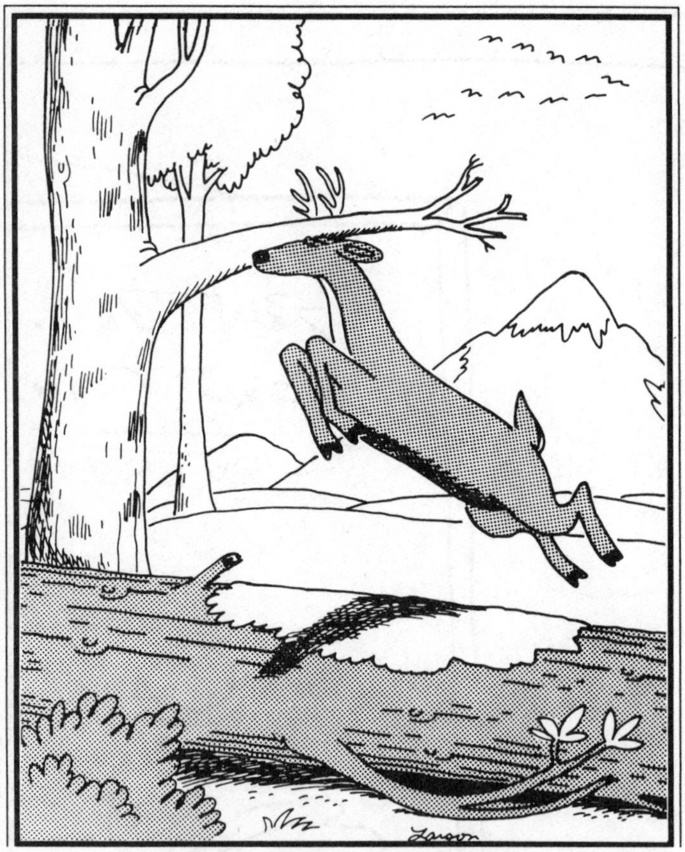
Larson

Nature scenes we rarely see

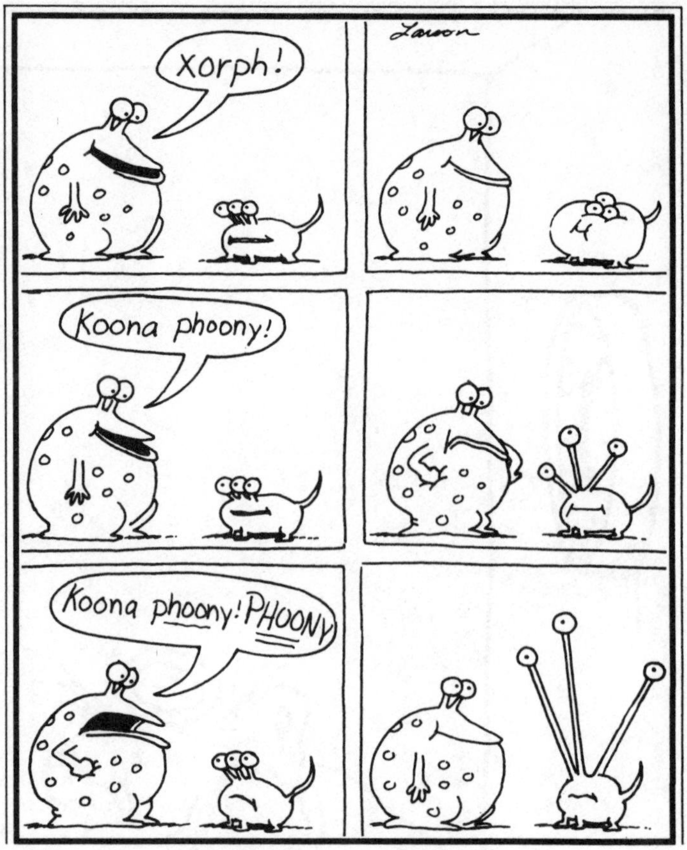
Larson
Xorph!
Koona phoony!
Koona phoony! PHOONY

Pet tricks on other planets

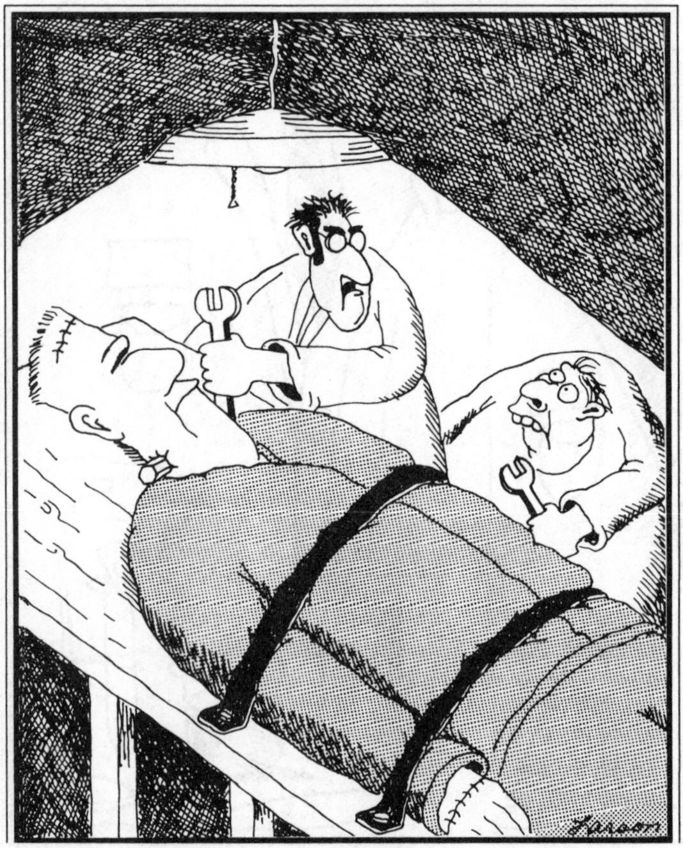
Larson

"Fool! This is an eleven-sixteenths . . . I asked for a five-eighths!"

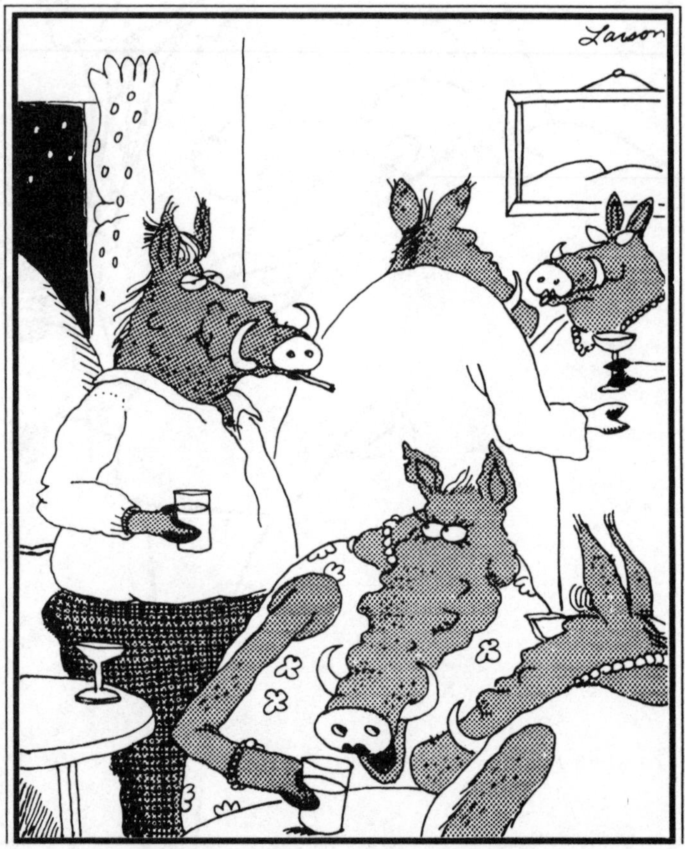
Larson

"Well, look who's here . . . God's gift to wart hogs."

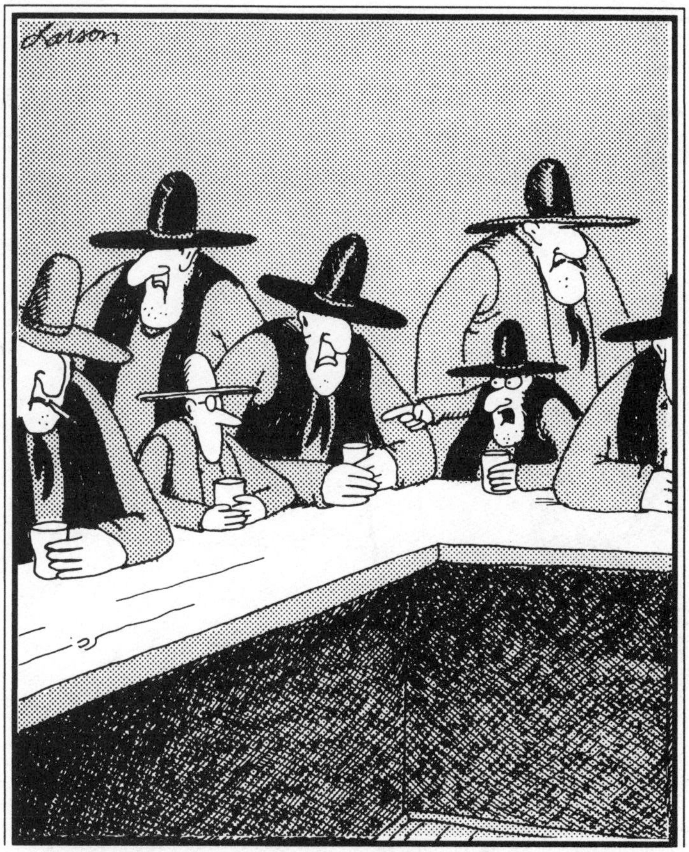
Larson

"Hey! You! . . . Yeah, that's right! I'm talkin' to YOU!"

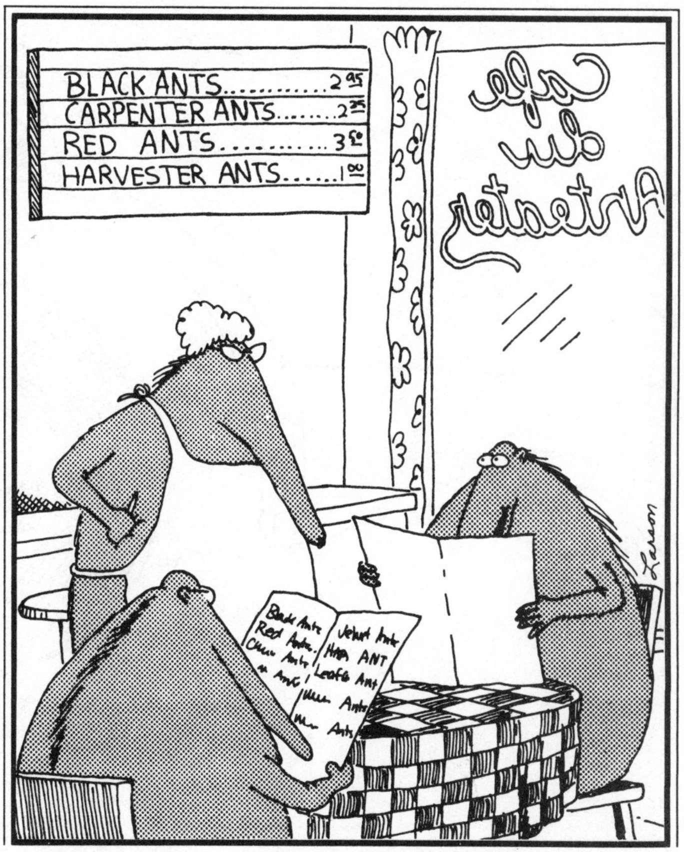
BLACK ANTS..........2.95
CARPENTER ANTS........2.25
RED ANTS............3.50
HARVESTER ANTS......1.00
Cafe du Anteater
Larson

"Hmmmmm . . . Are the red ants right off the hill?"

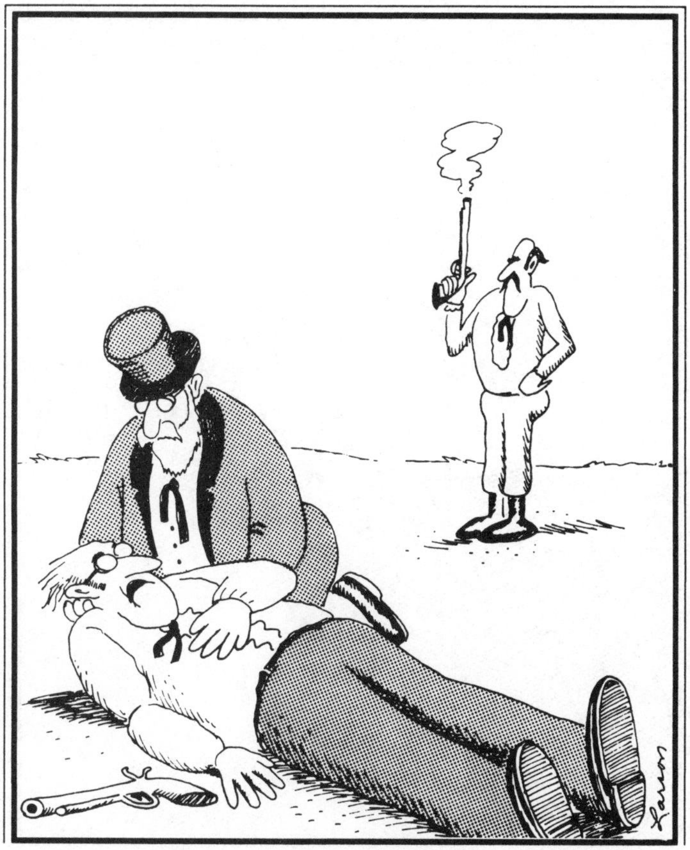
Larson

"I . . . could . . . have . . . sworn . . . you . . . said . . . eleven . . . steps."

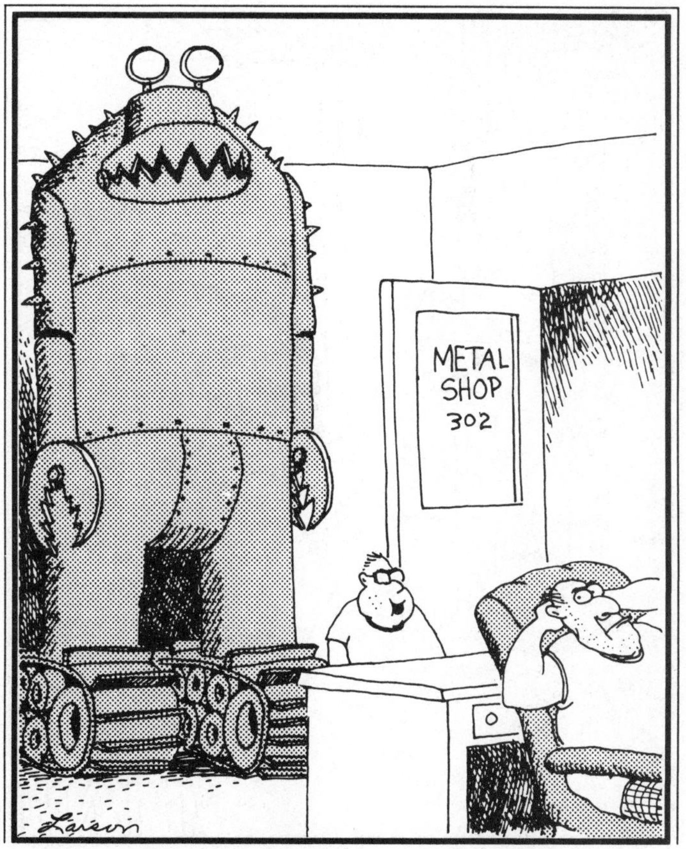
METAL SHOP 302
Larson

"My project's ready for grading, Mr. Big Nose . . . Hey! I'm talkin' to YOU, squidbrain!"

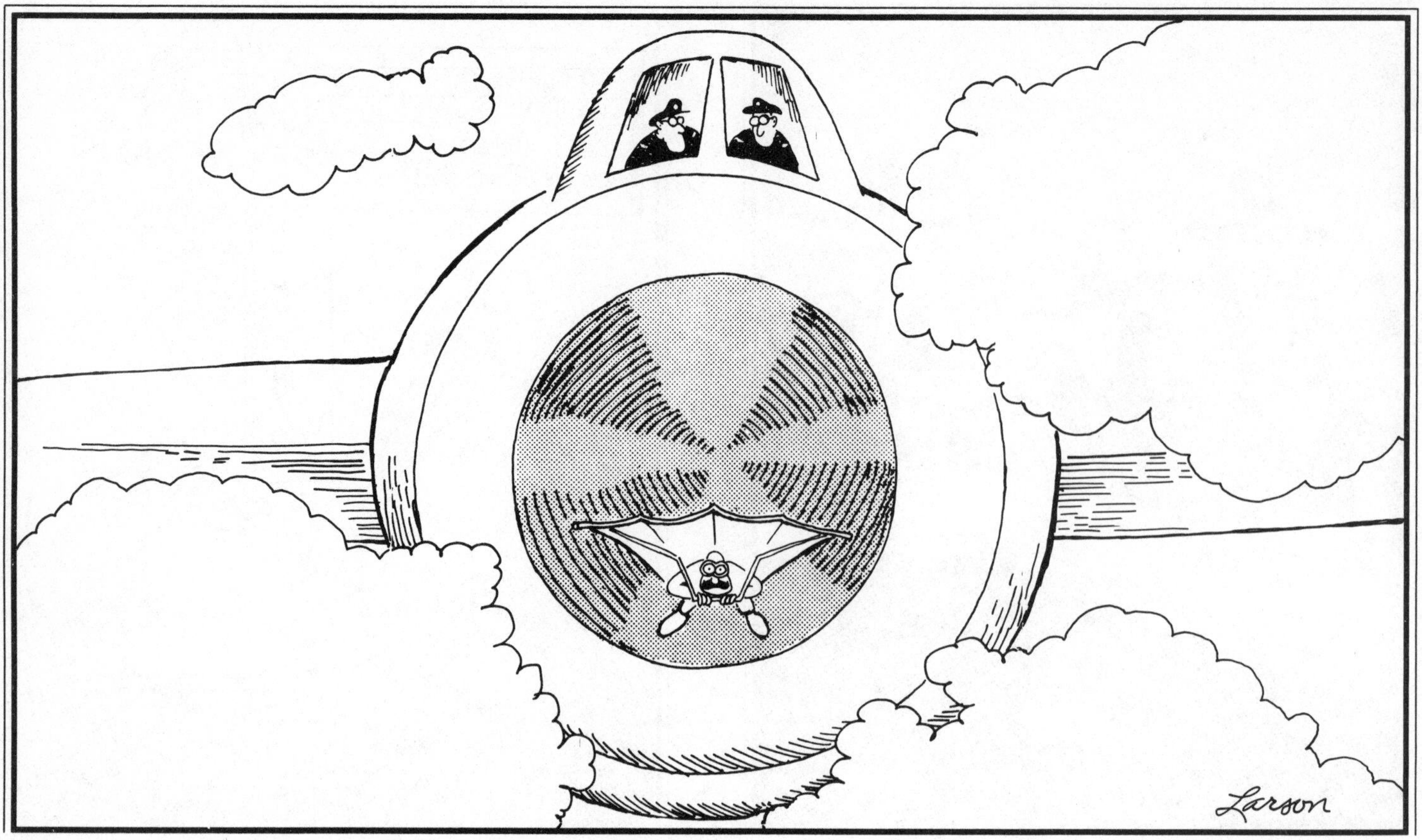
Larson

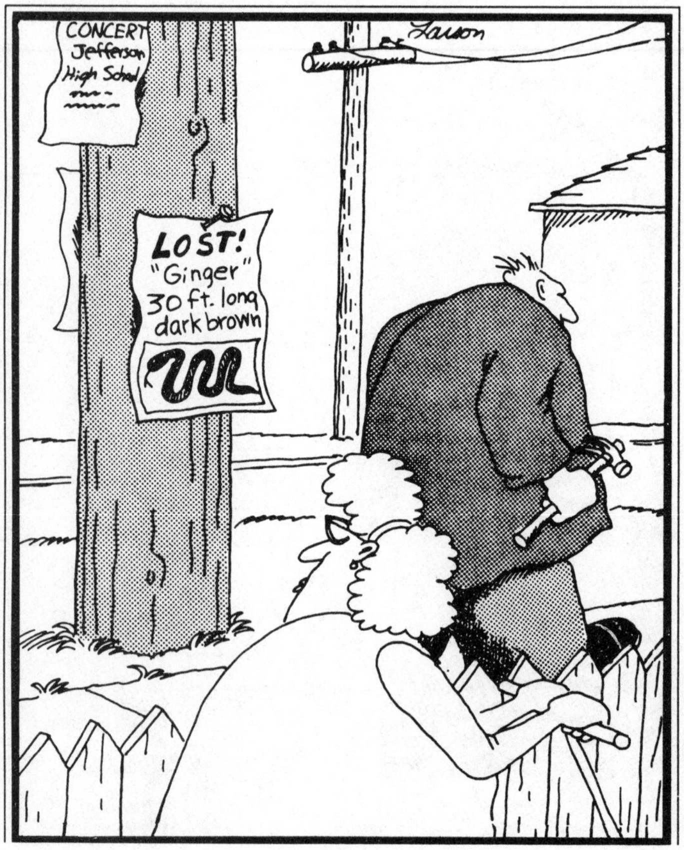
CONCERT
Jefferson
High School
LOST!
"Ginger"
30 ft. long
dark brown
Larson

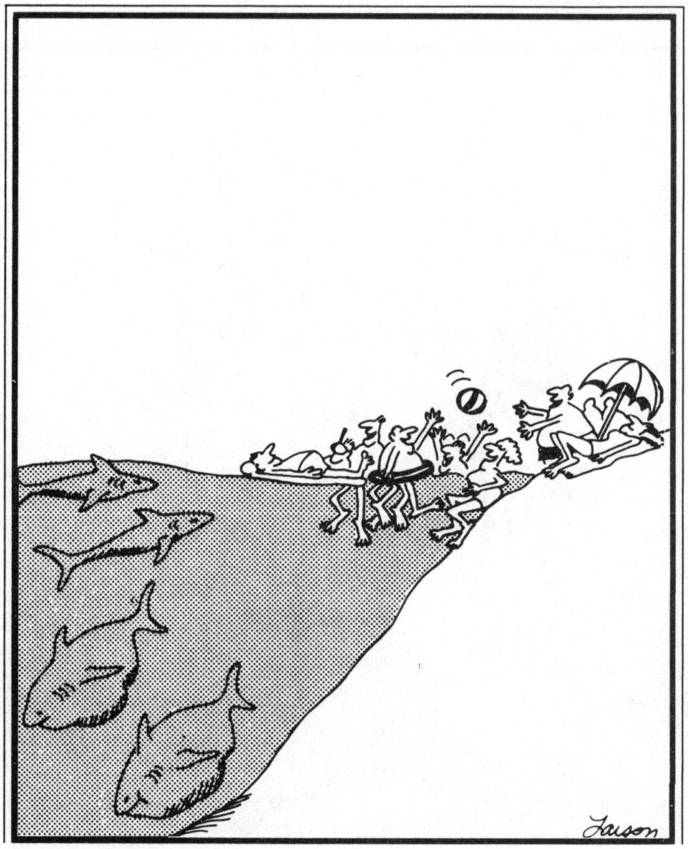
Larson

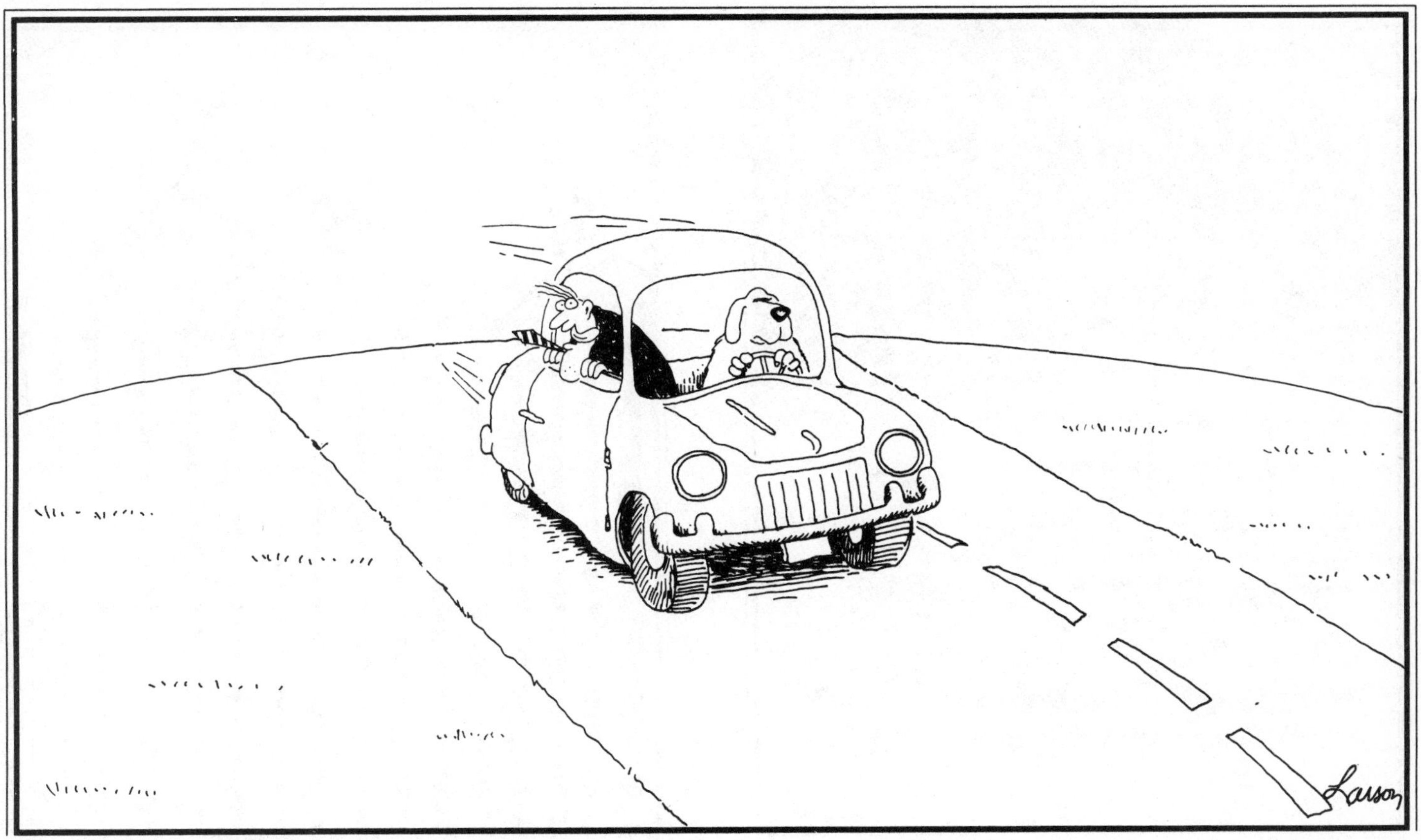
Larson

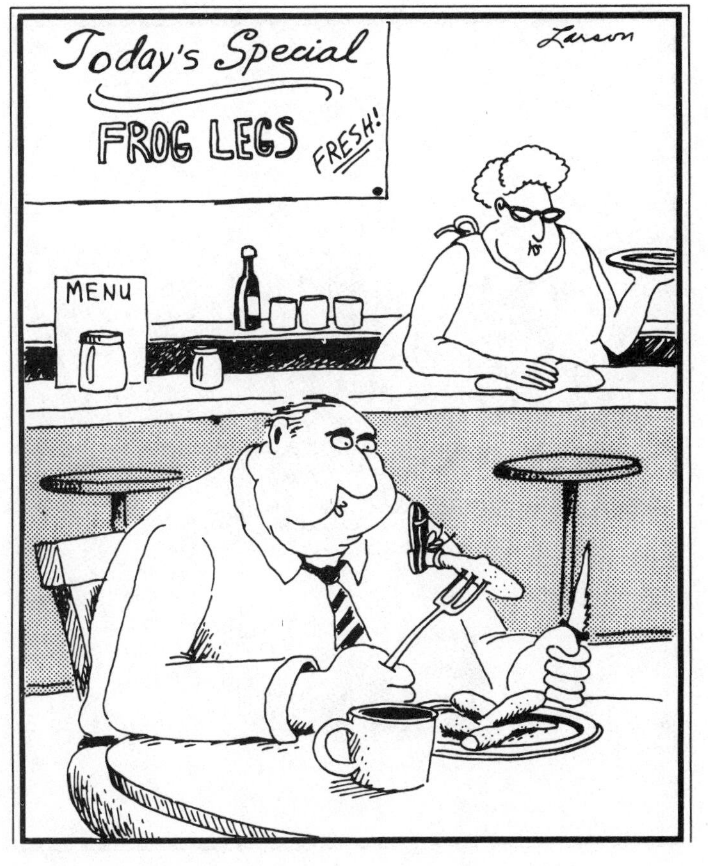
Today's Special
FROG LEGS
FRESH!
MENU
Larson

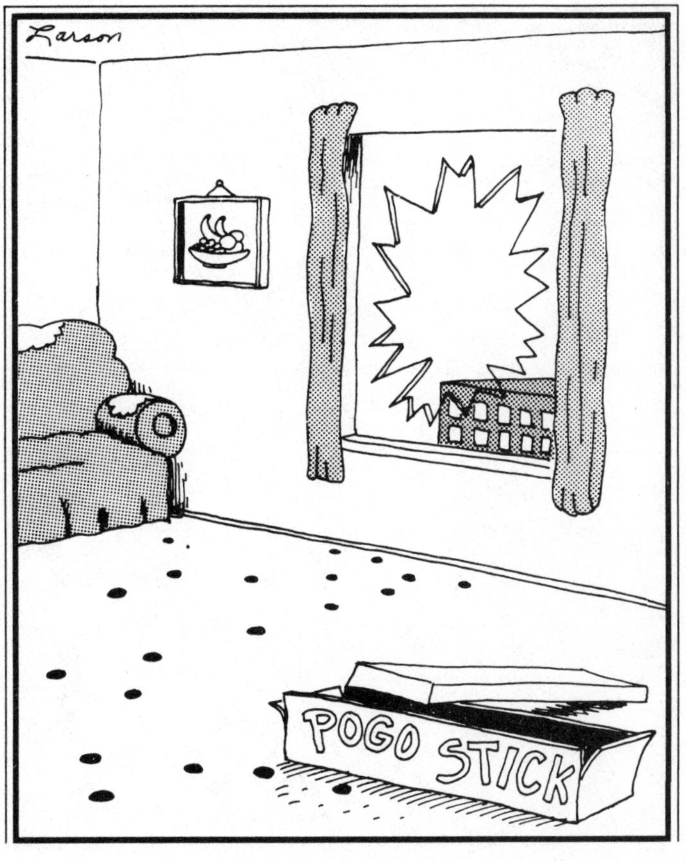
Larson
POGO STICK

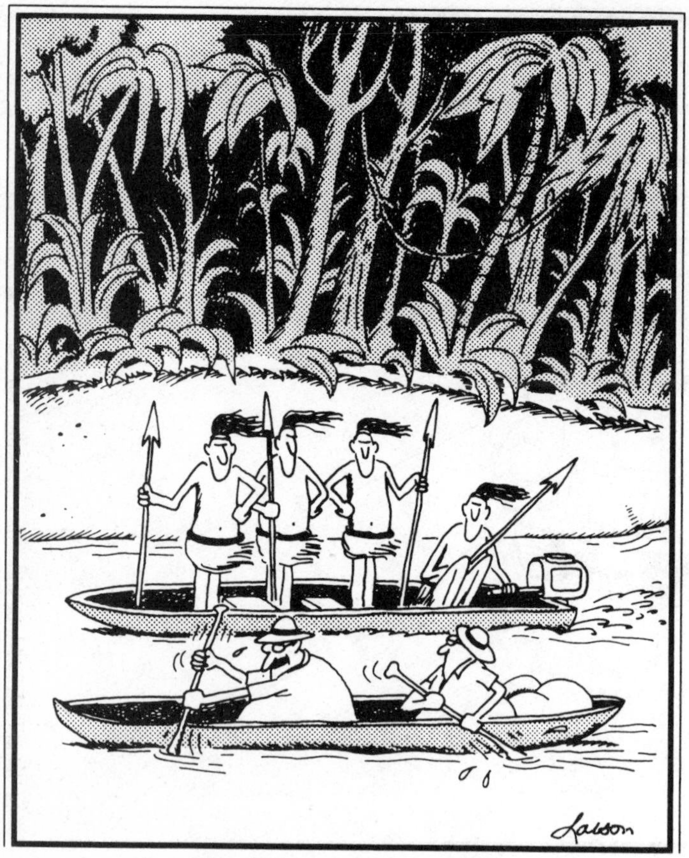

"Are they gaining, Huxley?"

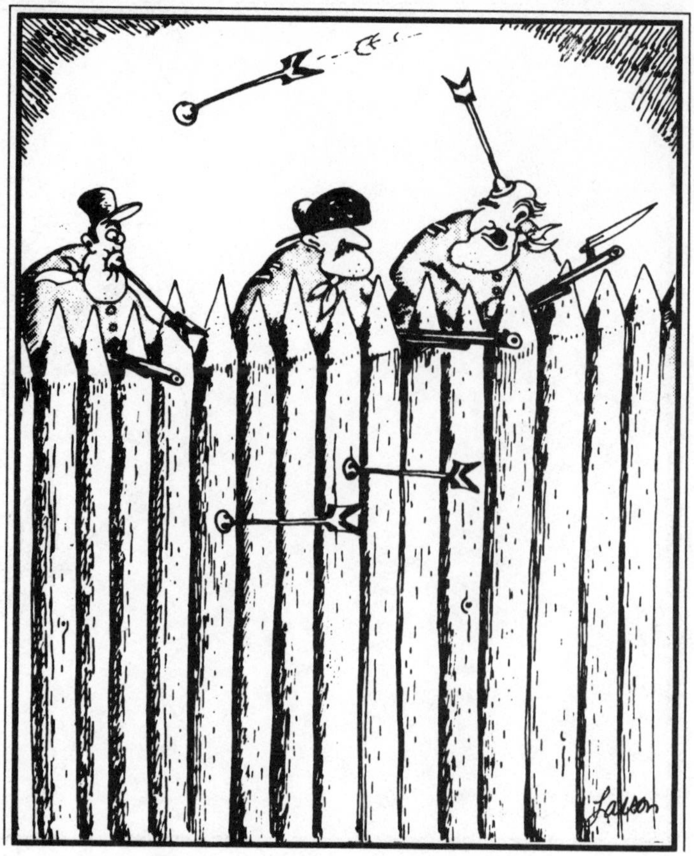

"Gad! . . . Not *these* Indians again!"

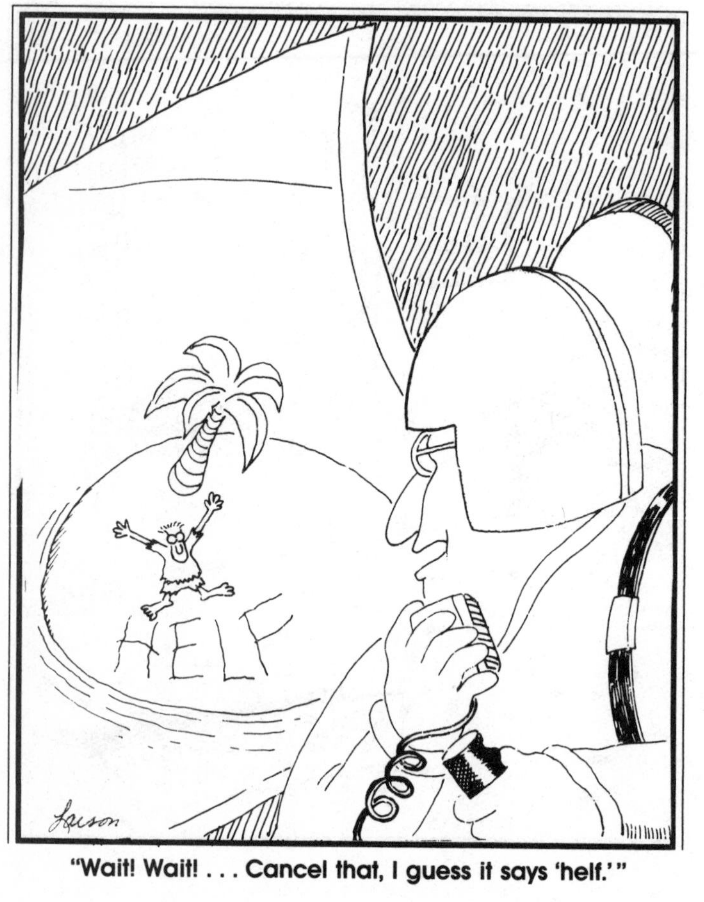
HELP

"Wait! Wait! . . . Cancel that, I guess it says 'helf.' "

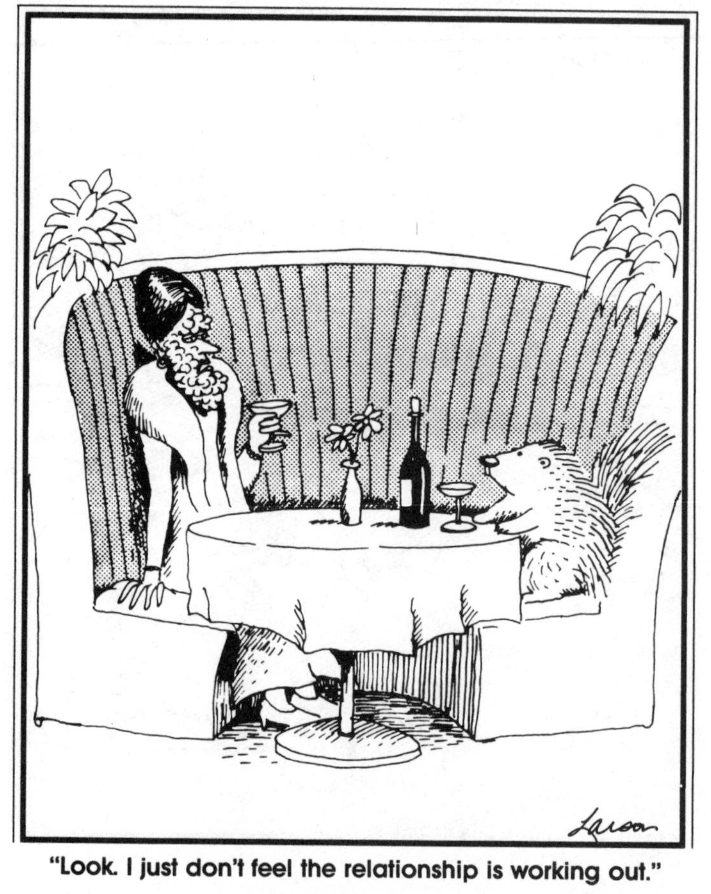

"Look. I just don't feel the relationship is working out."

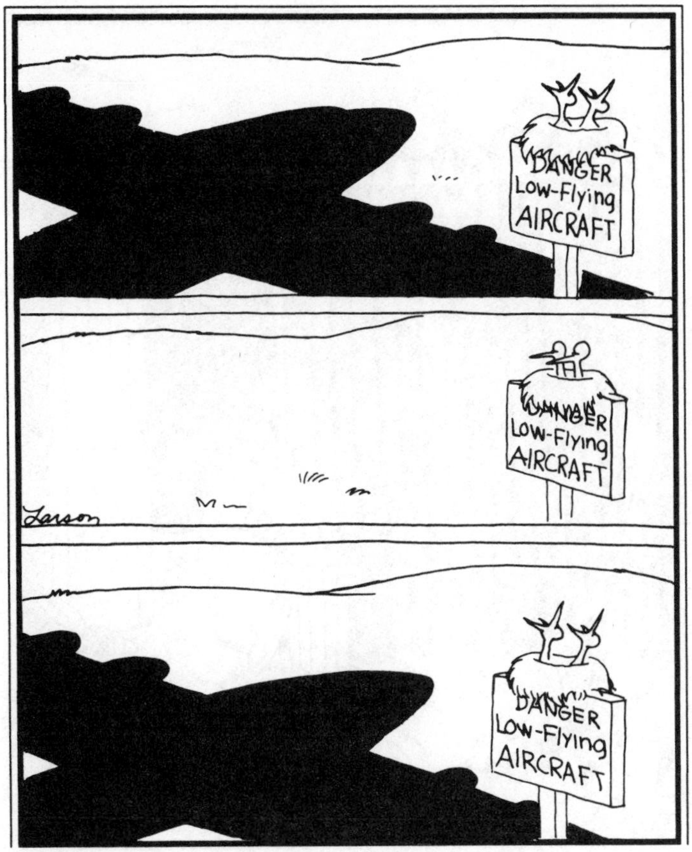
DANGER
Low-Flying
AIRCRAFT
DANGER
Low-Flying
AIRCRAFT
DANGER
Low-Flying
AIRCRAFT

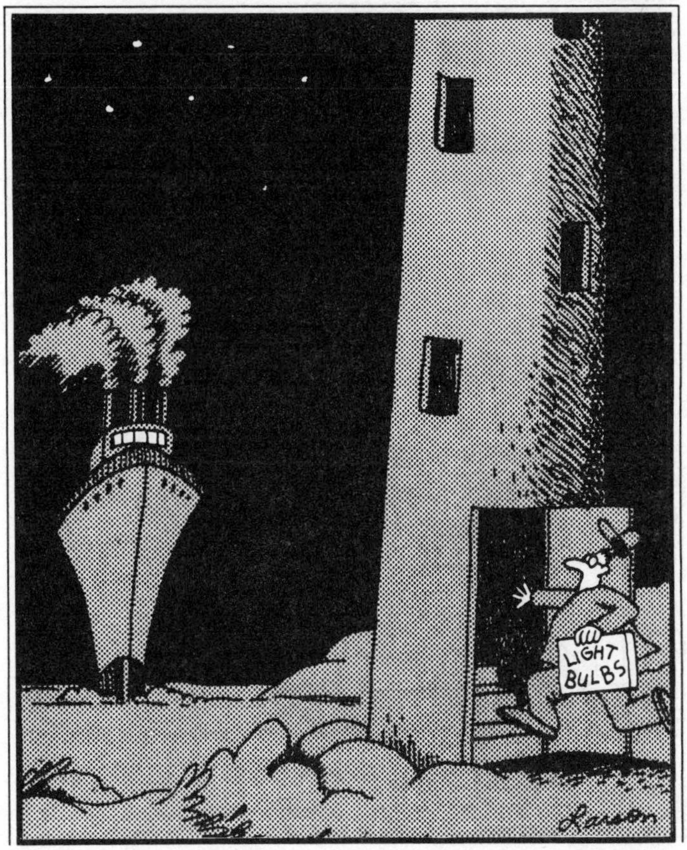
LIGHT
BULBS

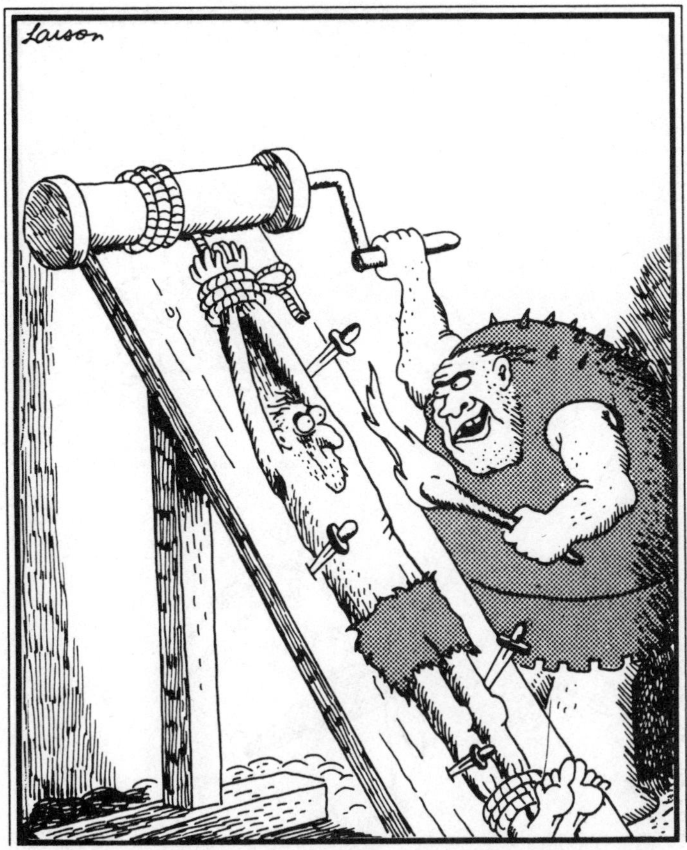

"Still won't talk, huh? . . . Okay, no more Mr. Nice Guy."

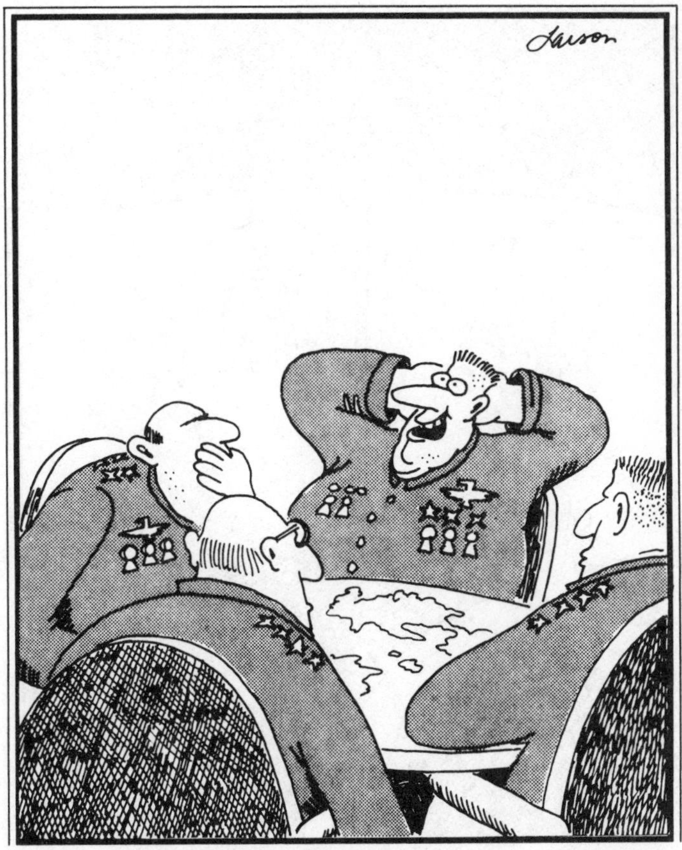

"On the other hand, gentlemen, what if we gave a war and EVERYBODY came?"

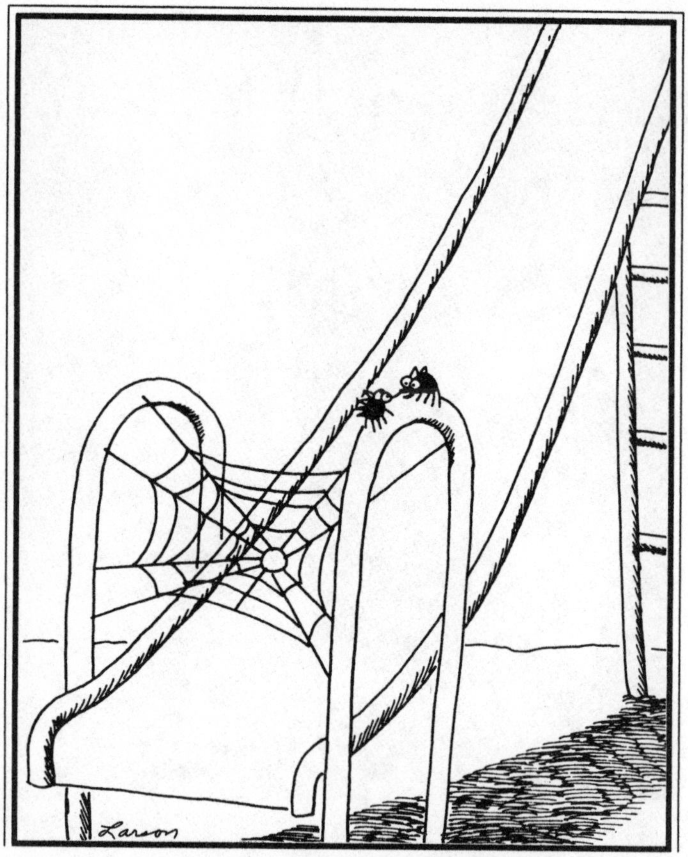
Larson

"If we pull this off, we'll eat like kings."

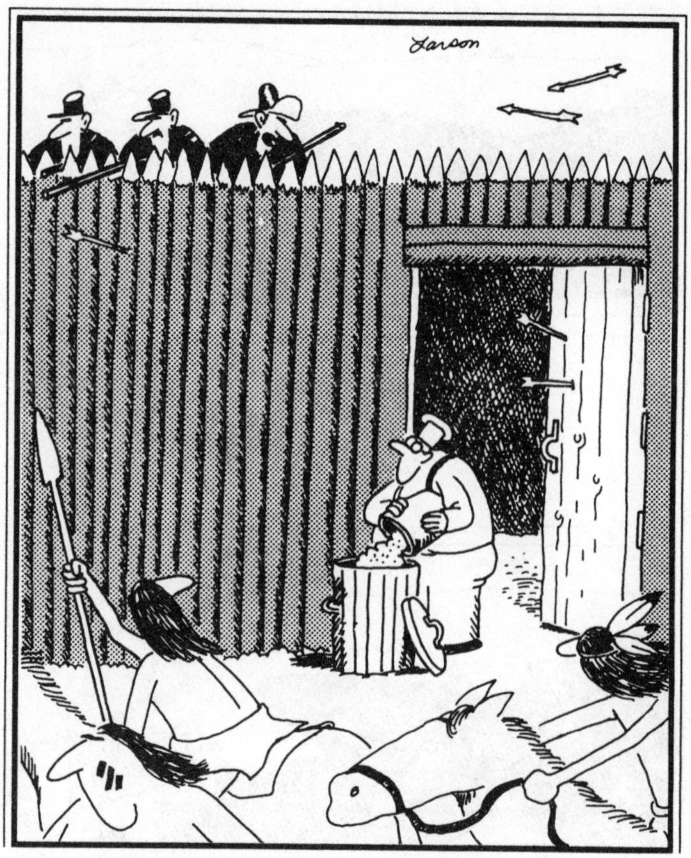
Larson

"Fletcher, you fool! . . . The gate! The gate!"

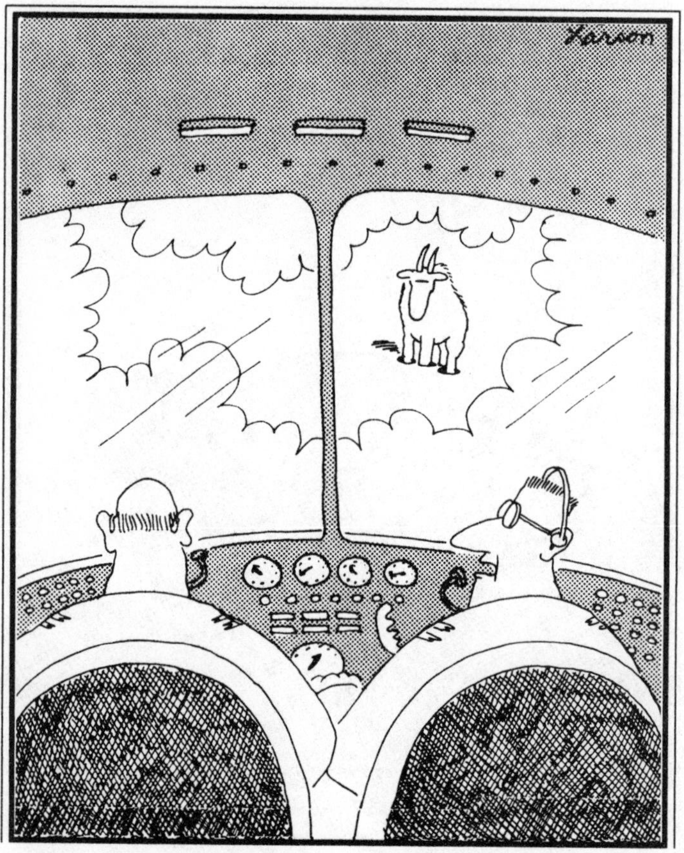
Larson

"Say . . . What's a mountain goat doing way up here in a cloud bank?"

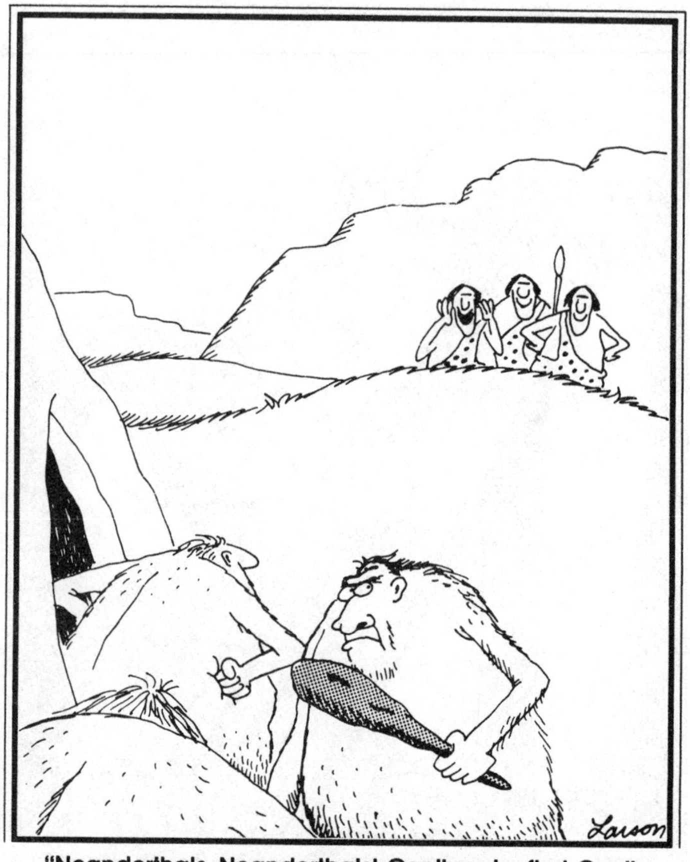
Larson

"Neanderthals, Neanderthals! Can't make fire! Can't make spear! Nyah, nyah, nyah . . . !"

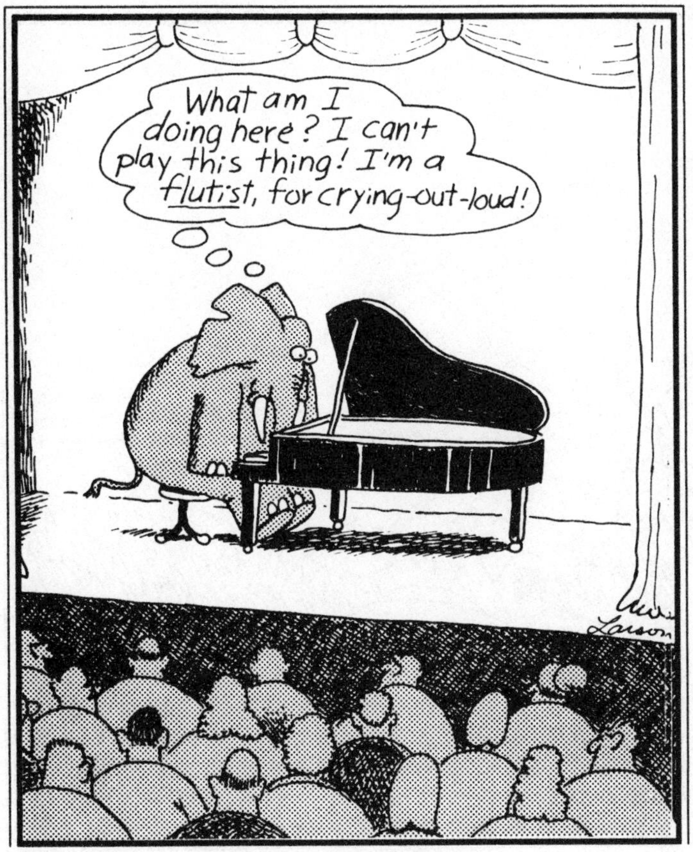
What am I doing here? I can't play this thing! I'm a flutist, for crying-out-loud!
Larson

The elephant's nightmare

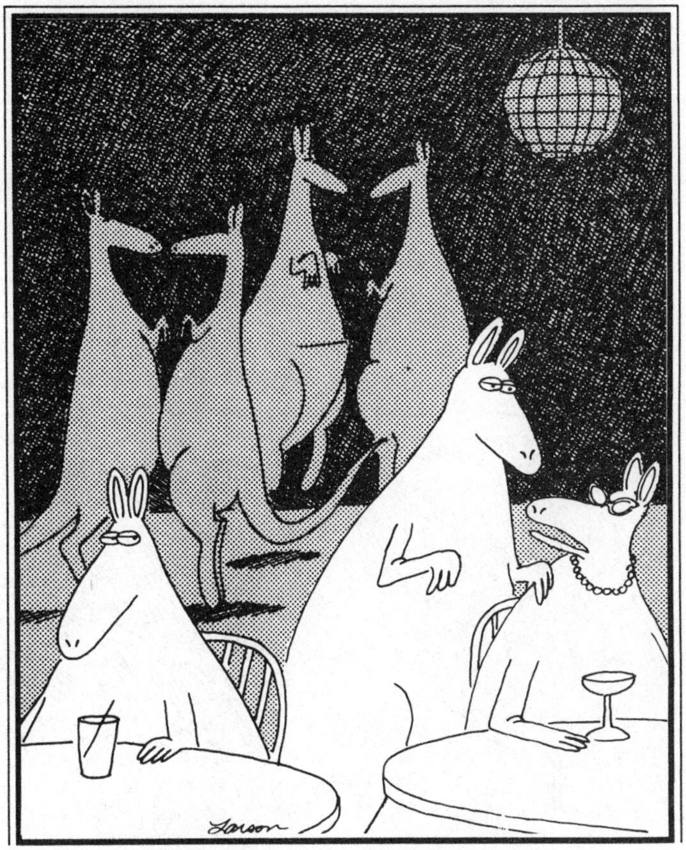
Larson

"No, thank you . . . I don't jump."

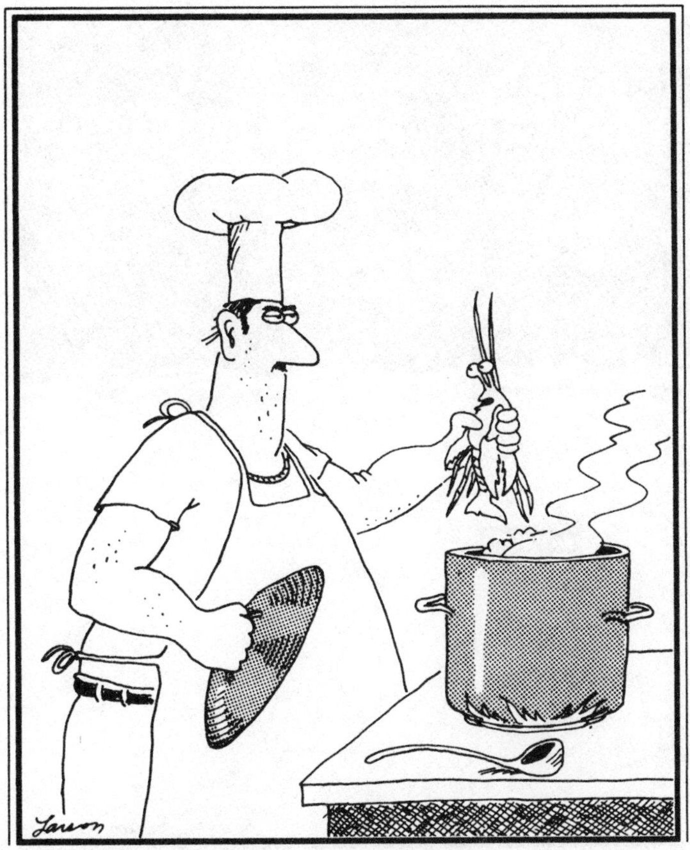
Larson

"Three wishes? Did I say three wishes? . . . Shoot! I'll grant you FOUR wishes."

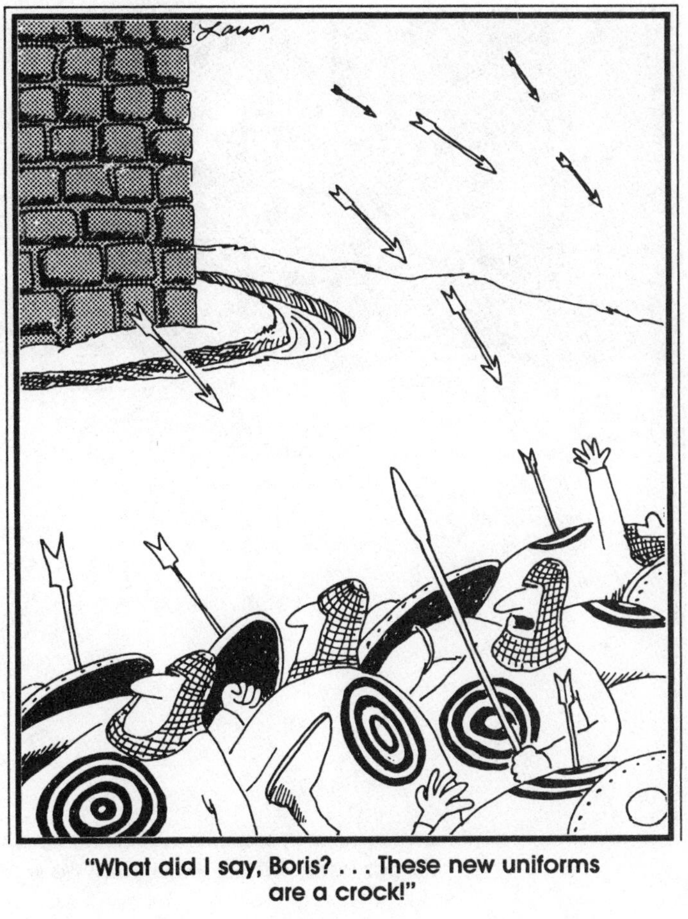
Larson

"What did I say, Boris? . . . These new uniforms are a crock!"

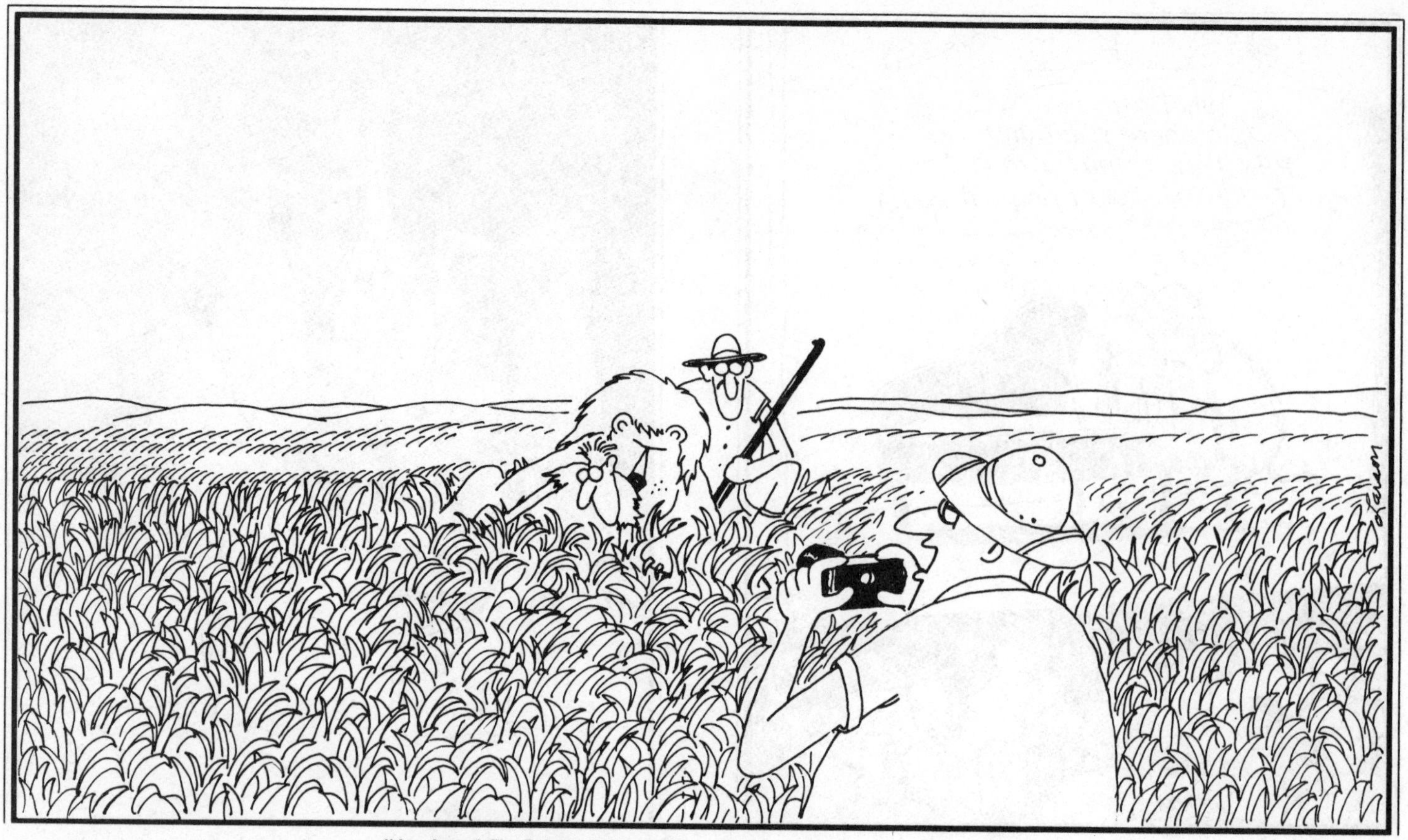

"Andrew! Fix Edgar's head! . . . It's not facing the camera!"

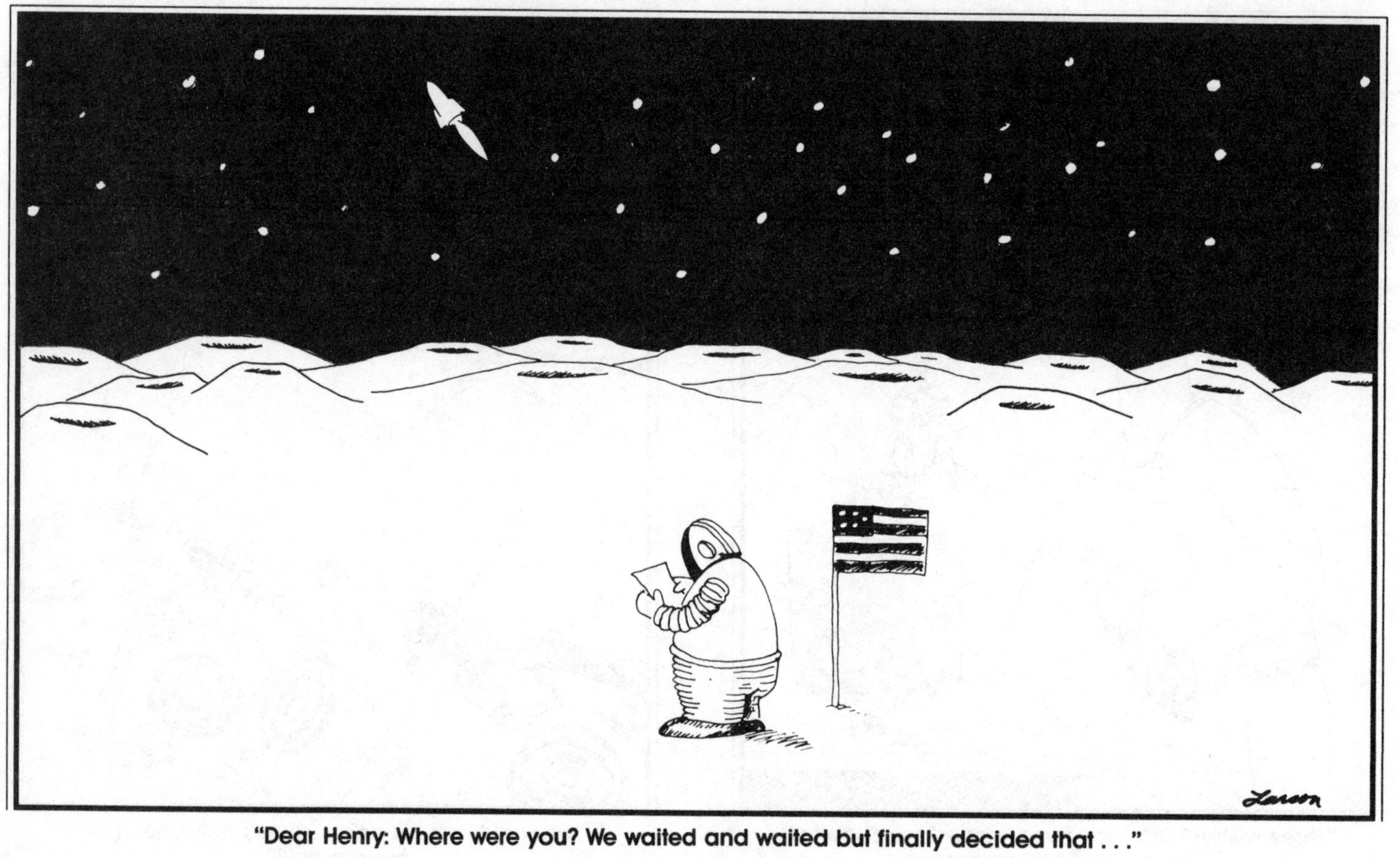
Larson

"Dear Henry: Where were you? We waited and waited but finally decided that . . ."

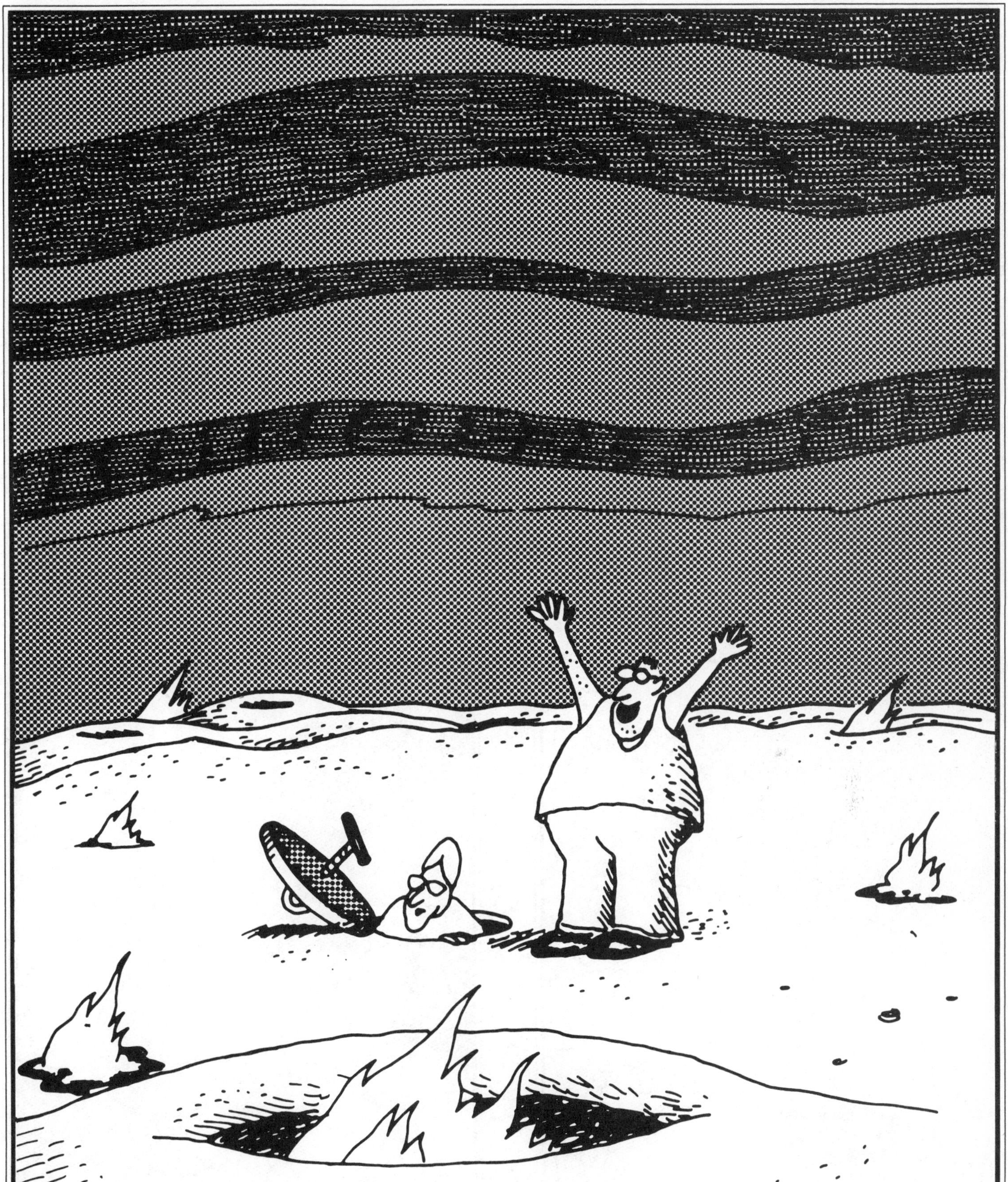
Larson

"Thank God, Sylvia! We're alive!"

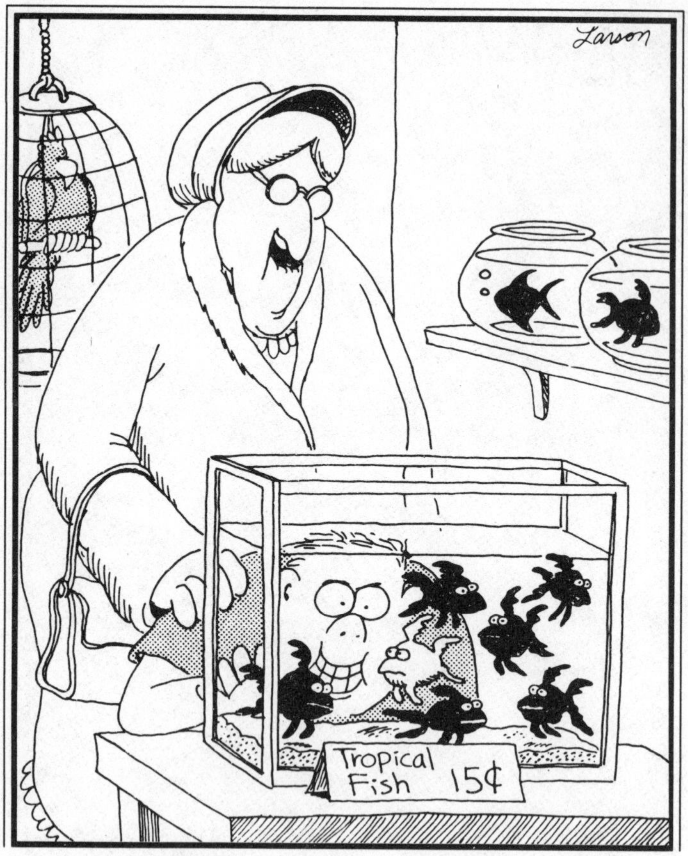
Larson
Tropical
Fish 15¢

"Well, little Ahab . . . Which one is it going to be?"

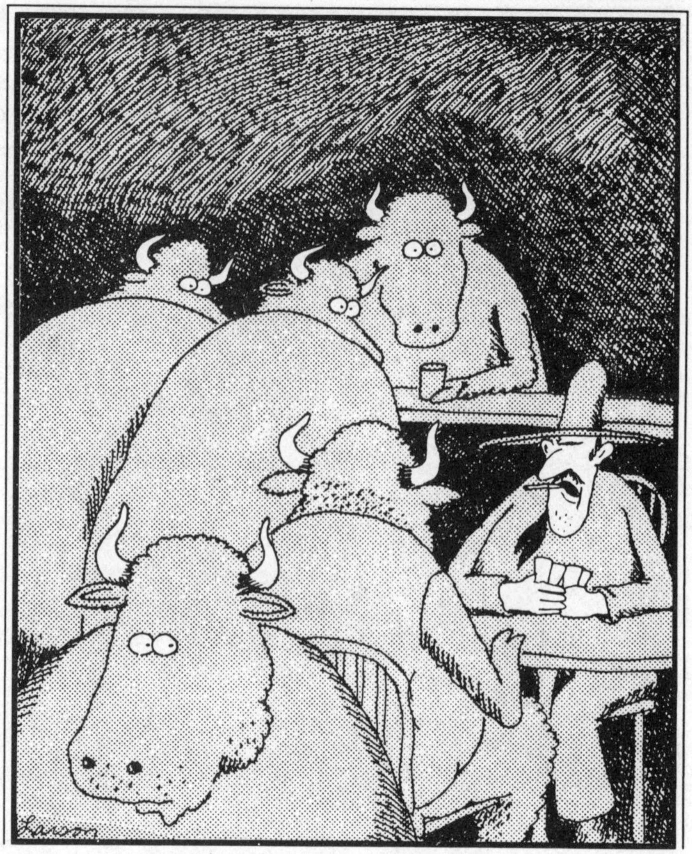
Larson

"The name is Bill . . . Buffalo Bill."

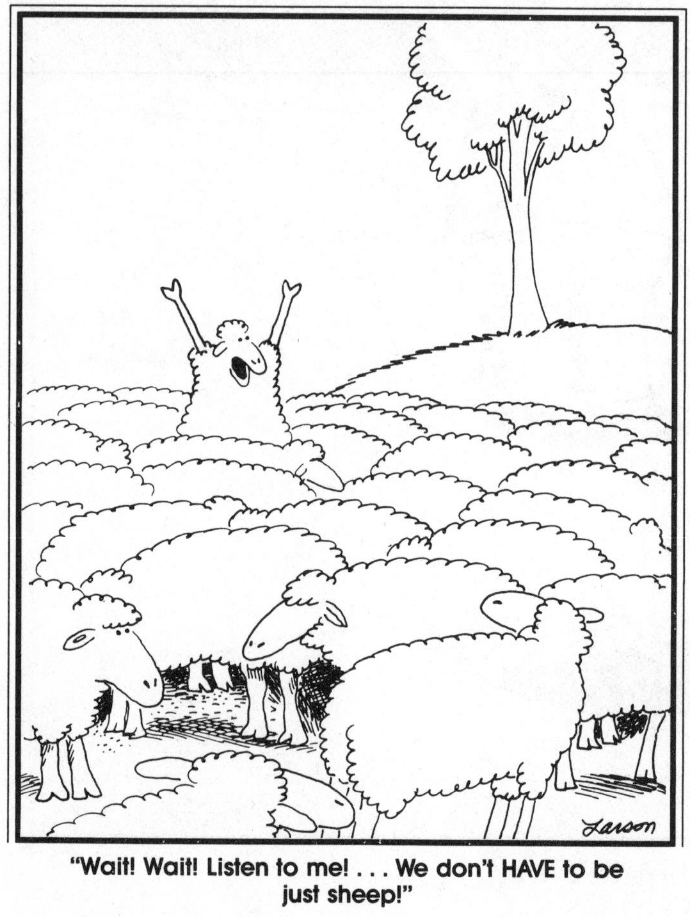
Larson

"Wait! Wait! Listen to me! . . . We don't HAVE to be just sheep!"

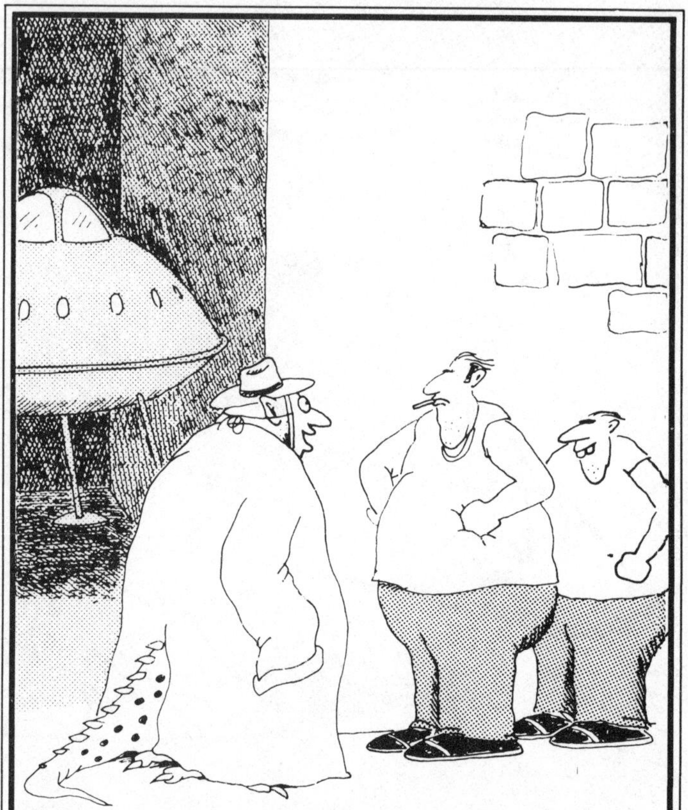
Larson

"Why . . . yes . . . thank . . . you . . . I . . . would . . . like . . . a . . . knuckle . . . sandwich."

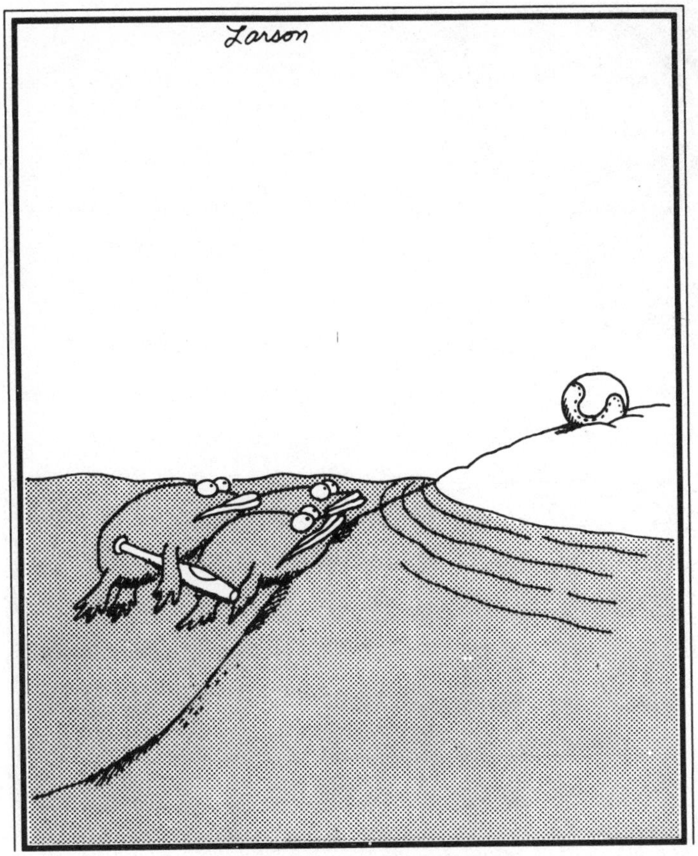
Larson

Great moments in evolution

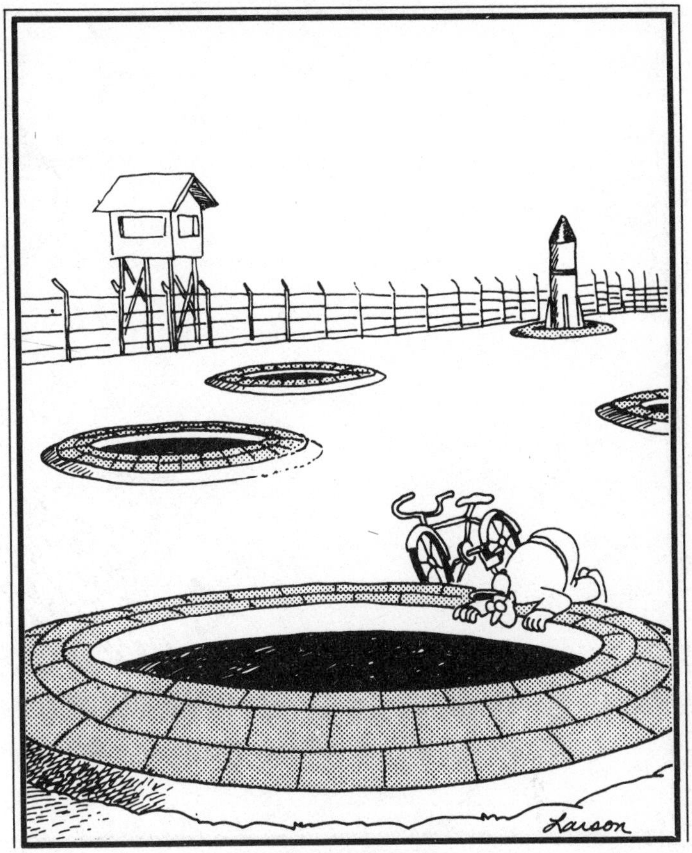
Larson

Never, never do this.

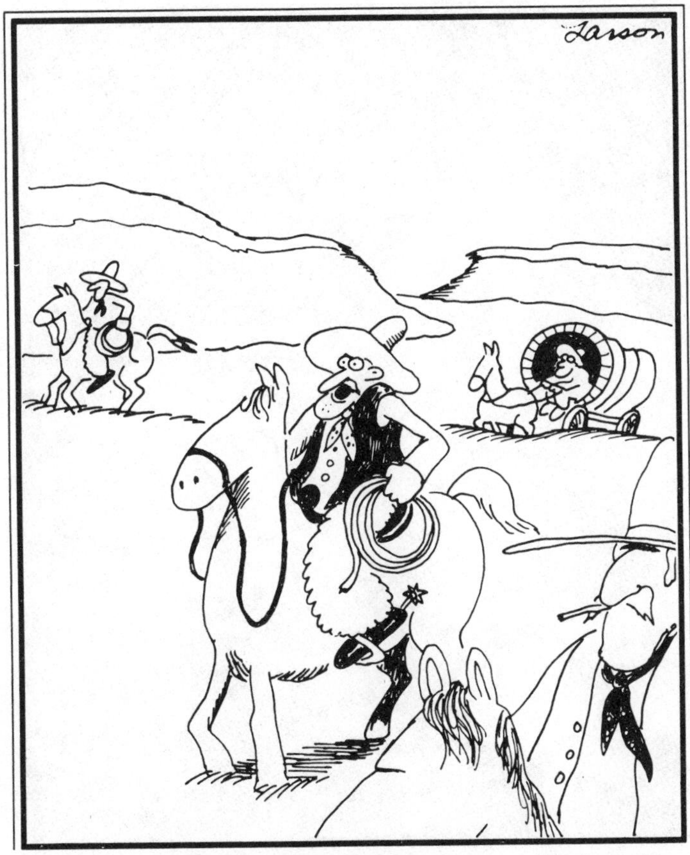
Larson

"Say . . . Wait just a dang minute, here . . . We forgot the cattle!"

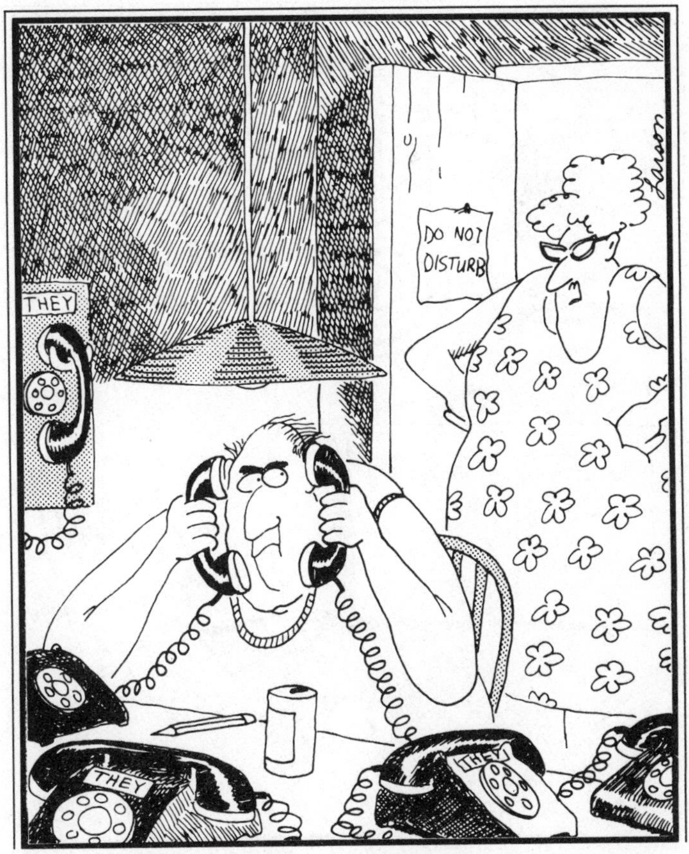
Larson
DO NOT DISTURB
THEY
THEY
THEY

"YOU, Bernie Horowitz? . . . So YOU'RE the 'they' in 'that's what they say'?"

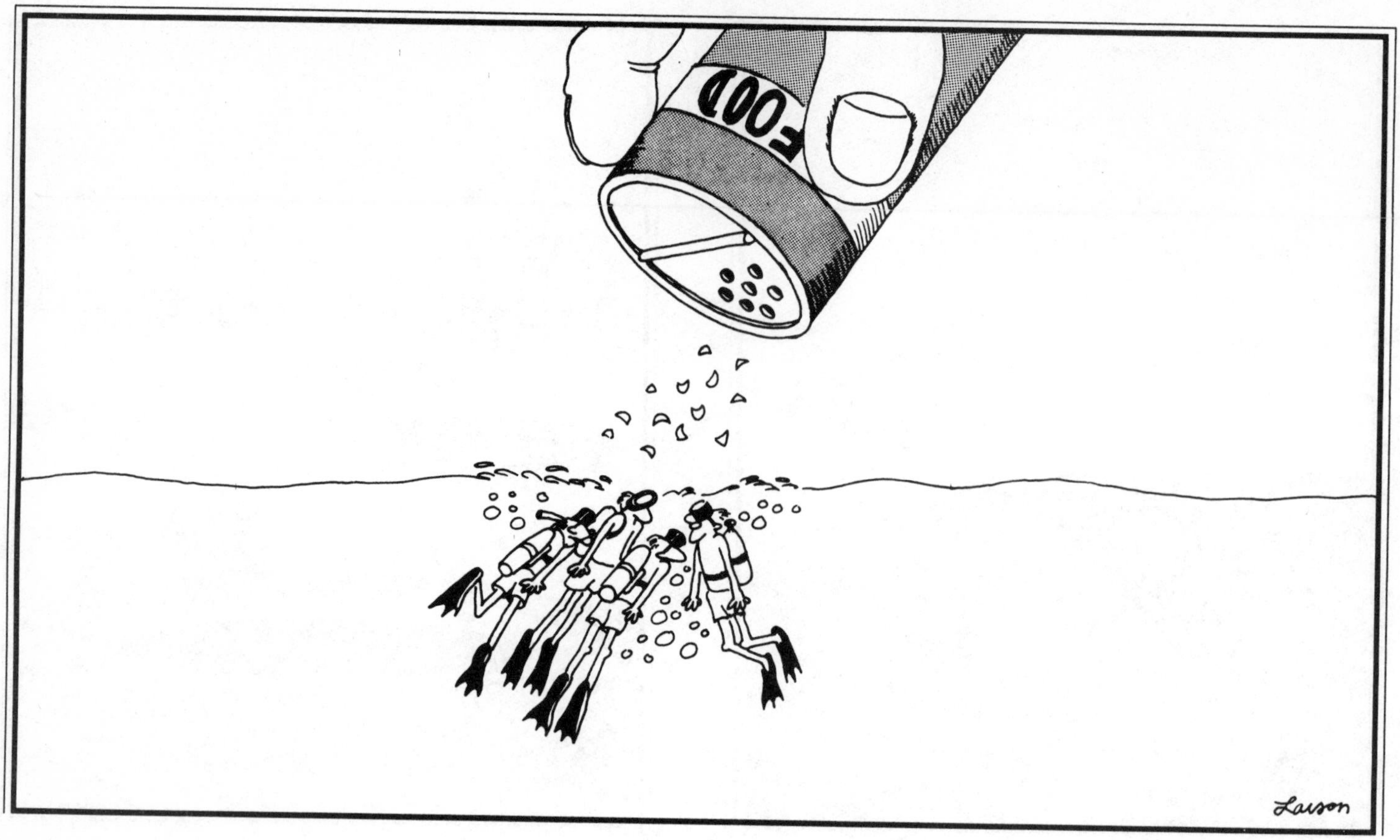
FOOD
Larson

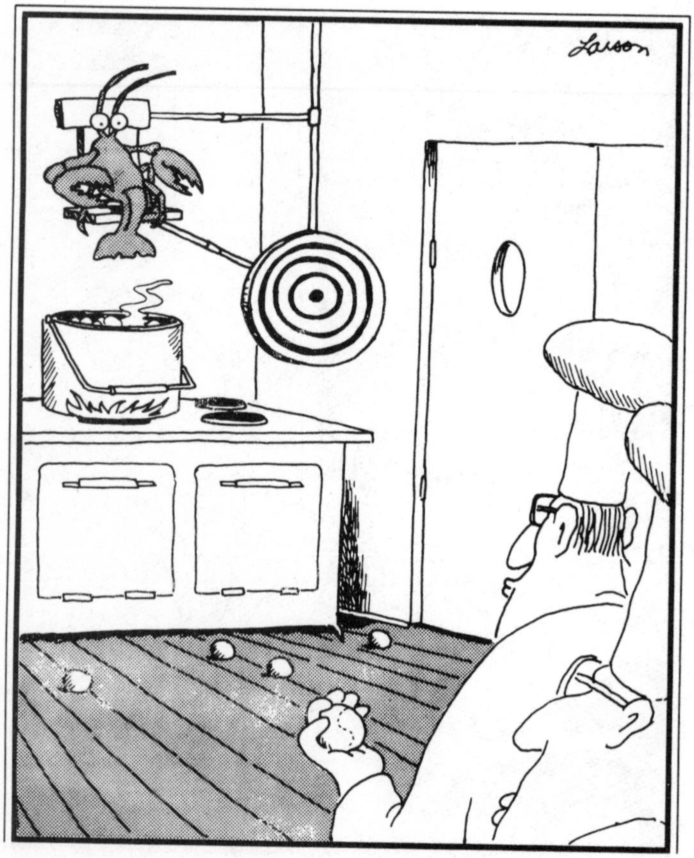
Larson

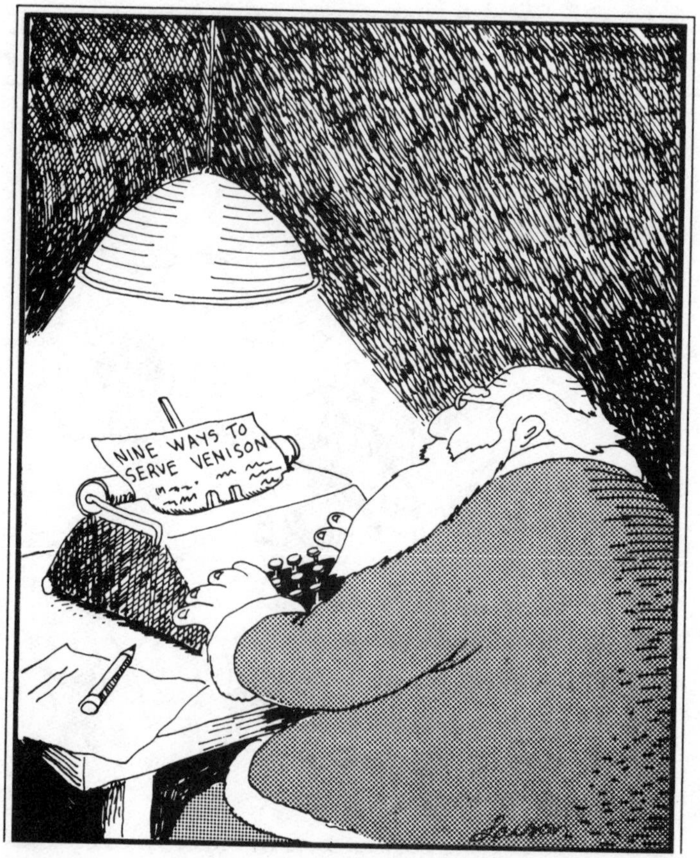
NINE WAYS TO
SERVE VENISON
Larson

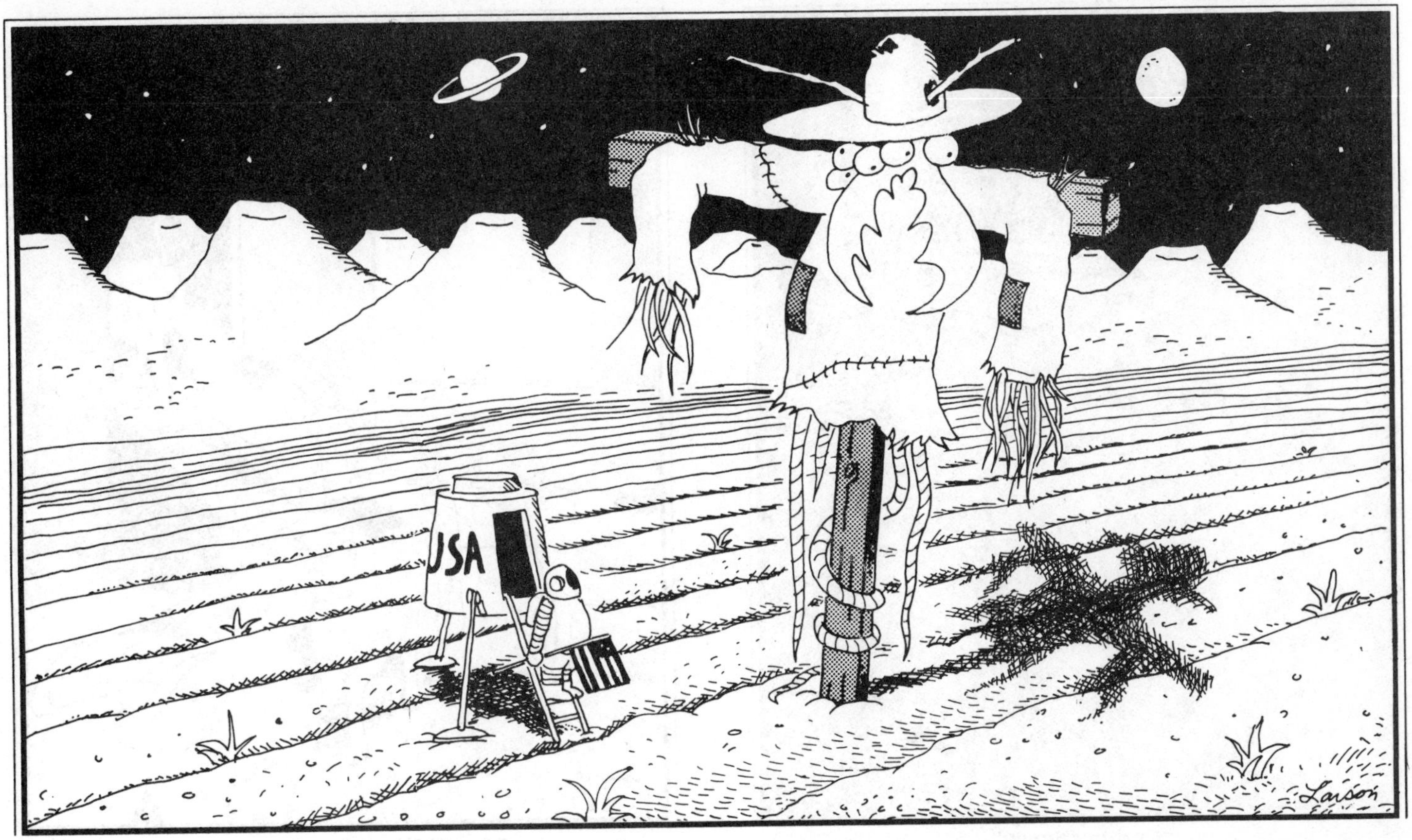
USA
Larson

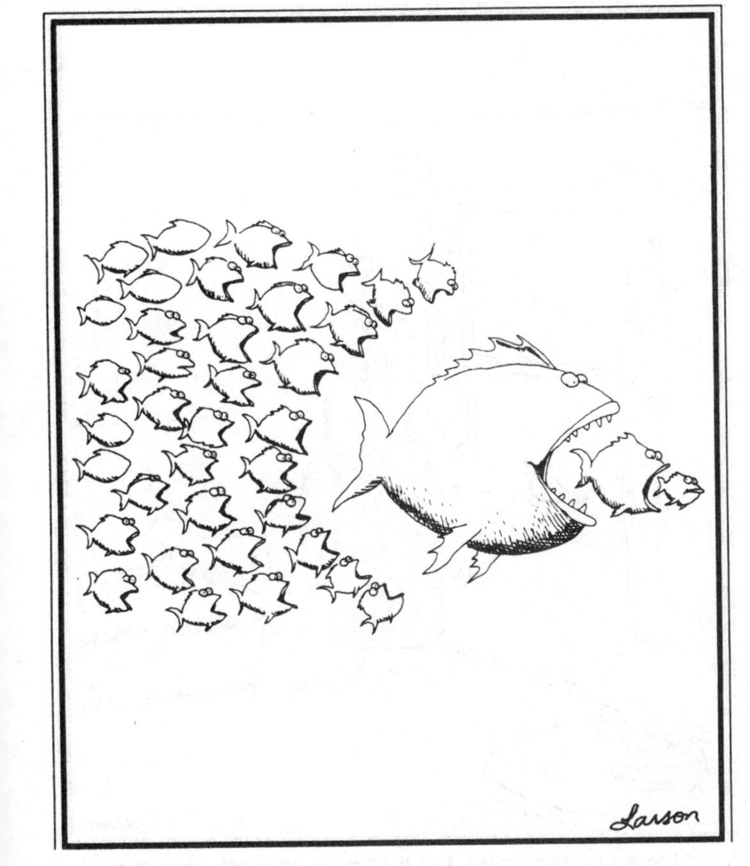
Larson

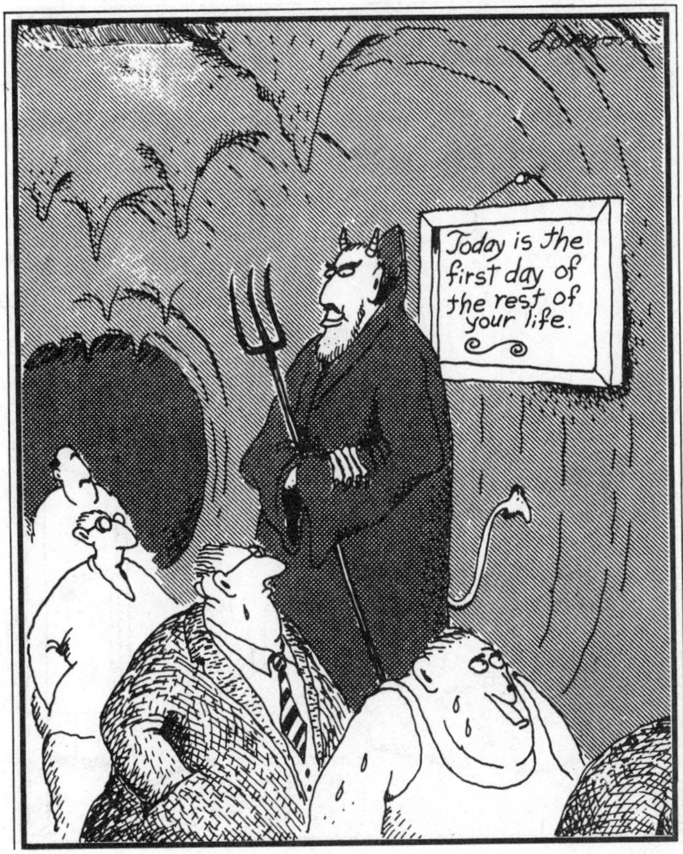
Larson
Today is the first day of the rest of your life.

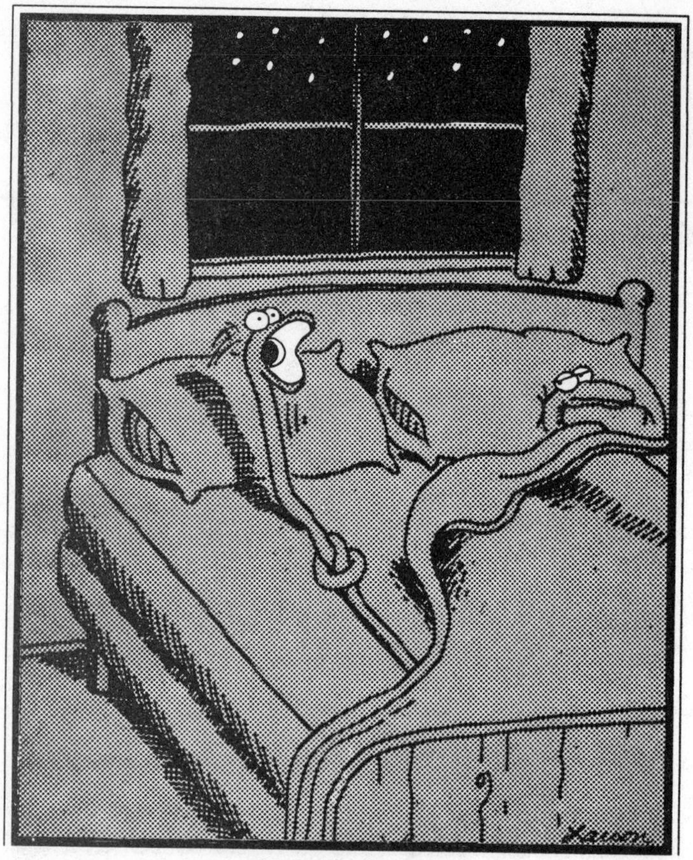
Larson

"Charley horse!"

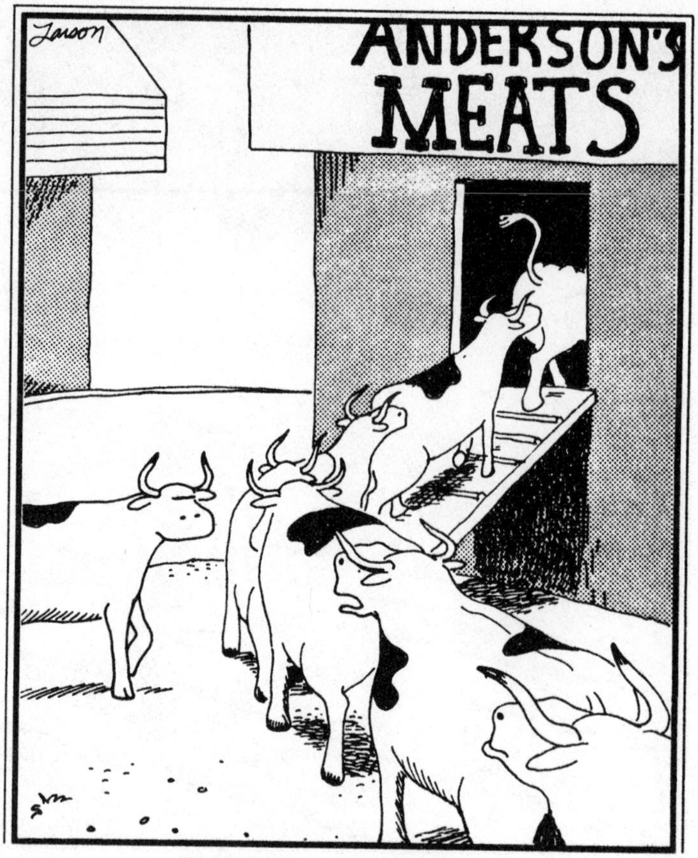
Larson
ANDERSON'S
MEATS

"Hey! You! . . . No cutting in!"

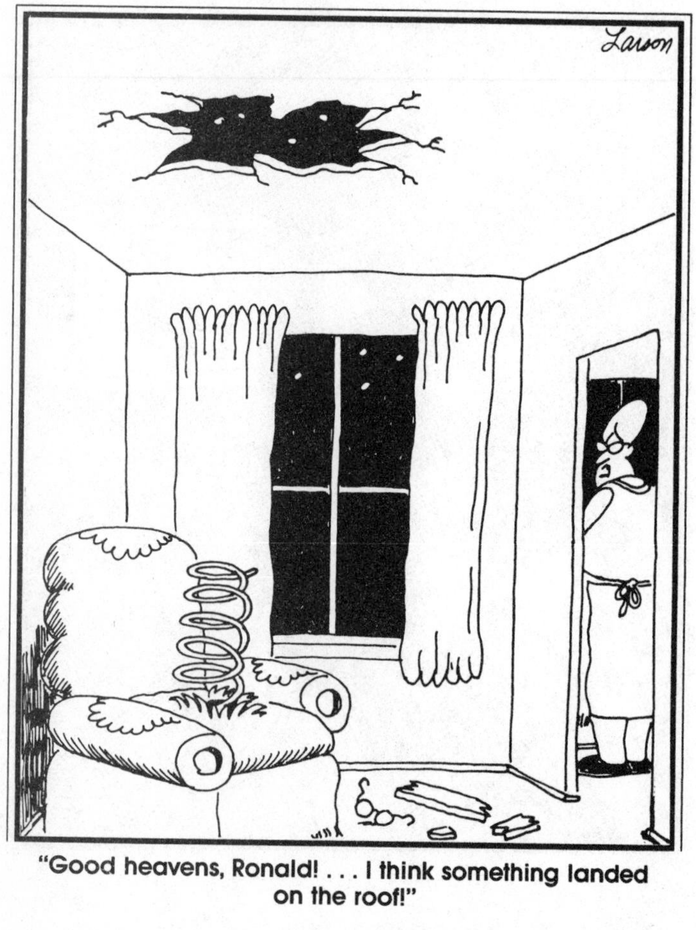
Larson

"Good heavens, Ronald! . . . I think something landed on the roof!"

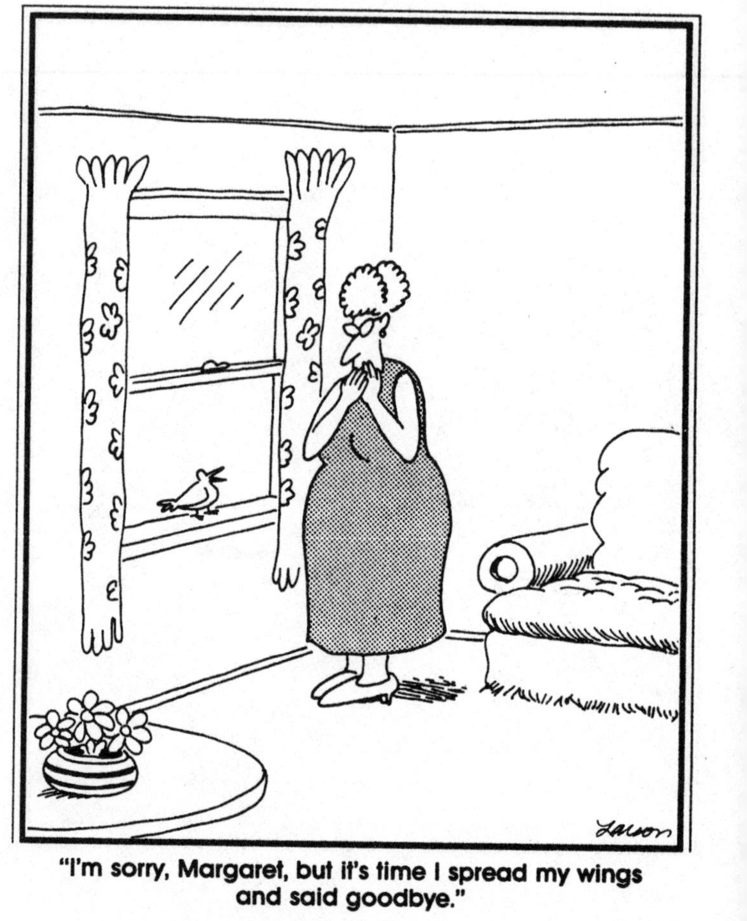
Larson

"I'm sorry, Margaret, but it's time I spread my wings and said goodbye."

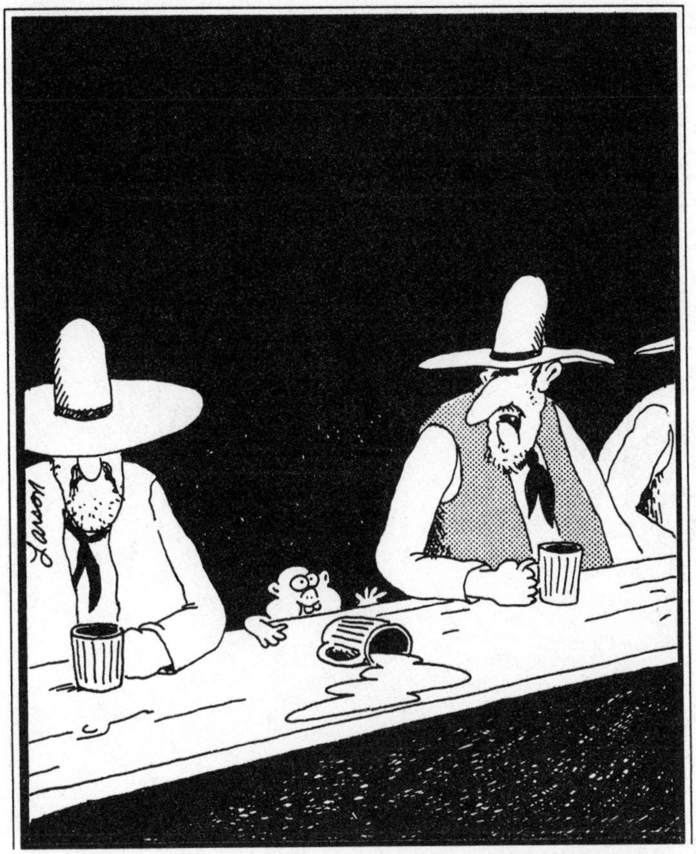
Larson

"So! . . . You must be the one they call 'The Kid.' "

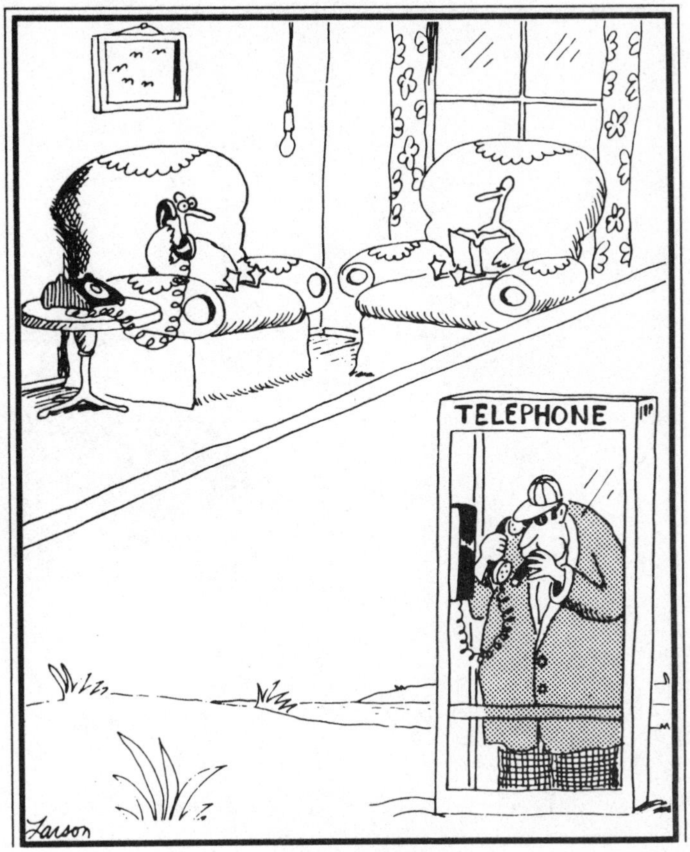
TELEPHONE
Larson

Obscene duck call

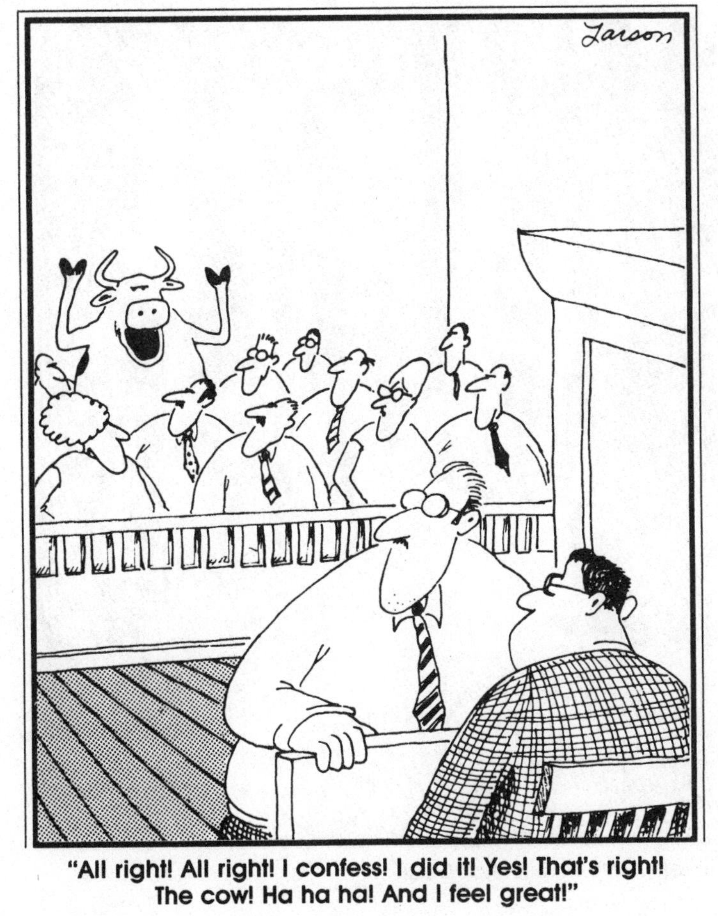
Larson

"All right! All right! I confess! I did it! Yes! That's right! The cow! Ha ha ha! And I feel great!"

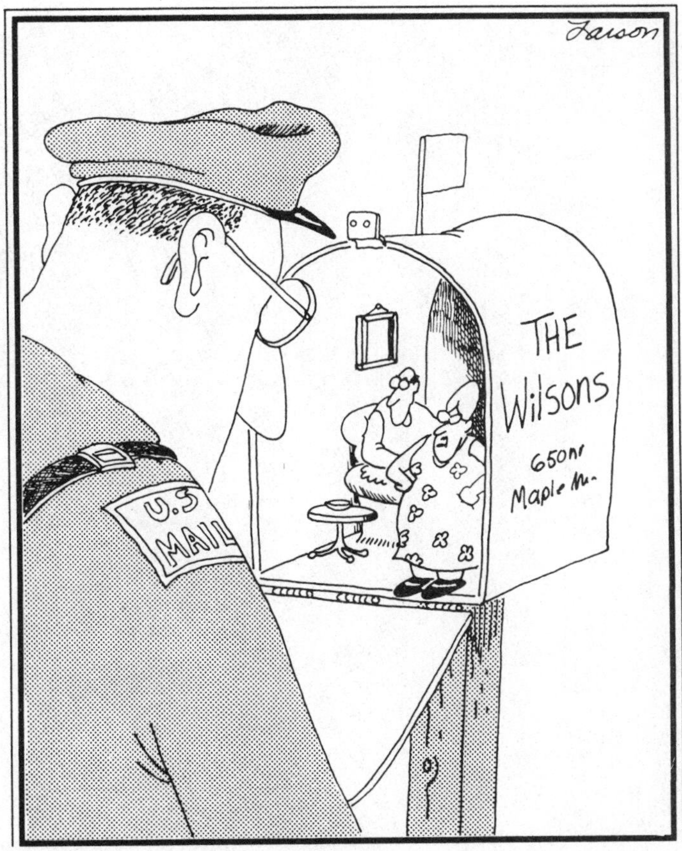
Larson
THE
Wilsons
U.S
MAIL

"We're the Wilsons, bozo! What's it say on the box?"

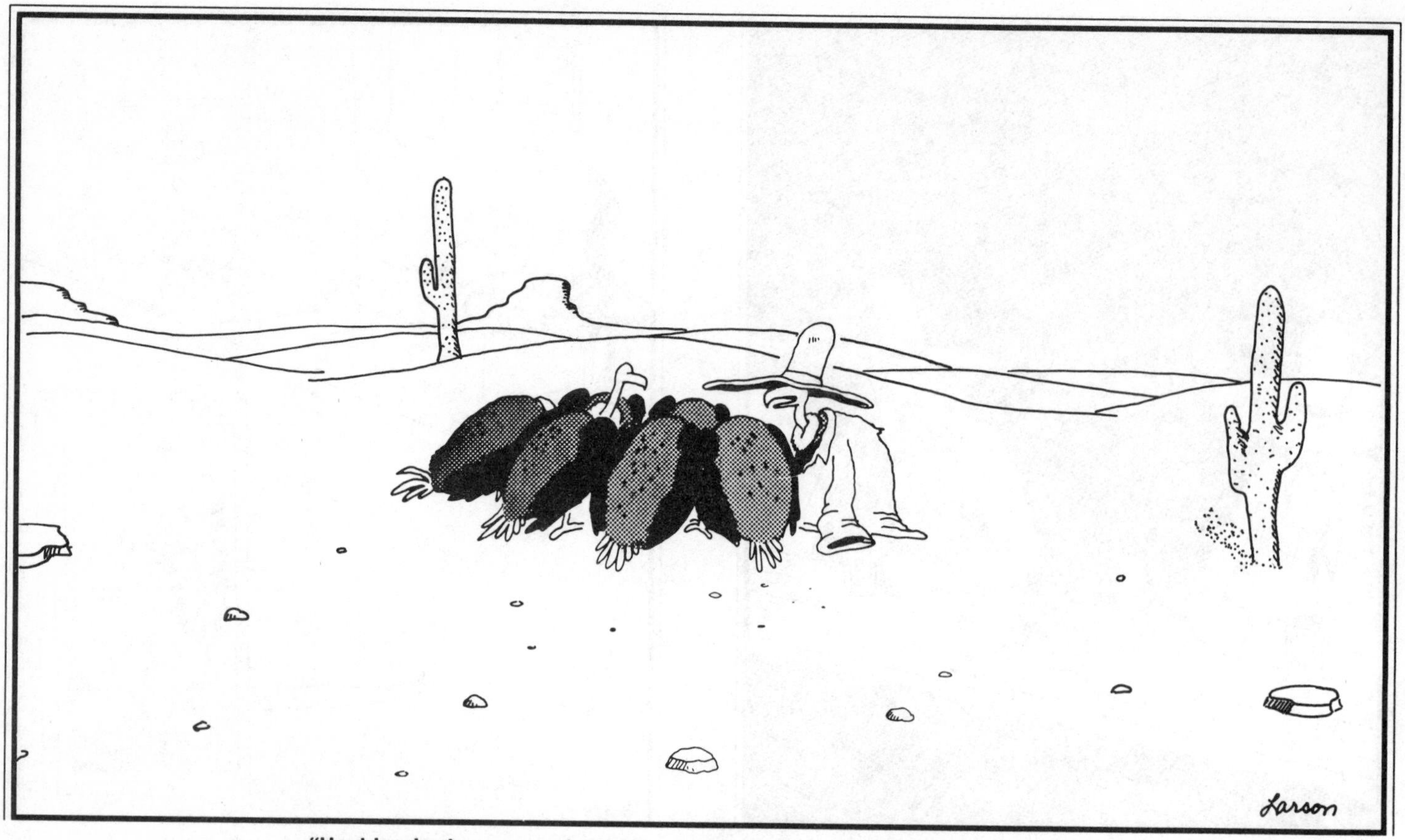
Larson

"Hey! Look at me, everybody! I'm a cowboy! . . . Howdy, howdy, howdy!"

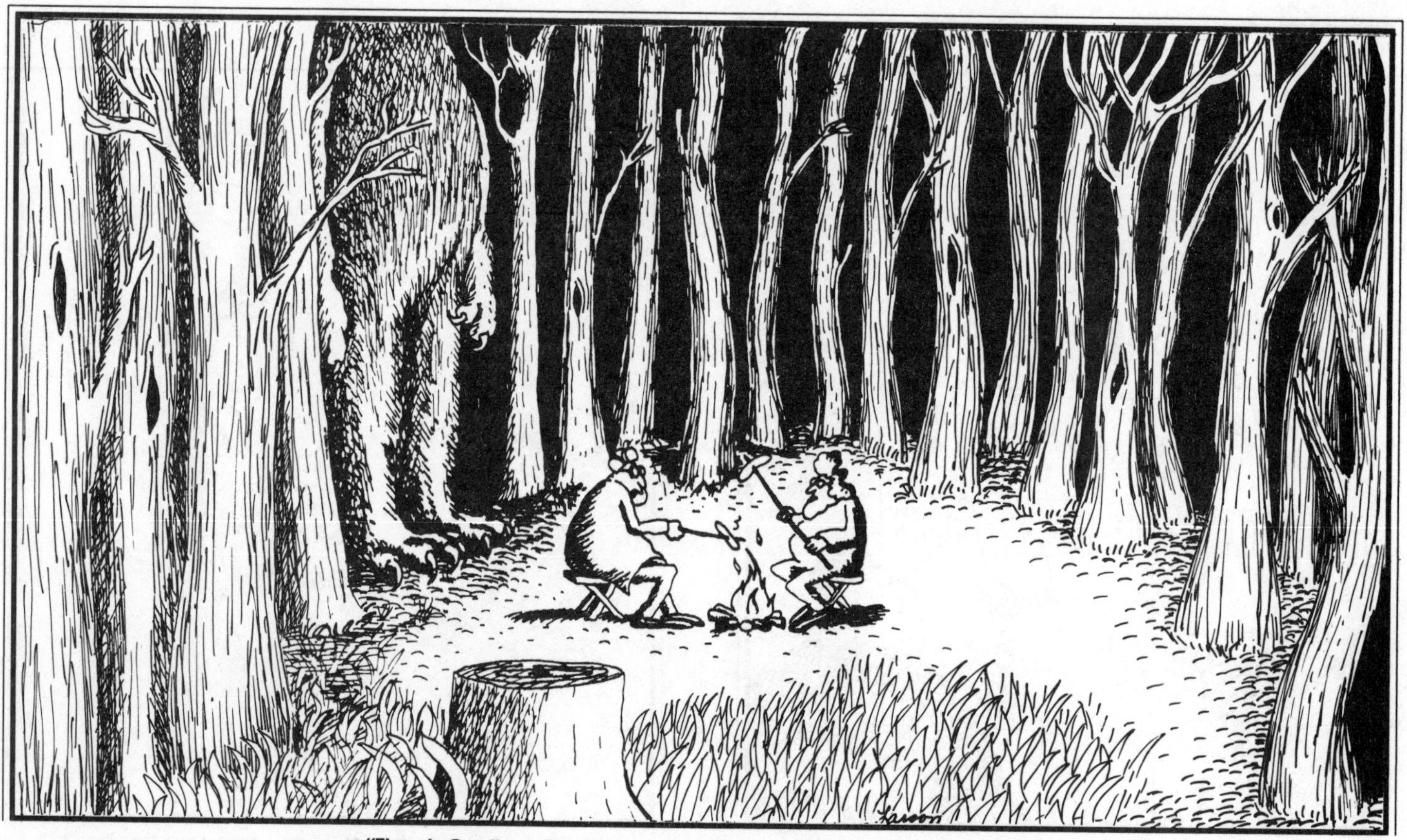
Larson

"Thank God! . . . Those blasted crickets have finally stopped!"

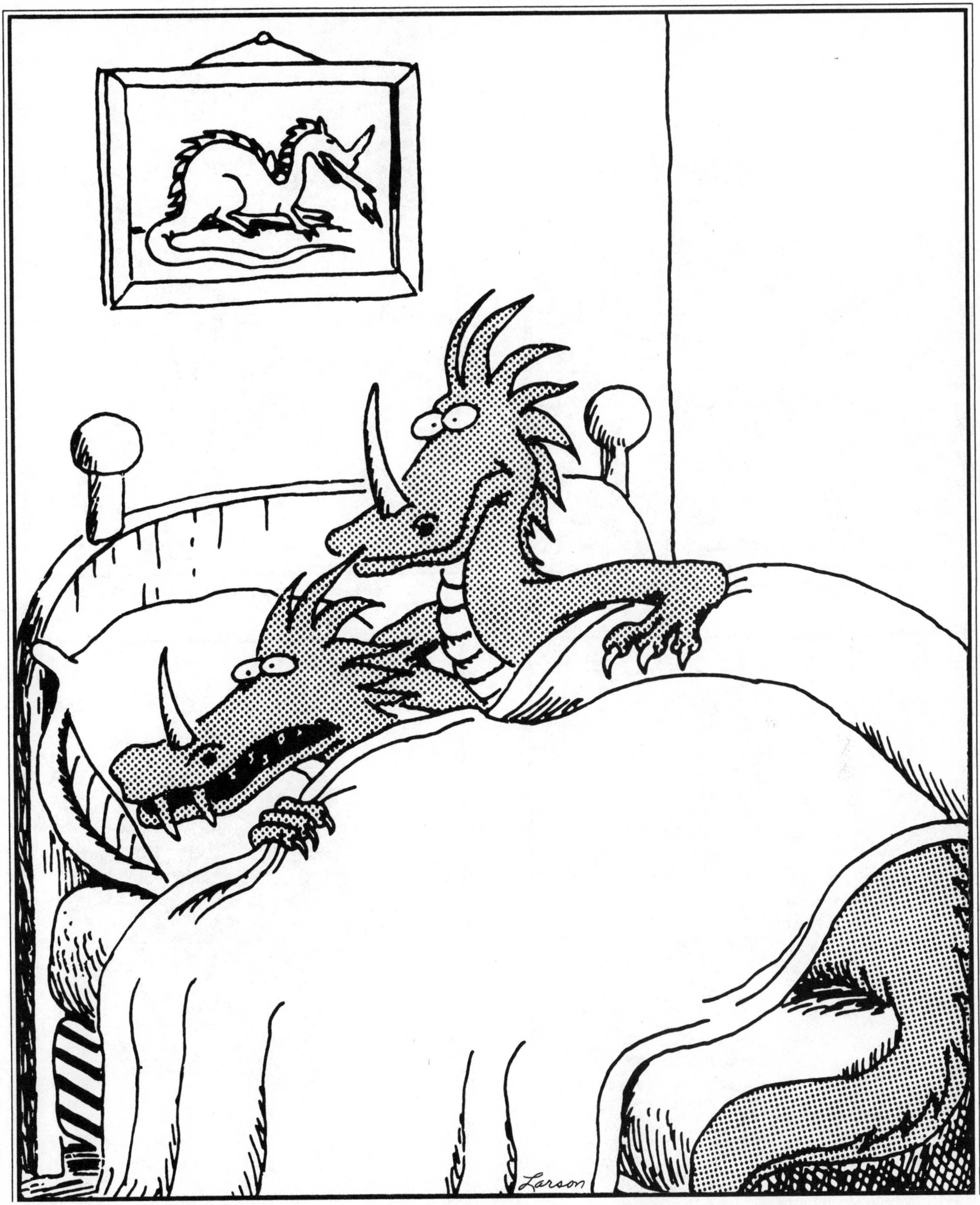
Larson

"I'm sorry, Irwin . . . It's your breath. It's . . . it's fresh and minty."

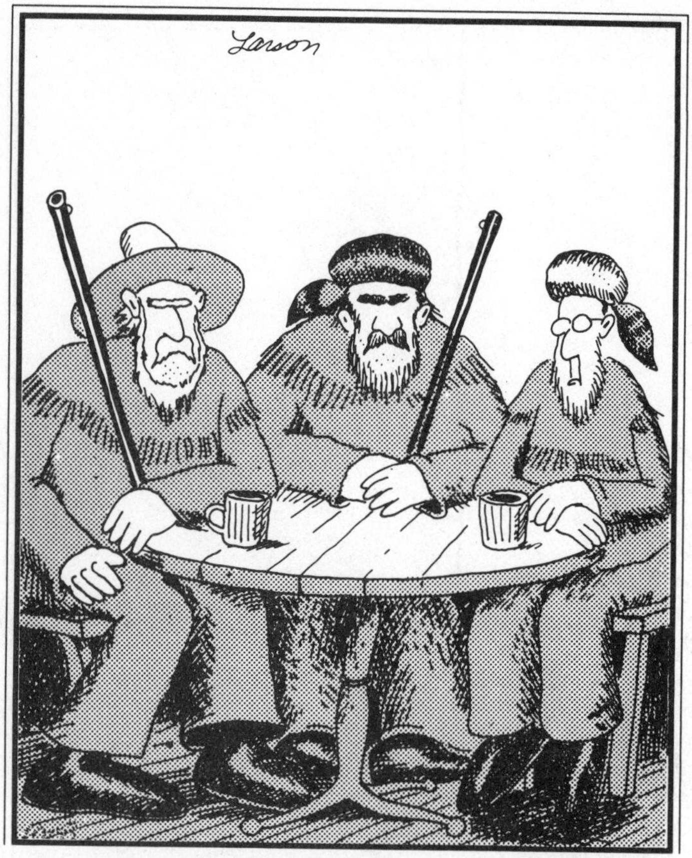
Larson

Buffalo Bill, Grizzly Adams and Pigeon Jones

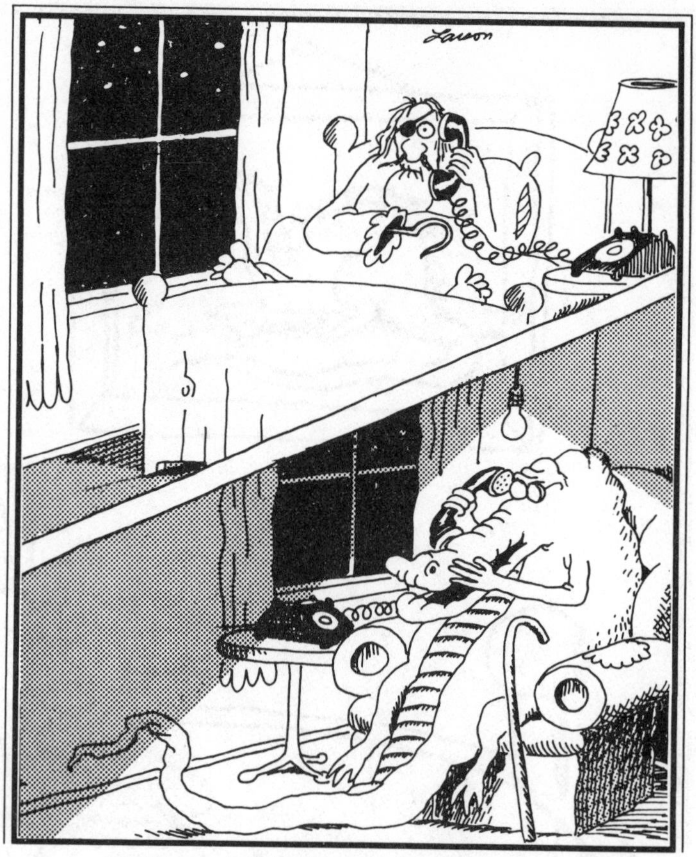
Larson

"Tick-tock, tick-tock, tick-tock, tick-tock . . ."

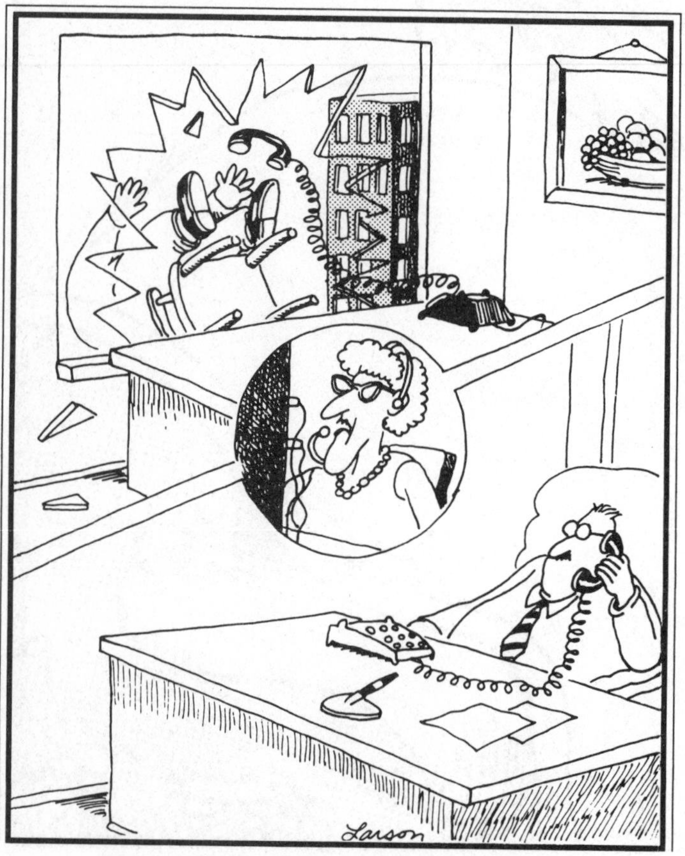
Larson

"Yes. Will you accept a collect call from a Mr. Aaaaaaaaaa?"

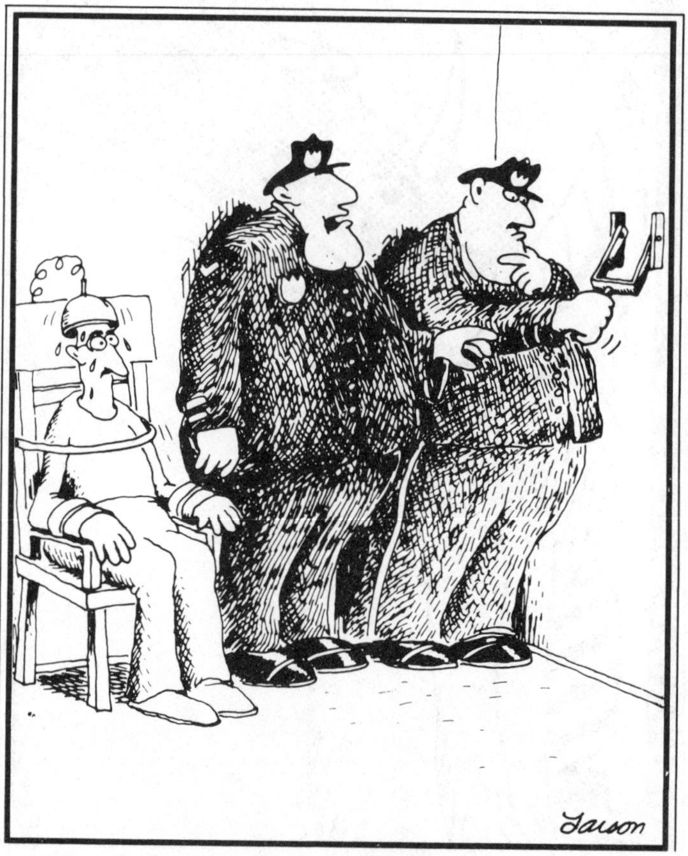
Larson

"The contact points must be dirty . . . just click it up and down a few times."

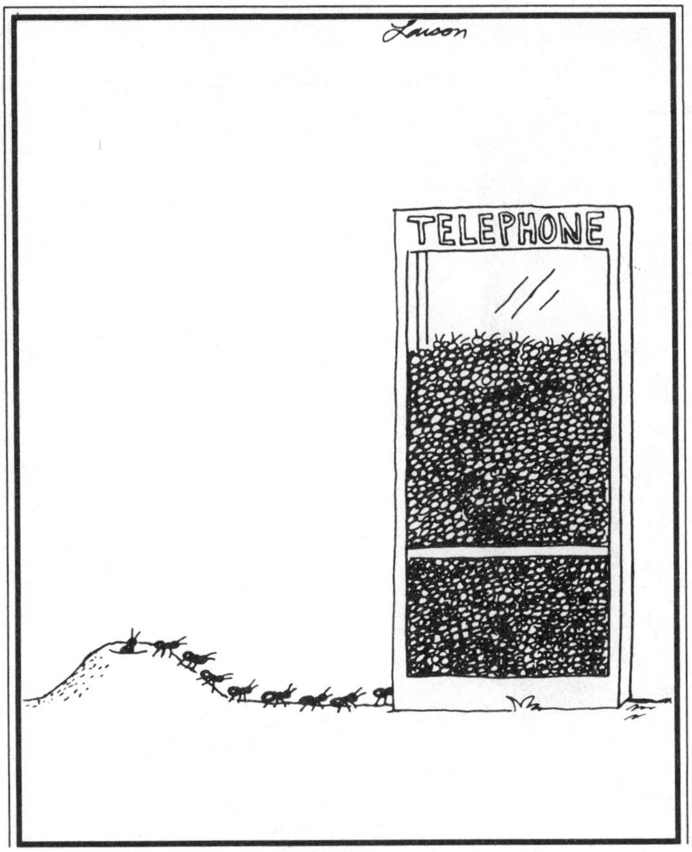

TELEPHONE

Insect games

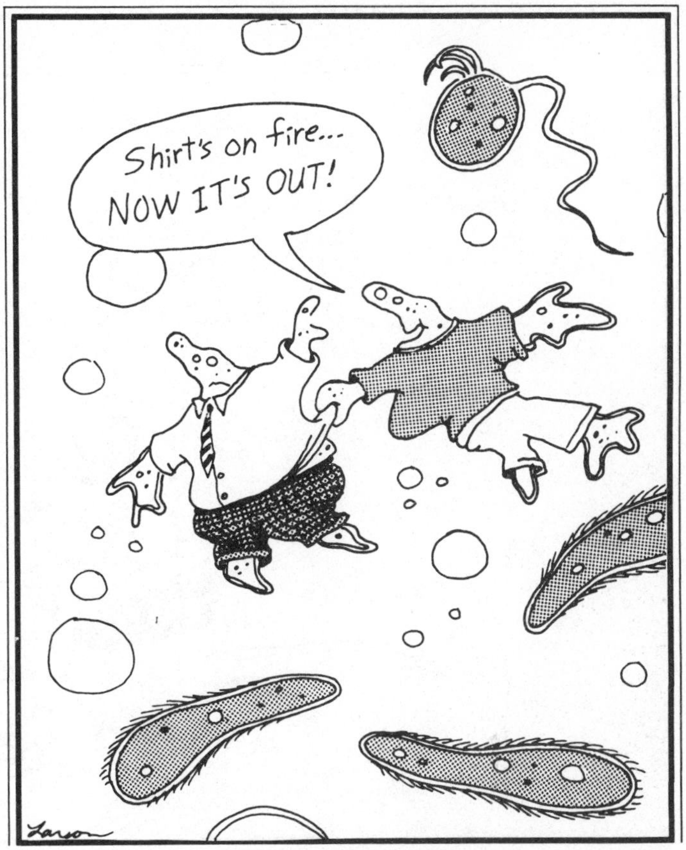

Shirt's on fire... NOW IT'S OUT!

Humor at its lowest form

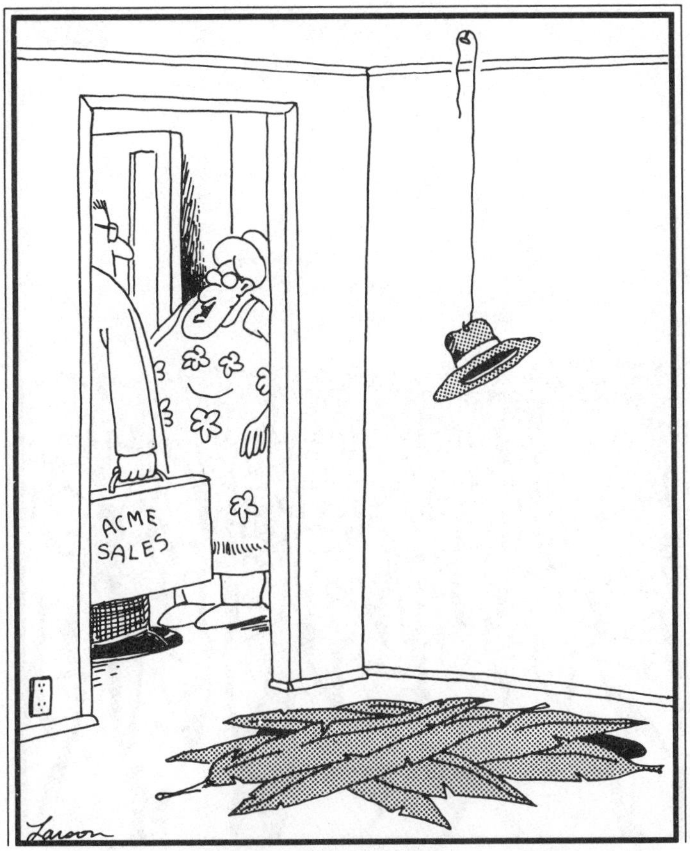

ACME SALES

"Oh, that's right! You DID have a hat . . . I believe you'll find it in the other room."

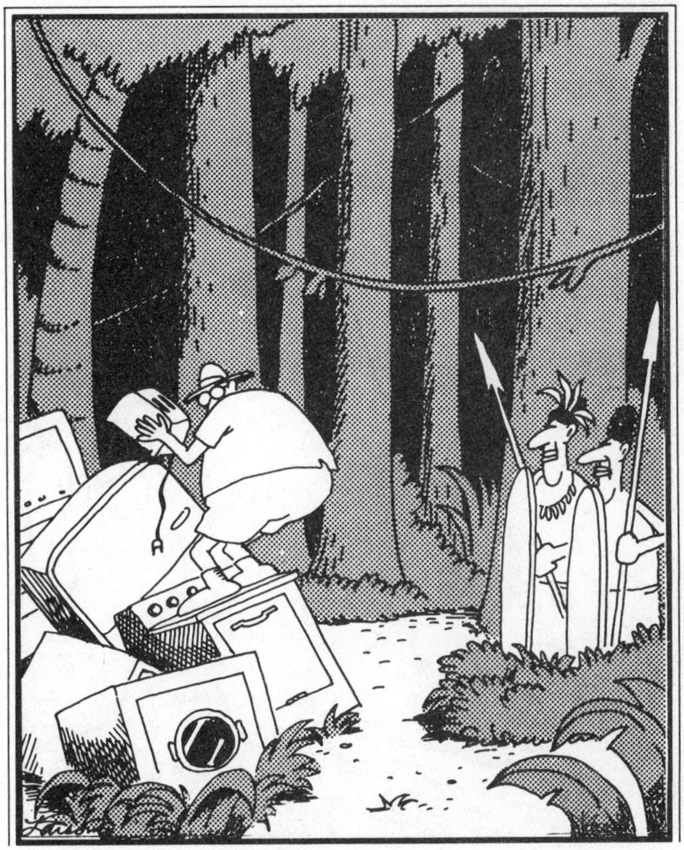

Murray is caught desecrating the secret appliance burial grounds.

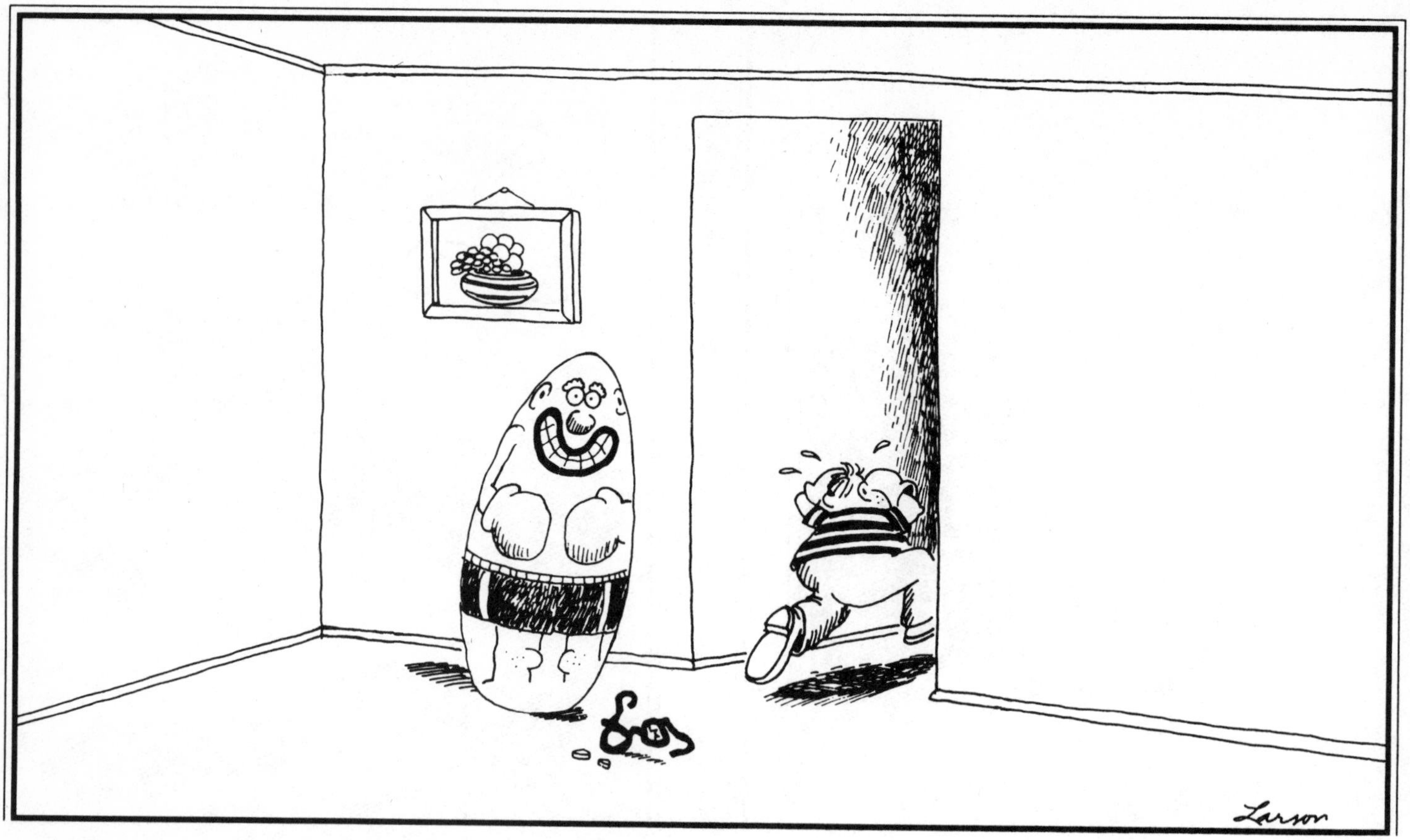

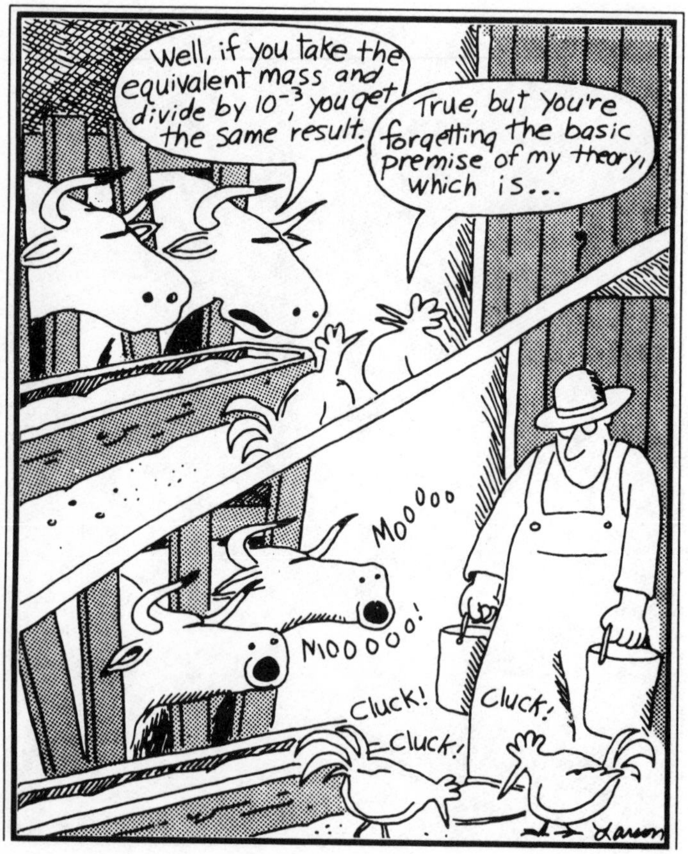
Well, if you take the equivalent mass and divide by 10^{-3}, you get the same result.
True, but you're forgetting the basic premise of my theory, which is...
MOoooo
MOOOOO!
Cluck!
Cluck!
Cluck!

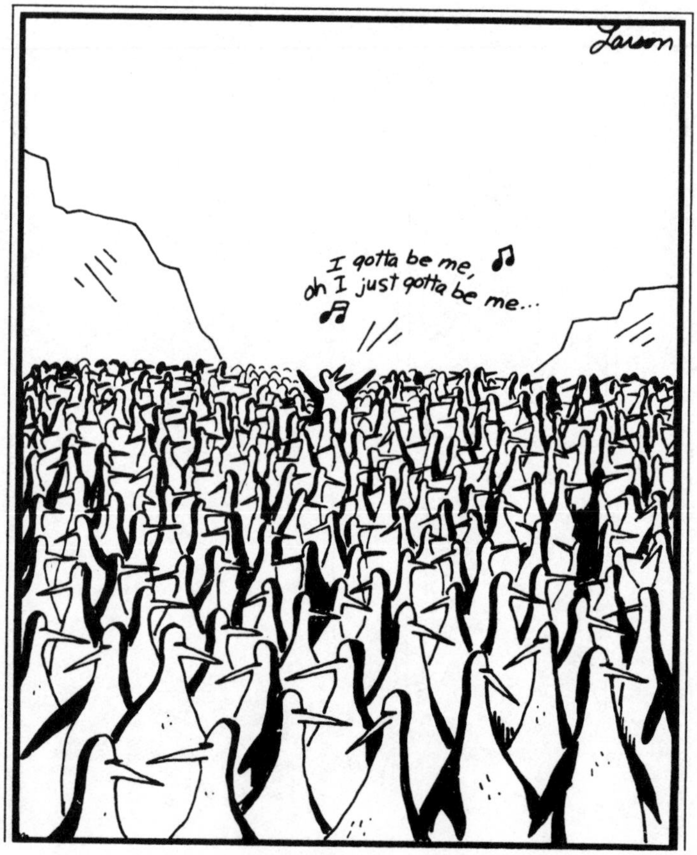
I gotta be me, oh I just gotta be me...

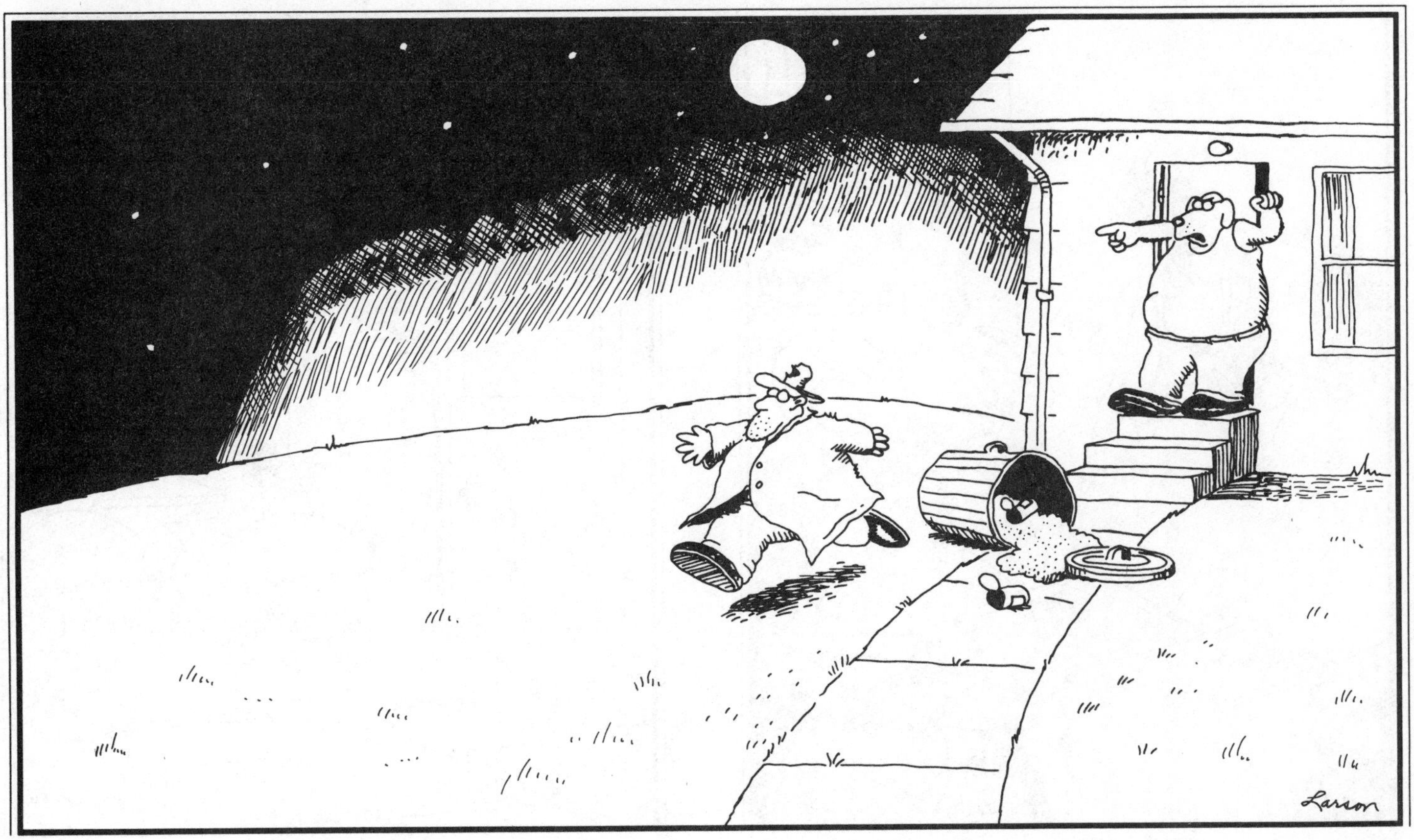
Larson

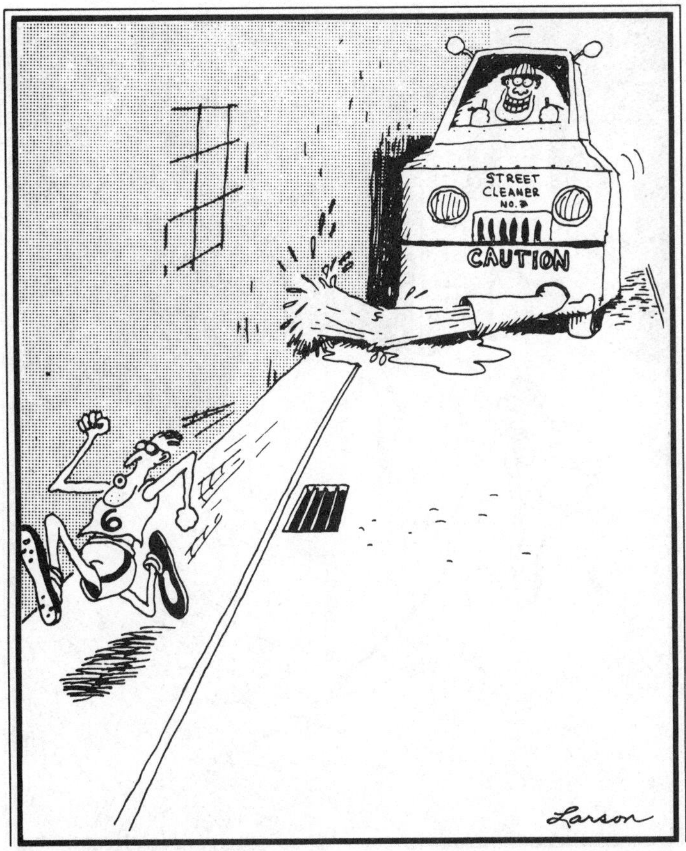
STREET CLEANER NO. 3
CAUTION
Larson

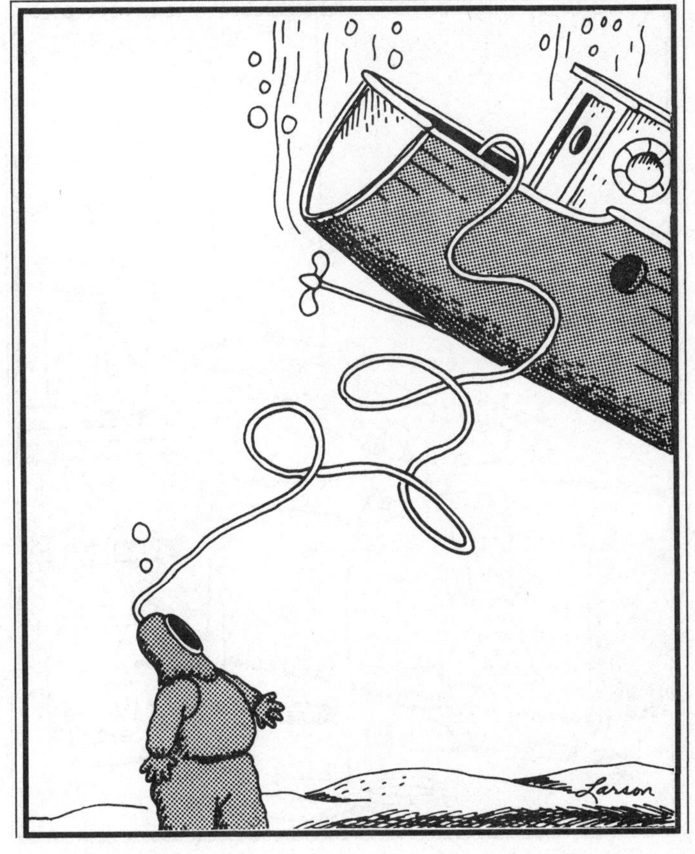
Larson

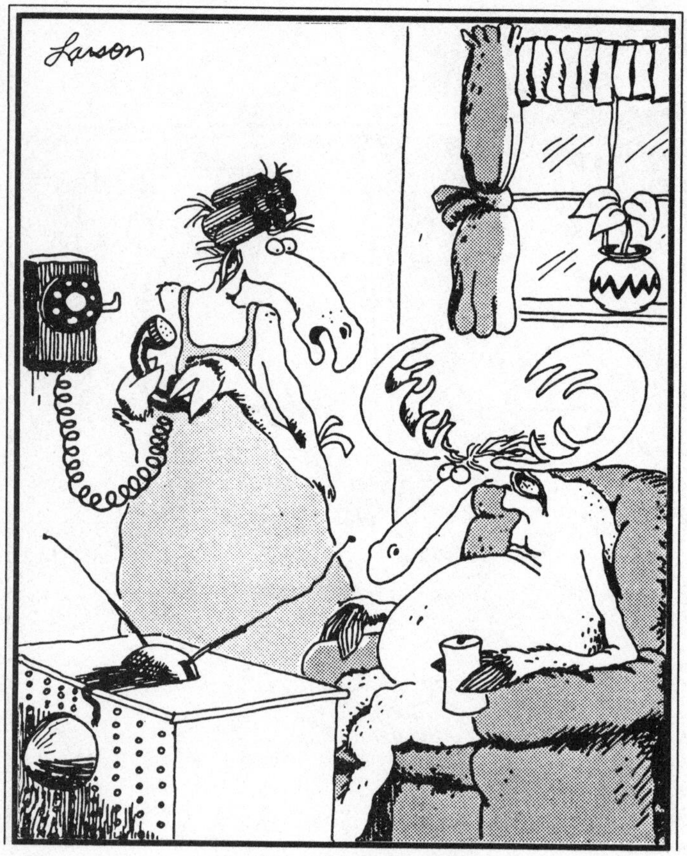
Larson

"It's the call of the wild."

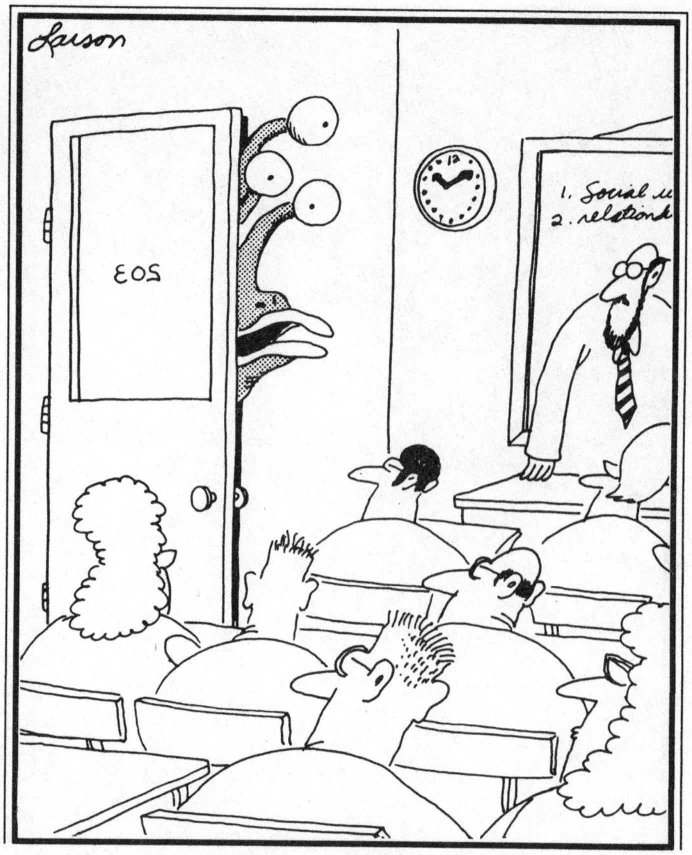
Larson

"Whoa! . . . Wrong room."

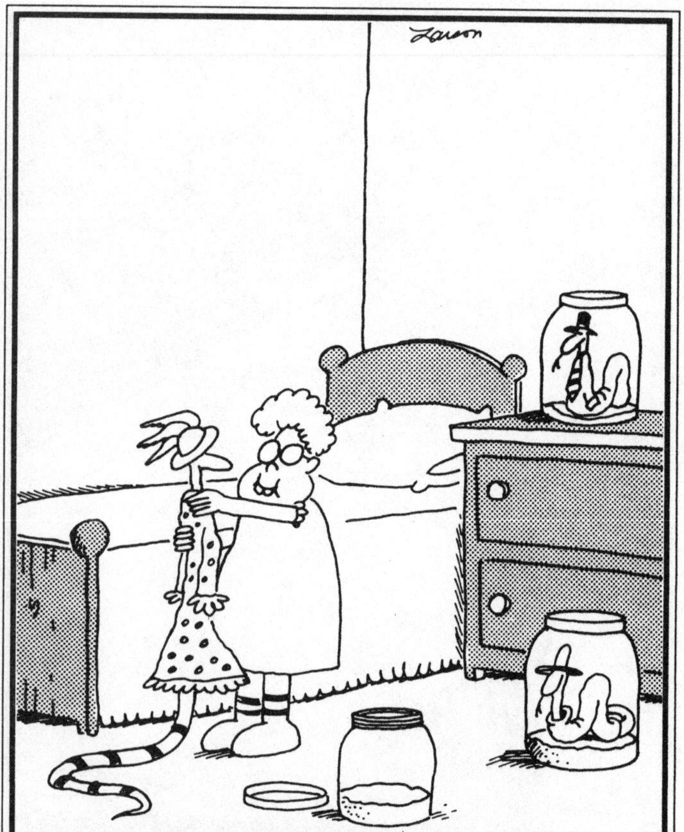
Larson

Frances loved her little pets, and dressed them differently every day.

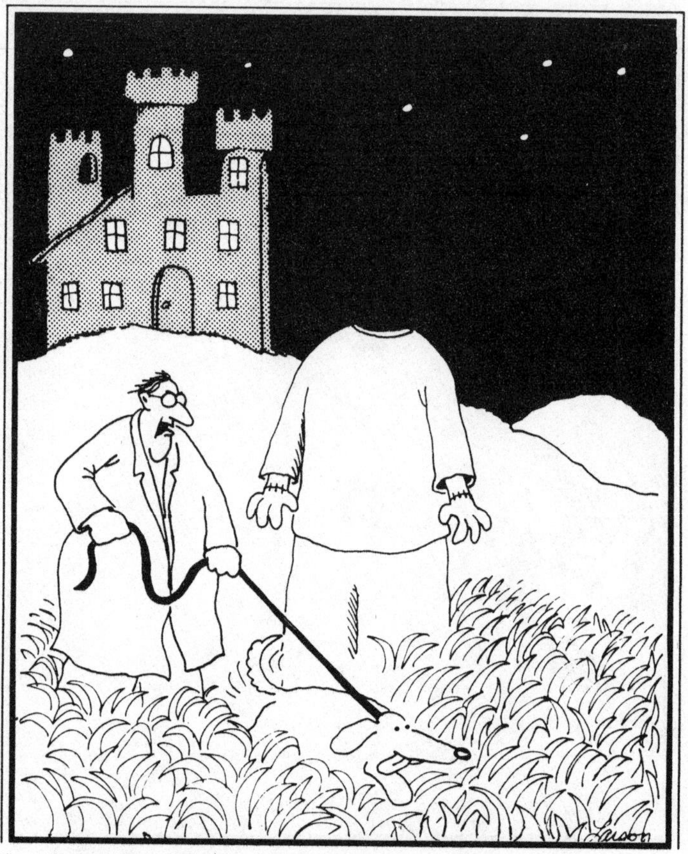
Larson

"Blast! This cinches it! . . . If we ever find it again, I'm gonna bolt the sucker on!"

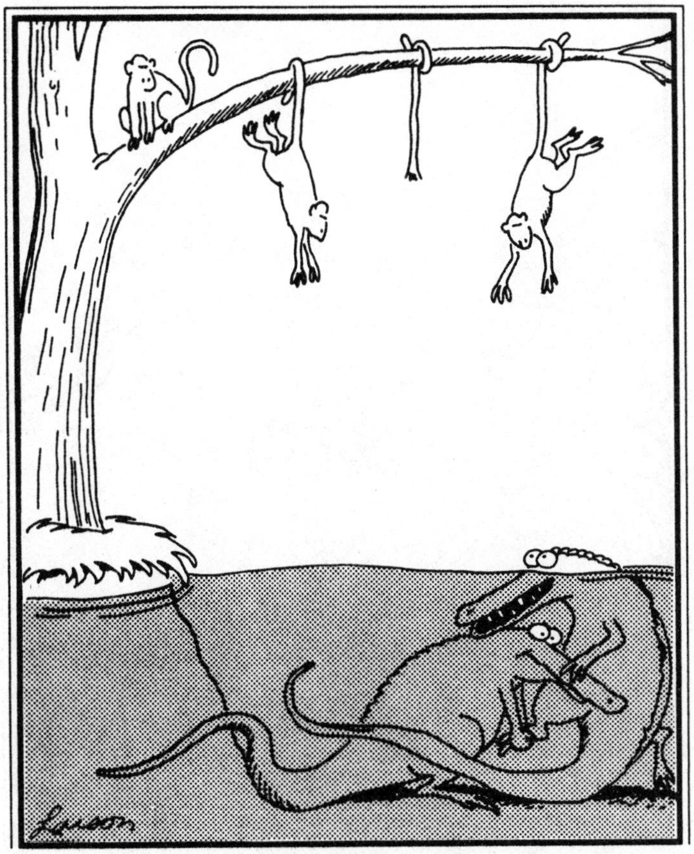
Larson

"Okay, here we go again . . . one . . . two . . ."

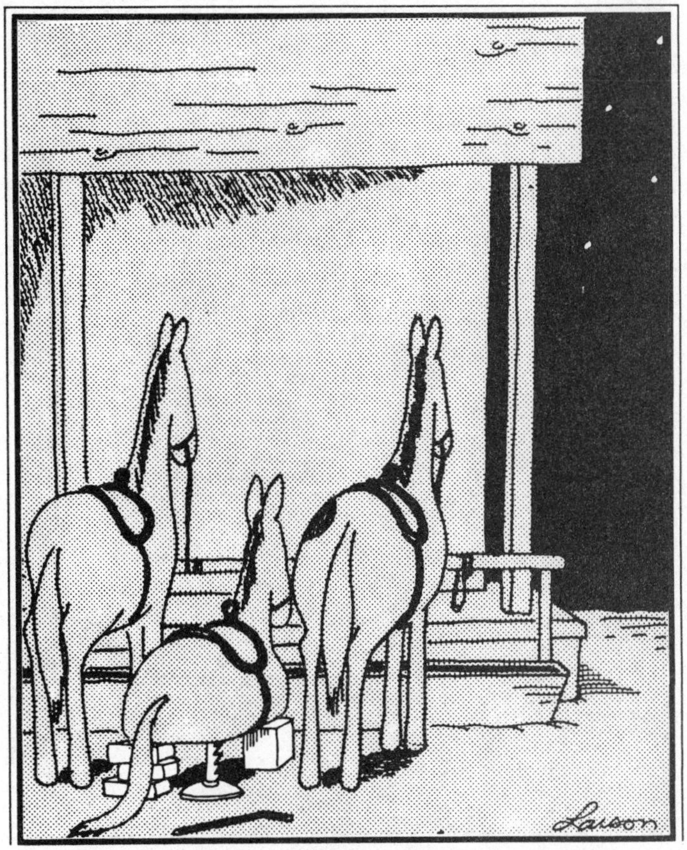
Larson

Never park your horse in a bad part of town.

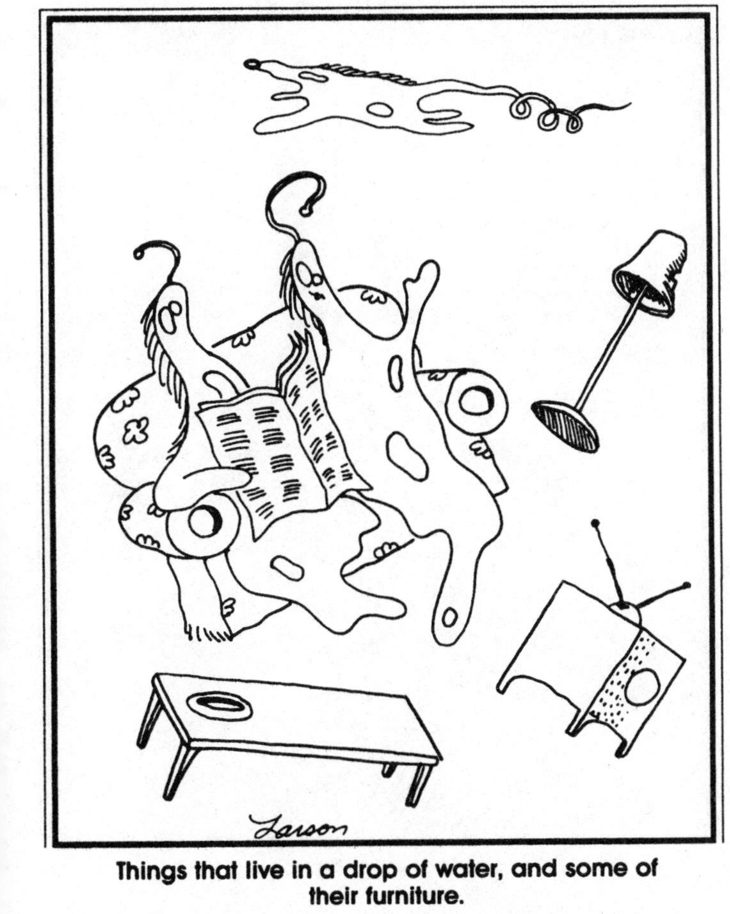
Larson

Things that live in a drop of water, and some of their furniture.

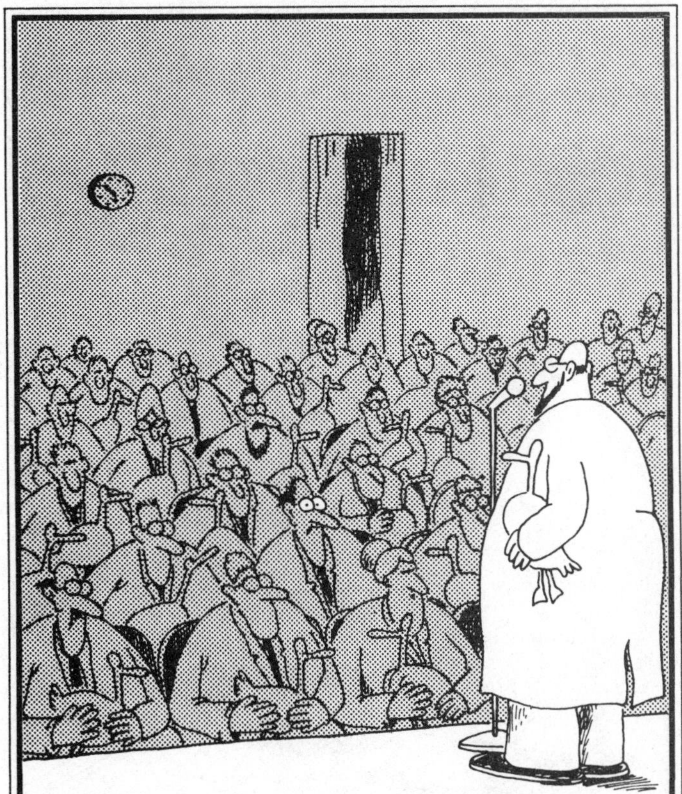
Larson

Suddenly, Professor Liebowitz realizes he has come to the seminar without his duck.

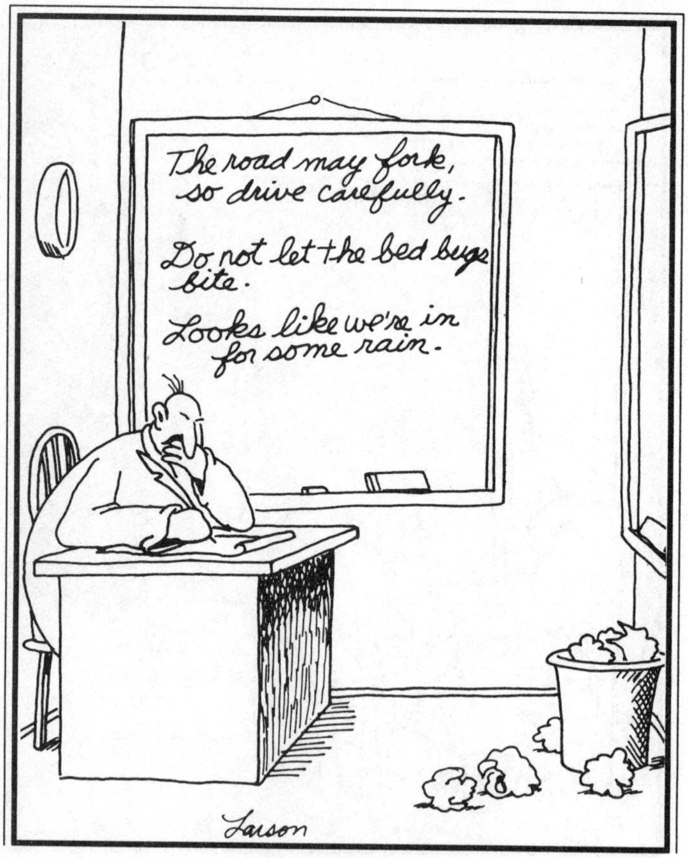

The road may fork, so drive carefully.
Do not let the bed bugs bite.
Looks like we're in for some rain.
Larson

Confucius at the office

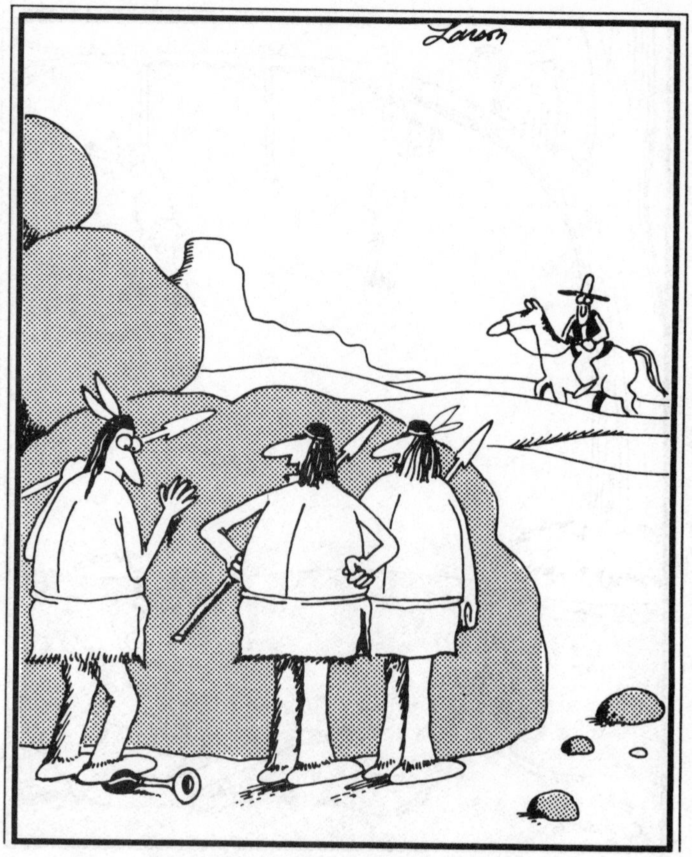

Larson

"And you call yourself an Indian!"

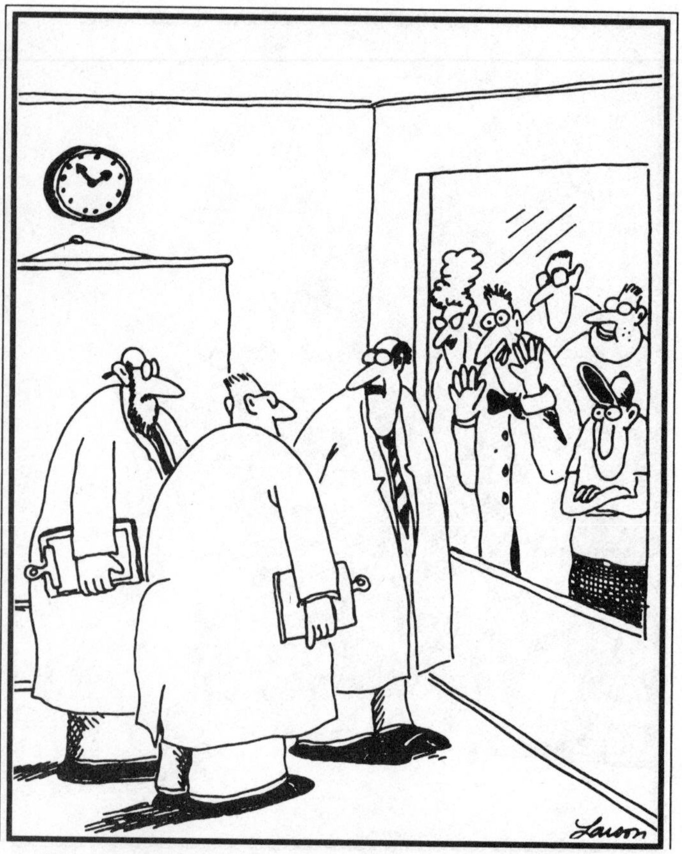

Larson

"Yes, they're all fools, gentlemen . . . But the question remains, 'What KIND of fools are they?' "

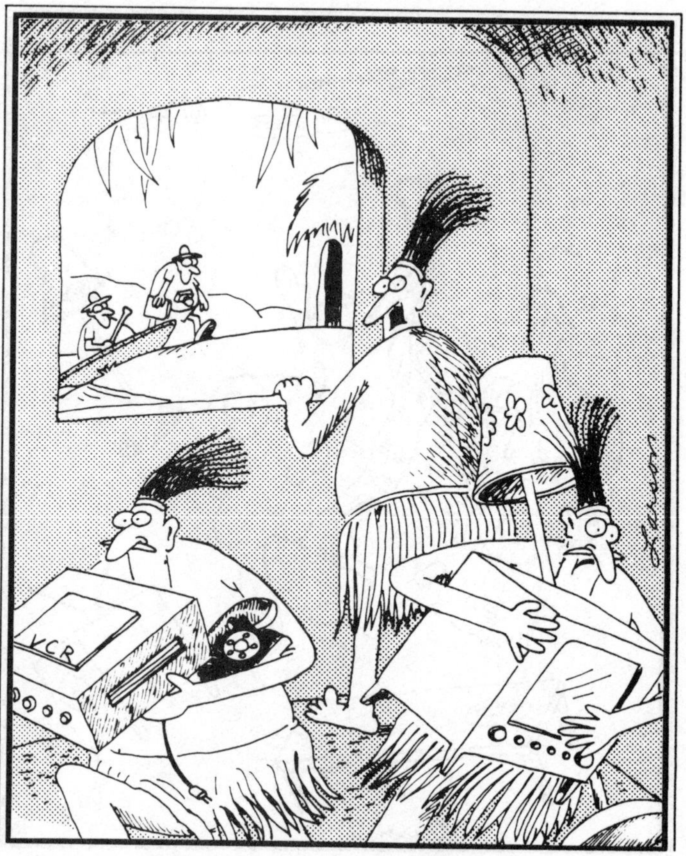

VCR
Larson

"Anthropologists! Anthropologists!"

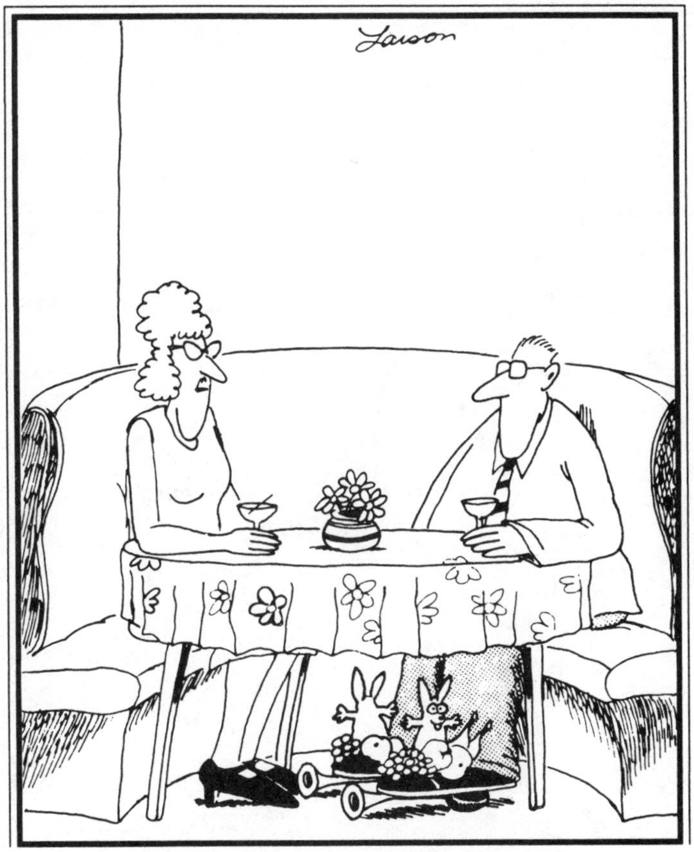
Larson

"I judge a man by the shoes he wears, Jerry."

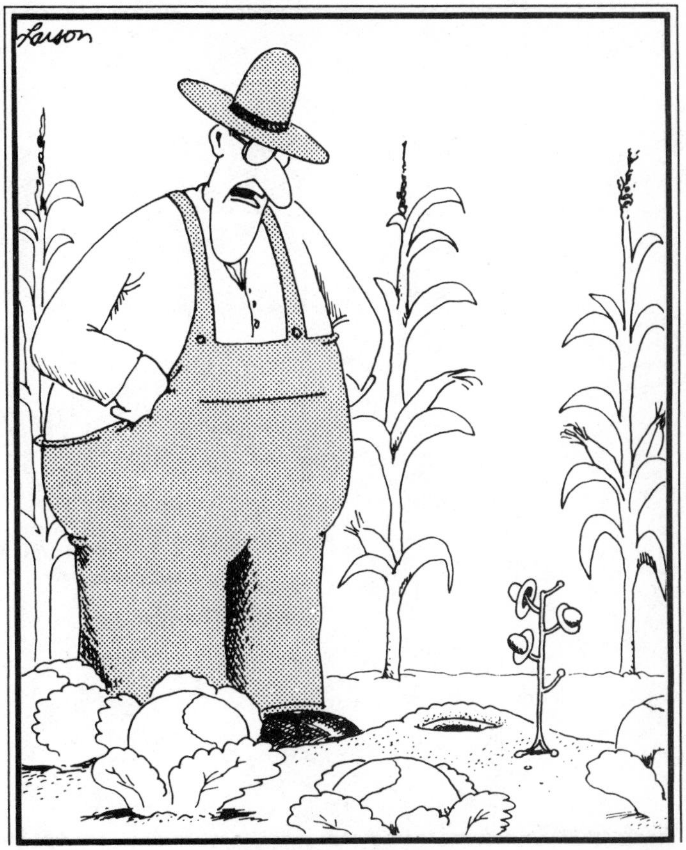
Larson

"So! They're back!"

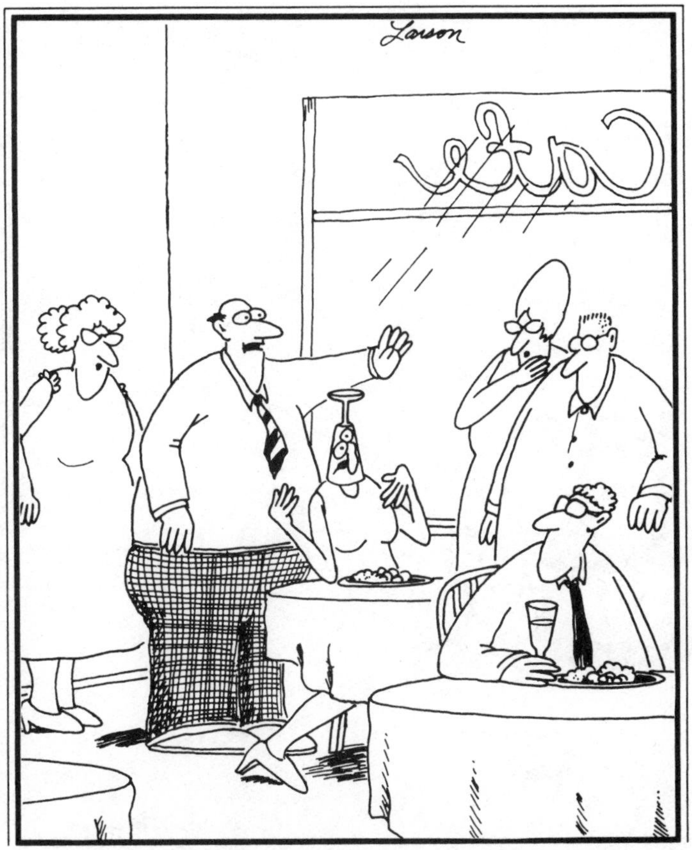
Larson

"Calm down, everyone! I've had experience with this sort of thing before . . . Does someone have a hammer?"

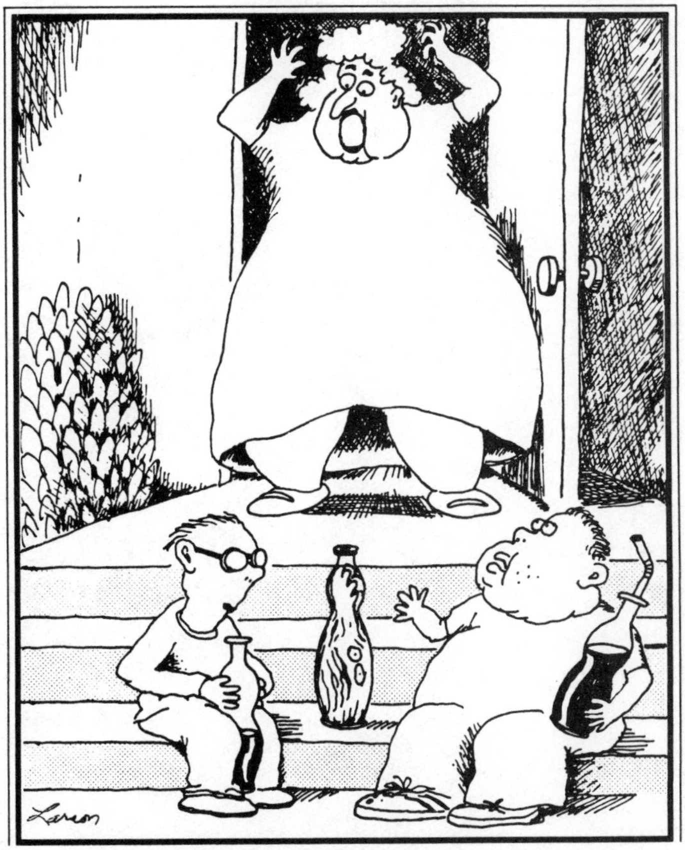
Larson

"Gee, Mom! Andy was just showing us how far he could suck his lip into the bottle!"

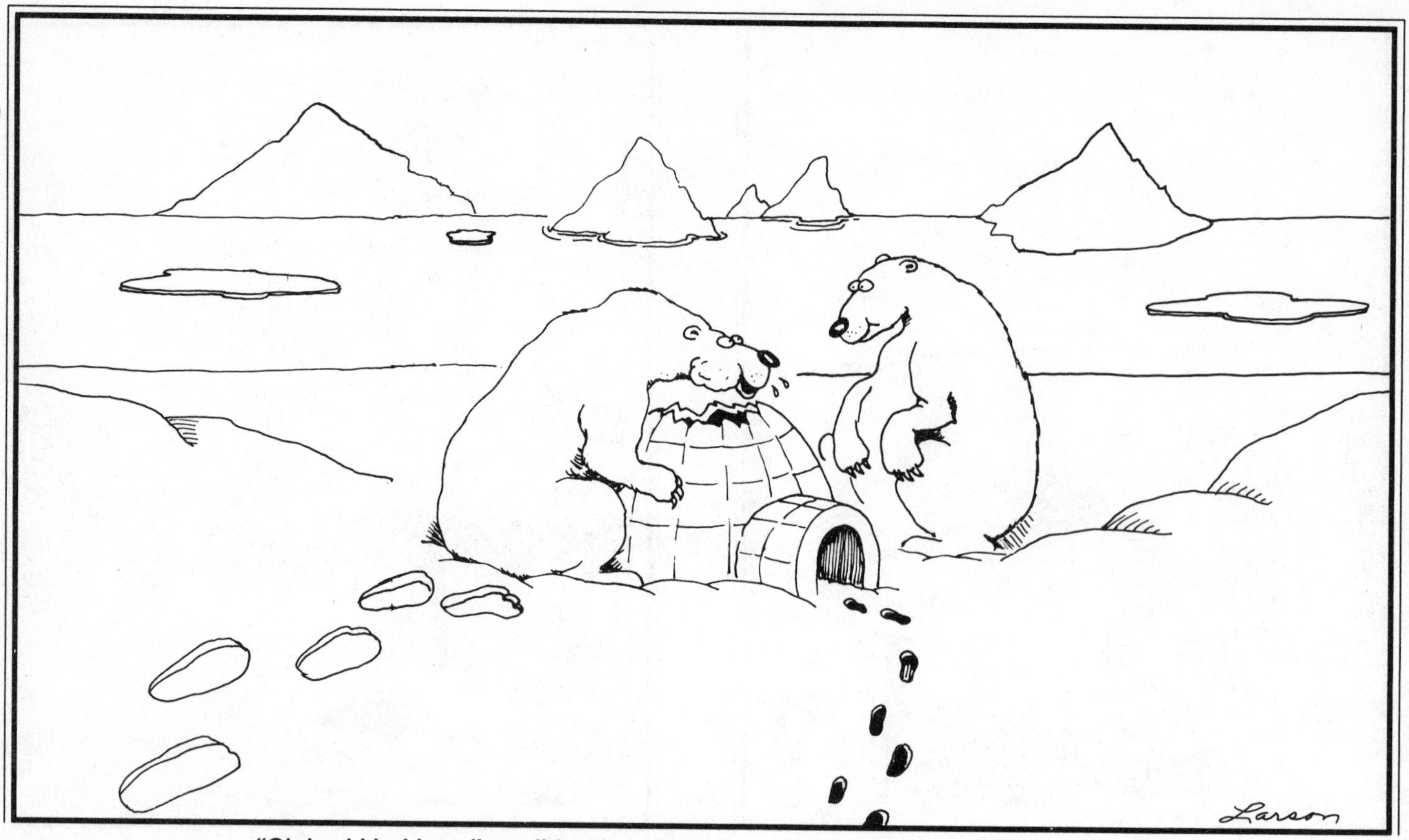
Larson

"Oh hey! I just love these things! . . . Crunchy on the outside and a chewy center!"

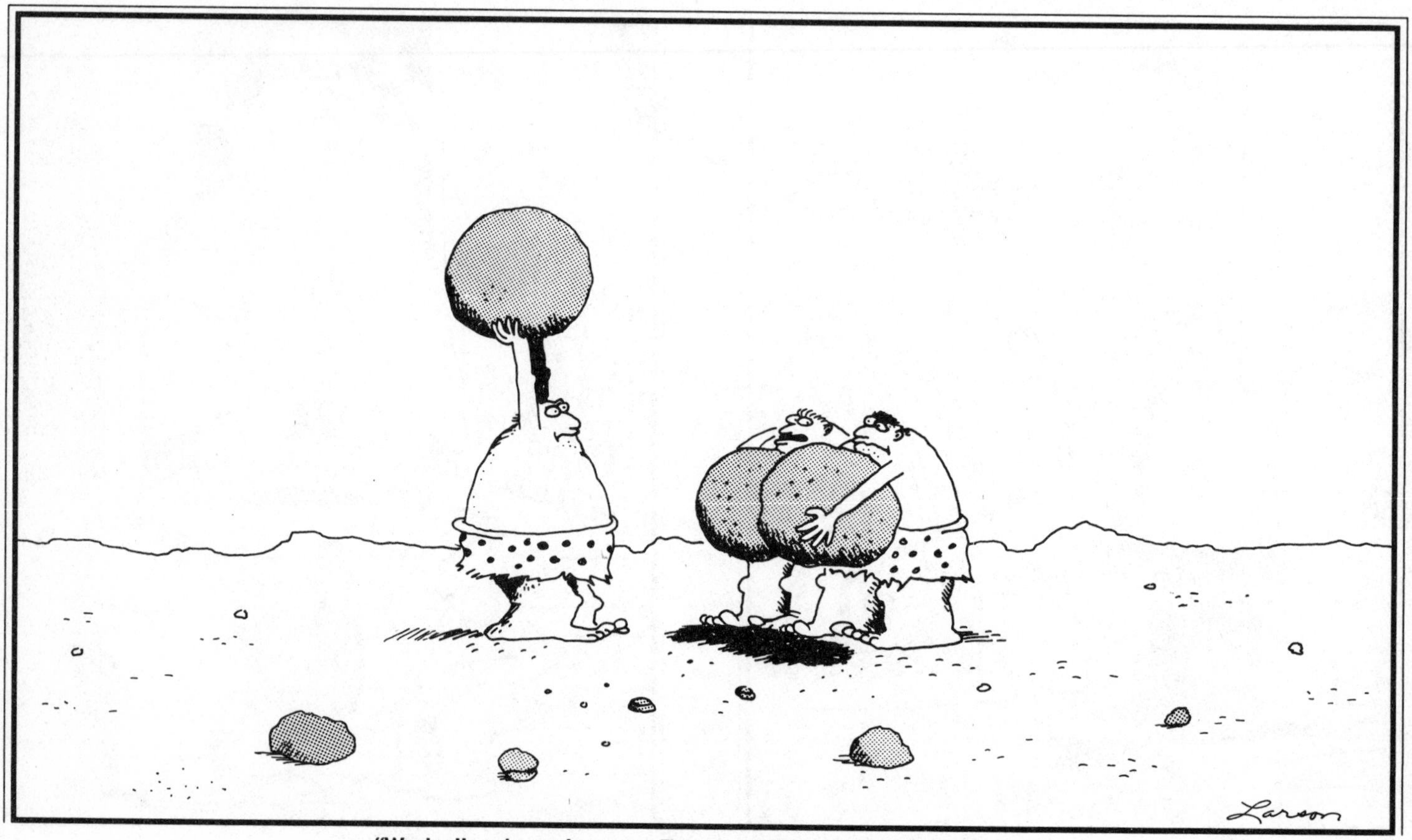
Larson

"We better do as he says, Thag . . . He's got the drop on us."

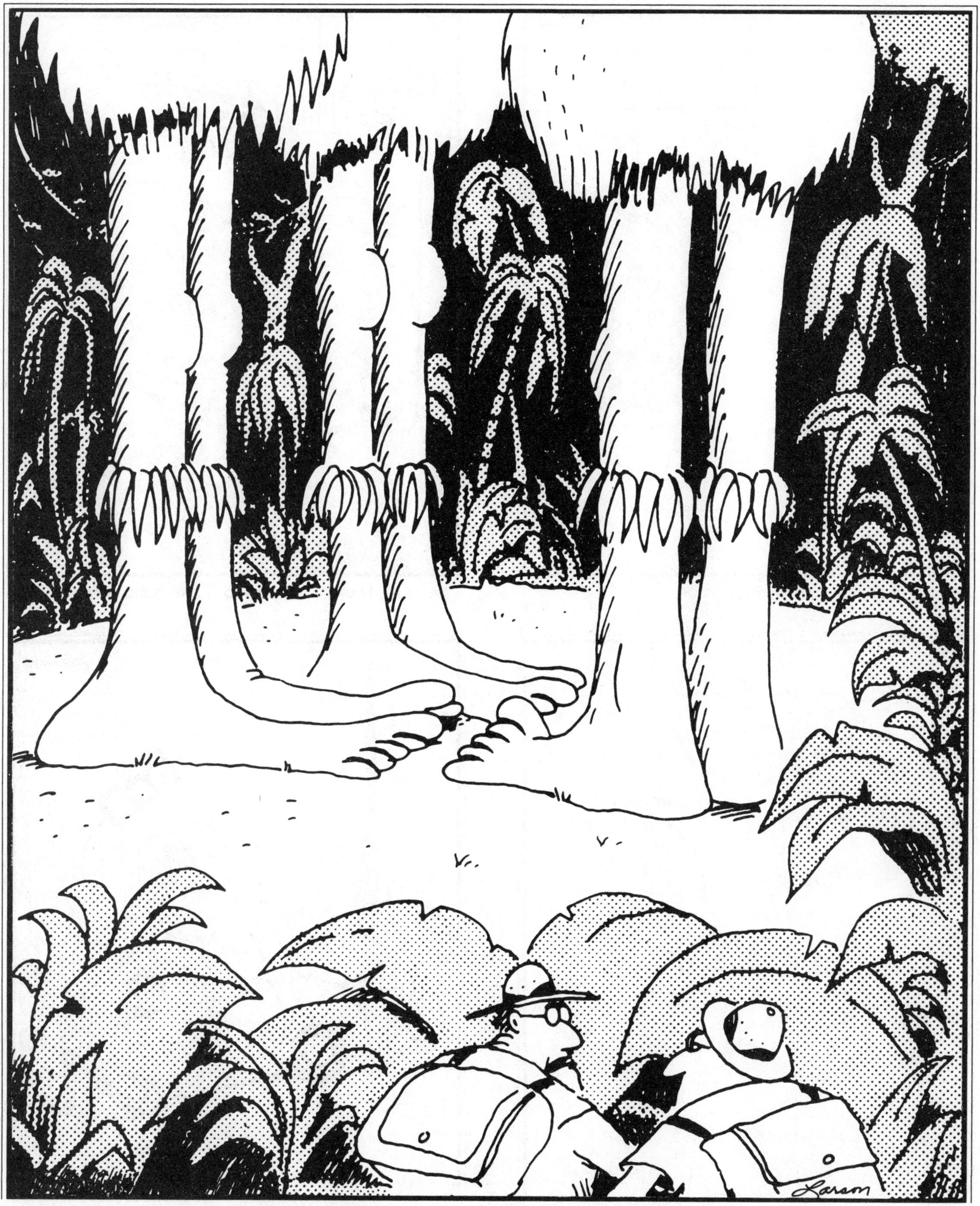
Larson
"With a little luck, they may revere us as gods."

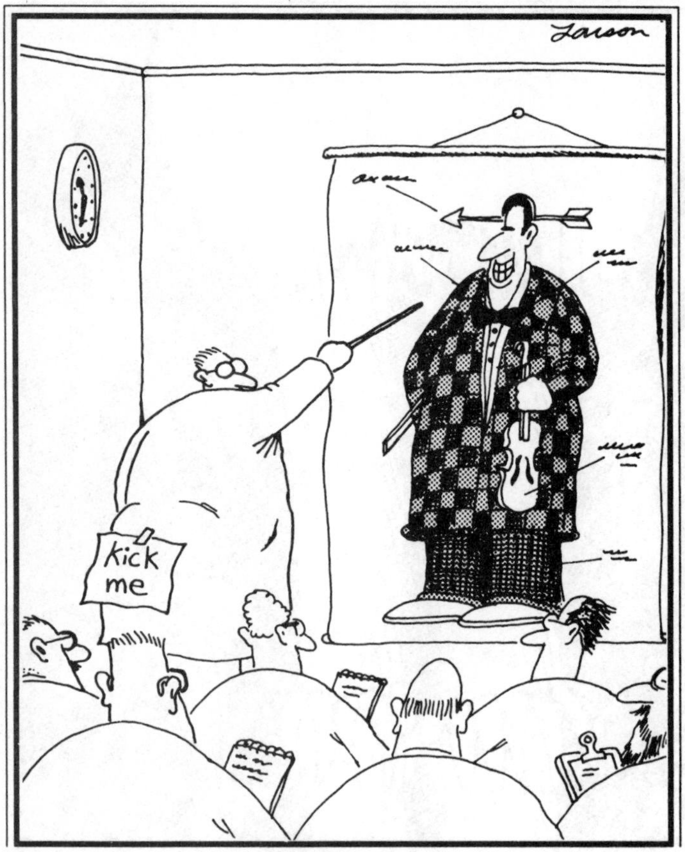
Larson
Kick me

Analyzing humor

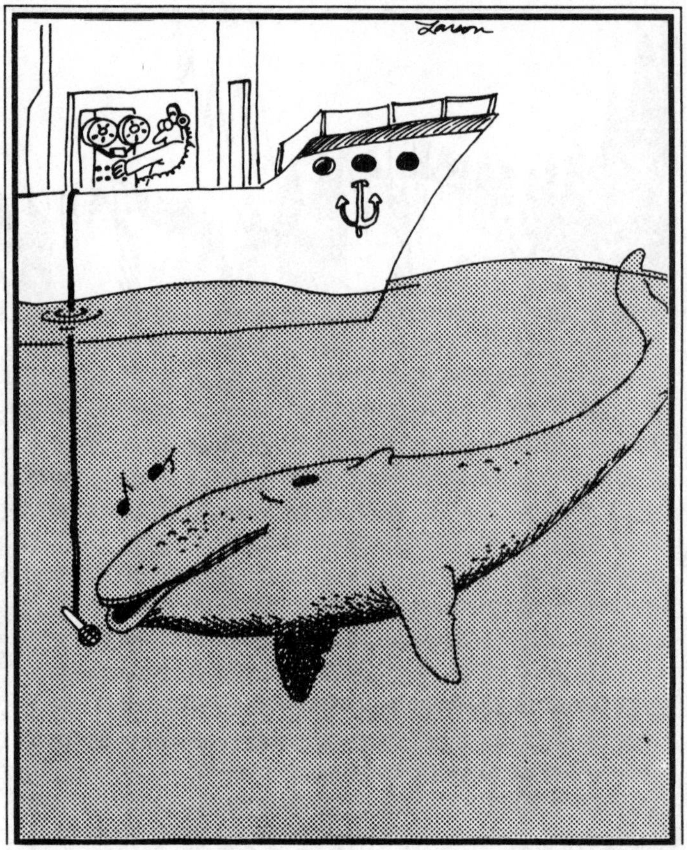
Larson

"A Louie, Louie . . . wowoooo . . . We gotta go now . . ."

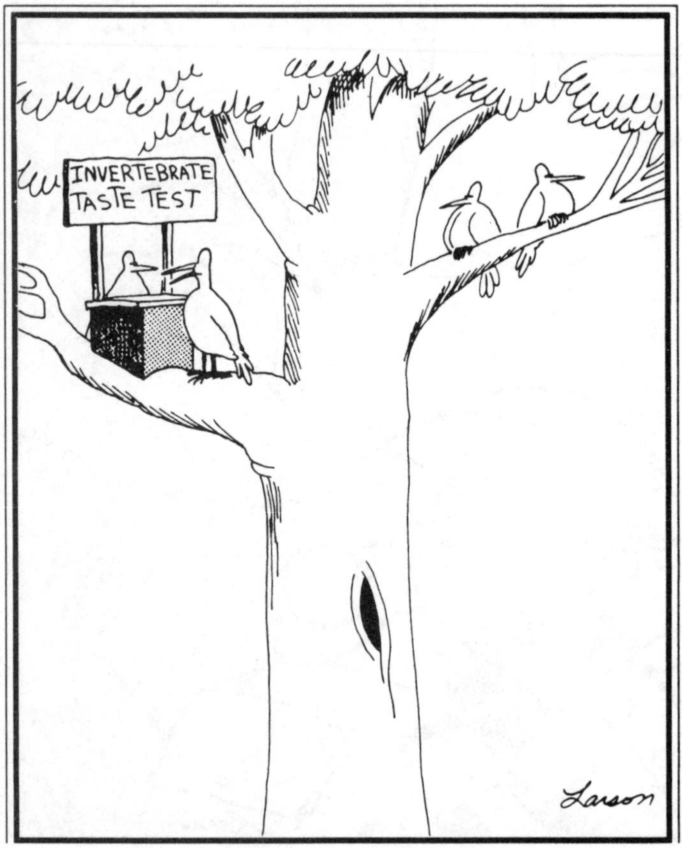
INVERTEBRATE TASTE TEST
Larson

"Mmmmmm . . . Nope . . . nope . . . I don't like that at all . . . Too many legs."

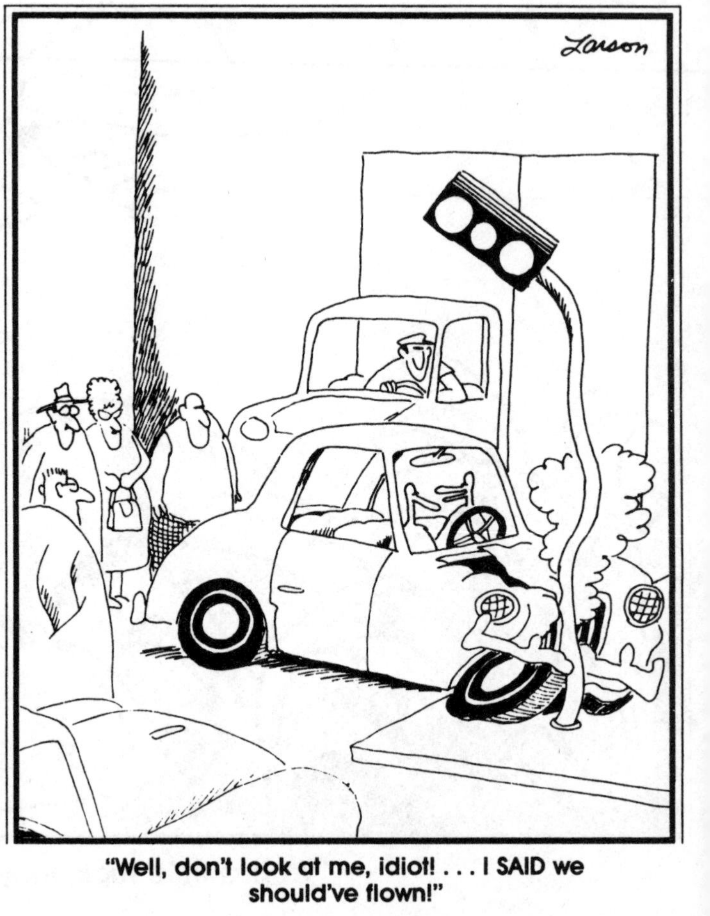
Larson

"Well, don't look at me, idiot! . . . I SAID we should've flown!"

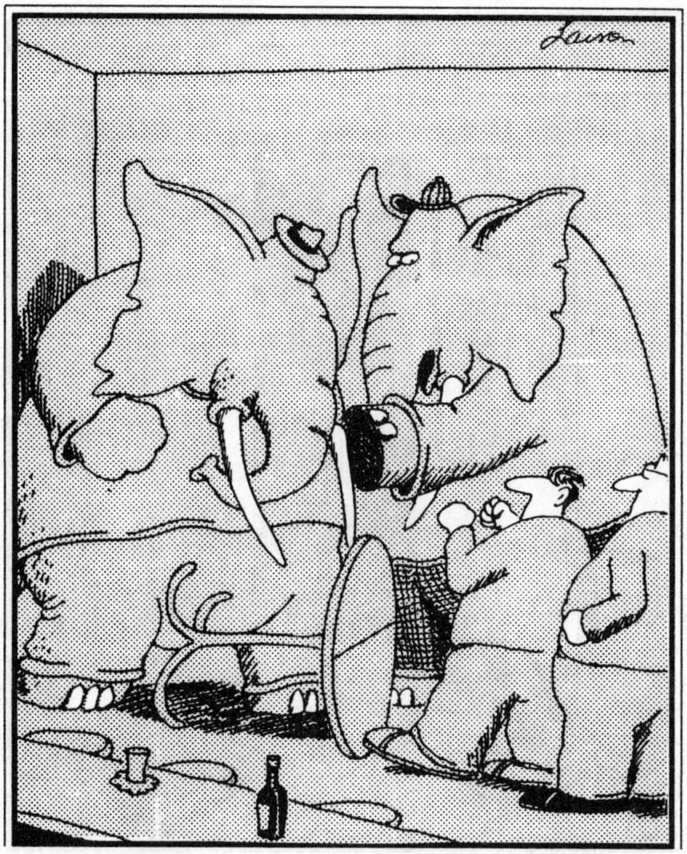

"Relax, Jerry! . . . He probably didn't know you were an elephant when he told that last joke!"

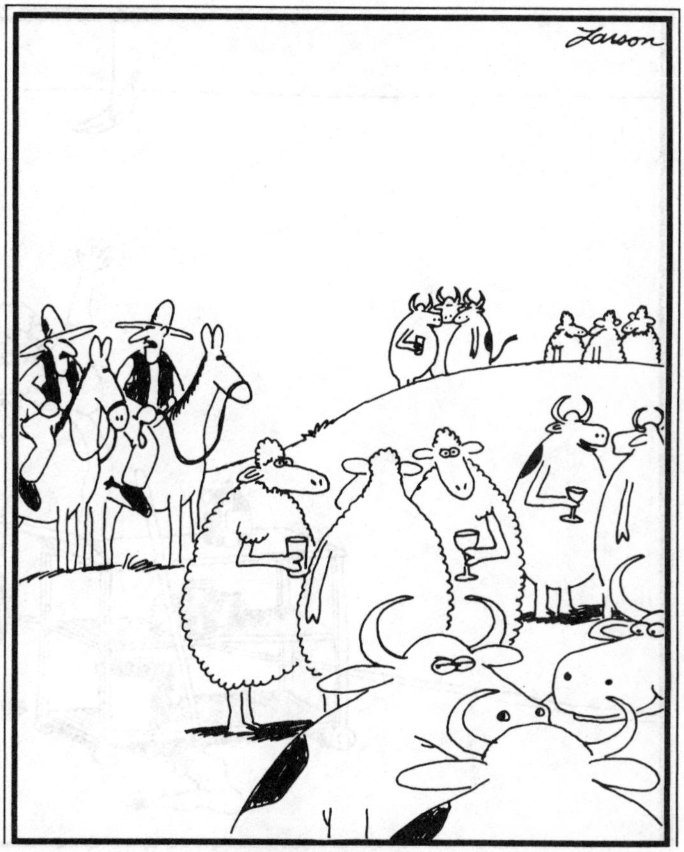

"Well, what have I always said? . . . Sheep and cattle just don't mix."

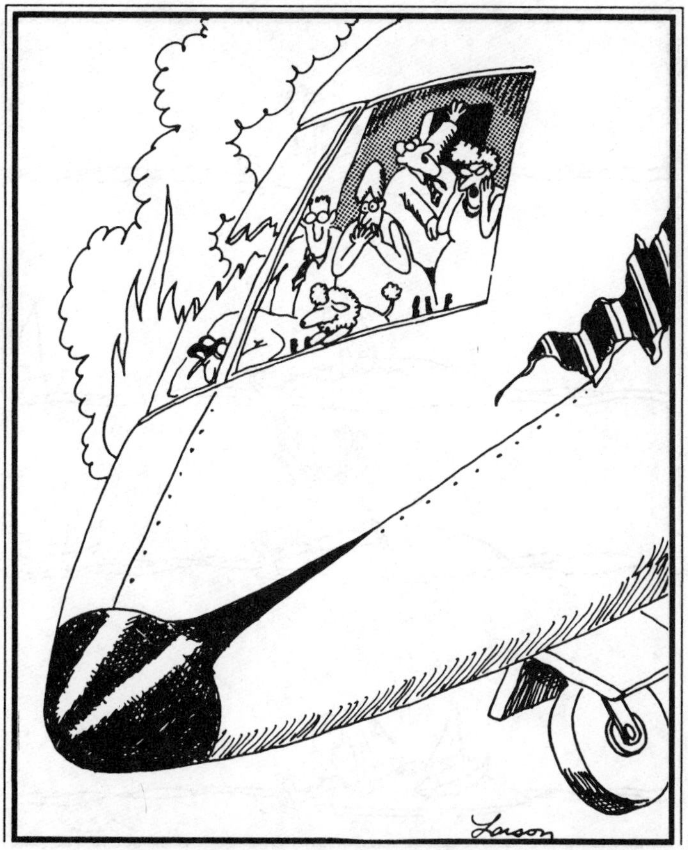

Suddenly, amidst all the confusion, Fifi seized the controls and saved the day.

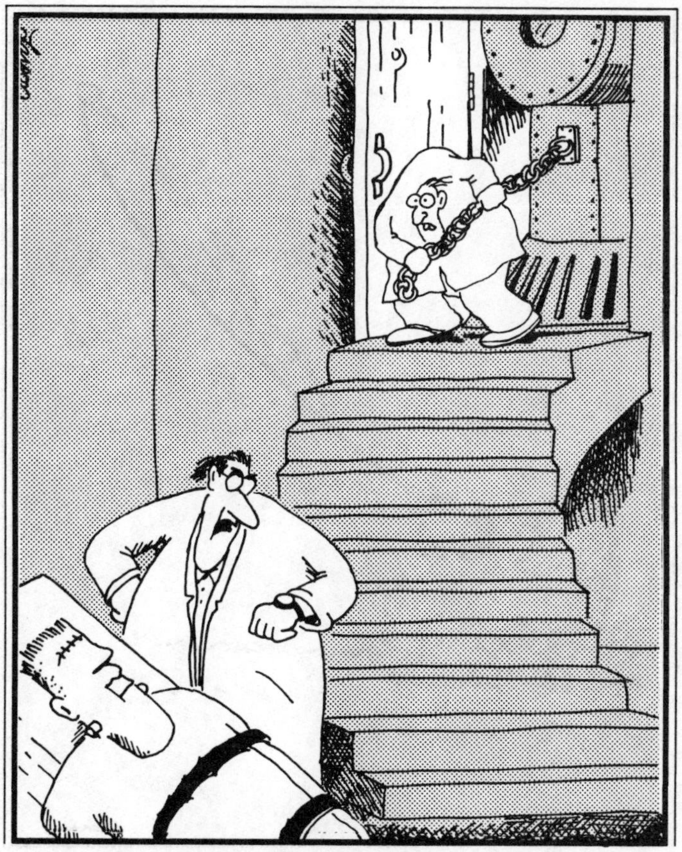

"Curses! . . . How long does it take Igor to go out and bring back a simple little brain, anyway?"

PRIMATE RESEARCH LAB
Larson

Larson

Larson

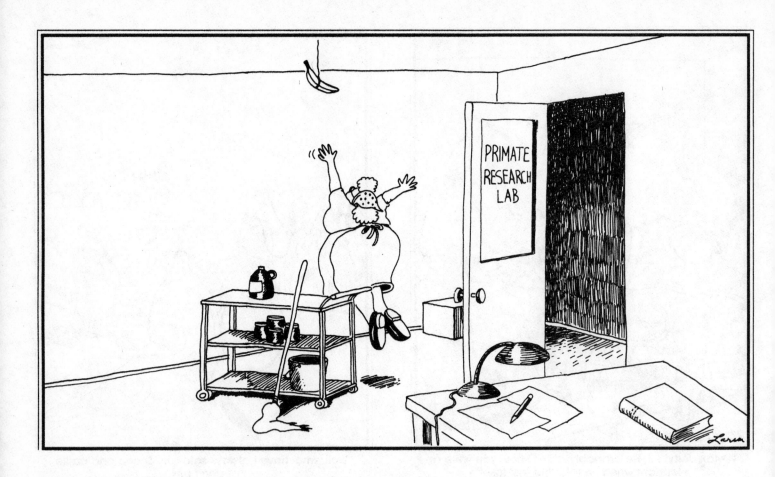

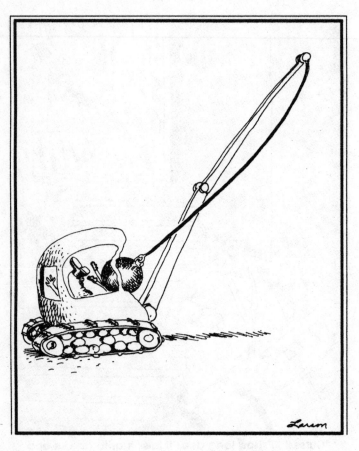

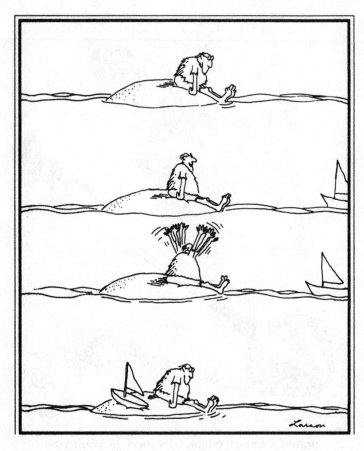

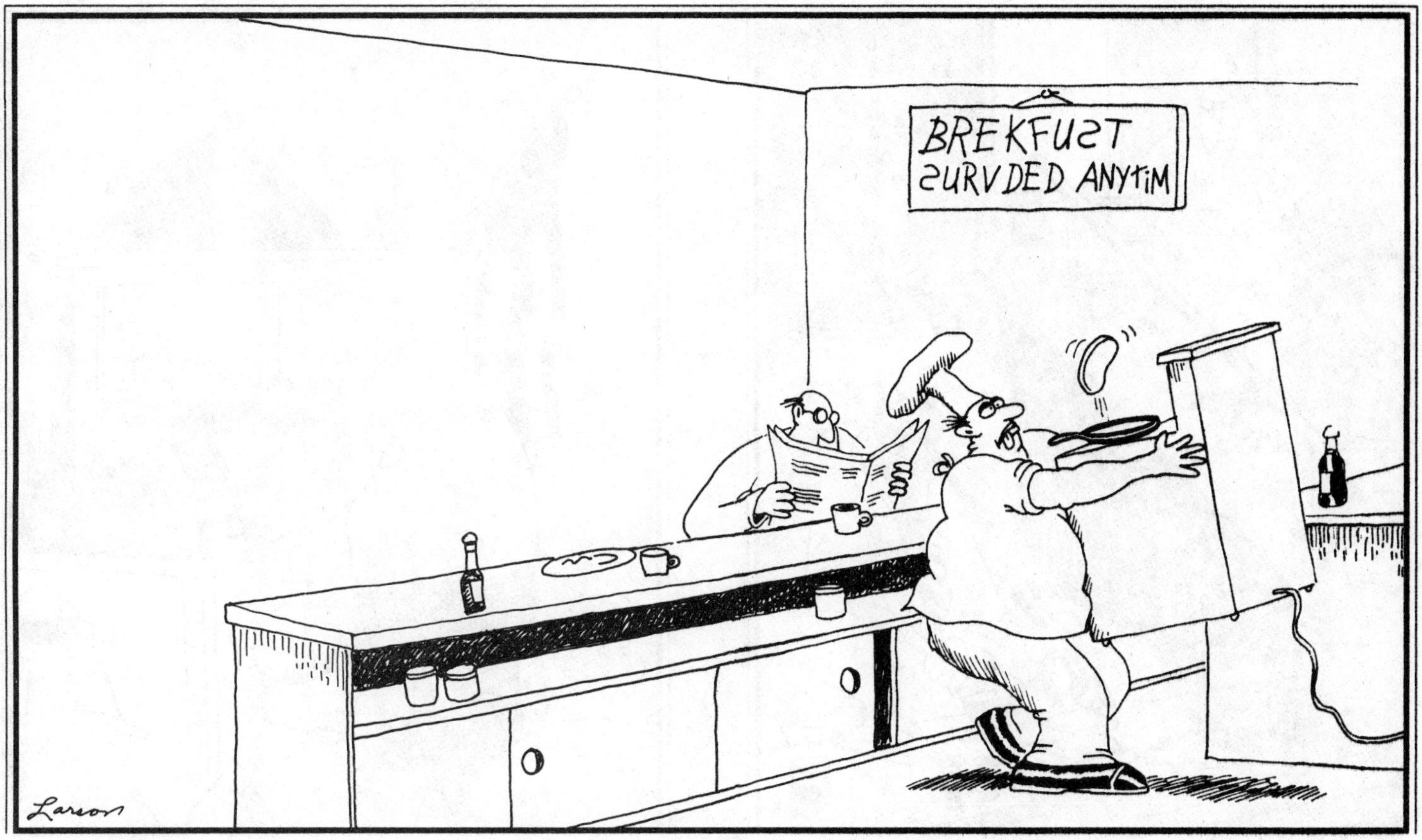
BREKFUST
SURVDED ANYTIM
Larson

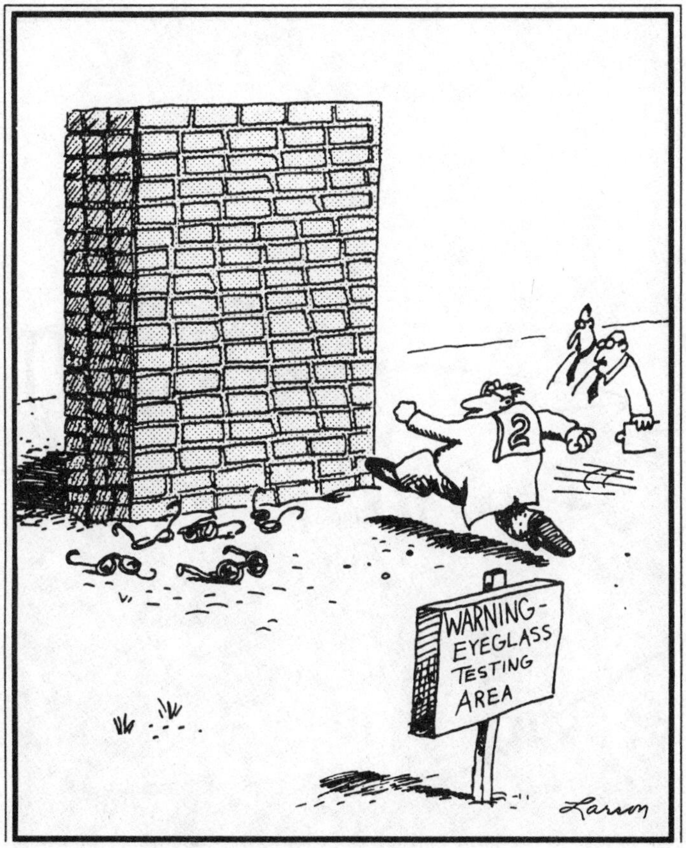
2
WARNING-
EYEGLASS
TESTING
AREA
Larson

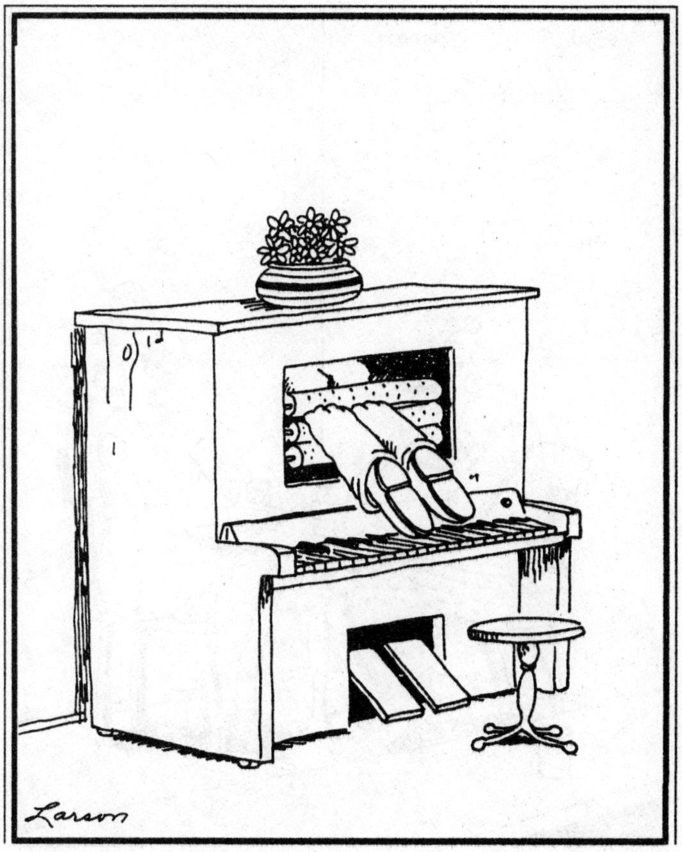
Larson

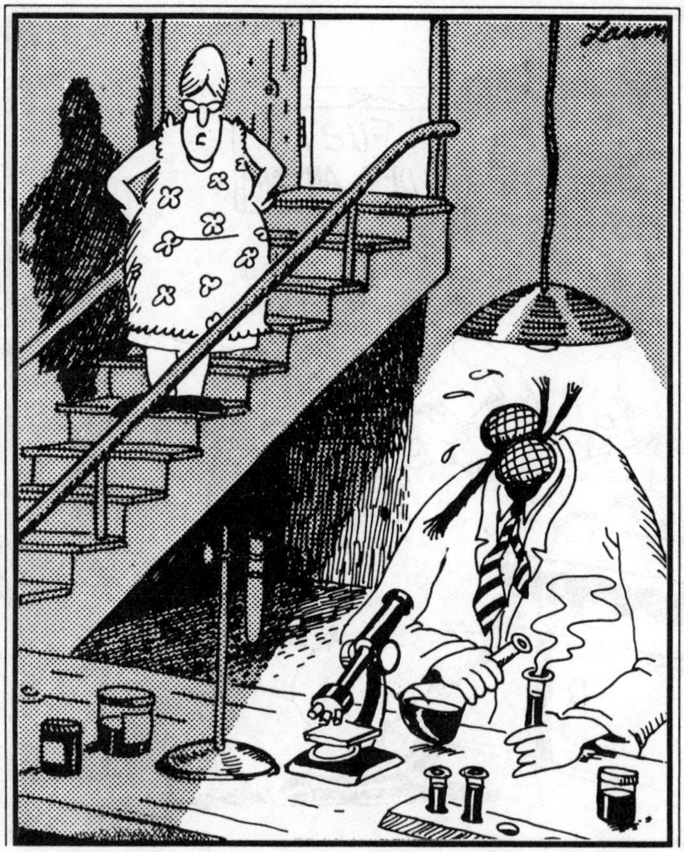
Larson

"Lunch is ready, Lawrence, and . . . What? You're STILL a fly?"

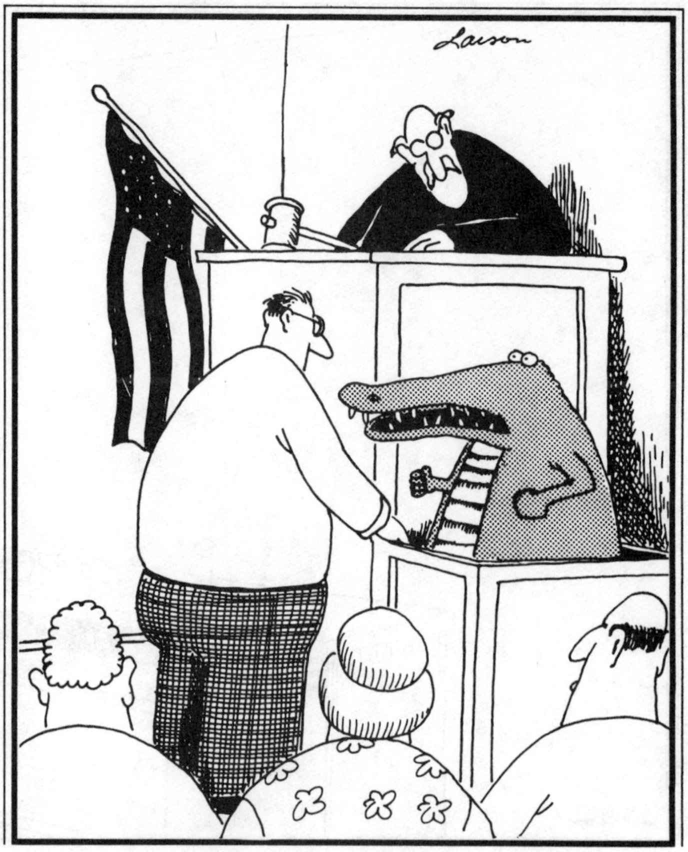
Larson

"Well, of COURSE I did it in cold blood, you idiot! I'm a reptile!"

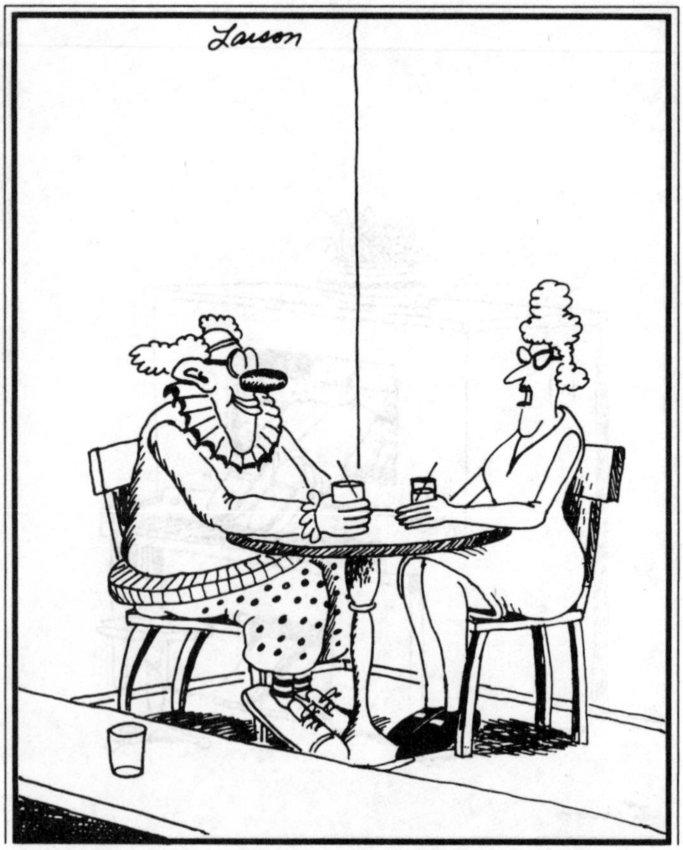
Larson

"And I like honesty in a relationship . . . I'm not into playing games."

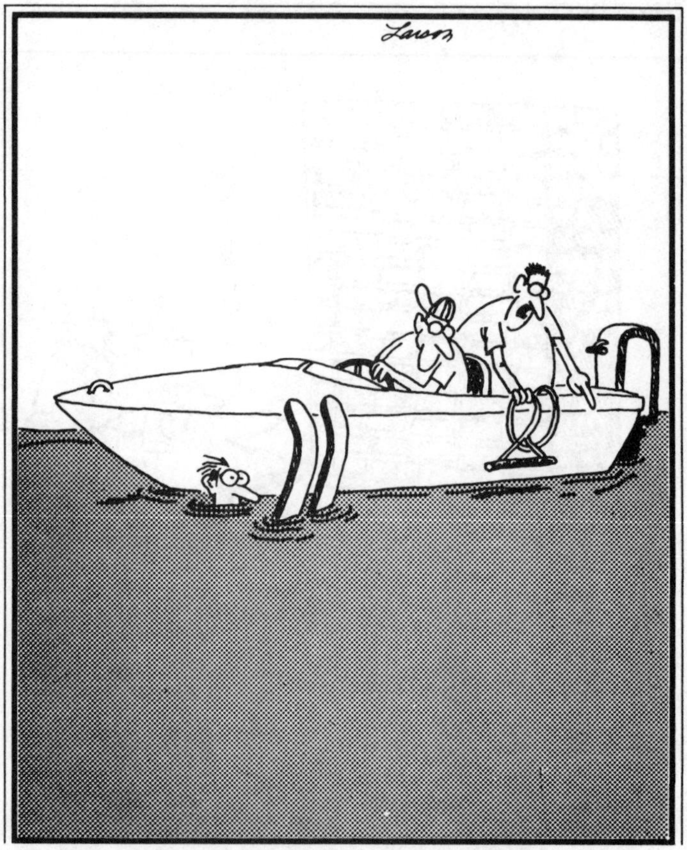
Larson

"There! Quick, Larry! Look! . . . Was I kidding? . . . That sucker's longer than the boat!"

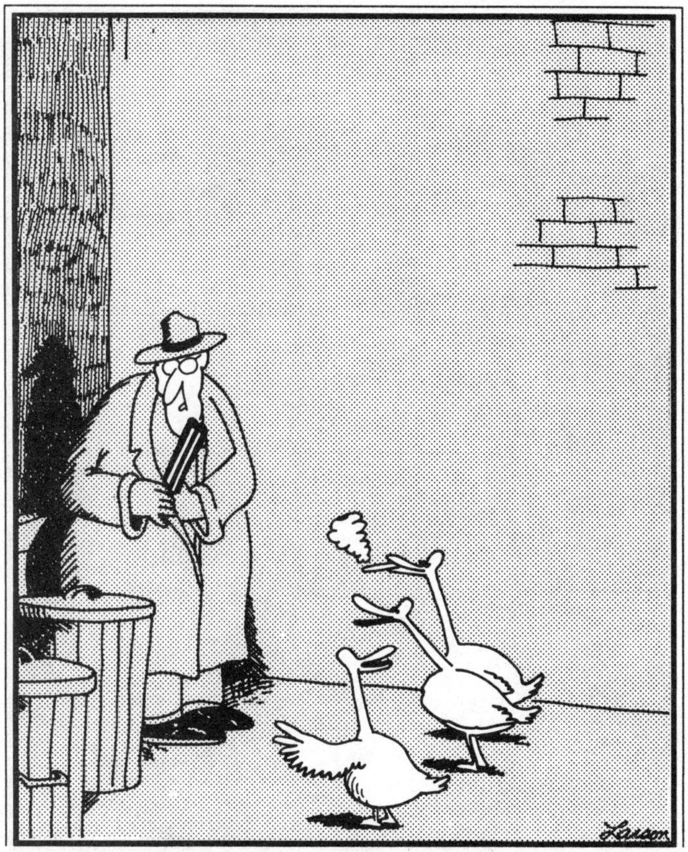

Cornered by the street ducks, Phil wasn't exactly sure what to do — and then he remembered his 12-gauge.

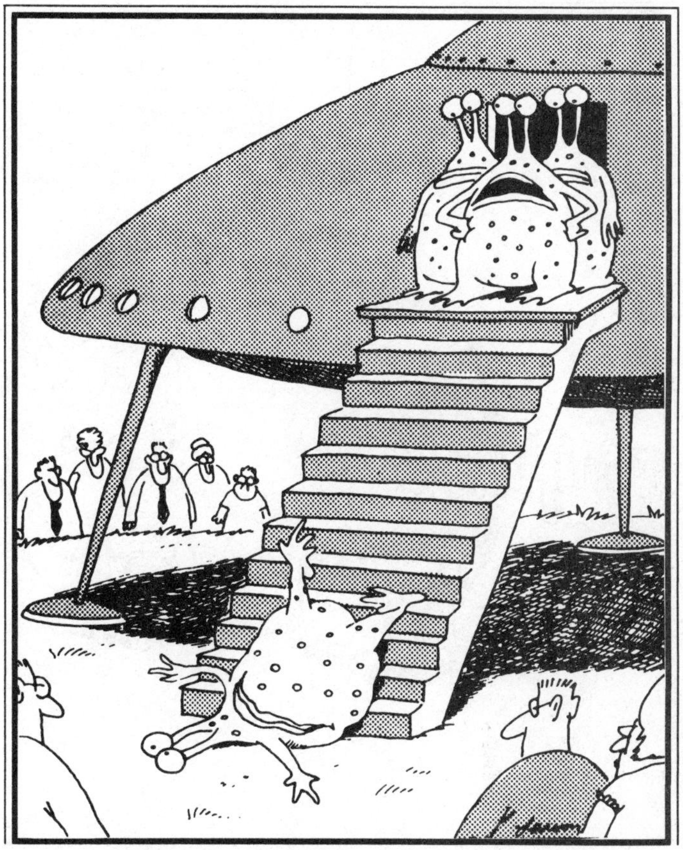

"Wonderful! Just wonderful! . . . So much for instilling them with a sense of awe."

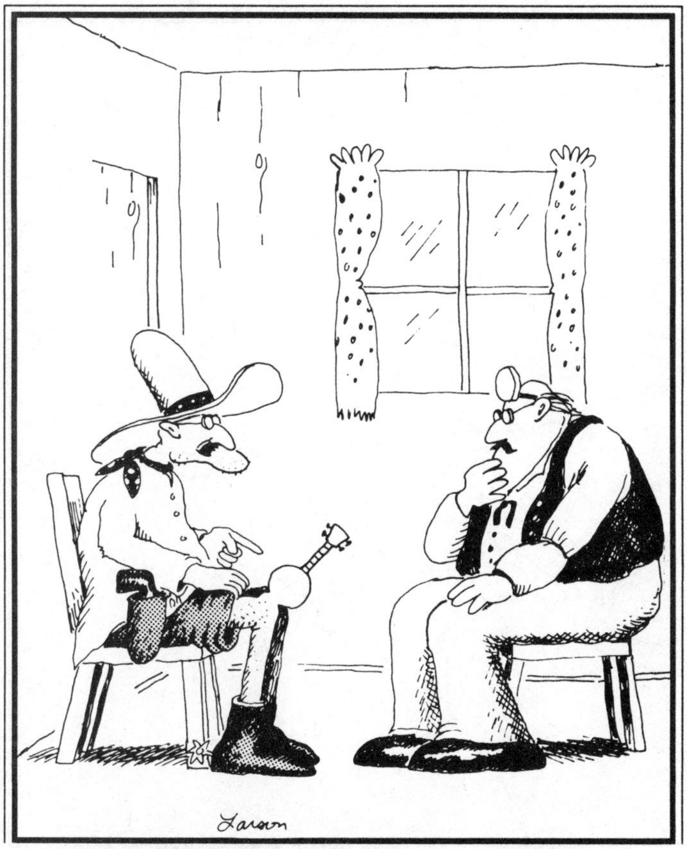

"I've had it, Doc! . . . I've come all the way from Alabama with this danged thing on my knee!"

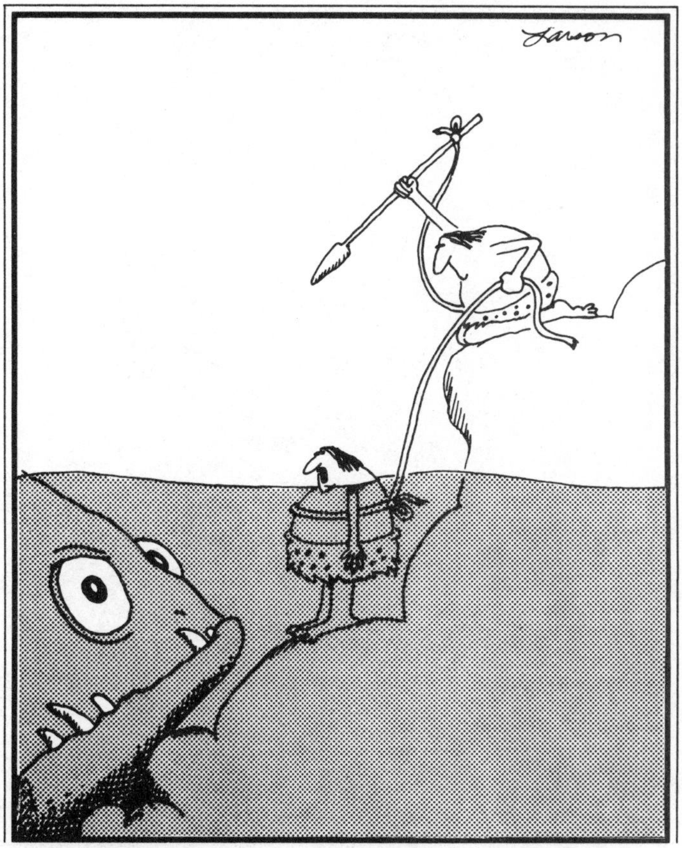

"Now, Grog! Throw! . . . Throoooooow! . . . Throw throw throw throw throw throw! . . ."

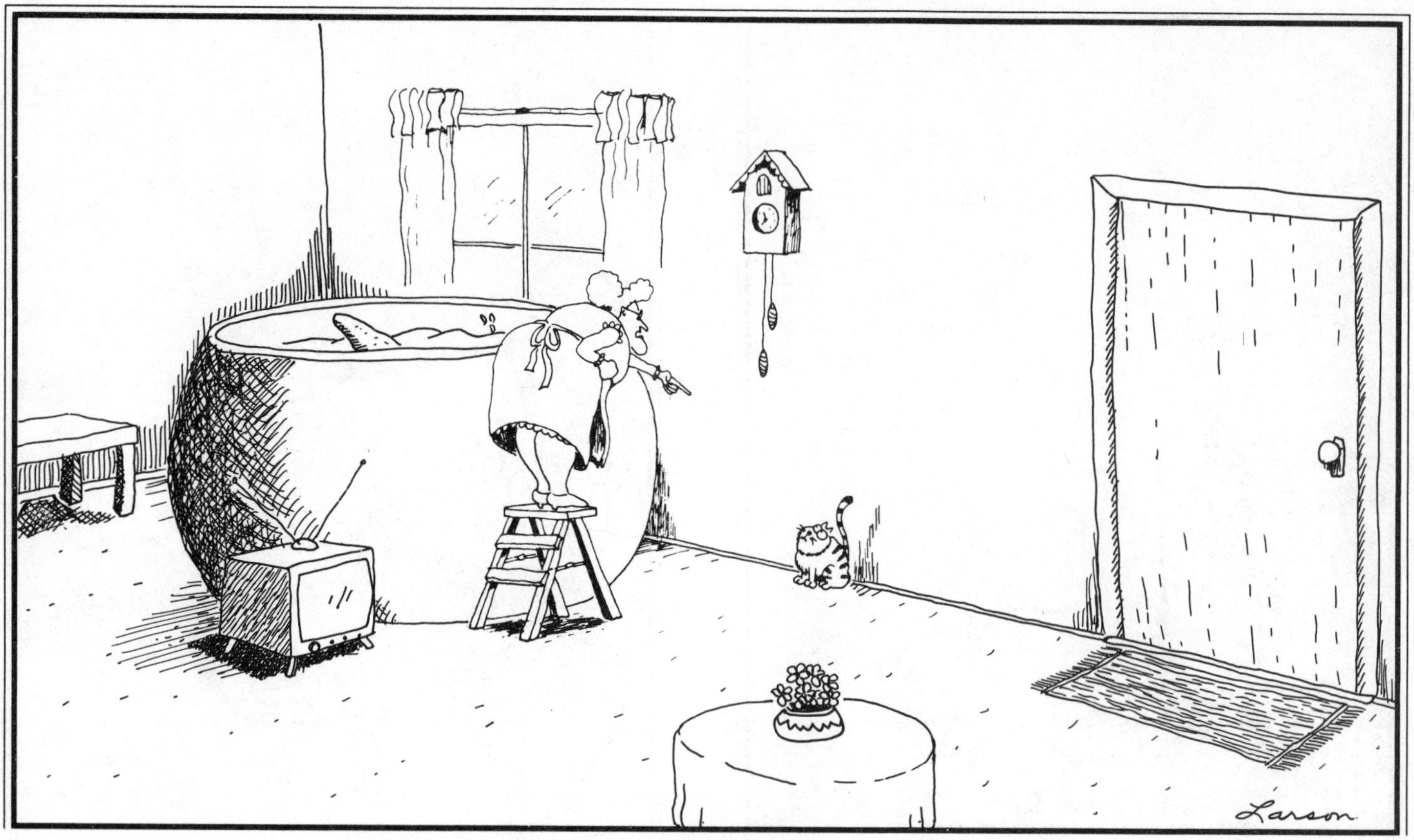
Larson

"And remember! . . . I don't want to catch you bothering the fish!"

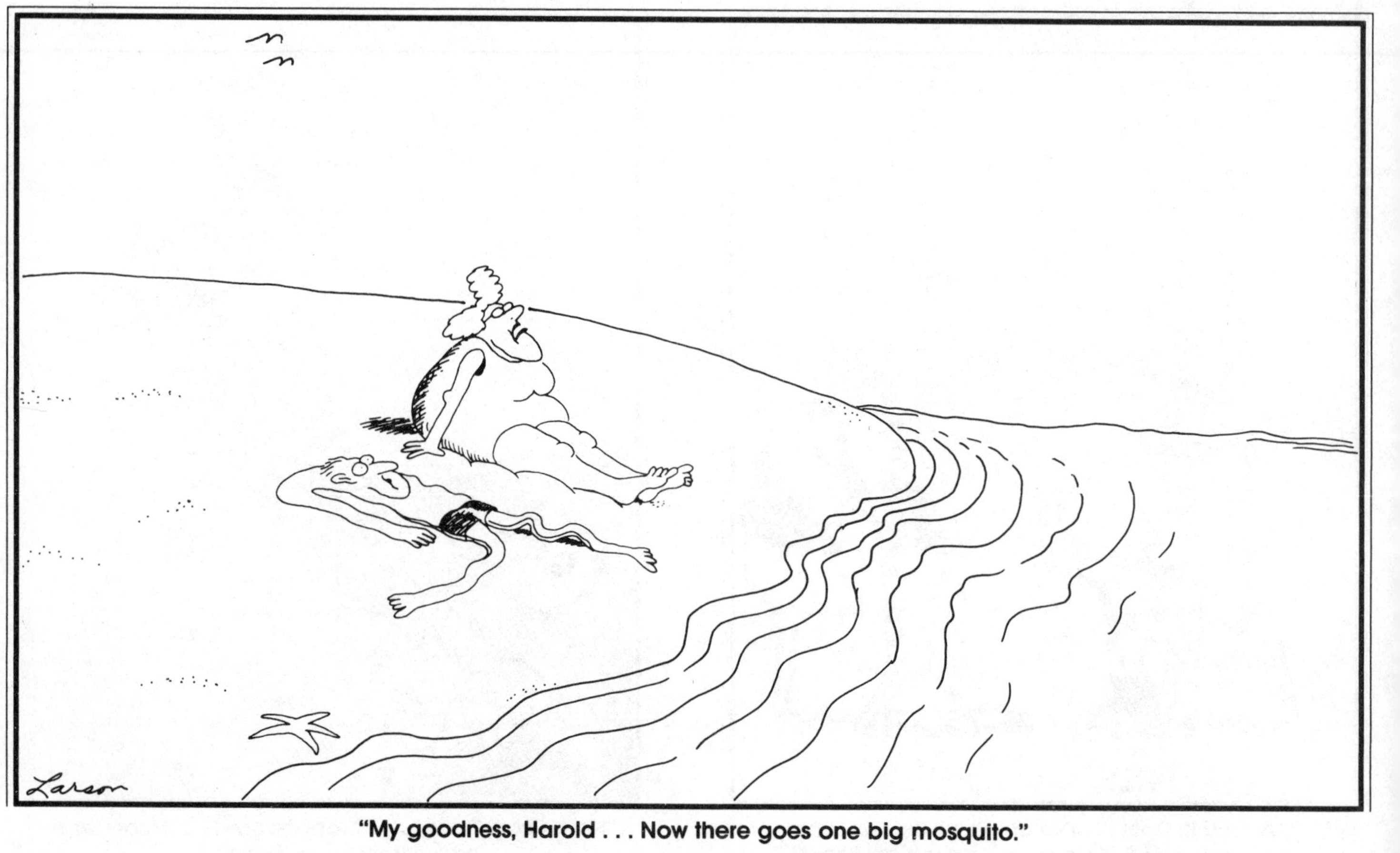
Larson

"My goodness, Harold . . . Now there goes one big mosquito."

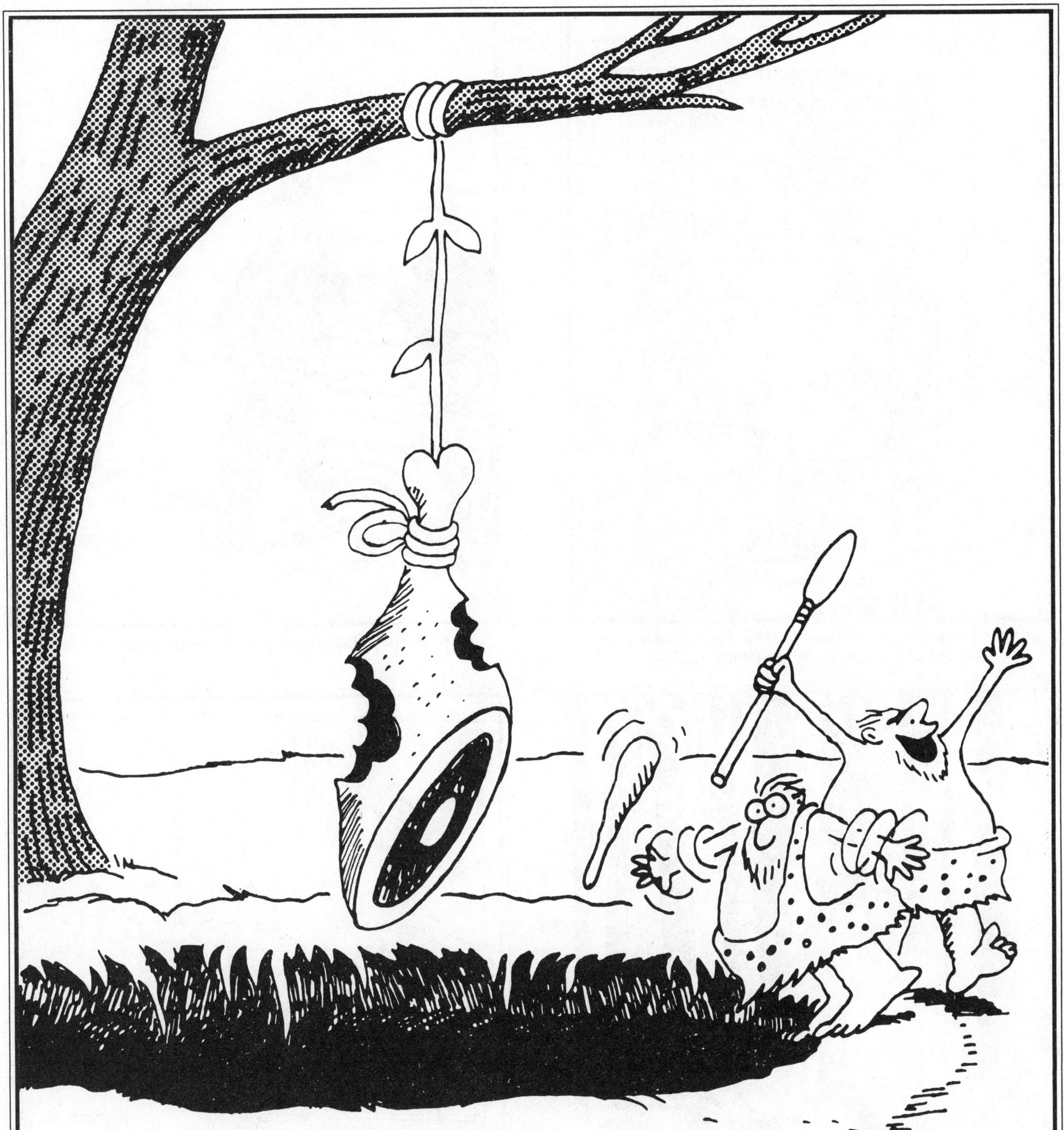
Larson

"Big one, Thag! . . . We caught biiiiiig one!"

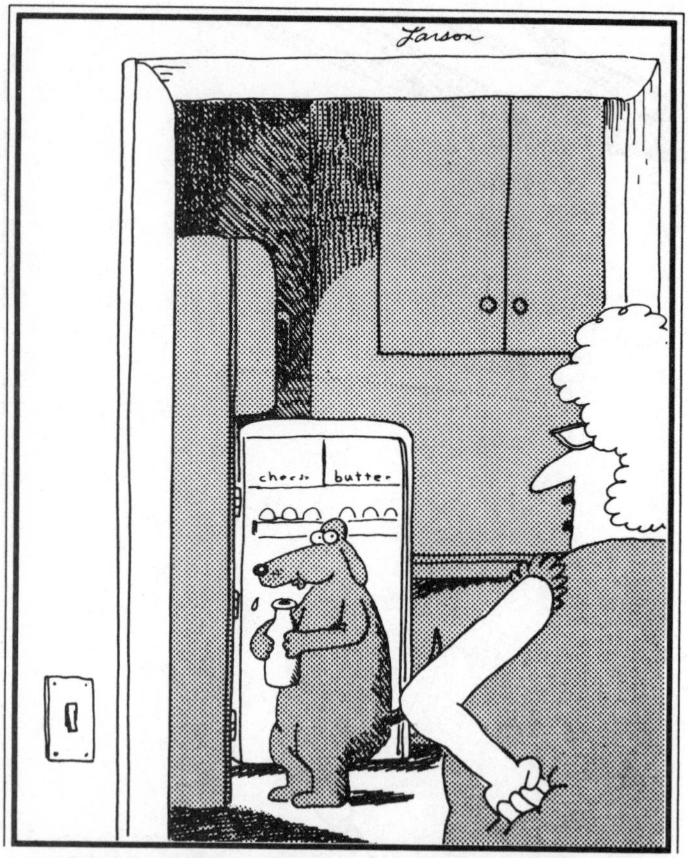
Larson

"Aha! As I always suspected! . . . I better not ever catch you drinking right from the bottle AGAIN!"

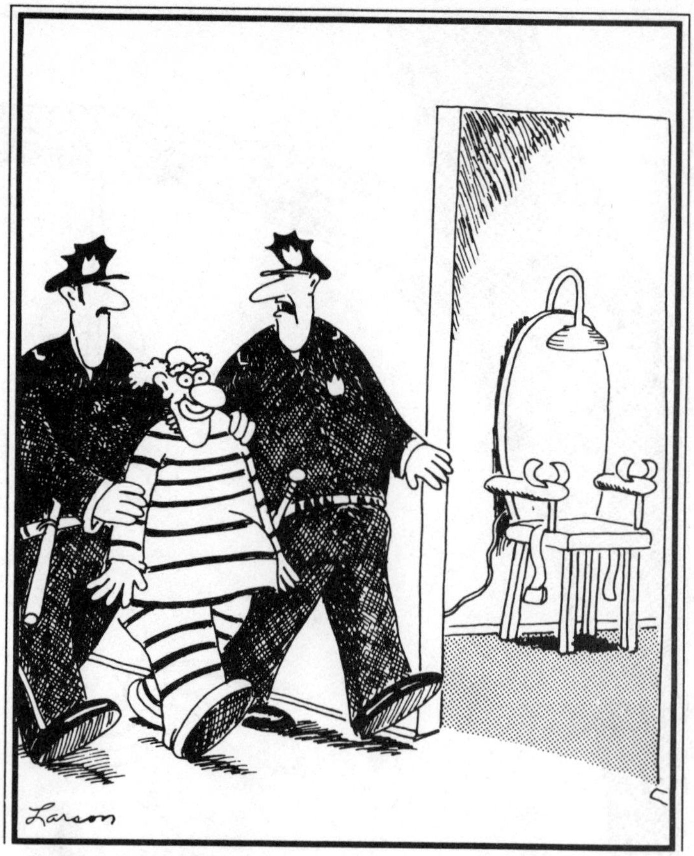
Larson

"I don't think I'll be able to tell the kids about this one."

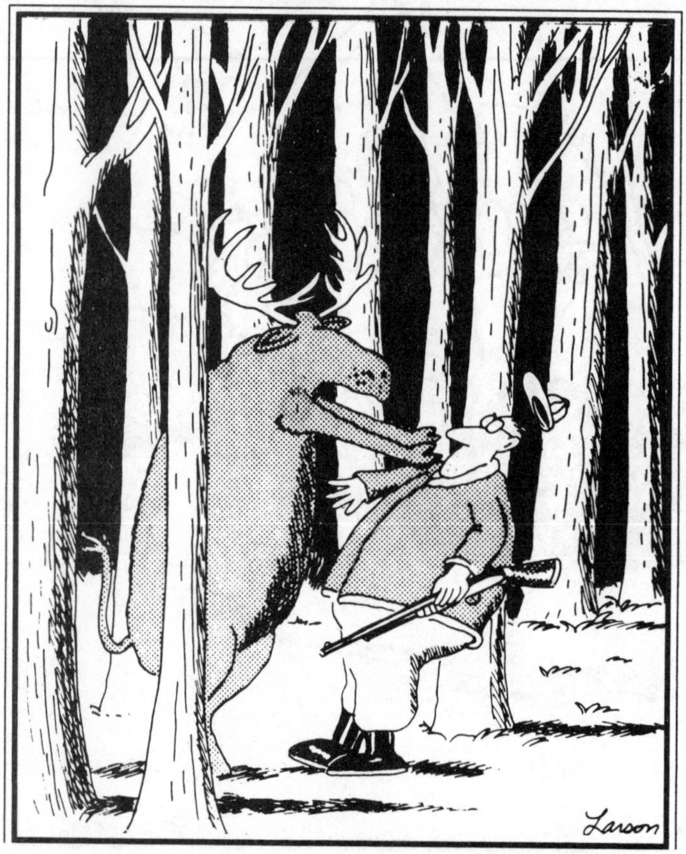
Larson

Carl shoves Roger, Roger shoves Carl, and tempers rise.

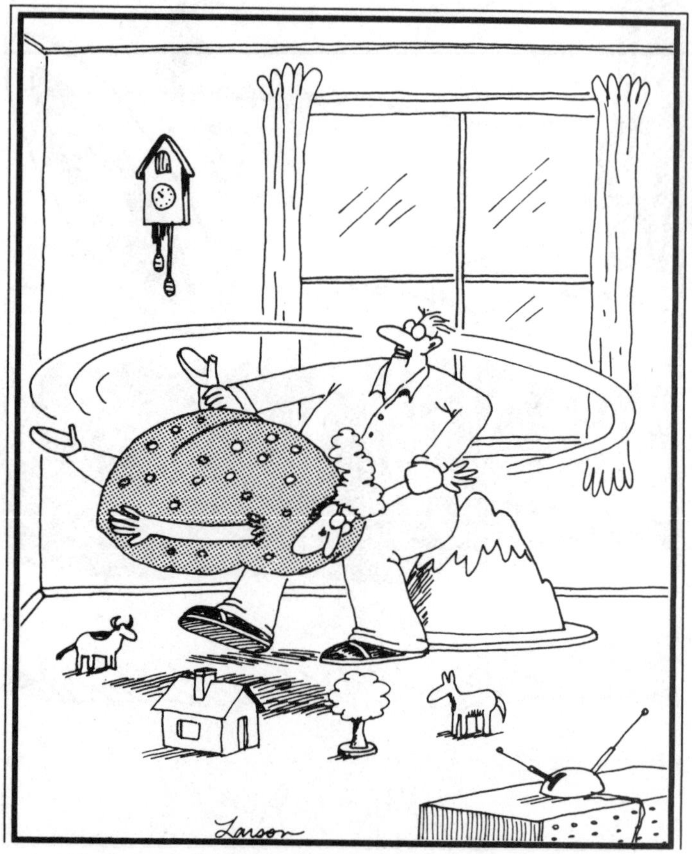
Larson

On the next pass, however, Helen failed to clear the mountains.

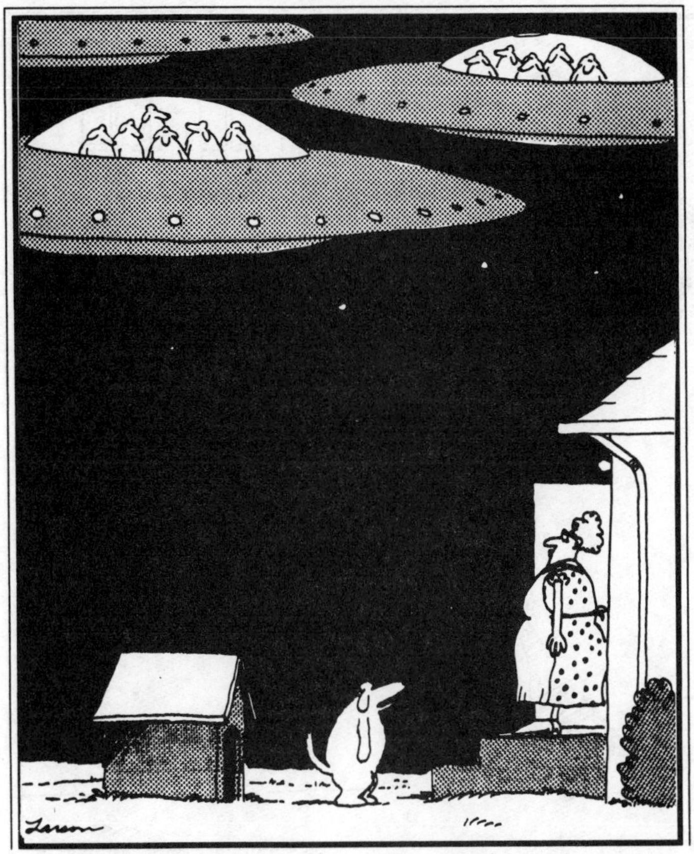
Larson

"Well, they finally came . . . But before I go, let's see you roll over a couple times."

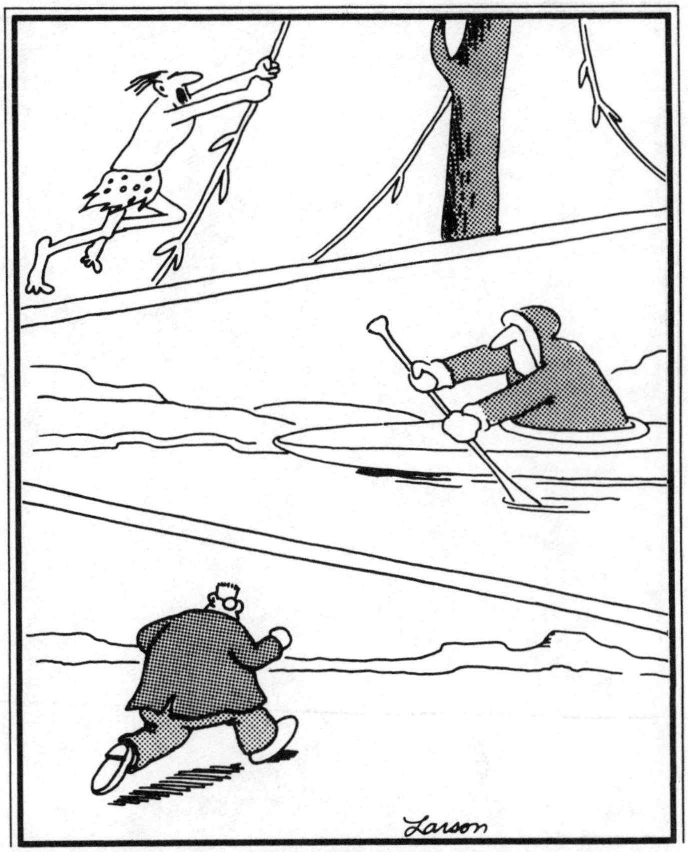
Larson

Tarzan of the jungle, Nanook of the North, and Warren of the Wasteland.

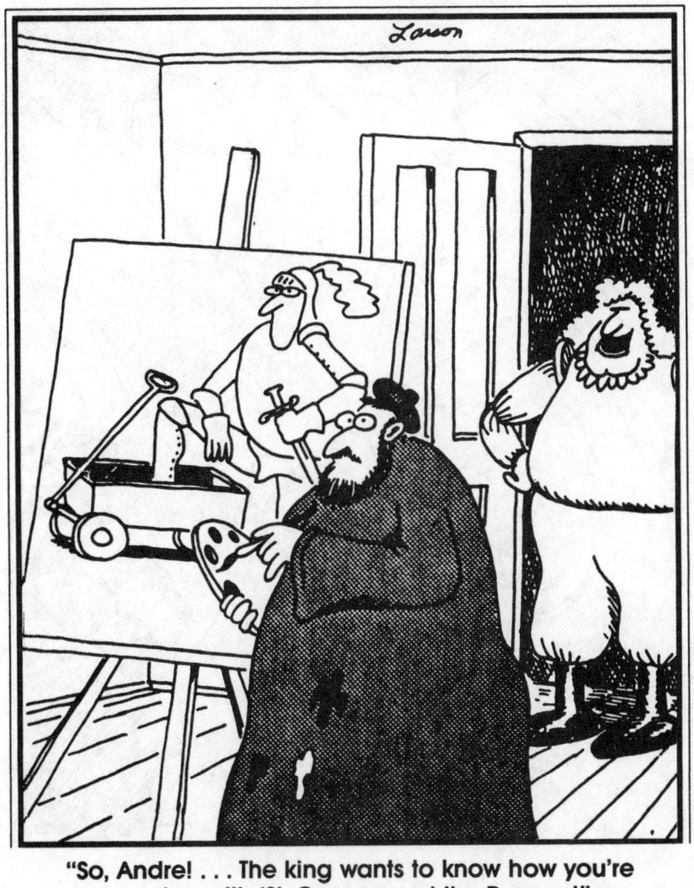
Larson

"So, Andre! . . . The king wants to know how you're coming with 'St. George and the Dragon.'"

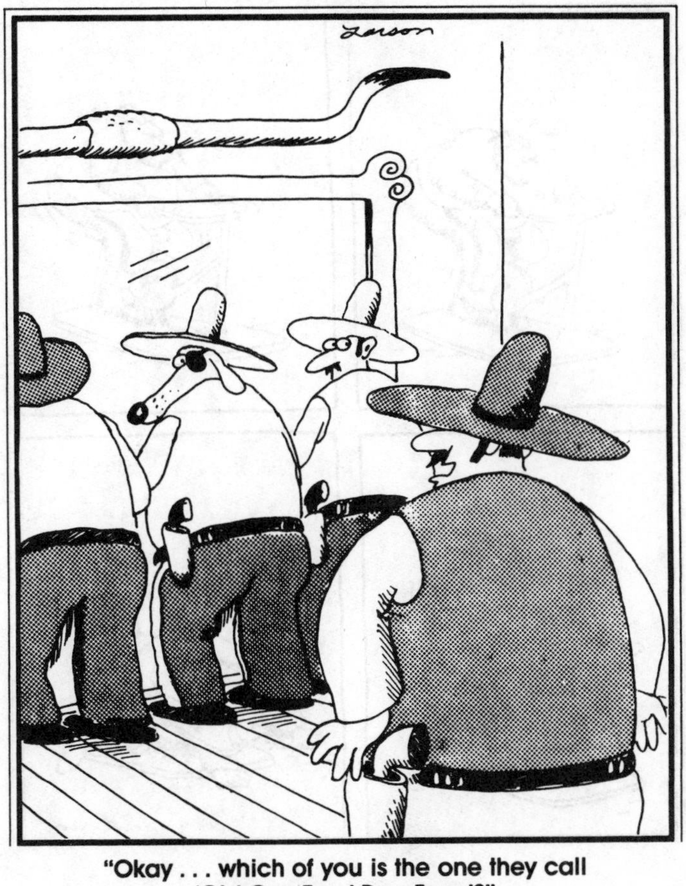
Larson

"Okay . . . which of you is the one they call 'Old-One-Eyed-Dog-Face'?"

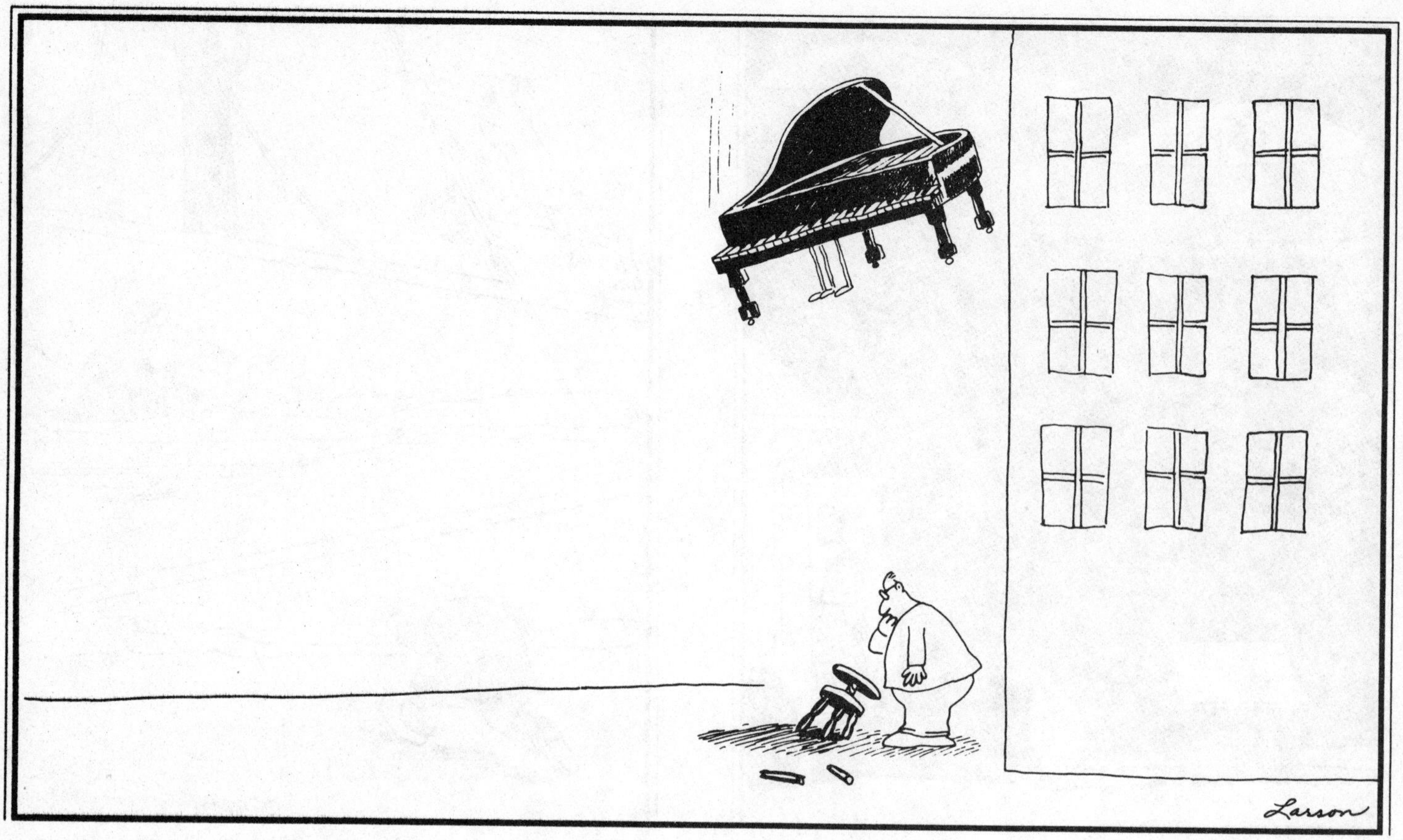

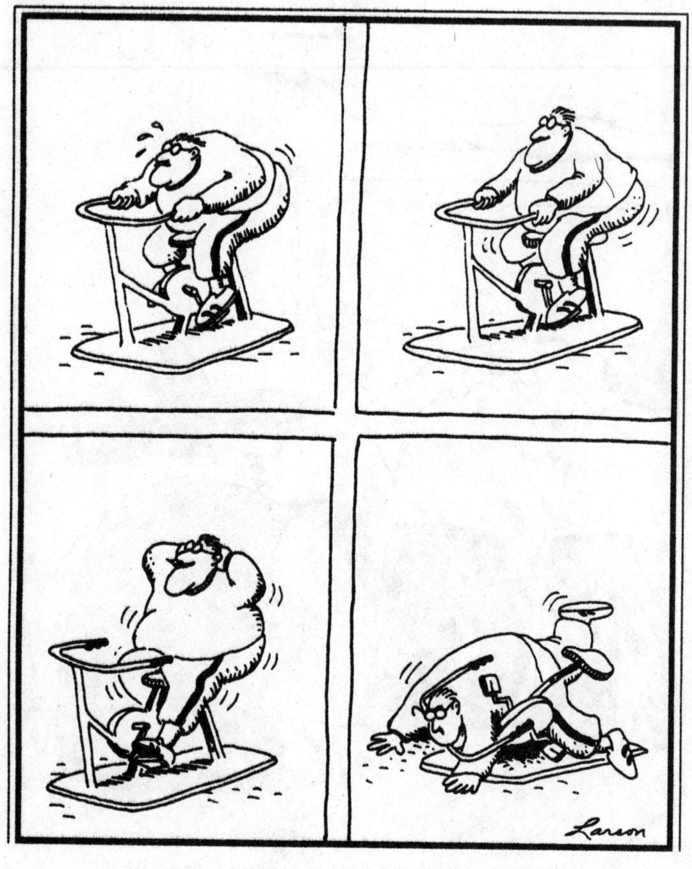

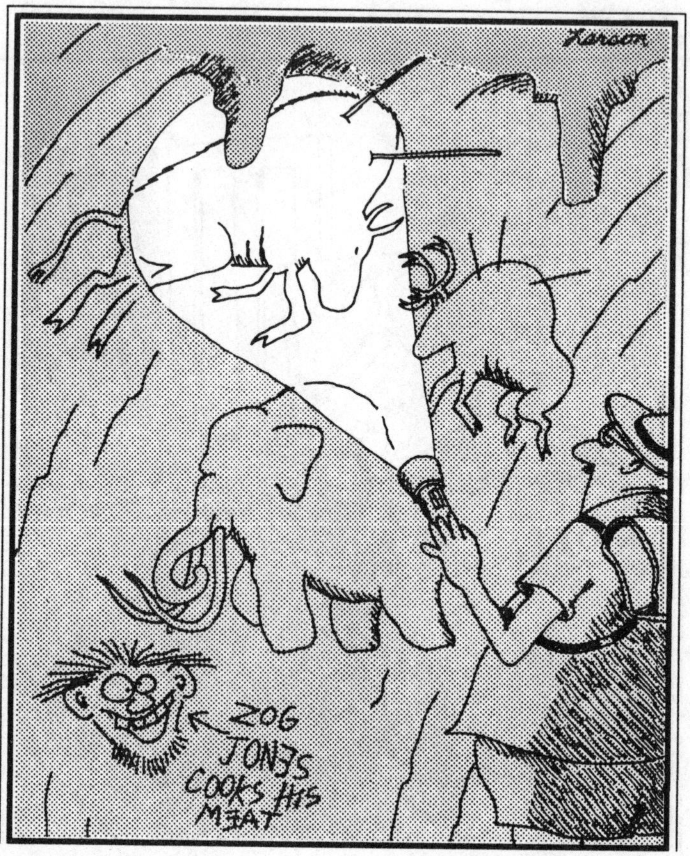

ZOG JONES COOKS HIS MEAT

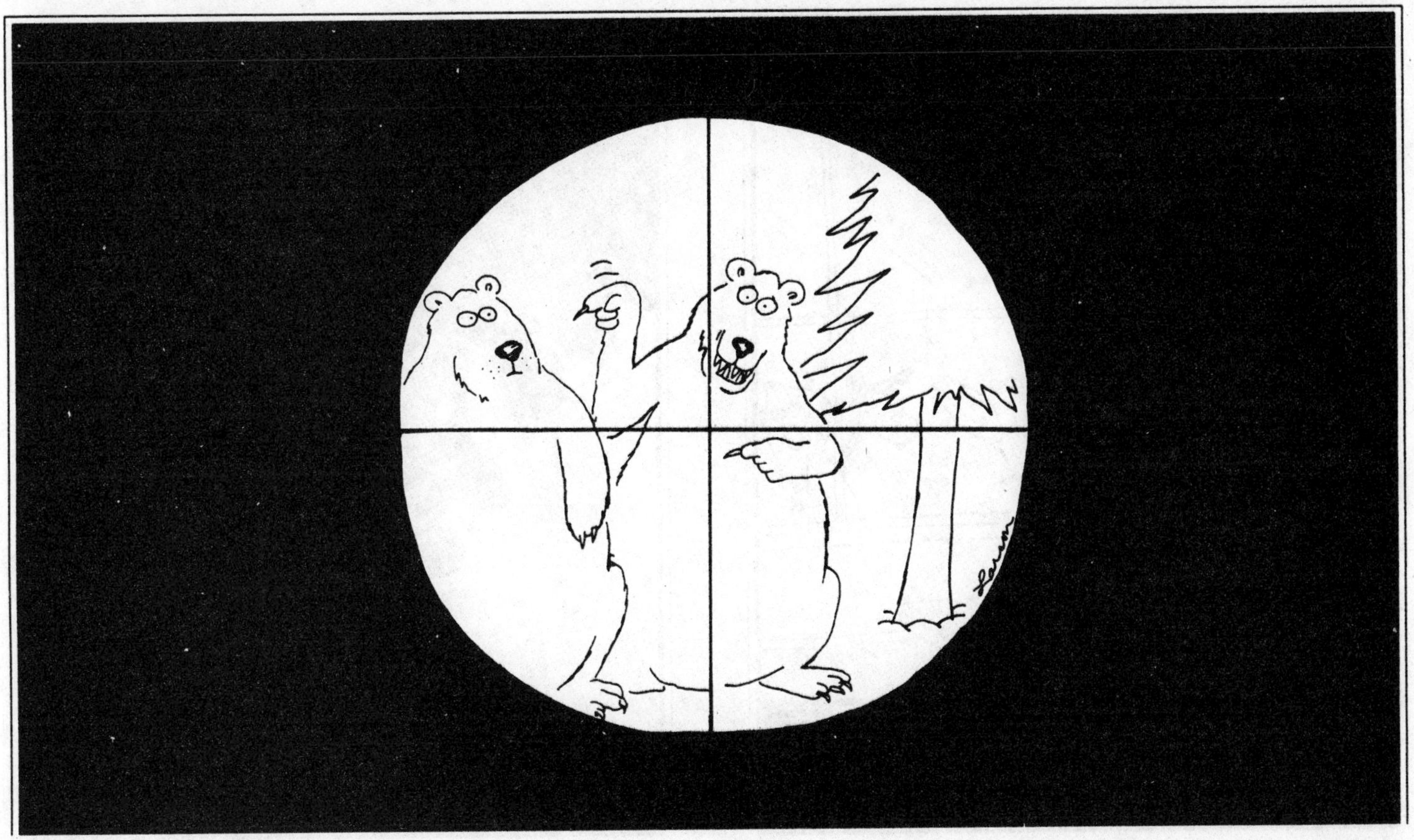
Larson

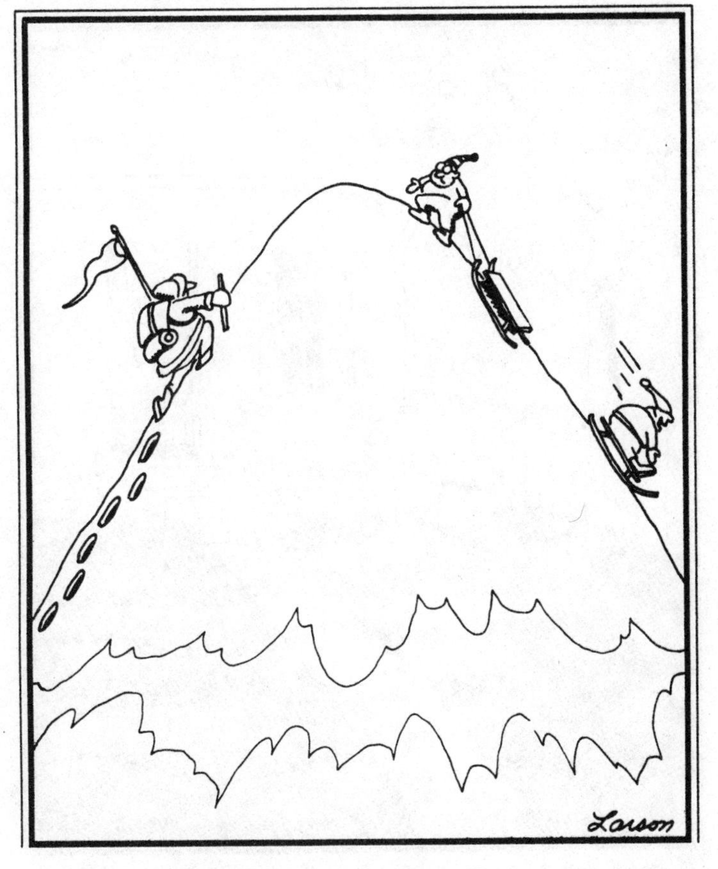
Larson

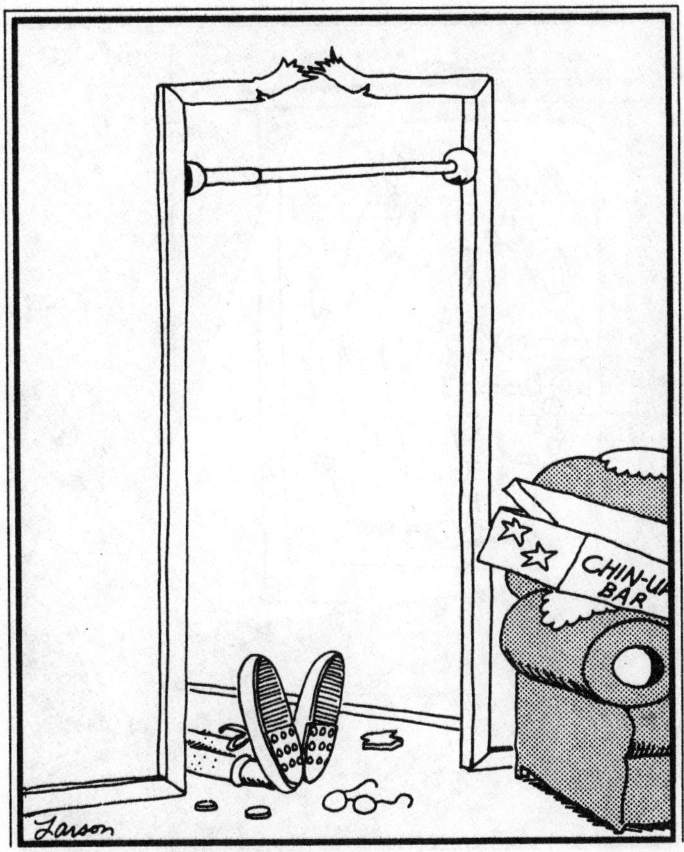
BAR
Larson

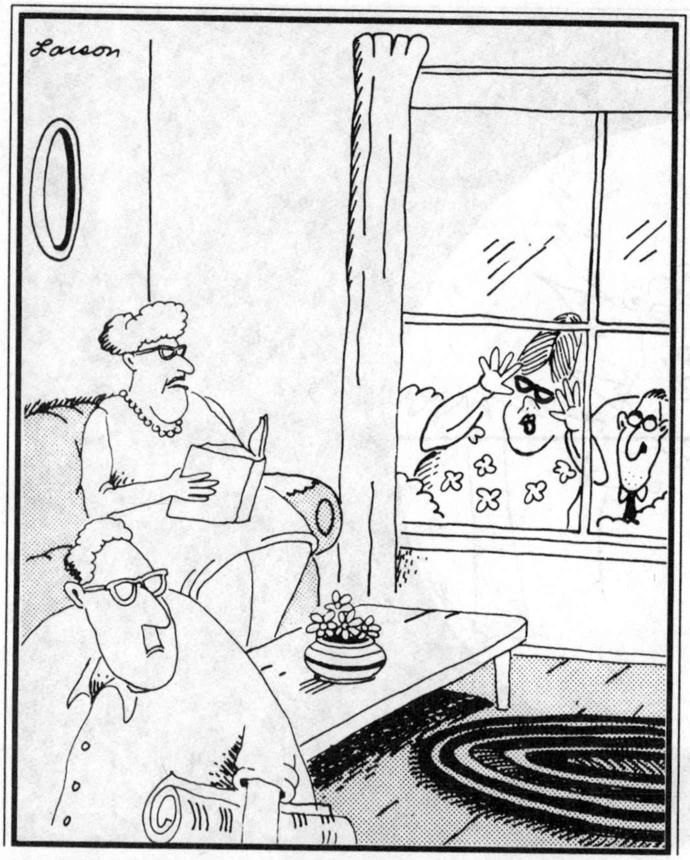
Larson

"Uh-uh, Warren . . . The Williams are checking us out again."

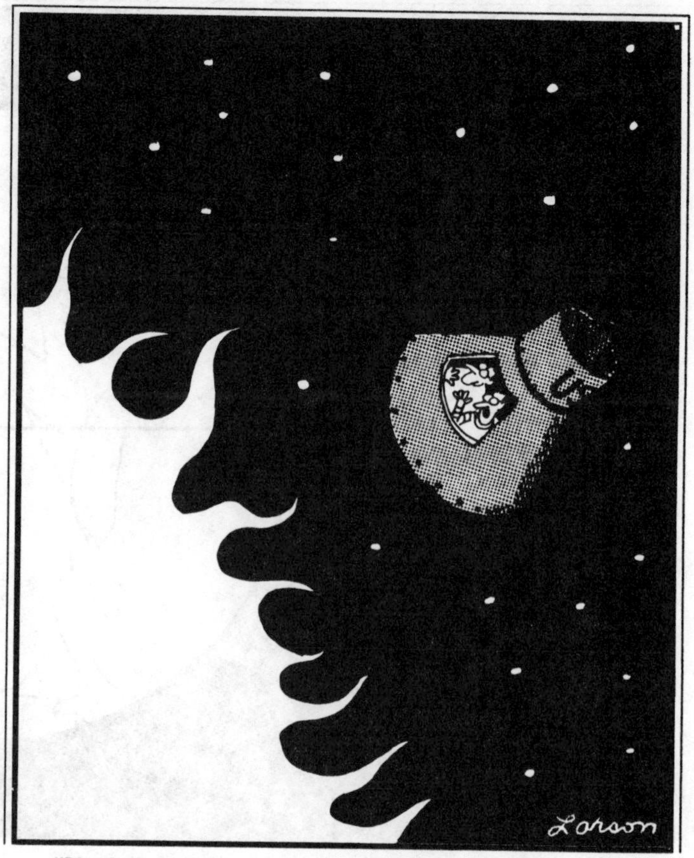
Larson

"Blast! The controls are jammed! . . . We're headed straight for Mr. Sun!"

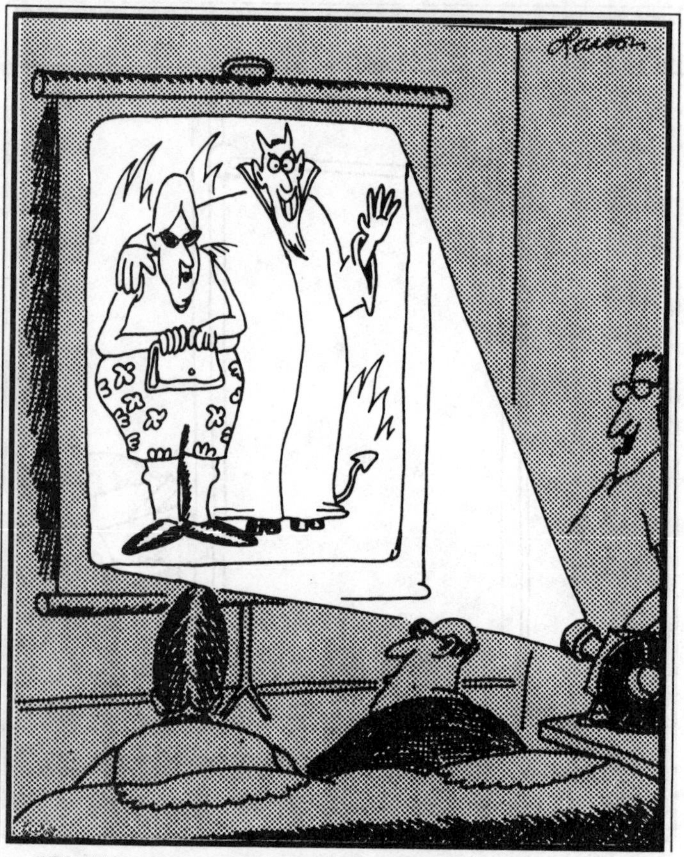
Larson

"Oh. Now this is from last summer, when Helen and I went to hell and back."

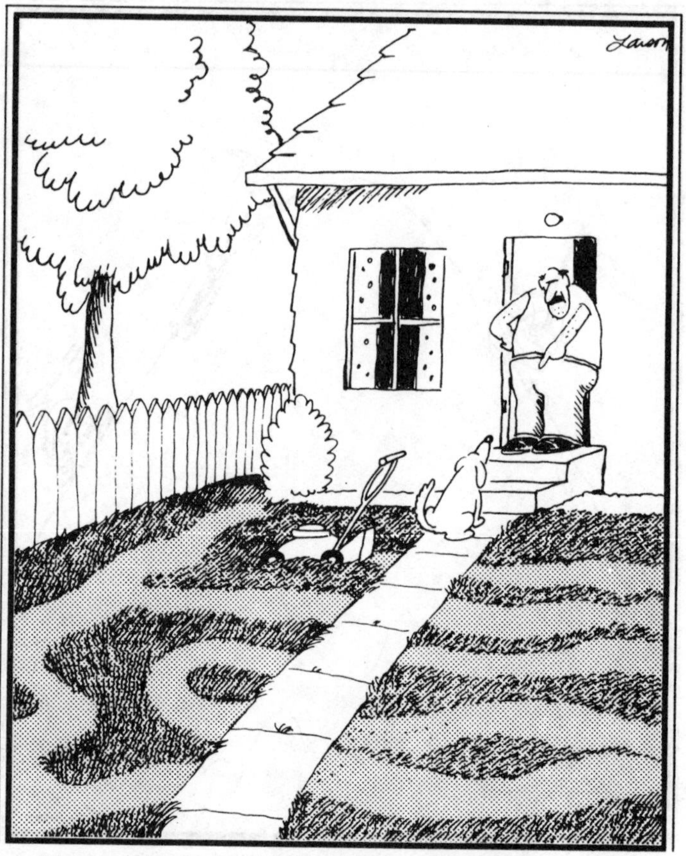
Larson

"You call that mowin' the lawn? . . . Bad dog! . . . No biscuit! . . . Bad dog!"

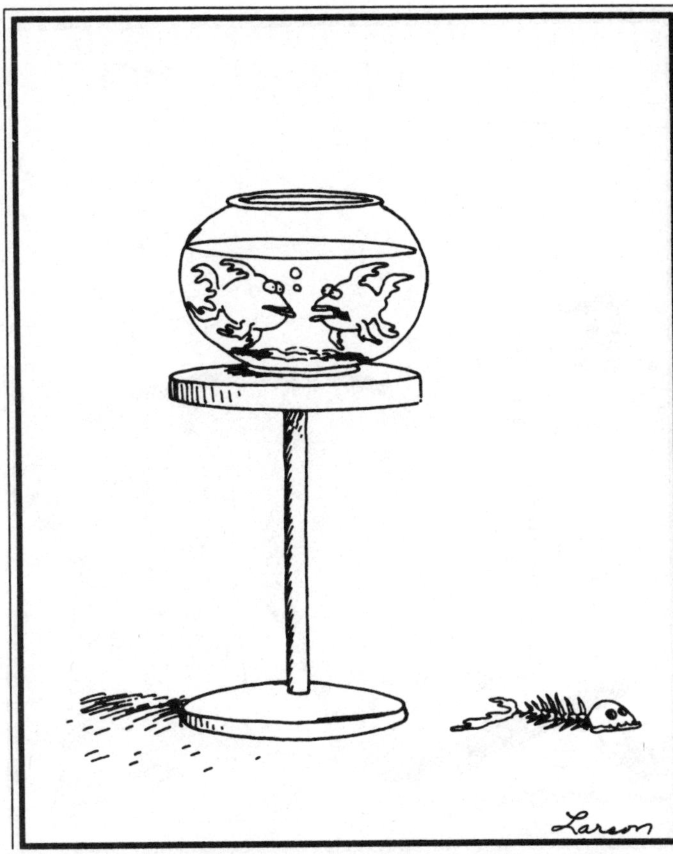
Larson

"I guess he made it . . . it's been more than a week since he went over the wall."

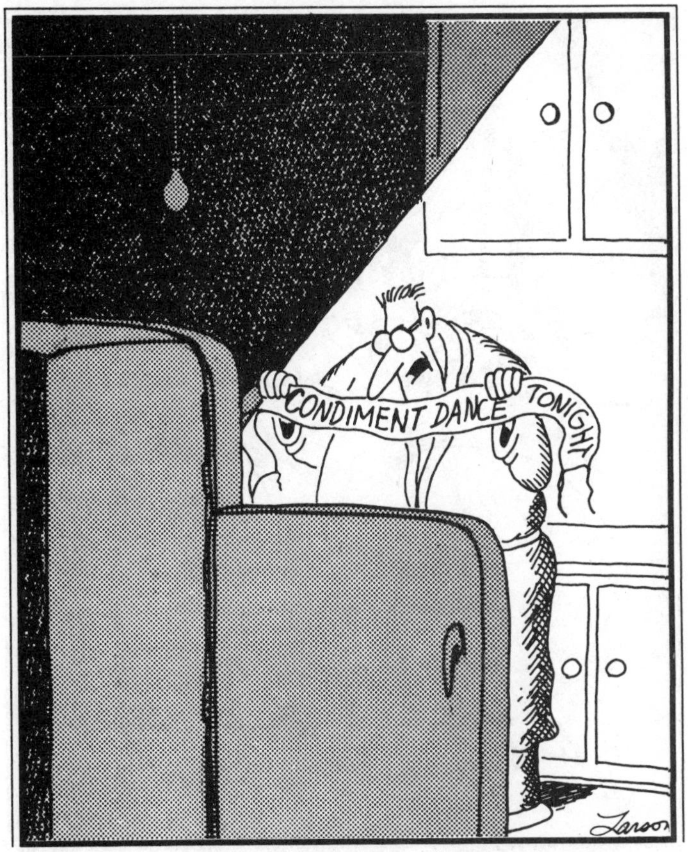
CONDIMENT DANCE TONIGHT
Larson

"I'll just take THIS, thank you! . . . And knock off that music!"

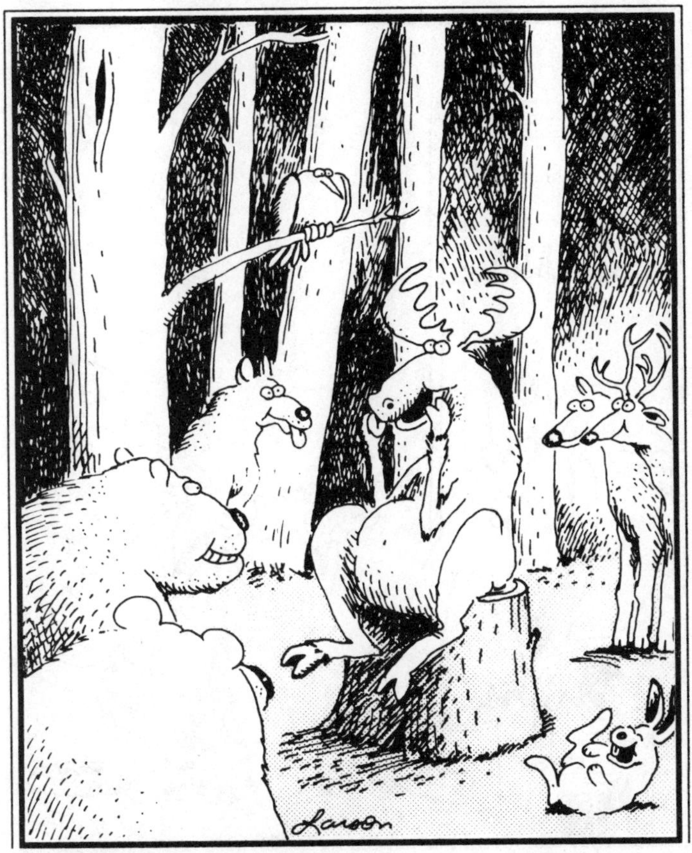
Larson

"Wait! Wait! Here's another one . . . the screams of a man lost in the woods."

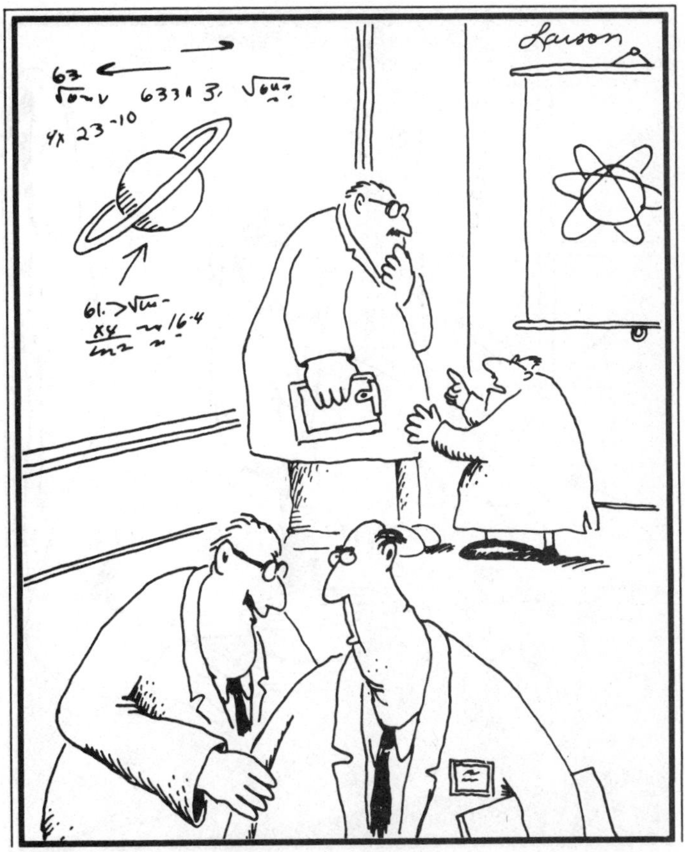
Larson

"There goes Williams again . . . trying to win support for his Little Bang theory."

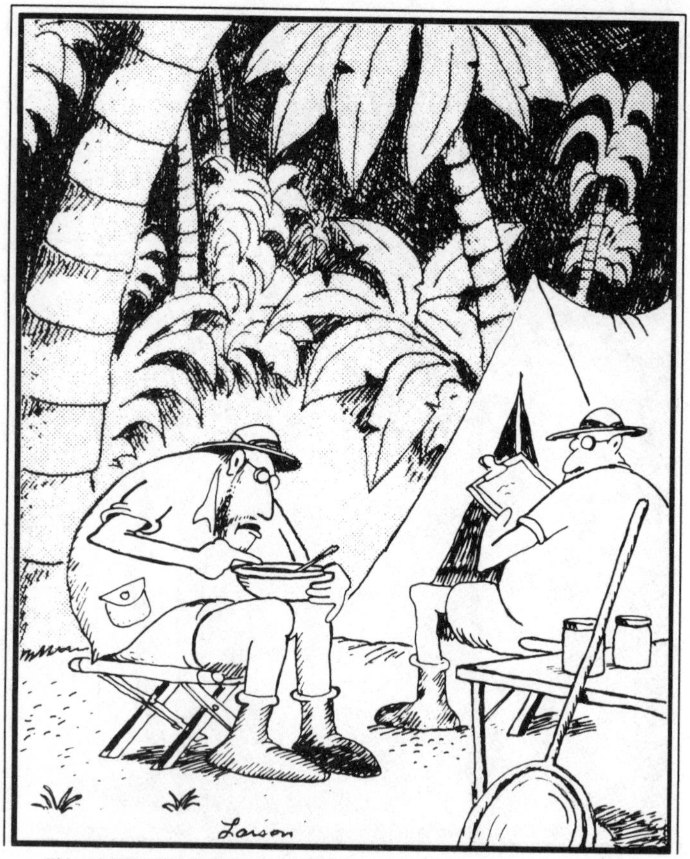
Larson

"Hey! What's this Drosophila melanogaster doing in my soup?"

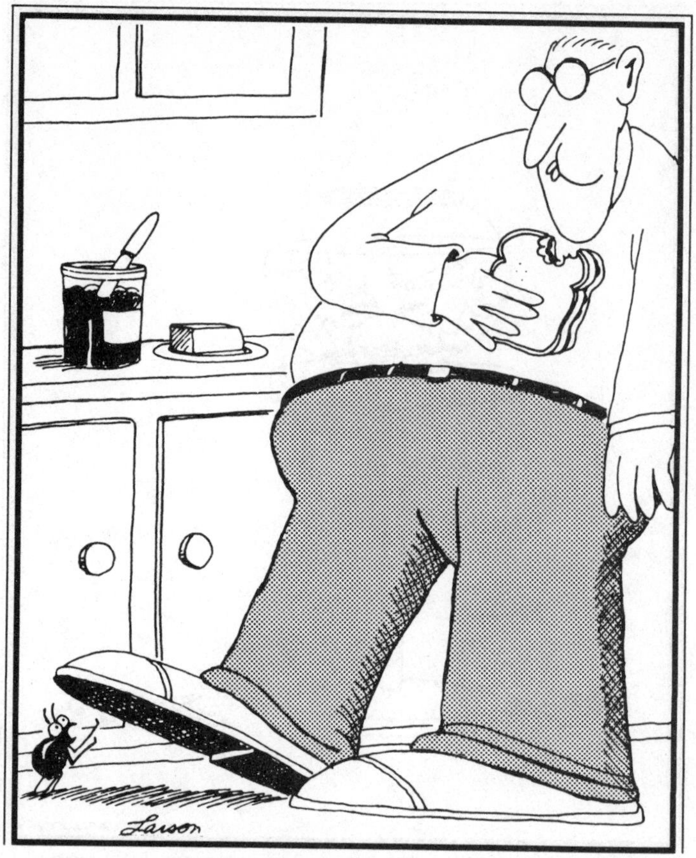
Larson

"Wait! Spare me! . . . I've got a wife, a home, and over a thousand eggs laid in the jelly!"

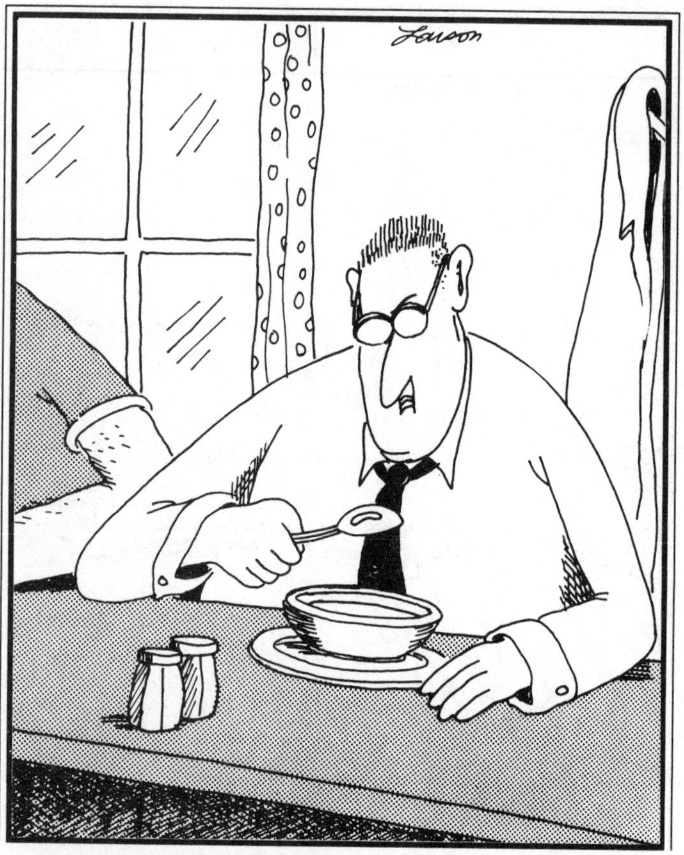
Larson

Darrell suspected someone had once again slipped him a spoon with the concave side reversed.

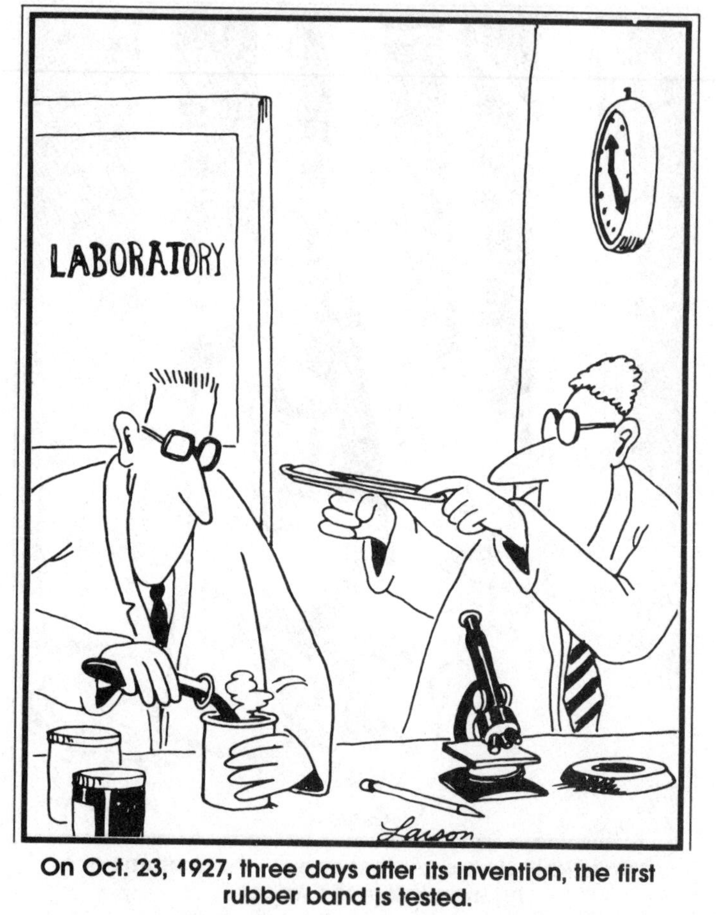
LABORATORY
Larson

On Oct. 23, 1927, three days after its invention, the first rubber band is tested.

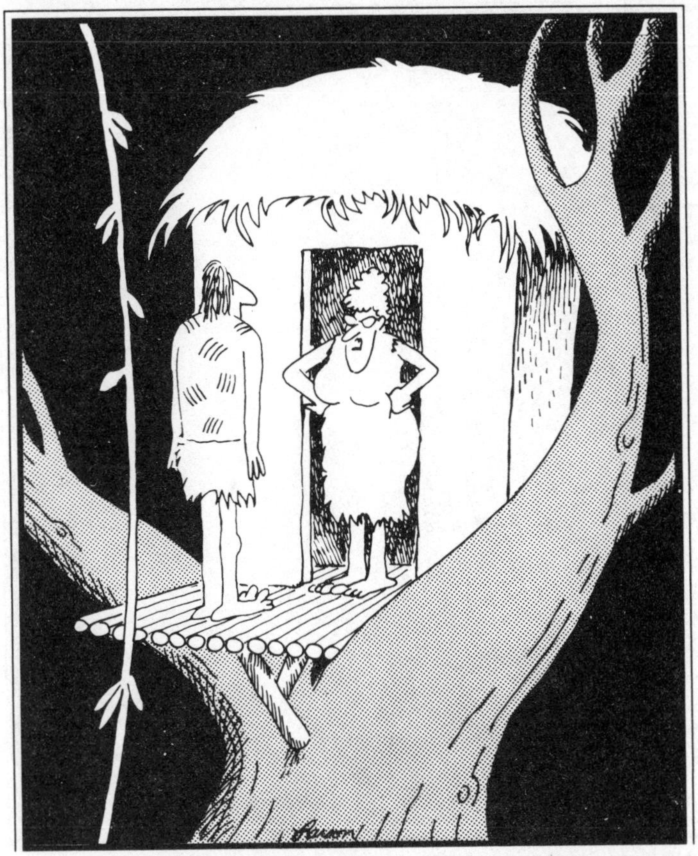

"Saaaaaay . . . I think I smell PERFUME! . . . Have you been over at the Leopard Woman's again?"

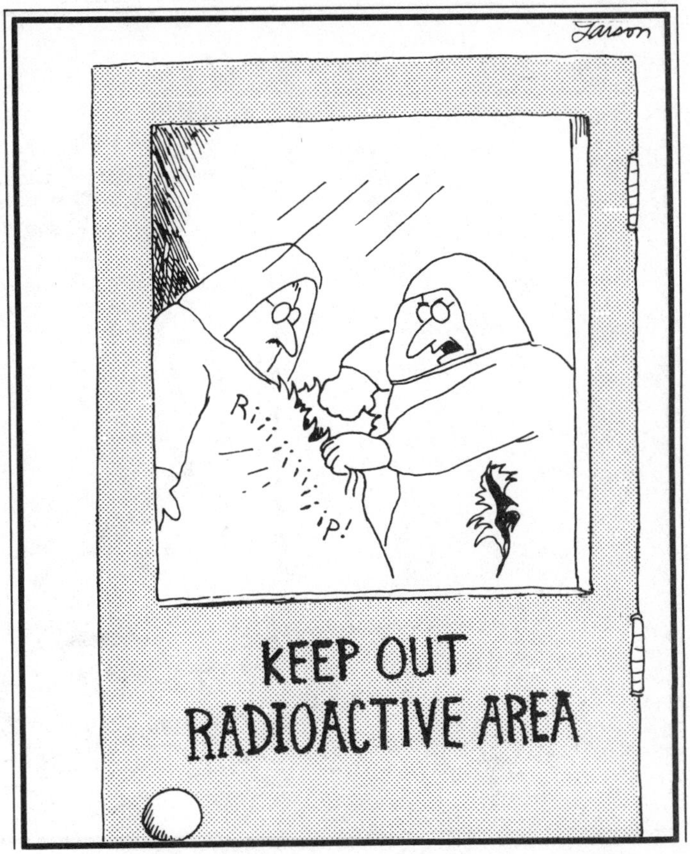
Ri...p!
KEEP OUT
RADIOACTIVE AREA

"So, Foster! That's how you want it, huh? . . . Then take THIS!"

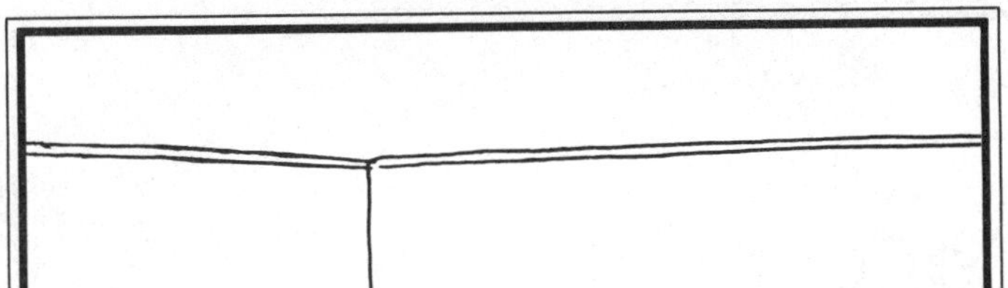
EXAMI

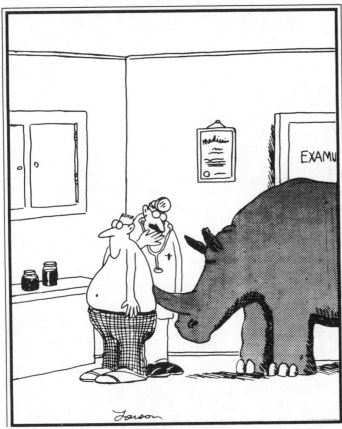

"Wait a minute here, Mr. Crumbley . . . Maybe it isn't kidney stones after all."

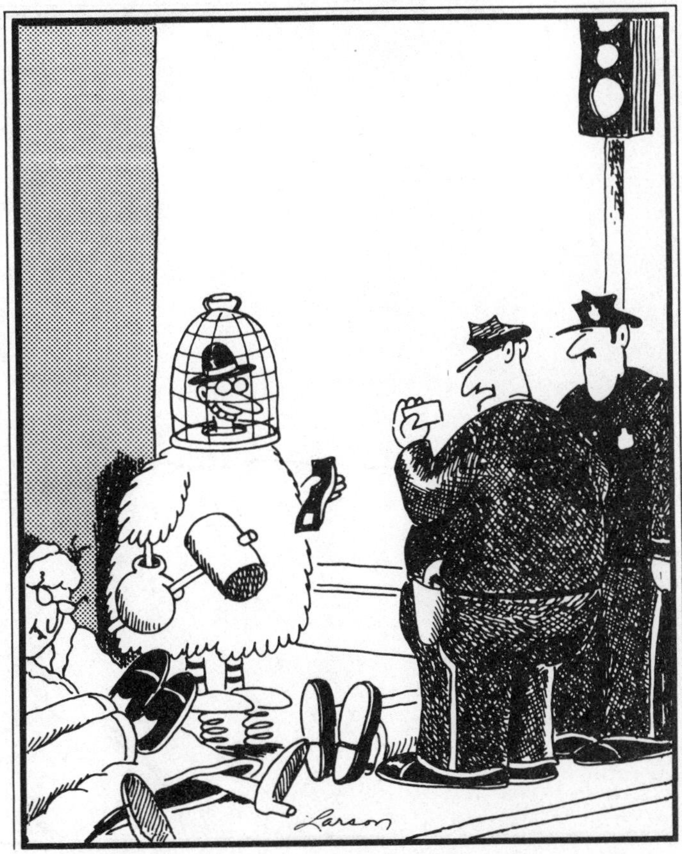

"Well, I'll be darned . . . I guess he does have a license to do that."

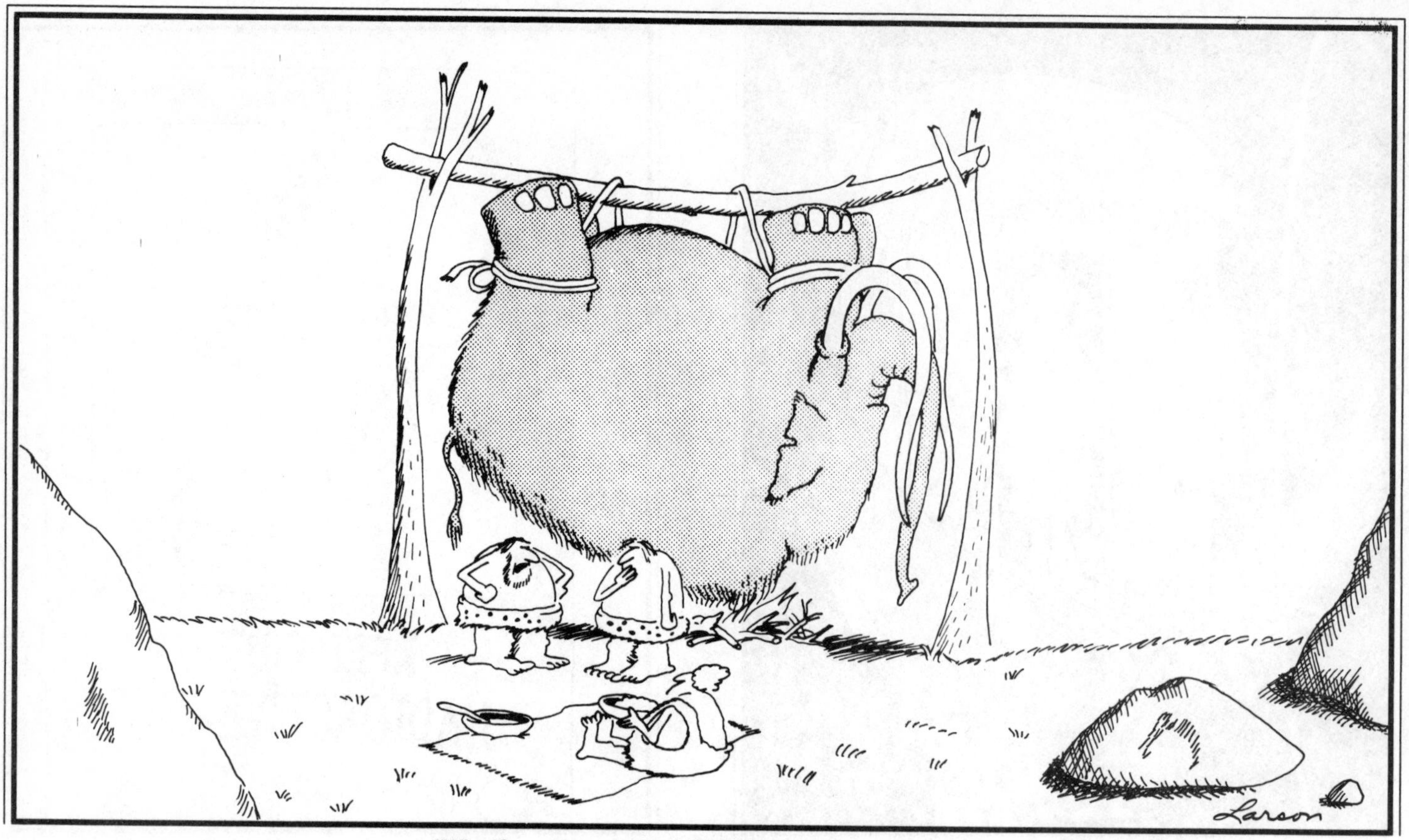
Larson

"What? . . . You mean NO ONE brought the buns?"

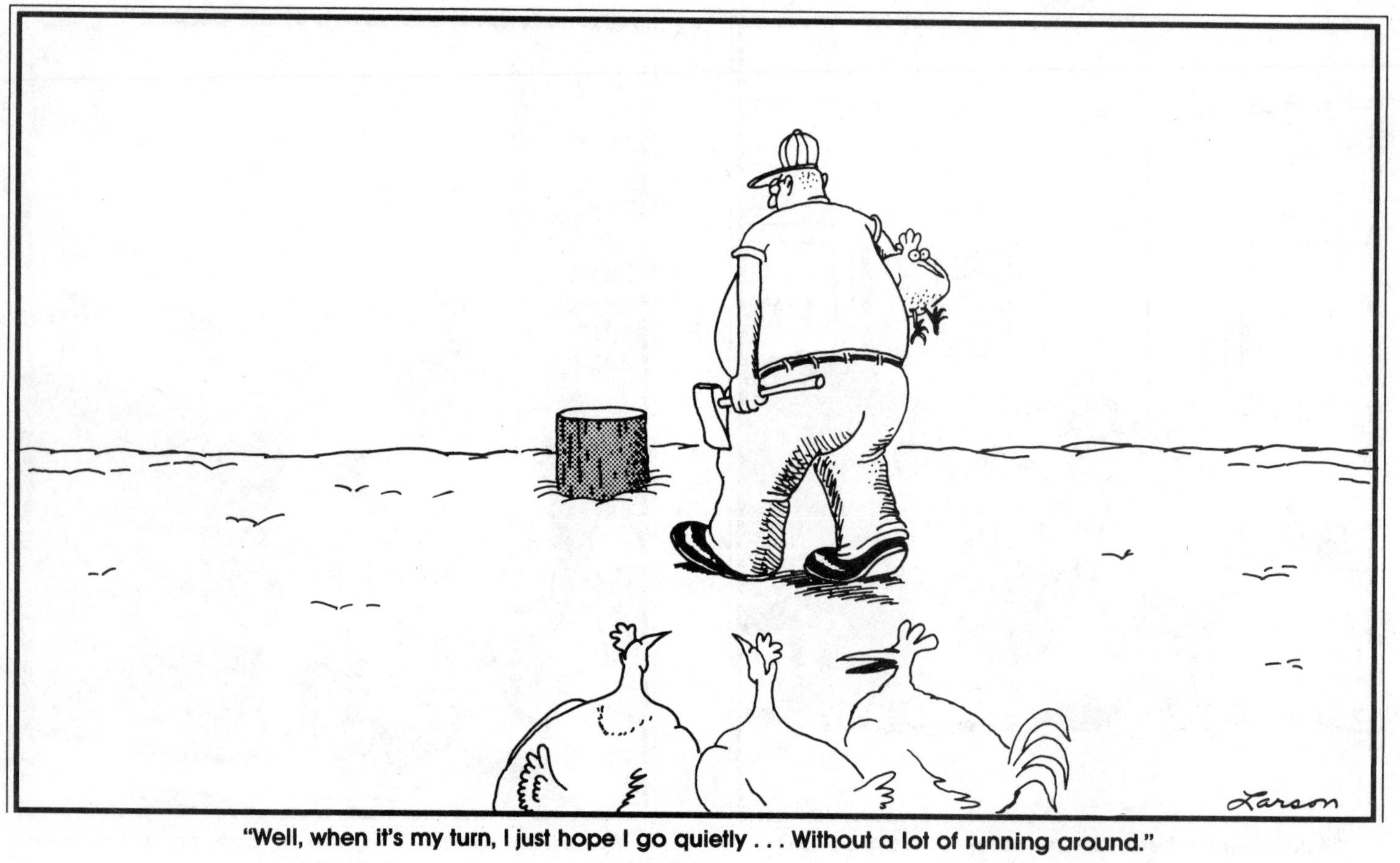
Larson

"Well, when it's my turn, I just hope I go quietly . . . Without a lot of running around."

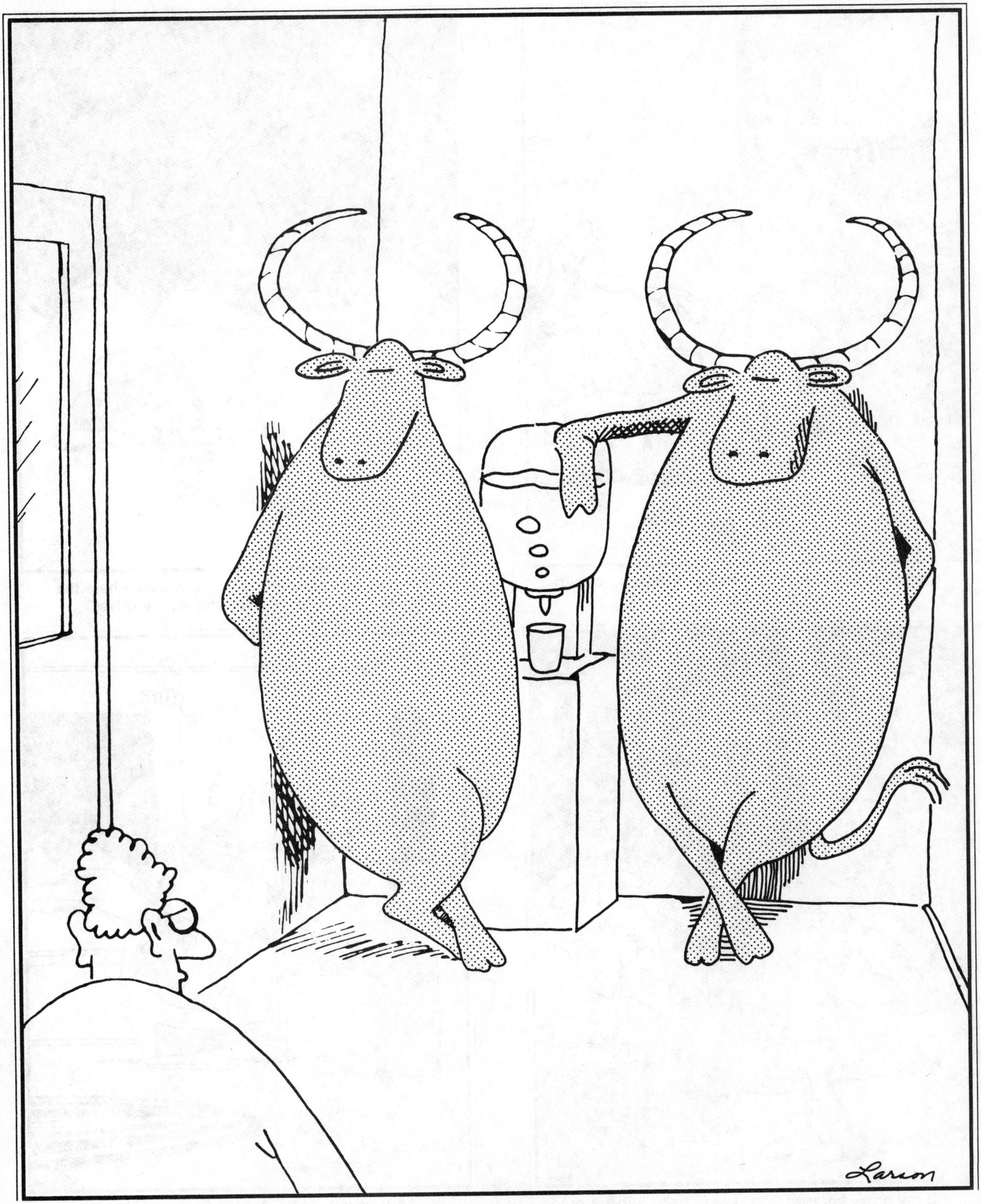
Larson

Water buffaloes

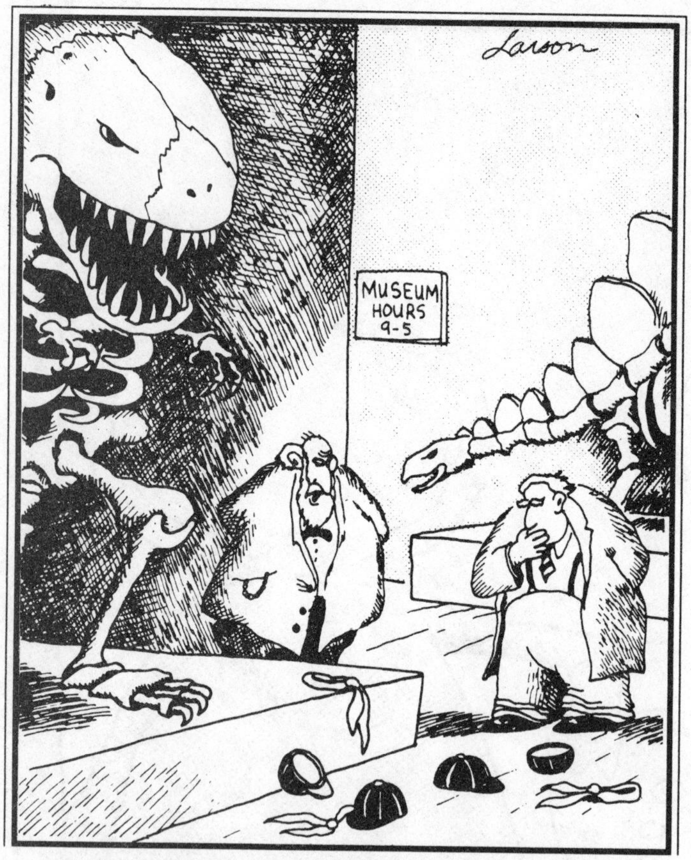
Larson
MUSEUM
HOURS
9-5

"Most peculiar, Sidney . . . another scattering of cub scout attire."

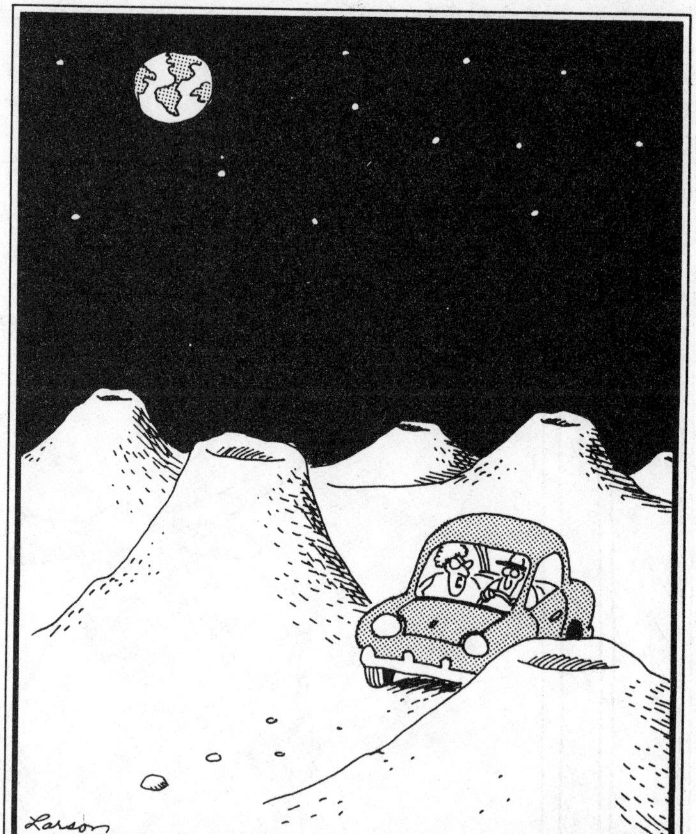
Larson

"For heaven's sake, Elroy! . . . NOW look where the earth is! . . . Move over and let me drive!"

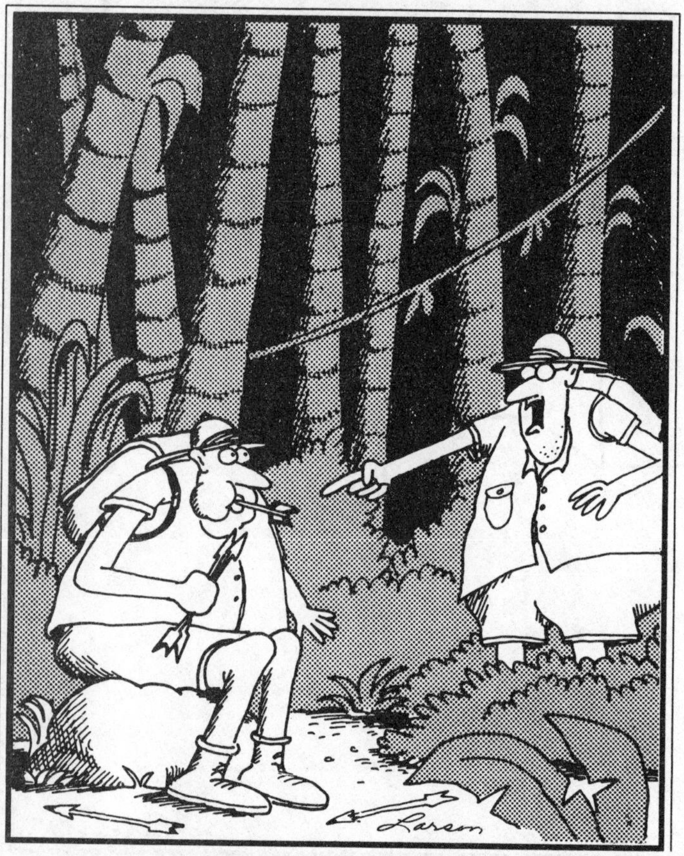
Larson

"Oh my gosh, Andrew! Don't eat those! . . . Those are POISON arrows!"

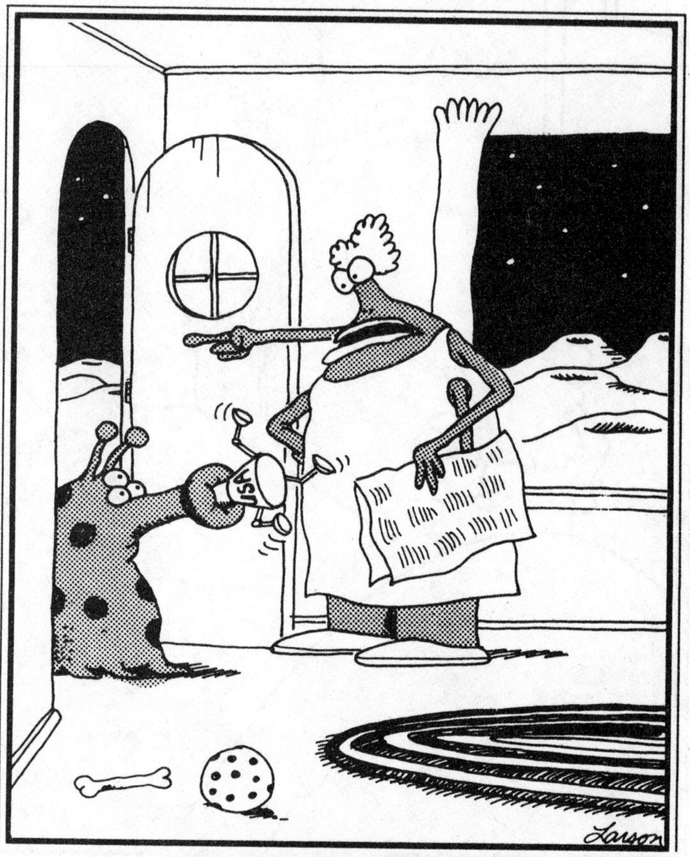
USA
Larson

"Aaaaaaa! . . . No, Zooky! Grok et bok! . . . Shoosh! Shoosh! . . ."

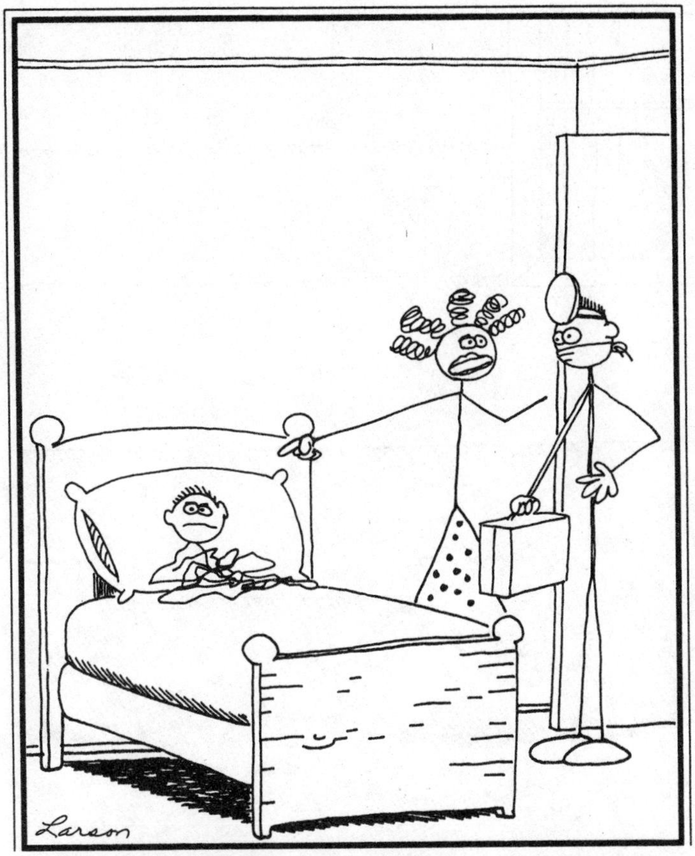
Larson

"Thank goodness you're here, Doctor! . . . I came in this morning and found Billy just all scribbled like this!"

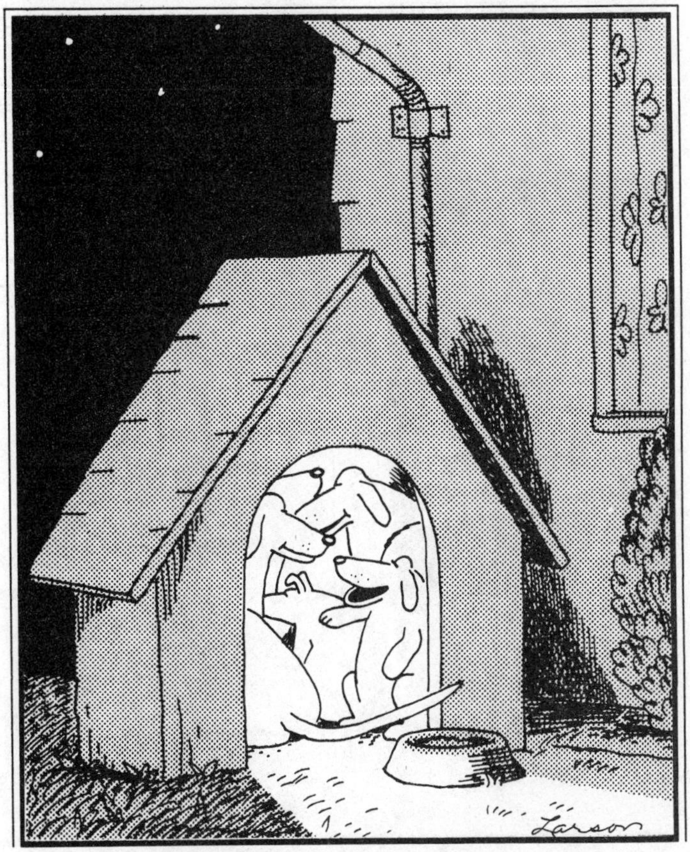
Larson

"Oh, hey! Fantastic party, Tricksy! Fantastic . . . Say, do you mind telling me which way to the yard?"

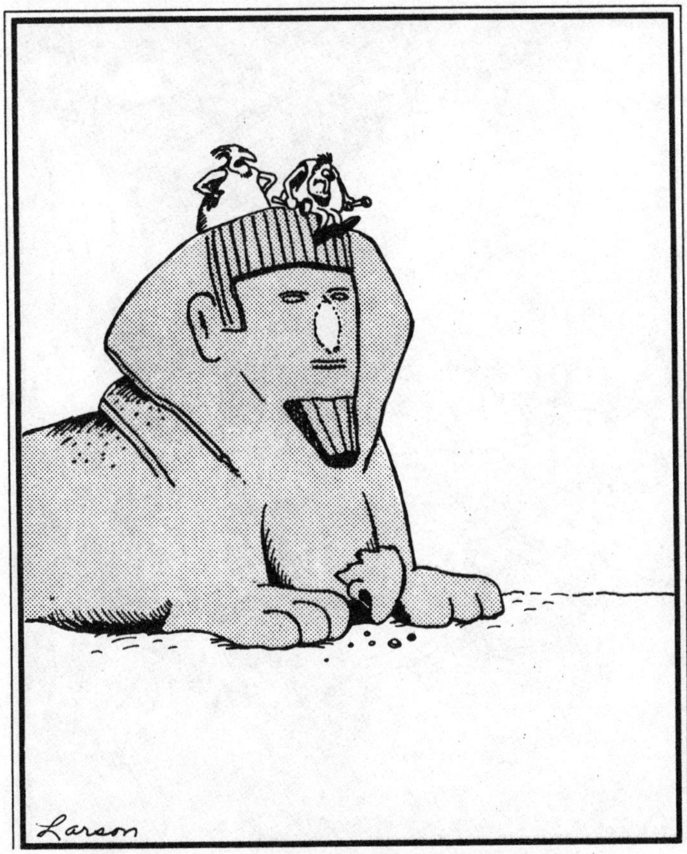
Larson

"'That's fine,' I said. 'Good nose,' I said. But no, you had to go and hit the chisel one more time."

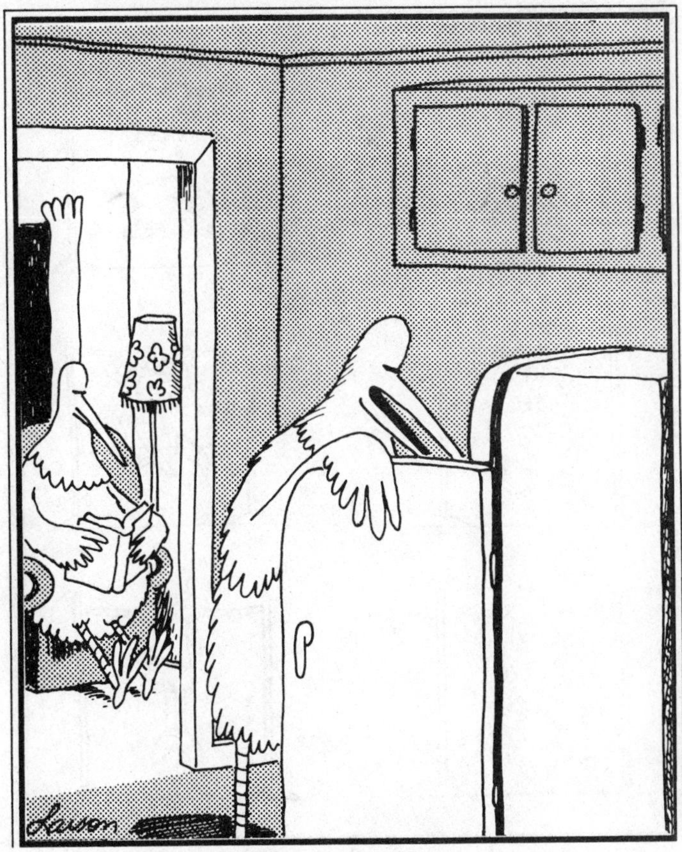
Larson

"Dang! . . . Who ate the middle out of the daddy longlegs?"

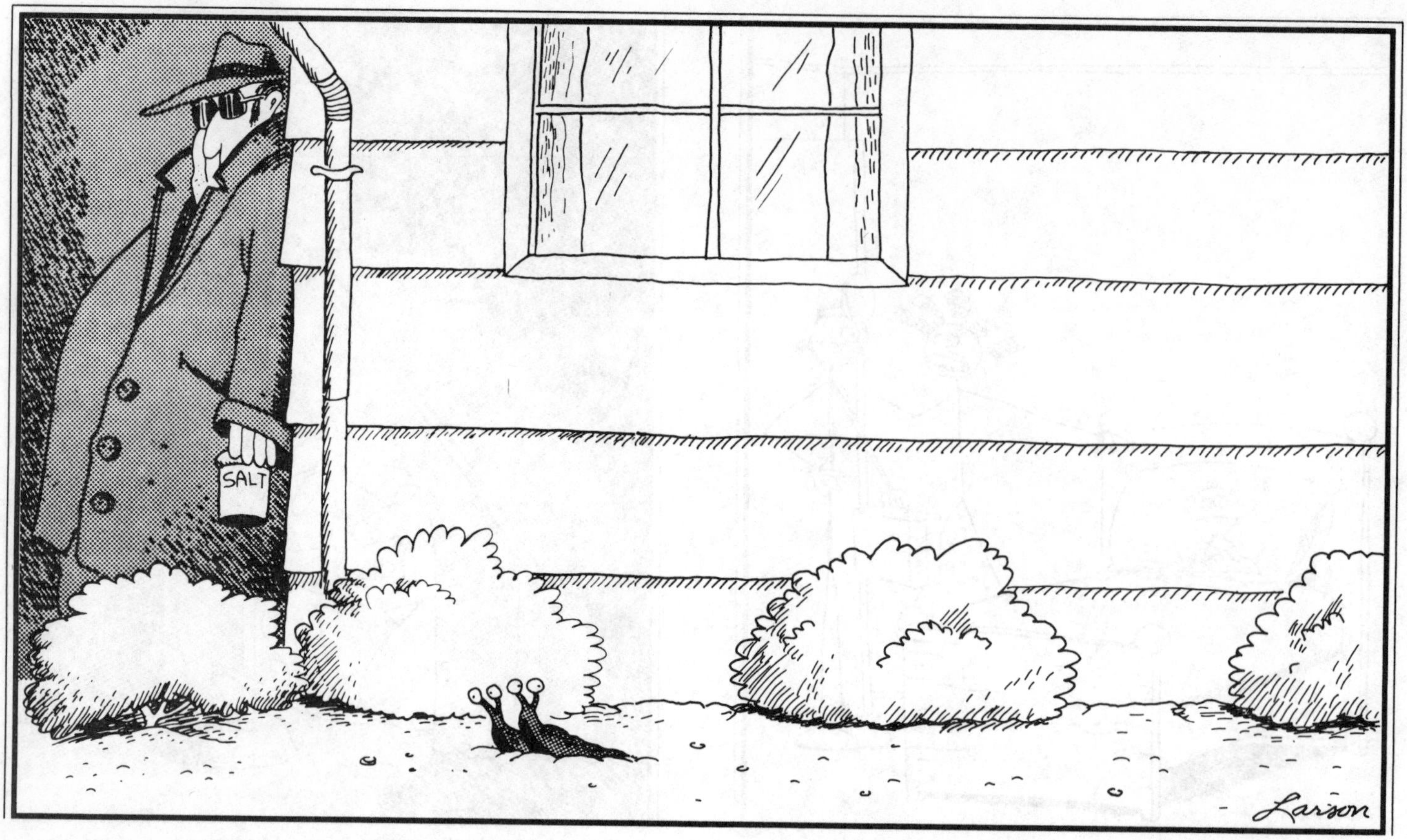

SALT
Larson

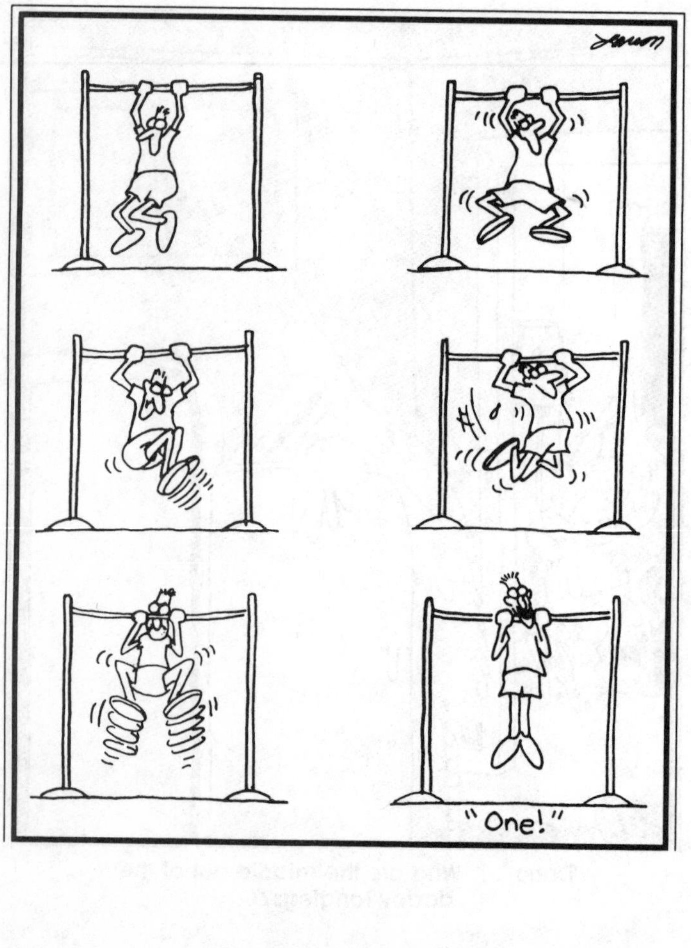

Larson

"One!"

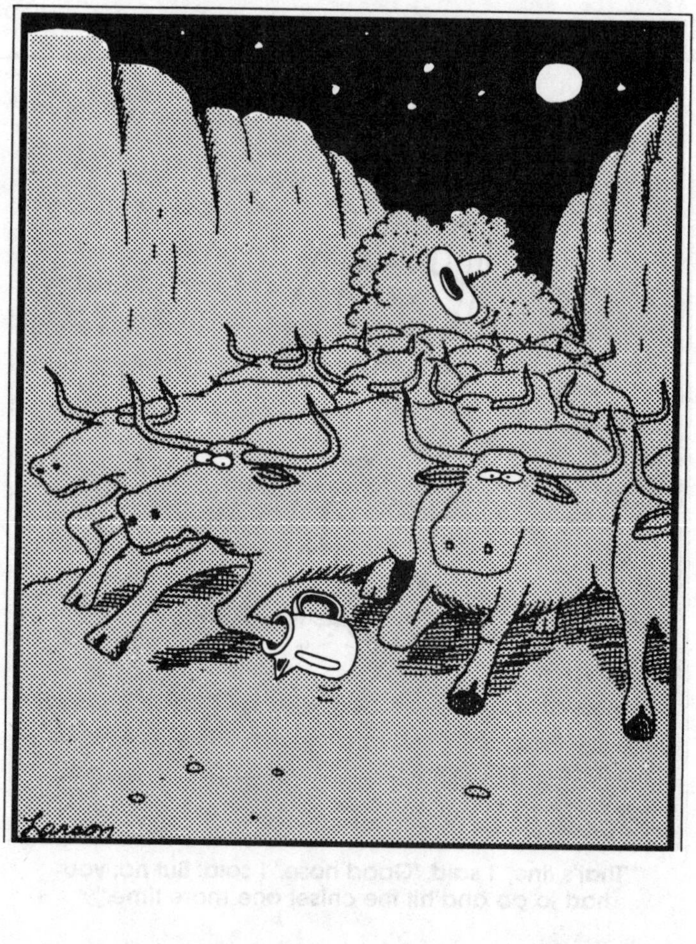

Larson

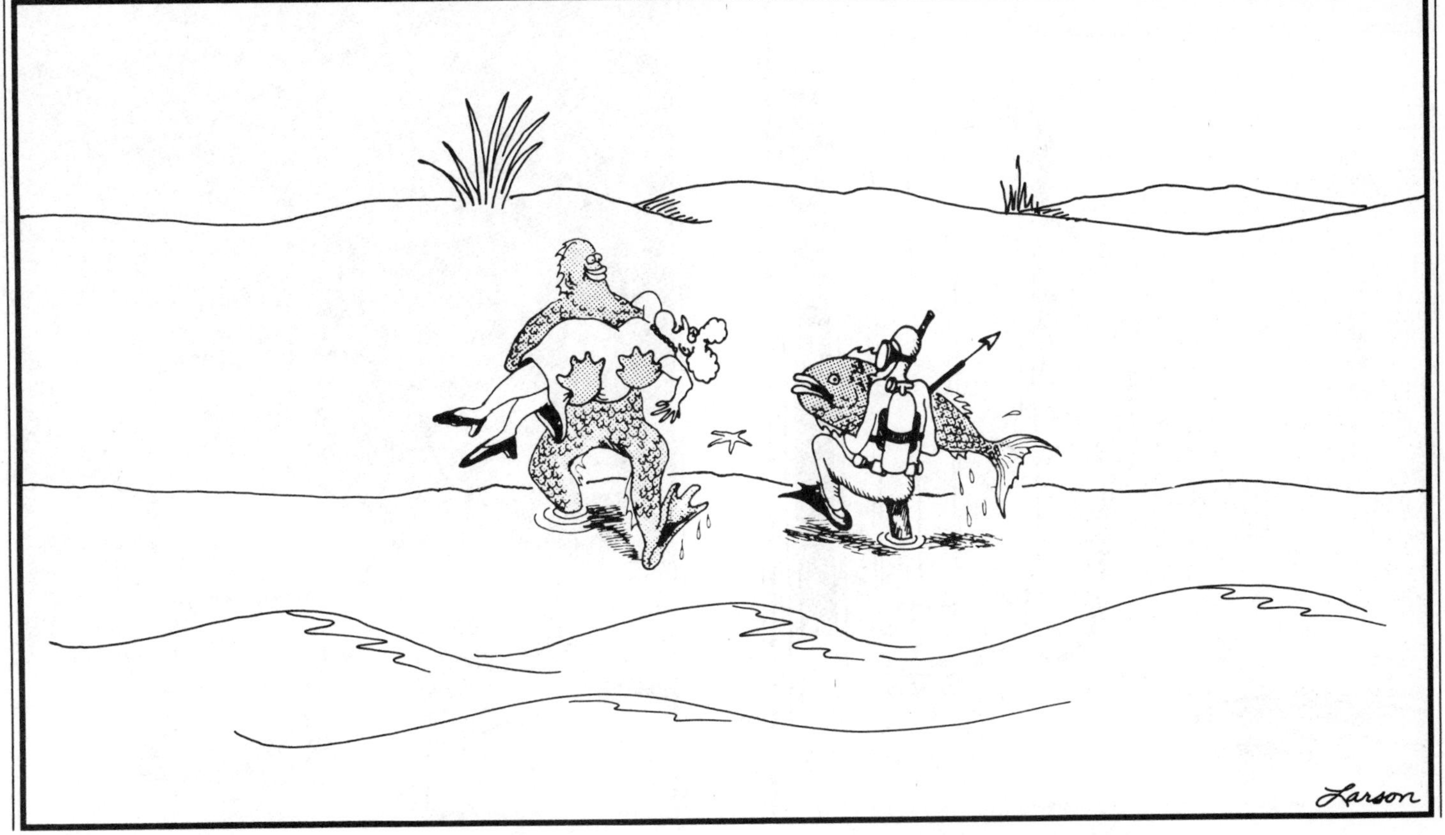
Larson

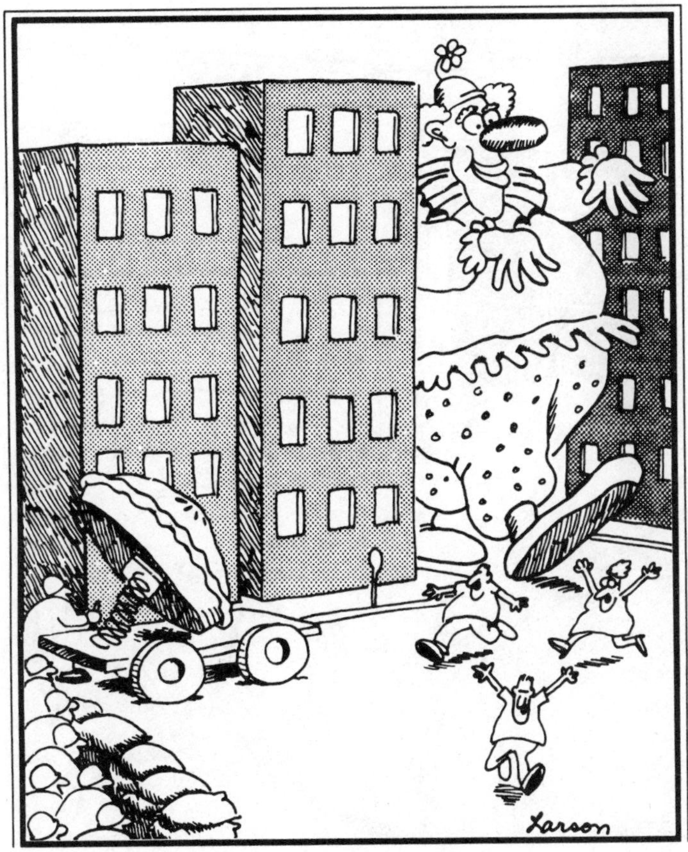
Larson

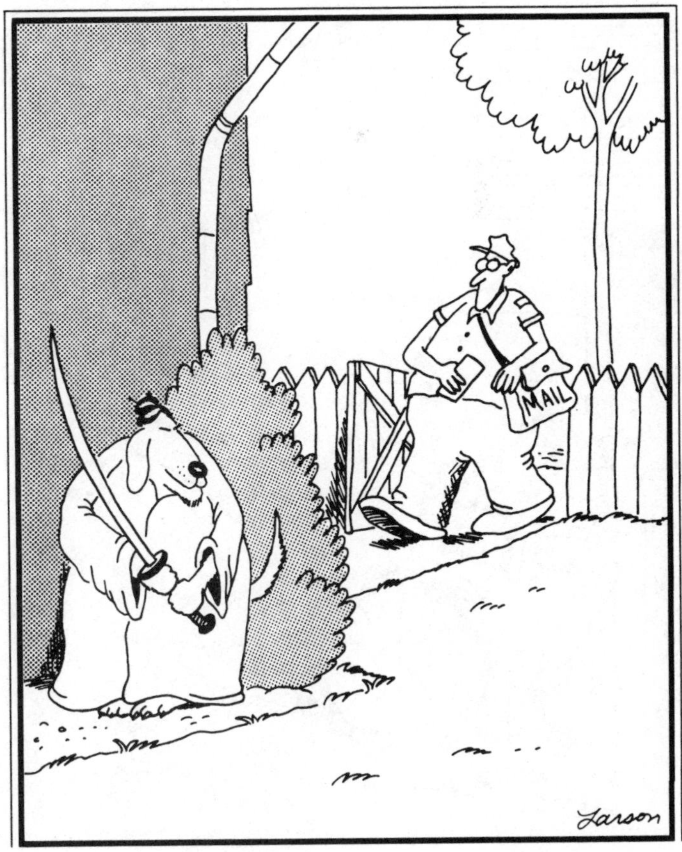
MAIL
Larson

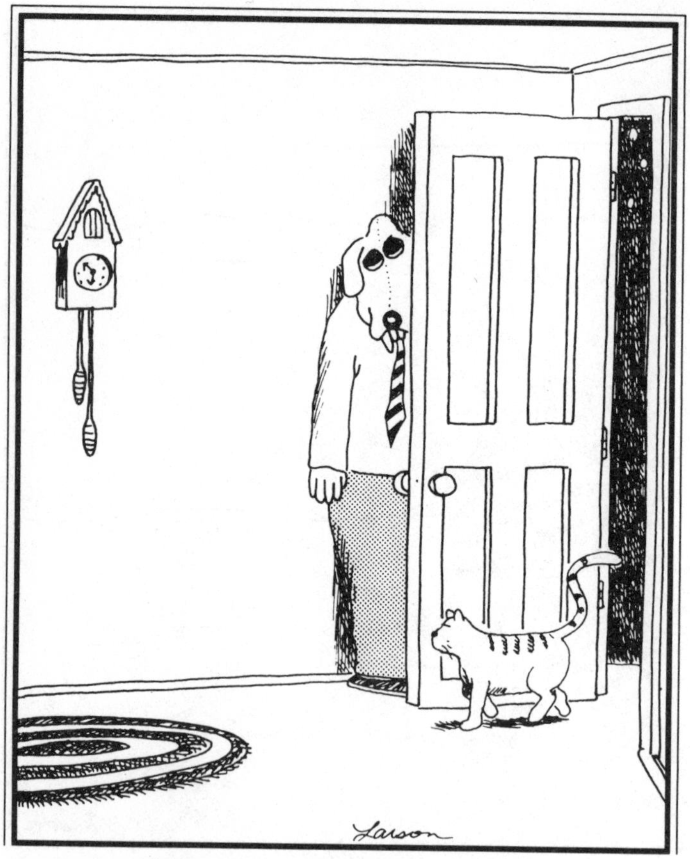
Larson

Games you can play with your cat

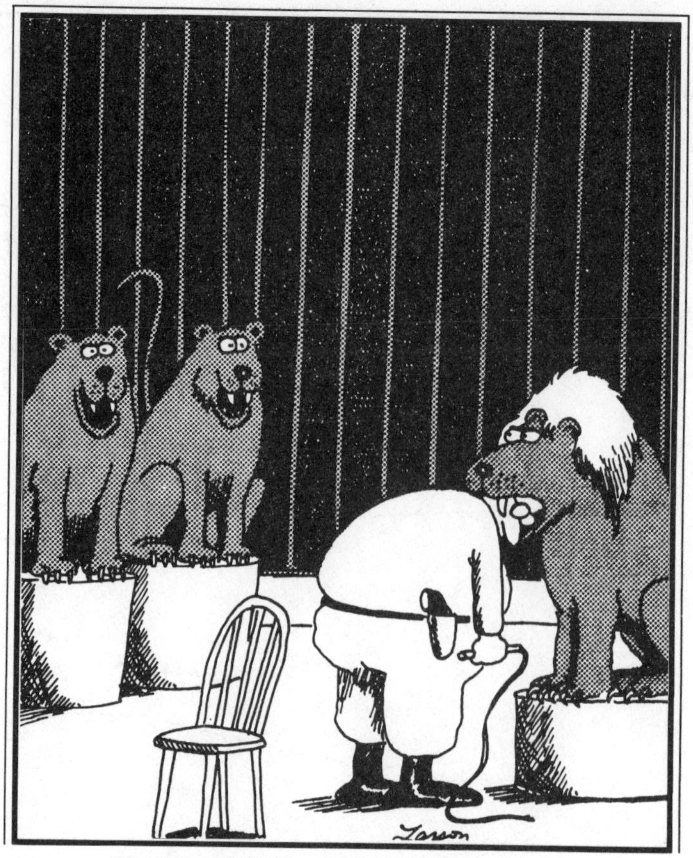
Larson

"Ernie's a chicken, Ernie's a chicken . . ."

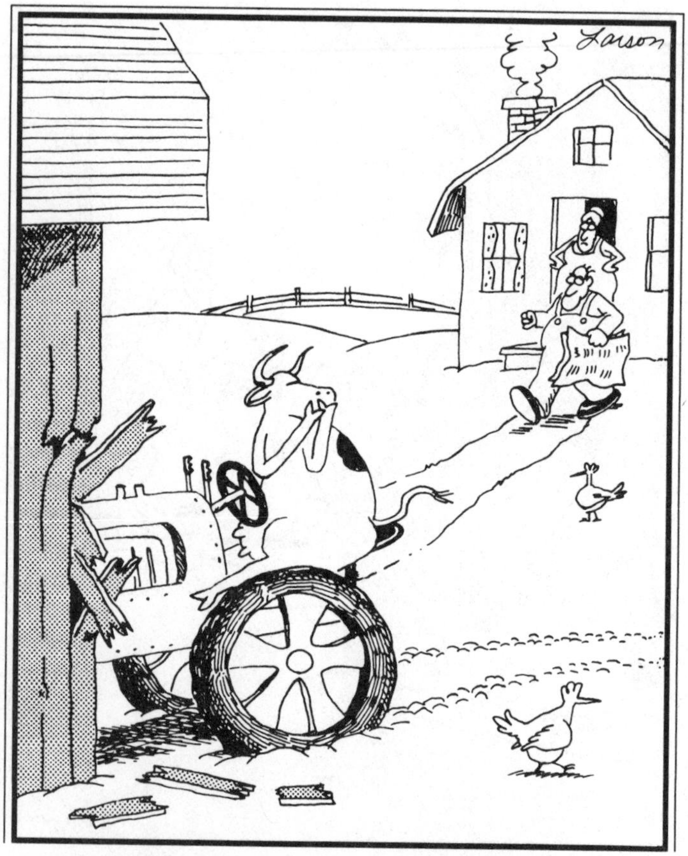
Larson

With a reverberating crash, Lulu's adventure on the tractor had come to an abrupt end.

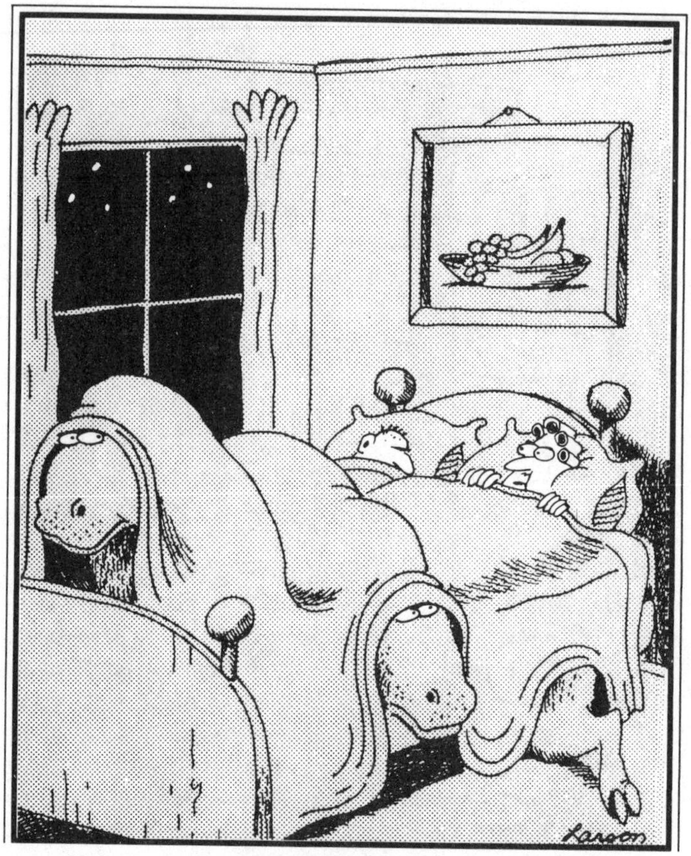
Larson

"For heaven's sake! Harold! Wake up! We've got bed buffaloes!"

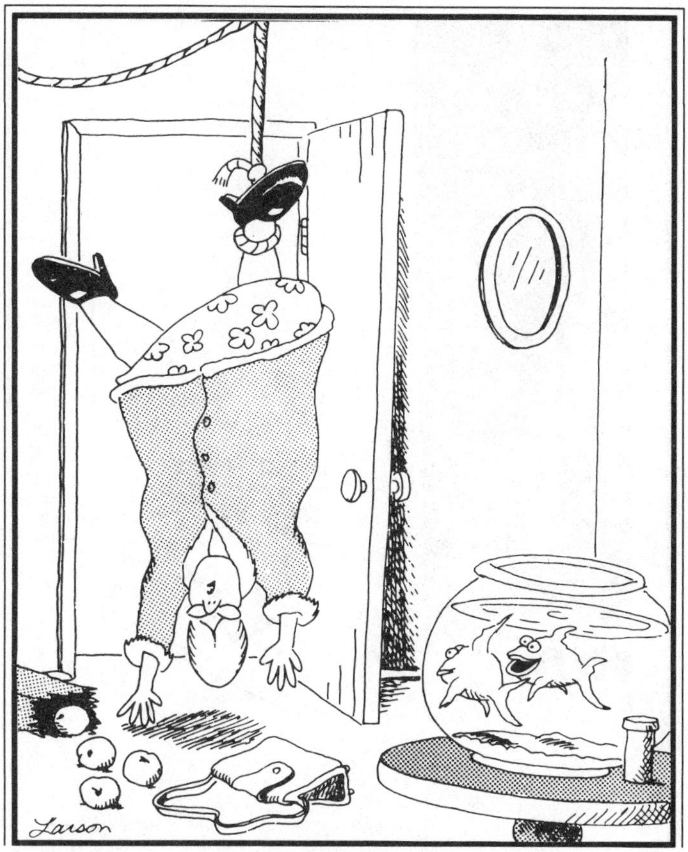
Larson

"It worked! It worked!"

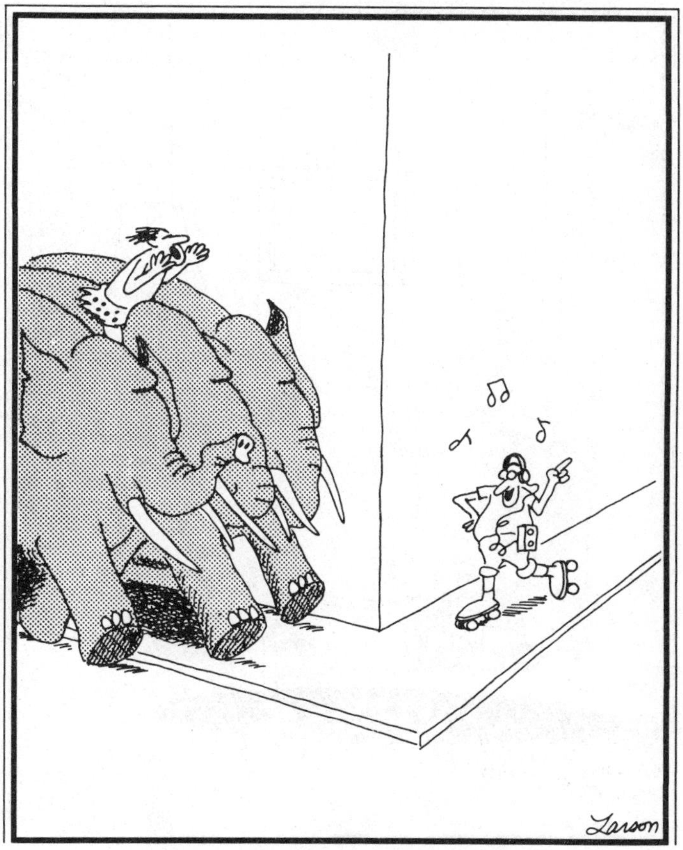
Larson

Brian has a rendezvous with destiny.

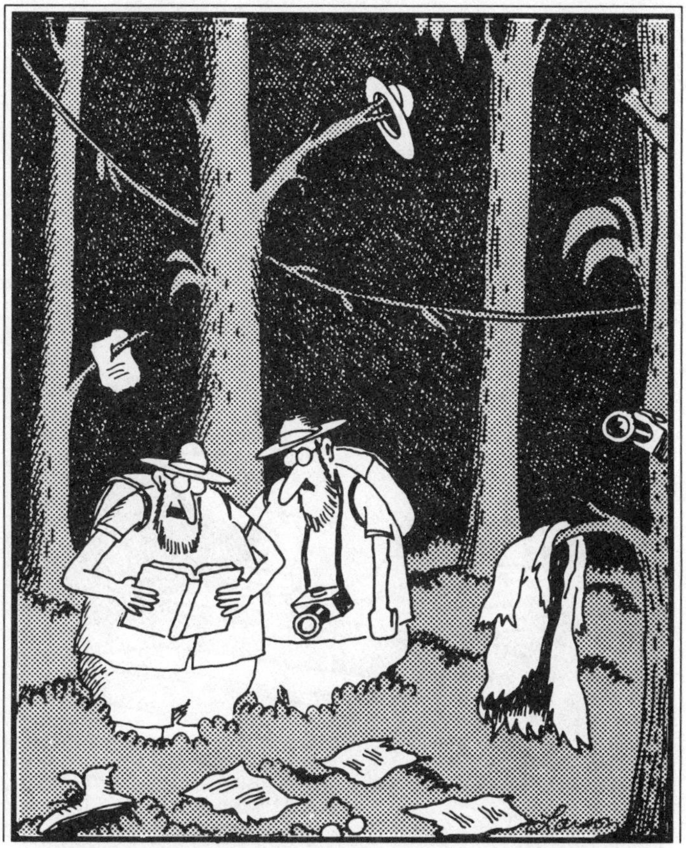
Larson

"Here's the last entry in Carlson's journal: 'Having won their confidence, tomorrow I shall test the humor of these giant but gentle primates with a simple joy-buzzer handshake.'"

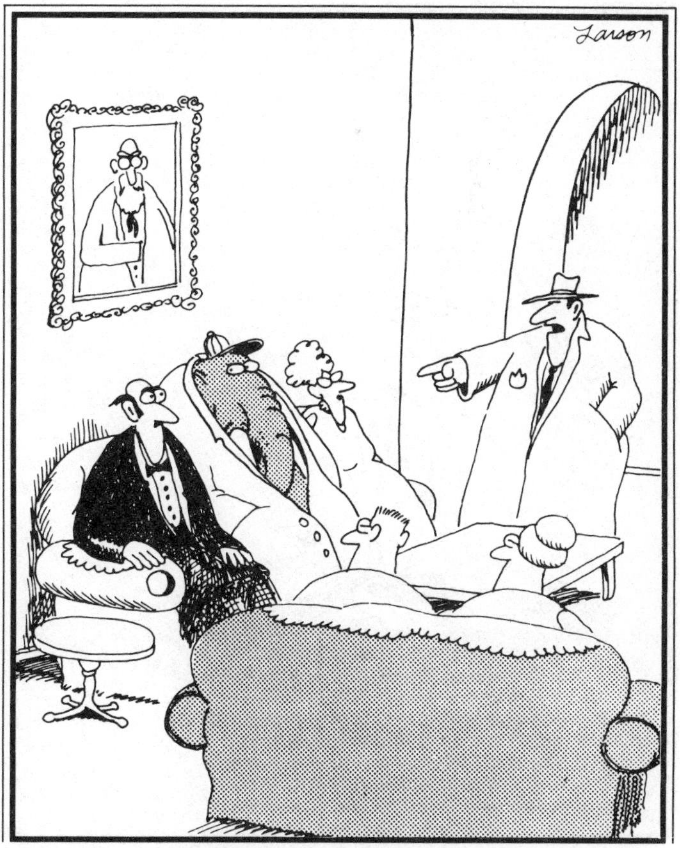
Larson

"And the murderer is . . . THE BUTLER! Yes, the butler . . . who, I'm convinced, first gored the Colonel to death before trampling him to smithereens."

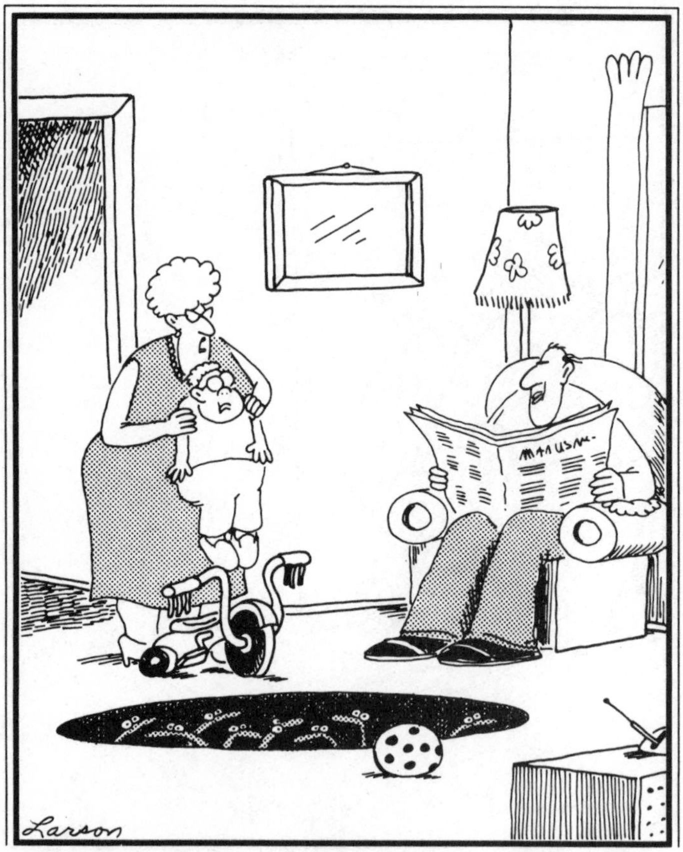
Larson

"That time was just too close, George! . . . Jimmy was headed straight for the snakepit when I grabbed him!"

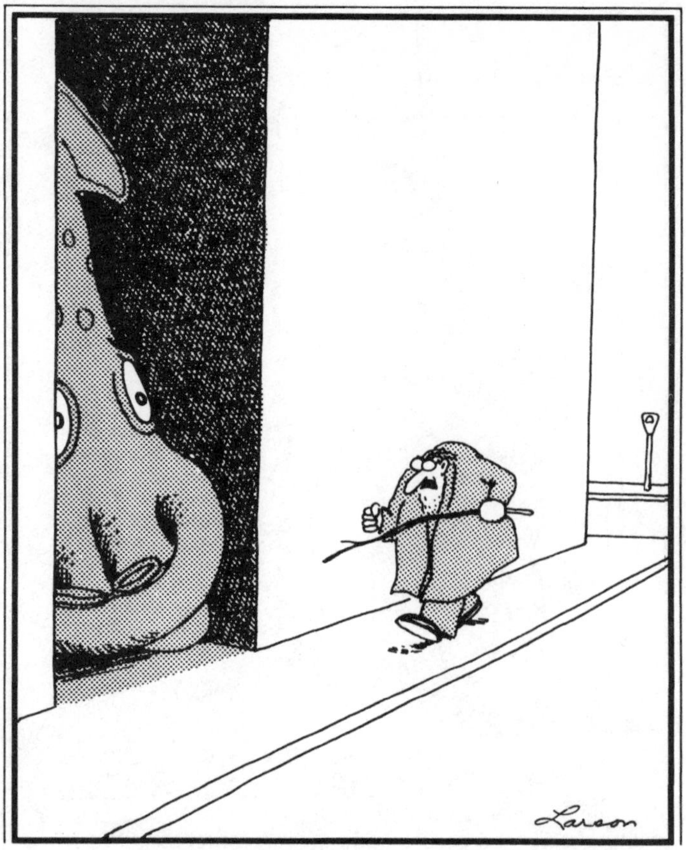
Larson

"I've had it! This time I've really had it! . . . Jump the fence again, will he? . . . Dang!"

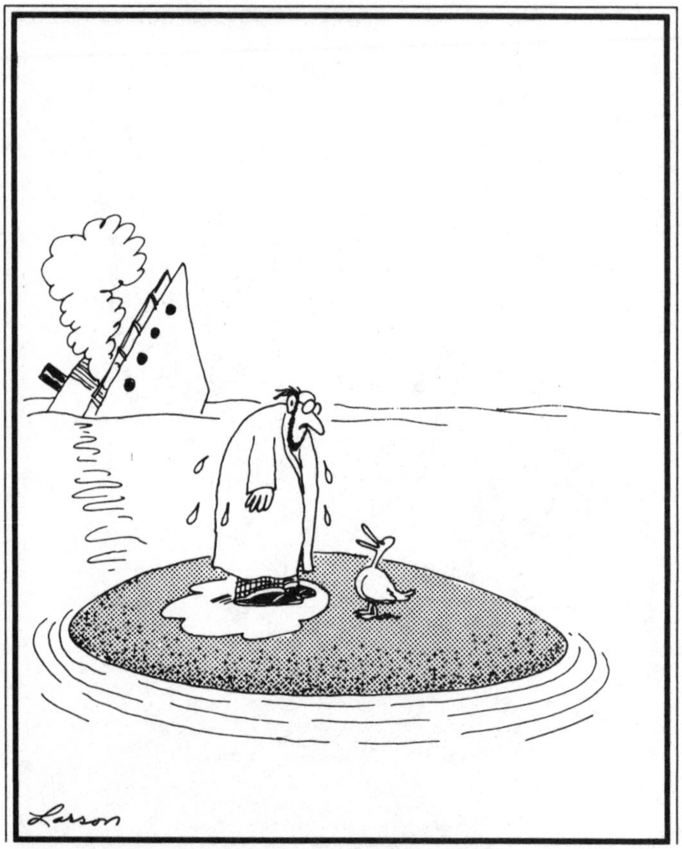
Larson

"So, Professor Jenkins! . . . My old nemesis! . . . We meet again, but this time the advantage is mine! Ha! Ha! Ha!"

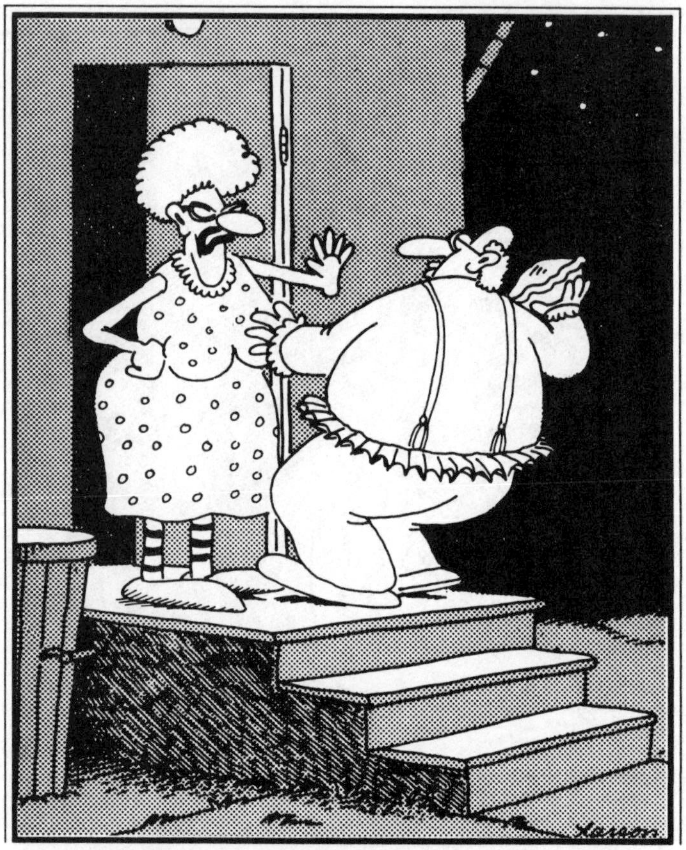
Larson

"Hold it right there, Charles! . . . Not on our first date, you don't!"

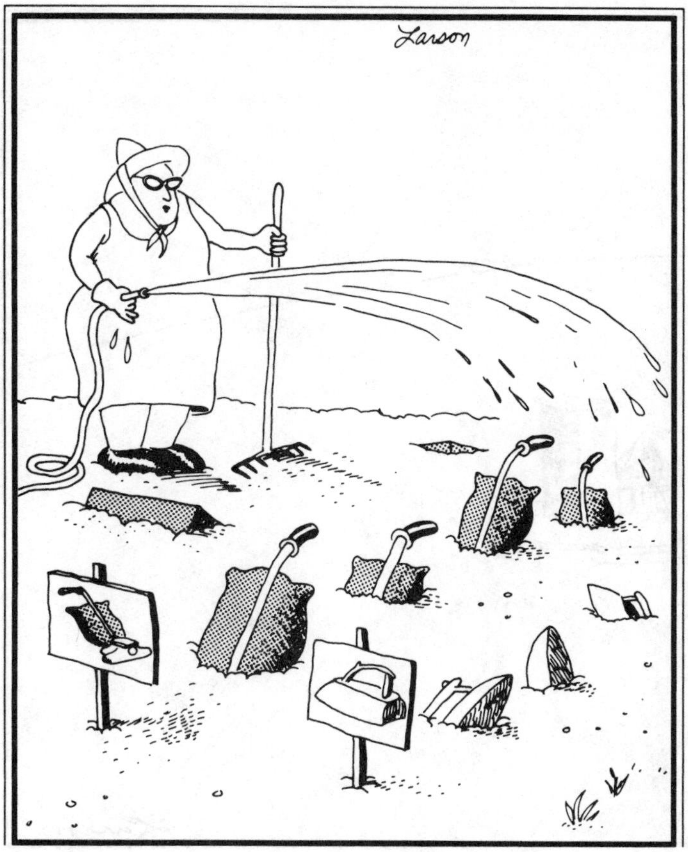
Larson

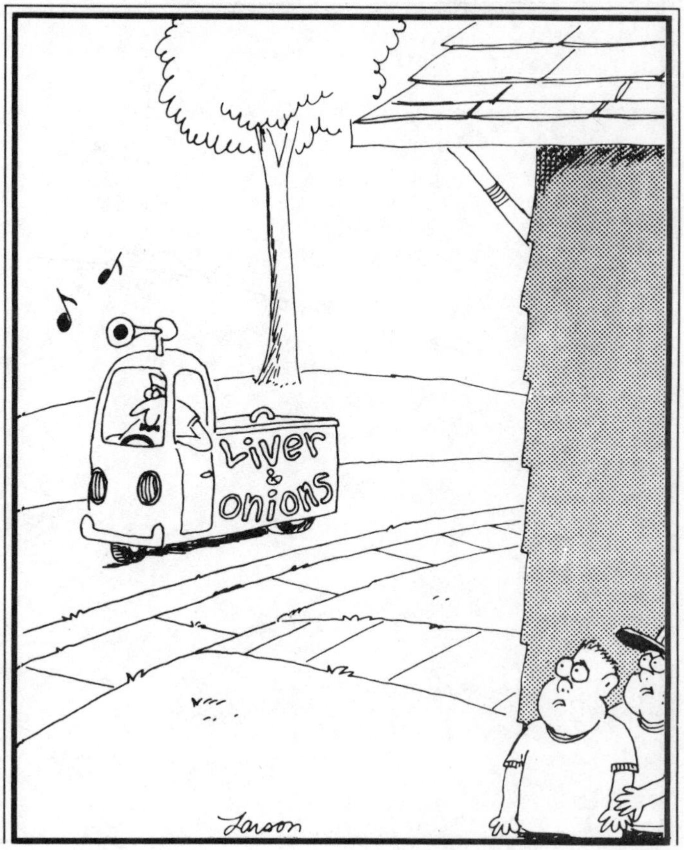
Liver
&
onions
Larson

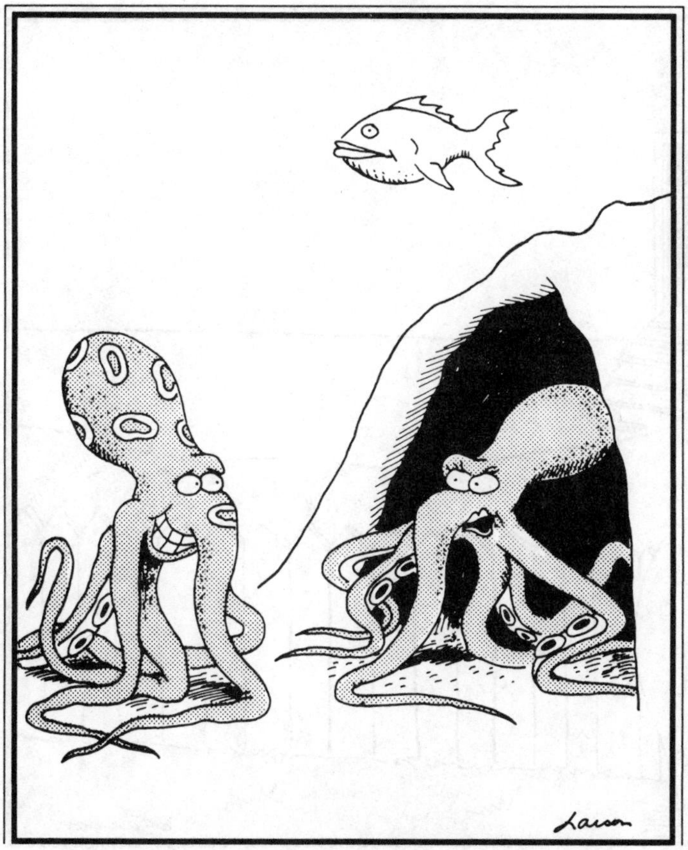
Larson

"Oh yeah? . . . And I suppose you got those suction marks at the meeting, too!"

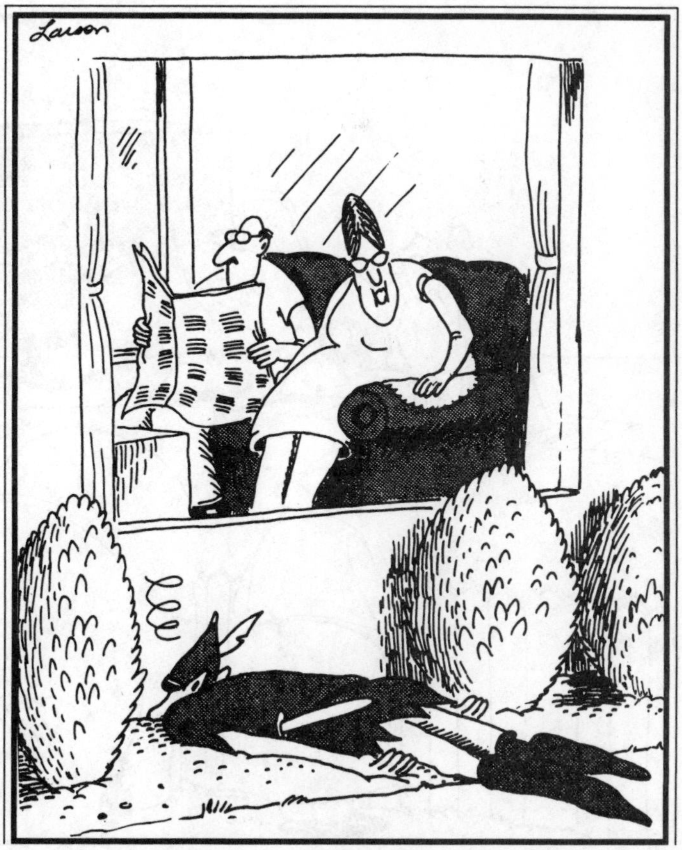
Larson

"My word, Walter! . . . Sounded like a good-size bird hit the window."

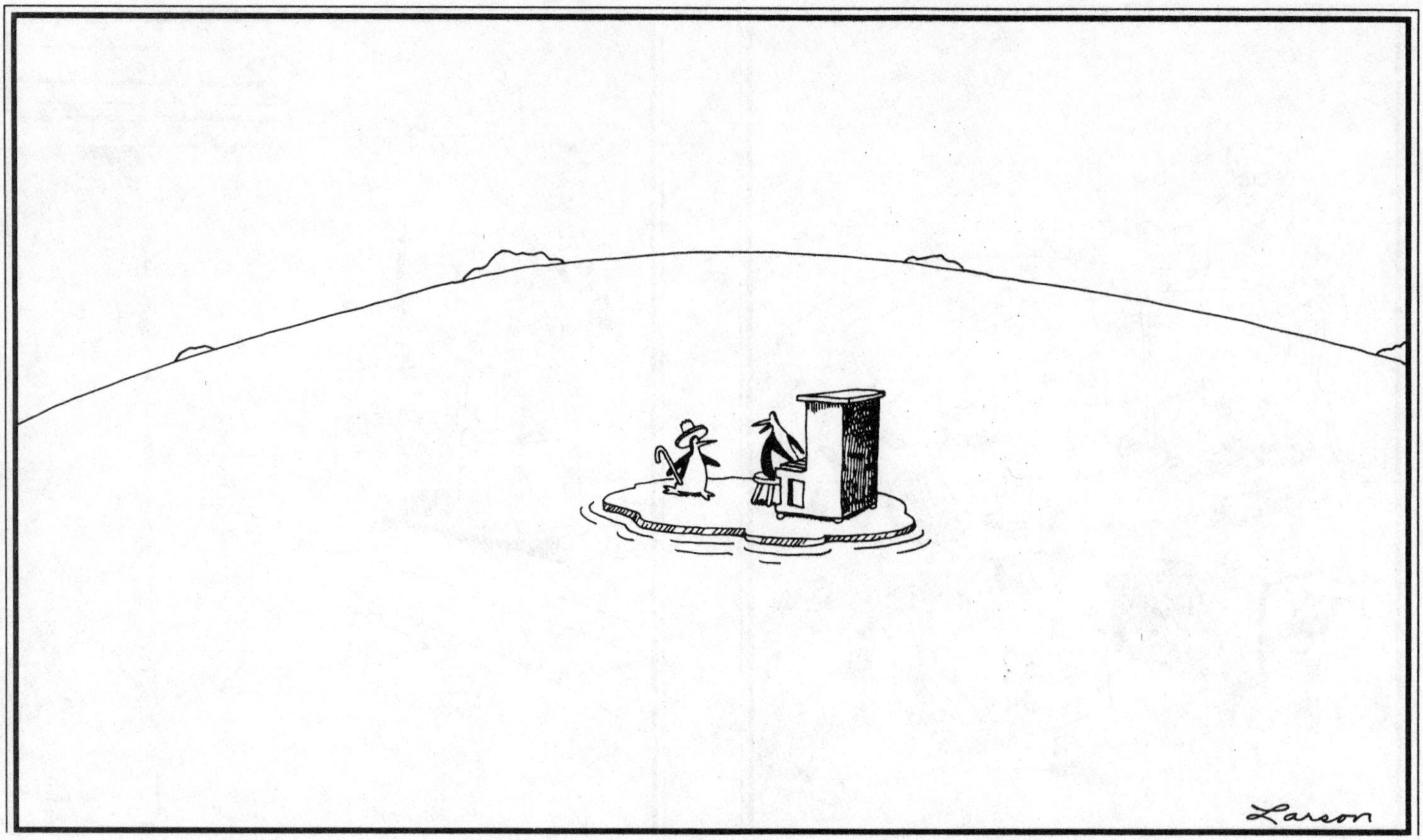
Larson

"No, no, no! Now, try it again! . . . Remember, this is our one and only ticket out of here!"

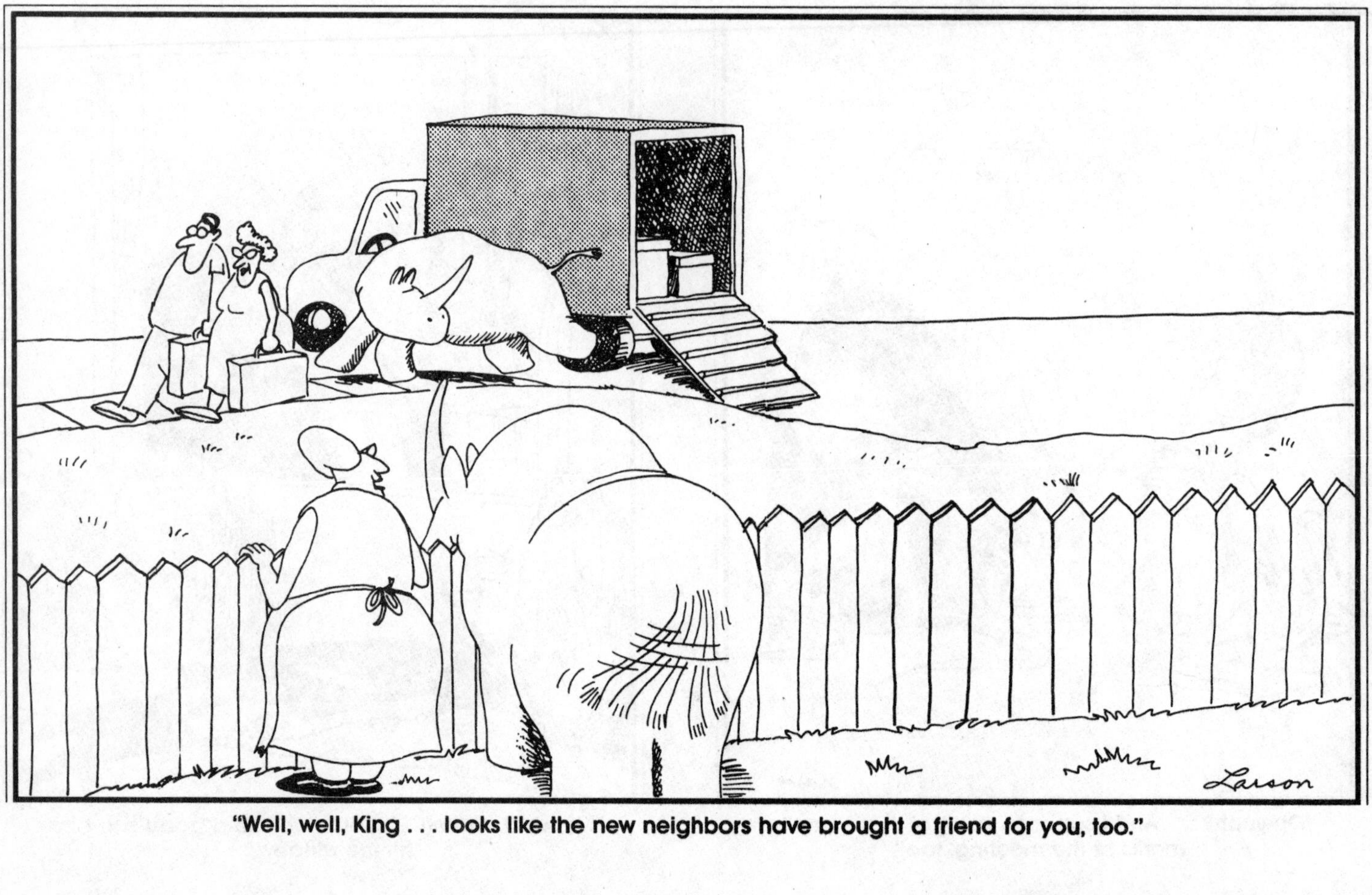
Larson

"Well, well, King . . . looks like the new neighbors have brought a friend for you, too."

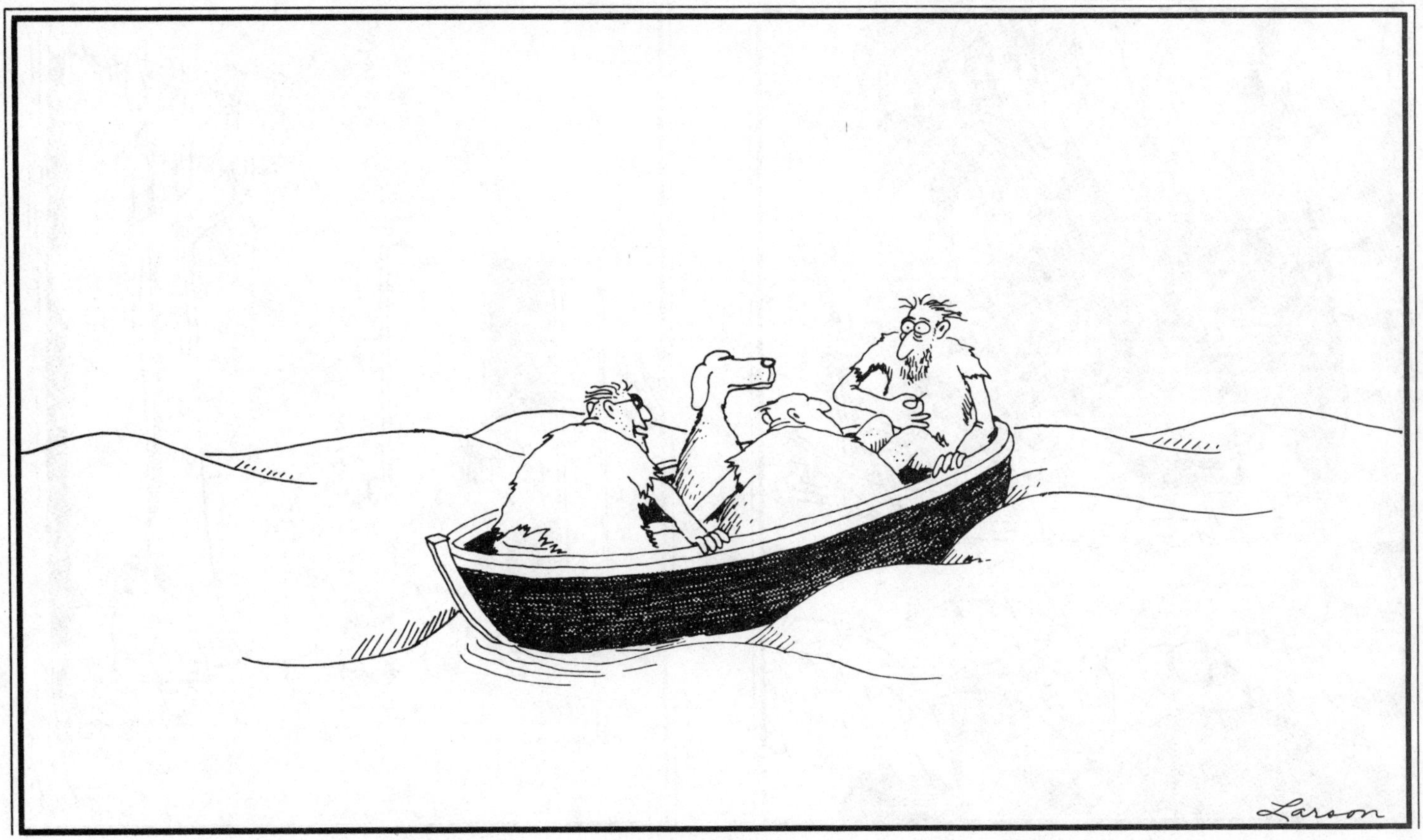
Larson
"Fair is fair, Larry . . . We're out of food, we drew straws — you lost."

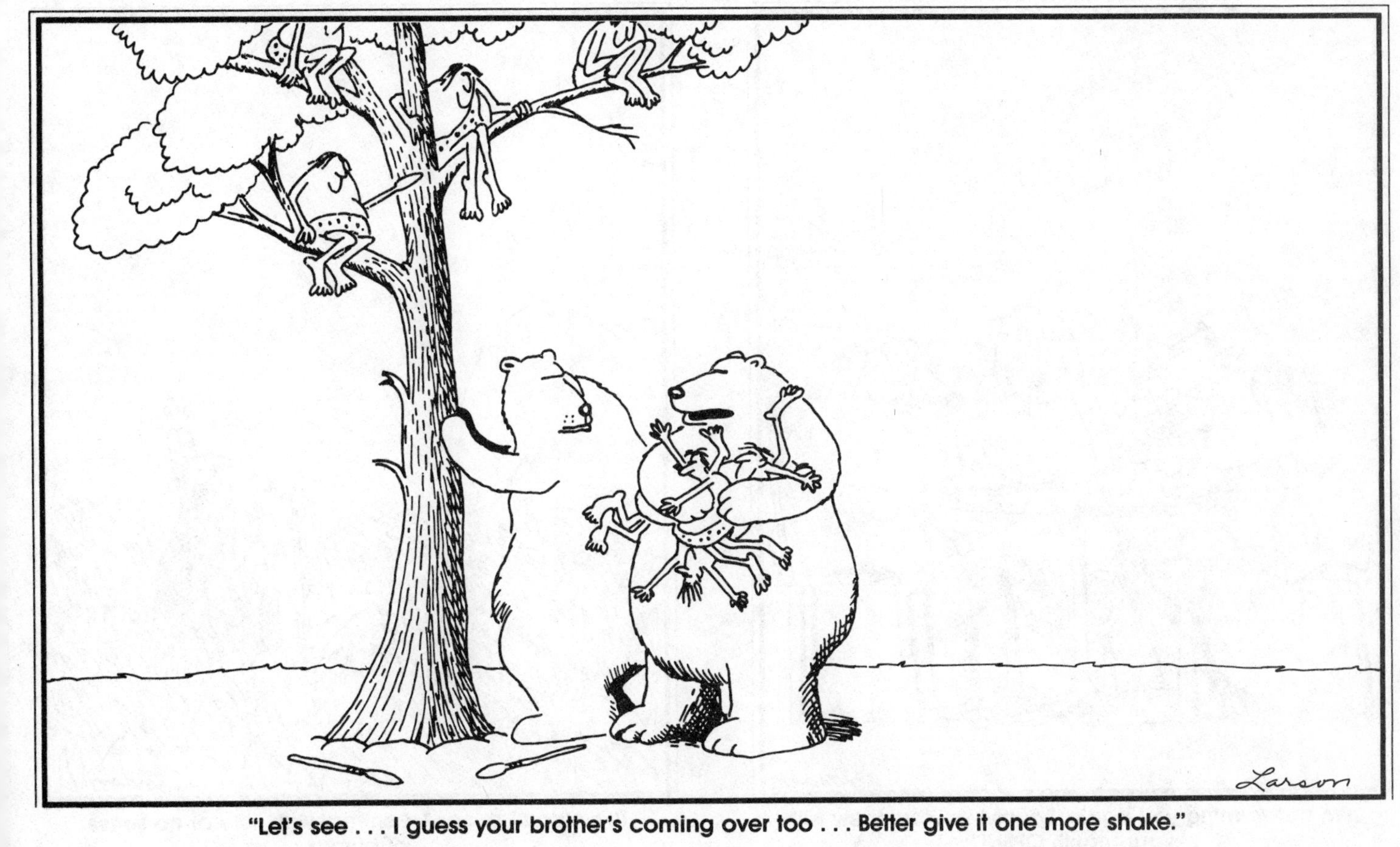
Larson
"Let's see . . . I guess your brother's coming over too . . . Better give it one more shake."

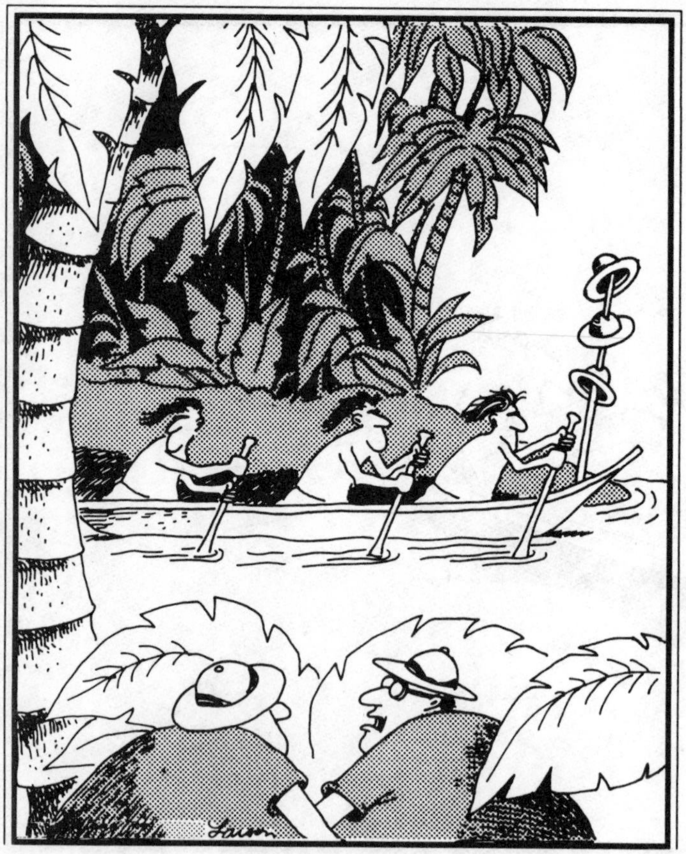
Larson

"Hathunters!"

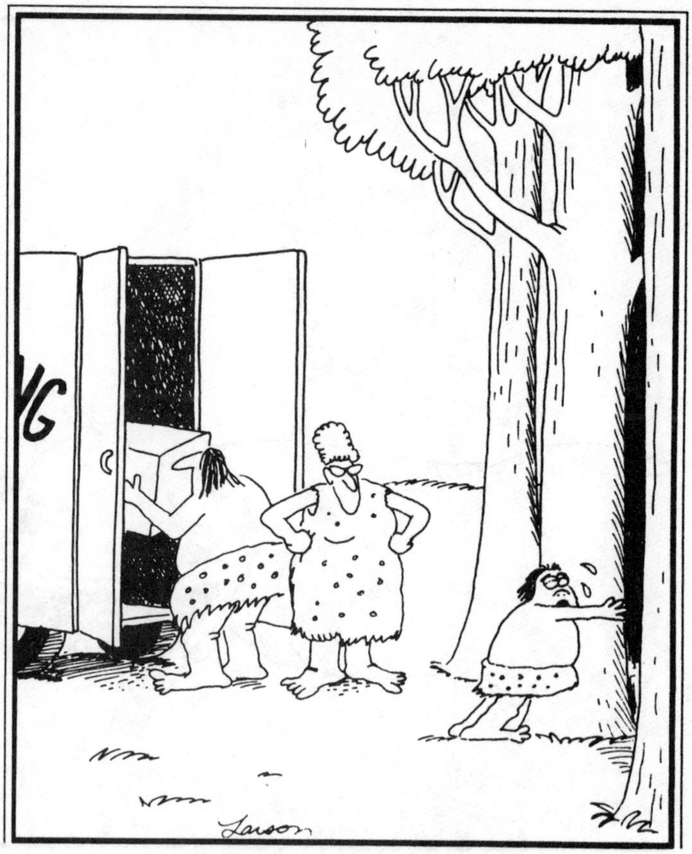
Larson

Primitive Man leaves the trees.

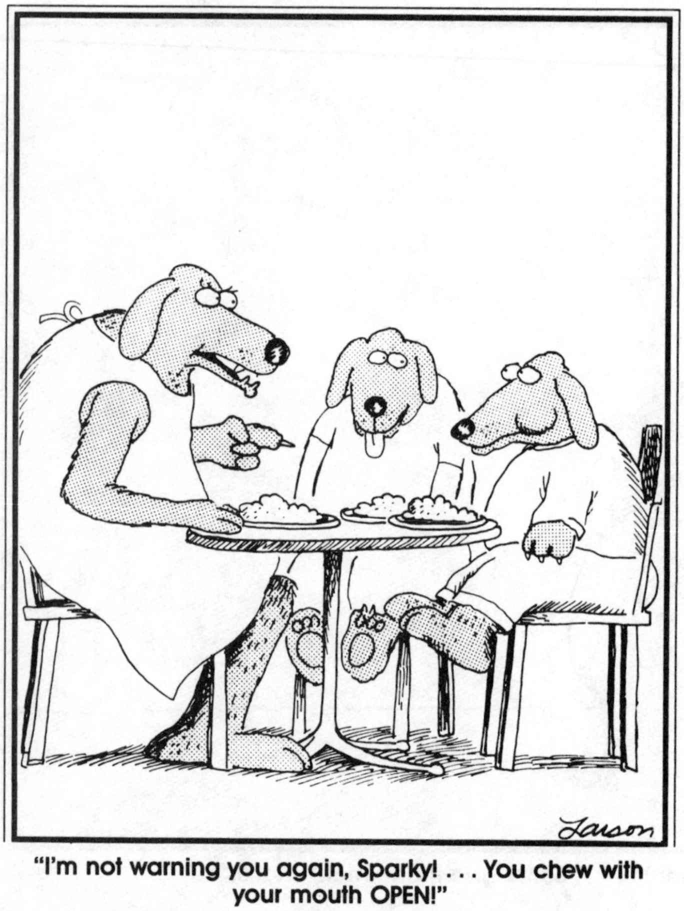
Larson

"I'm not warning you again, Sparky! . . . You chew with your mouth OPEN!"

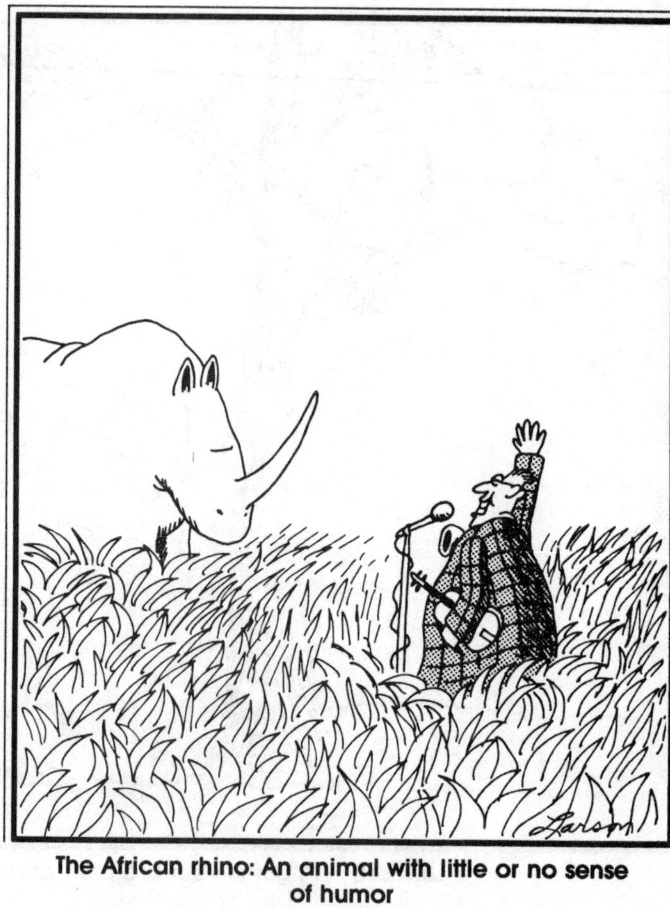
Larson

The African rhino: An animal with little or no sense of humor

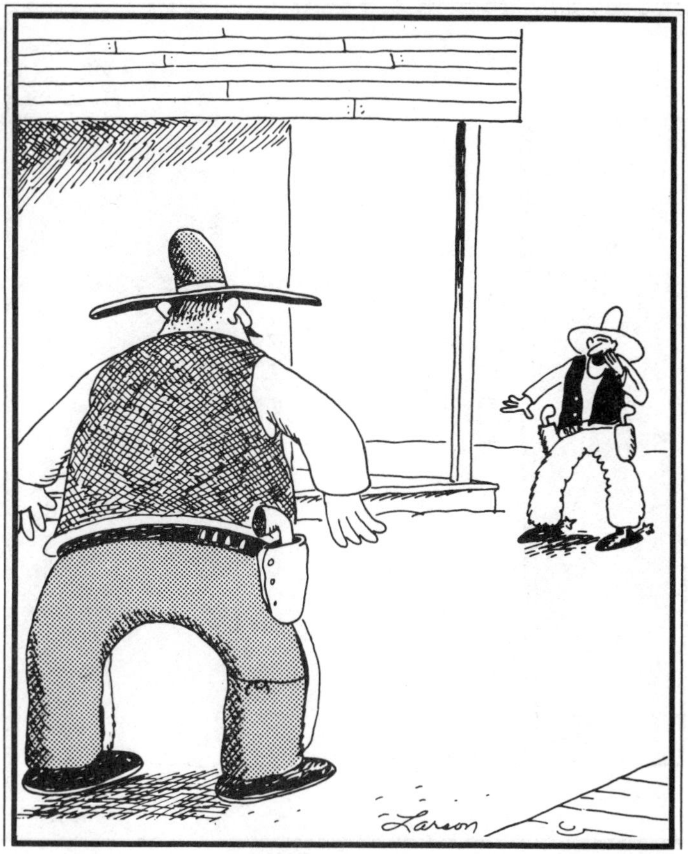
Larson

"Shoe's untied!"

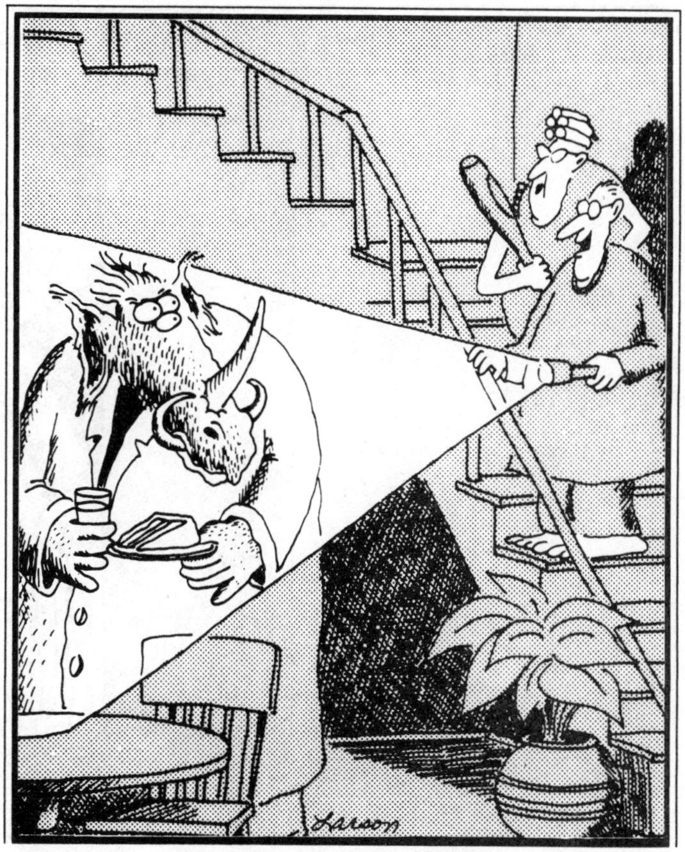
Larson

"See, Agnes? . . . It's just Kevin."

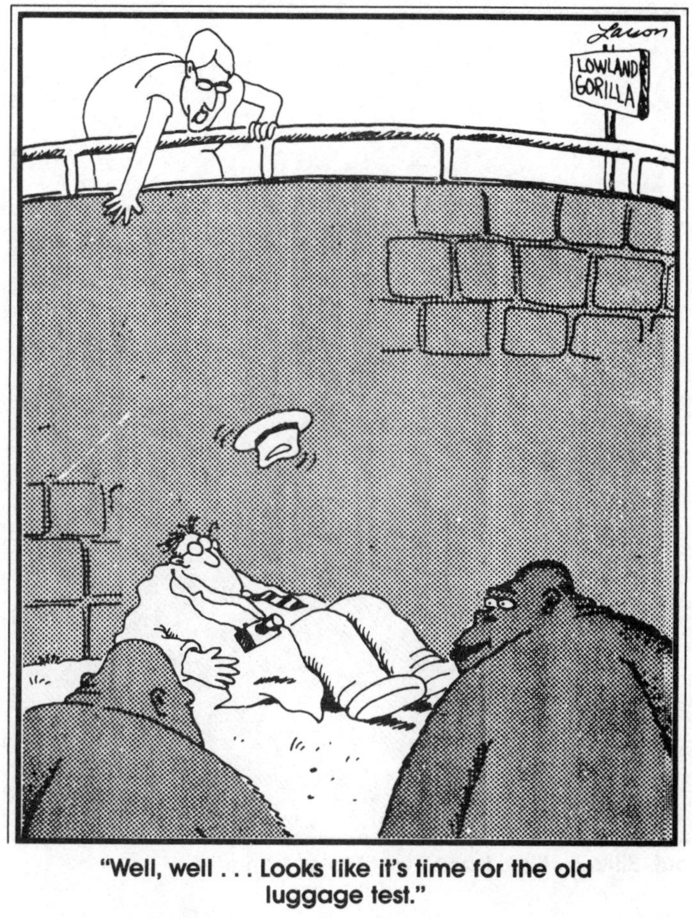
Larson
LOWLAND GORILLA

"Well, well . . . Looks like it's time for the old luggage test."

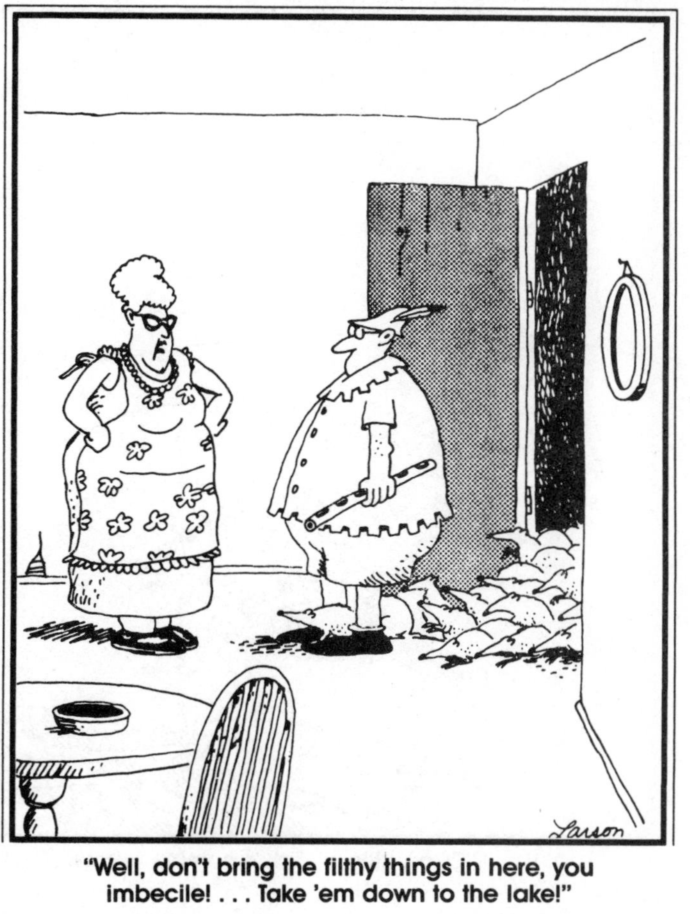
Larson

"Well, don't bring the filthy things in here, you imbecile! . . . Take 'em down to the lake!"

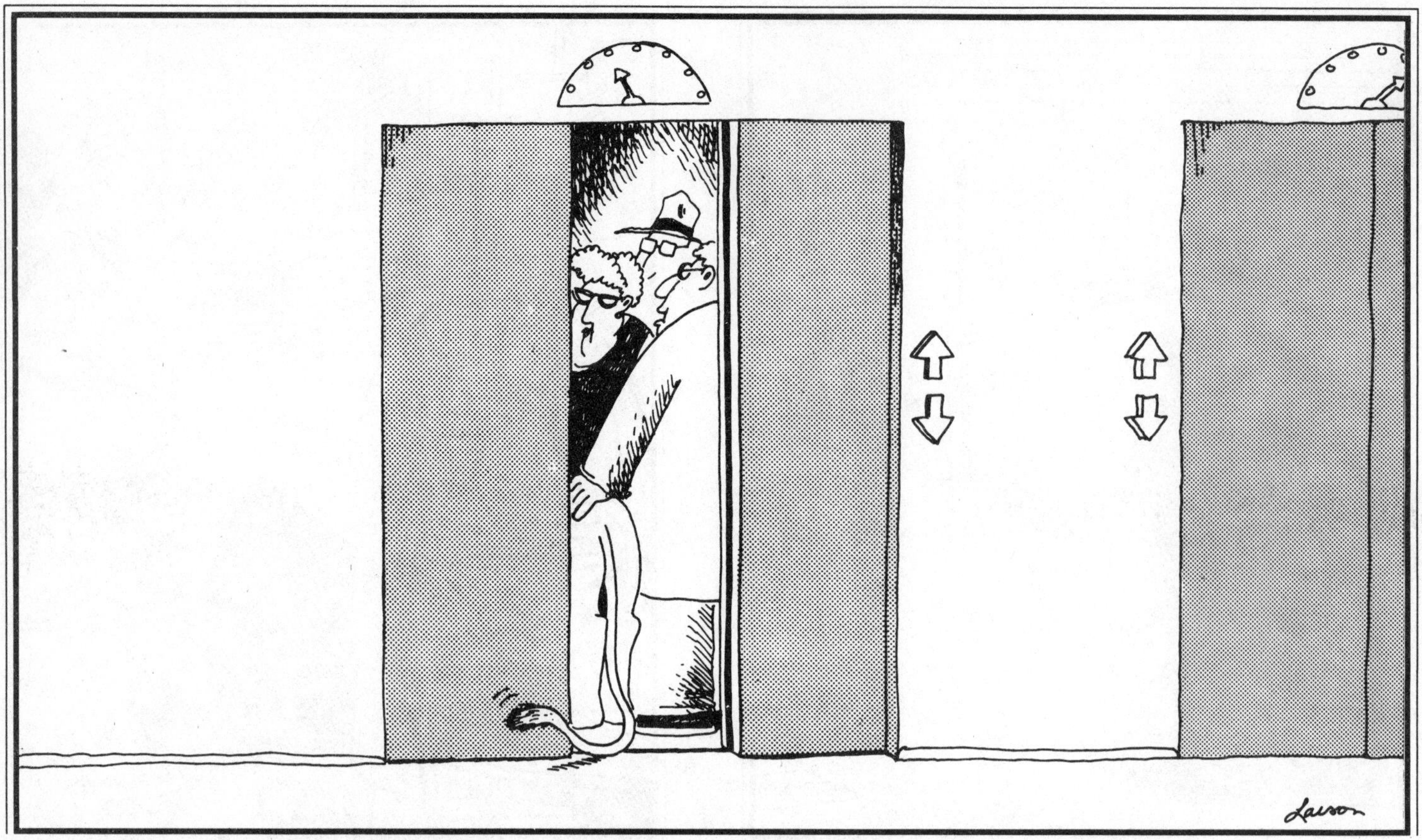
Larson

"Don't be alarmed folks . . . He's completely harmless unless something startles him."

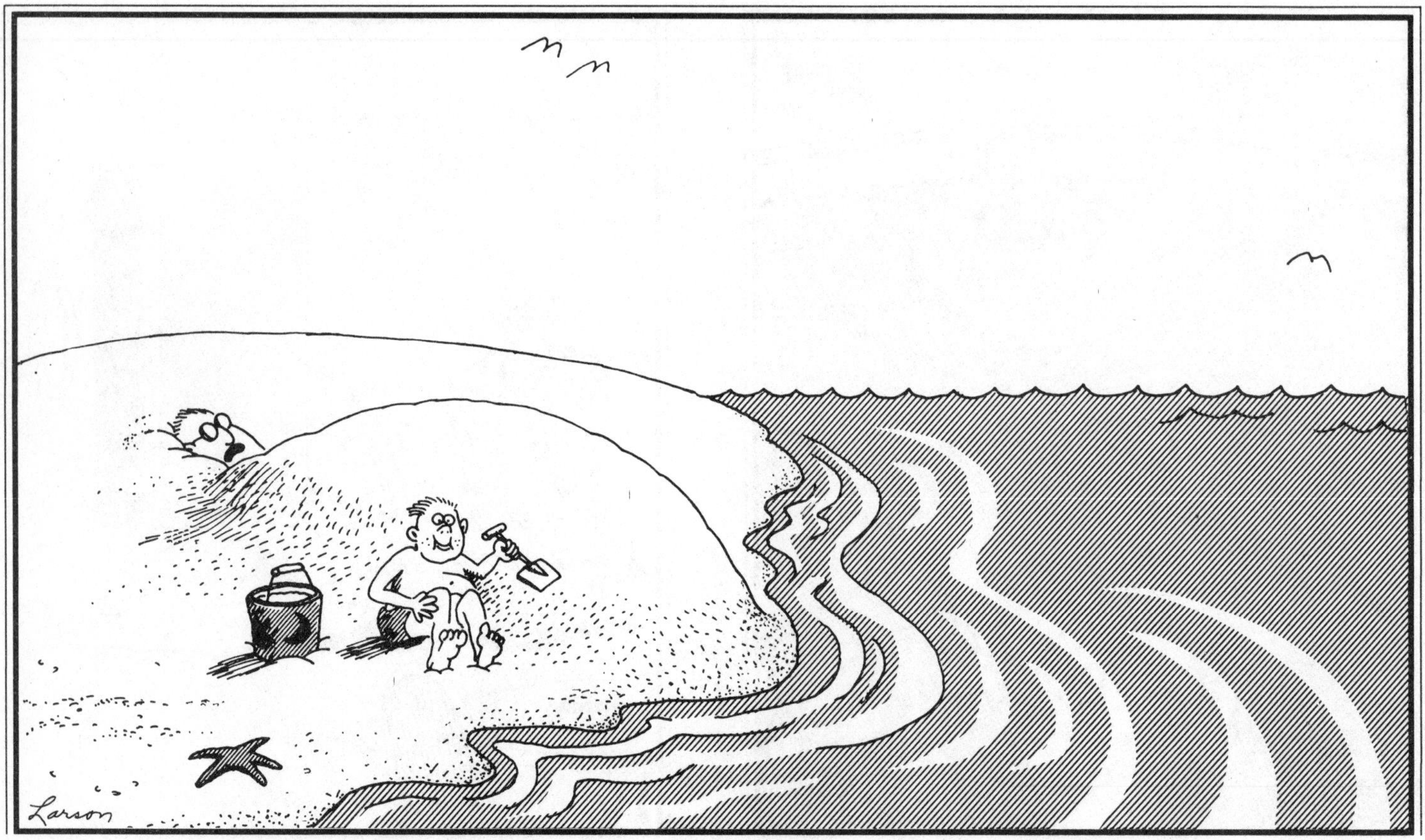
Larson

"Okay, Billy . . . Tide's coming in now . . . Dig me out, Billy . . . Billy, I don't want to get angry."